THE PRODUCT MANAGER'S DESK REFERENCE

THE PRODUCT MANAGER'S DESK REFERENCE

SECOND EDITION

STEVEN HAINES

New York   Chicago   San Francisco   Athens   London
Madrid   Mexico City   Milan   New Delhi
Singapore   Sydney   Toronto

3 4 5 6 7 8 9 0   DOC/DOC   1 2 0 9 8 7 6

ISBN: 978–0–07–182450–7
MHID: 0–07–182450–2

e-ISBN: 978–0–07–182581–8
e-MHID: 0–07–182581–9

This publication is designed to provide accurate and authoritative information in regard to the subject matter covered. It is sold with the understanding that neither the author nor the publisher is engaged in rendering legal, accounting, futures/securities trading, or other professional service. If legal advice or other expert assistance is required, the services of a competent professional person should be sought.

—From a Declaration of Principles jointly adopted by a Committee
of the American Bar Association and a Committee of Publishers

Library of Congress Cataloging-in-Publication Data

Haines, Steven.
    The product manager's desk reference / Steven Haines. — 2e [edition].
        pages cm
    ISBN 978–0–07–182450–7 (alk. paper) — ISBN 0–07–182450–2 (alk. paper) 1. Product management.
2. Marketing. 3. Product differentiation. 4. Business forecasting. 5. New products. I. Title.
    HF5415.15.H335 2014
    658.4'04—dc23   2014004899

To my mom, who had infinite editorial wisdom.
To my wife Debra, who holds my hand on this journey.
To my colleague Bob, to whom the baton will pass.

CONTENTS

Chapter 3

Leadership: Creating Influence   51

Chapter 4

Cross-Functional Product Teams: Getting Things Done   67

Chapter 5

Problem Solving and Decision Making: What's Next?   91

Chapter 8

Finding Markets to Conquer by Understanding Customer Needs and Market Segments   179

Chapter 9

Preparing to Set Your Mileposts: Forecasting for the Product Manager   207

Chapter 12

Is There Really a Business Here? Assessing Feasibility   313

Chapter 13

Appearances Are Everything: Defining and Designing the Product   345

Chapter 14

Justifying Product Investments: The Business Case   387

Chapter 15

Synchronizing the Gears: The Marketing Plan for the Product   419

Chapter 16

Execution and Oversight During Product Development   447

Chapter 19

Post-Launch Strategic Performance Analysis   525

Chapter 20

Post-Launch Strategic Mix Management   561

Chapter 24

Organizing for and Managing Product Management   645

MODULE 6

THE PRODUCT MANAGER'S TOOLBOX   671

ILLUSTRATIONS

TEMPLATES

Throughout the book, many helpful templates and tools are available. Additionally, in Module 6, the most important templates are encapsulated in a template library for you to recreate for your professional use.

Template Title	Figure Number	Chapter
Team Leader Assessment	4.6	4
Competitor Profile	7.5	7
Customer Visit Request	8.4	8
Customer Visit Plan	8.5	8
Organizing the Work of Data Collection	10.4	10
Strategic Product Retrospective and Baseline Evaluation	10.11	10
Product Strategy Review	10.18	10
Product as a Business Strategic Planning	10.19	10
Opportunity Statement	11.3	11
Value Proposition	11.8	11
Positioning Statement	11.10	11
Functional Support Plan	12.5	12
Resource Estimate and Approval	12.7	12
Product Team Resource Summary	12.8	12
Product Requirements Document (PRD)	13.6	13
Product Team Concurrence and Program Approval	13.14	13
Cross-Functional Product Team Meeting Minutes	19.16	19
Integrated Roadmap	20.4	20
Promotional Program	20.8	20
Product Discontinuation	22.1	22
Self-Assessment	23.2	23
Career Action Planning	23.3	23
Applied Learning Project	23.4	23
Product Team Hierarchy	24.1	24

TEMPLATE SECTION – MODULE 6

FOREWORD

PRACTICE WHAT YOU PREACH: A CASE STUDY ON STEVEN HAINES

I came to Steven Haines's consulting and advisory practice, Sequent Learning Networks, in 2012 after having been a client for several years. Philosophically, Steven and I had always been aligned in our thinking about Product Management. I was a huge fan of *The Product Manager's Desk Reference* and became an even bigger fan when I witnessed, first-hand within the company that I worked for, the tools and processes being translated from words on a page into real-life implementation and results. Needless to say, Steven and I got on famously, and when we made the mutual decision to work together not as client and consultant but as colleagues, I have to say that I was just a little bit nervous. Aside from leaving my corporate job to come work within what was, at the time, unknown, unchartered, otherwise uncertain vocational territory for me, I was also more than a little bit afraid to take a peek behind the curtain of this Product Management expert that I had come to admire through his writings and teachings over so many years. What would I find out about the real Steven Haines and the way he runs his own business? Did he really know as much about Product Management as he writes about? In short, was he really practicing what he preaches?

As I pondered these questions, right on the verge of making what I intuitively knew would be a life-changing decision, I was reminded of something that had been burned into my memory several years earlier. Having always been a big fan of a certain theme park that shall remain nameless, I was excited to have the chance at one point to go backstage and witness what went on behind the scenes. Mind you, it was a fascinating and educational experience, but I realized that I was a much happier person before that tour. There were big furry suits walking around with disproportionately sized human heads poking out of them, employees grumbling about what a bad day they were having, and actors and actresses out of character and out of costume. This was real life, and I knew it existed somewhere back there, but what I didn't know is that I never wanted to see it up close. Having stared it all in the face behind the scenes, I could never fully believe in what was happening on stage again. The whole experience was now somehow less enjoyable for me, and that company's main goal of fabricating this otherwise idyllic and euphoric environment could never be fully realized on me again.

Was this to be my fate at Sequent Learning Networks? Could I ever fully believe in *The Product Manager's Desk Reference* if I didn't see it all being implemented behind the four walls of the author's own company? I was as scared of that possibility as I was of leaving my corporate executive job to follow a passion that was largely inspired by this man who I was about to work side-by-side with for quite possibly the rest of my career.

So, at this point in the story, you might expect that I'll use the rest of my allocated space to tell you how everything was perfect, how Steven's company was doing everything right, and how we all lived happily ever after. But I can't entirely do that because (a) it would be far too obvious, and (b) it isn't entirely true. Certainly that would be the easiest, and perhaps the most "correct," path for me to take, but I believe that case studies are somewhat useless if they're written as nothing more than glorified advertisements for all the things companies wish they were doing but really aren't. Instead, I want to give you the unfiltered version because in that truth there are some really hard-earned lessons that don't deserve to be wasted. Not to mention the fact that I personally believe that anyone undertaking a Product Management transformation needs to know that it takes a lot of time, work, and effort—even for the experts.

So what is it that I found behind the Sequent Learning Networks curtain? Well, first of all, I can tell you unequivocally and without hesitation or doubt that Steven Haines, both as an author *and* a manager, really and truly is a Product Management expert. The things he writes about are not theories. They are facts. They are practices. They are experiences that he has not only witnessed but also lived himself. Steven is a practitioner. It is that voice that originally spoke to me in the first edition of *The Product Manager's Desk Reference*, and that tone, to this day, truly does reflect the real person behind the written words.

Next, I can tell you that Steven really does practice what he preaches. Sequent Learning Networks is a company of people who create, market, and deliver great products. And those great products were developed as a result of understanding customer's needs, comparing those needs to competitive offerings and industry trends, and producing products that fill the gaps between all of those things. In our world, our products are training workshops and learning events and advisory services and diagnostic tools, and even the very book that you are holding in your hands. All of these great products are a direct result of applying the principles that are discussed in this and Steven's other books, and I can tell you that we follow those practices to the letter. And the result of all that discovery and insight-gathering and listening to our markets is that Sequent has developed products that address customers' needs. And those are exactly the products that customers want to buy. So, in terms of Discovery & Innovation, Steven's company passes the test.

The next life cycle stage is New Product Planning. So how do we fare in that department? Large companies are typically challenged in this area, which is all about taking lots of ideas and filtering them down into only those things that are the most marketable and, as such, will give the greatest returns on investment. But the reason large companies are challenged here isn't because they lack the systems and processes required to filter out bad ideas. Instead, it's because they don't always know which ideas are actually the bad ones, largely because many of those ideas were born out of "innovating" without watching, listening, or learning about what customers truly want or do. Smaller companies, on the other hand, usually have fewer ideas to work with, but they may have more trouble filtering out *any* of those ideas because they tend to behave in a more opportunistic manner, particularly if every customer demand helps to pay the bills. And that is fully what I expected to find at Sequent Learning Networks. But, in fact, what I found was that, because we did a lot of listening, we also had a lot of ideas—many more than I expected. But between gathering market insights and filtering those ideas, Steven had developed a very clear and distinct strategy. So we knew, as a company, exactly who we wanted to be, exactly who we didn't want to be, and exactly how we would and wouldn't get to our ultimate destination. So it was easier to filter out those ideas that didn't make sense and fully develop those that were strategically aligned with both our customers' and our own company's needs. So another validating checkmark went in the box for Steven Haines.

Next I took a look at the third life cycle stage, New Product Development. Here, I was looking for products that were being developed and refined in accordance with initial customer requirements. I was looking for launch planning to happen concurrently with development activities. I was looking for actual product launches that were well promoted, on time, in budget, and in accordance with customer expectations. To illustrate what I found, I'll point to the launch, or should I say relaunch, of a product that I actually had something to do with—the Product Management Executive Board (or PMEB, for short). This began as a concept that Steven came up with several years before I joined his company to form an association of Product Management leaders who could share best practices, network, participate in research and benchmarking studies, and have a focused forum within which they could continuously grow and learn from one another. As a client of Sequent Learning Networks, I was actually the second member of the PMEB. Now, as an employee of Sequent Learning Networks, I was immediately put in charge of taking all of my experiences as a member and relaunching this association based on true and real customer wants and needs. Talk about "voice of the customer"! Having launched many products using the tools and concepts outlined in this very book, I already had a ready-made template to go about the business of reinventing PMEB. And we followed it to a tee. Using member insights to drive our development, we put together a project plan, complete with milestones and budget targets, we met weekly throughout the development process to make sure that all of our contractors, suppliers, and employees were aligned, and we concurrently planned out all of our launch activities, including the wheres and whens and hows and whats. Things evolved and changed and surprised us, but we were always able to manage scope changes and get ourselves back on schedule even through the worst of surprises. When it came time to launch the product, we planned a customer event at one of our Product Management leadership summits and captured it all on video to use for both future promotion and future learning. And the whole thing went off without a hitch. We now have a new association with a new membership website, a new certification program, and new research and benchmark reports that members really want to have and use and share with one another. And our membership just keeps growing, and growing, and growing. It works. This stuff really works.

So what about the fourth phase of Post-Launch Product Management? This is the part of the life cycle where you manage the performance of products in market. You track previously agreed-upon metrics and compare those results to previously established goals and forecasts, all the while using that data to reformulate, restrategize, and maximize revenue and profitability growth in accordance with your in-market life cycle state. On a product-line level, it can be very challenging for big companies to maintain this degree of focus on so many smaller products within the greater, very much larger, very much more expansive corporate portfolio. In fact, therein lies the main essence of a product manager's existence: to maintain small company–like focus within the much bigger machine. But, for small companies, this is where they have to live each and every day if they want to have any chance of paying their bills. Not that they all do it well, but it is much more common for small companies to get this part right out of pure necessity. And Sequent Learning Networks is no exception to that rule. However, what smaller companies do tend to overlook during this stage is, as the saying goes, "knowing when to fold 'em"—that is, knowing when to retire, change, or modify a product as it ages, matures, and begins to fall into decline. This is actually a trap for teachers, writers, and consultants like us. We have to stay fresh in our material, but if we are always so busy teaching that material, it can become all too easy to lose sight of the best and most current way to actually practice that material. Luckily, though, Steven had that little problem licked as well. Almost intuitively, he knew that we had to stay intimately connected with the most current best practices in order for our main products—that is, our workshops—to continuously be reinvented before they fall into decline. In fact, that's how the diagnostics and benchmarking part of our business was born. Analyzing and diagnosing the most current (successful and not so successful) practices of Product Management within companies allows us to stay connected with companies and learn from them in ways that we can use to continuously refresh and redesign our teachings. In fact, the very edition of the book you are reading was born from much of this same information. Armed with this constant inflow of new information, our business model has enabled our product portfolio to stay current, fresh, and alive—very much alive.

So, I've gone through all four life cycle phases and, so far, all of the fuzzy heads are still on all of the fuzzy characters, even from behind the curtain. So where, then, is that reality that I promised you?

Well, fortunately, everything I've told you so far is very, very real. But there is another reality that has unfortunately challenged us, just as it challenges many of our clients, and just as it will undoubtedly challenge many of the readers of this book. That challenge is time. We simply don't have enough time.

I've told you all of the things we're doing right, both practically and theoretically. And hopefully that will help to inspire confidence in your author. But your author, and I, and you, for that matter, are all human beings last time I checked. And human beings have finite capacities. We are all being pulled in a thousand different directions. And with each technological advancement designed to make our lives faster and easier, comes, at the same time and in the same form, a new distraction that, in reality, makes our lives feel more sluggish and overburdened. We all face this reality, and it is one that we must actively learn to overcome by reordering, reprioritizing, and rethinking the way we do every task, every way, every time.

As a small business, we face this reality each and every day, just as you will as you try to apply the tools, techniques, and principles that are written about among these pages. The biggest challenge you will have to overcome is the challenge of time. And although we do so much of Product Management right, it doesn't always feel that way because we are also busy writing customer proposals and dealing with administrative issues and trying to get paid. These little necessities of running a business—all of these little "fires," if you will—sometimes just seem to get in the way. So they do for us, and so they will for you as well. And with each little fire may come one less workshop that can be revised or one less webpage that can be updated or one less strategy that can be revisited. And then you fall behind.

But from this reality we must learn, and that is exactly what we have been doing. When we teach our workshops, we use the analogy that learning about Product Management is like drinking from a fire hose. I'm not sure to whom exactly this saying can be attributed, but it has been used many times in many different situations when people are feeling overwhelmed. Our response to this situation: prioritize. Unfortunately, there is no template for prioritization because each company and each person will have different strategies, goals, and objectives that they need to prioritize against. So it is difficult to give much more guidance than that without understanding an individual situation. But as you go through all of the incredible insights and advice that are provided for you throughout these pages, always keep that invisible checklist in the back of your mind as to which things resonate with you as most important to the success of your product lines or businesses. Chances are the ones that resonate with you do so for a reason. And then turn that invisible checklist into a very real and very visible one that will allow you to sort and resort that list with respect to the time you have available to you in any given day to actually bring these practices to life. This, quite honestly, is what we weren't doing so well. And this is what we are actively working on, every day, to ensure that the many, many, many things we have yet to do are actually getting done in the order in which those things will add value to our customers and, ultimately, to our business.

So Steven Haines really does know Product Management. And he has hired people who continue to challenge him to learn more about it every day. In the case of Sequent Learning Networks, what's behind the curtain really is very similar to what's in front of it, so you can apply these practices with the confidence of knowing the author actually does practice what he preaches. Not without mistakes or challenges, but always in character and always true to what you actually see in front of the spotlight.

I'm still a fan, and a client, and a coworker, and a friend. And all of these relationships continue to help make me, and Steven, better product managers.

Bob Caporale
President
Sequent Learning Networks

PREFACE

PERSPECTIVES

I wrote the first edition of *The Product Manager's Desk Reference* in response to an overwhelming need for a unified collection of business practices—a body of knowledge for product managers and product leaders. Since its release, tens of thousands of people have turned to this book for practical "how-to" guidance and applicable tools. I must say that it's incredibly gratifying when people send me pictures of the book with pages bent over, colorful stickers protruding from all angles, and other signs of daily usage!

The insights in this book are built around a core framework called the Product Management Life Cycle Model, which is designed to help Product Management professionals and others manage products holistically across their life cycles. It has been interesting for to me observe that this book, as a product, has a life cycle of its own. I have received a lot of feedback and many suggestions from readers of the first edition, and these ideas have helped me reenergize the look and feel of the content in this new edition.

Over the past few years, I've heard CEOs renew their call for innovative new products that get to market faster. They have overhauled planning processes and introduced rapid product development methods. Even with this emphasis, I've often seen the gears of organizations just not moving in lockstep with each other. This can result in a product without a competitive edge, or a bug that didn't get picked up by the people in Quality Assurance.

Even as executives make changes in their organizations, I've learned there is additional work to be done. Based on my research, I can see that more attention should be paid to the funding of market intelligence programs to help promote inspirational market insights. Yet, even if research is funded, insights alone won't help in the absence of a cogent strategy. To be able to craft the strategy, real financial and business data are required! Interestingly, more than two-thirds of product managers surveyed do not have adequate financial or market share data to help them assess their product's performance. This leads me to one of my greatest concerns: the lack of attention to the management and optimization of products currently in the market. If more data about current product performance was available, better decisions would be made about existing and future products. Furthermore, if product managers realized the psychological rewards that can be reaped when they take charge of a money-maker or breathe life into a stale brand, they might think twice about working on that next great technology!

While corporate executives intend for product managers to be more strategic, product managers say they direct their energy toward tactical, day-to-day work and "firefighting." Most of us know that this is due to the need to produce short-term results. Another reason that prevents product managers from being strategic-minded business thinkers is that often there are simply too few individuals on staff. A third challenge is related to the people in other functions who do not play their part, for whatever reason. Notwithstanding that some product managers need to up their game, this imbalance is not sustainable—and that's a tall order.

However, all is not lost! Now, more than ever, business leaders do care more deeply about efficiency and innovation. The "function" of Product Management *is* on their radar screen because they've come to realize that Product Management, done right, will contribute to their firm's ability to produce the great products and innovations that customers clamor for.

As a great example, over the past few years, a new role has emerged in many firms: Chief Product Officer (CPO) or an equivalent title. The CPO is a crucial leadership position and usually reports to the CEO. In a recent interview with a person at this level, I learned that she worked with the CEO to reorganize the executive cabinet to replace uncooperative executives (i.e., those with their own functional agendas and misunderstandings about Product Management) with a more collaborative leadership team. This leader also hand-picked product managers based on specific criteria, including critical thinking skills, the proven ability to solve problems in a collaborative way, and an overall solid business and operational understanding.

I am encouraged by the progress that's been made and am committed to continuing my efforts to professionalize the role of the product manager and to help leaders fortify the function of Product Management. As many are aware, I wrote two other books that extend my contribution to this area. *Managing Product Management* is designed to help senior leaders improve how they align the organization and support product managers. *The Product Manager's Survival Guide* is aimed at assisting newer product managers to be as productive as possible, as fast as possible. I am told that experienced product managers have found the *Survival Guide* to be a great resource to remind them of the work they should be doing!

WHAT'S NEW?

Now, let me tell you about the second edition of *The Product Manager's Desk Reference*. As Steven Covey said, it's important to "sharpen the saw," and that's what this edition is about. If you're curious to know how it's different from the first edition, here's a synopsis of the improvements:

1. The Product Management Life Cycle Model has been expanded to draw more attention to the areas I refer to as "Innovation and Discovery." You'll find that this can enhance your perspective on the

inputs required to plan, prioritize, launch, and manage products, services, and solutions.

2. In order to improve accessibility, all figures and tables have been updated. Process diagrams, workflows, templates, and checklists are easier to view and understand. I've also added directories at the beginning of the book for both illustrations and templates. A quick scan can get you to the right tool, just when you need it. In this book, you'll find more than 190 figures and more than two dozen templates. By the way, check out a major new template that I call a *Competitor Dossier*. It provides a terrific blueprint to understand your competitors in a more holistic manner.

3. I've provided a more finely tuned description of the role played by the product manager and how the product manager can effectively negotiate with and engage with people in other functions. The product manager plays the role of facilitator, partner, and orchestrator, and this context is threaded across many of the chapters. I've also included information that considers multicultural, globally situated teams.

4. Greater attention has been given to the need for the product manager to be able to garner market insights and craft strategies.

5. Improved perspectives on roadmaps are included, from both the historical perspective as well as from a more forward-looking point of view.

6. Across many of the chapters, I've mentioned the importance of storytelling as a way to improve communication, transfer knowledge, and ensure everyone is "on the same page."

7. As ideas are cultivated, I've recommended that product managers focus on experimentation and the development of prototypes so that opportunities can be vetted more quickly.

8. I've highlighted the need to pay closer attention to elements of the product's design and appearance during the phase when new opportunities are being considered. I've reinforced the need to make sure a designer is part of the team as product ideas are both considered and developed.

9. Succinct guidance has been provided in the Product Requirements Document (PRD). A new template and outline has been added. I've also included information to help increase uniformity and consistency in the product definition process through the introduction of peer reviews and inspections.

10. In Chapter 16, I've offered some context around rapid product development. I've portrayed the need for speed through iterative interactions both with customers and with your development team. This section is not a treatise on the *agile* method. Rather, it contains

a message about the need to consider rapid development techniques in your go-to-market strategy.

11. Module 4 on Post-Launch Product Management has been greatly expanded. Previously, one chapter was devoted to the management of existing products. Chapter 19 has been recast and is entitled "Post-Launch Strategic Performance Analysis" so that you can focus your efforts on how well your product is doing in the market and in its contribution to business results. Chapter 20 is entirely new and is entitled "Post-Launch Strategic Mix Management." It's designed to help you determine the type of investments that could be made to upgrade the product, reduce costs, improve the customer experience, and expand into new markets. I've also added sections that help you construct a strategically grounded and integrated *roadmap*, create a value-based market price, and improve your ability to influence programs to advertise and promote your product and educate your customers.

12. Module 5, as with the first edition, concentrates on the professionalization of Product Management. However, I've revised the product manager self-assessment to be a more user-friendly tool. You can explore this in Chapter 23. In Chapter 24, I've augmented the guidance provided for leaders so they have greater perspective on their role and so that they can be better coaches for product managers.

Overall, the second edition contains a lot of new content, significant revisions, and more engaging visuals. I trust that you'll use this resource for a long time to come!

CLOSING COMMENTS

If there's anything I've learned in my decades as a business person, it's this: without regard for organizational commotion and dysfunctional teams, product managers have the best job! One reason is because it's the only role that is "whatever you make of it." It's also the best job for people who want to be their best and contribute the most. We cannot know everything, and we learn continuously from the situations we encounter. We make our mark and earn empowerment by connecting the dots and seeing the big picture. We make sense out of amorphousness and the unpredictable actions of market players, craft and recraft our strategies, and get others to come along for the ride. That's leadership—and that's what product manager's do.

I hope that you will hop on board this dynamic machine of business and that the second edition of *The Product Manager's Desk Reference* will be the ever-faithful companion in your quest for innovative, market-defining products that will delight your customers and spark envy from your competitors.

INTRODUCTION

THE ACCIDENTAL PROFESSION

I teach Product Management workshops all over the world. At the start of every session, I ask if anyone has a degree in Product Management. Virtually all the time, there is no response. In the classroom, students represent a wide variety of backgrounds and college majors: marketing, finance, physics, engineering, computer science, English, philosophy, psychology, graphic arts—but no diplomas in Product Management. However, when asked how many have product manager as their job title, most participants raise a hand.

So the obvious question is, "If you're all product managers, but you can't get a degree in it, how did you get the job?" The answers often sound something like this:

- "My boss asked me if I wanted to do the job, and I thought it would be a good experience."
- "I thought it would be interesting."
- "I was in development, and since I knew the product, they thought I'd do well here."
- "I was in sales, and since I understood the product, I thought this was the next logical step."
- "It sounded like such a neat job."
- "I did marketing before, so this was a good fit for me."

Welcome to the accidental profession.

EVERYONE COMES FROM SOMEWHERE ELSE

You may have backed into Product Management from another field or business discipline. And you may be feeling overwhelmed as you try to figure out how to get an amorphous collection of urgent, important things done, right away. Dozens of distractions pull you in all directions—some important, some not—yet it seems essential to address each detail effectively. Things happen so fast you cannot structure them, cannot build in your mind's eye a clear picture of how things should be coming together. Everyone is placing tremendous expectations on you; chances are you have no idea how to meet some of the key expectations, nor are you even aware of all of them.

People in charge of products and services tend to manage them within the context of their own discipline (engineering, marketing, etc.). Faced with decision points, they simply choose the priorities that seem urgent to themselves or their management. When specialists from other areas plunge into the job, without adequate knowledge and support structures, they may end up operating a lot like Lewis and Clark. They become strangers in a strange land, guided by natives who speak strange languages and don't understand the importance or priorities of Product Management.

Adding to this confusion, Product Management has no well-defined framework and is often treated as a transient discipline in many companies. Consider a few obvious symptoms:

- No two companies seem to manage products the same way.
- Product managers report to different functions in different companies.
- Organizations and policies do not seem to line up in ways that support strong Product Management.
- Executives split important processes between too many departments, creating inefficient methods.
- A high percentage of typical product "practices" are either nonexistent, unnecessary, or made unnecessarily difficult because they are not based on proven, best-in-class methods.
- Most companies have neither a formal structure nor standardized internal Product Management professional development programs.

As a result, product managers unwittingly spend too much time on things that don't matter. Exceptional opportunities are missed, while mismatched, unwanted products seem to linger inexplicably in the marketplace.

The source of these troubles is not your lack of ability, nor is it your company's gross oversight. Individuals and companies struggle with Product Management because there has not yet been a codified body of knowledge available to the Product Management practitioner. Universities teach core business functions, and you should not underestimate the value of a solid business foundation. Every business discipline has its place, including a unique library of excellent books that make for a formidable education. Everyone should build that foundation because it provides a list of *what* to do. Absent from the curriculum, however, is an overall framework or "anatomical structure" to look at Product Management holistically—and there is no holistic framework within which to manage and grow your career.

A *GRAY'S ANATOMY* OF BUSINESS

I have written this book to remedy that situation and help transform a largely accidental profession into a successful, productive, and recognized discipline. There is a standard body of knowledge for Product Management, including a strong, holistic viewpoint of profession and career, along with a set of specific, learnable skills. My passionate goal—which this book reflects—is to provide that body of knowledge and, in the process, transform Product Management from an artificial, poorly defined slot in an organizational chart into its true and correct role: the pivot point for successful enterprise.

Think of this book as a *Gray's Anatomy* of business—a three-dimensional, in situ picture of how everything works when it's running right. Like the human body, business is a dynamic, living entity. It consists of overlapping, interlocking systems and functions that influence each other in very complex ways. Business generally responds slowly to corrective action and doesn't always respond predictably or consistently. Relationships between the players and the pieces are dynamic and situational, influenced by a fluid array of team decisions that address constantly changing circumstances. Business is not exactly a web, a mind-map, a flowchart, or a notebook full of checklists.

This is a reference written from the practitioner's perspective, for practitioners. Anchored by a standardized Product Management Life Cycle Model, this business "anatomy" book explains in detail:

- How to choose and justify which products to build
- How to plan for their profitable creation and deployment
- How to develop and launch them
- How to manage them once they enter the market
- How and when to gracefully retire them and replace them with new products
- How to use product portfolio management techniques to effeciently allocate investments across all of the products in an organization

To sum up, this book is designed to help you take the right actions, done the right way, at the right stage of the product's life cycle.

Along with these critical activities, a detailed primer on many of the fundamental business skills is provided to execute these methods successfully. Rounding out the collection is a broad range of best practices and examples, coordinated with a large library of templates throughout the chapters and in the toolbox in the back of the book.

Like a physician's handbook, this book is structured for dual use, as both a ready reference for decision making and for sequential self-education. Like doctors, product managers benefit greatly from a handy reference library of protocols that can be skillfully applied to various levels of risk. Considered as a holistic discipline, however, the art of Product Management has four fundamental pillars or "knowings" you must develop:

- Knowing where you are. To proceed productively, you must be able to answer the question, "Where am I now?" As a product manager, you need to assess your current career situation as well as the situation with your product. All journeys have a starting point.

- Knowing where you want to go and knowing how to compare your vision to your current environment. You must be visionary or at least learn how to cultivate and sustain a vision for what your product will bring to the marketplace. How far away is the vision? What needs to change? How should I react to the pressures of an environment that is pushing me to take some path that does not lead to my vision?

- Knowing how to get to where you want to be. You must have a large repertoire of processes, practices, and documents (i.e., know how) that you know *when* to dynamically apply to situations you've never seen before, but whose shadows you recognize through experience.

- Knowing how to use these skills with a centered, settled, quiet confidence in your ability to reach the right goals, predictably and repeatedly.

Studied sequentially, *The Product Manager's Desk Reference* is intended to help you to cultivate these four pillars incrementally. Within this framework, Product Management can be relatively straightforward and much *more* predictable.

HOW YOU SHOULD USE THIS BOOK

The material contained herein makes it *easier* to choose correct responses and make decisions, with much greater accuracy and effectiveness than simply "winging it." Ultimately, the situations you encounter may vary widely from one hour to the next. How you read this book really depends on your own experience. Read from cover to cover, it gives a good general orientation to Product Management. But also, based on your particular needs, you can:

- Use this book as a reference or "toolkit" to deal with specific situations for your product.

- Use it as a method to map your progression through your Product Management career.

- Use it as a way to link the "what you do" with the work that has to get done in each specific phase of the Product Management Life Cycle Model.

- Use it as a cross-reference to link practices to documents.

- Use it as a glossary of common terms so that everyone on your team speaks the same language.

Use it as all of these, and more. With a clear head and the right tools, it's possible to associate real causes with real effects so that you manipulate the *right* causes to gain the *desired* effects.

One of the key goals of this book is your growth and development as a product manager. In order to facilitate that growth, I have provided material at the end of most of the chapters, describing work you can do and experiences you can seek that will improve your knowledge, skills, and professional effectiveness. These are listed under the heading "Raising Your Product Management Experience Quotient (PMEQ)." These suggestions, keyed to the chapter contents, may be helpful in advancing your understanding or gaining an "edge" in your Product Management career.

DRAWN FROM EXTENSIVE BENCHMARKING AND EXPERIENCE

When I was getting my MBA, I used to get frustrated because the professors were preaching, not teaching. Distorted, low-probability case studies supported out-of-context views. Individual components of good product strategy, such as positioning, were touted as the single key to great results. I already had some business experience and was actively working at the time, so it was clear to me that there was plenty of data but very little relevant information.

I pictured myself in an entrepreneurial setting, managing my own business. I often said to myself, "If it were my money, what would I do?" As I moved forward in my career, the vision of a predictable set of methods was never far from my mind. Every time I solved a problem, the solution was captured in my private little notebook in my mind. Some of these are reflected in interesting stories I'll share with you as you read the book.

The Product Management Anatomy

Beyond a simple body of protocols, Product Management should be afforded an independent identity, similar to Accounting or Marketing. I strive to create that identity by offering a body of standardized knowledge that positions Product Management as an essential element of the organization's structure.

Many modern companies view Product Management in the same light that our ancestors viewed the practice of medicine. Think of Galen, the Greek physician who essentially organized modern medicine around 2,000 years ago. His story serves as a powerful example of what can be accomplished with an unswerving combination of passion and professionalism.

Galen was very much ahead of his time, successfully performing brain surgery and removing cataracts, feats unduplicated by medical practitioners until the twentieth century. His prodigious success seems to indicate exceptional natural ability, but by his own admission, he was an ordinary man who simply had an extraordinary passion for his profession. He did do one thing, however, that most of his contemporaries failed to do: he took good notes.

When Galen found something that worked, he finessed it until he understood it, and then wrote it down and added it to his protocol library. He recorded everything and anything he learned, and organized it into repeatable diagnoses, treatments, and standardized methods. His studies were so intense that he reportedly kept 20 or 30 scribes extremely busy while he worked. His knowledge of preparing medicines was so advanced that the Galenic Formulary is a still a bastion of modern pharmacy.

Of course, even with this broad collection of protocols, modern medicine is hardly a checklist-driven activity. Doctors use protocol mainly to quickly eliminate the predictable from the diagnostic process, leaving the mind free to focus on new and as-yet-unsolved problems. As with medicine, the practice of entrepreneurship is not 100 percent predictable, either. Like the physician, the product manager is primarily tasked with choosing the correct response to rapidly changing, complicated conditions or, in the best circumstances, anticipating and leading change.

Also like the physician, the product manager can proactively drive more predictable, positive, and repeatable results with a set of protocols that provide a standard response for at least *some* situations. This doesn't imply that there is a process for every activity or a pat answer to every problem. Business, like life, is at its core about response-ability, and the brain of this living system called "business"—or, at least, the creative side of the brain—is the product manager. However, the better you are able to recognize patterns and address them with validated methods, the more mindshare you can apply to unpredictable situations, and thus the better the business results, period.

A Career in Progress

Someone once said that if you don't know where you're going, you'll probably end up somewhere else. *Product manager* was nowhere on my list of career ideas. As a solid business generalist with strong leanings toward finance, operations, and marketing—an undergraduate degree in management science, a minor in organizational behavior, and an MBA in corporate finance—I had a host of jobs:

- I was a management trainee for a wholesale plumbing supply company, learning every job in the house. From picking pipe-fittings and selling toilets to sizing boilers and doing the books, I did it all.

- I was a cost analyst for a defense contractor, learning project management from the ground up, because that's what you do when your company works for the government.

- I worked as a budget manager for a women's clothing manufacturer, discovering ways to deal with suppliers, offshore manufacturing, and the quirks of a fast-moving fashion-oriented business.

- I joined finance and operations at a medical device manufacturer, soaking up manufacturing techniques, medical science, distribution management, reporting, Product Management, supply chain management, marketing, and a lot of other things.

None of these jobs, though interesting, made my list of jobs I'd like to have as my life's work. I didn't have a strategic direction; I didn't have a career coach; I didn't have a clue.

Eventually, I went to work at AT&T Bell Laboratories in business operations and finance. About three years into my career there, I encountered an unusual opportunity. Slated for a double promotion, my second-level boss asked me what I wanted to do. After more than a decade of work experience, there's nothing like finally hearing the question, "What do you want to do when you grow up?" I gave something of a vague answer, explaining that one day I wanted to be a general manager of a division of a larger company. Her concise, immediate response shocked me: "Oh. You want to be a product manager." That sounded too much like marketing, so I deferred. In spite of my skittishness, she insisted it was the right thing to do, so I enrolled in a week-long workshop, and that was that: I was hooked. Product Management really did turn out to be everything I ever wanted.

Not that it was easy. Instantly, I became a product manager, taking over the Japanese version of a "made for U.S." office telephone system. There were many problems, but the biggest one was my lack of product knowledge. My bosses expected that I would rapidly get up to speed, get to know all the players, learn the technology, and discover many other things that I didn't even know existed. I entered the job as a senior manager, when a lower-level job, with closer guidance, would have been more appropriate.

Someone else once said, "You haven't failed if you learned something new." Aside from my suspicion that the person who said that never tried anything big, I did learn a lot:

- To be a product manager, you have to start near the bottom, just like an apprentice serves under a master carpenter. No matter how much you think you know about business, you need to get the basics down, including products, people, systems, and methods.

- You can't learn, even at the bottom of the ladder, if you don't have coaching and mentoring. The smartest move I made as a product manager was reaching out to people and asking for help, and I asked a *lot*.
- Companies need a formal structure for professional development of product managers, modeled after their leadership development programs for high-potential employees, but few have them.

My next Product Management job was difficult for other reasons. I had a new boss who knew profit and loss but didn't understand Product Management. The result was a thankless cycle of doing what I thought was right, circumventing instructions and then secretly finding ways to fix business and customer problems. It wasn't quite as bad as being without a paddle, but because I had to come up with my own methods, it felt a lot like guiding an unbalanced canoe upstream in a drenching storm. Sooner or later, I worried, I would capsize, and then I'd have to swim for it—unless I put everything I had into getting things done.

As a matter of fact, an officemate once asked, "How do you know what to do?" I replied, "I just do what needs to get done."

In the end, though, I not only managed to keep the boat upright, I even garnered a "far exceeds" rating, luckily based on the results, not how I got there:

- I delivered a product on time, earning $5 million in revenue at a net profit of 50 percent.
- My solution had a compelling value proposition, filling a previously unmet need for a clearly identified market.
- Most of all, though, I used lessons learned from falling on my face many times over the years, because my commonsense approach often challenged conventional wisdom.

Considering my first *real* taste of product leadership, it was obvious that, while the school of hard knocks hadn't necessarily been kind to me, at least it had been talkative, and I had somehow managed to take a pretty good set of notes.

SEPARATING THE BEST FROM THE REST

Later on, and for five years, while still working at AT&T, I was assigned to a Product Management excellence task force. It was chartered to learn about the practices, processes, and methods used to produce successful products. Via practical research, we were to investigate how different companies in different industries carried out strategic planning, product planning, product development, and introduction; how they managed existing products; and how they managed portfolios of products.

With Bell Laboratories on our badges, we had an internationally recognized stature that opened doors. Thirty-six companies were benchmarked over a five-year period. The interviews were qualitative, based on Product Management practices used across the entire life cycle. We really wanted to find out what companies did to create and manage successful products, product lines, and portfolios. Each company in the research pool agreed to several days of presentations, tours, and interviews. Many of those firms agreed to follow-up visits and updates so that we could track their progress. The interviews were informative, exhaustive, and eye opening. As we worked through the responses, we started to see patterns that correlated specific activities with product success. Success was never guaranteed, but companies who applied certain methods were more likely to have successful products.

Here are some of the patterns discovered during this benchmarking investigation:

- Product and market success in these companies is linked to a keen focus on carefully chosen markets. In some cases, this focus may be obsessive. (Companies that focus on the marketplace tend to have a better chance of gaining an outside-in view of the world. This helps them recognize the needs of unique segments and important trends that influence product and marketing strategies.)
- Management *clearly* communicates its overarching strategic intent up and down the organization. This contributes to a reduction in organizational ambiguity and, most importantly, better alignment of product portfolio and product line investment decisions.
- These companies consistently use standardized product platforms. Organizations that use platforming as a part of their strategies benefit from improved economies of scale from reuse of common architectures, technologies and even components.
- Regular rationalization of product portfolios contributes toward more efficient allocation of investments to the most appropriate, strategically important product lines. Significant go/no-go project investments are made at the divisional or corporate leadership team levels based on portfolio strategies.
- Organization around products, not projects, using empowered, cross-functional product teams to run "mini-businesses" inside of these larger enterprises. When these teams are in place longer, they tend to perform better and achieve better results than teams that are

more transient. In the best performing teams, Marketing is always seen as a strong member. Furthermore, teams, not processes, are the glue that holds these organizations together.

- Most companies assign primary product or product line profit-and-loss accountability to the product teams.

- Almost all firms have some kind of phase-gate New Product Development (NPD) process *to make decisions* for product projects. As their experience grows, they adapt it based on the type of project and the market conditions driving the project. (As a side note, those firms that use the NPD process to manage project workflows tend to have less successful products, stemming from their "checklist" culture.)

- Funding for unplanned product opportunities is not made from annual budget money, but from a separate funding pool, and is vetted using the NPD process with funding and business justifications made using Business Cases.

- Success is linked to strong product team leaders and team members who respect one another. They have clear roles and responsibilities underscored by the consistent use of a common business language for processes and documents. Furthermore, these companies hold these product teams accountable for the achievement of business results using a small, manageable number of business metrics controllable by the team, not by individual functions.

- In terms of market focus, these organizations have a formal, centralized industry and competitive intelligence function.

- These organizations publish summaries or abstracts of select industry or competitive activity to interested internal subscribers.

- They create forums for information sharing. Product groups or marketing groups gather from time to time, either at lunch sessions, all-hands meetings, or the like, and present market updates or reviews so that everyone knows what's going on.

- They make the competition the main enemy, which tends to reduce internal conflict and draw teams together.

- They make market and financial data available to the Product Management and Marketing communities.

- They maintain communities of practice for product managers and marketers.

- Customer knowledge goes hand in hand with market focus. Connection to key customers is critical, not only from Sales but also from Product Management, Marketing, and Development.

- These companies use anthropological and ethnographic (live contacts with customers) techniques to understand customers' businesses.
- Chartered, involved executive leadership teams form governance councils or equivalent groups to guide the processes, methods, and tools used by product managers. They also have formal programs to recruit, select, and progress product managers.

Within these best-in-class companies, organizational structures typically have product managers reporting to the marketing department. Over the years, at the start of every one of my workshops, our facilitators ask, "Where do you report?" At this point, the majority of people indicate that they report to Marketing. The exception is in the software and technology sector, where product managers report to Product Development. However, a shift has taken place. A number of firms have established the senior leadership role of chief product officer (CPO). The ranks of CPOs continue to swell. In a number of firms, CPOs have a "seat at the table," meaning they are "C-level" leaders with the associated authority and stature of others in the C-suite.

The material you will encounter in this book has been fortified based on thousands of new data points. My firm continues to gather data on corporate and employee performance from our corporate diagnostics, assessments, and audits. These serve to reinforce the "best-in-class" norms against which leaders may be guided. Our Product Management Executive Board or PMEB (www.pmexecboard.com) conducts this research and provides a vibrant community of practice for senior Product Management executives. The PMEB has become a reliable go-to resource for senior product leaders from around the world.

SAFE JOURNEYS

Many years after my initial successes, I was explaining the situation to my daughter. She sagely observed, "Well, you didn't have a you." Precisely—I didn't have a "me," someone who had navigated the uncharted, rocky shoals of Product Management and survived, newly scrawled map in hand. It took a few more years for me to realize that I needed to share my discoveries, but eventually, I began to show others how to navigate this (sometimes treacherous) passage at the core of business and entrepreneurship. And now, I would like to do the same for you.

As a product manager, you are the quarterback, and on every single play there are dozens of variables to consider: field conditions, defensive formations, distance from the goal line, and so on. In your repertoire, there is a virtual mountain of information, from the playbook to scouting reports to last-minute instructions from the coach. Considering all these things, though, the final score and the ultimate result depend largely on your individual vision, competencies, and experience. If you have the right tools, correct information, and an appreciation for excellent workmanship, you can achieve superior results. And in the process, you can transform an unclear job assignment into a highly visible, well-respected career. The *caveat* is that it requires a long-term commitment.

Like Ulysses, if you burn your ships behind you (but not your bridges) and dedicate yourself to success as a product manager, it's amazing how quickly you can develop the magic touch. So if you are dedicated to success, here begins your work toward becoming a virtuoso of Product Management. Once again, welcome to the accidental profession. Here's wishing you fulfilling, productive, profitable journeys.

MODULE 1

FOUNDATIONS OF PRODUCT MANAGEMENT

INTRODUCTION TO MODULE 1

Most people live in a house of some kind. Every house has a foundation and a set of systems that sustain it, creating an environment in which people can comfortably live. Product Management, as you will learn, is not a job title or something that other people do. It's an element of a company's entire business model. In order to build the "house" of Product Management, a solid foundation is needed, as well as a working knowledge of the integrated systems that support Product Management. Therefore, Module 1 is about building this foundation.

Whether you are a new product manager, an experienced product manager, a product portfolio leader, or someone considering a career in Product Management, the topics covered in this module will give you a strong appreciation for what you need to know about Product Management. Furthermore, by fully grasping the importance of these foundational elements, people who perform other business functions will gain an important appreciation for the role of the product manager, and how each person can support the product and the product manager. After all, as you'll learn, everyone ultimately shares responsibility for the success of the product. Here's a quick synopsis of the chapters included in this module:

Chapter 1—What Is Product Management? describes Product Management by breaking down the expression *Product Management* into its two basic components, namely *products* and *management*. The two pieces are then rejoined to provide you with a view of the value of Product Management in an organization. Furthermore, the chapter helps you understand the vital role played by the product manager in the organization.

Chapter 2—The Product Master Plan gives you the wherewithal to create your official plan of record for the product. This "binder" serves as a repository for all product documentation, a communication vehicle, and a learning mechanism for all members of a cross-functional product team. The Product Master Plan keeps everyone on the same page.

Chapter 3—Leadership: Creating Influence provides you with the context for understanding the human dimension of your job. Most product managers don't have people from other business functions reporting to them. However, product managers are responsible for the success of their products. This chapter explores the people side of Product Management and provides helpful ideas to create a collaborative working environment—one in which all functional contributions can be successfully melded together, guided by the "vision" of the product manager in the creation and management of successful products.

Chapter 4—Cross-Functional Product Teams: Getting Things Done picks up cues from the previous chapter, and melds them into the primary work structure used to plan and carry out the work of the product as a business. First, it draws the distinction between a product team and a project team. Then, it provides you with the mechanics involved in clarifying roles and responsibilities so that the right team members get the work done. In the end, the cross-functional product team is the "board of directors" for the product and is accountable for optimizing the product's performance in the market.

Chapter 5—Decision Making: What's Next? The theme "what's next" appears many times throughout this book because it's exactly what product managers face every day. Across a product's life cycle, the product manager will be faced with situations arising day by day and hour by hour that require the assimilation of data, analytics, thought, and an action, namely, a decision. This chapter focuses on the product manager's challenge of assessing these situations and making the best decision possible on behalf of the product, the product team, and the company.

Chapter 6—Finance for the Product Manager: Keeping Score is the last chapter that rounds out the foundational areas upon which product managers must rely to plan and run their businesses. You won't get an MBA in finance here, but you'll get a solid dose of financial terminology. You will also learn the financial tools and methods used to plan and manage products across the life cycle.

With this in mind, let's start building the foundation!

WHAT IS PRODUCT MANAGEMENT?

Executive Summary

- Product Management is the "holistic business management of the product" from the time it is conceived as an idea to the time it is discontinued and withdrawn from the market.
- Product Managers play a central role in Product Management. They are business managers. With the mindset of a general manager or a "mini-CEO" for the product's business, they lead a cross-functional team to achieve the product's strategic intent.
- Organizations can achieve greater levels of efficiency if everyone uses a common vocabulary when referring to practices, processes, and documents.

The Introduction states that Product Management is the pivot point of successful business. However, the role of Product Management as a functional discipline in a company is poorly understood, and its associated practices are inconsistently applied. Before offering a remedy for this situation, it's necessary to explain precisely what I mean by Product Management. First, I will break down each of these words, *Product* and *Management,* and analyze their meaning. Then, I will define Product Management from a holistic perspective.

You will master the "how" much more quickly when you comprehend the overall context of the discipline of Product Management. Just like the assembly–disassembly demonstrations that apprentice mechanics are shown before learning to repair an engine, this chapter offers a rapid, break-down-and-reassemble orientation to Product Management. If you're using this book for sequential study, your grasp of the material will be deeper if you understand the foundational concepts covered.

Four questions must be answered to completely define Product Management:

1. What is a product?
2. What is management?
3. What is Product Management?
4. How does Product Management work to transform a business?

In this chapter, each of these questions will be explored in turn.

QUESTION 1: WHAT IS A PRODUCT?

In the *PDMA Handbook of New Product Development* (2nd ed., Wiley), the glossary contains the following definition for *Product*: "A term used to describe all goods, services, and knowledge sold. Products are bundles of attributes (features, functions, benefits, and uses) and can either be tangible, as in the case of physical goods; intangible as in the case of those associated with service benefits; or can be a combination of the two." Webster's online dictionary indicates, "A product is something that is produced."

These definitions are a good start, but there is much more to the story. Within a business context, a product is not always a single, stand-alone item; instead, within most companies, there is a hierarchy of products and services. A product may be part of another product or product line, packaged with a group of products, or offered as a solution or system to meet broad sets of customer needs. Products and product lines are usually part of a larger product portfolio—either in a single firm, in a business unit, or in a division of a larger company. Alternatively, products can be broken down into product elements, modules, or terms (as in a credit card). Products may be built upon product platforms or product architectures. In order to visualize this hierarchy, consider the model shown in Figure 1.1.

FIGURE 1.1

Typical Hierarchy of Products and Services

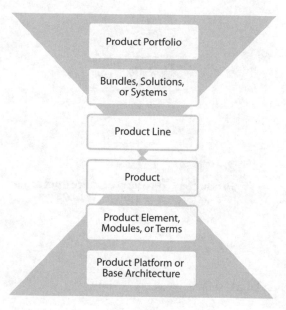

In the business sense, then, we need a workable definition of the word *product*: a product is anything that is sold, tangible or intangible. Businesses can create products to sell to other businesses (business-to-business, or B2B) or to consumers (business-to-consumer, or B2C). Businesses can also sell products to other businesses that then sell to consumers (business-to-business-to-consumer, or B2B2C). Some of these products are merely resold to end customers, while others are sold as parts of products.

Think of how an automobile parts manufacturer sells parts to an automobile company. The auto company is like an assembly business; in most cases, it doesn't even manufacture any of the parts. Auto companies sell to dealers (other businesses), who ultimately sell to consumers or other businesses.

Product Lines

Frequently, companies collect a number of related products into *product lines*. Very few companies carry isolated, one-off products. A product line, depicted in Figure 1.2, is a grouping of products geared toward similar markets or solving a particular type of customer problem. Typically,

FIGURE 1.2

Product Line Hierarchy

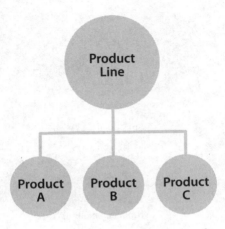

FIGURE 1.3

BMW Automobile Product Lines (source: www.bmw.com)

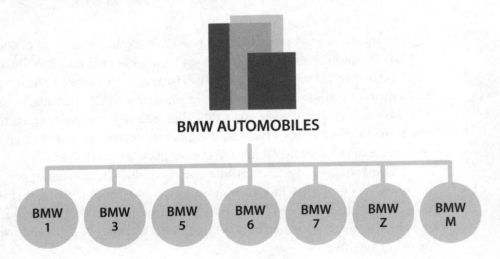

products within a line serve similar markets or can be produced via similar methods. In effect, a product line is a small product portfolio. For example, BMW Group has several different automobile product lines: The Mini brand, the Rolls-Royce brand, and the BMW automobile brand. The BMW Automobile Division has several cars in its product line. These product lines are depicted in Figure 1.3.

Product Portfolios

A product portfolio is the set of all products, product lines, or other groupings within a business unit or business division. Portfolios can include existing products, which may be at various phases of their own life cycles, as well as incoming products (those anticipated, actually in development, or in the launch phases). In smaller organizations, a single product or product line may in fact comprise the entire portfolio. A visual example of this type of product portfolio is shown in Figure 1.4.

In most firms, several products and product lines are grouped together to make up a product portfolio. Common approaches to organizing product portfolios include the following:

1. *The markets on which the products focus.* For example, a medical device firm may group a set of product lines—hearing aids, reading glasses, and motorized wheelchairs—into a "seniors" portfolio.
2. *Types of products produced.* In this case, a toy company might have a bicycle portfolio made up of three lines: tricycles, mountain bikes, and BMX bikes.

FIGURE 1.4

General Product Portfolio Structure

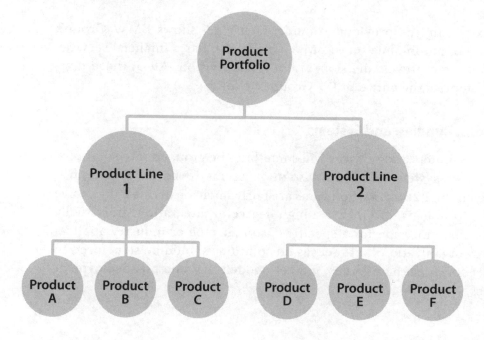

3. *Broad functional themes.* This structure is used by many technology firms that want to create tight linkages across the organization to minimize duplication and encourage collaboration. For example, a firm could be organized into three main areas: hardware, software, and professional services.

4. *Types of materials or development methods used.* An example of this organizational approach could be a cookware company that divides its product lines according to the type of metal used: cast iron, copper, and aluminum.

The choice of organizing principle for a product portfolio will vary widely from company to company. In some instances, one product line may be assigned to two different portfolios at the same time. For example, a major computer equipment vendor has a secure server product that sits both in the security portfolio and the multiprocessor computing portfolio. Ideally, this would not be the case, but in some instances this kind of dual assignment makes sense.

Product portfolio management and the related activities of portfolio optimization and balance are an important part of the strategic planning and strategic management of an organization, whether that organization is a company, business unit, division, or product line. The topic of product portfolio management is covered in more detail in Chapter 21.

Extending the previous example, Figure 1.5 shows BMW Group's portfolio of automobile lines. BMW Group also has a financial services division, a motorcycle division, and a retail division. All of those divisions comprise the entire BMW Group portfolio.

Solutions, Bundles, and Systems

Related products and services will sometimes be grouped into solutions, bundles, or systems. The word *solution* seems to be used more frequently in the B2B arena. Solutions are fairly intricate because they solve complex problems, often have a high degree of integration, and usually require customization for a specific customer type or industry application. An organization that focuses on solutions should be structured to support solutions-based sales, marketing, delivery, and postdeployment services.

FIGURE 1.5

BMW Group Automobile Portfolio

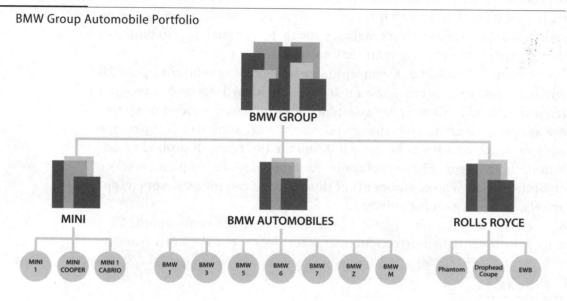

Companies that effectively organize for a solutions or systems business may utilize a solutions marketing group or even a professional services unit. These people can stay "close to the market" or be intimately
involved with a particular customer. Optimally, this enables the discovery
of opportunities that bring together the needed products, technologies,
and services, whether sourced internally or externally. There is typically a
large consultative aspect of every solution sale.

The term *solution* is sometimes used inappropriately. In principle,
every product should be a solution to some problem. If you assume that
every product is really a benefit-filled solution, then every company is
really in the solutions business. However, in reality, grouping products
together when they don't solve a customer's problem from start to finish
is merely the act of *bundling.* If a company wishes to sell a bundled solution, customers will eventually discover a weakness in one or more of the
components and look for another way to solve their problems. There is a
quick and easy way to determine whether a given solution is actually a
bundle. In a B2B setting, if purchasing agents can pick the offer apart to
shop the individual components, it is a bundle.

Bundling can, at times, represent an appropriate strategy, but bundles held out to be complete, seamless solutions might create excess

overhead for the organization. Companies should avoid adding overhead with a solution that doesn't increase profit or add value for the customer. Bundles do not generally contribute much to product profitability, so they may be more trouble than they are worth.

Figure 1.6 provides a conceptual snapshot of a solution in a B2B environment. In this case, several internal product lines and a product from an external company are assembled, to which value-added programs are supplied, such as consulting and operational support. The package adds value for customers because it offers the full range of problem resolution, including diagnosis, solution recommendations, implementation, and integration. The components of this solution cannot be shopped separately, so it is a genuine solution.

Here's an example of how a real solution might come about. IBM sells solutions. It brings products and services together, both from its

FIGURE 1.6

How Solutions Are Structured

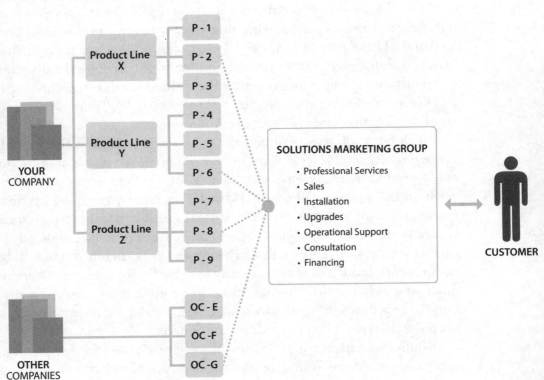

own divisions and other partners. IBM and its partners believe that there is tremendous added value to customers if it is *the* single face the customer sees, offering both diagnostics and problem solving.

Now, suppose a company makes medical devices and its customers are complaining of delayed shipments, damaged goods, and incorrectly labeled parts. This is costing time, money, and reputation. IBM has a consultative session with the stakeholders and executes a process discovery that reveals the company has a supply chain problem. It can be addressed with some physical products (from Cisco), some software (from Oracle), and some services from IBM Consulting. IBM offers to be the single point of contact for complete business analysis, customization, implementation, testing, turn-up, and postsales support. Because the medical device company doesn't have the people resources to analyze and fix complex problems like this, and they can't easily purchase this combination of products and expertise as separate line items, they purchase the solution.

Product Elements and Modules

Another key distinction in the definition of products is the idea of product elements or modules. For tangible products, these are product components that may be treated as "black boxes" inside the product. For example, if an appliance company buys electric motors from another firm in order to manufacture appliances, then the motor is a product element. If the motor is mounted in a larger housing with a wiring harness, then that could be called a "power module" or some equivalent expression indicating that it is a subassembly as a part of the product.

If another division supplies a product with a complex part at a suitable price, it may not be worthwhile to break down the part into individual components. For example, when developing software, modules of the code could be sourced elsewhere and then linked together later. There are also *intangible* modules, which might include features or terms. A bank's credit card line, for instance, may treat features, terms, or conditions as product elements. Whatever these modules, elements, or subassemblies are, they are building blocks of a product that may require individual Product Management oversight of their definition, design, and integration with a larger product or solution.

Platforms

The last piece of the product puzzle that needs to be defined is the product platform. The platform represents the underlying foundations, technology frameworks, base architectures, and interfaces upon which products are built. The platform provides commonality so that a higher degree of standardization can be achieved across a portfolio. This standardization contributes to larger economies of scale and greater flexibility in designing and styling products, so that the company can meet the needs of different market segments or customers.

As an avid automobile enthusiast, I often read about automobile companies to learn about the evolution of their models, designs, shared components, and platforms. Over the past few years, either because of competitive necessity, design flexibility, or needed scale economies, many automakers have embraced the platform concept. They are now rationalizing their platforms in search of greater efficiency as they expand globally. The degree to which firms share parts and other product elements or modules across their platforms is phenomenal (e.g., motors for electric windows, speedometers, and other components). In a recent article, one of the major automakers stated that it would reduce its number of global platforms by 50 percent within a few years. This type of platform rationalization will cultivate solid product foundations that can be designed for local markets or to suit local tastes. Figure 1.7 is a visual representation of this concept.

In *The Power of Product Platforms*, Marc Meyer and Alvin Lehnerd state: "Product platforms must be managed. If a platform is not rejuvenated, its derivative products will become *dated* and will fail customers in terms of function and value. If a company's platforms are renewed periodically . . . redesigned to incorporate new functions, components, and materials, the product family will remain robust through successive generations." They go on to say, "Robust product platforms do not happen by accident. They are the result of a unique methodology and of strategies for designing, developing, and revitalizing them over time."

Platform usage can be problematic for some large companies that have grown through mergers and acquisitions. Issues can arise when platforms are so complex (and old) that they are difficult to merge into a unified platform. Large banks, for example, may have many different platforms for processing credit card transactions or for managing deposits. If you contact a large banking company's call center, you may be asked about the state or region in which you live, so they know which

FIGURE 1.7

Platform Visualization Within the Product Portfolio

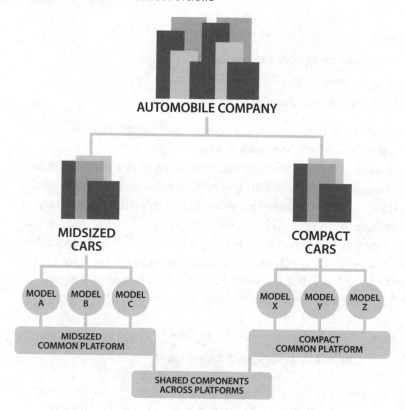

system to access. In one of my corporate jobs, we visited a wireless communications company that had gone through many mergers. Management was distraught because it had five different billing systems, and the bill-consolidating mechanism was "dropping" about 30 percent of the billing records, causing the company to lose millions of dollars in revenue.

QUESTION 2: WHAT IS MANAGEMENT?

Thus far, I've focused on products: I defined the different kinds of products and product offshoots, whether they are product lines, product elements and modules, platforms, solutions, or the product portfolio.

The second major part of this discourse on Product Management focuses on the art of management itself. The word *management* derives from Latin: *manu agere,* or "to lead by the hand." In most books about management, definitions generally include the usual cycle of business elements:

- Setting goals
- Directing human and financial resources
- Assessing outcomes
- Reassessing and/or resetting goals

I recall a professor from college saying, "managing means getting things done . . . period." Most business leaders would agree.

In Product Management, the person in charge is the product manager. However, considering the multifaceted definition of *product* established earlier, it is not safe to assume a one-to-one relationship between product and product manager. While that model may hold true at some organizations, a product manager can be partly or wholly responsible for all or part of a product platform or architecture, a module or series of modules, a single product, a product line (a small product portfolio), or several product lines (a larger portfolio).

What Is a Product Manager?

- The product manager is a business manager, appointed to be a proactive product or product line "mini-CEO," business leader, or general manager.
- The product manager leads a cross-functional product team.
- The product team's responsibility is to optimize the product's market position and financial returns, consistent with corporate, business unit, or division strategies.

What Does a Product Manager Really Do?

It is an accepted principle that product managers bear responsibility for everything under their purview (e.g., the range of operation, authority, control, or concern). This is an awesome level of responsibility and assumes the product manager has a number of distinct competencies. Although these competencies cannot be perfectly honed down to a finite number of abilities and expectations, there are some specific practices (things you need to do) that, when done well, will not only get your job done properly but also earn you credibility and enhance your stature—and contribute greatly to your success as a business leader. These practices include:

- *Integrating and synchronizing.* Across the life cycle, the work output of many people performing a wide range of functions must be orchestrated to achieve a common goal (e.g., the completion of a new product, the upgrade of a current product, or any initiative to improve the product's business or market performance). In order to deliver results and positive outcomes, product managers must be able to see the big picture; they must also be able to "connect the dots" among all aspects of the product's business.

- *Leading and influencing.* There is a distinct difference between managing and leading. Managing implies explicit authority over individuals. Leadership, on the other hand, means you must convince those individuals to follow your vision.

- *Cross-functional teaming.* Product managers cannot have their eyes on everything about the product that's important. Thus they need the help of many people, including those who bring specialized expertise from diverse areas and functions. Utilizing these skills and perspectives is critical to the product's success. The product manager organizes and leads a cross-functional team composed of people who can perform the tasks necessary to achieve success for the product. In addition to leading the team, the product manager must be able to facilitate discussions and debate, mediate conflict, and nurture a collaborative, "functional" cross-functional team that can ultimately act as the board of directors for the product.

- *Solving problems and making decisions.* Product managers must continually strive to make better decisions in near real time at every point across the product's life cycle. While good decision-making skills can be learned and cultivated, this education comes best from actual practice rather than following advice from textbooks.

- *Financial planning and analysis.* Planning for product profitability and assessing the profitability of existing products is an important dimension of Product Management. Companies invest money in products, and these products are expected to yield a positive return to the business. Product managers should be expected to fulfill the responsibility of planning for profitability; therefore they need a solid understanding of the financials.

■ *Assessing the industry and competition.* One of the jobs of the product manager is to interpret the environment within which the company participates, and where it may operate in the future. Furthermore, the company's products compete with other company's products across that industry landscape. Whether or not there are formal structures within the company that gather and archive this data, it is the product manager's responsibility to assimilate data about the industry and competitive environment. With this insight, a product manager can consider strategies for the product as well as understand how the company allocates investments across the product portfolio.

■ *Segmenting markets, identifying target customers, and uncovering customer needs.* Segmentation requires a joint effort that not only involves the cross-functional team but may also include outside research firms. Regardless of what needs to be done, the product manager often takes primary responsibility for directing this activity and keeping it on track. The product manager *must own this activity*, if for no other reason than to prevent bias typically associated with function-driven market research. Bear in mind, however, that customer-oriented market research and segmentation is no substitute for the hard work of discovering customer needs. Sometimes even the customer is unaware of a basic need; in other words, there *is* a "better" way. The product manager must drive this discovery process and own the results.

■ *Forecasting.* Forecasting volumes, market share, and revenue is an essential part of the product manager's job. Of all the jobs done in part by other groups, this is *the least likely to be owned elsewhere*. Frequently, a new product manager barely has a foot in the door before someone is asking for projections. The product manager must own this activity from start to finish.

■ *Formulating product and marketing strategies.* Establishing a vision for the product and crafting a path to the future rests with the product manager, who receives help from the cross-functional team. The most important responsibility of the product manager is to align the strategies for the product with those of the organization, and to make sure they interlock across the constellation of product portfolio investment possibilities.

- *Leveraging the Product Management Life Cycle Model.* Before explaining the model, it is important to note that the product manager must not only craft the strategy for the product but integrate that strategy such that appropriate systematic planning will support the product's development, launch, and management across its in-market life cycle. The product manager has the primary responsibility for creating and maintaining the various plans, documents, and other records required to give life to a product and keep it healthy. Furthermore, the product manager needs to make sure these plans are put into action. Product managers provide cross-functional oversight as product-related projects are carried out. Finally, product managers provide strategic and tactical management of products that are already in the market in different phases of the product's life cycle. This may include adjusting the levers of the marketing mix, influencing new product plans for enhancements or derivatives, or creating plans for replacement products. The work of the product manager here is to constantly collect and analyze performance data (e.g., market, financial, and operational) in order to identify new opportunities for the business.

Besides these practices, a number of important documents must be owned or heavily influenced by the product manager. These include the Product Strategy, the Business Case, the Launch Plan, the Marketing Plan, and the Product Requirements. These are explained, expanded upon, and exemplified in detail elsewhere within this book.

QUESTION 3: WHAT IS PRODUCT MANAGEMENT?

It is said that Procter & Gamble conceived of Product Management in the 1930s as a way to improve the oversight of its ever-expanding consumer products business. The concept of Product Management and its myriad interpretations has permeated the core of product and service companies around the world. It has long been a challenge for businesses to unify the disparate activities performed by people in different business functions under the umbrella of Product Management.

So what is Product Management? Based on the answers to the first two key questions, *Product Management is the business management of products, product lines, or portfolios, holistically, for maximum value creation, across their life cycles.* Managing products is akin to managing small businesses within bigger business. Sometimes an organization has one product; sometimes it has several. You will see references to the expression "product as a business" quite often throughout this book.

Now that the business world is moving at warp speed, many companies have arrived at an epiphany. Business leaders are announcing, "We're reorganizing the firm to focus on Product Management. We're going to revitalize our Product Management function." After investigating what these companies are planning to do and why, one thing is clear: they recognize that Product Management offers a way to improve their old style of management. They want to focus on their products as mini-businesses, that is, small businesses within their overall business. In addition, these companies are seeking to collectively manage all the products within a product line or portfolio in the way one might manage a portfolio of investments. There are a variety of drivers for decisions to reorganize, including poor product performance, product duplication in global markets, and even channel conflict. Reform is engendered by problems, and it is usually some business problem or challenge that leads an organization to Product Management as a way forward.

Product Management (big P, big M) is, at its core, a model for a business organization. *This model includes discovering, innovating, strategizing, planning, developing, introducing, managing, and marketing products.* In essence, Product Management alters the genetics of the organization up and down, as well as across business functions. Firms that employ this model generally focus on the market first and then concentrate on either the generalized needs of broad market segments or the explicit needs of target customer types. This kind of outside-in view of the marketplace will increase the likelihood of producing better business results and optimizing the value of the product portfolio. As mentioned earlier, implicit in this view is the fact that the business benefits when products are treated like investments in a portfolio of businesses (products), allowing for a more granular approach to strategic and tactical product planning. With this approach, the products become the building blocks of the organization.

> The function of Product Management is not necessarily a linear set of actions and work flows. Rather, it is a dynamic system that depends on the work of various people and many interconnected processes across the lives of many products and portfolios.

> (From my book titled *Managing Product Management*)

Does this statement imply that Product Management supports the entire organization? No, not at all. Though Product Management is genetic, it touches and influences all the organic supporting structures—all the business functions. Think of the human body: Product Management is in the genetic material; it's in the skeleton; it's in the circulatory system, the neural network, and, of course, the command and control center (the brain).

All actions of the body work together, holistically, toward a single goal: homeostasis, or balance. Therefore, everyone in the organization is (virtually, if not literally) in Product Management in some way or another, and everyone needs to understand the roles, responsibilities, commitment, and deliverables that make the business (body) work properly.

QUESTION 4: HOW DOES PRODUCT MANAGEMENT TRANSFORM A BUSINESS?

Answering the first three questions posed at the start of this chapter has yielded a detailed definition of Product Management. In order to gain a comprehensive understanding of this definition, however, it's necessary to illustrate the way that Product Management transforms good ideas into successful products—and how companies benefit from a well-organized Product Management structure.

The simplest way to achieve this is to use the Product Management Life Cycle Model, shown in Figure 1.8, and the four Areas of Work that help to surface ideas and then bring products from idea to final sale.

FIGURE 1.8

The Product Management Life Cycle Model and Four Main Areas of Work

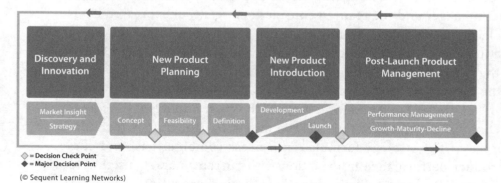

◇ = Decision Check Point
◆ = Major Decision Point

(© Sequent Learning Networks)

These four Areas of Work are Discovery and Innovation, New Product Planning, New Product Introduction, and Post-Launch Product Management (PLPM).

Out of necessity, the model is a linear, progressive, and static depiction of something that is actually three-dimensional, recursive, and dynamic—but for most purposes, it's a useful approximation.

Underneath two of the visualized Areas of Work undertaken by product managers (i.e., New Product Planning and New Product Introduction) is a standard phase-gate product development process—or as some refer to it, the NPD (or New Product Development) process. Companies seeking to improve cycle time or time to market have utilized phase-gate processes for decades. Venture capitalists also follow a similar methodology when selecting the best investments to optimize returns to their business. An explanation of this phase-gate process follows later in this chapter, with more details to follow in Module 3.

Discovery and Innovation

The Area of Work called Discovery and Innovation serves as a business canvas to capture data, derive insights, and formulate strategies. Consider what an explorer might think about when embarking on a journey into the unknown. Explorers are driven by an intense curiosity to learn and to share. In doing so, they also establish a pathway for others to follow. And so it must be for product managers, who serve to light beacons of possibility for others in the organization.

While the Discovery and Innovation box is fixed in the model, the work involved is never a one-time event. For example, insights are not derived from a single study, but of market-oriented observations that are captured over time. This ongoing signal processing is required for the product manager and the team to consider emergent, unexpressed challenges faced by customers, trends in a given industry, or actions taken by competitors. A continual stream of market and business snapshots provides the wherewithal to energize product managers and their teams. In turn, the insights or "aha" moments will reveal strategic possibilities for the product's business. Therefore, some of the most important outcomes from Discovery and Innovation are the inputs to the strategy formulation process. The strategy formulation process combines past and current product performance information with current market insights to set a direction and lay the groundwork for flawless execution.

New Product Planning Phases

The Area of Work called New Product Planning serves primarily as a backdrop for guiding decision making. It is also used to ensure that the proper cross-functional work gets done in the "phases" so that optimal product investment decisions can be made. Its physical size in relation to the other Areas of Work is intentionally larger to represent the amount of time and effort that should be devoted to planning by the product manager and the team. The expression "go slowly and carefully first so you can go faster later" is the mantra for New Product Planning. There is no mandate to use the word *new* to describe this Area of Work. However, whether the product being planned is new or an enhancement to an existing product, there is usually something new being considered.

There are three phases and three decision gates within this Area of Work: the Concept phase, in which new ideas are generated and screened; the Feasibility phase, in which they are qualified in greater detail; and the Definition phase, whereby products are designed and specified so that they can be developed. While a brief explanation of each of these phases follows, a more thorough discussion is available in Module 3.

Concept phase work includes assessment of ideas for new products as well as for line extensions, feature enhancements and product derivatives, and new market entry with an existing product. It is a process designed to rapidly screen ideas, assess revenue potential, and establish the context to achieve differential advantage for a good fit within the overall product line or portfolio. The output document of this phase is an Opportunity Statement. At the conclusion of the phase, a decision check point (DCP) is reached and a review takes place: Either the concept will proceed to the next phase, or it will be rejected and work will stop.

For ideas that pass the Concept phase, the Feasibility phase provides a more in-depth review of the business, market, and technical dimensions of the proposal. The input to the phase is the Opportunity Statement and the outputs are a preliminary Business Case, preliminary Launch Plan, and high-level Functional Support Plans from each function. (Functional Support Plans are defined and discussed in Chapter 2.) If a project is considered feasible after a deeper assessment of market, technical, human resource, and economic perspectives, it can move to the Product Definition phase. If the opportunity does not meet the established criteria for acceptance, the project is stopped.

The Product Definition phase represents the activities that complete the market research, technical, resource, and operational analysis of the prospective program. In this phase, the product requirements and business capabilities needed to actually develop and launch a product are more deeply considered, and the future state marketing mix is solidified. Major funding for development is tied to the successful outcome of this phase. A final Business Case, Marketing Plan, and set of baselined Product Requirements are the primary output documents. It is possible to reject the Business Case if the risks are too great or if the criteria for acceptance are not met.

New Product Introduction Phases (Execution)

The Area of Work called New Product Introduction (again, "New" is optional) focuses on taking the plans and getting the work done—in other words, executing. These phases are portrayed sequentially in most NPD models. This is not how work should be carried out during New Product Introduction. While the product is being developed under the watchful eye of the product manager, a cross-functional launch team carries out the work needed to prepare the product for the market and ready the market for the product.

The Development phase begins after the project is approved and funded. It is the critical point in program execution when the product and all supporting materials and documentation are built or developed. It can be characterized by a series of projects or subprojects (some of which are functional and some cross-functional). It could include software development, manufacturing, or other programs involved with the actual delivery of the product in accordance with product requirements.

Carrying out the Launch phase work actually begins early in the Development phase and involves the activities used to bring the product to market. This is exemplified by the inverted triangles of Development and Launch. The launch is an integral part of the Product Management process and is an intense, cross-functional team endeavor. However, management of the Launch phase is often heavily driven by the Marketing function or, at the very least, done in close partnership between Product Management and Marketing. It represents an orderly sequencing of activities and events to bring the product to market.

Post-Launch Product Management

After the product is launched into the market, the product manager begins to focus on optimizing the performance of the products within the context of the strategies of the firm, division, and product line. Furthermore, the strategic management of products and services characterizes PLPM, including adjustments to the marketing mix (e.g., product, price, promotion, and channels), with broad oversight of Customer Service, Finance, and Operations. In order to run the business of the product, product team leaders should be adept at leveraging the membership of the cross-functional team when products are in the market.

Often PLPM is characterized by "blocking and tackling," fire drills, and other urgent tasks and activities. This job frustrates many product managers and can often undermine their credibility on the team as they try to placate too many people and answer the ever-changing priorities of the day. PLPM is further characterized by intense information collection and sharing about the product's performance and the activities of the marketplace. The leadership of the team entails communicating and collaborating such that appropriate market-based decisions can be made as the product moves through the market. A premium is placed on team leadership and the collaborative skills of product managers in the encouragement of efficient, rapid communication among team members.

Product Management: A Holistic Activity

The phases in the life of a product do not have clean edges: early phases blend into later ones, while later phases have deep roots in earlier phases of the process. Best practices that appear to belong in one part of the life cycle are active across the product life span. Tools and techniques morph throughout the life cycle, and even best-in-class documents tied to a particular point in time have elements that touch everything, from beginning to end, so that they become living, breathing documents. In fact, Product Management is a living process: it evolves; it changes; things wax and wane in importance. It is an interconnected, living system.

While the Product Management Life Cycle Model does help establish a clear line of sight, creating fantastic products is not a linear or easy process. Any real business and market environment is dynamic, with many important things active at the same time. Decisions made now affect future elements of the life cycle; a seemingly small change in any given moment can make a world of difference later. Learning along the way changes the implementation of the life cycle, though the life cycle itself doesn't change structurally very much. Experiencing the product in the market can change the strategy or influence decisions about next steps. Actions taken by management or competition may suddenly change your immediate goals or operating environment.

There are times when certain actions or pieces become more important, times when other parts are dynamic, and even times when one or more elements of the product environment must absolutely be static and stable. The product manager simultaneously manages each of these pieces separately yet also manages all of these pieces together, holistically, in harmony. And that is the ultimate definition of Product Management.

SUMMARY: WHY PRODUCT MANAGEMENT MATTERS

In my book *Managing Product Management* I placed great emphasis on the fact that Product Management should not be considered a passing fad, something nice to have, or the strategic imperative of the year. In the modern world, businesses compete on a global scale and competitive forces are relentless. About a quarter of the firms that I study do an exemplary job of Product Management, and about one-third are headed in the right direction. The remainder of firms have a lot of work to do to properly implement Product Management practices.

While Product Management is on the organization chart in many companies, the roles and expectations of product managers tend to vary widely. In my experience, a lot of the confusion in this area stems from people trying to figure out Product Management on their own. They develop an approach based on their own operational or functional paradigms, which very often leads to inconsistent, ineffective business operations.

When Product Management isn't properly chartered, aligned, or scoped, people have to work harder to achieve the same goals. Therefore, Product Management must be established in organizations as a core capability, and organizational models must be altered to support the function of Product Management and to effectively utilize the capabilities of product managers.

With this in mind, here is why Product Management matters:

- Product Management provides a framework for consistency in the use and governance of key business practices across the organization.
- Product Management is uniquely situated as the only "horizontal" business function that serves to integrate and synchronize the work of others across the organization.
- Product Management serves to align cross-functional leaders around the business of the product, not their own functional agendas. In other words, Product Management breaks down functional silos!
- Product Management, and the use of the Product Management Life Cycle Model sets the stage for continuous improvement of all business practices that support or enable Product Management and the work of product managers.

RAISING YOUR PRODUCT MANAGEMENT EXPERIENCE QUOTIENT (PMEQ)

1. If you are new to Product Management or are considering a job in Product Management, visit the human resources department and ask them for some current product manager job descriptions. By reviewing them, you can recognize the kinds of tasks that product managers carry out in your company. You can also compare that description to some of the content in this book. This might help you devise some of your own professional development work.

2. A helpful method to learn about Product Management in your company is to have an information-sharing discussion with a senior member within the Product Management organization. Seeking out people and asking them about their career progression and how they gained experience along their career journeys will also give you a more interesting perspective on this job category. Further to this, ask to see an organization chart to see how Product Management is set up in the company.

3. If you're already a product manager, you have at least one product for which you are responsible. That product (hopefully) solves a unique customer problem. From time to time, you should be able to verify that the product actually does solve a customer's problem and that the product

carries a differential advantage in the marketplace. It may help you to reflect on or reevaluate some of the foundations on which your product is built, such as:

- The unique customer problem it helps to solve
- The type of customer who has this problem
- The reasons these customers choose your product over a competitor's

4. Within your company or division, there will be some relationships or connections between products. There could be shared platform elements, technologies, or components. Understanding these connections and documenting them in a visual way has value by helping you recognize a variety of factors that might influence your product. One idea would be to find out about the existence of product, product line, and product portfolio diagrams, as shown in samples throughout this chapter. If they don't exist, you might try to draw them yourself using a variety of resources such as your company's website, and by visiting the product managers or individuals responsible for those products to have them help you with those drawings.

5. If there are any true "solutions" sold by your company, perhaps you can learn about these in your discussions with Product Management leaders, marketing leaders, or perhaps in a professional services department in the company. Try to learn about how these solutions solve bigger customer problems, and ask if you can review any real case studies related to how these solutions actually solved customers' problems.

6. What type of thought or technical leadership does your company exhibit? Are there any documents or resources you can explore to help you learn about your company's distinctive advantage?

7. Your company may employ platforms or may have the opportunity to develop them. You can learn more about these product platforms by finding out if there is a platform organization. If there is, it is usually a chief platform architect or an equivalent group of people who have this responsibility. Visit these architects and have them describe the major platform elements as they are shared across product lines. This is critical if you are going to be creating product requirements for which you will need to rely on your ability to clarify systemic dependencies and interfaces. Additional work you might want to carry out in this area includes:

- Secure documentation to describe how the platform supports (or will support) current or future products.

- Review key drawings and documentation. Learn how the platform interfaces with the products. Learn if there are specific interface rules when defining products and writing requirements.
- Find out who, in your product development organization, is responsible for coordinating and testing interfaces with the platform group.
- Find out the process for making suggestions to the platform group to influence their evolution.

8. Find out about the product development process used in your organization. Get as much information and documentation as you can to learn about the terminology, documents, and protocols for planning, development, launching, and ongoing management of products. You can learn about this by working with a variety of people in Product Management and product development. Be sure you don't look at the development process from only the perspective of the Product Development department. Remember its functional process interlocks with the overall product development process.

CHAPTER

2

THE PRODUCT MASTER PLAN

Executive Summary

- All product managers needs a unified "plan of record" for the product or product line for which they are responsible.
- A Product Master Plan is the centerpiece meta-document that houses all product documentation.
- The Product Master Plan is the perfect "tribal knowledge" document in organizations where people may come and go but the product remains.

One of the questions I often pose to participants in workshops or to product managers during diagnostic interviews is this: "When you started your job as a product manager, was there any documentation to which you could refer in order to find out what was going on with the product you inherited?" Ask yourself this question as you read this paragraph. What goes through your mind? The usual answer is that there was little, or nothing, "on the shelf." The purpose of this chapter is to furnish you with a useful tool and introduce you to a methodology. It will help you learn which documents you need in order to better manage a product and the importance of having a single place to keep your current documentation. Ultimately these will become historical records for future product managers who may inherit your product.

THE PURPOSE OF A MASTER PLAN

When a state, municipal government, university, or other institution wants to establish a plan for facilities, human resources, equipment, thorough-fares, housing, or other elements of its infrastructure, "crisis mode" planning really cannot hold up. Devising a grand vision for a new community center, a major park, or a larger police force will not make it happen. What is needed is a complete strategy—one that covers near-term tactical plans plus long-term plans that often stretch decades into the future. Regardless of how well the strategy is conceived, every well-run municipality has a rigorous system or method to capture these plans and documents. This document repository and its archives serve as a plan of record for current and future activities. This collection of plans and information for a municipality, government, or institution is called the Master Plan. For the product manager, it is called the Product Master Plan. The content of the Product Master Plan serves as a mirror into the past, a bookmark for the product as it is currently situated, and as a roadmap to the future.

This plan of record is particularly important because so much is always going on. If you're busy implementing year two of a five-year plan, it's easy to forget that year three is coming and there are things to do ahead of time. Unless you keep good records, it is also easy to forget that you already solved a year four problem back in year one, and, therefore, not to budget for it again.

Note that *the Master Plan is not the strategy*. Many government development programs have a life span far beyond that of a single individual or administration, but the strategies may change with each election. So how do these projects and programs ever get completed? Obviously, long-range programs get completed because the previous administration not only did its homework but also captured that homework in some repositories for the next officials to inherit. The content of that repository is what makes up their Master Plan.

At the end of an implementation cycle (which could be a fiscal year), the Master Plan is updated, filed, and archived—never discarded. It needs to be available so that future generations of employees, residents, students, or historians—or anyone for that matter—can look back to see how the organization, institution, or municipality evolved over time. They can use it as a learning mechanism or as a way to communicate. They may even come back to it to implement some phases or activities that were never completed due to budget limitations, turnover, or unexpected changes in priorities.

Most organizations have some formal plan of record. Publicly traded companies should have one because they are not only accountable to their shareholders but also obligated to fulfill corporate governance guidelines. These larger plans are usually an amalgam of the more tactical plans and outcomes that guide the organization through a given fiscal period. Product Master Plans may also include the "official" visible plans used to communicate to shareholders, stakeholders, and other entities that have a vested interest in the success of the company, even if they don't contribute directly to the day-to-day operation of the firm.

Sometimes the plan of record is truly a strategic plan that serves to guide the organization into the future. Quite often these documents are used to demonstrate to industry analysts or securities analysts that the future of the organization is sound. More often these documents are created for a select group of executive team members as a decision-making platform, with the hope that objectives flowing from these plans will cascade to individual contributors and their managers for execution.

Plans Change

The Product Master Plan is a living, evolving collection of plans and documents. Let's face facts: plans are just that—plans. They change as new information and new events enter the picture; they become stale as objectives are missed or unsupported (i.e., bad) decisions are made; and sometimes they simply don't reflect a realistic approach to the dynamic affairs of real business operations. When those things happen, the Product Master Plan is simply updated to accommodate new information.

Although plans may change, a well-thought-out plan is generally less likely to be overcome by events than is a top-down plan that responds only to the most necessary elements of corporate planning. For example, a company requires forecasts and budgets. If that's all some managers provide, they stand a much greater chance of being viewed as "unsuccessful" by the boss compared with those who have a robust Product Master Plan that includes the best supporting documentation they can put forward. And if they have a plan of record that's at least fairly comprehensive, they are light years ahead of peers that have no plan of record at all.

This is very significant for your career and for the success of your product. When you are the "go to" person with the "well-oiled product machine" that's "highly visible," you reduce the chances that you or your product will face catastrophic cutbacks. But even if you aren't able to fight off a workforce reduction, documentation has value for your professional stature as a product manager—and for your own integrity and reputation.

When organizations eliminate experienced professionals, they lose mentors and coaches who take with them many years of experience and possibly critical product data. Offshoring continues to pull teams apart; so does turnover, a lack of time, chronic understaffing, and various exigencies of the moment. All of these issues, and more, contribute to the need for stronger documentation. At the end of the day, if you want to be recognized as a committed, professional product manager, you must take, keep, and share good notes—which means a strong, well-documented Product Master Plan.

THE FORMAT OF THE PRODUCT MASTER PLAN

The Product Master Plan is not a long deck of presentation slides. When I work with clients' product teams, I often ask them to produce documents like Marketing Plans, Business Cases, Product Strategies, and so on. These are typically requested as formal, written documents and are ideally signed by authorized leaders of the various business functions that have a vested interest. Over the years, I've asked various stakeholders to provide evidence of specific documents. At times people have been unable to produce any such artifacts. Other times, they offer something incomplete or provide a reflection on the work of various people that lacks a cohesive story line and appropriate context.

You cannot capture critical Product Management thought processes, arguments, and other important data in a deck of presentation slides. Yet because everyone is in a rush to get the job done, slides become the default. However, there are no back-up data. The only consistently applied standard follows the current corporate presentation format standards. Usually, with the use of a slide deck, people are neither able to adequately track changes to rapidly evolving documents nor create backups. When product people leave their jobs, they clean out their files, clear off the shelves, return their computers and electronic devices, and go on to their next assignment or another company. Everything they learned and any documentation they may have created all goes away. Then a new person comes into the job, occupies a new cubicle or office, and finds little or nothing on the shelf while facing the unhappy prospect of spending six months or more just figuring out where things stand. A product manager in a large pharmaceutical company once expressed the following (paraphrased) lament:

> I came into this job after three years in the field (sales). It took me six months to figure out what was going on and another six months to be productive . . . I just didn't know whether I was doing the right things right or the wrong things right . . . there's no one to learn from because everyone has the same issue . . . I can't wait to finish this and get back into the field.

The Product Master Plan represents the "must-have" platform to establish plans of record for a product organization and the cross-functional team driving product success.

THE VALUE OF A PRODUCT MASTER PLAN

An appropriate (i.e., proper and sufficient) amount of documentation for the planning, development, and management of a product or product line is critical to the product team's success. Notice the word *appropriate*; it is an important distinction. Having the appropriate amount of documentation helps to capture the product's business goals, clarifies roles and responsibilities, and serves as an archive for the product across the life cycle. A Product Master Plan is the perfect holding document—the meta-archive or master control plan for any product.

I often use the word *binder* to refer to the Product Master Plan. It conjures up an image of a ringed notebook whose pages can be updated, added to, or replaced. It's an evocative image that reminds us of how documents were stored in the past—even though many people still use them! Nowadays most documents are actually stored electronically, as users prefer the more sophisticated methods available. So, don't get hung up on the word *binder*. Rather, think of the best way to organize and store your documents so that they can be easily updated (with the appropriate changes to versions!) and made available to members of the product team, process owners, and the like. Whether you use a physical binder or an electronic repository, the product manager should control the stored material meticulously so it can serve as the definitive "go to" repository.

The product manager holds the complete master copy; however, all team stakeholders must be familiar with the entire contents of the Product Master Plan at all times. Depending on the organization, members of the cross-functional team should have ready access to the latest revisions and be notified of updates. Remember, everyone must see the same thing in order to make coherent decisions.

A single-source, up-to-date Product Master Plan is the best way to ensure consistent knowledge across the cross-functional team and beyond because the product manager, as primary steward of the Product Master Plan, is responsible for dissemination of its contents and any changes that are made.

In addition to the earlier arguments, some of the key benefits of a Product Master Plan are as follows:

- It's the perfect communication platform among cross-functional product team members because it serves as a standard way to capture their commitments, both to the team and to each other.
- It is a mechanism that enables effective decision making within the context of the Product Management Life Cycle Model, not just during the phases of New Product Planning or New Product Introduction.
- It is the ideal archive for major product-related documents such as strategies, Business Cases, Marketing Plans, financial documents, and project plans.
- Its importance and value ensures that product strategies are consistently reviewed and reconsidered as product plans and opportunities evolve.
- It can be constantly updated so that any team member can quickly sort out the current state of the product, which is especially useful for existing products.
- It is a learning mechanism for new team members or even a new product manager.
- It is an ideal starting point when creating a brand new product.
- It is a great continuity tool. Accumulated wisdom shouldn't be ignored. Families and tribes have practices, rules, and traditions that pass from generation to generation, sometimes for centuries. Cultures have memes, and societies have laws, myths, legends, and superstitions. All of these, however silly or apocryphal they may seem, transmit at least a little wisdom and a lot of continuity. With enough care, the Product

Master Plan can act as this "tribal knowledge" from one "generation" of products and product managers to the next.

- It is a perfect tool to build a "community of practice" among product managers in your firm because it contains information about process usage and performance management and inspires organizational learning in general.
- It clarifies roles and responsibilities of all product team members across the entire product life cycle.

The value of the Product Master Plan cannot be overemphasized. The Product Master Plan can be, and should be, the nucleus of everything related to the product. It is so fundamental to capturing the work efforts of a product team that it usually serves as the actual glue of the cross-functional product team.

AN INSURANCE POLICY FOR CONSISTENT COMMUNICATION

Document confusion is one of the key sources of inefficiency in organizations. While the documents mentioned in this book are named generically, each organization should create and maintain a consistent document library and applicable vocabulary. Each company or industry may have a standard nomenclature for some of these documents. Most of the documents held within the Product Master Plan are representative of the plans and activities being carried out by product managers or other cross-functional team members. There are some standard document names, including Business Case, Product Strategy, and Marketing Plan. Other documents may be referred to by a dozen different names. To achieve the goal of having a common set of documents you need to use each document's name consistently, making absolutely sure it is described adequately so that anyone can understand it.

THE BASIC CONSTRUCTION OF THE PRODUCT MASTER PLAN

The diagram shown as Figure 2.1 can be used like a table of contents or general outline for a Product Master Plan. The Product Master Plan is divided into three main sections:

1. Product and Product Line Documents
2. Organization Information
3. Product Business Information

FIGURE 2.1

Product Master Plan

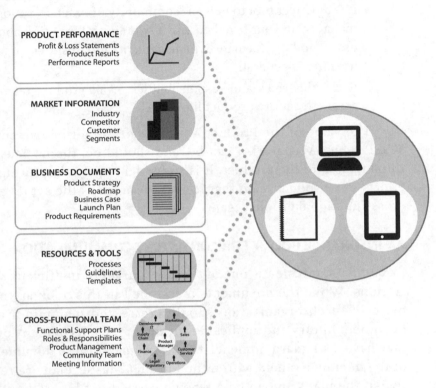

A discussion of each of these major items follows. Aside from these, however, there are many items shown in Figure 2.1 that you should consider including in your Product Master Plan.

PRODUCT AND PRODUCT LINE BUSINESS DOCUMENTS

This section lists and discusses the primary documents that most product managers will rely upon. There may be others that are used in your organization. I look at these main documents as fundamental to any product's business, regardless of life cycle state. You may find that there are many other product documents that are relevant to your company; be sure to include them too. In later chapters, these documents are discussed in more detail including how each should be constructed.

- *Strategic Plans.* It is important to have a place to hold the strategic plans for the product within the Product Master Plan. Effective Product Management considers the importance of strategy for steering products even during turbulent market activity. Furthermore, strategic plans represent the combined efforts of the cross-functional team to chart a path forward for products in the market. Successful organizations create, carry out, and modify their strategies on an ongoing basis. They continually seek to improve themselves by finding new and innovative ways to boost efficiency, streamline operations, and promote customer loyalty while adapting to market changes and new technologies.

- *Business Cases.* Product investments don't happen just because someone comes up with a good idea. Many ideas emerge across the product's life. The Business Case is the document used to clarify and justify investments for new products, product enhancements, and new market expansion. If these documents are not archived, future product managers and interested others will never know the Business Case history for the product. To put it simply, they won't know what you were thinking and why—especially if they are trying to assess a product's performance years into the future—when you aren't there to explain. Therefore, all Business Cases should be archived in the Product Master Plan.

- *Product Requirements Documents (PRDs).* All products have to be described so they can be developed, launched, and managed. PRDs describe how a product should work (how it functions) and the way in which its functionality is brought to life through its features, behaviors, attributes, or terms. PRDs reflect the needs of customers and provide a reference for technologists, designers, and developers who build products.

- *Product Roadmaps.* In order to set the direction for a product's business, strategic goals are spelled out in the Product Strategy. However, in order to clarify the path the product will travel, product roadmaps are needed. Product roadmaps reflect plans and programs that link strategy and market data with product business and technology decisions. Product roadmaps are also useful to help communicate business, strategic, and product plans to cross-functional product team members.

- *Product Launch Plans.* The Product Launch Plan establishes a product's path to market. It requires the alignment of many people who play important roles in the organization such as sales, marketing, customer service, and operations. The launch plan links the strategy to specific "go-to-market" activities, processes, and events that will ensure the product achieves its desired strategic, business, and financial objectives.

- *Marketing Plans created for the product.* There are myriad types of Marketing Plans. Some are done at the corporate level, some at the divisional level, and some at the product line level. There are even Marketing Plans for individual products within the product line. These documents have similar formats and flows, but their place in the organizational hierarchy means the focus of each plan differs slightly from area to area. Marketing Plans for the product are kept in the Product Master Plan because it captures the other marketing mix elements that support the product. These may include pricing programs, advertising and promotional plans, and distribution channel strategies for the product.

- *Product Discontinuation Plans.* Product managers invariably encounter products that have reached the end of their life cycle. For any product that must be brought to its conclusion, a Product Discontinuation Plan serves to guide the product team in the proper procedures and protocols to decommission the product and infrastructure that supports the product.

- *Functional Support Plans (FSPs).* FSPs represent the commitments by each business function to the cross-functional product team. They also serve as a primary mechanism for communicating among functional organizations and the product team. These plans describe the activities to be completed, the deliverables, schedules (project plans), resources, and budgets. FSPs are used during the phases of new product development, as the product moves through the market (across its life cycle), and in Business Cases. Each of the FSPs is critical to clarify roles and responsibilities. They will be described in other places throughout this book, but a summary of each is offered for you here:

  - *Marketing FSP.* The Marketing FSP represents the plan for inbound market data gathering and the support for outbound marketing plans and programs for the product or products in a product line. People in Marketing also provide descriptions of integrated marketing communication activities, sales kits, training, and other helpful material to the Sales team.

  - *Product Development FSP.* This plan contains information that may be needed about technologies, platforms, designs, and specifications so that the product can be produced or developed. Groups called IT, R&D, or Engineering typically provide this information.

- *Finance FSP.* The Finance FSP contains the commitments from the Finance department to the team. A representative from Finance typically works with product team members to consolidate the financial data. The data are based on product and market assumptions that ultimately appear in forecasts contained in Business Cases and budgets, and these ultimately make their way into financial statements. These financial documents will ultimately track how well the product is performing versus the established plans.

- *Sales FSP.* The Sales FSP may be a collaborative effort between the product manager, the marketing manager, and the representative from the sales function. Product managers and marketers usually work together to create assumptions about market size, segments, targets, and other market and competitive challenges that are communicated to Sales. The Sales team determines whether they have the staff and skills to support selling activities. The product team needs to have assurance from Sales regarding at least a few key issues:

    - Their commitment to sell and support the potential unit volume forecasts that they provide.

    - A sufficient number of sales staff on hand, or approved to hire, to support the committed volumes or to sell into given markets or geographic areas.

    - Their commitment to provide the staff who can get the training needed to support the agreed upon volumes or to sell into given market segments.

    - There is sufficient administrative support to manage the sales and sales operations activities.

    - They understand their dependencies on other team members, for example, Marketing and Product Management.

- *Supply Chain FSP.* The supply chain activities usually include issues related to sourcing, inventory management, and logistics. The Supply Chain organization may also maintain vital links to the firm's ecosystem partners. In order for this function to adequately support the product team, they should have a solid understanding of the product(s) currently being planned or already in the marketplace. Their support is critical in ensuring that the right materials are available at the right time and that goods can freely move through the company, to distributors and/or retailers, and, ultimately, to the end customer. If the product team is involved with the provision of tangible products to the market, this business function is vital. It requires information regarding unit and volume forecasts from the product manager and marketing team members as well as financial information regarding fixed and variable costs.

- *Customer service FSP.* The customer service department provides support for responding to service requests or complaints from customers, case management, and repair and return activities. Customer service also handles inbound ordering activities and has a responsibility for delivering a satisfying experience to those with whom they interact, whether on the phone, over the Internet, or in other sales and service support activities. Their FSP focuses on staffing, training, facilities, and technologies needed so that they can adequately support the product.

- *Legal and regulatory FSP.* There are important legal and regulatory issues facing some industries; these include product safety, packaging, labeling, marketing communications, and even corporate governance. Addressing these concerns is important for both domestic and international business. This FSP should be provided to make sure that any legal and regulatory issues are considered. Don't neglect to include the legal function for the following milestones: pricing reviews, regulatory updates, contract support (including negotiations), and bid support.

- *Operations FSP.* How does a business support its entire infrastructure? They do so through their business operations, including ordering, billing, fulfillment, marketing, selling, IT, human resources, and intellectual property management. Therefore, there should be an overarching plan for how any product or service is supported by typical day-to-day business operations.

CROSS-FUNCTIONAL PRODUCT TEAM AND OTHER ORGANIZATIONAL INFORMATION

Most people take organizational navigation for granted. However, I have learned through my research that most product managers spend an inordinate amount of time trying to learn their way around. If you are an experienced product manager, chances are you already know the back-channels and the main players. However, if you leave your job, it will take your replacement months to figure things out. Having this information in your Product Master Plan will help successive generations of product managers from having to reinvent the wheel in this area. While reorganizations seem to be commonplace, it's a good idea to do your best to keep this information up to date in your Product Master Plan. Here are some of the items that are important to include:

Product Team Information. You may be working on or leading one or more cross-functional product teams. If so, you should compile a list of "who's who" in the organization. Mind you, it is vital that each Functional Support Plan should contain this important information. In addition, any other relevant information about the major players should be housed here. Your product team list should contain:

- Name, title, and role
- All contact information
- Functional organization
- Work location

Organization charts. While you may be able to keep everyone's name who works on the product team on a list, keeping an organization chart is something much more complex. If you were to ask your Human Resources person for a current organization chart (or set of organization charts), you'd probably end up with a lot of out-of-date information. Modern firms are in a constant state of flux, and sometimes the organization charts are just not kept up to date. Therefore, it's up to you to make sure you can, through formal and informal means, keep your charts in order so that you know how to navigate your company in the most expeditious manner possible. Be sure to include information about:

- Key team players and their contact information
- Key business leaders
- Production locations
- Regional sales offices

Product team protocols and guidelines. You cannot participate in or lead product teams unless you have some clear cut rules and guidelines. These guidelines may establish roles and responsibilities for projects. They may also point out protocols used to evaluate data, produce documents, conduct reviews, and make decisions. Make sure your product team proto-cols and guidelines include:

- Guidelines for meeting attendance
- Rules for resolving conflicting priorities
- Methods to address risk
- Agreed-upon escalation paths when jeopardy conditions are encountered
- Comprehensive product team meeting information including a standard agenda for meetings, requirements for attendance, meeting notes, and action items

PRODUCT PERFORMANCE AND OTHER BUSINESS INFORMATION

Most companies have a lot of product business information. However, the challenge faced by many product mangers is that the product's business information is not in one centralized repository; it's distributed all over the organization. Therefore, product managers should, in their effort to maintain some semblance of control, learn where the documents are and understand how to harness them in their Product Master Plan. Even if the documents are not immediately transportable to the Product Master Plan repository, it's reasonable to establish or publish linkages to other systems or repositories where that information is housed or maintained. Here are some of the items that should be included in the product business information section of the Product Master Plan:

- *Product/product line description(s).* This section includes actual documentation on product descriptions consistent with publicly available documents. It could include actual positioning statements, value propositions, or any content that clarifies the purpose of the product.
- *Product performance data and scorecards.* It is critical to be able to keep track of the product's performance against stated, formal plans and budgets. This includes financial performance, market performance, and operational performance with the requisite financial statements and other formal performance documents and scorecards. Product managers will use various report cards and product health reports to keep track of the product's business and contributions across the life cycle. These scorecards provide the proper historical context for the product's business and life cycle analytics.

- *Financial data and reports.* The product performance scorecards mentioned above require a constant feed of financial data as contained in product profit and loss statements. This includes unit volumes, prices charged, product costs, gross margin, expenses, and product profit contribution. There may be other financial information that is correlated with other business data in key performance indicators used in product performance scorecards.

- *Product catalogs and product codes.* All products are placed in some type of product catalog, and each product has some type of code associated with it so that it can be ordered, billed, and serviced.

- *Operational systems that support the product.* This could include information about support systems such as billing, supply chain, IT, and configuration. It also includes procedural notes (e.g., how to add a product code, or maintenance of product availability ratings related to market status or "order-ability").

- *Win–loss analysis reports.* Many product managers will be involved in bids and proposals for business. Some are won, and some are lost. These should be utilized to gain insight that leads to purposeful action and improved win rates.

- *Post-Launch audit reports.* After products are launched, outcomes will be evaluated against the objectives stated in the launch plans. These audit reports provide the wherewithal to improve future launch performance.

- *Product gate and decision reviews.* Most firms use a phase gate product development process to evaluate product investments (with Business Cases) and to make decisions. The documentation used for these reviews should be preserved for reference and to help others learn about process usage.

- *Price lists and pricing programs.* All products should have a price that represents the value and benefits provided to customers. Product price lists and pricing strategies should be maintained by the product manager.

- *Promotional programs.* All relevant advertising and promotional campaigns and programs for the product should be kept in the Product Master Plan repository.

- *Sales and channel programs.* Sales people and distribution partners bring products to market. It is vital to ensure that these plans, programs, and outcomes be kept in the Product Master Plan.

- *Product service documentation.* The documents that customers or trainers may need for operating, installing, administering, maintaining, or using a product may include instruction manuals, online help guides, maintenance manuals, and operations manuals.

- *Outward facing programs and marketing materials.* These documents or programs may or may not be included in Marketing Plans but could include PR programs, industry analyst interactions, and documented conversations. This section should contain documents such as sales guides, sales collateral, and copies of advertisements, and so on.

- *Appendices.* Notes, additional supporting documents, resources, internal web links, detailed reports, and other relevant supporting items are included here. Examples of what might be kept in this section (or subsections, as needed) include:

  - Market research data and other research reports that are relevant to the product's history

  - Presentations to management, which might include strategy reviews performance updates, and others, that are important to preserve

  - Product price lists and product catalog (current and historical), which might include special discounting for specific bids and proposals

  - Escalation rules and contacts to resolve customer problems

  - Service-level agreements for customers

  - Sales guides, marketing collateral, and other documentation used for training sales people

  - Training plans and activities for other organizations, such as customer service (agent product training) or actual customer training

  - Customer presentations

  - Case studies and references

  - Bid boilerplates

  - Quality- and/or cost-improvement initiatives

  - Any other relevant, historical business documentation

MARKET DATA

It is emphasized throughout this book that market data and the insights gained should be stored for easy access by members of your cross-functional product team. As research projects, customer visits, and other activities are carried out, it's a good idea to make sure the methods, protocols, and outcomes are filed away and easy to retrieve. The most important market data might include:

- *Market segmentation models, customer profiles, and comprehensive information about customer needs.* This section captures information about desirable market areas (geographic or industry vertical breakdowns) and logical customer groups (demographics, behaviors, patterns of usage, etc.) on which the team focuses its efforts and why. It also contains documentation that describes timely information about customer needs within each segment or target area.

- *Customer research data and customer visit reports.* Across the product's life cycle, product managers will rely on a steady stream of customer data, analytics, and insights from customer visits. These are vital documents to form insights, track preferences, create or update "customer stories," and produce new product requirements.

- *Industry and competitive data.* Any data related to the industry and competitors are kept in this section. It also contains information from analyst reports, formal competitor analyses, and even competitive product analysis such as "tear-down" analysis, mystery shopping, and other techniques that capture the essence of competitor strategies and positioning.

RESOURCES AND TOOLS

As you'll see, this book provides many templates and tools that you and your team can utilize. These templates and tools serve to guide your thought processes and to inspire a collaborative culture. As documents evolve, the Master Plan repository can be used to keep track of various versions and to keep these linked to important business processes. Some of the templates and tools might include:

- Process documentation, including any important information on processes that guide work, such as the New Product Development process, product launch protocols, and discontinuation guidelines

- Business Case template
- Product Launch Plan template
- Product Requirements Document (PRD) template
- Customer Visit Plan template

What I have listed in the main sections are suggestions about things to include in the Product Master Plan; however, the primary goal is to keep the lens focused on the product's business, its position in the market, and its evolution across the life cycle. Any documentation, agreements, or supporting data needed to do that should be included.

A Personal Library

Although the Product Master Plan may not be entrenched (or even utilized) in your organization, it certainly cannot hurt the reputation or results of any product manager to start and maintain one. A Product Master Plan, used as part of your personal library, can easily become a nucleus for change, especially if management correlates a higher level of product and cross-functional team success to its use. In that light, here are some useful ground rules I would like to reinforce about the Product Master Plan:

- The product manager *owns* the Product Master Plan.
- The Product Master Plan should be located in a shared electronic repository or a central location.
- The entire team should know of its existence and its purpose and must know how to appropriately contribute content.
- The product manager should determine how versions will be maintained and how changes will be communicated to interested team members. With this, any team member should be able to contribute to its content, but other team members should understand what's being contributed, why a change is being made, and whether that particular contribution is at all relevant for them.

With those few rules observed, it's likely that a well-crafted, carefully maintained Product Master Plan will have a significant impact on the success of your product, the strength of your product team, and your career.

A PRODUCT MANAGEMENT LIBRARY

Everything I've discussed in this chapter has stressed the importance of using a Product Master Plan as the repository of everything relevant to the product or product line. Even if the Product Master Plan is not used routinely at your organization, it is still important to create a Personal Library. If, however, the Product Master Plan is a commonly utilized entity, where in the company are all the Product Master Plans stored? What about all of the documents, templates, processes, methods, and other information used by product managers, product teams, and others?

All Product Master Plans and all Product Management documents, templates, process information, and tools belong in a central repository or *Product Management Library*. There are many excellent systems (software, tools, etc.) that can be used to create work areas and file structures where all of these documents can be stored and easily accessed by designated people.

It is very important that senior leaders, through their Product Management governance board (or equivalent group), appoint people to properly maintain the Product Management Library. These may include process owners or those responsible for standard documents and templates.

SUMMARY

As discussed at the outset of this chapter, the notion of the Master Plan is not new. It's been used as a way for municipalities, governments, and institutions to document their work programs and historical information for many years. The amalgam of plans, programs, and budgets acts as a focal point, even when administrations come and go. This is why the Product Master Plan is the perfect meta-document for product managers and the teams they lead. New product teams can start out with a fresh set of documents that can be built up over time and act as a reference to guide current and future work activities. Teams managing existing products can begin to build any retrospective documentation and can also contribute as the product's evolution is planned and carried out. Finally, all Product Master Plans and associated documentation belong in a Product Management Library.

For more information on Product Management governance, refer to my book *Managing Product Management.*

And as people and teams come and go, one Product Master Plan, housed in a visible Product Management Library, will always be present to act as a centerpiece of best-in-class Product Management.

RAISING YOUR PRODUCT MANAGEMENT EXPERIENCE QUOTIENT (PMEQ)

1. Start now to create your own Product Master Plan, either in a physical binder or an electronic repository. You will not be able to complete it in an afternoon. Rather, you can set up the outline for the documents you wish to create based on the lists provided earlier in this chapter. If you can find any current or historical documentation, print or download it and place it in the Master Plan.

2. Because much of your work is done while collaborating with others, consider putting a list together with the names and contact information of all cross-functional team members. Include their managers as well. This should be inserted into the first section or folder, titled "Team Contacts."

3. Whether your cross-functional team is officially chartered, virtually constructed, or transient, try to find any documentation that demonstrates how teams made the commitment to take part in the work of the product. Try to understand the structure of the current relationships and commitments among the various organizations that support the success of your product. This can be achieved by talking to people who work in different business functions. This conversational roadmap starts with item 2 above.

4. Find out if there is a shared resource for all Product Management process documents, templates, and tools for your organization (equivalent to the Product Management Library mentioned earlier). There may be a Product Management process owner who can help you gain access to these important tools. You may also want to meet those process owners or document managers so that you can learn how to effectively utilize these tools.

CHAPTER

LEADERSHIP: CREATING INFLUENCE

Executive Summary

- Leadership is a critical skill that product managers can and should learn as they progress in their careers.
- For the product manager, leadership skills can be cultivated through a hunger for knowledge, ongoing learning, and the exponential effect of increasing business experience.
- Product leaders are able to transform ideas, facilitate debate, and process market signals into an actionable vision for a product.

We all have the capacity to inspire and empower others. But we must first be willing to devote ourselves to our personal growth and development as leaders.

BILL GEORGE, PETER SIMS,
ANDREW N. MCLEAN, AND DIANA MAYER
HARVARD BUSINESS REVIEW, VOLUME 85,
NUMBER 2, FEBRUARY 2007

How many times have you heard or read that product managers have to be leaders? How often does your boss discuss the importance of real leadership? How often does the topic come up in corporate pep rallies and strategy sessions? Leadership is an inescapable component of business and an indispensable asset for the product manager. Unfortunately, the qualities of genuine leadership are diluted by the overuse of the word and its many, many definitions found in business literature, the media, and human culture. The purpose of this chapter is to give you a basic framework for thinking about leadership as a product manager. Not all of us are "born leaders," but you can learn from the style of others to achieve your own success. This chapter guides you through some approaches and techniques that will enable you to evolve your own style of leadership.

There are many leadership concepts to be considered. There are those who make the distinction between the meaning of the word *leadership* as "an act of influence or inspiration" and the meaning of the word *management* as "an act of authority or direction." There are those who associate leadership with force of personality and charisma and, alternatively, those who agree with Emerson's lament on leadership and identity ("Who you are speaks so loudly I cannot hear what you say . . ."). The words *leader* and *leadership* are often defined by the context and nuance of the situation in which they are used. It is interesting to note that a recent search on Google using *leadership* as the keyword netted 168,000,000 references!

Every product manager should spend a fair amount of time studying and thinking about leadership. Most business curricula offer courses on motivation, leadership, and management. There are running debates on management versus leadership. This topic encompasses a broad field of study, as demonstrated by the plethora of articles, books, and schools of thought on leadership. However, the assertions of academics, pundits, oracles, and advisors should not trump your own reality and, above all, should not discourage further reading or discovery.

Leadership, like the role of the product manager, comes in many different shapes and sizes, covering an astounding spectrum. The reality is that when it comes to being a leader, some people have the innate gift of leadership, some are able to learn bits and pieces of it, and some just do not get it. Some people can be leaders in one part of their lives and followers in another area. My point is you should not assume that you cannot develop applicable, useful, leadership skills just because you believe you are not a born leader.

"Thou are a product manager." Product managers who are new to the profession or who take a position in a new organization arrive with great

FIGURE 3.1

The Product Team Leader as Superhero

expectations placed upon them. I often visualize an image in my own mind: a superhero, complete with cape, goggles, and T-shirt (with a big P on the front, as shown in Figure 3.1), charging onto the scene, saying, "I've come to save the product!"

This sardonic attempt at humor stirs some deeper questions. If leadership (specifically Product Management leadership) is key, why is it so difficult to attain? Why are there so many "secret recipes" of leadership? If leadership is what's necessary to be a product manager or product team leader, why isn't every product manager doing a great job as a leader?

The fundamental answer is pretty straightforward: *leadership is an acquired skill.* It's not a delegated power, an innate ability, or some black art that can be achieved by trial-and-error checklists. In short, job assignment doesn't imply leadership. Even some innate or "born" leaders (those thought of as charismatic) may inspire and influence, but unless they really understand how they're getting those results, they may falter or collapse at precisely the wrong moment. The person who knows that most elements of leadership are learnable (and who takes the time to learn them) will be able to thoughtfully address situations that many so-called natural leaders cannot handle.

There are several building blocks to improving leadership skills I intend to put in place for you. No matter where you are on the leadership development spectrum, you can always find a way to move from where you are and take a small step to further your leadership profile. In that light, it's valuable to put leadership and the product manager in perspective.

YOU ARE ALWAYS ON STAGE

"It's show time!" As a product manager, you are "on stage" each and every day. When I worked at AT&T, I had a boss named Bob who was an affable, sociable, outgoing person. He was a terrific manager and coach and played a vital role in my career development. When people saw him in the hall and said, "Hi Bob, how's it going?" Bob would always respond, "Great! Couldn't be better!" I often wondered how someone could be constantly at work, dealing with bosses, subordinates, outside suppliers, and customers, and always be "great." Even if he wasn't well, he never deviated: he was always never better! There were some things about his personal life that most people, had they known, would not have considered "great." But like an actor constantly in performance mode, Bob was always smiling, always happy, and always, always on stage, projecting that rosy optimism that radiated to everyone. This gave Bob's colleagues the confidence that all was "great" in their microcosm of the workplace universe.

In a way, the world of business is analogous to a theatre production, where it's the players backstage that make things run well so that everything up front looks—yes—great. In reality, almost all employees work hard to get their work done—and done well. But leaders have an archetypal role. And as a product manager, you're always in the public eye. In short, to increase others' confidence in your capabilities, beliefs, and vision, *put on a happy face.*

STAY CALM, EVEN WHEN YOUR HAIR'S ON FIRE

The life of a product manager is always complicated and never easy. It does not flow like the fluid movements of yoga or t'ai chi. Product leaders, like actual firemen, know what fire looks like, feels like, and smells like. *They put out fires all the time.* The last thing your peers, subordinates, or managers want to see is someone who goes berserk every time a crisis occurs.

For product managers with less experience or confidence, their anxiety or uncertainty is usually visible to others. However, after a few helpful interventions, they quickly learn this behavior is not effective. If they have enough on the ball, they must make a conscious decision to improve and get some coaching to better process and respond to unplanned or crisis events.

Usually after a couple of tries, here's what they tend to learn:

- Stay calm—even if your insides are jumping around.
- Process the "people signals" (e.g., watch faces and body movements).
- Calmly determine what's really going on.
- Evaluate what has to be done or what can be done.
- Make a decision and act.
- Calm everyone else down.
- Remember, you're always on stage, and act as everything will be great!

As the person who seems to be doing the processing, considering the options, and making the decision(s), when others see you're unfazed, they'll take their signals from you and feel like things are under control (even if you feel you just took air time on a roller coaster).

TRANSFORMATION

No matter where you stand within the leadership spectrum, you must find within yourself the will to learn and grow. For those who aren't naturals (and many are not), product managers and their bosses need to find an experiential roadmap that will enrich their ability to lead and influence. Leading requires an alteration in the way information from different sources is processed and acted on, which is part of the transformation.

Leading also has many faces. Your face to the company probably differs from your face to the community or your face to your family. You are in control of a vehicle (you) with many different dials or gauges that allow you to throttle forward or backward, depending on the situations in the past and those in the future.

To learn how to transform yourself, no matter your location in the leadership continuum, you need a good map. A very useful leadership map is shown in Figure 3.2. It contains elements from a variety of sources that are worthwhile to consider. These are discussed in the paragraphs that follow and may be helpful in creating a personal strategy for your own transformational leadership journey.

FIGURE 3.2

Leadership Transformation Map

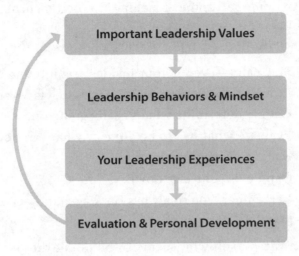

The Most Important Values

Values are an important element of your personal mission, your product's mission, and the mission of the organization within which you work. Everyone lives with an individual set of values. All companies operate with their own unique values. In short, values guide much of what people and companies do. Therefore, it is important to learn and understand the values and principles that form the fabric of the organization's mission and to integrate those values into what you do, how you act, and the face you put forward to your team, your managers, and your customers. Listed below are values that are vital to consider and develop—values that will inspire people to bind themselves to you:

- *Employ integrity in everything you do*. This is a core value that means you adhere to ethical codes of business and personal conduct. Integrity earns respect from others through consistency, reliability, and honesty. Integrity leads to trust.
- *Engender trust*. Trust is important because it is easier to influence others when people have faith that you will do the right thing and are consistently sincere.
- *Stand for something important*. People will identify with you if they know what you represent and that you stand for something meaningful. I often refer to this as "managerial courage"—product managers standing up for their convictions and beliefs.

- *Meet your commitments.* Meeting commitments to people with whom you work and to your customers means you will always be perceived of as responsible, trustworthy, and possessing integrity.
- *Act professionally.* Leaders have an uncanny ability to align personal and business conduct with ethical, professional standards.
- *Help or coach others.* Helping others is an important way to enhance your visibility while being perceived as altruistic and beneficial to your company. It also sets the stage for greater levels of trust, which builds closer working and, possibly, personal relationships. There are numerous ways to help. Be willing to help people learn more or work through problems; doing so will enable them to grow and optimize their capabilities. Set an example by acting as a role model or mentor in order to engender greater performance from others.
- *Include others.* When you include others in your vision for the product, in strategizing, in planning for the future, in leading the team, and in decision making, people are more likely to commit to your vision and work harmoniously with you to achieve it.

LEADERSHIP BEHAVIORS AND MINDSET

There are a number of internalized behaviors that are commonly evinced by effective leaders. Learning and development of these leadership elements may be difficult, but with focused attention and diligent coaching by experienced leaders, these behaviors can be cultivated.

Following is a list of the leadership characteristics that are important for product managers. If you do not have all of these now, don't worry; there's no hard and fast rule for how and when you acquire them. However, by considering this list of leadership traits and understanding how they can serve you and your organization, you have a chance to continue on your evolutionary path.

1. *Continuous learning.* Each and every experience you have as a product manager contributes to your repertoire of personal and professional resources. Learning all the time means that every environment in which you find yourself becomes a "learning laboratory" for building business savvy and people skills. The scope of all this learning includes learning about your customers' businesses and how they do what they do, and increasing your knowledge of the market environment in which your company operates.

After a while, others in your organization will see you as a knowledgeable "go to" person who shares insight as well as teaches, guides, and encourages others to learn continuously.

2. *Strategic thinking.* Best-in-class product managers, like good CEOs, are always weighing and planning, trying to assess the current state of business, how to optimize their products in the market, and beat the competition. There is an explicit methodology behind strategic thinking and plotting. It requires a keen sense of market nuance, a powerful focus on the product's business performance, and the formulation of ideas that will lead to new and interesting prospects for your product's business. *A strategic mindset is among the most important characteristics for a product manager* to develop and is inextricably linked to the next behavior and mindset: being a visionary.

3. *Vision.* Leaders have vision. They dream of possibilities—of what *could* be. People tend to pay attention when someone else's vision makes sense. This is because those who have a vision tend to inspire excitement about possibilities as well as a common purpose. The word *vision* is heavily used and is a quality expected of product managers by management. If your vision is not apparent to you, I offer you hope: there are "shades of gray"—variations that allow your vision to slowly emerge and become less dreamlike. This is discussed in greater detail in Chapter 10 on strategy. Vision can be improved just like a pair of glasses can give you the ability to see farther. This happens over time as you deepen your knowledge about the industry, competitors, customers, and your own organization.

If you recall the beginning of the book, my first Product Management job had me at a great disadvantage right from the start. I took over an existing product that didn't have a Business Case or a Master Plan. It didn't possess the competitive attributes needed to be successful, and I couldn't see any path to any kind of realistic future. *It took me six months to figure this out.* In the end, the only thing that came of it was my vision that the business was not viable and it was best to kill the product and withdraw it from the market. I moved on from there with a new set of experiences and a new appreciation for key Product Management building blocks.

4. *Networking and bridge building.* All great executives know a lot of people in a lot of places. The manager mentioned earlier, Bob, worked at AT&T for more than 20 years. Wherever business took him, it seemed like everybody recognized him, almost as if he was a celebrity. In fact, when he had a problem, faced a challenge, or needed some help, he always knew the right source to call. *Networking is part of the political process that helps you in building the bridges to resources that will help you get your job done.* Successful product managers constantly work to build a broad network, make friends, radiate their values, and ultimately know whom to contact and where to turn at every stage in their journey.

5. *The mensch factor.* There's a Yiddish expression with roots in German that means "human." In its American migration, it roughly translates into being a good and eminently decent person who exhibits the kinds of traits we would want in a good friend, colleague, or family member. The word *mensch* is almost onomatopoetic when used frequently enough that everyone gets it: be kind; be fair; be humorous; be helpful; do what's right. Be a mensch.

6. *Serving customers.* Although not on traditional leadership radar scopes, product team leaders (and product managers who feel deeply involved and want to be leaders) must be able to form working relationships with customers. These working relationships provide you with valuable insight into how they think, what's happening in their organization, and what's happening in their industry and with their competitors. They also educate you about your competitors. CEOs and other key executives in your company do this with their peers in customer companies. It stands to reason that product managers, as good leaders, should pursue the same kinds of relationships with customers who buy, use, or influence the purchase of products.

If you think this only applies to business-to-business (B2B) companies, let me give you an example. A couple of years ago, while flying on a major airline, I was approached by its chief operating officer. He came up to me, introduced himself, and reached out for a handshake. "You look like a guy who flies a lot. Do you fly with us often?" I replied that I did. After some polite conversation, he asked, "So how are we doing?"

I said, "I'm the right person to ask," and we had a heart-to-heart talk about being a business traveler. In this instance, in 15 short minutes he established a relationship with me, one of his consumers. Relationships can easily be brief, as in this example, and long lived, as well. Your relationships with customers teach you their way of life and allow you to see their world through their eyes. Bringing this back to the team when you've been the scout gives more people the opportunity and desire to listen to what you have to say about the marketplace.

7. *Facilitation and collaborative problem solving.* Good leaders grasp and consider the situation, ask a lot of questions, and bring people together to solve problems. Product managers as leaders can bring people together to clarify the team's objectives. The challenge arises when different people see things differently. Effective product team leaders are skillful at this kind of facilitation, which is usually needed as strategies are formulated and as plans are readied. Whenever the team is faced with a challenge and there are many differing paths to a needed decision, a product manager with superior facilitative skills will be able to steer the team in the right direction.

8. *Empowering others.* One of the most overused and misunderstood expressions in corporate life is the word *empowerment.* If a product team is chartered by a cross-functional executive leadership team, and has been provided with the appropriate authority, accountability, and resources for that team, and, if the team delivers great results with minimal oversight in a highly communicative environment, then that team will be said to have been empowered.

Empowerment does not, however, sit on its own island. Empowerment is a give-and-take process built on the trust between product manager and team members, the commitments that are continually met (demonstrating strong values), and the results that are delivered. A while ago, a marketing executive came in to kick off a Product Management training session, and as he went through his introduction, he talked about the importance of everyone's job. The most striking thing he said was, "From now on, you are all empowered." He wished them good luck and left the room. Everyone's jaw seemed to have dropped; the room was quiet. However, no one in that room felt empowered, and no one knew what to do with what had been said. Worst of all, the bond of trust between executive management, the product managers, and product directors was broken—and in less than five minutes. The ability to learn, and to ultimately feel empowered, comes from not only seeing good examples but also recognizing our own errors and the errors of others.

9. *Leading an organizational change.* At some point in your career, you will have gained enough experience and credibility that you may be called upon to participate in, or lead, a major organizational change. This can be a reorganization or restructuring, a major alliance or partnership, an acquisition, or a divestiture. Change happens, and your experience in this area will be of tremendous value to you because you have to, at a minimum, reconcile issues related to people, organizational culture, financial, and product portfolio impacts.

In my last corporate job, two of the things we needed were experienced people and some technology. Our objective was to acquire small companies to achieve this goal. As a product leader, I was part of the due diligence team for prospective candidate companies, and when a deal was done, I was on the transition team so that the people and product lines could be easily merged. This was an outstanding learning experience for me and one through which I gained significant leadership experience.

Within the Product Management realm, management, peers, and teams are constantly evaluating the product manager, either formally or informally, against these characteristics.

ADDITIONAL SKILLS AND SUBJECT MATTER EXPERTISE

Knowledge and experience are critical building blocks of the Product Management skill set. There are skills and experiences that you build throughout your career in specific fields, whether they're functional or technical. These could include computer programming, applications engineering, market research, operations analysis, manufacturing techniques, and finance. This is one of the reasons why, in Product Management, everyone comes from somewhere else and brings with them their particular subject matter expertise.

Many companies have management development programs in which people work in a variety of jobs unrelated to their core interest and within different business functions for a period of time. This kind of program helps people to experience and learn to understand how each part of the business works and how it all fits together. There are great benefits to this approach, mainly because you can see exactly how each and every department operates and interoperates. Because of these experiences, the product manager will be more likely to consider new things, new opportunities, or different ways of doing things.

EXPERIENTIAL DEVELOPMENT

One of the common themes of Product Management is the role that experiential development plays. Experiential development has tremendous value to both the individual and the organization. *Experiences are the enablers of your career, and the broader the scope, the more your growth and maturation.* They open up the doors for future opportunities—doors that aren't always easy to identify without a leadership transformation roadmap. When you understand the kinds of experiences on which you should be focusing, you are putting the lampposts on the road for yourself and others that you will influence.

Your growing self-awareness and experiential development sets the stage for you to be a role model to others. When others see "how it's done," they're more apt to follow your leadership, especially if they didn't know how much they didn't know or were afraid to admit they didn't know.

How do you know what to do? That's experience. As you keep "doing," you just start to know. Your mind is like a giant version of the central processing unit of a computer. You take inputs and signals, you process the data, and you draw conclusions. You learn to improve your inputs, process more efficiently, and improve your outcomes. This is why there is such a strong linkage between leadership and decision making and between leadership and the cross-functional product team—all foundational practices being discussed in this book. Figure 3.3 reinforces this extremely important point with a circular diagram.

FIGURE 3.3

The Cycle of Experience

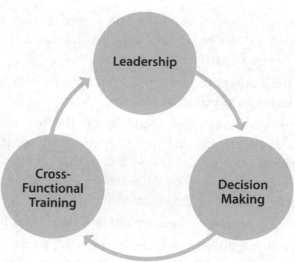

HOW DO YOU IMPROVE YOUR SKILLS AND EXPERIENCES?

The quote at the beginning of this chapter, from "Discovering Your Authentic Leadership" by Bill George, Peter Sims, Andrew N. McLean, and Diana Mayer, implies a mandate to continuously improve your leadership skills. There are two primary ways to improve your skills and experience. They are not treated individually, but symbiotically: instructional training and guided experiences on the job.

Instructional training can include formal classes delivered by training companies (like mine) or colleges and universities. Experience-based methods link work activities and tasks to performance development (formalized goal setting with your management) under the guidance of a manager, coach, or mentor, either on your current job or in a job rotation or special assignment. Whatever path you take, you should have partners (your coaches and mentors) who guide you and challenge you.

Product leaders can alter their behaviors and mindset and, by so doing, allow for examination of core values and of the next best experience to map out. Each experience changes your mindset, and each mindset adjustment may help you reassess your values until your mindset expands and your leadership profile adjusts.

Some of the actions you might consider for yourself include the following:

- *Be a student.* Study, observe, and be open to continuous learning. Don't glide along as you go; always take mental notes that may serve in some future situation.

- *Be a teacher.* Help others to learn and grow so they can develop the habit and knack of continuous learning.

- *Be a facilitator.* Encourage discussion about the business, the marketplace, and customers. Ask questions to stimulate thought about the business, the product, and competitive strategy in a manner that is engaging and contributes to your personal and professional growth and the growth of others.

- *Be a supporter.* Help or coach others, even if they don't work for you.

- *Be a recognizer.* Recognition validates. Recognize people's efforts by reinforcing positive contributions to the product team and providing feedback. This includes offering guidance regarding less than desirable behaviors.

- *Be a thinker.* Create your own "you" as you form opinions, gain wisdom, and become a sought-after adviser.

- *Be a product therapist.* Listen carefully and try to help others help themselves through questioning, guiding, and suggesting.

SUMMARY

Leadership in Product Management doesn't just happen. Those who believe leadership skills are innate don't understand the developmental nuances that build leadership. For the product manager, leadership is a vital skill and capability that can be learned over time based on the experiences you have, the guidance you are afforded by your coaches and mentors, and the inner belief that you want to influence and attain great business results. However, I leave you with the real key to your own personal growth as a leader, either of a small product team or an entire organization: *No one will bestow Product Management leadership on you. It is yours to own, to internalize, and to practice.* Over time, others will follow, and those signs are unmistakable.

RAISING YOUR PRODUCT MANAGEMENT EXPERIENCE QUOTIENT (PMEQ)

- If you find yourself at the point in your career where your focus turns to the improvement of your ability to lead, the first thing to do is create an inventory of the skills you believe you possess already. Using the ideas discussed in this chapter, try to take a realistic view of the areas on which you should concentrate. This exercise will enable you to create your own personal leadership skills development map. You can further reconcile some of your own personally derived goals by working with your manager to understand what he or she believes are the most valued leadership characteristics in your organization and the kinds of things you can do to further build your leadership skills inventory. In my book *The Product Manager's Survival Guide* there are other helpful hints to help you raise your game.

- In your human resources department, there may be a person or group of people focusing on leadership development. Perhaps they would be willing to talk to you so that you can better understand some of their guidelines. Furthermore, you could ask them to provide some examples, documentation, and perhaps other people in the organization with whom you could speak. These are the mentors who may be able to help you along your journey.

- As you progress, keep checking yourself to make sure you are putting your best face forward. This is somewhat of a leap of faith, but if you can visualize yourself watching you as you interact with others, you will come away with new perspectives. You could, for example, "see" how you interact with others when you work on a team to create a Business Case or work on some other planning document. Let's say you want to improve on always having a positive outlook. After the interaction or meeting, consider how you came off in the eyes of others. You can also enroll colleagues in your cause. Ask for feedback: "Do you think I came off as encouraging and positive to Joe in the meeting?" Keep a list of these interactions to show how you are making the kind of progress you wish to make, and compare this to your leadership skills development map.

■ If you happen to be more experienced, there are deeper transformational experiences on which you may wish to focus. For example, if one of your skill areas to develop is in "supporting people"—which could be in coaching or mentoring of others who either work for you or work for others—what can you do to further this goal? You can think about doing the following:

■ Mentor a person in another business function, with whom you work on a product team, who may have a difficult boss.

■ Lead a product subteam made up of less experienced people. Encourage them to set realistic goals and guide them in work activities that will build their confidence.

■ Maintain a positive outlook and keep people motivated under adverse circumstances such as during a reorganization, downsizing, or merger.

■ Help or coach an individual in your group or on your product team to reach a performance goal if that person doesn't know how to achieve that goal alone.

■ Leaders in product organizations (leaders overall, for that matter) understand how customers think. They visit customers frequently either in person or on the phone. Some of the ways you can achieve this are going on account visits with the sales teams, going on a tour of a customer's facility, answering the phone in the call center for a couple of hours or days, delivering training on your products to customers, or working in a booth at a trade show where your products are being demonstrated. Any or many of these things that put you on the front line with the customer will improve your insight and sensitivity to customers. Strong leaders have powerful customer insights built over years of talking, interviewing, teaching, and observing.

CHAPTER

4

CROSS-FUNCTIONAL PRODUCT TEAMS: GETTING THINGS DONE

Executive Summary

- Product teams and project teams are both cross-functional but differ greatly in purpose.
- A product team should run the business of the product like a board of directors.
- Product teams are accountable for the strategic, market, and financial success of the product.
- A product team leader is responsible for the success of the team and the success of the product.

For many people, teamwork can be the antithesis of productivity. How many teams and task forces have you worked on? Have you ever felt that the team was without direction, leadership, or purpose? Have you ever had to form a team of people from different areas but couldn't get them to commit to one another in a meaningful way? Was your team ever stuck because of some unresolved conflict? If so, you are not alone. The purpose of this chapter is to ground you in the basic work structure for best-in-class Product Management: the cross-functional product team.

67

Most people who work in companies have a good sense of what a team is and the purpose of a cross-functional team. This is borne out in organizational assessments and benchmarking exercises carried out with my clients. They recognize that cross-functional teams are made up of members from various business functions and that those team members commit to work with one another to complete the designated project.

CROSS-FUNCTIONAL TEAM DEFINITIONS

If you work with products, you have probably worked on a cross-functional team. A cross-functional team is typically defined as a group of people representing various functions involved in product planning, development, and launch.

Most definitions agree that members of a cross-functional team work on a *project*, even if the project is for work related to a product. Confused? Let me try to clarify, because this is where many issues arise: a cross-functional *product* team is different from a cross-functional *project* team.

The purpose of a cross-functional product team is to manage all the elements needed to achieve the financial, market, and strategic objectives of the product as a business. The cross-functional product team is made up of *delegated* representatives from their respective business functions. This team is the primary mechanism through which an organization initiates product strategies and plans. The team is responsible for making sure that plans are executed in a timely fashion. Finally, the product team is responsible for the profitability of the product in the marketplace. With these characteristics in mind, I want to reinforce the importance of thinking of the product as a *business*.

In my research, I've learned that product teams tend to take on one of three different profiles:

1. A team that stays in place from initial idea until the product is launched
2. A team that stays in place from the time a product is launched until it is discontinued or withdrawn from the market
3. A team that stays in place across the product's life cycle, from idea to discontinuation

The first structure, where members stay in place from idea to launch, is most prevalent, as products are continually updated and released. The second structure is found more often in firms with products that have been around for a number of years; the products are functionally "complete" and may profit from changes in how products are serviced and supported. The third structure, where the product team stays in place across the product life cycle, is the most desirable because it allows for a more balanced perspective that contributes to the optimization of products and product lines across their life cycles.

With that in mind, the challenge in most organizations is the transience of the cross-functional team. Team members often do not want to stay on the team long term, or frequent management changes affect their membership. When functional leaders change, they move their staff around; as a result, the product manager cannot rely on the kind of permanent membership needed to run the product as a business. This is why product managers often feel like they are the "dumping ground" for all the things the people in other functions fail to carry out. This is also why, when asked about what they do and with whom they work, product managers tend to respond with answers that vary widely. This is why the Product Master Plan and Functional Support Plans (FSPs) are so very important. These documents help to ensure that the commitments made by members from a business function to the team are met, even if members come and go.

DEFINITION: A CULTURE OF DISCIPLINE

> *Few companies have a culture of discipline. When you have disciplined people, you don't need hierarchy. When you have disciplined thought, you don't need bureaucracy. When you have disciplined action, you don't need excessive controls. When you combine a culture of discipline with an ethic of entrepreneurship, you get the magical alchemy of good performance.*
>
> —Jim Collins, From *Good to Great: Why some Companies Make the Leap ... and Others Don't*

As discussed earlier, a cross-functional *project* team is different from a *product* team. Both types of teams are made up of delegated team members. However, project teams primarily focus on *projects*. Projects, within the context of Product Management, are a series of activities and tasks that contribute to the *creation or support* of a product or service. Projects are organized within a systematic framework, utilizing appointed or allocated resources. Task completion is dependent on individuals fulfilling their commitment. If a person does not deliver as committed and on time, there may be risks and consequences for other team members.

In Product Management, a properly chartered cross-functional product team, with responsibility for products from beginning to end, will spawn many new *project* teams—small teams responsible for many discrete activities, such as evaluating opportunities, crafting Business Cases, and orchestrating product launches.

Project teams can also function in stand-alone mode. In the Development department, engineers, programmers, designers, and other technologists are always working on projects. Their projects, though, involve only people from within their function, which means they are not cross-functional projects.

Organized like a board of directors for a product, a cross-functional product team may focus on a single product, or it may be responsible for a product line or product portfolio. In its highest form, an executive-level cross-functional portfolio group charters the product team. The resulting product team will have its best chance of achieving success if led by a higher-level, experienced product manager or product line leader. Team members should be delegated by the executives on the portfolio team as representatives from their function. Either way, the product team is the primary means of assuring the ultimate success of a product or product line.

Product line teams should stay together across the life of the product because this allows stable (yet evolving) relationships with minimum conflict. This also allows for the teams to move through and appreciate all of the stages of team development, as formulated by Dr. Bruce Tuckman. These stages include forming, storming, norming, and performing. The definitions are almost self-explanatory.

When teams come together, they are *forming*. When forming, people on the team get to know one another and begin to understand their roles. In the second phase, *storming*, there may be some turbulence as new ideas surface and the team learns to deal with conflict. *Norming* implies that the team members are normalizing or stabilizing and becoming more productive. Respect for one another evolves as relationships become stronger, trust develops, and the team adjusts to each member's style as they deliver on their commitments. Finally, *performing* teams act as well-oiled machines, working smoothly, efficiently, and productively.

Figure 4.1 shows these four phases of team development. As you can see in the figure, there are two-directional arrows between each of

FIGURE 4.1

The Phases of Team Development

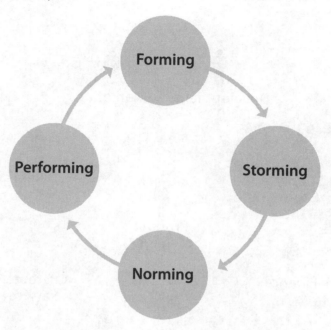

the nodes. This reflects what happens as teams move in and out of the phases as members come and go.

Many books have been written on the topic of team behavior and performance. One thing comes up as a common theme in all of this research: teams who stay together longer tend to perform better. When I worked on the product management task force, we observed a product team meeting as part of one of our benchmarking exercises. The meeting we sat in on was characterized by some very heated discussions including shouting and even name calling. We were aghast. Questioned about this later on, the team members said, "Oh, that—that was nothing—we've known each other for years." Such is the mark of an effectively "performing" team.

TEAM MEMBERSHIP

The actual team visual for a cross-functional product team is not new. The diagram exists in one form or another in many documented resources. In fact, you could say it applies to both product teams and project teams. Most likely, you've seen it before—it's a typical daisy

FIGURE 4.2

Typical Cross-Functional Team Members

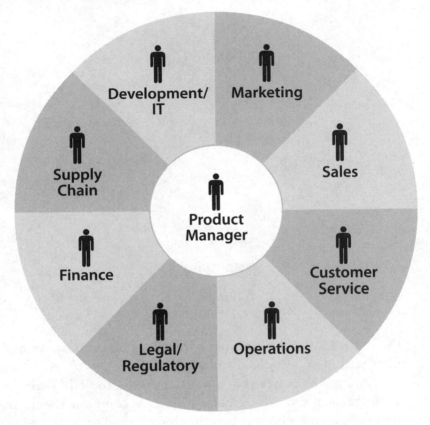

wheel or pie chart. I prefer the pie chart visualization (see Figure 4.2), but product managers should choose the type of graphic that works best for them.

The daisy wheel depicts the typical functions designated as the members of a core product team. No matter what visual representation is used, it should be applied consistently in the organization.

Teaming Is Not Always Easy

These descriptions of teams and team structures seem fairly straight-forward: team members are delegated; they act on behalf of their business function; and they contribute toward decisions that optimize the performance of their products. In practice, however, teams struggle to mesh well. When I think about teams and teamwork, I often think about a sandbox in a playground. The box is bounded, but the surface of sand inside the sandbox is uneven. Think about teams you've worked on and about the *unevenness* of team member performance—and further, how this uneven performance causes imbalance and inefficiency. These dynamics can play out in following ways:

- *Uneven commitment.* This happens when team members are hesitant about making significant commitments to the product team. They generally don't like to say "no" when asked if they are able to meet a commitment for a new or incremental deliverable. When they do consent to undertake the work to produce an incremental deliverable, they may be committing to more than they actually can deliver. They seem to feel that they must do everything because they don't want to let the team down or be viewed as inadequate. They work as hard as they can, but ultimately, they fall short of their commitment and the prophecy is fulfilled.

- *Uneven empowerment.* Many bosses tell teams they are empowered, but at the end of the day, they cannot make the decisions that empowered teams expect to make—usually because their bosses aren't committed enough to want to dedicate the required resources. The truth is even more complex. It's not really that the team member cannot commit the resources of that function—it may be that that there is no mechanism to properly manage intrateam projects and programs. This leaves the team members feeling they cannot possibly be accountable for business results.

- *Uneven alignment.* The team members themselves are not aligned with the priorities and needs of the team. Instead, they aim to further their individual agendas or the agendas of their business functions instead of considering the team's goals.

- *Uneven trust.* One of the most important foundations of cross-functional teams is the trust shared by team members. When people who work on product teams have trust issues, they tend to avoid confronting one another when encountering a difficult situation that may bring about a conflict. In these instances, there isn't an adequate trust mechanism that makes it okay for people to confront one another. There always seems to be a "hippo under the rug."

- *Uneven financial management.* Budget processes tend to take priority over other team issues. This leads to a generalized interpretation: "If it's in the budget, it's approved." What this means is when budgets lock for the year, teams feel they have all the money they need for product development projects. As a result, they don't use the New Product Development (NPD) process—or any decision-making method for that matter—to screen projects that may not make strategic, financial, or business sense. Failure to use a reliable process tends to result in short-term, project-oriented focus, not the big-picture, market-focused mindset that creates successful, lasting products.

- *Uneven accountability.* Management does not hold teams accountable for, or have any consequences for, ignoring mandated decision-making processes (NPD gate process, Business Cases, etc.). Along with this, many companies have great processes, but teams choose to ignore them or don't use them consistently. When problems arise, they tend to blame the process instead of the people issues that are usually the cause.

- *Uneven life cycles.* Very often, front-end planning is ignored. Teams are forced to react to executive- or customer-driven projects. The team must take its eyes off the marketplace, competitors, and other important dynamics because they're so focused on the short-term results. Furthermore, they tend not to push back to management for rethinking because management has not made it okay to do so, or the teams don't have enough formalized data to offer alternatives or assist in reprioritizing. The teams then have to rework, readjust, and fix all the things they should have anticipated by planning. Therefore, as they try to manage existing products, they are necessarily drawn away from running the business because they are fixing quality problems, dealing with functionality that doesn't work, adding missing features, or addressing other parts of the product's real value proposition that didn't make it into the product or were implemented incorrectly.

One of the best things about recognizing these poor team behaviors is that it affords us the opportunity to level the playing field by finding ways to better equip our teams—and ourselves. A high-level executive once complained that the corporate Product Management process was not working and needed to be fixed. Pushback data suggested a different issue: the teams were ignoring the process because they didn't think it *applied* to them.

CURING THE DYSFUNCTIONAL TEAM

Overall, poor team behaviors can be compared with those of a dysfunctional family. Poor behaviors lead to a lack of harmony and focus. Alert and focused product managers who identify these issues early can keep things running smoothly.

Effective product managers should strive to follow a different approach to cross-functional teaming. "Functional" cross-functional teams are focused and *goal directed*. The most efficient cross-functional product teams are those that share the following key characteristics:

1. The product team leader has the experience and stature to actually lead the team. Usually, this person is a product line manager or a product director.
2. The team is in place across the life cycle, which means that members may come and go but their business function remains bound to the business of the product.
3. The members are delegated and earn their "empowerment" through the actions and decisions they make and the results they deliver.
4. They enjoy the autonomy of being able to get the job done, working collaboratively, setting realistic goals, and communicating with one another when there is a risk.
5. Their primary loyalty is to the team, not to the function, and the team is properly rewarded for the results they achieve collectively.
6. They are tolerant of one another's individual differences, strengths, and weaknesses but still share their commitment to the team's goals.

Teamwork, team mechanics, and proper team documentation are needed to communicate, collaborate, and make decisions. The right tools will equip team leaders and team participants with the strategies to plan, negotiate, and carry out work, cross-functionally. They will also effectively monitor the work of the team.

BUILDING BLOCKS OF A CROSS-FUNCTIONAL PRODUCT TEAM

The Product Management Life Cycle Model provides a holistic framework and reference point for assembling the cross-functional team. The four primary areas of work—Discovery and Innovation, New Product Planning, New Product Introduction, and Post-Launch Product Management—represent the general areas of accountability for the product team.

Product teams that are in place across the product life cycle contribute most effectively to the management of the product as a business. Otherwise, product teams may just work on the product from idea to launch and then default to managing feature content and upgrades, with no regard for the other activities required to successfully manage the product as a business.

This error is often seen with highly technical products or IT systems that are managed by technology-oriented or engineering-oriented product managers. Moreover, in the technology business, many methods advocate rapid or agile product development. This launch-to-launch mentality makes it very difficult to actually manage the product because it leads to an internal project focus rather than robust, holistic, market-focused business management.

Full-stream, beginning-to-end Product Management means much more than simply focusing on a chain of product releases. The successful product team should also focus on marketing mix management, customer service and support, financial management, and operations management. In a best-in-class, cross-functional team setting, the product manager is the designated leader with responsibility and accountability for establishing the mission, vision, and overall strategic direction of the product. This leadership becomes the focal point for all product-related activities and actions as well as the gateway for all strategic and tactical decisions.

Every product manager must also work with other product managers, both in their immediate area within the product line and with other product lines in their divisions. This aspect is critically important because each product manager or product team leader should know the kinds of initiatives other teams are pursuing and how product investments are being allocated. Doing so avoids redundancy and establishes a context of elasticity across product lines (complementary, neutral, and cannibalizing).

Product team members are appointed representatives of business functions or functional organizations who have been given the authority to commit resources to a product and the resulting projects. If this structure does not already operate for an existing product, its implementation should be considered an urgent matter.

For entirely new products, the product team should be organized at the beginning of the product life cycle, during the Concept phase (the first phase of the NPD process). Although the team structure may be smaller at the beginning of the product life cycle, the team's membership will grow as the product concept matures and moves through each of the life cycle phases.

TEAM MEMBERSHIP

Membership on a cross-functional product team should not be taken lightly. It's not a role on a task force. The responsible business unit or division leaders must agree on those who are delegated to work on the team and approve of the members of the team. This assures that those team members will be accountable for their assigned responsibilities. That accountability is crucial to successful cross-functional teaming. Each member of the cross-functional product team must represent product issues and needs to their functional group and support the product manager and the product team as a whole.

Team members must be the key advocates and representatives from their respective functional organizations. They provide the interdependent link of functional expertise needed to support the product manager and the other business functions of the team. With this in place, the team can fulfill its primary responsibility, which is to meet all the performance goals of the product. The team members must, individually and collectively, assure that they fulfill their commitments to the team. Without this, the product may fail.

The focus and membership of the team may change as the product moves through its life cycle phases. Within each phase, it is the primary responsibility of the product team to carry out the fundamental work needed in order to make ongoing decisions about the product. When a product is in its NPD phases (Concept, Feasibility, Definition, Development, and Launch), the product team works together to decide whether to move a product opportunity from one phase to the next based on the results of actual work (research, product definition, and supporting documents).

These decisions and the supporting rationale are agreed upon with the product manager, so that the team can make the appropriate recommendations to executive management—which might be a product leadership or product portfolio council.

Not every functional group will have the resources or level of involvement to require a full-time member on the product team. Functional groups with specific resources dedicated to a specific product will typically have a full-time, or at least near-full-time, member based on the needs of the team and the current phase of the life cycle. Regardless of the membership status, each functional team member participates in both formal and informal supporting teams. These supporting teams represent the actual working teams (or project teams) that are responsible for planning and executing the agreed-upon tasks needed to support the individual projects that are spawned from the main product or product line team. Actual membership designations may vary among product teams, divisions, or business units of the same company and usually vary across industries. Functional areas of primary team members may include those listed below:

- Marketing or product marketing
- Finance
- Product development or engineering
- Information technology
- Sales
- Operations
- Supply chain
- Customer service or support
- Legal
- Regulatory
- Field operations
- Standards
- Security and safety
- Manufacturing

MULTICULTURAL PRODUCT TEAM ISSUES

Multicultural teams have long been a presence in many areas (such as consulting) because teams have to be every bit as global as the customers they serve. One of the things that all product teams need to deal with is that they too are becoming increasingly diverse and globally focused. In many well-run firms, employees are trained on cultural values and patterns that extend to meeting protocols, dress codes, and telephone etiquette. These organizations are trying to circumvent errors or missteps related to cultural differences. A team that thinks globally and is grounded locally will operate more smoothly and communicate more effectively.

When multicultural product teams run well, they portray a beautiful mosaic. Yet these teams present complexities for many product managers: communication styles vary, decisions are made differently, and there are language barriers. These issues can lead to misunderstanding and poorly designed products that don't deliver promised benefits.

In order to circumvent these issues, I strongly recommend working with your HR partners to find out how to bring your multicultural team together through training to improve communication and achieve common understanding among team members.

PRODUCT TEAM RESPONSIBILITIES

Product team leaders actively lead a product team, providing continuity and guidance. These leaders are team builders who develop shared goals and provide a balancing force for priorities, based on the required commitments and constraints of the various supporting business functions. Product team leaders are domain experts and market experts. They know the marketplace and the underlying needs of the market segments. Furthermore, they have good interpersonal and collaborative skills.

Functional team members provide needed functional expertise to the product team, but they are also responsible for coordinating the work of others in their functional organizations. This means that they must not only interoperate with other team members but also represent the capabilities and expertise of their own discrete business function as they negotiate across the business functions. If they cannot commit those resources to the product team, then they put the entire team in jeopardy. This pivotal point of contact is critical: they are ultimately accountable to the team for the implementation of their committed FSPs.

CROSS-FUNCTIONAL PRODUCT TEAM MEMBERSHIP

There are three different levels of cross-functional product team participation that help to describe the needed level of participation on the team: Dedicated Core Team members, Associate or Extended Team members, and Advisory members.

1. Dedicated Core Team members bring one member per functional organization, authorized to make commitments on behalf of their function, to the product team. These members are accountable for meeting the agreed-upon goals for their functional area.

2. Associate or Extended Team members are part-time (which could be half- to three-quarter-time) members. They are usually subordinates of Dedicated Core Team members and may be dedicated to a particular product or product project. They are not permitted to make final commitment on behalf of their function.

3. Advisory members are those who are called in to participate on an as-needed basis because they represent their organizations to many different product teams. Members from organizations such as Legal, Regulatory, PR, and Training are examples of Advisory members.

CLARIFYING ROLES AND RESPONSIBILITIES

A very interesting and useful method can help clarify roles and responsibilities in an organization, especially when it comes to task assignments for projects. It can also be a great tool for cross-functional product teams when there are cross-team dependencies and deliverables. The method is called RACI, and it's used to define which people in given functions are responsible for, consulted on, or informed about each milestone or deliverable required of the cross-functional team. RACI is an acronym, representing the four potential roles that a functional area can play relative to a specific milestone or deliverable. The components of the acronym have the following meanings:

1. *R*esponsible—the person who owns the deliverable, also known as the "doer." The doer is the person who executes a particular deliverable, or at least delegates and oversees its execution, and the single point of authoritative information on the current status and outcome of the deliverable.

2. *Accountable*—a person who has the authority to approve the completion of a task or activity. In general, the accountable individual has a larger stake in the outcome; thus, this person makes the final decision on execution.

3. *Consulted*—a person or persons who may be asked for assistance. The source of this is a group of people who may want or need to influence the final decision. These people are generally consulted before any major decisions are made and before a given deliverable is executed.

4. *Informed*—a person who is kept up to date on the execution, output, or status of the deliverable but who does not influence the result.

A RACI matrix is used to establish roles and responsibilities as shown in Figure 4.3.

All work tasks are typically characterized by some kind of goal or end point. It is important to be clear about these specific goals. This is achieved by considering reasonable methods for setting realistic, achievable goals. Psychologist Alfred Adler said, "We cannot think, feel, or act without the perception of some goal." When teams don't have concrete goals, indecisiveness and inability to move forward are amplified in proportion to the number of team members.

There are hundreds of studies in the field of Organizational Dynamics on how to set goals properly, yet there is no recognizable consensus. Many organizations set goals using the accepted SMART method—Specific, Measurable, Achievable, Realistic, and Time-framed. Applying SMART to task definitions can be extremely helpful in using a RACI matrix, but there are a couple of very important caveats we can learn from the academic study of goal setting.

FIGURE 4.3

A Typical RACI Matrix

	Task/Activity 1	Task/Activity 2	Task/Activity 3
Functional Team Member A	R	R/A	R
Functional Team Member B	C	R	I
Functional Team Member C	A	R	R

First, there is a tremendous difference between *approach* goals and *avoidance* goals—something the SMART mode doesn't move us to consider. Individuals and teams feel more motivated toward moving forward instead of holding position. In psychological terms, we are more motivated by things we approach, or go toward out of choice, than by things we avoid because life moves forward and requires us to do. While the effect may be marginal in high-functioning teams, the practice of setting approach goals, rather than avoidance goals, takes advantage of the human mind's natural motivational tendencies. For example, "grow market share 15 percent" is an approach goal; "avoid static market share" is an avoidance goal.

For most business elements of the cross-functional team, approach goals will seem obvious and routine. Development members of the team, however, may be more prone to set avoidance goals. For instance, in the software development and manufacturing realms, goals are often set for things such as "defect rates," giving the impression that things can only get so good. Bottom line: sometimes it's realistic to set avoidance goals, but most of the time the specific language of the goal should represent progress, growth, and forward-looking action.

Second, the structure of a goal often determines the level of commitment that a team member is willing to offer. Two factors play into this effect: goal importance (how challenging or visible the goal seems to be) and goal attainability (how realistic the goal seems to be). In fact, both individuals and teams find it easiest to commit to goals that are as challenging as possible without being unrealistic—sometimes (erroneously) called "stretch goals."

What does this suggest for goal setting? To put it simply, when setting SMART goals, maximum individual and team commitment is given to challenging, forward-looking, visible goals that state achievement in positive terms.

THE FUNCTIONAL SUPPORT PLAN

Knowing what we know now about cross-functional product teams, how should the team work? How does it get started, and how is continuity maintained across the life cycle? The simplest answer is that most of the team dynamics can be driven from the FSP. As discussed in Chapter 2, and as you will see extensively in the chapters covering New Product Planning, the basic building block of the Product Master Plan is the FSP.

FIGURE 4.4

Interrelated Elements of the Functional Support Plan

Function A (e.g., Marketing)

- The role
- Key responsibilities
- Major deliverables produced
- Other consumers of the deliverables
- Timing (when are the deliverables needed?)
- Possible risks
- Agreed-upon escalation paths (how to communicate to executives that a project is in jeopardy or there is a missed deliverable)

Function B (e.g., Sales)

- The role
- Key responsibilities
- Major deliverables produced
- Other consumers of the deliverables
- Timing (when are the deliverables needed?)
- Possible risks
- Agreed-upon escalation paths (how to communicate to executives that a project is in jeopardy or there is a missed deliverable)

Perhaps it would be better called the "cross-functional support plan" because that's more descriptive of its purpose.

FSPs are created as action planning, horizontal contracts across the cross-functional product team's membership. FSPs describe the activities, deliverables, dependencies, and schedules for each team member across the entire life cycle, especially the new product development phases. High-level versions are created for each FSP during the Concept Phase of the NPD process and are updated in each succeeding phase. You may recall our earlier summary of the typical FSP in Chapter 2. We'll go into detail on each of the different FSPs as we get to later sections of the book, but for now, you need to know that the FSP is the primary vehicle for giving the cross-functional team cohesiveness. As such, it must be able to describe what the function is giving and getting, to whom, and when. To help you visualize the interrelated elements of the Functional Support Plan, refer to the diagram shown as Figure 4.4.

TEAM MEMBERSHIP ACROSS THE LIFE CYCLE

As products move from one area of work to another (from New Product Planning to New Product Introduction, for example) or from one phase to another, team membership will evolve. The matrix shown in Figure 4.5

FIGURE 4.5

Cross-Functional Team Membership Across the Life Cycle

		Discovery & Innovation		New Product Planning			New Product Introduction		Post-Launch Product Management		
		Developing Insights	Formulating Strategy	Screening Concepts	Assessing Feasibility	Shaping the Definition	Developing the Product	Launching the Product	Encouraging Growth	Managing Maturity	Handling Decline
Core Team Members	Product Manager										
	Marketing										
	Development										
	Finance										
	Sales										
	Operations										
	Supply Chain										
	Manufacturing										
	Customer Service										
Advisory Team Members	Legal										
	Regulatory										
	Compliance										
	Human Resources										
	Org. Development										
	Training										

provides a way to identify team members who need to be associated with the team at various phases across the entire life cycle. This template can be modified for your own environment and include the names of the business functions that are specific to your organization. It is also a great tool to use to create a RACI framework for your team and to identify cross-functional relationships so you can negotiate FSPs.

Further to the point on team evolution, the right number of people should be assigned to or associated with the team. This is referred to as *team sizing*. An appropriately sized product team should have its core membership identified. Those members would be the Core Team Leads, Associate or Extended, and Advisory members, as mentioned earlier. Some of these members may need only to be consulted or informed about relevant changes. Establishing this team is the responsibility of the executives or senior business leaders who are cross-functional themselves and who have portfolio oversight for several product lines or product portfolios. After all, those who allocate investments across product teams should be able to allocate the human resources as well. Can you remember a team meeting where a particular technical or financial discussion completely derailed the agenda, only to be resolved later as a nonissue being pushed by someone with too narrow a focus? Choose the attendance at each team meeting, and in each life cycle phase, carefully.

The key point is to always maintain *relevant* membership in the cross-functional product team; any functional area that has a vested interest in—or needed expertise for—a particular phase should participate in the team. Anyone whose only contribution is pressure toward an unbalanced process or a side agenda should be excluded, or at least reintroduced to the rules of the cross-functional team.

CROSS-FUNCTIONAL TEAMS IN THE GLOBAL ARENA

As globalization continues its march, team members may rarely meet in person. These virtual teams are linked together by technologies that are intended to remove boundaries. Even with these great technologies, some hurdles remain. These include:

- *Time zone differences.* The quick exchanges that can move things along are not so easy to accomplish. Often, people in one time zone have to be available late at night or early in the morning.
- *Cultural miscues.* When team members don't appreciate or understand cultural nuance, misunderstanding and tension can arise.
- *Lack of chemistry.* When team members can't meet face to face and develop relationships, the team may not be as productive as it could be.
- *Insufficient access to information.* When team members don't have access to a repository of information, or don't have access to common processes or templates, things can get out of sync very quickly, leading to suboptimal decisions.

Fortunately, there are some great ways to improve global cross-functional team performance! Let me get down to the details so you can easily engage and empower your team.

1. *Use networking tools to build communities.* To overcome the challenge of physical separation, there are many types of social and other networking tools at your disposal to build one or more

communities of interest to collaborate, exchange ideas, and share knowledge and information.

a. When people can post information about their activities and interests, it creates gateways for conversation. Conversations can then be picked up in premeeting updates. Imagine a product manager asking a developer in another country, "I noticed that you took your family to Disneyland in France. How did you enjoy it?" These door openers can lead to further discussions about ideas and insights because you're not always talking about the business at hand.

b. A virtual cross-functional team is more likely to be productive and inventive if it includes some people who already know each other. These preexisting relationships can be vital to rapidly building networks among the team members.

c. Lastly, when virtual cross-functional team members have a shared online workspace, their work product and work progress is visible to all team members. This allows team members to gauge where they are in relation to each other and to the team's overall goals. This also provides the product manager with the information and insight to keep things moving along.

2. *Identify and appoint cross-organizational delegates.* Cross-organizational delegates are individuals who have the right networks and connections from across the organization to help get the team's work done. If you have one or two of these people on your team, you might be able to improve your team's performance when you need it most. If your cross-organizational delegates have preexisting relationships, your team is all the more advantaged.

3. *Evaluate and distribute project tasks.* Many of the work activities for which a cross-functional product team is responsible can, and should, be divided among team members. If you understand how work flows within a given process, and what the goals are, divide the work among people who can move quickly and independently toward that goal.

4. *Use video technology.* The cost and availability of video systems make them affordable for everyone. Being able to see people and interact with them creates a valuable sense of connectedness.

CROSS-FUNCTIONAL TEAM LEADERSHIP

An important theme ties together two important foundational chapters in this book, namely, Chapter 3 on leadership and this chapter on the cross-functional product team. All cross-functional product teams need a leader. The product team leader inspires a shared sense of purpose—the success of the product. The product team leader brings the team through the phases of team development and acts as the catalyst for action, which helps the team focus on the tasks at hand. At times, the product team leader is the coach, the teacher, and even a negotiator when conflict arises or priorities need to be adjusted. As such, team leaders use the suggested tools like FSPs, RACI, and SMART goal setting to make sure that both pairwise work activities and deliverables are clearly agreed upon, and then they make sure that those deliverables take place. During meetings, product team leaders encourage participation through inclusion with a shared, standard agenda, agreed-upon times for discussion, rules to take "other things" offline, negotiating discussions, and facilitating the team to consensus. This is all done with an unwavering focus on actions of the industry, competitors, and, of course, customers.

SUMMARY

Every company has teams because teams are a primary structure used by organizations to get work done. Teams are put together because they have the collective skills to best achieve a common goal. In business, there are many team types. Most important, and related to the topic of Product Management, you should understand the difference between project teams and product teams. Most project teams you are familiar with are cross-functional. Product teams are cross-functional as well. Project teams focus on the completion of explicit tasks and deliverables and then they disband. Product teams are responsible for running the business of the product. A product team in place across the entire life cycle can have a positive impact on the product's performance across the entire life cycle. This distinction between team types is so significant because it tends to confuse many people. Even if team members come and go, the product team requires leadership, and that team leader is a product manager or product line manager. The cross-functional product team can, when appropriately led, be a highly effective work structure for strategizing, planning, and managing the product.

RAISING YOUR PRODUCT MANAGEMENT EXPERIENCE QUOTIENT (PMEQ)

1. If you are newer to Product Management, ask your manager if you may observe how he or she runs product team meetings. Observe team members and how they participate, the subject matter expertise they bring, and how the meeting is structured. You can compare the way the team operates with the guidelines provided in Chapter 19. (A template for capturing meeting minutes is also included in Chapter 19.)

2. When you lead a team, or if you work on a project team, make sure that you can clarify roles and responsibilities. Use SMART as one approach and use RACI as another. You can also use the FSP to clarify roles as needed (refer to Figure 4.4 as a guide). If a team member's role is unclear, work collectively to both uncover the aspects of his work that are unclear and to learn where his roles or responsibilities may overlap with other team members'. You can use this discovery process as a way to bring the team together while negotiating about who does what and when. If the team member's role is still unclear, then you can use this data to ask for help from management.

3. Ask your manager or an impartial person in your organization to observe you leading a team meeting to determine your facilitative style and how you build trust, remove barriers, and inspire purpose.

4. Check to see which documentation is used by the teams you work on. Try to adapt the FSP format as used in this book to the clarification of roles and responsibilities, deliverables, and dependencies.

5. Carry out a quick self-assessment to determine where you are in your evolutionary development as a product team leader. Figure 4.6 provides a template to use. On a scale of 1 to 10, 10 being the best, where do you think you are and what might you be able to do to improve?

6. Work to resolve conflicts that invariably occur by recognizing the conflict, carrying out fact finding with key team members, mediating disputes, and having affected team members participate in finding alternative solutions.

7. Focus on building trust among team members. Trust is established first at the personal level. Additionally, try lending a helping hand in the building of relationships between team members so that they feel more comfortable with one another. Relationships have a degree of personal engagement—it's not always about work, so when you spend time with people, it should be not just in team meetings.

8. Since effective teaming and team leadership are about understanding people (team participants), think about having the entire team go through a personality or behavioral profiling exercise, such as the Myers-Briggs Type Indicator (MBTI), the Keirsey Temperament indicator, or some other type of instrument. The goal is to gain better insight into why people do what they do and use this insight to establish better working relationships.

FIGURE 4.6

Team Leader Assessment Template

	RATING	ACTION PLAN
Clarifies the product's strategy and makes sure others buy-in		
Builds relationships with other core team members and understands what each member brings to the table		
Plans and organizes purposeful product team meetings with agreed-upon agendas and desired outcomes		
Provides a forum for making sure that team roles and responsibilities are clear using FSPs		
Solicits input and inspires others to contribute to problem solving		
Creates a collaborative working environment to focus on the product and the market instead of individual team agendas		
Focuses the team on the production of results		
Keeps the team on track so it meets its commitments		
Provides positive reinforcement to team members for their participation		
Regularly reviews the product's business results, and inspires team members to contribute to the analysis of variances and the identification of solutions		

5

PROBLEM SOLVING AND DECISION MAKING: WHAT'S NEXT?

Executive Summary

- The building blocks of good decision making considers agility of thought plus the rapid assessment of opportunities and their consequences.
- For product managers, decision making is a nonstop series of pivotal inflection points across the life of a product.
- Effective product managers are adept at problem solving, which is at the heart of all decision making.

Decision making, in a nutshell, is how we solve problems. Throughout your career in Product Management, you will be continuously called upon to process an endless stream of information and to make decisions. Some are easy and don't affect many people or require much in the way of resources. Some decisions are very complex and their impacts can be long lasting. Decision points abound, whether during the New Product Development process, when deciding to enter a new market, or determining the best way or best time to launch a product.

Entrepreneurs have active, constantly moving thought processes and are always trying to consider options, opportunities, and consequences. Sometimes they must pivot at a moment's notice. For all businesspeople, product managers included, the biggest challenges are often to decide, "What will we do next? Why? What if we choose one option over another?"

THE IMPORTANCE OF DECISION MAKING

One of the most important things that product managers need to do, no matter what their job level in the company, is recognize there are always decisions to make because there are always problems to solve. Agility of thought and comprehension are of supreme value for any manager, and this includes product managers and the members of the teams they lead. Experienced product managers are thinkers who *decide* their way forward, always strategizing and restrategizing. They constantly ask, "What's right for the customers, the teams, and the business? What are the resources involved? What's the impact on the portfolio?" Successful product managers are continually reviewing situations in their minds and considering the available options second by second.

For the experienced product manager, good decisions are all about assimilating the varied cadences of the industry, evaluating the competition, considering the financial state of the product, and assessing other performance indicators to properly frame a situation.

The greater the product manager's familiarity with these indicators, the more rapidly the indicators can be processed in her mind and on spreadsheets. This leads to greater rapidity in the decision-making process—and greater speed is a key differentiator for good decision making.

In larger companies, many different people have to be included in the decision-making process, which involves dealing with many different personality types. Some of these people need an endless barrage of data, which unduly extends the decision-making process. Others are seemingly comfortable with less data because of their "third eye" into the other more nebulous areas of the business environment. Some call the extended process "analysis paralysis." An unwanted outcome from extended analysis is a failure to act, opening you up to being beaten by a competitor. Balancing the need for speed and the need for data is essential. As a matter of fact, the need for speed and data will continue to exert pressure on managers at all levels of the company. How do you deal with this constant state of urgency?

If decision making is the fulcrum, then what exactly are we trying to leverage? The multitude of variables in the equation for product managers includes known product strategies and tactics; cross-functional team expertise; finances; competitor knowledge; competing initiatives; and your (and your team's) time, just to name a few. Accurate and timely data is your friend, and that data should be as accurate and available as possible, so that the decision maker is able to do what needs to be done.

DECISION MAKING AND PROBLEM SOLVING

The crux of decision making is that it leads to solving problems. The word *problem* shouldn't necessarily have a negative connotation; it just means there is a situation to deal with that requires attention. Part of the decision-making process is built upon determining the problem's root.

Throughout your career in Product Management, you will always be talking about determining customers' needs. A need is an apparent problem, whether it causes pain or discomfort or is just a situation that can be improved. A commuter's need is a reliable way to get to work, via a car or some other method of transport. A problem can arise when the car is in the repair shop and an alternative is needed: work at home, take a train, ride a bicycle, and so on. Speedy decision making solves the problem of how to get to work.

To identify problems and evolve alternatives, you, as a product manager, will have to do a lot of the digging and research yourself. If you are working on or leading a cross-functional team, as I advocate, you cannot get your team members to listen and participate in problem solving and decision making if you are not the orchestrator of the problem-solving process. In order to smooth the way, you may want to take advantage of a simple model to guide the problem-solving process, as shown in Figure 5.1. This process acknowledges that there is an observed situation followed by an opportunity to clarify and solve the problem.

FIGURE 5.1

The Problem Solving Sequence

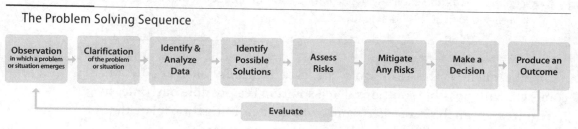

When I worked at Oracle, I led four product groups focused on solving problems related to the operation of call centers. As the leader who owned the portfolio, I saw a disconnect between the sales teams and product teams, which was the result of a lack of understanding by salespeople and inadequate sales training. Specifically, I needed to clarify the role of the software that ran inside of "black boxes" and figure out just how to prove the value proposition—so that it was more visible to salespeople and to customers. I pondered the idea and then the vision came to me: "If only the salespeople and customers could actually see into the black box." I had limited spending authority. I shared my vision with my team and said I wanted to create a "day in the life of the call center" video that would showcase what people did and how all of our products together helped them solve a much bigger problem.

I contacted a firm to produce the video for $15,000, which I knew wouldn't sit well with the corporate marketers who already told me "we weren't in their budget." I also didn't really want to call any attention to my stealthy project because of the impact I wanted to have on those who always said, "we just don't do that here." It took us about three months to produce this video sales tool. It was fantastic!

Then, it was show time! At the semiannual divisional offsite, I delivered my presentation, and then I lowered the lights and fired up the video for the 50 people in the room to see. Jaws agape and smiles were just a couple of the reactions I observed. "How did you do that?" "Where did you get the money?" "Who did this?" were only some of the questions. The next day, several people came in to ask me for the contact information for the video production company.

You see, sometimes you just have to make a decision (in this case, it was several decisions) to do something differently, stimulate ideas to turn people's heads, and demonstrate that things can be done differently for greater effectiveness with creativity—and outside of older paradigms.

The lesson I want to pass on to you is this: When you see that a problem has to be solved, you have to feel strongly that you are the one to solve it and then take the risk that you can deal with the consequences—positive or negative. By the way, the sales guys loved it—they "got it"—and they thought that it was a great way to begin a consultative dialogue with a customer, based on comparative scenarios. I was told explicitly that it wasn't a boring product demo that said, "Click here and look at this great feature!"

Subsequently, the team gets the data it needs, analyzes it, and comes up with possible solutions. Each solution is a possible outcome, so it requires an analysis of risks, and with that, a mitigation plan that, when acceptable by all, leads to the agreed-upon outcome.

SAVING GRACE: A CASE STUDY ABOUT DECISION MAKING

In order to illustrate some of the complexities and challenges related to decision making, I am providing you with a case study, presented as a story. At the end of this story, some questions will be posed for you to think about and answer. There are no right answers. Subsequently, parts of this story will be threaded through the end of this chapter to illustrate the relationship between this story and some of the other dimensions that contribute to your understanding about the decision-making process.

Jason, the product manager of a loyalty credit card program for a large regional bank, was waiting for his computer to boot up one morning when he *decided* to scan the monthly customer complaints report. Something jumped off the page: he noticed an increase in calls and an increase in card cancellations over the previous two months. Jason *decided* that this required more immediate attention.

The decision to introduce the card was made over a year before to appeal to a specific group of art collectors. It had been *decided* that the launch would take place at the start of the auction season, which had been nine months earlier. There was a big advertising campaign, and 75,000 new accounts were opened in the first two months. The number of new customers for the card grew 15 percent per month for four more months. Jason's product team noticed that late fee revenues were growing faster than expected and interest income was also higher during the previous two months. Of course, that is a good sign for a banker, but only up to a point, because you don't want people to default on their obligations.

Jason *decided* to ask the customer service manager for a more detailed complaint report and then *decided* an immediate meeting with the customer service manager was needed. When he called the customer service manager on the phone, she was too busy and said that her agents were getting tired of being yelled at by so many customers who were then canceling their cards. It was time for more deliberate action, so he thought about the situation while driving to work.

Jason wasn't scheduled to have a team meeting for two weeks, but he wanted to find out what was really going on and get to the heart of a problem he thought might get worse. He asked the customer service manager to lunch and said, "I really need your help to solve this problem—because by helping me, I can help you solve your problem and maybe another, bigger problem, which is unhappy, defecting customers." She took notice and said, "Okay, how can I help?" They both brainstormed and *decided* on a few things they could do:

- They could review the detailed agent reports. The customer service manager agreed to get these out of the CRM system immediately.

- They *decided* to each spend a couple of hours listening to the interactions on the call center recordings to determine exactly what was happening. What they heard was quite startling. Customers were complaining about getting charged late fees and interest that shouldn't have been charged because their bills were paid within the stated grace period.

- Jason and the customer service manager *decided* that there should be an emergency meeting of the cross-functional team.

At the meeting, representatives from Marketing, IT, Customer Service, Risk Management, Regulatory, and Operations discussed the situation, which was based on actual, verifiable data. After further analysis and diagnosis, the team *decided* that the issue was caused by a Marketing oversight.

Apparently, the new person in Marketing (who didn't have a Functional Support Plan and checklist) was asked whether she had put the billing system change on the IT project list the previous year. Apparently, she had not done so. Marketing neglected to secure the cross-functional team commitment from IT to change the grace period in the system. Instead of the grace period being the promised 25 days, it was set to 19 days, so the system billed fees and interest charges to those account holders who chose to use what they believed was their total grace periods to their advantage.

IT held part of the key to the solution but was adamant that it could not spare any programming resources for at least six weeks to make the adjustments in the system. IT stated that it was working on a big merger project, and besides, this situation wasn't really its problem. Jason was not too happy about this, so the team brainstormed and wrote down some options:

- Option 1—Train each of the 100 call center agents about how to deal with any customer who calls with a complaint. The solution would be for the agent to reverse any charges immediately and apologize to the customer.

- Option 2—Same as option 1, but add 5,000 loyalty points to the customer's account.
- Option 3—Same as 1 and 2, and suspend the annual fee for two years.
- Option 4—Escalate to the VP of IT and push the schedule up by four weeks.
- Option 5—Do a direct mail campaign to the 98,000 remaining accounts to explain, apologize, and promise to rectify the situation in 60 days.
- Option 6—Complain to the VP of Marketing that the error was costing the bank too much money.

Now it's time for you to examine the questions below so that you can evaluate the information and make some decisions about the pros and cons of each option. Remember, each option should be considered within the context of cost, schedule, resource availability, impact on customer loyalty, and brand reputation for the bank.

1. What option would you choose and why?
2. Is there enough data to make a decision? If not, what additional data would you want to have?
3. What would happen to the bank if competitors found out about this internal oversight?
4. What other dimensions would you think about in making the most appropriate decision?

The scenario just reviewed is fairly simple because it is presented in a linear fashion. However, problem solving and decision making are generally a bit more complex because the process requires careful consideration of a variety of variables. The flowchart or problem-solving map in Figure 5.2 shows, in a little more detail than that shown in Figure 5.1, some of the internal recycling that may take place. It considers discussion, debates, missing data, other organizations, customer impacts, and other questions about cause and effect when considering possible outcomes, risks, and mitigation in making the best decision possible.

It is important for you, as the product manager, to create decision-making maps using this flowcharting technique. The essence of this technique is breaking down problems into smaller and smaller pieces,

FIGURE 5.2

Documenting a Decision Process

Observation of a problem or situation

Data is needed.

Other people may have the data you need.

The situation is analyzed further—perhaps with the help of the cross-functional team.

QUESTIONS OR MISSING DATA
- How important is it?
- Does it exist?
- Can we get it?
- Can we afford it?
- What if we don't?

OPTION 1
- How does it fix the problem?
- Does the outcome associated with this option create any other problems?
- How would you measure the success of the outcome of this option?

RISKS
- What are the possible problems that could be a result of this option?
- What are the impacts elsewhere if we choose this option?
- Who else would be affected and how?

MITIGATION
- What would you do about it?
- How would you prove to your team and/or management that the benefits of this decision outweigh the risks?
- What would you do if no one agreed?

OPTION 2
- How does it fix the problem?
- Does the outcome associated with this option create any other problems?
- How would you measure the success of the outcome of this option?

RISKS
- What are the possible problems that could be a result of this option?
- What are the impacts elsewhere if we choose this option?
- Who else would be affected and how?

MITIGATION
- What would you do about it?
- How would you prove to your team and/or management that the benefits of this decision outweigh the risks?
- What would you do if no one agreed?

THE DECISION
- What was decided?
- Why?
- How did the team deal with the risk assessment?
- Who agreed? Who dissented?
- How were they acknowledged?

THE OUTCOME

Evaluate

and then going back and forth through the process so that you can discern the following:

1. Is the problem you see the real problem?
2. What is the importance of the problem?
3. Why is this important and deserving of your or your team's attention in relation to other issues you're addressing?
4. What additional data do you need?
5. How comfortable is everyone with the amount of data (that's a decision in and of itself)?
6. What are the potential outcomes, or other problems, that could emerge from this decision?
7. What would you do about those other problems if they emerged?
8. How will you document what you did so that others might learn from your experience?

By cycling through this process, one can usually whittle the problem down to, at most, three options, if not two.

DECISION-MAKING TECHNIQUES

Ideally, perfect solutions tend to show up by continued iteration, but often there are at least two options that fit the combination of risk and urgency presented by the problem. Ronald Howard, a learned explorer in the area of decision analysis, wrote, "Decision making is what you do when you don't know what to do." Therefore, we focus on a variety of techniques that are designed to support decisions and provide a degree of perspective or insight into how the problem might be solved. There are four additional techniques that can help identify the best option, or at least refine your options so that a choice is easier:

- Combining options
- The morphologic box
- The decision matrix
- The decision tree

It's worthwhile to take a brief look at each of these tools.

Combining Options

If you have only two options, it's critically important to consider the possibility that they aren't mutually exclusive; that is, they can both be executed without working against each other in any noticeable way. In many cases when problem solving, the choice of whether to execute two or more options simultaneously comes down to one of marginal cost and marginal value. When you're making a decision, and you get hung up on two or three finalists that don't seem to stand out each other, try applying the following tests:

- Is there any reason why we can't do all of these?
- Can we find a way to afford them all?
- Do we have enough resources to execute them all?
- Do they interfere with each other?
- Is there marginal value in doing all of them?
- What is the marginal cost of simultaneously executing the second option? That is, what costs will the second option incur that the first option doesn't already cost us?
- What is the marginal value of simultaneously executing the second option? That is, what additional benefits will it bring that the first option alone won't achieve?

These marginal costs and benefits aren't always measurable in dollars, so be sure not to focus exclusively on budgetary impacts or benefits.

The Morphologic Box

When facing more than a couple of options, you will have to look to linkages between individual criteria. In Jason's case, for example, was it customer retention, customer satisfaction, product revenue, or some other aspect that he was trying to improve—or some combination of them, or maybe all of them at once? For most decisions, there are just one or two aspects that are really important. Sometimes making up your mind is as simple as identifying these aspects, then evaluating each option after you have done so.

In the late sixties, Fritz Zwicky, a Swiss astronomer, developed a way to simplify problems that were too complex for making a simple decision. It's called the "morphologic box," a digestible, easy-to-evaluate form for analyzing a problem and evaluating its possible solutions. The

FIGURE 5.3

The Morphologic Box

	Customer Satisfaction	Customer Retention	Product Revenue
Option 1			
Option 2			
Option 3			
Option 4			
Option 5			
Option 6			

table in Figure 5.3 is a simplified version of the morphologic box for this particular problem and its options, considered for just three possible aspects.

The goal is to simply choose the aspects of the problem that each option truly affects. For example, if you think that Option 6, which involves complaining to the VP of Marketing, will really improve the customer satisfaction characteristic, then you would check the cell in the row for Option 6, under the column "Customer Satisfaction." In many cases, you'll be able to decide right away that one or more options do not contribute to a solution aspect. In this specific case, for example, it's clear that complaining about the situation will not actually improve any of these aspects—so why keep it? While some of the answers you get may be intuitive, this method gives you better clarity in explaining why you chose a particular option. For example, if a senior manager were to ask, "Why didn't you just complain to the VP of Marketing?" you can more clearly state that you couldn't see how that would improve customer satisfaction, customer retention, or product revenue. Maybe you didn't need a chart to tell you that, but the chart helped you clarify your thinking so that you gave a wiser, more cogent answer.

The Decision Matrix

Sometimes options can't be easily reduced by either combination or morphologic analysis, usually because every remaining option has some level of desirable impact on every problem characteristic; that is, they're all good choices. That's where a decision matrix can be helpful. The decision matrix is constructed similar to a morphologic box, with one

FIGURE 5.4

Decision Matrix

	Weight 1 Customer Satisfaction		Weight 2 Customer Retention		Weight 3 Product Revenue		Total
	Your Score (1–5)	Rank Times Weight	Your Score (1–5)	Rank Times Weight	Your Score (1–5)	Rank Times Weight	Sum of Rank Times Weight
Option 1	1	1 (1x1)	5	10	3	9	20
Option 2	2	2 (2x1)	2	6	5	15	23
Option 3	5	5 (5x1)	3	4	4	12	21

very important difference: it assigns a weight to each solution characteristic and asks you to evaluate, on a simple numeric scale (e.g., 1 to 5), how much each option contributes to each characteristic. The table in Figure 5.4 shows how a decision matrix would be run for the example used in this chapter.

Just to run through the mechanics of this quickly, the important part is to assign higher weights to characteristics that you feel are more important. In this case, it was arbitrarily decided that product revenue was more important than customer retention, which was more important than customer satisfaction. Having thus assigned the weights, one then just proceeds down the table and inserts the best estimate of how much that option will improve each characteristic, ranked according to the "1 to 5" ranking scale we've used here (you could use 1 to 10 if you wanted, although larger numbers sometimes get ridiculous to score and compute).

In the example, Option 1 was scored a "1 out of 5" in terms of customer satisfaction, while Option 3 was scored a "5 out of 5." Once you've ranked all the options on all the characteristics, you then multiply your rank times the weight and write the result in the "Rank Times Weight" column for that characteristic of that option. Continuing the example, we ranked Option 1 as "1 out of 5" against customer satisfaction, which has a weight of "1," so the "Rank Times Weight" is 1×1, which is 1. Finally, you add up all the weighted scores (i.e., all the "Rank Times Weight" entries) for the "Totals" column at the end of each row.

It seems complicated, and sometimes (as in this case) it produces options that don't differ much from each other. But if you study the chart for a minute, you realize how much better you can explain your choice. Suppose, for the sake of this example, that you chose Option 1, which doesn't have the highest score but has better results in your highest weighted characteristics (Customer Retention and Product Revenue). Now you have a much better answer when the boss asks, "Why did you choose an option that made all these customers complain so much?" You can say, with a little more wisdom and forethought, that while the option you chose had much lower customer satisfaction, the options with better customer satisfaction scores had abysmal customer retention and product revenue possibilities, so you chose the option that gave you better customer retention and product revenue results, knowing that customer satisfaction is a fleeting, changeable characteristic. Sounds smart, but the fact is, with the decision matrix, all you have to do is pretty much "read" your scored chart.

Ultimately, you may or may not choose the option with the highest score, as we showed in our example. The point is to understand clearly why you're choosing a specific option and what you believe to be the most significant impact(s) of your decision.

The Decision Tree

An effective decision analysis technique used to clarify and visualize decision options (alternatives) and possible outcomes is called decision tree analysis. It uses a diagram that looks like a tree with branches (outcomes) and nodes (decision alternatives). It's a good technique when the decision analysis is serial; that is, one decision and alternative leads to another set of alternatives.

A good way to start using a decision tree is to create a scenario or a story. The use of scenarios is important because of their relationship to the creation of assumptions when a Business Case is being prepared to analyze a product investment or when a market share forecast is being made. This linkage is critical because Business Cases and forecasts represent structured decision-making techniques, within the context of the New Product Development process, which is also a decision-making framework. Figure 5.5 shows an example of a simple set of activities involved in deciding when to launch a product, and where. In this simple case, you could almost imagine the cross-functional launch team meeting in a room, thinking about the impact of launching a product early or later, and having reached a decision of later, how they may have discussed the location and why. Each situation involves a series of scenarios, which helps the team envision the consequence of the outcome of an alternative.

FIGURE 5.5

A Decision Tree

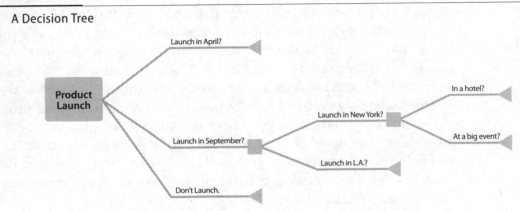

ANALYSIS PARALYSIS AND RATIONAL IGNORANCE

Sometimes, the more options you have, the worse your decision—or you might not make a decision at all. Curiously, overanalysis, or analysis paralysis, is easy to fall into when the possible negative impacts of a bad decision (the opportunity cost) seem much greater than the potential gains made by deciding. For example, if one stands to lose $3 million with a bad decision but gain only $500,000 with a correct one, it's very easy to spend more time than necessary analyzing the problem.

The root cause of this paralysis is the overwhelming negative view that causes you to naturally focus on only one side of the equation (unfavorable outcomes), which can limit your creativity. A simple technique to break this type of deadlock is to assume the worst case and then work upward from there. For instance, in the previous example, a seasoned decision maker will quickly recognize the onset of paralysis and approach the problem differently: "Assume we've lost $3 million. Now, how can we improve on that situation before it happens?"

Another deadly sin of decision making is rational ignorance, which, in some cases, is actually useful. When it's very expensive or difficult to gather facts for an informed decision, you need to consider the possibility that an informed decision might cost more than any benefit you'd gain from getting the facts. Hint: there aren't very many of those situations in corporate life. Some real world examples of appropriate rational ignorance might be (1) just getting everyone out and running away while you still have time, rather than trying to figure out which wire to cut on the bomb; (2) avoiding asking personal questions when someone seems to be in a bad mood; or (3) not bothering to find out, by experiment, just exactly how much tolerance a state trooper adds to the radar reading before pulling you over!

Rational ignorance can also hinder decision making, usually when people (or cross-functional teams) feel their voices won't be heard. Rational ignorance is often applied to presidential elections, using the reasoning that one vote is so small that, in the scheme of things, it just isn't worthwhile to be informed on the issues. As a product manager, if you suppress the voice of certain members of your cross-functional team, you run the risk of seeing rational ignorance begin to affect their decision-making behavior. For a very common example (especially in the software industry), if you don't adhere to schedules, and you ignore complaints or questions about slippage, you run the risk of everyone falling into denial about schedule risks. Before long, the product is either second to market or canceled altogether. This doesn't mean you should blow issues out of proportion, but you can't ignore or denigrate them either.

In short, if you want to make better decisions more often, you must avoid focusing too much on negative consequences (analysis paralysis) while ensuring that issues are not unduly suppressed (rational ignorance). You can't succeed as a Pollyanna or an Eeyore in the Product Management role—the glass is neither half full nor half empty—simply something that must eventually be washed.

This brings us to an important point: product managers and the teams they lead continue to earn greater credibility by having a higher percentage of better decisions than worse decisions. Often management one or two levels above you may become focused on one key characteristic of the solution—such as customer complaints—failing to recognize that you are making the right long-term choice for revenue, retention, or gross margin, for example. In other words, your management may get caught up in a weird combination of paralysis (short-term negative consequences—customers might call again) and rational ignorance (just get these calls to stop now). If you use a documented decision process, do enough evaluation to explain your choices credibly, and keep good records in the Product Master Plan, these "local anomalies" and decision-making fallacies are easier to address and control. And if you keep thorough, well-thought-out decisions in your Master Plan binder, you can continuously look back at your results and improve your decision making.

The New Product Development process (discussed in more detail in later chapters) is a somewhat structured decision-making process.

On the whole, though, day-to-day product management is a massive exercise in decision making. There will be some things you just have to do, some mini-decisions that will be easy to make, and some difficult problems to solve that have significant consequences; in the end, you must deal with all of them.

GUT-FEEL DECISION MAKING

As explained above, decision making has many objective methods, but a great deal of *subjective* content. Some of that subjective content can be qualified with rational thought, while some of it is based purely on instinct, intuition, or emotional reaction. In fact, decision making based solely on reason may not lead you to the most effective option. Often a well-rounded decision requires "going with your gut," otherwise known as *gut-feel decision making.*

Psychologists have come to understand that we generally have two neurologic reactions to any problem. Our rational reactions employ logic that is structured in slow, clear, linear argumentation that may continue for hours, days, or weeks. Usually in only microseconds, however, we use *somatic markers* (our basic survival instincts) to holistically analyze and pass judgment on a situation. These markers are often expressed directly through our physical reactions, such as embarrassment, anger, fear, fight-or-flight responses, and excitement.

FIGURE 5.6

Gut-Feel Decision Making

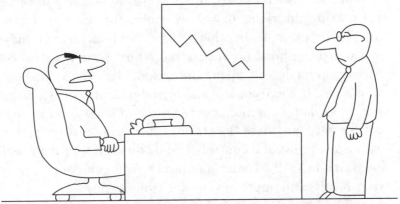

"It would appear, Hopkins, that your gut feel was only indigestion"
(Used with permission of the artist, Timo Elliot)

BUSINESS INTELLIGENCE

In order to make optimal decisions, product managers and their teams must digest ever-increasing amounts of data—both historical and real-time. This section provides some perspective on an evolving field of analytic techniques. I urge you to stay current on these methods, systems, and practices so that you are always equipped with the most appropriate sets of data and analytics with which you can make optimal decisions.

Business intelligence dates back many decades. As originally envisioned, business intelligence focused on technologies that gathered, processed, and presented information about business operations. These sets of data focused on sales, production volumes, and operations. The overall purpose was to provide business people with a comprehensive, structured set of easy-to-understand metrics. This operational business intelligence usually uses transactional data to provide current views so that the business can be "steered."

Data-gathering techniques continue to evolve. Vast amounts of data from transactional systems and business applications may be combined with data from click streams, system logging tools, publicly available data, and the like. This wealth of data presents business people with rich pools of data to evaluate products, customers, and the supporting infrastructure of the firm.

In a nutshell, for every decision you make, the more data you have (within reason), the better your chances of making a good decision. As you've already gathered, I am a strong advocate of gathering a lot of good data from every possible source. Once you have that data, however, it's crucial that you convert it into relevant information—then use that information as an *input* to how you arrive at your decision. As BI systems and other tools and techniques become more sophisticated, there may be a tendency to "let the data speak for itself" rather than to use the data within the context of other decision-making parameters or business signals. Remember that there are rarely times when you should not apply a little reason, along with a healthy dose of instinct, to your decision. Do stay focused on the right data set to help you reach the optimal conclusion, and help your team steer clear of analysis paralysis!

SUMMARY

Decision making is an evaluative process that product managers must cultivate throughout their careers. Every moment, every day, every week, dozens of decisions will need to be made, some simple and almost unconscious and some requiring complex data analysis. In the New Product Development process, you'll have to decide to move an opportunity from one phase to another, or whether to terminate a project. When you create a Business Case, you will need to decide whether a product investment is worthwhile. When evaluating product line financials, you'll be deciding how to respond to unfavorable outcomes. And of course, you will always have to ask, and answer, "What's next?" For now, it's important that you recognize the importance of decision making and begin to develop some skills in this key area. The tools and methods in this chapter will certainly help you get started.

RAISING YOUR PRODUCT MANAGEMENT EXPERIENCE QUOTIENT (PMEQ)

1. Keep a journal of the number and kinds of decisions you make each day. Classify them as personal and business. Use this method to examine your thought processes, the data you used, the assumptions you made, and your own satisfaction with the outcomes. Over time, you may be able to spot some patterns in how you process data, how comfortable you are with missing data, and what you might do to improve the speed and/or quality of the decisions you face.

2. When evaluating a situation, you need to get to the root cause. Ask "why?" There is a technique, roughly known as "why analysis." When you encounter a situation or problem that you believe requires a decision, you need to figure out what decision to make based on the basic problem. If you focus on the wrong problem, then you may make the wrong decision. I recommend you use a journal for this, too. Identify the problem or challenge in several steps. Here is an example:

   - Unit volumes are below plan. Why?
   - There has been an increase in customer complaints and an increase in product returns. Why?
   - The contract manufacturer used a substandard part, causing the product to fail. Why?
   - The product specification did not adequately describe the type of material to be used. Why?

- The product requirements did not clearly identify the performance needs for the customers based on how the product is to be used. Why?

- The customer analysis research did not capture the most appropriate usage scenarios. Why?

3. The next time you believe you are faced with a key business decision, start out by clarifying the problem to be solved—or the decision that must be made. You must have a clear idea of what the problem is; otherwise, this exercise will not work. A white board or other larger visual display might help inspire creative thought. Next, make a list of things you think you might do to solve the problem. At first, the obvious possibilities will surface, but each possibility might lead to a consequence, either desirable or undesirable. This begins to eliminate some ideas and raise new ones. You can step away from the exercise and come back to it, or you can invite others to help you, especially if others have a more diverse set of experiences. You may also find that you need to do further analysis or secure more data. These are all positive actions designed to help you reveal possibilities and narrow alternatives, as you work toward the best possible outcome.

4. You will invariably have to evaluate new product project ideas using a structured decision-making technique. Discussed in detail in Chapters 11 through 17, decision "screening" is used to determine which product ideas are to be acted upon and which will be rejected. It is suggested that the technique you ultimately use be documented and used as a learning tool for the cross-functional team. By capturing the decision-making process and the data used, you will create the artifacts that describe how and why you and the team arrived at the decision. If you ultimately present a recommendation to management, you will want to document the outcome in the Product Master Plan.

CHAPTER

FINANCE FOR THE PRODUCT MANAGER: KEEPING SCORE

Executive Summary

- Product managers should have a solid understanding of the "numbers" in order to plan and manage products.
- Product managers who understand the mechanics of financial statement construction can readily evaluate the performance of their products, their own companies, their competitors, and even the industries in which they compete.
- Product managers work to cultivate successful products that provide a positive economic contribution to the company.
- The product life cycle curve is a graphical representation of the product's stream of revenue and/or profits. It provides a powerful tool to illustrate the product's overall progress and performance.

The product manager must make sure that the product's actual financial performance fulfills expected financial and market performance targets. Making good decisions on behalf of the product requires financial data. However, I have learned from my ongoing benchmarking that many

111

product managers do not have any formal education or training in financial management. Furthermore, they don't have access to important and timely financial details about product performance, product costs, and product profitability. Financial principles, along with the associated financial and accounting vocabulary, should be a vital part of the product manager's toolkit.

THE LANGUAGE OF BUSINESS

Finance is the common language of business. If product managers are responsible for running the business of the product, they need a good foundation of fundamental financial skills. They must be able to understand and assess how a product's financial returns affect the business and the product portfolio. In addition, they need the financial acumen to manage future investments in their product wisely. Product managers need grounding in the fundamentals of business finance.

This chapter provides you with that essential financial foundation. Basic financial statements and vocabulary will be defined. These include Income Statements (sometimes called the Profit and Loss Statement, or P&L), Balance Sheets, and Cash Flow Statements—and an explanation of the importance of discounted cash flow and net present value (NPV).

These key techniques are aligned with the Product Management Life Cycle Model and are then applied in two broad categories: *planning* and *managing* the "business of the product." Each of these topics will be developed as the chapter evolves.

THE BASIC FINANCIAL STATEMENTS

Product managers should be able to review and analyze financial statements. When business and financial people talk about gross profits, depreciation, working capital, and cash flow, they must comprehend the meaning of these terms and feel comfortable when discussing financial matters. The language of business is derived from the accounting field. Your familiarity with this critical business vocabulary will increase your stature as a product manager and earn you greater respect from your cross-functional team members as well as from management.

Financial statements are the most important and universal documents utilized by businesses. They are the functional instruments used to manage the business, make decisions, and communicate results to various interested parties.

Since products are "mini-businesses" for which product managers and their teams are responsible, it is important to understand that these same financial statements are used at the product level. Product managers use these statements to create and communicate product budgets, analyze results, and make decisions when results don't align with projections. The product manager should also understand how these tools are used to disclose information about the product's performance to stakeholders, namely your cross-functional team members and your management.

Additionally, the product manager should make sure there is strong financial expertise and representation on the product team. Understanding and applying financial techniques does not automatically bestow the underlying knowledge about the mechanics of corporate financial management and accounting. The financial representative to the team provides critical insights when Business Cases are created, forecasts are derived, and analyses are carried out. In the following sections, I'll describe the characteristics and usage of each financial statement.

THE INCOME STATEMENT

The Income Statement is sometimes called the Profit and Loss Statement, or just P&L. Since the P&L tracks product or business performance over a given time period such as a month, quarter, or year, it is referred to as a *periodic* statement. The P&L helps to determine whether the product has contributed a *profit* or *loss* over the specified time period. Each product should have its own P&L. The basic P&L format for a product is shown in Figure 6.1.

There is an easy way to view the P&L: divide it into two halves. The top half of the P&L considers *revenue* and the specific costs to create that revenue. The bottom half includes the *expenses* incurred by the functional departments as they support the business or carry out their daily activities.

The top half of the P&L opens by accounting for the revenue brought in from the sale of products or services to customers. Revenue is calculated by multiplying the unit selling price by the number of units sold:

$$\text{Revenue} = \text{Unit Selling Price} \times \text{Units Sold}$$

FIGURE 6.1

Projected Income Statement for Product ABC for the Upcoming Year 20XX

	Budget
Sales (Revenue)	
Number of Units	10,000
Price per Unit	$6.25
Total Revenue	$62,500.00
Cost of Goods Sold (COGS)	
Materials	7,500.00
Labor	4,500.00
Overhead	$9,800.00
Total COGS	$21,800.00
Gross Margin	$40,700.00
Gross Margin%	65.1%
Expenses	
Marketing	5,400.00
Sales	3,300.00
R & D	3,235.00
General & Administrative	2,100.00
Total Expenses	$14,035.00
Earnings Before interest & taxes, depreciation, and amortization (EBITDA)	$26,665.00
Depreciation & Amortization	500.00
Interest Expense	350.00
Income Taxes	2,631.00
Net Income (Profit)	$23,684.00
Net Income %	37.9%

If your company produces tangible goods, a variety of costs are incurred to produce them. (Note: Service-based businesses or software companies do not have material costs; however, you should always check with your finance department to determine if there are any costs in this category.) These production-specific costs, in total, are referred to as *cost of goods sold* (COGS) and represent the *direct* costs incurred to produce the product and any overheads allocated in the production of the product. COGS is generally composed of the cost of raw materials, the associated labor to assemble the product, and various direct and allocated overhead costs like rent and electricity for the facility used in the production or assembly of those products:

Material + Labor + Overhead = Cost of Goods Sold (COGS)

Gross margin (sometimes referred to as *gross profit*) is the money earned directly from the sale of the product. It is derived by subtracting COGS from revenue. Gross margin is very significant because it represents an important measurement of product profitability. For product managers and their cross-functional product teams, gross margin is often the only measure of product profitability that can be reasonably applied. The gross margin must be significant enough to cover the expenses incurred by other departments that support your product—and deliver a net profit at the end of the financial period. Gross margin in absolute dollars, and as a percentage of revenue, is also an important measurement when comparing one product's performance to another's (within the portfolio), and in comparing your company's results to its competitors':

Revenue − COGS = Gross Margin

Gross Profit / Revenue = Gross Margin %

The bottom half of a P&L is where the different functional departments' expenses are listed. These expenses are categorized by functional departments, including Sales, Marketing, R&D, Customer Service, IT, and other operating expenses. There is usually an allocation for "general and administrative" expenses, which are borne by all products and distributed to product line P&Ls by the company according to predetermined algorithms. However, these expenses are often beyond the control of the product manager and the team.

If it is possible to establish budget line items for expenses that are budgeted in Marketing Plans, and to be able to track those incurred expenses against those plans, the product team will better visibility into the impact of those marketing investments on the product's market performance and profitability. This could be accomplished as a collaborative effort with the Finance department. The team could thus "absorb" its marketing allocations and, as a consequence, be able to recognize the direct expenditures for product-related marketing investments.

After operating expenses are accounted for, the next level of product profitability must be calculated. That is called the *earnings before interest, taxes, depreciation, and amortization,* or EBITDA. In some companies, this might be referred to as "income from operations." This allows for the separation of interest and taxes from the actual operating P&L for the product:

$$\text{Gross Margin} - \text{Operating Expenses} = \text{EBITDA}$$

There are some additional expenses that are often charged against product P&Ls: interest and taxes. Interest is sometimes allocated to a product or product line to cover a proportion of the cost of the company's borrowing money to finance its operations. Taxes are levies by federal, state, provincial, and local governments on profits earned by a company.

All of these categories are typically beyond the extent of control of the product manager and the product team. However, in many cases, positive gross margin or even EBITDA can "evaporate" because of other allocations or charges, such as interest, taxes, depreciation, and amortization.

The true profit of a business as well as a product's "bottom line" or net profit can be calculated by subtracting all expenses, interest, and taxes from EBITDA by the following calculation:

$$(\text{EBITDA}) - (\text{Interest, Taxes, Depreciation, and Amortization}) = \text{Net Income}$$
$$\text{Net Income} / \text{Revenue} = \text{Net Income \%}$$

Net income (or net profit) is the whole reason that your company is in business. If the bottom line isn't greater than getting a return on investment such as interest from a bank, why run the risk of operating a business at all?

Your product may be dependent on "assets" such as machinery, equipment, facilities, computer systems, patents, trademarks, or other assets. A portion of an asset's value is taken each year as "depreciation or amortization." If your product is dependent on "assets," these assets are depreciated or amortized over time. Depreciation and amortization is how companies indicate the use and declining value of assets. Since the company lays out the money for the equipment or facilities in advance, it lists those assets on the Balance Sheet (more on Balance Sheets later). The company already paid the "cash" for the equipment when it was purchased. Therefore, your product is "charged" each year for a portion of the normal wear and tear caused by usage of the equipment (depreciation) or the remaining life of a patent or trademark (amortization).

Depreciation and amortization are not really a current cash expense because the team (or company) didn't spend any money. However, the team does have to absorb a cost for the portion of the asset actually utilized in that year. Depreciation and amortization have to be captured and accounted for somewhere. Therefore, they are recognized in a line item of the P&L by being treated as if they were a cash expense. Depreciation does not affect cash flow for the company.

THE BALANCE SHEET

The Balance Sheet is a financial statement that takes a "snapshot" of the *assets* and *liabilities* of the company at a specific point in time and depicts the overall *net worth* or *equity* of the company at that particular point in time. It is different from the P&L, which shows results for a financial period.

The Balance Sheet depicts the assets owned by the business and how those assets are financed with money from creditors or the capital of its owners or shareholders, or both. The Balance Sheet states that the business is in balance. Like the human body, the Balance Sheet *must* be in a state of balance, or homeostasis, if it is to function properly. The Balance Sheet has a basic arithmetical formula or equation:

$$\text{Assets} - \text{Liabilities} = \text{Owner's Equity}$$

Assets are the items of value that a firm controls, all of which are measured or *valued* in terms of money. Assets are employed by a company's management to create value. For example, a manufacturing plant is an asset that enables the company to build products. Consider the forms and sources of assets: assets are more than just cash in the bank; they can also be money that's owed to the company by customers, called *accounts receivable*.

Current assets are those that can be easily converted to cash within one year and include cash in the bank, marketable securities, accounts receivable, and inventory. *Quick assets* (as they are sometimes termed) are the subset of current assets that are essentially already in *liquid* form, such as cash and marketable securities.

Fixed assets are those that are more difficult to quickly convert to cash: buildings, manufacturing equipment, and land. Collectively, these are also referred to as property, plant, and equipment (PP&E).

Intangible assets are a financial representation of intangible items that nonetheless have some monetary value. These include patents, brands, intellectual property (acquired knowledge), and goodwill. Intangible assets are considered difficult to measure and value, but companies, as well as accounting governance bodies, are focusing more and more on finding ways to account for them.

Liabilities generally represent the means by which assets are financed. When your company incurs a liability, it is obligated to pay for it at some point—either in the near term, or over the long term, so it represents a future cash outflow. Just like assets, liabilities are divided into two categories: current liabilities and long-term liabilities or debt.

Current liabilities are those obligations that must be paid off within one year. These include payments for operating expenses, supplies, and materials as accounts payable. Current liabilities may also include short-term loans, the interest on those loans, the current portion of loans required to be paid within one year, and taxes owed.

Long-term liabilities (often called long-term debt) describes obligations that mature beyond a year. Many companies incur long-term debt (or issue bonds) to finance capital expansion or to finance other business activities. This is where the term *leverage* often comes into play. When a company is "heavily leveraged," it is said to have a lot of debt—money it owes to others (I'll give you an example shortly).

One of the derivative financial principles and terms you often hear is the expression *net working capital*. Net working capital is what you get if you subtract current liabilities from current assets. It's called "working" in the sense of "doing work," *not* "available to do work," since it's the share of the owner's equity that's actually tied up in day-to-day operations and could be extracted within one year if the company ceased operations and paid all outstanding bills. *Working capital* is a particularly sensitive subject for many financial team members, because its application and use has to be carefully balanced. If there is too little working capital available, the company won't be able to meet its monthly financial obligations such as payroll and rent. However, if the balance sheet shows too much, it can indicate certain problems such as excess or slow-selling inventory, slow payments by customers, or even uncollectible accounts. Any one of those situations needs to be immediately analyzed and rectified.

Owner's equity is the collection of assets that actually belong to the owners or shareholders. Also known as net worth, it is the difference between assets and liabilities, and therefore a representation of the true "book value" of the ownership of the company. A simple comparison could be your ownership of a home. The value of the home could be $500,000, but if you have a $200,000 mortgage, the amount of your true ownership, or equity, in the home is actually only $300,000. The forms and sources of owner's equity include contributed capital (money invested in the company by its owners, private investors, or shareholders) and retained earnings (the company's accumulated net income over its time in business). A sample Balance Sheet is shown for you in Figure 6.2.

As briefly described in an earlier paragraph, financial leverage refers to the situation in which you use borrowed money to purchase an asset (to create value), and then repay the money with an overall net gain that exceeds the return you would get on your own capital.

For example, let's say you could buy pencils for a dollar each and sell them for $1.25—but you only have $1 of working capital. Without leverage, you can buy one pencil, sell it, and keep $.25 profit, for a gain of 25 percent. After four such sales, you could afford two pencils, and so on, each time making only 25 percent return on your investment. On the other hand, you could borrow $3; add it to your dollar to buy four pencils; sell them for $5; return the $3 loan; and reap 100 percent profit on your original investment of $1. Even if you had to pay 10 percent interest (i.e., $.30), you'd still net 70 percent profit from your original dollar.

Product managers may not be concerned about how the chief financial officer (CFO) or controller finances equipment or other assets used in the creation of their products. However, when analyzing their competitor's situation, product managers may find it is important to know whether they are overleveraged. Whereas overleveraged organizations (those with too much debt on the Balance Sheet) may be limited in whether they can invest in new products or new marketing programs, companies that are not heavily leveraged (don't have a lot of debt), and have cash on their Balance Sheets, have the luxury and advantage of being more financially agile, which counts in competitive situations.

In general, the Balance Sheet is usually a reference tool to the product manager. However, in certain instances, assets would be an area of interest. For example, if new equipment or facilities are needed to support product investments, the product manager would be concerned about the investment required as well as the future depreciation of these new assets allocated to the product.

FIGURE 6.2

Sample Balance Sheet: December 31, 20XX

	Past Year	Current Year	Increase/ (Decrease)
ASSETS			
CURRENT ASSETS			
Cash	250,000	325,000	75,000
Marketable Securities	335,000	420,000	85,000
Accounts Receivable	650,000	700,000	50,000
Inventory	725,000	240,000	(35,000)
TOTAL CURRENT ASSETS	$1,510,000	$1,685,000	$175,000
Property, Plant, & Equipment	$2,750,000	$2,850,000	$100,000
TOTAL ASSETS	**$4,260,000**	**$4,535,000**	**$275,000**
LIABILILTIES & OWNERS EQUITY			
CURRENT LIABILITIES			
Accounts Payable	635,000	720,000	85,000
Short-Term Loans	24,000	19,000	(5,000)
Taxes Payable	125,600	138,000	12,400
TOTAL CURRENT LIABILITIES	$784,600	$877,000	$92,400
LONG-TERM DEBT	$625,000	$550,000	($75,000)
TOTAL LIABILILTIES	**$1,409,600**	**$1,427,000**	**$17,400**
OWNERS' EQUITY	**$2,850,400**	**$3,108,000**	**$257,400**
TOTAL LIABILITIES + OWNERS' EQUITY	**$4,260,000**	**$4,535,000**	**$275,000**

Product managers should also have an interest in the inventory position of the product. If too much inventory builds up, it is an indication that sales are not materializing, which indicates that production forecasts are incorrect and the underlying causes need to be addressed. If there is too little inventory, it might mean that a lag in production will result in lower-than-projected sales. Such problems are within the purview of the product team and are the responsibility of the product manager.

CASH FLOW

Every month, the company receives money from sales of products and services (revenues) and disburses money in order to operate the business (expenses). The best parallel to use is based on our own personal lives. We receive money from salaries or other sources and disburse money for our living expenses. In a nutshell, this describes cash flow.

It is not a typical responsibility for the product managers to know every nuance of cash flow management. It is largely the responsibility of the CFO or treasurer of the company. However, a fundamental understanding of cash flow is important for the product manager. The reason is because all forecasts (and the underlying assumptions in those forecasts) involve the translation of market share estimates and sales projections into financial information. This information is synchronized with the calendar so that the appropriate plans can be made coincident with the expected arrival of money from sales, and the outflow of money to support operations. The CFO reviews the forecasts of all the product teams within the company to determine how much money to anticipate to finance business operations. If shortfalls are predicted, the CFO needs to work out where to get money to pay the bills. If there is an excess of cash flow, then the CFO has to have a plan in place to invest the money so it doesn't sit idle.

This scenario can be an example. If the product manager predicts a product launch in May, first orders in July, and payments from July orders in September, the team's financial member informs the CFO about the product forecast and the CFO inserts this into the cash flow plans. (By the way, if you are producing a physical product, your factory forecast is also tied to the assumptions about when your product will be selling).

Now, suppose the launch is three months late (August) and the first orders don't actually materialize until October. It is possible the company will be paid either late in the year or perhaps not until early the next year. This could be a dilemma if the product manager does not understand two things: the company's sales cycle and the *order-to-cash* cycle (which tells the product manager how long it takes to get paid after an order is received). The late launch problem could also have a negative impact on product inventory because the factory's production forecast was tied to the sales forecast.

Inventory build-up takes cash away from the CFO's checkbook because instead of funding operations or investments, the money gets tied up in nonproductive inventory.

When you create a forecast in a Business Case, the potential cash inflows from product sales must exceed the investment that the company has made (in advance of those sales) plus some premium for the cost of capital and a return on that capital.

In the accounting concept known as *present value,* the basic premise is that a dollar (or unit of currency) today is worth more than a dollar tomorrow. For those who are not financially trained, this is sometimes a difficult concept. Thus, another reason cash flows are important is because of present value: the further out into the future the cash comes in, the less value it has to the company. In financial planning, money received today has more value than money expected to be received two years from now.

However, not all product investments are the same. In order to put this into perspective, we need to talk about *discounted cash flow.*

DEMYSTIFYING DISCOUNTED CASH FLOW

Throughout the year, many product teams ask management for investment money for their products. The CFO, working with the executive leadership team, is supposed to take a portion of the company's profits, after providing for normal working capital requirements, and invest it. One way to do this is to reinvest in the business. If the product team wishes to "borrow" money from the CFO, it must be paid back with interest (providing a rate of return). This interest has another word in the corporate world: the *discount rate*. The discount rate is based on what is called the "cost of capital." (If you're interested in this, you can read more about it in most finance textbooks.) Companies supply their checkbooks with money from a variety of sources, and each source has a different "cost." The discount rate is also considered a function of the company's risk of loss—for example, if your product team doesn't pay it back when expected. The discount rate may be increased for investments perceived as riskier. Suffice it to say that the CFO charges you a discount rate that accounts for the fact that money expected to arrive further into the future is discounted back to the present. Hence we have the financial expression *discounted cash flow*. Here's a simple example of how this works:

Suppose your product team needs $100,000 for a new product. The finance representative feels that the Business Case has a low risk of failure and that the discount rate of 12 percent will be sufficient to cover the cost of capital and the relevant risk of the investment. Figure 6.3 shows how the cash flows are actually discounted.

- In the current year (CY), the team gets $100,000. In the first year, the net cash flow from product sales is $45,000. However, because it's one year into the future, the $45,000 needs to be "discounted" back to the present. In our example, it would be calculated as [$45,000 + .88 = $39,600], with .88 allowing for the discounting of the cash flow by 12 percent. In the second year (CY + 2), the product contributes $60,000 to the company.

- In the second year, the money is discounted twice (that's compounding the discount rate), which means it's discounted by 12 percent two times, calculated as [$60,000 × (.88 × .88 = .7744) = $46,464].

- In the third year (CY + 3), the money is discounted three times and the discounted cash flow is calculated as follows: [$75,000 × (.88 × .88 × .88 × .6815) = $51,110]. Each future cash flow is discounted "back to the present" and then added up.

FIGURE 6.3

The Mechanics of Discounted Cash Flow

	CURRENT YEAR	CURRENT YEAR + 1	CURRENT YEAR + 2	CURRENT YEAR + 3	TOTAL
CASH INVESTED	−$100,000				
REVENUE		$45,000	$60,000	$75,000	$180,000
DISCOUNTED CASH FLOW		$39,600	$46,464	$51,110	$137,174
CUMULATIVE DISCOUNTED CASH FLOW		$39,600	$86,064	$137,174	

Adding up the future discounted cash flows is called the cumulative discounted cash flow (CDCF). Most financial analysts will take the CDCF and subtract the original investment to arrive at the net present value (NPV) for the investment. Positive NPV means that the investment will generate a return to the business. The CFO and the portfolio review board will likely compare different NPVs based on timing (cash flows received sooner are generally viewed more favorably), risk, and the absolute amount of the initial investment. This is an expression you will probably hear many times during your Product Management career and while you are involved in the world of business.

When product managers learn the fundamentals of financial statements, they are better able to apply these financial tools and techniques to the business management of the product—that is, to create plans and to manage those plans based on a good knowledge of fiscal requirements.

FINANCIAL PLANNING FOR PRODUCT MANAGERS

Now that you've had an introduction to understanding the financial statements, let's talk about financial planning. Product managers, at some point in their career, have to carry out the following:

1. Create Business Cases for product investments
2. Assemble forecasts
3. Test planning assumptions (sensitivity analysis)
4. Derive product cost models
5. Establish pricing models
6. Prepare product budgets

Each of these planning activities is critical to setting up the business of the product so that its results can be tracked and compared against those plans. I'll briefly discuss each one. However, these topics are discussed in more detail in other chapters.

Creating Business Cases for Product Investments

The Business Case is the primary document used by product managers to justify investments in new products or product enhancements, or even marketing investments. The term *investment* is revealing. It means that the product manager is requesting money from management (typically the product portfolio review board) and is going to prove that the product team can deliver a positive return to the business. There may be other product managers in the company who are competing for money, so realistic, believable Business Cases usually garner greater levels of support from management. Product managers should try to create the best, most complete Business Cases possible because these documents help to establish the product manager's credibility and business acumen in the eyes of management and the cross-functional team members with whom they work.

Assembling Forecasts

A forecast is an estimate based on assumptions about the future. As you will learn in Chapter 9, product managers are responsible for forecasting market share, sales volumes, and demand or production forecasts. Each of these forecasts is based on a host of variables, ultimately linked back to the strategy for the product. Forecasts are built on assumptions formulated by members of the cross-functional product team. Their goal is to determine "future state" market situations that are ultimately translated into unit volume forecasts.

Forecasts are also created to determine the market share the product can capture. Market share postulations and assumptions are built on a solid foundation of industry and competitive research, and needs-based market segmentation models. For example, assumptions for sales volumes are evaluated in conjunction with the Sales department, because Sales needs to be able to commit to delivering those volumes and, of course, needs to be appropriately compensated for selling the product.

Assumptions are also linked to demand forecasts for tangible goods so that the factory's production schedules can be created. In addition, forecast assumptions are linked to the work of the Marketing department since marketing programs must be appropriately timed to stimulate interest in the product and drive sales activity. If the sales forecast is too low, there won't be enough product available and customers will go elsewhere to satisfy their demand. If sales volumes are too low, inventory positions will build, wasting company money.

Of course, each and every assumption about the future in any forecast is expressed in financial terms.

Testing Planning Assumptions Using Sensitivity Analysis

As you begin to consider investment decisions, forecasts in budgets, and Business Cases, it does not take long to reach the point of asking, "What if . . . ?" What if the cost of materials goes up in six months? What if we increase the price by 10 percent? Eventually, as a product manager, you will want to create various assumption sets and then see what *might* happen. Testing assumptions means that you change a variable (unit volume, a product cost element, or a unit price) to assess the impact on future product profitability. When you change a variable in the formula based on a revised assumption, you're trying to see how "sensitive" the impact is on profitability. This process is called *sensitivity analysis.*

When carrying out sensitivity analysis, you should not be changing many variables at the same time. You change one variable to see the overall impact on gross margin or net income. If you believe that the most likely market situation will yield a unit volume of 1,000 units at $250 per unit for one year with revenue of $250,000, what happens if the volume is 20 percent less and the price is the same? Then, revenue would be $200,000. Would that be enough to sustain the business and deliver the targeted product profitability and market share?

Deriving Product Cost Models

As suggested earlier, all tangible products have costs associated with their production. Businesses that make or buy goods to sell deduct the COGS from their revenue in computing gross margin. This information applies if the business is a manufacturer, wholesaler, or retailer, or if the company is engaged in any business activity involving the buying or selling of goods to ultimately produce revenue. This does not generally apply to businesses that provide intangible services.

Product managers should have some ideas about the cost models used to plan and manage products. The three methods discussed here include standard costing, target costing, and activity-based costing.

Standard costing of a product is based on the company's cost of direct material, direct labor, and overhead. During planning or budgeting, many companies don't assign an actual cost of material, labor, and overhead to the product. Rather, they establish a standard cost by estimating the costs based on what's already known, or based on products that have already been produced (especially if there is inventory that has a cost associated with it). Product managers can think of the standard cost as the "cost used for planning purposes." Typically, the standard cost is set at the outset of the fiscal year, and then as new costs are realized for producing the product (in different volumes), these actual costs will be compared with the standard costs. If there is a difference between the actual costs incurred and the standard costs, they can be analyzed and attributed to variations or fluctuations in volume, material costs, or overheads. As products evolve across their life cycles, product managers will always be looking to reduce the costs of producing the product and will rely on having relevant reference points from which to carry out their cost analyses.

Target costing is a method whereby the proposed product costs are specified so that a targeted gross margin or product profit can be realized. The process of target costing begins with the product definition, and clearly encompasses the product's functionality, performance, and quality. The underlying assumption, in tying costs to the product definition, is that it considers the market segments or target customer types for whom the product is to be developed. If the product manager establishes a gross profit goal of 75 percent and the market price of the product is $100, then the targeted cost cannot exceed $25.

Activity-based costing is a technique that logically allocates overhead to products based on actual usage of factory facilities or machinery. The best way to describe this is with an example where there are two products in one product line: product A and product B. Product A is a product ordered by customers in low numbers. However, for product A to be produced, it requires some additional engineering, testing, and many machine set-ups. Product B is ordered frequently by customers and the production runs are longer and are not interrupted by set-ups or other activities. If your company applied standard costing, it would probably allocate the overhead based on the number of hours of machine time. This means that product A would have little overhead because it uses less machine time, and product B would have a lot of overhead because it uses a lot of machine time. Activity-based costing considers not only machine time, but other costs such as engineering, testing, and set-up, which are activities used in conjunction with the production of the product. Therefore, product A's overhead would be higher by utilizing activity-based costing. Product B's overhead will likely be reduced because there is less overhead to be spread over a larger amount of product and will only be charged for machine time, not those additional costs incurred by product A. Activity-based costing is not always easy to implement and track in many organizations, but it is an option if these cost-recognition mechanisms are available in the corporate accounting systems. Activity-based costing can be a helpful approach when really looking at cost reduction or process improvement initiatives.

Establishing Pricing Models

Every product, within the context of a carefully crafted marketing mix, has to be priced. Pricing models abound. The most appropriate model is a value-based approach, although many companies use cost-plus pricing, which I do not advocate. Pricing is both art and science, but is built upon a solid foundation of well-researched and understood customer needs and competitive pressures. This basis determines how the product is ultimately positioned in the market. Pricing is also determined based on the strategic goals set for the product. Introducing a new product at a lower price can "buy" market share. If your product is sold in the luxury consumer segment, your prices are usually priced at a premium. Some companies price for short-term gains in revenue or profit; some try to sell as many units as possible.

Strategic pricing often requires some assistance from a financial specialist based on some of the intricacies involved. In carrying out strategic product planning, an assessment is created that baselines how well the product has sold, at what prices, and under what conditions and to which customer types. Although list prices may reflect what is believed to be the product's value proposition, actual pricing performance, as in special bids, discounts offered for purchases in specific quantities, and so on, may have brought about shifts in the average prices paid for the product. These pricing details need to be factored back into future pricing strategies. For pricing planning, the product manager (along with a financial specialist or pricing specialist) should continually be thinking about pricing within the context of financial planning and the desired future financial performance of the product. Your product revenue forecast is dependent on the pricing model and your gross profit is ultimately calculated based on the units you sell. The price, therefore, is the linchpin in the product profitability formula.

Preparing Product Budgets

Product managers need to create budgets for their products. The budget sets up the product's business to fulfill its near-term goals. Typically, budgets cover the next fiscal or calendar year. They are spending roadmaps that link the near-term business of the product to the product's strategy. Therefore, budgets are used for short-term planning, coordinating functional activities, communicating to management and other team members, and tracking progress. Functional Support Plans, for example, contain spending estimates. When all the spending estimates for all the functions are "rolled up" into the budget for the product or the product line, they can be carefully evaluated by management to make sure that the spending plans are both affordable and achievable— based on the financial resources available to the company. Not only do product budgets need to link to the product strategy, but product budgets are linked to the cash flow requirements used by the CFO to make sure there is enough money to run the company.

When you submit your budget in October and it comes back to you with a directive to pare it back, it's typically because it is deemed not affordable or it does not contribute enough to the company's net income. The reason the budget is such a great communication tool is that it uses the language of money to describe to management or other stakeholders the action plans of the product team. It also provides a medium that enables management to communicate back to the product team. As will be discussed shortly, the budget column in the P&L provides the reference point for being able to track the product's actual financial progress, and to be able to explain variances between actual spending and agreed-upon budgets.

MANAGING THE BUSINESS

Up until now, we have discussed the basic financial statements and how finance is applied to product planning activities. Next we focus on how finance is used by product managers and their teams when the product is in the market and is "living its plans."

There are two general categories to be discussed. First, the product manager must make sure that that the product is achieving its stated business goals as budgeted, or in relating the product's performance against the original Business Case. Second, the product manager should be able to determine where the product is situated on the life cycle curve.

Making Sure the Product Is Achieving Its Financial Goals

Given a basic understanding of financial statements and product budgets (plans), it's appropriate to expect that the product manager can understand and explain how actual outcomes compare with the established plans. Tremendous insight can be gained from this analysis. One of the most important methods applied to analyzing the performance of the product and the business is *variance analysis*. Variance analysis looks at a financial plan or budget and compares that plan to the actual results as shown on the product's P&L. Variance information is a starting point for the product manager, usually with the help of a financial specialist, to analyze what has taken place, why, and what kind of remedial action might be needed. The key in this kind of product level financial analysis is to determine the relationships between unit volumes, costs, and product profitability. Every line item in the product P&L provides a glimpse into the business performance of the product. All variances, either positive or negative, must be explained. Each explanation should have some kind of action plan to remedy any deficiencies. We start with the sample P&L budget from Figure 6.1; now we'll look at Figure 6.4, which shows actual results that are now revealed, along with the associated variances.

To properly evaluate the product's financial performance in an orderly fashion, three general questions have to be asked, and answered.

1. What is the variance?
2. What happened?
3. What is the action plan for remedy (or to further exploit) the situation?

These questions can lead you to uncover possible problems to be addressed by the cross-functional team, the resolution of which may

FIGURE 6.4

Income Statement for Product ABC for the Year Ended December 31, 20XX

	BUDGET	ACTUAL	VARIANCE	VARIANCE %
Sales (Revenue)				
Number of Units	10,000	10,450	450	4.5%
Price per Unit	$6.25	$5.88	−0.37	−5.9%
Total Revenue	$62,500.00	$61,446.00	−$1,054.00	−1.7%
Cost of Goods Sold (COGS)				
Materials	7,500.00	7,612.00	−112.00	−1.5%
Labor	4,500.00	4,250.00	250.00	5.6%
Overhead	9,800.00	10,412.00	−612.00	−6.2%
Total COGS	$21,800.00	$22,274.00	−$474.00	−2.2%
Gross Margin	$40,700.00	$39,172.00	−$1,528.00	−3.8%
Gross Margin %	65.1%	63.8%	−1.4%	−2.1%
Cost of Goods Sold (COGS)				
Marketing	5,400.00	5,105.00	295.00	5.5%
Sales	3,300.00	3,410.00	−110.00	−3.3%
R&D	3,235.00	3,875.00	−640.00	−19.8%
General & Administrative	2,100.00	2,140.00	−40.00	−1.9%
Total Expenses	$14,035.00	$14,530.00	−$495.00	−3.5%
Earnings Before Interest, Taxes, Depreciation, and Amortization (EBITDA)	$26,665.00	−$24,642.00	−$2,023.00	−7.6%
Depreciation and Amortization	500.00	500.00	0.00	0.0%
Interest Expense	350.00	350.00	0.00	0.0%
Income Taxes	2,631.00	1,985.00	646.00	24.6%
Net Income (Profit)	$23,684.00	$22,307.00	−$2,669.00	−11.3%
Net Income %	37.9%	36.3%	−1.6%	−4.2%

ultimately improve market performance and profitability of your products and services. The structure for carrying out the analysis and reporting to management during a product review session is demonstrated in Figure 6.5.

FIGURE 6.5

Product Profit and Loss Variance Analysis

WHAT IS VARIANCE?	WHAT HAPPENED?	WHAT IS THE ACTION PLAN/REMEDY?
Unit volume is 450 units (4.5%) greater than plan.	There was a sales contest in the last quarter.	Consider using this to boost sales in the future.
Unit prices were $0.37 or 5.9% below plan	Apparently, the sales team had to do intense discounting in the fourth quarter to promote sales. Sales volumes would have been lower than plan. Sales said that the competitors were also pushing deals in the fourth quarter	Consider using this to boost sales in the future.
COGS are slightly above plan by an average of 2.2%. Material costs were greater than plan by 1.5%, and overheads were 6.2% higher than plan.	Upon further analysis, the supplier raised prices due to higher shipping costs and overhead was higher because electrical costs went up. Both material and overhead variances were due to fuel costs. (The utility said that oil prices went up 30 percent, and they raised some of their rates accordingly.) The higher costs for materials and overhead were offset by lower labor charges due to a productivity enhancement on the production line.	Purchasing is looking into local suppliers to minimize shipping costs, and Operations is exploring changing lighting to energy-saving bulbs. It is also looking to change the hours of the plant from 9–5 to 7:30–3:30. Starting 1.5 hours earlier will reduce electric usage by 6 percent and, the production workers union agreed.
Gross margin is slightly below plan by 3.8%.	The problem with gross margin is the lower average selling price (even with higher volumes) as well as higher COGS, as explained earlier.	Remedial action is being taken with Sales, Purchasing, and Operations. Results will be provided at the next review session.
R&D expenses were 19.8% higher than plan.	R&D said that two of its top engineers left the company and went to work for a competitor. A major project deliverable necessitated the hiring of contract workers.	This is a temporary variance and was approved by the head of R&D and the CEO.

Financial Ratios

Financial analysis can extend beyond variance analysis to find relationships between items on financial statements. If you've spent a lot of time evaluating results, you'll discover that there are many useful relationships between some of the line items in the statements. Expressed as ratios (division formulas), these relationships can give a quick, often intuitively obvious read on the financial health of a business by revealing the financial condition of an organization as well as the efficiency of its business and marketing activities. Ratios can also be abstracted to the product, product line, or product portfolio level. They are especially useful in comparing results between time periods for the same product, between different products in the portfolio, and even in comparing competitors' products' financial performance with your own (although this can be particularly challenging). There are even ratios that may be considered common within a specific industry.

Perhaps the most important ratios for a product manager are the two profitability ratios, gross profit percent and net profit percent. These are derived using the following formulas:

$$\text{Gross Margin / Total Revenue} = \text{Gross Margin \%}$$
$$\text{Net Profit / Total Revenue} = \text{Net Profit \%}$$

Another profitability ratio that would be of interest to the product manager would be *return on investment* (ROI). ROI is often calculated for many purposes when an investment is made. It asks, "How much will I, or did I get back from the investment?" ROI can be calculated for a marketing investment (Marketing ROI) or a product investment that was justified by a Business Case. The ROI for the product as a profitability ratio looks at the overall investment made in the product and the actual profits generated by the product because of that investment. It is strongly advised that product managers be very careful when trying to use ROI because it is often very difficult to isolate the exact return for the investment made. As such, it can be abused and can lead to over-exaggerated results and future over-optimistic forecasts. Work closely with your financial team when considering these measurements.

In financial analysis, there is another type of ratio. It is called an *activity ratio*. One of the activity ratios measures the number of days it takes to get paid after issuing an invoice. This ratio is called "days receivable outstanding" and affects overall corporate cash flow. A product manager may be interested in this ratio because it helps put future forecast assumptions for a product investment into perspective. If you know that most customers pay their invoices in 90 days, then assumptions about future cash flows and discounted cash flows for the product should follow the typical pattern of payments to the company.

Another important activity ratio that product managers really should be concerned about is called *inventory turnover*. This is a measurement of how many times the inventory is refreshed because of ongoing sales. Higher inventory "turns" are preferred as they indicate a high level of business activity. This is because the ratios measure how fast you're moving the product. How fast should your inventory turn over? That depends on your industry and how quickly your products "get stale" or become obsolescent. Inventory turnover is computed as COGS divided by average inventory:

$$\text{Inventory Turnover} = \text{COGS} / \text{Average Inventory}$$

A commonly accepted practice is to calculate average inventory in order to smooth out dramatic changes in inventory over a given evaluation period. To apply this method, you would add the inventory figures from various times from the beginning, through the end of the period being measured, and divide that figure by the number of inventories included to get a rough average.

Lastly, one of the types of ratios that I find particularly helpful measures a cost or expense category as a percentage of revenue. For example, marketing or R&D as a percentage of revenue helps determine whether the company is investing heavily enough, or too heavily, in each of these areas. It's also a good way to see if you're doing better or worse than your competitors.

Last Words on Ratios

Knowing about ratios is one thing; knowing how they're used is the key. Ratios alone say little. They should be used within the context of industry or business averages, thereby providing a measure of the relative position of your business against others in similar business categories. *They can also be used to show trends in your business over time.* For example, they can show seasonal variations in product profitability. If your product is showing increased profitability over a period of several quarters, but then begins to deteriorate, you know that your product is facing some challenges. However, if you observe that there is a general economic downturn and other companies in your industry are experiencing the same profit pressure, your conclusions and actions might be different.

One final note on ratios: As you manage your products through their life cycles, you'll note that your product performance indicators may require fine tuning. The performance levers you'll adjust correspond to the marketing mix (product, pricing, promotion, and place or channel), which can be adjusted upward or downward, depending on your business goals. Financial statements and ratios tell you very quickly whether such adjustments are having the desired effect and allow you to make further adjustments as the product evolves across its life cycle.

Maturity Assessment: Placing the Product on the Life Cycle Curve

One of the ways product managers can use financial data is to organize the data so that the facts shown tell a *story* about the product's history. A new product begins its life in the concept phase and absorbs money as the company invests in it. After the product is launched, it hopefully begins to earn a profit and contributes to the financial health of the company. Since there may be many products within the portfolio, each product's performance should be tracked against the original objectives as articulated in the Business Case.

Financial data, particularly revenue, gross margin, and even cash flow (which could be difficult to track at the product level), can tell a story about the product's history. If the product remains viable for a long period of time, its history can be tracked beyond the monthly or quarterly numbers and back to its early years. By tracking the product's performance in a table or spreadsheet and graphing those numbers, even years back, you create the depiction of the product life cycle curve. That graphical portrait can be a very powerful tool when used by product managers to analyze the product's performance. It can also be a great way to communicate results to the product team or to management. The curves that result are not always the "S" curves you might see in marketing texts. But they can provide true visual clues about how the product's performance was impacted by marketing investments or enhancements, or how it responded to the pressures from the competition or the economy.

Figure 6.6 provides a view for us into the value of graphing the product's performance on a life cycle curve. For this simple example, a fictional product's life is charted over 36 quarters. The depiction portrays a product experiencing approximately 7 quarters of revenue growth, 6 quarters of slow growth, and then a decline in revenue somewhere around quarter 13 into quarter 19, followed by 8 additional quarters of renewed growth.

FIGURE 6.6

Tracking the Product's Life Cycle in a Graph

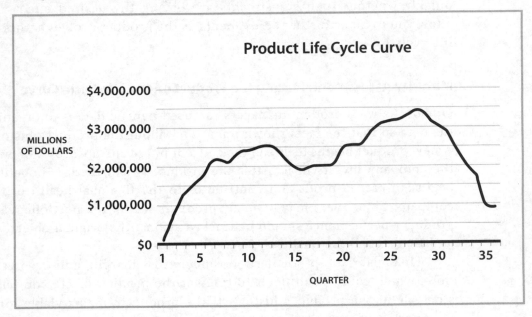

If the product manager keeps good records, he or she will have a valid ongoing analysis of customers who buy, competitive activity, and other relevant financial and operational analyses to correlate the product's performance (portrayed graphically on a life cycle curve) with explanations as to what happened and why. This is important because future investments will need to be calculated by the product manager to match the life cycle state of the product within the context of its evolving strategy, plus the evolving investment profiles for other products within the portfolio. Can you imagine trying to manage a product without the most basic financial data? It would be a nearly impossible task.

Using Scorecards and Other Evaluative Tools

There are some measurements of the product's performance results that you and your management may want to keep track of on a monthly basis. Some are financial and some not. Such a monthly scorecard or dashboard can help you understand how all of the numbers and other business indicators come together to form a picture of the business.

Whether it's a single product or an entire product portfolio, it's important to make sure that the business is evaluated from a holistic standpoint, not just by the financials alone. In Chapter 19, which focuses on Evaluating the Performance of the Product, I've provided some very detailed examples showing how to construct and use scorecards.

SUMMARY

The objective of this chapter has been to illustrate the basic elements of finance, in order to provide you with a perspective to help you plan, manage, and market products and services across the product life cycle. Product managers don't necessarily need to be financial experts, but since product managers function as "mini-business" owners or general managers for their products, they should have some degree of financial acumen. Furthermore, product managers as leaders must be able to draw their teams into the "numbers game" so that every team member has the ability to process the data regarding the product's performance. This would mean that they are equipped to participate in capitalizing on positive outcomes or to overcome financial challenges.

RAISING YOUR PRODUCT MANAGEMENT EXPERIENCE QUOTIENT (PMEQ)

1. If you have never had any formal financial training, you may wish to enroll in an Accounting 101 class and a Finance 101 class. This will give you the basic tools to navigate the world of finance. I don't recommend the quick one- or two-day "finance for nonfinancial managers" type of classes.

2. Make an appointment with your financial representative, or someone from your finance department, who can help you understand the format and structure of your product financial statements. Find out how frequently they are produced so that you can have the most up-to-date financial data about your product.

3. Ask a financial manager to attend your product team meeting to explain the financial tools used by the organization so that you're all speaking the same financial language inside your company.

4. Begin working with your financial representative to help analyze variances in the product P&L. Understand the steps that take you from perceiving the variance and asking the question, "What happened?" That will take you to a place where you are better able to either carry out the investigation, or to work with your financial team member to discover the cause of the variance.

5. Work with your management during the annual budgeting and planning process. Help define, or at least understand, the assumptions to be used in the creation of product budgets.

6. Identify the top metrics most appropriate for your product where they rely on financial inputs. As mentioned in this chapter, use gross profit, an expense to revenue ratio, inventory turnover, or other financial analysis tools as may be required for your organization. Use these metrics as part of the product reporting or readout regimen.

7. Set up a monthly status session for your cross-functional team, or an even broader representation of team members where you "go through the numbers" so that everyone knows what's happening with the business. Describe the positive contributions as well as the challenges where they are indicated by numbers that are below plan.

MODULE 2

BUILDING INSIGHTS AND DRIVING STRATEGIES BY MAKING THE MARKET YOUR PRIMARY FOCUS

INTRODUCTION TO MODULE 2

Module 1 provided you with the foundation to support the knowledge, skills, and structure needed to be a product manager. With this framework established and in place, it's time to consider the more specific techniques that allow product managers to turn their attention to the "markets" in which their products are sold.

Most fundamental texts about marketing or economics cover the topic of markets. Modern marketers and business people often talk about their strategic intent to focus on the market and on customers. However, some of the terms most commonly used to discuss strategic intent have numerous interpretations. These terms include *market focused, customer focused,* and *customer oriented.* To eliminate confusion, it is crucial to have a firm definition of the word *market*. Simply put, a market is where buyers and sellers come together. If an organization is market focused, then it devotes its efforts to understanding the dynamics of the place where buyers and sellers come together. Buyers are customers, and sellers are competitors. A particular market area where both buyers and sellers come together is called an industry.

Keeping in mind this basic definition, I want to discuss the importance of the chapters in this module. In a nutshell, they are designed to guide your thought process. While the chapters are arranged in a linear fashion, the practices are dynamic in nature. This module will teach you how to collect and evaluate data, and then stitch it together using a dose of critical thinking. With this knowledge, you can create and refine strategic goals that are easy to understand, straight forward to carry out, and produce the desired results.

Why Insights Matter

Many product managers and others lament that they don't have enough time or resources devoted to the research required to secure industry, competitor, and customer data—the data that can be combined and synthesized in order to derive relevant insights. There seems to be a nearly universal belief that when a customer describes what they want, or a competitor takes a given action, then that's the path that has to be taken. While these knee-jerk reactions to market movements may have positive short-term effects, they are often poor product investment decisions that have negative long-term consequences.

To provide a comparison, think of an engine in an automobile. It must run on a balanced formula of fuel and air so that the engine can properly perform. A business requires an engine that runs on a balanced formula of market insights and product performance outcomes. When the business engine is starved for insights or product performance information, different people in the organization may "tinker" with the engine. They may get it to "work," but they won't be able to optimize its performance. To be competitive, a company cannot afford to have its engines just sputtering along; it needs to ensure the engine is getting a steady supply of the proper fuel. Based on my research, I am optimistic that business leaders are moving in the right direction. They continue to discover that useful data rests in many places. This data can be tapped and organized. Executives are working hard to rebuild the engines that provide needed insights. Decisions that once were based on budget cycles can now be hastened due to newer capabilities to detect and monitor market activity. Some of these new capabilities include increasingly powerful systems, analytic software, and evaluative tools. Regardless of the machine that produces the content or the speed with which it processes data, *product managers must be able to effectively utilize the principles of discovery and creative thought to spark innovative ideas and product strategies.* This is the reason that Discovery and Innovation are shown in the Product Management Life Cycle Model (Figure M2.1) and why the content covered in the chapters in this Module is so important.

Market insights not only are vital inputs to the strategy formulation process but also stimulate thoughts and ideas about how to fine-tune business operations and manage risk. Product managers and their cross-functional product teams play a crucial role in this process. Team members must bring their functional expertise to the table to evaluate increasingly complex questions based on connections that must be made between disparate pieces of data. Cross-functional team members must also play an active role in product and market planning, which may transcend traditional feature development or incremental product updates. They must focus on efforts to continually optimize customer experiences, improve product designs, or streamline business operations to gain competitive advantage. Moreover, their ecosystems are more complex. Players from across the business, as well as outside the business, must be brought to the

FIGURE M2.1

The Product Management Life Cycle Model (© Sequent Learning Networks)

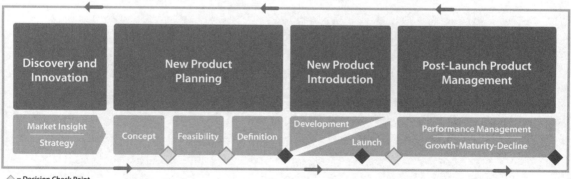

table to help solve problems. *It is the product manager who must have the vision and clarity to bring these dynamic forces into focus.*

Market and business insights are formed by product managers and others when they have sufficient depth and breadth of understanding about their product's business, market, and the domain. Broad yet deep perspectives are formed and reformed as new experiences are gained and as new situations are encountered. Figure M2.2 displays the linear flow from data to insight to strategies along with the opportunities that might emanate from those insights.

While it is simple to elucidate the insight process flow, it can be difficult to map out how a person forms an insight. Each person is unique in how he processes information and draws conclusions. Because of the complexity involved in drawing conclusions and reaching the magical "aha" moment, I urge you to become deeply familiar with the four chapters in Module 2.

Chapter 7, "The Playing Field and the Players: Analyzing the Industry and Competition," provides sharp focus on *sellers*—in other words, the competitors you face. It also establishes a context for those competitors who face off in a given sector or industry arena. You will learn what it means to become an industry and competitive expert who knows how to evaluate trends, track competitor movements, and lay a foundation for true competitive strategy.

FIGURE M2.2

Market Insight Process Flow

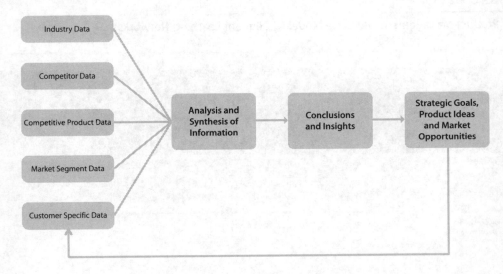

Chapter 8, "Finding Markets to Conquer by Understanding Customer Needs and Market Segments," puts the spotlight on the *buyers*—who they are and where they are. You will learn the importance of effective segmentation models so that customer groups can be logically organized and evaluated. You will also learn how different customer types are characterized so that you can uncover their underlying needs, which in turn will help you create and develop products that customers truly want to buy.

With the sellers and buyers identified and the market insights put into perspective, Chapter 9, "Preparing to Set Your Mileposts: Forecasting for the Product Manager," will help you figure out how many units you can sell and when.

Ultimately, you want to figure out what to sell, who to sell it to, and which competitors you will face. In order to get there, you need to know how to formulate a strategy for your product and the related marketing mix elements. This process will be described in Chapter 10, "Strategic Product Planning: The Inflection Point."

THE PLAYING FIELD AND THE PLAYERS: ANALYZING THE INDUSTRY AND COMPETITION

Executive Summary

- One of the key responsibilities for product managers is to establish and maintain competitive advantage for their products in the marketplace.
- Good intelligence about their industry and the competition gives product managers and their teams the edge and expertise to strategize and act with purpose and clarity.
- The more product managers know about their industry and the competition, the greater the credibility they have as product team leaders.

An organization's ability to learn, and translate that learning into action rapidly, is the ultimate competitive advantage.

—JACK WELCH

In order to chart an astute strategy for their goods or services, product managers need a comprehensive perspective on the marketing strategies of their competitors: a lens through which to view these competitive actions. This lens, when focused properly, allows product managers to observe how industries are classified, how and why they evolve, and how the competitors, as participants in these industries, carry out their work.

A fundamental understanding of the playing field and the players enables product managers to better anticipate what a competitor might do, how a regulator might intervene, and, more significantly, how customers respond. With so much at stake, the importance of the content in this chapter cannot be overemphasized. The goal is to help you formulate the best decisions to plot your product's journey to success.

BECOMING THE EXPERT

Successful business people and entrepreneurs are knowledgeable, totally involved, and passionate about what they do. They are constantly seeking cues and clues from the markets in which they operate.

Product managers in sporting goods companies are usually ardent about sports. They are aficionados who keep up with and even actively engage in particular sports. They have a hunger to know as much as they can. I'm an avid skier and expect the product managers of companies that produce skis to have enough expertise about the sport to offer skis designed for the demands of skiers like me. People who feel strongly about something—a sport, a hobby, or even their professions—understand passion. If you keep that level of enthusiasm in mind, you'll be motivated to develop the analytic and evaluative skills needed to compete successfully in the marketplace. The more you keep your eye on what's happening and why, the better you'll be at generating the best strategies for your products and services.

When colleagues and team members see periodicals and research documents on your desk, and hear you discuss industry activity knowledgeably, they'll realize the benefit of such strong focus. This may motivate them to seek and integrate their own observations into their work routines. Your posture as a leader will grow as you are perceived as "the" expert about the industry and the competition. Others on your product team will take their cues from you. The more you pursue and assimilate market signals and take action, the better you will be at creating the best strategic options for you and your team to grow the business.

WHAT IS AN INDUSTRY?

Definitions of *industry* vary. I think of any industry as an arena or playing field made up of companies that focus on solving the problems and serving the needs of discrete groups of customers.

By another definition, an industry is composed of companies who focus on the same market segments with similar solutions within a sector. Governments look at broad categories of the economy to determine areas of expansion and contraction, and these categories are called *sectors*. If you follow the world of investments, you'll hear or read about sectors.

Most industry classification schemes focus on two dimensions: production and market demand. The production dimension is simple to understand because it takes the producer's perspective and is based on the types of products that are created to meet the needs of given market segments or customer groups. As the scope of business has become more global, and tangible products have given way to intangible services, perspectives have evolved and greater emphasis is placed on the end-customer or consumer.

One hard fact you can depend on is that industry is constantly changing. Sometimes the changes are fast; sometimes slow. Change depends on many aspects: politics, the regulatory environment, the economy, social trends, consumer preferences, the state of technology, and other factors. The primary rule of "blocking and tackling" is that you, as a product manager, be always vigilant about what's going on in your industry and decide what you want to do with your products based on insights about the customers you're competing for.

INDUSTRY CLASSIFICATIONS

Here are some essential resources that product managers should know about and be able to utilize:

- In North America, there is an industry classification structure called the North American Industry Classification System (NAICS). It lists only manufactured products. There are several dozen NAICS codes for different industries.

- There is the North American Product Classification System (NAPCS). This U.S. Census organization created 71 product lists for a variety of industries.
- There is also a Global Industry Classification Standard (GICS), established in 1999 by Standard & Poors and MSCI Barra. The GICS acts as a framework for industry analysis used by investment researchers and other financial professionals. According to its website (www.msci.com) there are 10 major sectors, 24 industry groups, 68 industries, and 154 subindustries.

In Figure 7.1, extracted directly from the MSCI Global Investable Market Indices Methodology, you can clearly see how an industry hierarchy might be portrayed.

Figure 7.2 is a summary taken from a publicly available download available at the MSCI website. It shows the 10 major sectors, the 24 Industry Groups, and some of the related industries (not the complete list).

How you describe and classify an industry is important. It will help you understand what your research yields, to analyze how industries change and evolve, and the ways that competitors within each industry change. Now let's talk about how to analyze an industry.

FIGURE 7.1

Telecommunications Services Sector Hierarchy (from MSCI)

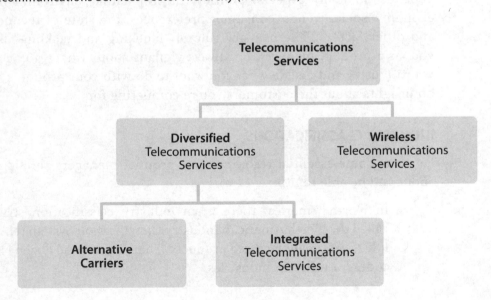

FIGURE 7.2

Global Industry Classification Standard Summary

SECTOR (10)	INDUSTRY GROUP (24)	INDUSTRY	
Energy	Energy	• Energy Services & Equipment	• Oil & Gas and Consumable Fuels
Materials	Materials	• Chemicals • Containers & Packaging	• Metals & Mining • Paper & Forest Products
Industrials	Capital Goods	• Aerospace & Defense • Building Products • Construction & Engineering	• Electrical Equipment • Industrial Conglomerates • Machinery • Trading Companies & Distributors
	Commercial & Professional Services	• Commercial Services & Supplies	• Professional Services
	Transportation	• Air Freight & Logistics • Airlines • Marine	• Road & Rail • Transportation Infrastructure
Consumer Discretionary	Automobiles & Components	• Auto Components	• Automobiles
	Consumer Durables & Apparel	• Household Durables • Leisure Equipment & Products	• Textiles, Apparel, & Luxury Goods
	Consumer Services	• Hotels, Resorts, Restaurants, & Leisure	• Diversified Consumer Services
	Media	• Media (Advertising, Broadcasting, Movies, Publishing, etc.)	
	Retailing	• Distributors • Internet & Catalog Retail	• Multiline Retail • Specialty Retail
Consumer Staples	Food & Staples Retailing	• Food & Staples Retailing	
	Food, Beverage, & Tobacco	• Beverages, Food Products, Tobacco	
	Household & Personal Products	• Household Products	• Personal Products
Health Care	Health Care Equipment & Services	• Health Care Equipment & Supplies • Health Care Providers & Services • Health Care Technology	
	Pharmaceuticals, Biotechnology, & Life Sciences	• Biotechnology • Pharmaceuticals • Life Science Tools & Services	
Financials	Banks	• Commercial Bank	• Thrifts & Mortgage Finance
	Diversified Financials	• Diversified Financial Services	
		• Consumer Finance	• Capital Markets
	Insurance	• Insurance (Brokers, Life, Health, Reinsurance, etc.)	
	Real Estate	• Real Estate Investment Trusts	• Real Estate Management & Development
Information Technology	Software & Services	• Internet Software & Services • IT Services • Software	
	Technology Hardware & Equipment	• Communications Equipment • Computers & Peripherals	• Electronic Equipment Instruments & Components • Office Electronics
	Semiconductors & Semiconductor Equipment	• Semiconductors & Semiconductor Equipment	
	Telecommunication Services	• Diversified Telecommunication Services • Wireless Telecommunication Services	
Utilities	Utilities	• Electric Utilities • Gas Utilities • Multi-Utilities	• Water Utilities • Independent Power Producers & Energy Traders

PUTTING INDUSTRY EVOLUTION INTO PERSPECTIVE

Industries evolve because market forces evolve. Think of most industries today and how low-cost global communications, the Internet, transportation, and technology have affected how people do what people do; how companies make and deliver products; and how customers' preferences change.

A good way to analyze an industry and its evolution is to select two that are highly visible in their morphology. One is the U.S. airline industry within the Industrials sector; the other is the U.S. commercial banking industry within the Financials sector.

The U.S. airline industry has gone through a host of changes since its deregulation in 1979. The industry was once controlled by the Civil Aeronautics Authority (CAA). The CAA controlled routes and ticket prices because its role was to serve the public interest. Today, the deregulated airline industry operates in an environment where competitors set prices and domestic routes are based on market demand. The industry is characterized by falling prices, concentration (mergers), some overcapacity, and some inefficiencies of operation. Major "legacy" carriers have not taken full advantage of deregulation, but smaller, lower-cost, efficient carriers like Southwest Airlines, JetBlue, and others have done so.

Contrast this with the commercial banking industry, which has also gone through many changes. In the late 1980s and early 1990s, commercial banks were operating in a world of economic and financial difficulties due to poorly performing loans, thousands of bank failures, and a recession (1990–1991). Many foreign banks opened branches or subsidiaries in the United States, adding complexity to the competitive climate. Most banking companies in the United States weren't allowed to expand beyond state lines and needed more latitude in order to compete. In response to these issues, the government began making regulatory changes that allowed banks to open branches in other states and removed the restrictions on interstate bank acquisitions. Furthermore, the regulations were altered to allow banks to expand their businesses into wealth management and sales of insurance, securities, and mutual funds through subsidiary operations. The changes in the banking industry have been tremendous. As always, there are new challenges. In the early twenty-first century, many banks opened a huge network of retail branches to gain access to more customers. Whatever their size, they also face enormous competitive pressure across all their business lines. These two short examples characterize the evolution of two different industries and their changing competitive profiles.

Product managers in these businesses must be vigilant about industry capacity and downward pressure on prices. Their strategies tend to focus on outdoing competitors in service and convenience, cost management, productivity, and greater efficiency. In this market environment, they need to make sure that their product portfolio strategies help them maintain profitability and avoid erosion of margins.

Furthermore, in these heavily competitive environments, product managers should factor into their strategies other marketing mix elements to support their products. As a product manager, you will need to foster greater levels of cooperation between product line groups and work together to prune product lines and focus on continuously clarifying customer needs. You would probably want to provide broad solutions packages or bundles, and other creative measures to surmount the possible problems of these overgrown, maturing industries.

CARRYING OUT INDUSTRY RESEARCH

Knowing that industries constantly change, product managers must develop highly sensitive industry radar. Such ongoing monitoring provides a steady stream of data that you can translate and apply to potential opportunities and action plans for the product.

As the product manager, you are an important catalyst for effecting profitable and productive change. It is up to you (and most likely, your marketing counterparts) to obtain this vital data on a timely and ongoing basis. You have to be aware of the need to keep current and to process all data so that meaningful possibilities and successful future strategies for the product will emerge.

It is also your responsibility to share what you learn with all others involved, from your team to other organization stakeholders. In benchmarking activities carried out while I worked at AT&T and through research carried out with Sequent's clients over many years, I found that when product managers and/or marketers share research findings with other team members—whether dealing with the state of the industry, the competitive environment, or customer research—the collective energy of the team enhances their efforts and produces more positive and rewarding results.

There are many resources for learning the basics of industry research, along with many useful and important models. Esteemed academics such as Michael Porter have written extensively on these topics and warrant tremendous respect and admiration. These tools and techniques are absolutely invaluable.

To start an industry research project, you need a plan of action. First, create an inventory of the data you have. You may have industry reports, past research projects, and other data. Colleagues in marketing, other product managers, or your own manager can offer some valuable and pertinent information.

Next, what is it you want to study and what do you want to do with the information you glean? If you are preparing to update your product strategy document, you can limit your research to the past year. If you're creating a new product strategy, then you may need several years' worth of data.

After identifying what you want to learn, you have to determine where to obtain the data and what to do with it. Here is a listing of potential resources:

- Industry trade journals
- Business periodicals
- Internal reports on trade shows or industry events attended by others in your company, from shows you attended or from analyst coverage of those events
- Trade or industry and professional associations
- Governmental agency reports and websites
- Standards groups
- Financial market analyst reports
- National, provincial, and state industrial development agencies
- Syndicated research
- University-based research on regional development
- Keyword searches on the Internet
- Field research and interviews

Once you acquire the data, you might want to begin filling in a table (as shown in Figure 7.3). This enables you to construct a chronology of prior-year industry observations, current observations, and future possibilities, some of which may be articulated in the writings and forecasts of analysts, editors, and other industry specialists.

FIGURE 7.3

Putting Industry Activity into Perspective

Past 3–5 Years	Past 1–2 Years	Current Year	Future

There is a technique that creates a useful, macroscopic view of a given market area. It examines the political, economic, social, and technological factors affecting a market or a geographic area. PEST is the acronym used in most marketing books that prescribe this standard analysis. However, in many market environments there are regulatory controls and some other instances that may not fall into any of the other categories, so the letters PRESTO encapsulate and offer a better approach. It's useful to consider each of these factors individually:

- *Political*—The political environment of a geographic area is vital because you will learn about government's treatment of business, governmental stability, attitudes about employment, and so on. Obviously, a business would not want to create products for or in markets (e.g., countries, states, regions) that are hostile to the kind of products available to sell.

- *Regulatory*—What are the laws that govern health, safety, and welfare? What are the rules that drive corporate governance? What are the tax laws in each area? The regulatory environment will often cause market barriers to be raised or to be lowered. It's wise to understand the cause and effect of regulations on various sectors, especially from a historic perspective, to determine overall market attractiveness and receptivity.

- *Economic*—A positive, well-managed economic system is critical to business success. Countries or regions with poor economic fundamentals, such as high unemployment, high interest rates, unbalanced trade activities, or poor consumer confidence, are less conducive to business formation, new product introductions, and overall business success. Businesses and consumers may not have enough money to spend on the product. Solid economic fundamentals improve the probability for business success. Economic issues are also important because many businesses are publicly traded companies. Macroeconomic influences on stock prices in a group of companies may be relevant. For example, a rise in oil prices may add profitability to an oil company but will play havoc with an automobile company selling fuel-inefficient vehicles.

- *Social or societal*—Discrete market areas are distinct from others due to characteristics such as income distribution, age distribution, attitudes about work, number of two-earner families, number of children, and other lifestyle issues. For example, as people become more concerned about harm to the environment, they increasingly wish to buy products from companies who share their concerns. Societal indicators are directly connected to market segmentation and the needs expressed by different groups.

- *Technological*—Some market areas encourage investment in technologies, and some do not. California's Silicon Valley tends to breed companies that experiment in new technologies. Venture capital firms are situated there, and many engineers and scientists are also located there. Pharmaceutical or biotechnology companies may situate themselves in other areas with a rich resource pool. Some governments may provide tax incentives for some types of businesses in some areas. Another issue related to a particular market may be the pace of acceptance and adoption of newer or different technologies

- *Other*—Not every observation fits neatly into one category. You may find other dynamics in industries similar to the one in which you operate. For example, an industry may be characterized by a series of mergers, none of which fit neatly into the categories you are looking at. Therefore the "other" category can be applied when you can't readily identify an industry.

PRESTO is also a helpful tool when you need to create a framework for a bigger picture. As you use this technique, it will become apparent that each dimension of the model relates to another. Political party changes may lead to shifts in regulatory policies, which in turn may stimulate or retard economic growth. Further, each time you conduct a PRESTO analysis, you and your team will be enlightened with a unique market context. This will contribute to what you explain to others about the direction you wish to take, and why.

There are other methods to assist you in studying industry-based activities. Michael Porter's Five Forces Analysis is one of those methods. For example, you can examine the industry environment based on its attractiveness and/or ease of access. Although there are theoretic underpinnings, there are some dynamics and business realities you should be familiar with:

- Customers in some market segments can exert power over competing companies when it comes to buying readily available products. When there are many competitors and many choices for customers, they may group together, like a food co-op or a hospital supply–buying group, and by doing so, hold vendors in check and achieve favorable pricing or other benefits.

- In business-to-business firms, some vendors are so embedded in a company's infrastructure that the cost of switching to a competitor is too great. A communications equipment supplier may have a strong foothold with communication companies (e.g., Wireless Carriers and Internet Providers) because the infrastructure and equipment took years to build and cost hundreds of millions of dollars to develop. An alternate vendor cannot attempt to offer a replacement unless the value proposition is overwhelmingly compelling—and even then, the political infrastructure in a company may offer its own entry barrier.

- If you are in an industry that hasn't really kept up with the times, your company may be vulnerable to new, creative competitors. If you work in one of those companies, be on the alert for niche players who may have products in the better, faster, cheaper category. Low-cost airlines, communications service companies, and firms that provide business applications are some good examples.

- Some industry areas are very thorny to penetrate. Their customers won't switch to another product or company due to strongly entrenched suppliers who can counter the incursion of newcomers. Governmental regulations can present some hefty barriers, too. An example of this could be an effort by an upstart, low-cost airline to work out of a major airport where one embedded carrier is dominant. The low-cost airline believes that a low-fare approach will win passengers. All the entrenched airline needs to do is offer a host of low fares; within a few months, the upstart may be bleeding red ink.

A model that guides your thought process about competitive activities that produce usable clues is made even better when you continually have your market radar on. The more experience you have from "living" in the market, the more you are able to make sense of what you hear, see, and read. To illustrate this, think about the following points:

- More participants in a market mean more competitive activity. Soft drink companies vie for quarter-point gains in market share when they reduce the prices of their colas by 30 percent for a week through a chain store grocer.

- When the general economy slows down, the remaining suppliers struggle to maintain market share. When homebuilders enjoy explosive growth, there is plenty of business to go around. But when the real estate market slows, builders must compete more vigorously for a smaller, more cautious group of homebuyers.

- When a company has a strong brand, they may not have to compete quite so vigorously.

Additional research and articles covering economics, competitive analysis, and strategic planning are not elaborated upon here. I cannot emphasize enough that there is tremendous benefit to continual learning in these areas.

SECURING ADDITIONAL DATA

The astute product manager will look to colleagues in the Industry and Competitive Intelligence group or Market Research department to augment the arsenal of data. There are also many industry research organizations (syndicators) that do a lot of the legwork for you. Their value lies in offering detailed data collection and maintaining relationships with many companies in the industry. The drawback is that they sell the same information to everyone. Their reports can be fairly expensive, and there may be subscription fees for updates. Also, in their 120-page (or so) annual or semiannual update report, half the text may be recycled information from previous reports. Despite any shortcomings, it's smart to keep current by using some combination of these resources to help create and maintain comprehensive industry profiles to support strategic product planning, forecasting, and other activities.

It's up to the product manager and the marketing members of the cross-functional team to decide on the most relevant set of data points that can be used to evaluate strategic and tactical options for the product. When you know which data is most relevant, and the rate at which data should be collected, you can then work more collaboratively with the people who are responsible for data collection in your company. Alternatively, if there aren't others assigned, you may have to devise a plan to do some of the legwork yourself or with select team members who have the capability to support such efforts.

In many corporations, product managers (or others in Marketing or other corporate areas) maintain relationships with analysts in several industry research companies. They also purchase (often expensive) subscriptions from these companies. Industry research companies are much like consumer products rating organizations. A company must constantly prove to analysts in these research companies that their products are competitive and worthy of consideration. The analysts set the bar high and continue to raise it as you share more information. They sell their findings to other subscribers, purchasers, and prospects who are considering your products or competitor products. Many sales can be lost due to a poor rating from an outside industry analyst firm. Even with any flaws, however, they often provide relevant, useful data on market size and growth rates.

If you have five reports from five different industry analyst firms, and they're all providing a growth curve that looks about the same, you can take the data points and average them. For example, one research company estimates that the total market space will be composed of 20,000 distinct customer types in two years and 40,000 in five years. Another company claims that the market will be 18,000 in two years and 43,000 in five years. Given the PRESTO environmental indicators plus the data from these two syndicates, you can reasonably forecast a market size between 15,000 and 22,000 in two years and 35,000 and 45,000 in four years. This is a rough "guesstimate," but it would give you a sense of possible market size for a forecast that's in the ballpark.

If you find that you don't have enough data, or don't have enough time, you may have to hire an outside research firm. If you make that decision, be sure you have an explicit goal for your particular project. Know exactly what you want to learn, and specify the format you require. Be sure to specify a full and thorough analytical commentary. The research company should provide you with a detailed statement of work, a project plan, and a project estimate.

Be prepared to devote a fair amount of attention to managing their work, and meet often with the research team to make sure they're on track. It's your money, your research, and your reputation that may be on the line for spending what could amount to a lot of money.

Another research source is the Internet. Do a Google search using the keywords "industry review" and see what you come up with. Click around and explore. List a specific industry. Try "chemicals industry" or "electronics industry" or "communications industry" or anything else. You will find free resources and those that charge a fee. Or, set up a Google Alert (or equivalent alert) that notifies you when a keyword or set of words is used. Try an experiment: set up an alert for a couple of your competitors based on their company name and see if you learn anything new. Alternatively, try the name of a competitor product, or even the name of a key executive in a competitor firm. You'll be surprised at what you'll learn and how you can refine your strategy for this type of data collection to suit your own curiosity and available time.

Since some of my clients operate in the Telecommunications sector, I have developed a keen interest in their business challenges. One of the resources I use is the International Telecommunications Union (www.itu.int). The ITU website is filled with data and reports that point to specific trends in market penetration and proliferation of services, devices, and other interesting dimensions of industry activity. Recently, I was inspired to review some information with respect to mobile device penetration because I *observed* that many people have two or more devices. I also *noticed* that many people are using an increasing variety of applications. I *wondered* what service providers and device makers would have to do to meet the demands, both from a product and an infrastructure perspective. I *discovered* a chart that was produced by the ITU to portray two interesting market dynamics: mobile subscriptions overall and mobile subscriptions per 100 inhabitants. Thus, the data confirmed what I had observed. Investigating further, I found that mobile penetration was picking up in certain parts of the world, while it

FIGURE 7.4

Global Mobile-Cellular Subscriptions, Total and per 100 Inhabitants, 2001–2013

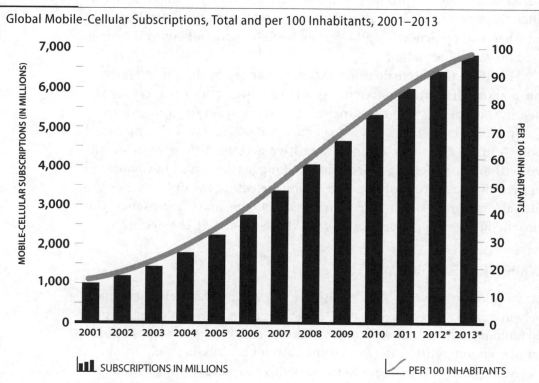

III SUBSCRIPTIONS IN MILLIONS   PER 100 INHABITANTS

NOTE: *Estimate
Source: ITU World Telecommunication/ICT Indicators Database

was slowing in others. Figure 7.4 shows some of this data. If you were to write an introduction for a consumer technology product or an application for a mobile device, and wanted to establish a probable trajectory for your forecast, the data in this chart could prove helpful.

When you assemble multiple related data points, you might uncover some useful clues. For example, forecasting assumptions, as you will learn in Chapter 9, may rely on the market penetration of similar products or technologies. Therefore, a chart like this may help as an analogy in validating assumptions about market sizing and trends.

PROCESSING THE SIGNALS

"What to do next" is what product managers think when a problem arises. If a competitor introduces a product update, cuts a price, or begins a national advertising campaign, the signals are unmistakable. It's investing monies in its products or in the company. Conversely, if a competitor issues a recall of a defective product or announces a layoff, you know that it is under pressure and is vulnerable. These are simple examples, but they show that when you recognize a problem, you need to work out your next move based on your observation.

However, proactive decision making is far better than reactive decision making. It's often better to be a first mover and a market leader. Keep the competitors on their toes and let them react to your actions.

In business, nothing is so clear-cut or ideal. You will also be called upon to make decisions about competitive actions, offensive or defensive, without complete data. Decision making (as discussed in Chapter 5) requires the evaluation of alternatives and selecting the one that has the optimal outcome. The better your data, and the more experience you gain, the higher the comfort level you'll have in making the decision.

COMPETITIVE ENVIRONMENT

Many industry "players" work untiringly to *position* themselves competitively in a market area or domain. Pursuit of profit, market share, prestige, and building their brands drive your competitors. Product managers need to identify the competition and form some basis for positioning their products.

Much of what is written about competitive advantage deals with *corporate* competitiveness, but not with individual competing products or services. Product managers must be champions for their products, and find effective strategies to compete vigorously. However, this may not be feasible for the individual product manager or an individual product or product family. In certain cases, the product is successful because the company's brand or entire product portfolio pulls the product along. The following extract from a story in the *Wall Street Journal* gives the large brand perspective.

Leaders of the nation's biggest banks often boast that bulk and breadth are best. They say their far-reaching collection of businesses will insulate their profits from upheaval in financial markets better than other financial companies . . . [T]hese so-called universal banks, which support massive balance sheets, are also well-positioned to withstand Wall Street's unrest . . . Most recently, the big banks have started to demonstrate that their diversified business models can give them flexibility to be opportunistic when their rivals are focused on managing their smaller balance sheets.

Source: *Wall Street Journal*, September 6, 2007, page C1

Interestingly, a year after this article appeared, the financial system almost imploded because of taking on too many risky investments. When you have broad perspectives on market movers, and assume the role of "industry and competitive historian," your wisdom and insights may contribute to better decisions.

Product managers contribute to their firm's competitive advantage by making the decisions and taking the necessary actions to solve specific customers' problems—and doing so better than anyone else. However, over time products tend to commoditize, but that doesn't mean that it's inappropriate to continue to compete. To retain customers, product managers must "go the extra mile." Offer customers service and support them with care, which helps maintain strong customer bonds and memorable customer experiences. Your extra efforts to make the product distinctive—a special design, packaging element, or style—may give your product an edge over the competition.

COMPETITIVE POSITIONING

According to Al Ries and Jack Trout in their book *Positioning: The Battle for Your Mind*, "Positioning is not what you do to a product. Positioning is what you do to the mind of the prospect." They have a point, but realistically, a major goal of positioning is to ensure that your product can be favorably compared with your competitor's product. Often the positioning of competitors' products can be evaluated through their advertising or promotional activities.

In order to create an initial profile of a competitor and the company's product or products, it's a good idea to determine how various competitors position their products in the market against other competitors' products, including yours. One way to determine the positioning of a competitor's product is to use the Positioning Statement template shown in Figure 11.10 in Chapter 11.

GAINING AN EDGE: PERFORMANCE COUNTS

Competing vigorously and winning in the market should be ascertained by specific performance comparisons. How can the members of a sports team know if they are winning or losing if they don't know the score?

For a product's performance, some of the measurements include revenue, gross profit, market share, and customer satisfaction. For a portfolio, it could be product line breadth or depth, or the mix of sales across that portfolio. More abstractly, it could include the degree to which a product complements other products in a portfolio. It is possible that your product either *pulls through* sales of a complementary product, or *is pulled through* by another product. Your product's sales may be cannibalized by another product if there is competition within the line.

How does this happen in competitors' companies? How does each competitive product compare with yours? How do their portfolios stack up against yours? There are other factors you can look at as well. For example, how large is their direct sales force versus yours? How much do they spend on R&D as a percent of revenue? Do you know what percentage of their revenue is from products that are less than 12 months old? The more you can compare your product's performance measures versus your competitors' products, the more you add to your competitive arsenal.

COMPETITIVE INTELLIGENCE IN YOUR COMPANY

Before we delve into the diverse steps necessary to obtain the competitive intelligence you need for your strategies, check if there is a formal Industry and Competitive Analysis group in your own company. In most companies there is an actual Industry and Competitive Intelligence group at the corporate level. Typically, they focus on higher-level competitive actions within an industry area. Your company may also have a market research department with funding for industry and competitive research. Many of these groups tend to focus on broad aspects of an industry and do not focus as much on product-level research. You certainly need both perspectives. Product managers must evaluate both in order to figure out the best competitive path to take for the product. And of course, this information must be maintained in the Product Master Plan! The following are some of the competitive intelligence items that you should include:

- A glossary of industry terms
- Subscriptions that your firm has to industry publications (or at least a list of them) and how to access those subscriptions.
- Academic case studies where your company and/or its competitors has been studied by business students
- Relevant government reports about your industry

- Population or census reports
- Bibliographies or lists of relevant reference books (e.g., technologies, practices, and methods)

Other resources often subscribed to by corporate offices include services provided by the following companies:

- Hoovers (www.hoovers.com) provides information about companies, industries, and people. (Hoovers is owned by Dunn & Bradstreet [D&B].)
- European Securities and Markets Authority (ESMA, www.esma.europa.eu) provides investment rating, governance policies, and market analysis.
- Standard & Poors (www.standardandpoors.com) provides credit rating information, indices, risk evaluation, investment research, and so on.
- Thomson Reuters (www.thomsonreuters.com) provides information and services for financial management, academic, government, corporate, and related areas.

I strongly suggest that you check into the resources and expertise available to you within your own company and decide whether these resources are right for your research. Here are some criteria to apply:

1. Who are the key personnel in that organization?
2. What research services do they offer?
3. Which subscriptions do they have for industry or competitor news that can be sent to your computer?
4. Do you have the latitude to request that special research projects be carried out for your specific purposes?
5. Can you gain access to outside industry resources or organizations, trade groups, and the like?

COMPETITIVE INTELLIGENCE IN YOUR WORLD

Competitive intelligence is all around you, and it's yours for the taking. Look at the job board on your competitor's website. Talk to your salespeople to see what competitors' products they see in their labs. Walk through your supermarket and see who's selling what or how packages

are changing. Read trade magazines to see which competitors are advertising. Visit regulators' websites, including:

- Federal Communications Commission (fcc.gov)
- Food and Drug Administration (fda.gov)
- Federal Deposit Insurance Corporation (fdic.gov)
- Federal Aviation Administration (faa.gov)
- U.S. State Banking Departments, Insurance Departments
- U.S. Securities and Exchange Commission (sec.gov)
- Securities and Exchange Board of India (sebi.gov.in)
- Australia Securities and Investments Commission (asic.gov.au)
- European Securities and Markets Authority (esma.europa.eu)
- European Directorate for Quality of Medicine and Healthcare (edqm.eu)
- European Aviation Safety Agency (easa.eu.int)

Visit the website of the U.S. Patent and Trademark Office (www
.uspto.gov), the European Patent Office (epo.org), or even the Thomson
Reuters website (thomsonreuters.com) for scholarly and scientific
research. Check your competitors' D&B reports. There are clues everywhere as to what your competitors are doing. As the product manager, it
may be a bit more of a challenge to get down to the product level in these
general sweeps of the competitive horizon, but there are certainly many
indicators of competitive activity available to you. Seek and you shall
find. You don't have to be a spy, but you certainly need to have your
competitive radar working, and it should be scanning the horizon all
the time.

To modify some of your competitive intelligence paradigms, here
are a few things to consider. First, *it's easier to find out about competitive
activities in regulated industries* because, very often, they need to publish or request permission to sell a product. A second factor is to evaluate the degree to which a product's category is changing or evolving. For
example, advances in technologies are continually written up in trade or
industry periodicals. Third, competitive intelligence is widely available
for businesses such as cable TV companies, phone companies, and
money center banks, among others, which are highly visible by reason of
what they do.

Review the securities industry required reports (10-Ks, annual shareholders' reports, and others). In these reports, the companies discuss their product development activities, the competitors they face, and the challenges within their industry.

ETHICS IN COMPETITIVE INTELLIGENCE

However you seek competitive intelligence, it should be done in an ethical and above-board manner. Leonard Fuld, in his wonderful book *The New Competitor Intelligence*, states there are "Ten Commandments of Legal and Ethical Intelligence Gathering." He suggests that intelligence gatherers should not misrepresent themselves, should not do things that are illegal, shouldn't bribe, shouldn't eavesdrop, and shouldn't seek information from someone whose employment could be jeopardized.

Here are two more important things to do:

1. Regardless of what you have learned, make sure to share the information with your team members. Your findings and data should be written down and filed in a central repository or the Product Master Plan.
2. Get everyone on the product team in the competitive intelligence game. For example, when you hold a cross-functional product team meeting, ask your teammates to share what they have learned.

If you continually gather and share industry and competitive information, the entire product team benefits because it has a better perspective from which the members either accept or reject product strategies and tactics. Furthermore, everyone on the team will be encouraged to speak with the voice of the market—and that can represent a tremendous shift from their own functional agendas!

WITH WHOM DO YOU COMPETE?

Now let's get down to the actual work of characterizing competitors. Characterizations will help you to personalize the impersonal nature of competitors so that you can create stories about them and determine your product positioning strategy.

Begin with the basics. Classify them by company name, the products you are competing against, and the market segments into which they sell. In my work, I have found that many product managers do not have this fundamental information written down (let alone in a Product Master Plan). In order to effectively codify this data in your Product Master Plan, a section should be instituted for formal competitor profiles. Figure 7.5 shows a simple competitive profile template. I also created a more comprehensive tool: a *Competitor Dossier Template* because it's a great way to organize your research—and you can review each section from time to time to ensure it is up to date. (It's included in Module 6 of the book.) Each competitor can and should be identified by using a common set of characteristics. Furthermore, based on the known data, observed market actions, sales force feedback, and a host of other inputs, these competitor profiles should be kept up to date.

COMPETITOR SWOT

One of the "weapons" in your competitive data arsenal is the ability to understand how your strategies can be used effectively to either attack a competitor's vulnerability or defend against its strengths. A valuable methodology to apply is a variation of a SWOT analysis (SWOT is an acronym for an analytical technique meaning strengths, weaknesses, opportunities, and threats, discussed further in Chapter 10) for each relevant competitor. Just examine and chart the strengths and weaknesses of the competitor's products, as portrayed in Figure 7.6. This helps identify effective methods to plan attack strategies that focus on competitor vulnerabilities or defensive postures to counteract competitor strengths. The secret to accomplishing this is to look for all the common denominators across the field of competitors in order to get some indication of the areas on which you can focus.

HOW DO THEY DO WHAT THEY DO?

As noted above, a competitive profile is a great way to provide an overarching summary for each of your competitors and the products with which you compete. The challenge for the product manager and the product team is to determine how your products compare with the competitors' products so that appropriate product strategies or game plans can be devised and implemented. In other words, *how do competitor companies deliver value to their customers?*

FIGURE 7.5

Competitor Profile Template for a Product or Product Line

Name of competitor	
Date of profile	
Address of main office and other locations	
Web URL	
Publicly or privately held	
General statement about the company's or brand's reputation in the market	
General observations about the financial condition of the firm and any relevant financial data at the product level or at the level of the division of that company where your products compete	
Divisional or business unit structure plus a description of each division's market focus, market segments, and market share. Additionally, include key customers and/or key wins, if relevant	
Relevant organization charts and key executives supporting the divisions that sell the products you compete with	
Number of employees (by division)	
Names and model numbers (or other identifiers) of every product with which you compete. Include feature, function, and other attribute comparisons	
Market segments on which they focus	
Key accounts or customers to whom they sell (especially B2B)	
Pricing strategies and discounting activity for each product	
Channels used to move products from source to customer	
Promotional mix profiles (how do they advertise and promote, where, and when)	
Selling models (direct sales force, web, etc.)	
Value propositions represented for those products	
How the competitive products are positioned against other competitors as well as your own products	
Employee morale or other employee indicators	
Key strengths for the products with which you compete	
Key weaknesses for the products with which you compete	
Known competitive strategies of this competitor. What are the most visible activities of this competitor over the past year or two, and what might you expect in the future?	

FIGURE 7.6

Competitor SWOT

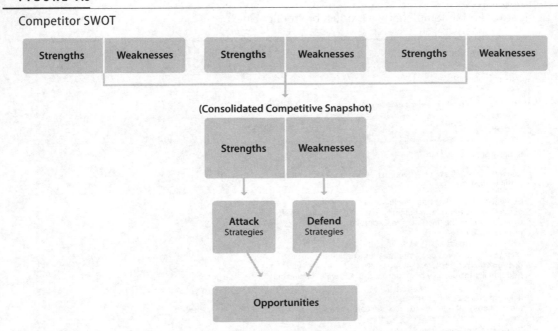

(Consolidated Competitive Snapshot)

There are some challenges with this because we don't always have the basic competitive data to help us dig beneath the surface—except for a comparison of competitors' features, or whatever may be revealed in general data contained in the competitor profile. One of the ways to overcome such challenges is to enlist the support of the members of your cross-functional product team. Engineers, marketers, and others may be helpful in filling in missing information. They all read different material, talk to different people, and may have data that will help construct a more complete story. In some firms with tangible products, reverse engineering studies may help in creating a bill of materials and a cost model for a competitor product

The factor that makes a competitive analysis valuable for a product manager and team is knowledge of what happens in a competitor's company. Simply defined, it's what they do, how they accomplish what they do, and why. Furthermore, how does your company do what it does in comparison with what competitive companies do? There are eight groups of questions (and some subquestions) I have found effective in finding what lies behind the locked doors of a competitor company. Hopefully, you will be able to extract some meaningful guidelines that assist you to carry out your own competitive analyses.

FIGURE 7.7

Competitive Analysis and the Business Model

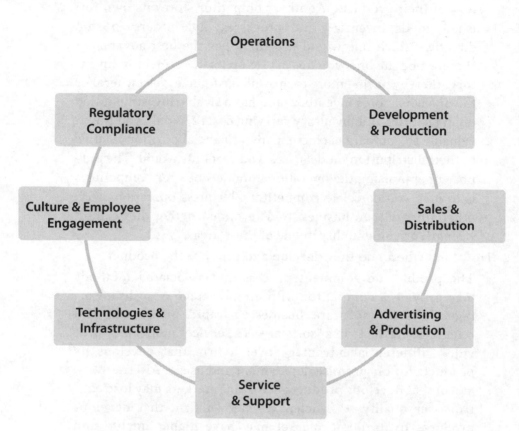

Figure 7.7 provides a visual representation of how any firm, including your own, might portray their *business model*. This is another useful way to guide your thought process when it comes to the evaluation of competitor strengths and weaknesses.

1. How do they operate their company?
   - Every company has a basic operating model. There are operational support systems and elements of infrastructure that either afford them a competitive advantage or leave them vulnerable. These procedures include:
     - How they procure, move, and manage materials through their supply chains
     - The methods they use to process orders and collect money from customers

■ It is important to know about each of these areas. Here's why: Suppose one of your competitors uses a retailer to hold inventory of their products. Another competitor stores its own finished goods inventory and processes bulk orders to ship directly. Which one would you think has the best advantage? Would it be the one who doesn't tie up its investment in inventory (thereby having more cash available to invest elsewhere) or the one who stores inventory (and has a sizable investment tied up in facilities and inventory carrying costs)? Would you find it valuable to compare each company's financial position relative to their distribution models? Yes, you certainly would. The purpose of appraising the operational models of your competitors is to help you correlate competitors' business operations with other areas of their business to determine whether they exhibit strength or vulnerability in one of these areas.

2. How (and where) do they develop and produce the product?

■ The product development process and associated methods may provide a competitor with an advantage or a disadvantage. In some software businesses, rapid production and release of products in a "software as a service" model may provide a differential advantage over a firm that develops its products for on-premise deployment and usage. Alternatively, a firm that develops products in distant markets may lose control over quality or efficiency, where a firm that develops products in its home market may have higher quality and demand premium prices as a domestic supplier. As a product manager, you need to be able to relate the competitor's methods in product creation to your own product's production or development methods. How you develop and produce directly influences your cost structure. It affects your ability to price your product profitably and your ability to reinvest at the product or portfolio level.

■ The production of the product can be examined in many ways. For tangible products, you'll want to know where they make their products and how. Twenty years ago, when General Motors or Ford saw competitors building factories in the United States, they were probably concerned that these companies were invading their home markets and would capture some of their market share. More recently, there has been a shift to the outsourcing of computer programming, customer service, the manufacture of noncritical product parts, and product assembly to other regions domestically and overseas. When your competitors are outsourcing and lowering their costs, and you are not, what does that mean for your company and your products?

■ Another dimension of the production puzzle involves the cost of goods of a tangible product. You should have a version of every similar product your competitor sells in your laboratory or other product development area. Tangible products should be torn down to their basic components, and all of the components' costs should be calculated based on assumed volumes and production locations. In some companies, the process of reverse engineering helps put cost models and pricing models in perspective. In many tangible goods businesses, from industrial machines to sophisticated communications gear, low labor cost markets like China are producing lower-cost (and possibly lower-quality) products, and creating tremendous downward pricing pressures on higher-cost competitor products. Such factors could cause your company to consider other options in materials, labor, and production facilities. You could even decide to completely outsource your production in order to have products that are markedly more competitive while preserving your margins.

3. How do they sell and distribute the product?

■ Although operational models and production techniques continue to be streamlined, product distribution can also be a major source of competitive advantage or disadvantage. Distribution (also called "place") is one of the *marketing mix elements*, and usually distribution cannot be changed without some other elements of the mix being changed as well. For example, you know your product needs to move through a channel, but no product is going through a channel without a price or some promotion to build awareness and encourage sales. Distribution must leverage one of the other mix elements in order for that element to serve as a key competitive advantage. Take the company Research in Motion. That company capitalized on its product's wireless e-mail capabilities (its key strength) and gained a lot of favorable treatment by wireless service providers. This was a huge advantage for them because they built their credibility with those channel partners. This, in turn, provided more monies for R&D in order to continuously improve its product. Currently, it retains a powerful competitive advantage due to its distribution network, which also helped promote and establish its brand.

- What you learn about your competitor's distribution method and what those facts tell you about their methods (direct versus indirect, wholesale versus retail, etc.) will tell you a great deal about how efficiently they get their products to their end customers. By now, many firms have capitalized on use of the Internet as a core competitive advantage. Anecdotally, one of the large networking equipment companies reported that 80 to 90 percent of their reorders were processed online, thereby removing a direct sales interface for ordering.

- Another question to be answered is, "How do they sell their products?" Some companies maintain a direct sales force, while others rely on manufacturers' representatives or value-added resellers. Some salespeople foster great account relationships, and some do not go this extra mile. Your research should focus on building as much of a sales force profile as possible. You need to work with your own salespeople so they can help you learn who else in the competitor's sales force works on the account, who they interact with (e.g., middle management or upper management), and who makes the purchasing decisions. Furthermore, you may be able to pinpoint the geographic areas where they are strong and where they are not so strong. You may be able to find out why customers buy their products versus yours, or why they buy yours versus theirs.

4. How do they advertise and promote their products?

- Most companies advertise and promote their products and/or brands using a variety of methods. This is the promotional mix, or, as some say, integrated marketing. Do as much investigation and research as you can on your competitors' promotional programs. Be aware of their use of changing marketing communication methods, which encompass both traditional and digital methods. Some companies will actually hire research firms to go to different geographic areas to find out which competitors are advertising locally. Recently, a fairly new product manager of a retail bank asked me how to learn more about competitors' retail products. I asked her, "If you were a consumer, how would you compare the banks you were considering doing business with? Go hunting." She called me back a couple of weeks later to tell me she had gone to all of the competitors' branches, browsed all their websites, and came up with a matrix of products. I then suggested she phone their call centers to see what else she could deduce. After a while, she "got it." She may have known it all along, but doing a competitor product comparison appeared more complicated than it needed to be. A good way to learn more about your competitors' products would be to act like a customer or a prospective customer seeking a vendor. If you had a specific need you wanted to satisfy, how would you go about shopping for the product and what promotional material would you find? Shopping for the product can be so helpful, many companies hire market research firms to do "mystery shopping" of competitors' stores and websites, and even act as a customer of a company.

5. How do they service and support their customers?

- One of the best ways to find out how competitors support customers is to be a customer of a competitor (if you can) and try to report a problem, lodge a complaint, or request information. Then, be a customer of your own company. Compare the experience and try to determine the differences between your experiences. Many times in my career I have been amazed at how difficult it was to get product data from my own company. Whether you hire a researcher, call to request information, or go into their retail outlet, try to walk in the customer's shoes (which, by the way, is a great way to listen to the customer's voice). You would do this when researching your own consumer needs, and you can apply this method to one dimension of competitive research. Your goal is to find the vulnerability in the competitor's armor in order to attack that weakness and play up (or build up) your own strengths.

■ Some of the subtle nuances you want to discern are the degrees to which their customer service agents are empowered to help you and the feelings they engender. Do they make you feel they're interested in your satisfaction? Do they apply good problem-solving skills? If there is a repair and return policy, what is it and how does it compare with yours?

■ Finally, at some point, the industry analysts will issue comments on the manner in which a company services and supports its customers. In the current computer marketplace, HP and Dell are constantly being monitored by independent firms for the purpose of correlating service-related performance and product quality to customer satisfaction and revenue or market share.

6. What are the primary technologies or infrastructure elements employed?

■ When you understand the technologies employed across the competitive landscape, one of the things you learn about is how companies utilize technology for competitive advantage and why. Often, patent intelligence allows you to find this out. There are a host of resources available. The Science unit of Thomson Reuters maintains databases of world patents, impending product launches, and other technology industry trends. Google now offers a patent search option that can yield very usable data.

■ University research programs offer another interesting resource. You can determine which companies are funding which kinds of research (through grants). This information is usually available through the Office of Projects and Grants and the Office of Technology Transfer (or other similar departmental names) in organizations within the university.

■ Technology and systems can be a major competitive weapon. Walmart can determine which product is selling down to the store level within 10 minutes. Their ability to react and move merchandise in and out of stores in a timely fashion gives them the advantage of moving the hottest goods to the most favorable locations on the floor.

7. What is their corporate culture and are employees engaged?

■ Every company has a culture. When I talk to people from Southwest Airlines, they don't say a negative word about their employer. After flying on Jet Blue, I chatted with the pilot after I saw him collecting trash in his plane. He told me he had agreed to do whatever it took to help the airline. When I hear employees at a bank complain that they're worried about their jobs, I wonder how productive they may be under such circumstances. The old adage that your employees are your most valuable resource can differ in value to various companies. Your competitive advantage can be better secured when the environment in your organization is progressive and communicative and people feel connected to their leadership. This is why product team leadership is so important—it helps to create an environment of "can-do" collaboration and cooperation.

■ Keep an eye on your competitors and their employee activities. In some industries, people move among competitor firms, so your friends in your current company may leave one day and work for a competitor—and you don't usually stop being friends. Recently, while visiting a banking client in a southern U.S. city, I heard about a baseball game to be played that evening. The teams were from big bank W and big bank B. Most of the players were friends no matter which team they played for. Friends talk to each other.

8. Are they compliant with the regulatory authorities or securities regulators?

■ Each publicly traded company files reports with the SEC or CESR. These reports discuss its businesses, its financial performance, its investments, and its performance. It's not unusual for these reports to discuss competitors—sometimes by name. They even cite legal actions taken for or against rivals, and the reasons why (think about looking for vulnerabilities). These documents are a great resource for competitive data.

THE FINAL ANALYSIS

The industry in which you work and compete, and the competitors you face, represent the playing field for the products you manage.

Throughout your career in Product Management, you will be asked to provide industry and competitive profiles. These profiles will be used in your product strategy documents, your Business Cases, and Marketing Plans. You don't want to have to go back and do a completely new analysis each time you need to create a document. Since storytelling is an extremely effective method to describe and characterize a situation, developing a competitive story is a good idea. Then, when you need a standard format and structure to tell the story about what is going on in your market area with your competitors and their products, you are well prepared to do so. This is also desirable because at a moment's notice, you could be called upon to render a fairly up-to-date interpretation of the market. This story about the industry and the competition is built around the following data-derived story structure:

1. A historical perspective of the industry that describes what has happened in each market area where your products have been sold.

2. A discussion about who the competitors are, what they have been doing with their products, and why. Moreover, you will likely need to provide individual competitor snapshots as well as some type of description about how your product or products compare with those of the competition, and why those competitive products are performing the way they are.

3. Finally, you'll need to be able to synthesize the data into a cogent story about what's going on overall within your business playing field, what your next steps are going to be, and why.

SUMMARY

Any successful product strategy seeks to construct the most viable and durable competitive advantage. Compelling value propositions and superior positioning must be built on the foundation of an astute understanding of industry landscapes that often change like the chameleons and competitors whose products seem to morph overnight. Product managers should be self-motivated professionals who seek to continually evolve their industry and competitive assessment knowledge base—and keep good records on an ongoing basis, using industry and competitive profiles.

The basic collection of data and its ultimate translation into usable information provides the true basis for deriving industry and competitive intelligence. Analysis of information by correlation, inference, extrapolation, and just gut feel helps you create the intelligence that provides you with the ability to strategize and to act. In the end, it's not about the actual reports or documents you generated, it's about what you do with the data you have garnered.

RAISING YOUR PRODUCT MANAGEMENT EXPERIENCE QUOTIENT (PMEQ)

1. Create a visual, historical gallery of your product or product line. Use pictures or just text boxes or diagrams (if you have intangible products). Call this the "retrospective visual product roadmap."

2. Take what you did in item 1 above and overlay it onto your competitor's products or product lines.

3. Create a storyboard for items 1 and 2, describing how industry and competitive forces, as well as other business, regulatory, economic, technological, and other market drivers, motivated these product line changes.

4. Generate a list of industry and trade periodicals and analyst organizations that are the most relevant for your organization or product line. To find out what exists, talk to as many people as possible in Marketing, Sales, R&D/Engineering, and anyone else you may learn about who might have this information. Subscribe to as many of these industry, trade, and analytical publications as you can. Some of these publications will respond favorably to requests for complimentary subscriptions. Furthermore, every publisher is expanding their digital media distribution, so ask if you can be allowed complimentary access. Use your funds wisely when you do have to pay.

5. Subscribe to every internal and external news feed or information summary service in the relevant areas covered by your products. Scan them frequently.

6. Create a physical bulletin board or an online resource with information you've learned from what you have scanned or read. This will act as a reference library. People in the organization will take notice of these "leadership" indicators.

7. If there is an existing corporate information library or electronic repository, visit it often. Incorporate what you learn into periodic team reviews. Find out what you can do to add to its content and/or commentary.

8. Every month or so, or as often as practical, invite your team members to an informal industry and competitive review session. This means you have to actually put together a 15- to 30-minute presentation. The best time is before the workday starts or at lunch time. Bring food. The object is for you to share the latest industry and competitive news and to announce any

major wins or losses. You'll quickly find that when meeting with the attendees, some of them may have read or heard about things you were not yet aware of. Be sure you record what you heard and keep copies of all the items discussed in your Product Master Plan.

9. Prepare a detailed industry and competitive analysis report. Keep it updated as often as needed (depending on the speed of product life cycles in your industry). You will find that when you are called upon to prepare a document, decide on a feature trade-off, or make a presentation, you'll always have one "ready to go." Use the Competitor Dossier Template as a guide.

10. Establish a contact in your Competitive Intelligence group and ask her to notify you when new content is available. Follow up by calling her every month or two to be updated on what's been happening.

11. Join a trade association for the industry in which you work. Attend conferences and expositions where you can view competitors' product information or attend a speech they may be giving. Networking at these events is vital. You can glean a surprising amount of information.

12. When attending trade or industry conferences, be sure to write up a synopsis of what you found or learned, and share it with members of your cross-functional team as well as with your peers. When you attend a conference, you are the eyes and ears for others, too.

13. Reach out to your Industry and Competitive Research organization, if one exists. Find out what it does and what its sources of information are. Perhaps you can encourage experts on the corporate staff who may be involved in corporate development or corporate strategy to talk to your product team from time to time to share some of their findings and observations—and some of their strategic plans.

FINDING MARKETS TO CONQUER BY UNDERSTANDING CUSTOMER NEEDS AND MARKET SEGMENTS

Executive Summary

- The more you know about the needs that motivate customers, the more successful you can be at attracting them.
- Understanding the benefits that customers value most can help you create the most potent product positioning.
- Market segmentation models are highly transient and volatile because customers' needs continually evolve. Product managers need to keep up with those changes so they can more appropriately evolve their products with the necessary agility.

"In search of answers to questions untold . . ."
—JOHN DENVER, "CALYPSO"

For product managers and marketers, if you don't know who you intend to sell your product to, and you don't know what they value, you will likely not make the sale. Successful business people have known this for eons, as philosopher Lucius Annaeus Seneca once said: "If one does not know to which port one is sailing, no wind is favorable."

In basic terms the "market" is made up of buyers and sellers. The previous chapter defined sellers as companies who compete for customers within industry areas or sectors. With this chapter, we turn our attention to the customers. Market segmentation is the classification method that helps product managers and marketers identify customer groups based on specific categories such as common needs or similar buying behaviors. When product managers and marketers actually understand the needs and motivations of specific customer types (consumers or businesses), they can create optimal marketing mix strategies targeted to these customer classifications. The marketing mix, described in various places throughout this book, comprises four categories:

1. The product and its capabilities that provide proven value and benefits for targeted customers
2. The value afforded to targeted customers from the product as expressed through the prices charged
3. The way in which value is communicated to targeted customers through promotions and education programs
4. The methods by which value is delivered to targeted customers, or how customers access a company's products, through diverse sales and distribution channels

Like many business and marketing terms, the phrase *market segmentation* seems easy to understand. However, when you are applying it in a real situation it may be somewhat fuzzy and imprecise. The reason is that the common sets of needs and attributes for specific customer types or targeted customers are not clearly understood. Different companies in different industries have different ways to classify customers and the markets in which they are situated. In this chapter, these issues will be addressed and clarified.

THE COMMON DENOMINATOR IN SEGMENTATION: CUSTOMER NEEDS

In the world of fast-moving consumer products and services, there are many opportunities to take market and customer snapshots in rapid succession. Such snapshots reveal helpful insights into why customers buy certain products and how they use those products. In businesses with fast-moving products, the performance results of product and marketing strategies need rapid responses so new strategies can adjust to meet new needs. In complex business-to-business (B2B) industries, even with rapid customer and market feedback, companies sometimes move at a glacial pace. It can take a surprisingly long time for strategies to be reformulated.

Whether your products target consumers or serve businesses, product managers have to ask, "Who buys our products, and why?" The next logical question would be, "Who is it we *want* to add to our customer base, and why?"

The "why" is the most significant question. The answers will help product managers understand the overarching problems or needs of specific customer types. What determines a customer's motivation to actually buy or use your products? What leads customers to seek products that haven't yet been created? The stronger your commitment to understanding and acting on customer needs, the better your chances for meeting or exceeding their expectations.

In my workshops, I ask, "What needs does your product address?" The participants offer a wide variety of responses—and most of them are off the mark. In most instances, the answers from people in the group describe their product's great features. "Our product has a quick start button." "Our product has an easy-to-navigate user interface." "Our product works faster." None of these answers points to the needs that these features are supposed to address.

Within the realm of Organizational Behavior, a defining work on human needs was presented by Abraham Maslow, in his 1943 paper, "A Theory of Human Motivation," in which he proposed a hierarchy of needs model. It's a great way to take a look at needs at the most basic, fundamental, psychological level. Even though academics debate the theory and others challenge the idea of a sequencing of needs (if indeed there is a satisfaction sequence), the fact that there really are ways to explore human needs offers an opportunity to reflect on how to view market segments.

Maslow posited that there are several layers of needs, beginning with primary *physiologic* needs such as the need to eat, to survive, to be sheltered from the elements, and to rest so that we can rejuvenate. At the next level, he indicated that there are *safety* needs. Safety allows people to stay safe from physical harm, from illness, from pain, and more. Next, there are *social* needs, which may be satisfied through affiliation with others, including the need to be supported and to participate in productive, rewarding relationships. He further proposed that there are needs that contribute to *self-esteem* and *self-respect* and suggested that there are also cognitive needs, which require that we learn, grow, and become more aware of the world around us (which, by the way, is what's needed for good decision making).

These very basic elements have merit for our discussion on market segmentation and how *true* needs form the building blocks for appropriate segmentation models.

Just a quick note on another topic. Invariably, you will find that some people use the words *wants* and *needs* interchangeably. There is no damage done if you mix them, but I see them as another expression with a blurry semantic delineation. For purposes related to product management, we'll use the expression *needs*.

In order to accomplish the work of market segmentation, you must understand the difference between underlying needs and product features. Figure 8.1 provides some clarifying examples.

FIGURE 8.1

Distinguishing Between Features and Needs

Feature	Need
A personal identification number (PIN) for a debit card	Safety and security—to protect your money and your identity
A telephone with an amplified handset	To be able to hear clearly
A telephone with large push buttons	To be able to see clearly
A chair with an easy-to-use height adjuster	Comfort
A fast-loading computer game on an airplane	To be entertained during long flights (to avoid being bored)
An intuitive, easy-to-navigate user interface for a website	To be informed quickly when there is little time

HOW MARKETS ARE SEGMENTED

Markets can be segmented based on a variety of characteristics, but of utmost importance is the difference between *consumer* and *business* markets. Consumer markets tend to be distributed within the traditional marketing categories that characterize each segment based on the following:

- *Demographics* guide the product manager or marketer to classify people by age, gender, education level, ethnicity, culture, income, and other dimensions. You probably wouldn't target twenty-something's if you were a luxury auto company.

- *Geographic* indicators designate where consumers live and work as well as local tastes and conditions. If a major coffee chain sets up a store every few blocks in a big city, it must know something. People who live in Florida have very different needs for furnaces and air conditioners than people who live in New England.

- *Values and beliefs* are important gauges because they relate to the characteristics of needs-oriented affiliations. For example, some customers may have political or religious affiliations. Some may support causes, such as protecting the environment or treatment of animals. These customers represent, as the marketers like to say, psychographic profiles, which may indicate what sorts of companies' products they may wish to affiliate with (e.g., environmentally oriented people may only buy "green" products). Values and beliefs are also very important for brands: if your customers don't like your stand as a corporation, they may not buy from you no matter how much they like your product—think Nike and sweat shops.

- *Loyalty indicators* help to determine how often a customer buys a product or uses a service. Frequent buyers, frequent flyers, and heavy users may be our favorite customers. Again, brand is important here.

Business markets may share similar characteristics with consumers, but more often are focused on the following:

- *Geographic* areas in which companies operate serve as useful delineations. This partitioning into local, regional, national, or international categories allows you to determine their degree of market coverage and, therefore, potential opportunity for your product. The number of facilities and the business carried out at each specific facility are also of concern to the B2B product manager. This is especially important for international business operations.

- *Company size* would include sales, market share in an industry, number of employees, assets on the balance sheet, profitability, market capitalization, and other traditional business measures.

- *Industry or industries served* offers you the chance to get a sense of the trends and activities in this area. (To find more about different industry types, refer to Chapter 7.)

- *Market segments on which these companies focus* allow you to identify who their customers are, or even who their customer's customers are (in more complex business-to-business-to-business [B2B2B] or business-to-business-to-consumer [B2B2C] enterprises).

- *Loyalty indicators*, as mentioned in the earlier consumer bulleted list, are important because you want to understand the buying patterns of these businesses. A hotel chain may offer a local business better rates and amenities when the company commits to having all its traveling employees stay at that particular hotel chain.

In addition to categorizing customers as consumers or businesses, there are a host of subsegments within each grouping. These subsegments are typically known as customer segments or customer targets. The term *target customer types* refers to the detailed makeup of constituents within a broad market segment. Whether classified within a consumer or business market, they comprise, typically, people who *use* a product, *influence* its purchase, actually have to *buy* the product, or are the *decision makers*. This consideration is particularly important when it comes to identifying shoppers or buyers—whether or not there is an intended willingness to pay (e.g., to write the check or part with the cash) for a specific benefit. Each of these customer segments has its own distinctive set of needs, and product managers or marketers can be caught off guard if they don't consider these distinctions.

Theodore Levitt, a noted author in the area of Marketing, said, "If you're not thinking segments, you're not thinking. To think segments means you have to think about what drives customers, customer groups, and the choices that are or might be available to them."

Several years ago, I was negotiating with a communications company in Italy about the purchase of a major automation tool. This would have helped the company reduce its workforce by about 2,000 people. The arithmetic of the value proposition was compelling to the purchasing manager. But we lost the deal! The value proposition was really great, but the target was wrong. The decision maker had not informed us beforehand that the workforce was heavily unionized; a fact we failed to consider. We wasted a lot of time in support of an unsolicited proposal because we didn't properly recognize how the would-be customer operated and consider the customer's particular needs, even though the company was in the right market segment. In other words, we missed the target!

Over the years, I've learned some important lessons about these different customer types. In many cases, the customer you plan to target is not the customer who actually buys the product. The automobile industry is filled with examples of this phenomenon. In one case, a major brand designed a compact sport utility vehicle targeted at 18- to 24-year-old males. After the product introduction, it became clear that the vehicle was being purchased by people in their 30s and 40s—people who might be working on home and garden projects. Although the vehicle was designed to attract the original target customer, functionality won out and the product roadmap for the vehicle had to change—an unintended consequence for the auto maker. The good news is that automobile companies have learned valuable lessons and are attuned to these changes. They're better equipped to pivot when necessary, which is an important lesson for all product managers to understand.

MARKET SEGMENTATION AND THE MARKETING MIX

Product managers need to know about each of the market segments so that they can define which customers they should focus on. They also need to know that different customer types provide different amounts of revenue or profit to their business. Market segment definitions, as discussed previously, divide customers into groups with similar characteristics. That's fairly simple to grasp. However, the axiom is very significant. The reasoning is that a business should not formulate an identical marketing mix for different customer types (although it seems like that is too often done).

Segmentation models should allow product managers to tailor the marketing mix to specific market segments or target customer types, thereby affording the business a greater opportunity to satisfy the needs of that specific group. A marketing mix strategy should also focus on the customers within those segments who have enough purchasing power to be profitable to the business. This means that if you have aimed at the right target, the customer types in the chosen segment should favor a specific *product* (especially if it is correctly positioned), be inspired by advertising and *promotional* messages, believe that *prices* reflect the value delivered, and acquire the product through the most convenient *channel* (or place, e.g., a retailer, representative, supplier, manufacturer, over the Internet, or through an intermediary).

Take that big coffee retailer. Its target customer is a coffee lover who appreciates the amenities of the store's environment. The coffee retailer knows this target, prices the products at a premium, and promotes the product through media outlets most likely to reach its targeted customer. That's a marketing mix of product (coffee), a value-based price (at a premium), advertising and promotion (through the optimal media), and place or channel (the retail outlet and other places that sell that brand of coffee). That's a marketing mix most suited to a particular customer type. The coffee retailer won't pursue other coffee drinkers who don't value the ambience or appreciate the premium-quality coffee.

DESCRIBING THE TARGET MARKET

When a product manager prepares product strategies, Business Cases, Launch Plans, and other product or marketing documentation, it is necessary to describe why a specific segment is chosen. These particular segments represent the *target market*. Industry trend data and competitive activity levels provide clues that determine the size and desirability of a segment. Thus, market attractiveness is selected based on several factors:

1. *The degree to which the segment is growing.* For example: the large number of baby boomers in the United States is creating sizable opportunities for companies offering services focusing on convenience, travel and leisure, and health care. The segment is also attractive because demographic data suggest that there is a tremendous amount of wealth built up by this part of the population, and because they're not all retiring and sitting around

(many continue to work and save), they have more money for discretionary items.

2. *The number of competitors vying for the space.* If there are too many competitors in a given market area, customers may have too much choice and it may be more difficult to establish a differential advantage with your product. However, companies with sufficient financial resources can often advertise their way forward, leveraging their brands and recognized names. Witness the presence of retail banking branches in major cities.

3. *The manner in which a segment is accessible by known distribution channels.* The Internet redefined the world of commerce, making products and services available for purchase 24/7. Retail stores are open longer hours. Warehouse stores serving consumers and businesses abound. Everyone is mobile and connected electronically.

4. *The profit to be gained by bringing products and services to those segments.* No matter how attractive or accessible the segment, if it won't make enough money, it isn't attractive enough.

Suppose you worked in a bank as the product portfolio manager for all credit card products. When you looked at your market segments based on credit card balance, what kinds of segments might you want to preserve and which ones would you want to *target* to build up? If the banking industry is characterized by intense competition, then you would want to do at least two things:

1. Ensure that other banks do not lure away your current customers—for example, those with good balances who pay large fees.

2. Take market share from your competitors, perhaps by pursuing large-balance accounts.

To achieve this, you have some decisions to make about what to do. Figure 8.2 presents this example in a matrix format showing five general groupings of credit card customers, segmented by the size of the balances they keep on their cards.

By using this simple model, a product or portfolio manager may be able to consider different options, based on which segments offer the best opportunity, while managing the risk profile of the portfolio.

FIGURE 8.2

Segmentation Example

Segments by Credit Card Balance	Number of Accounts	Accounts Profitability	Segments Vulnerable to Competition	Strategic Options
Less than $1,000	40,000	Low		Maintain
$1,001–$2,000	90,000	Low-Medium	x	Grow
$2,001–$5,000	56,000	Medium	x	Grow
$5,001–$10,000	39,000	Medium–High		Grow
$10,001–$15,000	19,000	High		Maintain

Good segmentation models help bring the world of the customer into better focus so that product managers and marketers can focus their efforts on the communication methods most effective at impelling usage among their customers. Such models stimulate more granular thought regarding the needs of each segment and cultivate a fertile ground for potential new product features or attributes.

THEY DON'T KNOW WHAT THEY DON'T KNOW

Up to now, I've talked about the foundational elements of market segmentation. However, the real challenge for the product manager extends further—to the discovery of the real needs of customers in chosen segments.

All too often, we struggle with trying to understand needs. Customers are frequently asked questions like, "What keeps you awake at night?" or "If you could have three wishes, what would they be?" Companies use focus groups and ask consumers which cola they like better. More positive answers for one cola must mean that everyone likes that cola. "Would you buy this one or that one?" asks the interviewer. "I'd buy that one," says the interviewee. What is often missed in the controlled interview environment is, "If you were walking down the aisle of the market, would you actually buy one?"

When people are interviewed in a controlled setting with other people present, they may be reluctant to reveal their true feelings.

An article in *BusinessWeek* (November 15, 2005) called "Shoot the Focus Group" states, "There's peer pressure in focus groups that gets in the way of finding the truth about real behavior and intentions . . ." There are certainly new methods that can be applied to expose and capture the customer's true needs. The *BusinessWeek* article describes how a senior packaging designer at Kimberly-Clark did something novel to learn more about mothers who changed diapers:

> . . . a camera mounted on a pair of glasses to be worn by consumers at home, so researchers could see through their eyes. 'Letting us see what they see, rather than pointing the camera at them, proved more comfortable for them and useful to us,' . . . It didn't take long to spot the opportunities. While women in groups talked about changing babies at a diaper table, the truth was they changed them on beds, floors, and on top of washing machines in awkward positions. The researchers could see they were struggling with wipe containers and lotions requiring two hands. The company redesigned the wipe package with a push-button one-handed dispenser and designed lotion and shampoo bottles that can be grabbed and dispensed easily with one hand.

The product manager must be able to determine how to enter the minds of current customers or get inside the heads of desirable new customers. Consumer examples of capturing the customer's voice abound. However, many product managers don't work in consumer goods industries. They are employed by industrial companies, medical device companies, insurance companies, banks, investment firms, software companies, and other service industries. What they have in common is the need to know what's in their customer's mind. But which customer?

The Business Value Delivery Model Helps You Understand Who the Real Customers Are

Earlier in this text, I indicated that customers can be business customers or consumer customers. Many people in the B2B world use the word *customers* when they are really talking about companies. A *customer company* is made up of a number of different individuals: users, influencers, decision makers, and the like. However, sometimes the needs of a particular *customer type* in a customer company may not represent the most important needs to address. Let me explain.

If your B2B company aims to sell a product to a person in a customer company, that product may actually be a part of a larger product that is ultimately sold to another company or a consumer. For example, let's say your company makes transmissions for automobiles and your firm sells to an automobile company who assembles the car for a distinct customer type. That customer type could be a person who needs economical transportation or someone who is a sports car enthusiast. If the transmission company only makes one transmission for both end customers, the sports enthusiast may end up with an underperforming vehicle. That customer's need will not be met, even if the procurement person in the automobile company thinks it will be the right product for both cars.

To ensure that you have the right customer in sight, you need to have a viable *customer value delivery model*. The customer value delivery model is based on the idea that product managers and their teams must know every customer type—from the point of product creation to the point of actual usage. This is portrayed by the visual in Figure 8.3.

There are five main reasons you and your team need to completely embrace the business value delivery model:

1. It will help you to understand "who's who" in any of these customer milieus. Product managers must be customer experts with respect to all customer types, not just a customer company or a consumer household.

2. It will help you on the road to uncover the unexpressed needs of buyers, users, influencers, and decision makers. When you are able to share these customer perspectives with cross-functional team members, they will be better able to rationalize their own work. Moreover, when you're preparing product requirements or considering the product's design, you'll be able to better characterize *user stories* or use other techniques to portray the "day in the life" of a customer.

3. When you develop the proper perspective for each customer type, you will be able to derive relevant, *needs-driven value propositions*. These value propositions will be vitally important in the derivation of competitive pricing models, which I'll discuss in Chapter 20.

4. Marketers must also understand the needs and motivations for each customer type along the business value delivery chain so they can target the right messages to those customers for optimal impact.

FIGURE 8.3

Customer Value Delivery Models

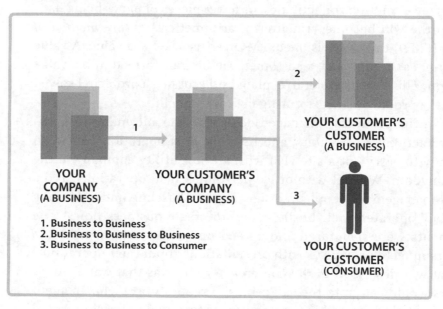

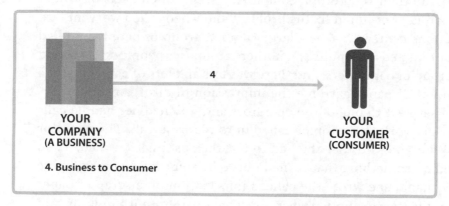

5. With the increased emphasis on consultative or value-based solution selling, salespeople must be brought into the customer analysis process. Further, salespeople must be adequately trained to look for business anomalies, which they accomplish through their intimate familiarity with customer business operations and workflows.

When an operational workflow is understood, it can be seen as a *present method of operation* (PMO). When the work is broken down into basic tasks and the task durations and activities can be measured, then each granule of work can be looked at as an opportunity for operational improvement. When a sleek, new operational paradigm can be discerned that offers fewer motions or activities, or fewer pieces of paper being handled, then the win becomes a matter of arithmetic. A *future method of operation* (FMO) can be envisioned: FMO versus PMO = a value. A value worth noting, assimilated by a customer, can be transformed into a value proposition. This may be easier to explain by discussing a problem I solved when I was a product manager during my corporate life.

One of the products I managed dealt with the automation of customer interactions, call centers, and field dispatch operations. I had an opportunity to carry out a site visit with a water utility company in the United Kingdom. We met with office personnel, field operations, and a variety of management people in order to gain a baseline understanding of how they operated their business and to create business flows. The arrangements were structured and agreed upon in advance, with customer personnel to provide us with presentations about their operations.

What was described in the conference room was that water utility customers would call in to the call center to report a problem, an agent would look up their record in a computer system, and a decision would be made about who should fix the problem and when. Then we went into the operations center. In a very large room, a group of people huddled around antiquated computers; another group of people sat around another group of computers; and there was lots and lots of paper. Just the sheer amount of paper gave me the impression of disorganization personified. I sat next to one of the operators and watched her handle calls and her paperwork. A customer called in to report a leak. The operator did a look-up and said that she had to put the customer on hold. Then she looked up something that turned out to be some kind of geographic coding. By hand, she wrote the caller's information on a scrap of paper and brought it over to another operator. That operator did a look-up and found the record. The first operator transferred the call to the second operator, who then took over. After the second operator entered some of the information into the computer, a service order was printed. She then verified the data with the customer and scheduled an appointment.

The second operator then walked about 100 feet to another bank of computers and handed the service order to an operations supervisor. The supervisor looked it over and walked it over to another person who then faxed the service order to a field operations office who would then assign a field repair person to fix the leak. This was just on the receiving end.

The dispatching operations turned out to be inefficient, too. The field repair crews came to work and waited until they got the service orders. There were no measurements or standards for how long jobs should take or their level of complexity, and there was no tracking of what the field people did. The operations manager expressed concern about field crews' wasted time.

After my review of their operations, I knew I had "heard" the customer's voice and perceived the real needs that underlay their problems. I fired up my laptop to a graphics program and diagrammed the business flow in excruciating detail. After showing the program to the operations manager and the sales representative, we discussed it further. With a few tweaks, we created a flowchart that analyzed time intervals (once called a time and motion study). This profile provided me with a wealth of information about systems, people, operational rules, work tasks, and timing. The resulting analysis helped us to define an improved FMO. By being able to derive an extraordinary value proposition, I helped the customer defend its investment while I defended my investment.

Moreover, this profile provided me with a wealth of information about systems, people, operational rules, work tasks, and timing. I gained a better understanding of the PMO. This gave me the basis for characterizing discrete customer types: the users, which in this case included the operator, dispatch supervisor, and field service crew people, and the influencers, whom I classed as the operations manager and his manager, the chief operating officer. Finally, by mapping the PMO, I had a solid basis for communicating the value to the customer and deriving the most effective pricing strategy.

PLANNING AND CARRYING OUT CUSTOMER VISITS

The preceding example shows why it is important for product managers and marketers to really understand how customers operate. To do this, you need to get into the field. Product managers often face travel restrictions, which is doubtless a challenge. However, if a product manager asks to visit the customer, there's a very good chance her manager will heed the request.

The correct documentation for this vital element of market research is a *customer visit plan*. Many salespeople use a somewhat similar technique to chart which customers they're going to visit and in what sequence, but this is not quite the same. A product manager can plan a visit with a salesperson or account manager. Procedurally, you can't initiate this alone—you need to respect the salesperson's domain. When you have a clear plan for what you want to accomplish for a visit requiring travel, you improve the odds your travel request will be approved, restrictions or not.

Customer visits are generally carried out when your products are sold to other businesses. B2B organizations have target customer types, which include buyers, users, influencers, and decision makers.

If you were to put the customer segment representatives around a table (the buyer, the user, etc.), you'd probably find that your customer's company has a cross-functional team. Now extend the model a little further. If you're in the "vendor" company as the product manager, you too work on a cross-functional team.

With so many interests on both the customer side and the vendor side, the benefit of structured customer visits cannot be emphasized enough. The customer visits I carried out were always enhanced by including someone from Engineering or Development, a sales specialist, an operations or systems engineer, and a product manager. Sometimes, a marketing person would be on our customer visit team.

Single visits don't necessarily provide you with the context and benchmarks to compare one customer's environment to another. Therefore, visit strategies should consider a variety of visits over time. Some visits will be to the same customer over time and some will center on a multiplicity of customers over a period of time. Some visits take place because there's a problem with the product. Some are to showcase new products. Some even happen when the customer comes to visit you at your location for a demonstration or customer advisory group meeting. The kind of customer visits being advocated here are for fact finding, observing, looking for potential opportunities, and, of course, to identify or validate customer needs.

Before starting out, you need to gain approval from management for the visit using the form shown as Figure 8.4.

Once you gain approval to carry out the visit, you will want to use a more detailed, formal visit plan document to plan and guide your work activities. This should be produced in concert with your cross-functional team members because it creates the framework for carrying out this important on-site research. As with the many templates that are provided, filling in the blanks is less important than scoping the work and execution. For example, the objective is critical. You can't lead a team of people if you don't know what you hope to find out. You will probably learn more during the visits from what you observe and hear. Those outcomes will become more apparent and can be captured during the visit.

FIGURE 8.4

Customer Visit Request Form

Name of Customer	
Address of Customer	
Industry Classification	
Account Manager Name & Information	
Product Manager Name & Information	
Travel Required? (Yes/No)	
Travel Budget Needed	

- Purpose of the visit
- Customer's names and titles
- Team members who will accompany you and their roles
- The type of activities to be carried out (interviews, observations, tours, etc.)
- When you expect the debrief to be completed

Approved: _____

Date: _____

Tied explicitly to the objectives of the visit are some structured activities that could take place while carrying out the visit. They are divided into the following areas:

- *Interviews with key stakeholders.* Structured interviews can be highly revealing. Interviews with users might include categories like ease of use, problems, and suggestions. Interviews with decision makers could range from complaints heard from users to billing problems. These interviews might even talk about the customer's future strategies. Interviews are not "in-person surveys." You and your team are involved in a *conversational exploration* with an expert. Therefore, you need to have someone on your team who can establish a rapport with the interviewee(s). Curiosity and a general context for the business, as well as a clear objective for the visit, set the stage for asking open-ended questions that allow the customer to talk. "What are the biggest competitive challenges you face?" is an example of an open-ended question versus "Are you more concerned about competitor A or competitor B?" Then, you need to be prepared for the next follow-up probing question.

- *Tours of facilities.* (e.g., factories, call centers, and distribution centers). An amazing amount of data can be gleaned from a guided tour, hearing from a functional expert, and seeing how your customers carry out their day-to-day activities.

- *Observing people at work.* Watching people in a factory, operations center, call center, distribution center, or in operating departments provides great insight into company culture, mood, and other attributes of an organization. Recently, I visited a client's administrative offices and there was an immense amount of pride shown in each department's contribution to the business: Operations, Quality, Sales, Finance, and so on. There were impressive charts, graphs, and explanations. Everyone knew what was happening in their department, and the mood was very collegial. A quick look at the charts was even more revealing. There was a general upward trend in orders; customer satisfaction was high; product quality was improving. However, the one thing I observed was that all the charts and dashboards used data derived from *disparate* "systems." If I were a product manager for business intelligence automation software, I'd be thinking about selling them something!

- *Presentations.* Initial visits may begin with people from business functions providing overviews of "what they do." This provides an excellent foundation for asking good questions. Consultative selling techniques depend largely on this type of questioning to uncover potential problems. You can also structure presentations around your customer's perceptions of industry and competitive trends they're watching. This gives you some insights into their customers and possibly even their customers' customers.

There are a few other things to cover. Ground rules need to be set in advance with regard to confidentiality, safety, and other aspects that demonstrate respect for the customer's environment, privacy, and security. Furthermore, each team member will have a role to play. Someone should be assigned to record notes and *verbatims* from interviews; some will draw flowcharts, and others may use other available techniques to record what took place.

During a visit, and at the conclusion of the visit, the team should meet and review what they saw, observed, heard, and learned. In-process debriefs are like football game huddles. They give the team the opportunity to ascertain whether they're on track, or, conversely, whether they need to make any modifications in interview questions or to validate participant perceptions.

Analysis of the visit should be carried out with the team and perhaps other cross-functional stakeholders. The discussions should concentrate on themes, findings, and information that can benefit unmet customer needs.

Furthermore, the findings should be more than a set of stand-alone notes. They should suggest meaningful ways to think about improving the product, operational support, and other business, technical, and operational dimensions of the product. This is easier said than done because observational and qualitative data are taken from perception and interpretation, which is subject to human bias and functional paradigms. One way to deal with this is to have the visiting team members write up individual reports. Then, have the group meet together in a separate session during which team members present what they saw and heard. This gives the team leader (the product manager) and perhaps a marketing counterpart the opportunity to summarize, generalize, and come up with the most valuable conclusions.

Lastly, everything should be captured in written documents—the functional reports as well as the group reports. All this data should be kept in the Product Master Plan binder so it becomes part of the permanent plan of record for the product, and for all the supporting product activities. Of course, the Product Master Plan is a great repository for this documentation.

A caveat: all of these steps, even if carried out in the right sequence, may not yield the optimal or "expected" findings. Results are often related to the experience of the team members. My experience suggests that the best visits are carried out by the most experienced cross-functional visit teams. However, experience begets experience, so do not let inexperience be a deterrent.

In order to fortify this planning sequence for you, a customer visit plan template is provided for you in Module 6 of this book. A visual for this customer visit plan template is shown as Figure 8.5.

THE VOICE OF THE CUSTOMER

The reason for customer visits as a form of market research is to learn more about customer needs. Customer visits and field research allow product managers and their teams to search for the customer's voice. *Voice of the customer* (VOC) has emerged as a well-worn expression that may have a variety of interpretations.

Observing customers can be compared with the work carried out by anthropologists in their study of humanity. One of the offshoots of anthropology is ethnography, which covers human social interactions through research carried out in the field or *in situ* (from the Latin words "in the place"). For product managers and marketers, being in the field means being with customers where you have the opportunity to work with them or observe them doing what they do, that is, carrying out their daily activities.

Merely understanding the concept of VOC is different from being able to effectively apply it. Therefore, just because you can go into the field doesn't make you a skilled observer. When I open the refrigerator and ask, "Where's the ketchup?" my wife quickly points it out—which is typically right in front of my face. She's a better "observer" than I am.

It's the same thing with field research. Field research provides the product manager with the opportunity to hear the customer's voice, whether they express it vocally or not. The product manager should not be the only one who "listens" for the customer's voice or observes customers in action. Many people on the cross-functional team hear and see differently. The customer service agent takes complaints or orders and hears *tone of voice* of customers on the phone. The responses to a customer survey may be biased—depending on mood and other conditions—or how you phrased the question. ("Were you happy with the outcome?") The salesperson sees the customer at work *carrying out daily tasks*. The engineer may see an IT person in their lab. A web analyst *observes* website entry points and navigation.

FIGURE 8.5

Customer Visit Plan Template

Name of Customer's Company	
Address of Customer's Company	
Name of Primary Contact	
Phone Number	
Email Address	
Account Manager Name & Information	
Product Manager Name & Information	
Date of Planned Visit	

Objective or Purpose: Why is this visit being carried out? What do you want to learn? Is this visit a singular visit to one customer, a series of visits to one customer, one customer visit in a series of multiple customer visits?

Customer "targets" to be visited: (e.g., names of people and job titles)

Guidelines and ground rules: (e.g., voice or video recording, picture taking, security rules, nondisclosure)

Team members who are attending: Names and titles (e.g., product manager, engineer, marketing manager, account manager). Also, what role will each play (observer, interviewer, video recording, workflow diagrams, photography, etc.)?

Agenda and structure: How will the visit be structured (e.g., introductory session, presentations, tours, on-site employee visits, interviews, and observations etc.)?

Capture the visit: Use this space to write down what you heard or observed. Note work flows, skills used, timing, difficult activities, or actions by different customer types or users as they "do what they do."

Debrief: Capture all observations based on what all visitors learned, observed, or inferred. Use this data to prepare a final visit report or presentation for cross-functional team stakeholders.

Additional notes, actions, or follow-up: (e.g., thank you note for customer and for team members)

Go to Where Customers Do What They Do

In my research, I spend time with people who work in product design firms. I do this to better understand how they view customer activity and how their efforts ultimately result in more interesting designs. Randy Rossi of Bally Design provided a short case story to exemplify my point about the importance of going where customers are and understanding how customers do what they do. This is a story about a hospital operating room:

> Approximately 5,000 times a year in the United States, something is left inside a patient during surgery. The average cost of this mistake is $250,000 per incident. More than two thirds of the time, it's a surgical sponge. When this happens patients suffer great pain; some even die. Our client, ClearCount Medical Solutions, created a solution using a radio frequency identification device (RFID) to address this problem; the RFID tag is implanted in the sponge. At the end of a surgical procedure, before a surgeon closes the wound, a person in the operating room (OR) passes a wand (like a metal detector) over the patient. An audio–visual alarm indicates whether a sponge remains inside the patient. That's a great solution to one problem.
>
> However, my team spent hours watching surgical procedures and talking to scrub technicians—those responsible for keeping track of sponges. We observed that sponges were counted at the start of a procedure and at the end so that the number of sponges taken out and discarded equaled the number at the beginning. We also noticed that the used sponges were thrown into a steel bucket, which doesn't really sound like much—until we had our "aha" moment!
>
> We took our observations about what we saw and created a series of cartoon storyboards to portray the workflow of how the wand was used and how sponges were tossed into this bucket. It seemed like there was wasted effort in taking the inventory of sponges, counting the sponges in the bucket, and in the use of the wand. Our idea was to design a "smart bucket!" We'd design the bucket with an RFID detector so that as sponges were tossed out, they would be counted and the total number of sponges at the end of the procedure would be compared with the total number of sponges at the beginning. With this perspective, the OR was considered a "system" of interactions, not just a set of independent actions and activities. Now, sponges at the start of a procedure are scanned by the smart bucket, and as they are used, they are counted, so if one is missing, the bucket sounds an alarm and the wand isn't used.
>
> Once accepted, the idea was properly vetted, the value proposition was proven, and the product was developed. ClearCount Medical Solutions provides this product and is considered a provider of a "sponge management system" that improves patient safety and operational efficiency.

Capturing the customer's voice is not a once-and-done visit and report. It is an ongoing part of the market research process, and it is an inherent part of the "market radar" used by the cross-functional product team. Readouts from this radar should be taken in regular team meetings, where people report what they heard or observed. All of those should be recorded in research notes, which, as noted before, belong in the Product Master Plan.

USING PERSONAS (OR CUSTOMER CHARACTERIZATIONS) AS A WAY TO CAPTURE NEEDS

Many companies have found success in defining products around user models, which are referred to as personas or customer archetypes. An archetype, as characterized in the dictionary, is a "perfect person." A created persona may be a good model because it represents a common set of characteristics, motivations, affiliations, or other traits that makes that group unique, like a market segment or customer target. As such, the persona is not a basic customer, but a representation for a group of people or customer types. A persona isn't a segment, per se, because it is too general, but the creation of a persona can be complementary to the segmentation models you create.

To create realistic, usable personas for your own company or for your product, you will have to do some serious legwork. This involves the creation of a number of *customer profiles*. A customer profile is an actual characterization and description of a day in the life of a customer. The homework required to create these customer profiles and keep them up to date can be intensive and may require many in-market field or site visits. The creation of a customer profile also offers a wonderful opportunity for cross-functional product team members to collaborate and gain a common perspective on customers.

The rationale behind the customer profile is simple: you want to understand the influences on the customer's "way of life." In other words, you want to understand how customers of a company or consumers in a household do what they do—and why. This involves some anthropomorphic research that you and/or your team members must carry out. This research may include interviews and observations of individuals "in action." With the right groundwork and diplomatic protocols, this can be easily arranged.

Here are the basic steps involved to create your *customer profile inventory* for a business customer:

1. Identify a "receptive" customer company.
2. Create an organization chart of a department where people work, who either use your product or are in some way associated with what your product does.
3. Indicate each person's name, role, and capacity (e.g., user, influencer, or decision maker).
4. List the main tasks or goals for which each person is responsible with whatever information you have, and then create a storyboard or flowchart that identifies the work activities of that person— again, to the best of your ability.
5. Pay close attention to how this person interacts with their environment and how they work with each person or group. This may include employees, managers, people in other functions, customers, and suppliers. It may also include administrative tasks such as writing e-mail and recording information into company systems.

Creating personas (or customer characterizations) using customer profiles enables you to look at broad groups of customer types as clusters of people who exhibit common traits or characteristics. These people may operate or interact in one or more operating environments. When you start to see similar characteristics within one cluster of people, you have the basis for the creation of your first persona. The persona is the representation of the cluster, not the individual. This allows you to build various personas for buyers, users, influencers, or decision makers. To reinforce this approach, the persona represents the common denominators of behaviors, preferences, or attitudes of a similar group of people in one archetype.

Lastly, if you consider customer operating environments or household units, you should look at their surroundings from a holistic perspective, where every dimension can be melded; it can help you form, in your mind's eye, a unified, systemic view of the customer's world.

YOUR RESEARCH STRATEGY

This chapter is not meant to be a primer on market research. Its goal is to provide you with some relevant, usable techniques to characterize customer groups and to understand customer needs. Generalized market research practices are carried out within a company in the context of the organization's business challenges. Therefore, your own portfolio of complementary techniques will be useful for your purposes, whether your company offers products for businesses or for consumers.

Product managers are not responsible for all corporate market research programs. Mostly, they rely on the efforts of personnel from the marketing department or market research department to plan and carry out this work—some of which should be done on behalf of your product team. That said, I cannot emphasize enough the importance of ongoing research and market surveillance as a way for product managers to understand customer-related trends.

Your research should include constant scanning of business literature and syndicated research reports. It should include frequent customer visits, review of customer satisfaction data (such as call center reports or customer satisfaction surveys) and preference surveys, and so on. You may need to support advisory panels, focus groups, and even mystery shopping.

To start with, use what you have. If you need more data, then structure the research projects accordingly, but in harmony with your market research counterparts. If you cannot secure the cooperative attention or financial resources for your specific projects, you may need to use some ingenuity and find other resources.

In some cases, you may need the help of an outside firm to carry out customer or market segment research. As with any project employing an outside firm, you have to be prepared to clarify the goals of the project and the format of the project's output, and of course, you have to manage the project and the budget. These types of research projects tend to eat up a lot of money and sometimes don't provide the desired outcomes. Customer research must always focus on end results that yield what you need to learn, why you seek such data, and how you will use what you glean.

SUMMARY

This chapter focused on finding the right customers in your quest to cultivate an effective marketing mix strategy targeted to your most desirable set of customers—and to recognize their voices and needs. Why else would a product manager develop relevant market segmentation models? Ultimately, you will create new value propositions and product positioning or have to revise or validate the existing ones. The fundamentals of both the value proposition and product positioning depend on the following variables:

1. The target customer.
2. The implicit or explicit needs or problems that customer seeks to solve.
3. The product's attributes or features that solve the problem or meet the need.
4. The benefit or advantage that the target customer would gain from using that product or feature.

Another reason you need valid market segmentation models is that product managers are often responsible for training salespeople so they gain a solid understanding of their customers, which is conveyed in marketing material, sales training manuals, and other documents that contain value propositions and product positioning. Segmentation models will appear in other documents as well, including marketing collateral, product requirements, and the many elements contained in the Product Master Plan.

RAISING YOUR PRODUCT MANAGEMENT EXPERIENCE QUOTIENT (PMEQ)

1. What are known market segments for the products you're associated with? How would you characterize the common set of needs for each segment? Use a table like this as a guide.

Name of Segment	Characteristics and Underlying Needs

2. Based on the established segments, check if there is any market or customer research validating that the customers your company focuses on are actually in those segments.

3. Find out who is responsible for the existing segmentation models for your product area. You may need to visit different people, including your boss, your peers, and people in the Marketing Department. With this information, create a profile for each of the segments based on their accepted characteristics, plus any other needs you deem relevant.

4. In a B2B environment, and within the segment groupings, who are the people who represent the buyer, user, influencer, decision maker, or other individual involved in the buying process? Are there adequate descriptors for each of these customer types? Update these if necessary and keep them current in the Product Master Plan.

5. When you review the functionality and features of your product, you should be able to make a direct connection between the feature that exists and the need it satisfies. This system substantiates whether your product's features satisfy the needs of a specific customer type within a segment. Use the following table to make a direct connection from feature to need to name of the segment.

Feature	Need Satisfied by the Feature	Target Customer Type Within a Segment

6. Review all the sales training material and product marketing collateral to ensure the wording is appropriate for the correct validation of market segments and target customer types on which your product is focused. Read carefully for verbiage that embodies the value proposition and positioning of the product. Be sure the focus is on the right target customer type or market segment.

7. Participate in the planning and carrying out of a customer visit, if you haven't done this previously. If you are experienced, try to involve a product manager who is less experienced so he can gain the benefit of your experience. Use the visit planning template as a guide.

8. Arrange to interview one or more people at a customer's location. Prepare a series of open-ended questions to guide the customer to answers that are most valuable to you. Prior to the visit, invite some of the visit team participants to help you role-play so that you have a good sense of where the conversations might go, and develop strategies to ensure that you can expertly guide the interview.

9. Set up periodic meetings with team members (or even with executives). Be sure to include up-to-date market segment overviews that illustrate how customer groups are changing over time. Show "Who's buying what," where they're buying, how, and for how much. This demonstrates to others that you are vigilant about the markets in which your products are sold, you understand your customer's needs, and you care about delivering value-oriented benefits.

CHAPTER

9

PREPARING TO SET YOUR MILEPOSTS: FORECASTING FOR THE PRODUCT MANAGER

Executive Summary

- Without accurate forecasts, a product's potential cannot be determined.
- Forecasts link the research of the marketplace to the strategic possibilities for the product.
- Forecasting is used by product managers to calculate market potential, depict sales, and meet demand.

Every business has to figure out how it is going to invest its limited resources. Product managers manage the investments made in products, and therefore need to derive forecasts and deliver the expected returns. Unfortunately, most forecasts are wrong. Because incorrect forecasts happen so often, there is a need to find a better way forward. This "way forward" is the purpose of this chapter. The goal is to provide you with a commonsense, data-driven approach to the creation of more realistic forecasts, either for new products or for existing products.

Another reason this chapter is so important: It's critical to allay some of the fears and anxieties that product managers and their teams may feel when the boss says, "I need your forecast by next Thursday." Based on some of the topics I've discussed thus far in the book, and those that will be discussed in future chapters, the availability of timely data on which to base your forecast and its underlying assumptions is critical. You may not have all of the data you need, but your heightened sense of urgency about data collection and analysis will put you in a better position in the future.

Lastly, before I proceed, I want to assure you that I am not going to deliver a complex series of statistical or econometric models with detailed mathematical formulas. There are many other resources that you can use to gain that perspective. Your company may even have an economics office, or there may be other specialists, either at the divisional level, corporate level, or other levels, where complex future state models are developed and maintained. I urge you to find those resources to learn all you can about how forecasts are developed in your company. The techniques applied in this chapter, and those most product managers depend upon, are typically referred to as *judgmental*. With this in mind, let's get into forecasting in the product manager's world.

FORECASTING BASICS

To begin, a general set of definitions is needed, as well as a sequencing of events. These are summarized below and discussed in more detail later in the chapter. Product managers are typically responsible for the following:

1. Determining the total size of a desired market, which is called the total addressable market (TAM)
2. Deciding what portion of that market the product can penetrate, or the attainable market share (AMS)
3. Figuring out the number of units or the volume that the sales team can commit to sell
4. Calculating the number of units of tangible product that can be produced, which is called demand planning
5. Determining realistic pricing for the product and how that pricing will vary over time
6. Translating the sales and demand forecast into a realistic budget for the product

This list of responsibilities is depicted as a simple sequence of events in Figure 9.1.

You will notice that there are two different columns in Figure 9.1. One column shows the sequence for new product forecasting, while the other depicts existing product forecasting. Notice that each column includes the same categories and essentially the same work. The main distinction between the two has to do with the availability of data. New product forecasts may not have a robust suite of data available to help you figure out the size of the market or determine whether the market is worth pursuing. In fact, later on in the chapter I've created a simple case study to demonstrate how this forecasting sequence can be applied.

Now that you see the general sequence, I want to link this sequence to the Product Management Life Cycle Model, since *all* work activities across the product's life can (and should) be equated to the model.

In Figure 9.2, notice how the forecasting sequence is aligned with the area of work called New Product Planning (NPP). As discussed throughout the book, NPP is relevant to more than just brand new products. New products can also include enhancements to existing products. The arrow

FIGURE 9.1

Forecasting Sequence

FIGURE 9.2

Aligning the Forecasting Sequence with the Product Management Life Cycle Model

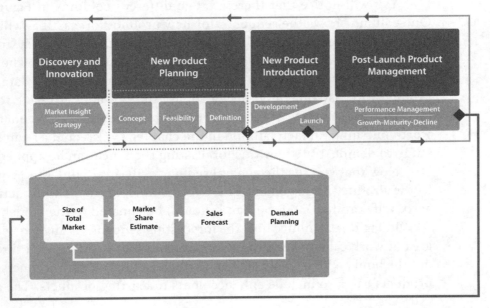

that connects the Post-Launch Product Management area of work (Strategic and Tactical Product Management) and wraps back around to the forecasting sequence shows the recursive nature of the product life cycle as the business management of the product is carried out. This is important because when you already have products in the market, you have to reforecast, using the same sequence. Hopefully, you'll have much more data, and with any luck you can compress the work associated with forecasting market size or attainable market share. This will allow you to focus on working with the sales force to develop more realistic sales forecasts, and free you up to work with your Demand Planning organization (if you have tangible products).

FORECASTING IS A CROSS-FUNCTIONAL EXERCISE

Product managers do not create forecasts in a vacuum. There are many interrelated activities that have to be carried out in order to derive a forecast—one that people in the supporting business functions can live with. This is important because all forecasts drive the cross-functional commitments that lead to execution. Therefore, the cross-functional team helps put the underlying assumptions into place. Questions that will have to be asked and answered by the cross-functional product team include:

- Will Marketing invest enough to stimulate demand?
- Will Sales have the right number of salespeople who are appropriately compensated to sell the product?
- Will Manufacturing produce enough units to meet the demand?
- Will Finance have timely sales data to evaluate performance?

Furthermore, other documents are produced that capture the forecast elements. The Business Case must have a forecast section and a series of assumptions that justify the investment in new products or product enhancements. The Marketing Plan for the product will support the business scenarios that, in turn, support ongoing business operations. For example, suppose an existing product isn't being enhanced or upgraded in an upcoming year. Or, suppose during midyear you have to recast and update the sales forecast and budget for the product. In any instance, you will use the same general thought process to validate or improve your initial set of assumptions. All of these are driven from the heart of the cross-functional team, led by the product manager.

VALIDATING MARKET AND DEMAND POTENTIAL

Evaluating the attractiveness of a market requires that you consider many factors. It is critical to determine future product or business viability. Once this attractiveness is understood, the product team is in a better position to decide if the market is substantial enough and accessible enough to continue pursuing, or, at least, to pursue in the future. There are two approaches to completing this evaluation:

1. Determine or understand the *market potential.*
2. Evaluate and recognize the *demand potential.*

I'll talk about both momentarily, but you should be aware that even if you believe the market potential is high, a host of other factors must be considered to both encourage demand (i.e., adequate sales and marketing investments) and "deliver the goods," or get the product to the end customers through the most efficient distribution channels. Lastly, the product must be priced appropriately such that it will deliver the promised benefit to the customers you're focusing on.

First, I'll talk about market potential. Market potential, or, "What could we possibly sell?" is driven by the possible size of the total market, attractive market segments, and the growth rates of those segments. These "upper-limit" estimates are complex to derive unless you have some evidence of market variability, along with some idea of the size of the markets themselves. Some of the methods used to capture this data require that you:

- *Use a statistical model that takes some percentage of a segment's size and allocates the market share estimates across the segment.* This could include a percentage of the population within a segment or percentage of units sold across the number of competitors.

- *Consider past unit sales volumes as a way to evaluate market potential.* If your sales volumes (in units) for the preceding years have been growing at 5 percent per year, for example, and you believe that your competitive market share will not shift as you make a series of product enhancements, you might want to continue your 5 percent per year growth rate.

- *Examine distribution channel performance, assuming that you are able to track product sales through each channel.* A company that uses traditional, direct methods may expand their channels to include the Internet or indirect distributors, or expand to a series of international resellers. Any of these approaches may help you garner greater levels of market share.

- *Consider a variety of analyst perspectives, based on research reports, to determine how to characterize market potential.* You can use industry analyst research reports and abstract some of the most salient characteristics and trends in the market to estimate potential sales. This can be a great way to navigate the marketplace and to determine your share relative to the competition within the context of the direction of the overall industry.

- *Evaluate generally available governmental resources.*
  - For the United States, I often refer to U.S. Census data because it's easy to get population numbers by age, region, and other demographics (see www.census.gov). Another such resource can be found on the website "Survey of Current Business" (www.bea.gov/scb/index.htm) to understand a variety of information related to gross domestic product, price indices, and other economic data.

■ For the European Union, I frequently scan the European Commission's Eurostat website (epp.eurostat.ec.europa.eu/portal/page/portal/eurostat/home), which contains a vast amount of statistics about the European Union.

■ If you're thinking about business expansion in Asia-Pacific markets, you might want to take a look at the Asia-Pacific Economic Cooperation website (statistics.apec.org) for some helpful information about countries along the Pacific Rim, both in the Eastern and Western Hemispheres. Further, the United Nations maintains interesting statistics on the Economic and Social Commission for Asia and the Pacific (ESCAP) website (www.unescap.org/stat/data).

■ *Utilize evaluations and analyses from industry associations.* Many industry associations carry out their own research to monitor trends and activity in those domains. Refer to Chapter 7 for information about industry categories. Once you've narrowed down your categories, you can search for current associations and find out about research and reports that are available.

■ *Determine the level of competitive intensity in a market area.* This is an important context to have. You want to know whether there is stiff competition with many products. If you're already in that market, then you understand the dynamics of that environment. If you are considering a new product entry in a crowded market, then you must make sure your product is highly differentiated. Michael Porter's "Five Forces Analysis" is a good method to use.

Now, someone might ask you whether you are doing a "top-down" or "bottom-up" market or sales forecast. These are two different general methods for evaluating market potential. If you start with a population as a whole, and then drill down or keep segmenting until you reach the customer demand, this is top-down forecasting. If you start with a single customer and try to determine the customer's demand from the customer's perspective, this is bottom-up forecasting. Which one you choose to do will be a matter of preference for your business organization and dictated by the data you have available. If you can do both, and they agree, then your confidence is increased. The success of each forecasting technique is dependent on the availability of adequate market segment information. Moreover, bottom-up forecasting requires a significant amount of customer data.

Now, let's talk about possible demand, or "what would customers actually want to buy?" This can be characterized using the following general approaches:

1. Determine what portion of the overall population (based on demographics, geography, etc.) could actually buy the product.

2. Identify the number of people who actually buy or use the product or product type. For example, think of toothpaste: If each person in a market area buys an 8-ounce tube of toothpaste four times a year, and if you multiplied that number by the number of people in a segment, you would get an overall number based on product use by segment.

3. Measure "intent to purchase." In many companies, the Marketing department frequently carries out surveys that ask respondents directly whether they would buy a product, and if so, when their next need-state might emerge.

4. Discover analogous product performance. This is another very effective method. If you are able to understand the pattern of sales or market uptake for similar products in your company, you may be able to identify adoption patterns. For example, if your company introduced a similar product in the past, how well did it fare against its forecasts? What problems did it encounter? What has been the company's track record in capturing market share? Of course, past performance won't guarantee that your product will achieve the same results, but it does serve as another useful reference point for your forecast. It also provides an indication of how well your company can perform, averaging many factors. If you can obtain the data of performance versus forecast, you have a reliable way of adjusting marketing, sales, and other input to the model.

5. Finally, you can use a competitive analogy. Although somewhat difficult to derive, there may be some available industry analyst data to determine competitor market penetration rates, volumes, and other indicators for their new product introductions.

FORECASTS ARE BUILT ON BELIEFS ABOUT THE FUTURE

Forecasts are based on data, knowledge, and, ultimately, assumptions. Essentially, when you do not have a fact that you need, you will use an assumption. Assumptions are particularly applicable to the sequence of events depicted in Figures 9.1 and 9.2. You're taking a large data set and continuously narrowing it down, subject to known and assumed parameters. If you have an existing product, you have data about your current market segments, customer needs, product volumes, and financial data. When your boss says you have to raise your sales forecast by 5 percent next year, barring a lack of investment to drive marketing, sales, and other supporting structures, you do the arithmetic and you're done—regardless of whether the forecast is rational and achievable. It's usually a management edict that ends up contributing to missed numbers. Real, usable product forecasts are dependent on not only meeting the existing needs of known customers but also anticipating needs of existing *and* new customers, so you'll need to take that into account.

A proper forecasting mindset begins with a clear understanding of how expectations should be framed; only then can the product manager create a useful and relevant forecast. But what are those expectations? The correct set of expectations for any product decision, investment or otherwise, is based on what you derive when you formulate the product strategy and its associated "strategic mix." This strategic mix is a combination of marketing mix elements and a host of operational support activities, which you'll read more about in Chapter 10. Hence, the purpose of forecasting is *to improve the probability that a given product investment decision will achieve the strategic goals of the division or of the company.*

Needless to say, it is very important that all assumptions are clearly identified. First, the market, your company, and the competition are not static. Assumptions can change over time and must be fed back into the forecast. Second, these assumptions are often the major factors in understanding the risk surrounding a product investment decision. At some point, a changed market forecast or risk level may indicate that a new product introduction be changed or abandoned.

VALIDATING ASSUMPTIONS AND APPLYING CUSTOMER PREFERENCES

Most forecasting techniques are based on numerical or statistical data elements. Sometimes you don't have all the data you need, and sometimes you might just need a little help—a second opinion. Whom do you go to? If you lived in Greece about 3,500 years ago, the Oracle of Delphi was the place you went. People came from all over Greece and beyond to have their questions about the future answered by Pythia, the priestess of Apollo. Pythia's answers were often cryptic, not unlike some of the input you will receive from your cross-functional team. However, these answers were interpreted in ways that helped determine when farmers planted their crops or even whether another empire might declare war. In business, experienced executives and mentors may be able to help, either formally or informally.

The *Delphi Technique* brings together a panel of experts, usually in a facilitated session, to consider future state scenarios and to provide additional insight into the forecasts you're considering. Sometimes you can use your customers or a representative sample of targeted market segments. The goal of this technique is to elicit preferences from these customer (user) groups, customer councils, or advisory panels, either in a focus group setting or in prearranged meetings, with the explicit purpose of determining their preferences. Where there is broad agreement, those inputs are more readily accepted, and the product manager can focus on those insights where there is broad disagreement.

Another method used by marketers is *conjoint analysis*, in which customers are surveyed to determine their preferences for combinations of product attributes or features (burgers and fries; a burger, a salad, and a drink; a burger, fries, and a drink?). Remember, just because you use numerical data does not mean you cannot adjust the numbers based on qualitative data or inferences you draw either from what you've observed first hand or from others who can offer a second opinion.

HOW MUCH CAN WE REALLY MAKE? DERIVING MARKET SHARE ESTIMATES

With the fundamental context about forecasting in place, let's tackle the first two areas in the forecasting sequence described earlier. These include:

- Determining the total size of a desired market, the TAM
- Deciding on the portion of that market that the product can penetrate, or the AMS

Let's walk through the steps to accomplish these goals.

- *Step 1. Assess TAM.* If you had no competitors, and you could sell all the units of your product to each and every possible customer within a segment, how many units would you sell and how much money would you make?

Total Possible Market Volume × Average

Unit Price = TAM in Dollars (or Currency)

- *Step 2. Segment the market based on TAM.* These segments are subsegments of TAM or customer types of TAM based on typical market segmentation characteristics such as geography and demographics (see Chapter 8).

- *Step 3. Derive assumptions.* Assumptions represent possible combinations of future outcomes. Remember, assumptions are used in other Product Management documents, including Business Cases, Marketing Plans, product requirements, and product strategies. Assumptions may consider market attributes such as technology, competitors, industry, and shifts in customer preferences. A PRESTO analysis (see Chapter 7) could help refine some of the market attributes.

- *Step 4. Estimate the AMS.* How much share could you attain, in unit volumes, pricing, and revenue? Each market segment has a historical profile and future size based on the parameters established by you or by outside research sources. If you have existing products, you might be able to use some of that historical data.

These four steps, which describe what you do to create a market share estimate, are the easy part. Actually creating it may be more of a challenge. In order to ease the way forward for you, I am going to provide you with an example that can be used to derive the market share estimate, a sales forecast, and then a demand plan. The case will be divided into two sections. The first part of the case will provide the contextual data and lead you up to the attainable market share. Then, I'll explain more about sales forecasting and demand planning, after which I'll conclude the work on the case.

The case example uses a fictitious company and easily identifiable market segments. This is not meant to be an academic study, but rather a simplified example, so that you may be able to construct similar forecasts on the job. You will also find, as you read this, that there may be some missing data or issues you might have wanted to know more about to validate the assumptions. My suggestion is that in your own forecasting work, you create a list of data elements you think would be important and then reach out to other data resources in your company or search on the Internet to find more about each data area. Forecasting is a craft you learn over a period of time in your career; the nuances of the situation and variables you consider will always vary.

CASE STUDY: FORECASTING

You are the product portfolio director for the BetterLife Company. Your company's mission is to improve the lives of an aging population of adults. This population is unique because of two factors. First, the current population is staying active for longer periods and living longer overall, and second, the population continues to swell as baby boomers come of age. According to the Alliance for Aging Research, by 2030, one in five people will be age 65 or older. There are three basic underlying problems exhibited by this population. People who get older have problems with dexterity, vision, and hearing. With this in mind, BetterLife products are designed to meet these needs with functionality that enables ease of reading, hearing, and handling. BetterLife focuses on two explicit market segments: people aged 55 to 64 and people aged 65 to 84, all living in the United States.

In 2006, BetterLife introduced the EZ Phone, a corded home telephone with larger buttons, a larger display, and a high-quality speakerphone with a good amplifier. The phone sold well through the BetterLife website and retail outlets. The phone sold for $75 in the United States, and sales have been nothing short of phenomenal. In 2009, the company added a new product called the EZ Remote, a universal remote control for televisions and other audiovisual systems operated by remote control. It uses voice recognition for guided oral programming of television and audio system controls, and it uses a small number of large, easy-to-see buttons. This product has also achieved great success.

The company is highly profitable and has been working to create the next big product, which will be introduced in 2014, called EZ Mobile. Consistent with its strategy, it wants to introduce an easy-to-use mobile device with larger, well-lit buttons, a high-quality speaker, and an easy-to-use touch screen display, all in a slightly larger form than today's slim, multifunction mobile devices, so that it is easy to handle.

Your goal is to derive a unit volume forecast for 2014 to 2018 that you and your team can agree upon. As you get started in this forecasting exercise, you have a historical business profile prepared and put into the form of a snapshot. Figure 9.3 provides you with the BetterLife business situation from 2006 to 2013, showing unit volumes, average prices, and revenue. It also shows the overall population of the chosen market segments. A graph of EZ Phone sales is also shown in Figure 9.4. This helps you put the business into perspective.

FIGURE 9.3

BetterLife Historical Snapshot

	2006	2007	2008	2009	2010	2011	2012
EZ Phone Units	212,740	329,747	456,700	599,190	799,918	1,075,890	1,366,381
EZ Phone Average Price/Unit	$75	$75	$75	$75	$75	$75	$75
EZ Phone Revenue	$15,955,500	$24,731,025	$34,252,470	$44,939,240	$59,993,886	$80,691,776	$102,478,556
Revenue Growth Rate	N/A	55.0%	38.5%	31.2%	33.5%	34.5%	27.0%
Volume as % of Total Population	0.352%	0.531%	0.716%	0.916%	1.192%	1.563%	1.963%
EZ Remote Units	N/A	N/A	N/A	47,000	83,500	91,000	126,000
EZ Remote Average Price/Unit	N/A	N/A	N/A	$29	$29	$29	$29
EZ Remote Revenue	N/A	N/A	N/A	$1,363,000	$2,421,500	$2,639,000	$3,654,000
Revenue Growth Rate				77.7%	9.0%	38.5%
Volume as % of Total Population				0.072%	0.124%	0.132%	0.181%
Total Revenue EZ Phone & Remote	N/A	N/A	N/A	$46,302,240	$62,415,386	$83,330,776	$106,132,556
Total Cost of Goods Sold: All Products	$6,701,310	$8,903,169	$9,590,691	$13,242,441	$18,162,877	$24,832,571	$33,431,755
Gross Profit All Products	$9,254,190	$15,827,856	$24,661,778	$33,059,799	$44,252,508	$58,498,205	$72,700,801
Gross Profit %	58.0%	64.0%	72.0%	71.4%	70.9%	70.2%	68.5%
US Population by Segment (000)							
Age 55–64	25,050	26,600	27,850	29,100	30,350	31,575	31,700
Age 65–84	30,925	31,000	31,240	31,460	31,700	31,950	32,500
Age 85+	4,425	4,550	4,715	4,850	5,075	5,300	5,400
Total Population by Segment (000)	60,400	62,150	63,805	65,410	67,125	68,825	69,600
Population Growth Rate	2.9%	2.9%	2.7%	2.5%	2.6%	2.5%	1.1%

FIGURE 9.4

BetterLife EZ Phone Unit Sales History

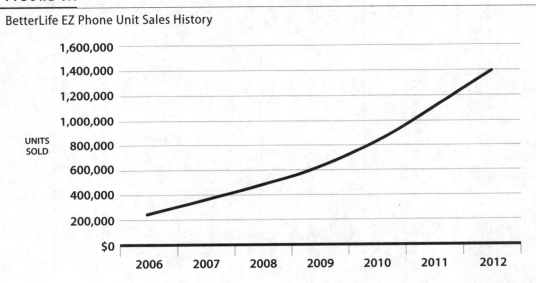

With some of this data under your belt, you are in a position to reevaluate the TAM as well as the AMS for the new mobile product. Using the population data shown in Figure 9.3 and the data points of two different product lines launched within the past several years, you believe that you can make some calculations.

Certainly, the population figures and the data from the two products are helpful. However, as the portfolio director, you decide that you want to know how much money is available to be made on these high-value products in a category called "assisting electronics," a phrase you coined. You are not concerned about customer targeting, for example, using a finer level of granularity by age groupings, and you are not concerned with income and affordability. These form the basis in your mind for your assumption set. Your assumptions will be supported by the growth rates of the populations in those segments and the belief that people will continue to spend, especially as they continue to be more mobile.

TAM calculation: One of the research reports you read stated that "the market for consumer-based therapeutic and well-being products is expected to grow by 20 percent per year." You believe that the total population of people between the ages of 55 and 85 + in 2007 of 69.6 million might spend between $300 to $600 per year on assisting electronics, or, roughly, between $20 billion and $40 billion. It is certain that you will not get *that* kind of business, but it's the starting point; it validates that there is indeed enough money in the pockets of the customers in this segment. The next step in the process is to identify characteristics about the market segments. You know that the population was growing in the early 2000s at a rate of about 2 percent overall. The 55-to-64 segment is growing more slowly than the 65-to-85+ segments. That's the conclusion described by most economists and the Census Bureau. In fact, the total population is predicted to grow from 69.6 million in 2007 to 85 million in 2015, which is a 22 percent increase; annualized, it's a little under 2 percent per year, but it suggests that there is an inflow of more than 1 million people into this population grouping (net of "outflows").

You also want to put your market share assumption set in place. This will serve to reinforce what you believe to be true about the market. Based on the research derived with your company economist, and equipped with some additional information from an outside research firm, you make the following assumptions:

1. People who buy these types of products seem to be less influenced by external economic factors than other groups. This means that these products tend to be recession resistant.

2. People aged 80 and over may exhibit a stronger demand for these products but may also have affordability issues, as suggested by one of the industry analysts. Some of your direct research argues that point because of an increase in the net worth of people aged 75 and over.

3. You believe that competition will be limited because most large companies don't want to pursue this market segment for this category of products. There is only one other company, which is based in Europe, and their products sell at a 25 percent premium because of the strength of the Euro.

4. Consumer electronics are going to become more complex, and instructions will continue to be difficult to understand, so the underlying needs for this segment will continue for the foreseeable future.

5. Retail outlets want to meet the needs of this segment and are clamoring for devices that are simpler. They are even willing to work with you on design and functionality.

6. The electronics retailers have said to you that they believe their sales to people aged 55 to 64 will rise at 21 percent per year for the next five years because this segment has more discretionary income, and that sales to 65- to 75-year-olds are expected to rise at 14 percent per year for the next five years.

7. The wireless service providers told you that they are spending too much time in their retail outlets and on the telephone trying to work through setup issues. They said that they need to increase sales per person, that simpler devices would be given their own display areas, and that they would provide cooperative advertising funds for promoting the product.

With this context in place, you can begin your work on figuring out the AMS. AMS can be calculated based on your market share in relation to your competitors, or it can be calculated on the basis of your share of the population within the market segments on which you focus. Right now, you're not focusing your efforts on the current products, but you want to focus your efforts on the EZ Cell product. You are entering a very crowded market with leaders such as Nokia, Lenovo's Motorola brand, Samsung, and Apple, who own 80 percent of the market already. That leaves BetterLife battling in each space.

You learned recently that only 75 percent of people aged 55 to 85 had mobile phones or devices. So you calculated that 75 percent × 69.6 million = 52.2 million people in the targeted segments actually have mobile phones or devices. Your Market Research department also learned that 8 million people aged 62 and over want mobile devices but are afraid of the technology. You have to come up with some assumptions about AMS based on what you know so far.

1. There is an opportunity to take market share from the market leaders, but most subscribers are locked into two-year contracts.

2. You learned that about 10 percent of the market churns annually. There are many other variables, but you decide to make the assumption that 5 million people or approximately 10 percent of the competitor's customers are "up for grabs" on an annual basis.

3. You also believe that advertising and word of mouth will lure 10 percent of the techno-phobic seniors into the stores—or that their adult children will want to purchase EZ Mobile devices for them.

4. The total assumed population is therefore 800,000 techno-phobics plus 5 million available customers, giving you a possible field of

5.8 million customers to reach. But this is not the market share that you can actually attain, especially in the beginning. You have to make an assumption about what you believe AMS *could* be.

5. Talking to the retailers and other sources, it is believed that you could reach between 2.5 percent and 4 percent of the field of possible customers in the first year. In the second year, you could reach between 3.5 percent and 5 percent, and in the third year, between 4 percent and 7 percent.

With these numbers in mind you are ready to begin having conversations with the people in the Sales organization and in Marketing.

SALES FORECASTING

Ultimately, you will want to know roughly how many units will be sold and how much money the company will be able to make. Of course, you'll want to know whether you can create, produce, and deliver the product, which is part of the next section on demand planning. Typically, your management will suggest to the Sales executives, Marketing executives, and other leaders that sales rise at a specific percentage over the prior fiscal year in order to deliver the results to stakeholders, who are usually shareholders. The underlying assumption is that there is a history of sales activity. However, you should always remember that sales forecasts, like all forecasts, are usually subject to industry activity and competitor actions.

One of the important contextual elements for sales forecasts is that they be expressed in ranges of possible outcomes. When you prepare a Business Case, a budget, or even a production forecast, you will want to make sure that you consider best-case, expected, and worst-case scenarios. The more alternatives you try, the more tedious the work. *Sensitivity analysis*—the testing of a set of assumptions—is particularly helpful in this case. I suggest that product managers always have what I call the "worst-worst" case in mind. For example, if you think that the best case is achieving 100 percent of last year's sales volume, and your worst case is 85 percent of last year's sales volume, you need to consider what might happen if you only had 50 percent of last year's sales volume. What would the P&L look like in that case?

What you need most, when compiling a sales forecast, is the actual sales force. Sometimes salespeople are asked to create their own sales forecasts by product. These are rolled up, and then a sales executive carries out a negotiation with the salespeople in order to negotiate the final quota. However, if this is done without product managers involved, then there may not be a connection with the reality of making sure that product is available. Furthermore, Marketing input is needed to determine if lead generation or demand generation programs are on the marketing investment docket. Finally, how good is Sales (and the company) at meeting sales forecasts?

Product managers can triangulate this internally derived data with surveys and other observations carried out during customer or field visits. Understanding buyer intentions can truly help in capturing the most likely buying scenarios.

MAKING THE SALES FORECAST USEFUL

Sales forecasting is not a once-and-done series of tasks. Forecasting is a continual work in progress. The job of the product team is to continue to build its knowledge base and database of market activities. Economists are always looking for new data, analyzing cause and effect, and working to improve forecast accuracy; so, too, should the product team. Best-in-class companies maintain repositories of market, customer, and competitive data to enable this constant refresh to take place. Product teams help in data collection and analysis. The Product Master Plan is an excellent repository for this data as well.

As suggested in the previous section, useful forecasts try to provide several scenarios about the future, which give needed validity and integrity checks. That's why best-case, worst-case, and even likely case scenarios are so important. To put these checks into place, consider four actions that help you validate your assumptions:

1. Make sure that you *identify your data sources*. Note whether information comes from past sales data, economic data, government data, and so on. Refer back to the earlier section on "Validating Market and Demand Potential."

2. *Constantly update the data* with an ongoing program of product sales and market performance reporting as well as ongoing market research.

3. *Write everything down.* If you don't document the situation for each assumption set, you won't remember what you meant. This

is important for not only sales forecasts but also any forecast that winds up in a Business Case, Marketing Plan, or other document.

4. Finally, *consider any other external constraints* that might put a damper on potential sales. A larger reality may provide some kind of limitation because of a dynamic of the market. Recall the PRESTO model discussed in Chapter 7 where political, regulatory, economic, societal, technological, or other market indicators may constrain your assumptions. This reality check is critical, especially if there are limited customer budgets. Willingness to pay is different from ability to buy. Beware of adopting growth rates that result in unrealistic market sales estimates.

DEMAND PLANNING

After the sales forecasts are prepared, the company's demand planners step in. Demand planning is different from sales forecasting. Sales forecasts ask, "How many will we sell?" Demand plans describe how the company will make sure that it can produce or supply the product at the needed time at an acceptable cost.

Demand planning is a very dynamic process. As with many Product Management processes, demand planning benefits from a strong dose of cross-functional support. Specifically, you need to include members from the supply chain organization, Manufacturing, Finance, Operations, Sales, and Marketing. The demand plan starts with the sales forecast. This provides the demand planner with the "how much is to be sold" scenario. From this, supply chain elements must be considered. The company must either source raw materials or procure product elements and components so that the product can be produced. A service provider such as a wireless company has to not only procure mobile devices from other suppliers but also link its subscriber forecasts with supplier forecasts so it has enough units on hand to sell. It also has to make sure it has enough network capacity. A supply of mobile devices and the network capacity comprise the demand plan for that particular industry. Ultimately, the product has to be available so that it is orderable and can be shipped and delivered. Remember that the mobile device includes more than just the device itself; there are many accessories that must be made available such as chargers and cases.

Furthermore, the demand planning function needs to make sure not only that there are enough goods to sell but also that inventories can be replenished as needed based on sales cycles, inventory turns, and other measurements. Demand planners benefit from performance data from within the firm, including:

- Return rates
- Number of products destroyed and not returned
- Inventory turnover
- Obsolete inventory numbers
- Sales forecast accuracy
- On-time shipping rates

The more your demand planners are able to synchronize their efforts with sales and market forecasts, the more closely they can influence the supporting functions of procurement, manufacturing, and distribution. This is very important because if these functions are out of sync with the rest of the organization, operational inefficiencies will develop, resulting in the misuse of valuable financial and human resources.

Now that you have the final pieces of the puzzle, namely the sales forecast and the demand plan, let's work on the sales forecast for the BetterLife EZ Mobile product.

CONCLUDING THE CASE

Since the inception of the company, with the sales of EZ Phone and EZ Remote, the company achieved sales in 2012 of over $106 million. For the most part, BetterLife has barely begun to penetrate the population of people aged 55 and over.

You and the Sales organization, with validation from retailers and service providers, predict that the possible number of customers is about 5.8 million in 2013. You take that as your TAM for now, using it as a point from which to negotiate with Sales.

You have all agreed to a conservative growth rate for this TAM (in number of possible people) of 1.4 percent per year for the next five years. This conservatively approximates the growth in the entire population. You all agree that it is only going to serve as a guideline to validate that there is a big enough, interesting enough market for you.

Based on assumptions about possible market share, according to retailers and other sources, the following table was constructed. With an average wholesale price of $75 assumed, three projected sales scenarios are shown in Figure 9.5.

FIGURE 9.5

EZ Mobile Projected Forecast Scenarios

EZ Mobile Sales Forecast	2014	2015	2016	2017	2018
Base Scenario					
Population	5,800,000	5,881,200	5,963,537	6,047,026	6,131,685
Percentage of people who might buy	2.50%	3.50%	4.00%	4.00%	4.00%
Number of possible customers	145,000	205,842	238,541	241,881	245,267
Total retail revenue (list price $149)	$21,605,000	$30,670,458	$35,542,679	$36,040,277	$36,544,841
Total EZ Mobile revenue (wholesale price $75)	$10,875,000	$15,438,150	$17,890,610	$18,141,079	$18,395,054
Forecast total population 55+ (in thousands)	70,500	71,650	73,000	74,120	75,380
Unit volume as a % of senior population	0.206%	0.287%	0.327%	0.324%	0.325%
Scenario 2: Best Case					
Population	5,800,000	5,881,200	5,963,537	6,047,026	6,131,685
Percentage of people who might buy	4.00%	5.00%	7.00%	7.00%	7.00%
Number of possible customers	232,000	294,060	417,448	423,292	429,218
Total retail revenue (list price $149)	$34,568,000	$43,814,940	$62,199,689	$63,070,484	$63,953,471
Total EZ Mobile revenue (wholesale price $75)	$17,400,00	$22,054,500	$31,308,568	$31,746,888	$32,191,345
Forecast total population 55+ (in thousands)	70,500	71,650	73,000	74,120	75,380
Unit volume as a % of senior population	0.329%	0.410%	0.572%	0.571%	0.569%
Scenario 3: Worst Case					
Population	5,800,00	5,881,200	5,963,537	6,047,026	6,131,685
Percentage of people who might buy	1.50%	2.00%	3.00%	3.00%	3.00%
Number of possible customers	87,000	117,624	178,906	181,411	183,951
Total retail revenue (list price $149)	$12,963,000	$17,525,976	$26,657,009	$27,030,208	$27,408,631
Total EZ Mobile revenue (wholesale price $75)	$6,525,000	$8,821,800	$13,417,958	$13,605,809	$13,796,291
Forecast total population 55+ (in thousands)	70,500	71,650	73,000	74,120	75,380
Unit volume as a % of senior population	0.123%	0.164%	0.245%	0.245%	0.244%

After the estimates are prepared, you hold a cross-functional team meeting to discuss the assumptions with all concerned stakeholders. Here's what you conclude at the end of the meeting:

1. Sales commits to selling 125,000 units in year one, with a stretch goal of 150,000 units.
2. Demand Planning, Development, and Procurement have commitments from the manufacturer to ensure that a solid supply

will be in the channel 45 days before launch, and a 15 percent safety stock will be added before the official launch. The cost per phone will not exceed $35 for two years.

3. Two major retailers and two wireless service providers are going to stock the phones and will assist with advertising expenditures.

4. The team agrees to meet every week to review sales targets, complaints, and other issues that may arise.

5. The team commits to revise the sales forecasts within 30 days of launch and to meet every two weeks to make sure that the business stays on track

The bottom line for BetterLife is that everyone agrees that the forecasts are achievable and commits to fulfill the business and market scenarios in the Business Case, which is almost complete. The team believes that a "go" decision is warranted and that all cross-functional team members are ready to go, once the executive committee provides the funding for all wheels of the corporate machine to begin turning.

As the case for BetterLife demonstrates, a fundamental amount of validated research and a solid assumption set is going to pave the way for its introduction of a new product that focuses on a specific market segment—a segment characterized by proven, fully understood customer needs.

At the end of the analysis, as the sales forecast is finalized, the timing of the first orders and the timing of order to cash (order to payment) will be incorporated into the operating budget for the product line. If, in the case described here, the product is announced in February, some orders for product will have already been processed because the distribution channels will have been "loaded up" with inventory. You will learn about launching products in later chapters in the book.

SUMMARY

Forecasting is, at the very least, extremely complex. As I described earlier in the chapter, product managers typically use judgment techniques, based on a variety of data sources, to identify the TAM and the AMS for the product. The forecasting sequence aligns with the Product Management Life Cycle Model.

Forecasting is a continuous process that requires product managers to think about markets and understand them, which is why the chapters on industry environment and market segmentation were presented prior to this chapter. The product manager and the cross-functional team must keep as much current data as possible about the product, its finances, the market environment, and anything else remotely relevant about the existing product's performance as a way to maintain a perspective on the business, and to be able to create or revise forecasts as often as necessary.

Finally, the thought processes involved in forecast creation can be fine-tuned over time. The more experience you have in working on forecasts, or in deriving forecasts, the better you become at the practice.

RAISING YOUR PRODUCT MANAGEMENT EXPERIENCE QUOTIENT (PMEQ)

1. If you have never done a forecast before, talk to your manager or peers to learn about the forecasting activities that have been carried out within your organization.

2. Collect some of the forecast data and outcomes. Find out how well the forecasts have fared against the actual performance and what analyses were carried out to determine the cause of any variances.

3. Find out about the forecasting cycle in your company. What kinds of forecasts are product managers responsible for, and when do they work on these forecasts?

4. Work with other product managers to describe the techniques they use for product forecasts. What exactly did they forecast? Who did they work with? How did they arrive at the final numbers?

5. There are usually corporate economists or others in corporate-level positions who are responsible for corporate forecasting. Try to introduce yourself to them, and ask if they would be kind enough to explain their forecasting methods to you. Ask them about the data they incorporate and any models they might use.

6. If your company has a Demand Planning department, make sure you know how they do what they do, when they do it, and with whom they work. You will learn much from people who also work in Manufacturing, Procurement, and other vital areas.

7. As you improve your forecasting proficiency, begin to fine-tune your efforts in terms of establishing sets of assumptions for upcoming work, which might include a Business Case or a budget. As you improve your assumption formulation skills, you will begin to find it easier to draw conclusions. You will also develop a more astute approach to understanding risk and, hence, be more aware during future-state scenario planning.

10

STRATEGIC PRODUCT PLANNING: THE INFLECTION POINT

Executive Summary

- All strategies for a product must answer three vital questions: How has the product performed thus far? What is its envisioned market position? What can be done to achieve that vision?
- When product managers can depict their long-range vision for their products, they fortify their own positions as central business figures and can more effectively bring together cross-functional teams.
- Integrating the cross-functional product team into the strategy formulation process produces more effective, realistic strategies.

The future influences the present just as much as the past.
—FRIEDRICH NIETZSCHE, 1844–1900

The purpose of this chapter is to introduce you to the basic elements of the strategic planning process for products. The fundamental components of the strategic planning process combine related marketing mix elements, including pricing, promotion, and place (or channel). Therefore, the product's journey begins when the product manager envisions the product's future.

Well-developed strategies also focus on competitive advantage. Where would Southwest Airlines or Ryanair be without their low-cost, low-fare strategies? The product manager and the product portfolio manager *must* have a workable strategy—a game plan—for every product or portfolio. A product's performance depends heavily on the quality and range of its core strategy.

Strategies formulated by a product manager propose the execution parameters for a product or for the portfolio of products. Well-formulated strategies set the stage for robust, ongoing planning and decision making throughout the product life cycle.

A strategy defines *what* is going to be done and *how* it's going to be done. Product Management can be compared with a football game (i.e., American football). The coaches work out game plans (strategies). During the game the quarterback (team leader) and the coach (boss) continually monitor field position, weather, players, and other variables and restrategize on the spot. The plan is constantly updated in case of unforeseen events, such as an injury or change in weather. Winning depends on strategies, and strategies apply to most endeavors—a game, a war, a business, or a product's success.

STRATEGY IS A DYNAMIC CONTINUUM

Strategy is an amalgam of two Greek words: *stratos*, meaning "army," and *ago*, meaning (roughly) "to lead." Centuries ago, Sun Tzu, a Chinese general, wrote a book called *The Art of War* that focused on effective war strategies and tactics. One of its major themes is the futility of seeking hard-and-fast rules instead of fluid, adaptable strategies.

For the product manager, the relevance of the phrase "leading an army" means defining a holistic but flexible strategy and being the "general" (or CEO) of the product team.

Product managers, like generals, direct a series of actions over the long term. They may or may not have a clear picture of enemy strength and disposition, but as good leaders, they have built a number of broad contingencies into their strategies.

For product managers, as in all business, it is important to differentiate between strategies and tactics. They sit at opposite ends of a continuum, and you can't have one without the other.

As in all game plans, strategies:

1. Require a plan of action that encompasses a future time frame
2. Address an entire chain of events or actions that may be separated in space and time along the value chain
3. Must have more flexibility and less dependence on specific events or processes
4. Have an inherent capacity for greater reactivity to patterns of events or outcomes
5. Focus on gaining advantage that is tied to a desirable future vision (such as an advantageous market position)
6. Are less concerned with actions that make up the individual, day-to-day operational components of the product manager's work

The characteristics of tactics are opposite to those of strategies. They depend on specific resources or external actions and are not intended to take into account contingencies and unanticipated obstacles. Tactics do not take the broad view, nor do they deal with major changes. They only address the immediate problem. In baseball, when a batter swings, his focus is on the hit. He doesn't watch the shortstop "step into" a possible infield ball. Like that batter, whose action is only in the moment, tactics deal mainly with the present. There is no time to ruminate on future gains or to pause and evaluate status. The next action must only deal with the immediate situation: the next punch, the next step, surviving the next round.

From a business perspective, tactics involve taking action and help us achieve competitive advantage. Tactical actions can be tracked and measured. These contribute to the feedback loop that helps to "steer" the product's business and in the refinement of strategy. In addition, tactical activity tends to expose opportunities to improve a process or processes.

USING A GENERIC STRATEGY

One of the most influential voices on competitive strategy is that of Michael Porter, the father of the *value chain*, along with *strategic groups, generic strategies,* and a host of other key concepts in this area. Pivotal among his observations is the idea that structure *follows* strategy. Rather than impose strategies over existing business structures and organizations, companies should create groupings that embrace the cascade of strategies. This principle is the core of many of my recommendations in this book, including the heavy use of cross-functional product teams and my belief that product managers should be at the epicenter of their enterprise.

Another valuable observation from Porter is the idea of *generic strategies,* defined as broad classifications of strategic thinking. He suggests three types of generic strategies: cost minimization, product differentiation, and market focus. However, companies must choose *only one* generic strategy, because generic strategies work against each other when mixed.

For example, imagine a heavily commoditized industry wherein a CEO focuses on cost minimization (appropriate to the market). Then, in midstream, he begins a program to differentiate the products. The cost of additional R&D, customization, and market research would likely undo the gains made by cost cutting, while the commodity nature of the industry would indicate that differentiation could only gain marginal results. As a general rule, using more than one generic strategy tends to be counterproductive.

STRATEGIZING IS LIKE SOLVING A PUZZLE

When I was a kid, I would visit the Museum of Natural History in New York City. The dinosaur skeletons always fascinated me, but I couldn't figure out how the museum assembled a complete dinosaur because the bones seemed fused together. It was a puzzle. Later, I learned that the paleontologists assembled the material they had (real data) and fused it with clay (theory, hunches, or other "smarts").

Strategic planning for products is akin to assembling dinosaur bones. It means solving a complex series of problems (assembling the skeleton or solving the puzzle) based on (the bones, clues, or ingredients) of past performance, current indicators, and other pertinent data.

As a product manager, your challenge is to solve these multivariable "puzzles," allowing you to make coherent, appropriate decisions about the future of your product. You have to look at all the components to understand what's happening, deduce why it's happening, and decide what should be done next.

Every product or business opportunity has a starting point and an objective. You cannot devise a realistic strategy for your product unless you know where you've been, where you are right now, and where you want to go. A strong strategy answers the questions, "How do I know I'm on track to achieve my vision, and how will I know when I get there?" This is strategic planning in a nutshell.

My goal is to bring strategic planning to your world. I want to offer you a perspective that makes strategic and tactical planning a reality for you. Let's go forward and try to create this perspective.

THE WATERFALL EFFECT

Within the corporation, there must be a cascading continuum of strategy from the top down. Corporate strategy must interlock with division or business unit strategy, which must, in turn, cascade into portfolio, product line, and product strategies, as shown in Figure 10.1.

Sorting out (or even adjusting) this cascade is one of the larger responsibilities for the product manager. Organizational strategy variations sometimes make these cascades challenging to diagram.

In an ideal cascade, corporate strategy sets the position in terms of market dominance (industry, technology, or demographics); financial objectives; and corporate "identity" positions such as culture, values, mission, and overarching goals.

Divisional or business unit strategies define more specific advantages tied to more specific markets, industries, technologies, or segments. They

FIGURE 10.1

The Waterfall Effect Strategy

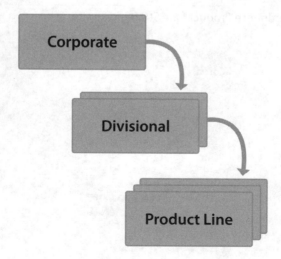

also include financial objectives that focus on an optimal portfolio of investment options, as well as components of a divisional budget, so that product managers may more effectively evolve the strategies for their products.

When companies have carefully crafted strategies and methods to achieve them, they tend to have higher levels of product success and higher levels of employee engagement. Who doesn't want to play on a winning team, and who doesn't get caught up in bringing passion and extra effort into a successful endeavor? When companies are more successful with their products, they tend to invest more in innovation, advertising, promotion, people development, and infrastructure. Carefully planned investments tend to improve the probability that new-to-the-market, category-defining products can be conceived and brought to customers.

Even with increasing specificity, however, strategy is still a creative exercise. While there is a somewhat stepwise strategy formulation process, it is not about rote analytics. Developing strong product strategies still requires a tolerance for ambiguity and nuance and careful handling of vagueness and uncertainty in the form of contingencies, decision timing, and a bias for meaningful, triggered action.

Product Management is not confined to its own niche and performance. It is contingent on dealing with the functions of the corporate entities within the cascade. Figure 10.2 provides a simple visualization illustrating how other business functions continually try to influence what happens at the product line level.

FIGURE 10.2

Other Functions Try to Influence Product Line Strategies

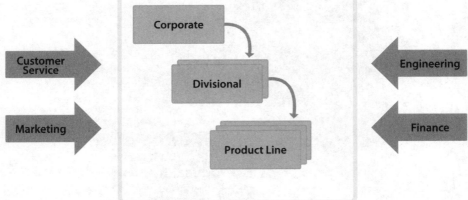

These functional strategies are orchestrated by other department members with an agenda that attempts to cast the best possible light on the overall performance of *that* function in fulfilling *its* charter. Functional strategies tend to introduce elements that result in sub-optimization, which is the bane of good strategy because it inhibits overall performance. The simplest example is the soccer player who "hogs the ball." Even though this "hot shot" might make three individual goals, sharing the ball could allow more goals by better integrating the skills of the other players into the mix. The net result of this kind of grandstanding could easily mean the star player breaks a record while the team loses the game.

A business example might be a product that consumes a disproportionate share of the overall advertising budget or one that consumes more engineering resources, producing products with only marginal returns. While the product does extremely well, sharing could allow more sales for the portfolio or the company. Net result: the company loses money because a key resource became saturated by one product.

DYNAMIC STRATEGY FOR THE PRODUCT MANAGER

Successful products owe their stellar achievements to *dynamic strategy.* The product managers of these high fliers are always aware of the dynamism of strategic events. They are constantly alert for and responsive to the continuous change in the oncoming, constantly morphing stream of actions, reactions, opportunities, and capabilities. Such dynamic strategic thinking helps product managers to process and accommodate higher levels of risk and uncertainty. They can react more effectively to "patterns" in the marketplace. The potency of such a full-spectrum strategy has a much deeper impact on advantage and position than any traditional operational strategy, no matter how extensive. What does all this mean? Your strategic plans for your product are all about future position. *Dynamic strategies evolve the future vision over time by addressing marketplace changes.*

The effective product manager is responsible for creating a full-spectrum operational and dynamic strategy that merges formulation and implementation while accommodating all elements of the marketing mix.

STRATEGY IN YOUR WORLD

All too often, strategic plans are created to satisfy some corporate edict. It's August and you have to "hand in" your strategies to the corporate office. Everyone rushes around trying to get the forms filled out and into

Finance, where the numbers get crunched. In my view, strategic planning for products should not be a once-a-year event if your goal is success.

This begs the question, "What is the right time to restrategize and replan?" My answer is, "It depends on a number of factors—the industry you're in; competitor activity; how the product is doing from a financial perspective; how fast the product moves across the life cycle; plus any other unforeseen factors. But the important thing is that you have to consider them within the framework of what's happening at all times."

That's a pretty long list of things to think about and act on. However, it's not a good idea to skip over any details or to consider only a few variables in such an extremely complex equation—and therefore make decisions on too inadequate a basis. You need to know a lot more about how each variable influences the desired outcome and how it affects your vision for the product.

Another challenge for product managers and other business stakeholders in the organization is reconciling strategic product planning with the annual budgeting process. The pressure on you seems to demand that you make advance decisions and budget forecasts for what's to be done and when, and what financial outcomes are expected.

The budgeting process is supposedly all structured for you; all you need to provide are your numbers and some facts to support them. However, numbers are easy to list in August and difficult to reconcile when April rolls around and the actuals aren't in line with the budgets (and then you're told you can't travel). Some organizations really do a great job with this, but I've seen enough results to know that when missed forecasts are traced back to the root cause: "plug numbers" were in the spreadsheet.

I don't expect to change the world in terms of fully disconnecting the budgeting process from strategic planning. In many organizations, the use of budget as a throttle overcomes a significant challenge: How do you know where you are? Without a budget to set some parameters, how do you make comparisons between the current situation and the past or the current situation and the future? What paths did the product take in the market and within the portfolio, and where will it go in the future?

THE PRODUCT AS A BUSINESS: A STRATEGIC PLANNING MODEL

The diagram in Figure 10.3 shows a business model deconstructed into its components. Using it will help you produce a meaningful analysis of what should take place in each phase. But first, you have to get the data

FIGURE 10.3

The Product as a Business Strategy Model

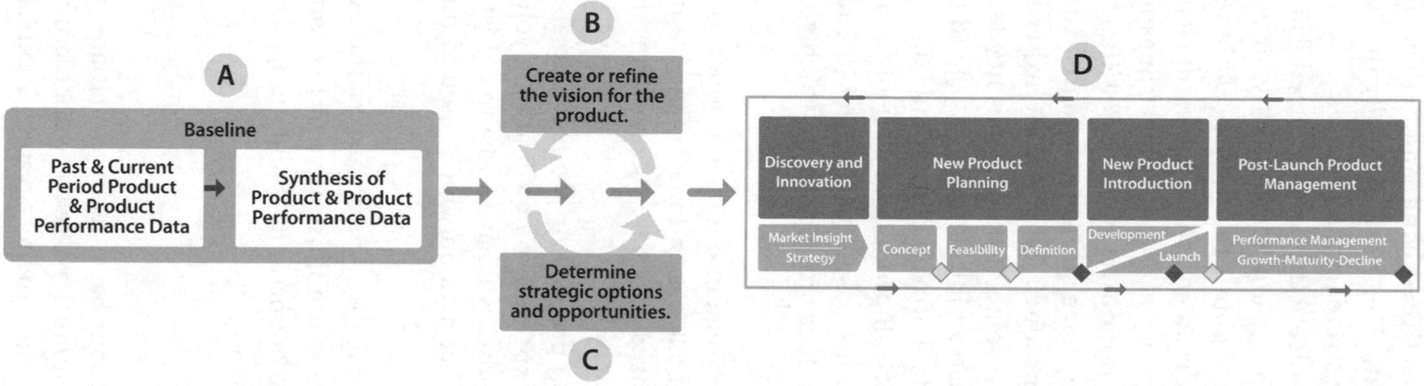

needed to get the right perspective; second, and perhaps more difficult, you must decide on the "what." The "what" is really the "what to do" in order to plan the appropriate strategies and tactics.

The model's elements indicate the data you need. Having pertinent data helps your mind form images and ideas about your business. These elements also represent linkage points to other parts of this book—some are in chapters you've already read and some will be in chapters to come. For instance, when I suggest you need an industry snapshot, you simply need to look up Chapter 7, on industry and competition. If you've read through to this point, you may have already considered some of the suggested work to raise your product management experience quotient (PMEQ) and given thought to some of the analysis needed to formulate the strategy. Note: there is also a bidirectional linkage to the outline for a Product Strategy in a template provided in Module 6.

This is not a one-size-fits-all product as a business strategy model. There can be myriad variations based on a variety of factors, among them, the maturity of the product or industry in which you operate. For example:

- If your strategy focuses on a brand new product, you need to create a snapshot of the business and market environment in which you plan to operate based on where the market is now and how it arrived at its current state.

- If you have an existing product or product line and you're going to evolve the line or expand into new markets, you must create a similar snapshot. But now, you have a wealth of historical product performance and market data on which to build future strategies for the product.

As this chapter progresses, we will focus on the evolution of an existing product because it is more illustrative of the work of data collection, synthesis, and future opportunity evaluation, all of which comprise elements of strategic planning.

An Overview of the Model

This model (Figure 10.3) has four basic sections that are tagged with the letters A through D. A brief summary of each will be provided, and then I will describe each in detail. The Product Strategy Template in Module 6 recapitulates this model as well.

- *Step A. Establish a baseline for the business of the product.* This gives you a focal point that allows you to compare where you've been with where you are so you can determine where you want to go. Setting the baseline demands that you have the most relevant product and business data available because such data is to be synthesized into a product snapshot. Baselining isn't a once-and-done exercise. It needs to be reset from time to time depending on the variable influences of the market and within your organization, the same way the line of scrimmage moves in a football game.

- *Step B. Formulate or reformulate your vision for the product to cast it as the driving force for the product or portfolio.* You must be sure you know where you intend to focus your efforts to accomplish this and the reasons *why* you chose that focal point. You may not have to *create* your "why" from scratch if you have an existing product, you may just need to refine "where you want to go."

- *Step C. Identify strategic options* by identifying the possible future elements of the marketing mix, the desired industry and competitive posture, and any other supporting business functions that need to be brought into the future state equations.

- *Step D. Link the strategic options to the Product Management Life Cycle Model* so that you see whether you have the right balance of investments supporting current products, products in development, and products in the process of being launched. Also to be included are ideas for new products or enhancements to existing products that need to be vetted across the product planning phases.

The Model in Detail

You've gotten an overview of the model. Now we have a context from which we can extrapolate the details. Most important to the entire model is the baseline. Follow me through all its complexities.

Step A. Baseline the Business of the Product

The baseline is the essential tool to help you get the clearest understanding of your product, product line, or portfolio's current circumstances. It *is* a reflection of everything "business" about the product, including the characteristics of the industries in which you operate, the competitors you challenge, the resources your company brings to the business, and the product's financial, operational, and market results. The creation of a baseline actually amounts to a big data collection project. If you have not done this before or have only done portions of this, or even if you're new to your job in Product Management, consider this one of the most important activities you will ever carry out.

Before moving on to the data itself, there are some points about the logistics to be considered. Gathering data involves considerable effort, so you may want to think of a place to store this data once you have assembled it. Certainly an electronic repository should be a necessary consideration.

But you may also want to think about creating a physical location for the data, not just for now but for the future as well. Rather than a one-time-use area, this should be an ongoing repository—perhaps a "strategy room" with space for tables, white boards, and places to tack things up. You will be collecting data from many cross-functional constituencies, and the repository will make this data available to all product team stakeholders. By creating this location, you can bring your Marketing counterparts and other cross-functional team members together to share the results of some of their efforts. It's also a great place to have team meetings because it creates a visual, contextual environment where your marketplace can be seen and felt by all team members.

Although this could present a challenge for virtual teams, the idea of the central repository for all product, marketing, financial, and business data cannot be emphasized enough. Recall that the Product Master Plan serves as the ultimate repository for the product's documentation.

Organizing the Data

The organization of this data on paper is one of the most challenging procedures for creating a baseline.

Figure 10.4 is a template that shows how to get organized in order to collect data. Breaking big work projects into smaller pieces or chunks within a "cell" allows you to make progress steadily so that you don't feel overwhelmed by the work.

1. The left column is the product or business element being analyzed.
2. The column on the extreme right is for the current year (CY). In the CY cell, you would record the most relevant data corresponding to the product or business element being analyzed. The two columns to the left of the CY represent the CY less one

FIGURE 10.4

A Template to Help Organize the Work of Data Collection

Product or Business Element Being Analyzed	CY–2	CY–1	CY

CY = Current Year

year (which would be last year) and CY less two years (which would be two years ago). You can (and perhaps should) go back many more years than just one or two if you are really trying to create a retrospective view of the product.

These cells are not financial spreadsheet cells (although in some cases, financial data would populate the cell). They allow you to map out your work so you know where to record the results, and, therefore, the outcomes of the work yield the perspective you need. At this point, you may be thinking, "It's so much work to do." But I assure you that once you do this the first time, updating it at regular intervals will be much easier—and you'll be glad you have it.

Collecting data about the business of the product is organized into the following broad categories:

1. Acquiring external data about the industry and competitors
2. Obtaining customer activity data (validating segmentation models)
3. Capturing data about how the organization evolved in terms of capabilities and resources as well as its underlying financial health
4. Securing data about the product's market, financial, and operational results

External Data: Industry and Competition

Your competitors across the industry landscape affect your product as day-to-day business activities are carried out. That is one of the components of your baseline analysis, and you would use the structure of Figure 10.4 to record this data.

Figure 10.5 is an example that illustrates how to use the table effectively. It shows how you can populate your chart with the most appropriate current and recent historical data.

FIGURE 10.5

Organization of Industry and Competitive Data

PRODUCT OR BUSINESS ELEMENT BEING ANALYZED	CURRENT YEAR–2	CURRENT YEAR–1	CURRENT YEAR
Industry Environment	• Fuel prices fell 10%. • GDP grew 3%. • Regulators not concerned with fuel economy standards.	• Political environment is stable. • Regulators focus on safety issues. • 3.5% GDP growth. • Fuel prices are stable. • Automobile inventory build-up worries economists.	• Election year politics favors business-friendly candidates. • Regulators begin to discuss importance of fuel economy standards. • Economists feel a recession is on the horizon. • A major automobile firm was taken private. • Demand for fuel-efficient cars has increased.
Competitive Environment	• Intense competition for SUVs. • Compact car sales have fallen. • Auto firms have not introduced many new or interesting compact car designs. • SUV production is at capacity. • Compact car inventories are higher than normal.	• Major competitor introduces stylish hybrid with heavy advertising. • Competitors show SUV hybrids at auto show. • Analysts praise the new SUV designs and technology. • Excessive compact car inventories.	• More hybrids offered by more companies. • Competitors advertising "safe and small" fuel-efficient cars. • SUV sales are on the decline. • Factory capacity is lower than forecast demand.

CY = Current Year

Using the practices shown in Chapter 7, let's apply this to the automobile industry—and specifically to compact automobiles—based on known industry and competitive activity. This is for illustrative purposes. I'm certain that given some research time, this table could be populated more extensively.

Customer Activity

As your product is marketed, you will want to learn more about the customers who purchase your product and their motivations. The market segmentation models you read about in Chapter 8 can be applied in order for you to discern whether your product's attributes fulfill their intended needs.

If you are in a business-to-business company, you classify your customers by industry, geography, size, and the volume of business carried out. If you work in a company whose products are sold to consumers, you classify your customers by demographic variables such as age, income, gender, and so on. Each customer type or grouping is characterized by a common set of *needs,* and your customers buy your product because its benefits fulfill that specific need.

All customers go through some kind of selection process when deciding to buy any product. Some make impulse decisions, and some go through complex buying decision processes with many influencers and users. Your job in this phase of the strategy formulation process is to highlight and characterize your key market segments and customer types, and to understand how their needs and characteristics may have evolved to the current point and why that evolution took place.

Let's use the information in Figure 10.6 to organize our past and current customer profile. The table helps describe one market segment for the automobile company's compact car by characterizing the needs of that segment.

Securing data about evolving needs and preferences of customers in a given market segment can be achieved when there are multiple data points. In the simple example used in Figure 10.6, the product team involved could secure data from dealers and customer surveys to gain insights into those evolving needs. It should be noted that when a current perspective on these needs is not available, the assumptions we put into our product strategies and supporting future forecasts will likely not be useful, and the decisions made could expose the business to unnecessary risk.

FIGURE 10.6

The Evolution of Needs of Customers in a Market Segment

PRODUCT OR BUSINESS ELEMENT BEING ANALYZED	CURRENT YEAR–2	CURRENT YEAR–1	CURRENT YEAR
Market Segment: • Young families • Age range: 24–36 • Income range: $60,000–$80,000 per year • Region: Mid-Atlantic States in the U.S.	• Need reliable, safe transportation • Want comfort for long commutes • Require safety to protect families and perceived threat from so many large SUVs on the road • Young families need ease of access for child seats	• Need reliable, safe transportation • Concern for the environment—desire for clean air • As families grow and as prices for cars increase, resale value is important • Minimal time available for maintenance procedures	• Need reliable, safe transportation • Concern for the environment—desire for clean air • Growing, active families need more space for their gear • Other cost-of-living elements are increasing, and families are looking to carefully manage expenditures

CY = Current Year

Organizational Capabilities and Financial Health

It is the role of the company to provide a population of competent, capable engineers, designers, marketers, and other employees. The company should also have adequate financial resources to support future investments in products, people, and operational support systems. Product managers should be aware of and understand this financial data because their future opportunities depend on having funding for resources to support future product and marketing activity.

Let's continue using our data collection model to create a snapshot of the financial health and organizational capabilities for our automobile company example. The table in Figure 10.7 provides this perspective. Figure 10.7 indicates to the product manager and his team that there are more favorable internal business conditions in the current year. The improved status suggests a greater opportunity for the pursuit of new initiatives with which to address specific customer needs. Perhaps, in this case, a new CEO instilled new spirit into the company. The heightened optimism can act to stimulate creativity by inspiring a renewed sense of purpose in everyone.

FIGURE 10.7

Data About Organizational and Financial Health

PRODUCT OR BUSINESS ELEMENT BEING ANALYZED	CURRENT YEAR–2	CURRENT YEAR–1	CURRENT YEAR
Financial Health and Organizational Capabilities	• Revenue is falling due to the recession. • Company is operating at its biggest loss ever. • Morale is low because of layoffs in Marketing and Engineering.	• Revenue is stabilizing as the economy begins to recover from a recession. • Company is still losing money. • The union went on strike for two weeks to protest cuts in benefits.	• Revenue is slightly higher. • The first quarterly profit in two years. • The new CEO created a strategy for the firm to focus on the creation of stylish compact cars. • New designers and engineers have come up with compelling hybrid automobile designs that industry analysts love.

CY = Current Year

Capturing Product Performance Data

The activity of forming the baseline for the product as a business is ultimately built on the basis of how the product is currently performing in the market. These performance indicators are made up of both financial and nonfinancial measurements (which I'll talk about in Chapter 19). This part of strategy formulation is, by far, the most complex when you are constructing the database of current product performance data.

Invariably, you may find that you do not have all of the data needed or prescribed here. You may find that other data may be important too. At this point, you have to take over and determine what's right to do for the problems you uncover or the challenges you face—and ultimately, the decisions you will need to make. In order to secure this kind of product-specific performance data, you need to know which data to gather. Think of this as taking an "inventory" of the product—not a physical count, but for the purpose of gathering a significant amount of data about the current product as a business.

To take this kind of inventory, you need a solid checklist of things to do in order to assemble the needed data. When you have the data, it is then used to depict the current product by following the path it traveled through the market up to the present—and you and your team are armed and enabled to rethink the future of the product.

Some of the data elements are posed as questions you can probably answer, while others require research or data collection.

- When was the product introduced to the market?
- How has it evolved functionally?
- How has it changed aesthetically?
- What technologies were incorporated?
- What materials were used?

There are many more questions to ask that, when answered, can help define the current state of the product. Whether you are starting out as a product manager for the first time or inheriting an existing product, you can create this *retrospective roadmap* that describes the path the product has traveled up until the current time. This retrospective is a reflection of the "strategic intent" of the company or business unit, up until this point. If you never did this before, here's how it works: First, create a chart like the one shown as Figure 10.8. I've provided some descriptors for you—some hints to help you to find the relevant categories needed for your product's relevant retrospective roadmap.

You can create your own table with rows and columns that show various dimensions of the product's evolution. You can then summarize the rows in key product attribute categories to yield a diagram similar to the one shown in Figure 10.8. You might include items such as technologies, platforms, and competitive positioning points. You can trace the product back for as many years as data may exist to tell a story of how product investments were deployed and results obtained.

You'll find that when you show people in Product Development, Marketing, Operations, or other departments what you're working on, they'll probably be glad to share what they know. Hopefully, you'll be able to talk to the product managers who were the stewards for the product. You'll be glad when your additions to the Product Master Plan are available to others.

FIGURE 10.8

Product Roadmap Retrospective

ROADMAP ELEMENT	CY−2 FIRST YEAR	CY−1 ADDITIONS	CURRENT YEAR
Safety Features	Airbags	Anti-Lock Brakes	GPS Navigation
Models	Base DX Version	LX Upscale Model	LX Luxury Edition
Designs/Styles	Four-Door Sedan	Two-Door Coupe	Hatchback
Colors	Black, White, Red	Blue	Silver Metallic
Engine	4-Cylinder Gasoline	6-Cylinder Gasoline	Plug-In Hybrid
Acceleration	0–50 mph in 12 seconds	0–50 mph in 9 seconds	0–50 mph in 8 seconds

CY = Current Year

If you are involved in the creation of a brand new product, this retrospective approach may not work for you. There are other practices you can use to determine a future product roadmap, and they will be discussed shortly. (To learn more about future-oriented product roadmaps, refer to Chapter 20.)

Additional work is required to continue assembling this baseline analysis. This includes the assembly of information to help you gain perspective on three important areas: the current product's life cycle state, how the other marketing mix elements have been used, and the other areas of the business that affect the baseline.

1. *It is essential you know where the product is situated in its life cycle.* That's the only way the most appropriate product investment options can be considered for the future. Investment allocations must be aligned to the appropriate life cycle phase to avoid wasting scarce human and financial resources. To review:

the main phases are growth, maturity, and decline. Growth is characterized by sales that increase rapidly with growing market share and growing profits. Maturity is characterized by revenue that grows more slowly or where product revenue may modulate slightly. Mature product profits may follow a similar pattern or shift with increasing or decreasing costs. Decline phase products exhibit sales or profits that decrease at an increasing rate. (More information about identifying the product's life cycle state is included in Chapter 19.) In addition, the product's historical and current market share should be tracked against originally established forecasts. Our retrospective method can be used to construct a product life cycle profile. This profile will give you the needed perspective to characterize the correct phase in the product's life cycle. The chart in Figure 10.9 offers another method that can be used to build a retrospective. The difference is that instead of a table on its own, a table and graphics are used. Visualizing data related to product life cycles provides a very illuminating portrait of the past financial and market performance of a product.

2. The other three marketing mix elements—price, promotion, and place (or channel)—provide important input to the baseline analysis. The goal in your retrospective analysis is to understand how pricing adjustments, promotional investments, or channel shifts contributed to or influenced changes in unit volumes, revenue, cash flow, and product profitability. If, for instance, a new model was introduced but required heavy promotional advertising and extensive discounting to encourage buying activity, then perhaps the model's value proposition was not compelling at the envisioned price point. These analytics are a vital part of the retrospective review because you don't want to be introducing new models or versions if they don't deliver the envisioned benefits. Using the example of the automobile company once more, the evolution of the other marketing mix elements is shown in Figure 10.10.

3. In the creation of product retrospectives, there is an ancillary list of "things to examine" for the product manager. This list cannot necessarily be distilled into a chart or graph. It has to do with the

FIGURE 10.9

Product Life Cycle Data and the Life Cycle Curve

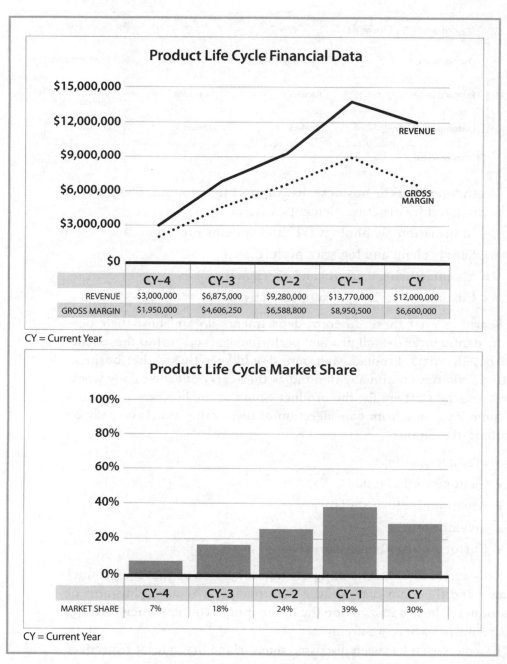

Product Life Cycle Financial Data

	CY–4	CY–3	CY–2	CY–1	CY
REVENUE	$3,000,000	$6,875,000	$9,280,000	$13,770,000	$12,000,000
GROSS MARGIN	$1,950,000	$4,606,250	$6,588,800	$8,950,500	$6,600,000

CY = Current Year

Product Life Cycle Market Share

	CY–4	CY–3	CY–2	CY–1	CY
MARKET SHARE	7%	18%	24%	39%	30%

CY = Current Year

FIGURE 10.10

Evolution of Marketing Mix Elements

Marketing Mix Element	CY–2	CY–1	CY
Pricing Activity	Rebates of $1,000	0% Financing	$179/month lease
Promotional Activity	Radio, TV	Direct Mail, TV	Tech magazines, sponsorships
Distribution Channel	Dealers	Dealers	Dealers

CY = Current Year

other parts of the business that support the product. These operational infrastructure elements include:

- Information Technology (IT) and systems evolution
- Supply chain and logistics performance
- Manufacturing capacity and efficiency
- Customer Service and support activities

Learning what these different departments do and how their performance influences overall product performance is critical to the assembly of baseline data. Product Managers should keep these other business function activities continually in mind as they carry out their daily work. In evolving the strategy for the product, some of the business indicators that come into view from consideration of these other functions may be important to examine:

- Product quality
- Customer satisfaction
- Repair and return statistics
- Inventory turns
- Customer experience scores

This section is concentrating on data collection so that the product manager and the team can gain the right perspective on the business of the product. These data provide the foundational content when forming the baseline of "where we are now."

Based on what has been discussed thus far, and that our retrospectives were built on the CY, CY−1 year, and CY−2 years (aside from capturing the product revenue and gross margin), we can now assemble all of the captured data into a unified profile. In reality, it would be unrealistic to capture all the data on one page. However, the template in Figure 10.11 provides a visual snapshot of how all of the data collected might actually be organized. This can serve as a helpful guide to ensure that the intrinsic meaning behind the

FIGURE 10.11

Template for a Strategic Product Retrospective and Baseline Evaluation

Product Element	CY–2	CY–1	CY
External Indicators			
Industry Activity			
Competitor Activity			
Customers/Segments			
Internal Indicators			
Company Financial Situation			
Skills/Capabilities			
Retrospective Roadmap Information			
Features			
Models/Versions			
Designs/Styles			
Colors/Sizes			
Technology Used			
Performance Levels			
Safety Elements			
Competitive Positioning			
Product Life Cycle Performance			
Revenue			
Gross Margin			
Market Share			
Pricing Programs			
Promotional Activity			
Distribution Channel Activity			
Product Operational Performance			
Product Quality			
Customer Satisfaction			
Repair & Return Data			
Inventory Turns			

CY = Current Year

sum of all the data can be more easily understood. Furthermore, it serves as a good indicator that there may be data missing (if one or more of the cells remains unpopulated). Overall, this sets the stage for the next work activity: synthesizing data into meaningful information.

Synthesizing Data and Creating Useful Information

Collecting the data up to this point is only part of the journey to the *baseline*. Referring to the Product as a Business Strategy Model (see Figure 10.3), the next step is to synthesize the data—or to knit the data together in a way that creates informational tip-offs, which can help you visualize and think of new ideas and opportunities.

The acronym SWOT stands for strengths, weaknesses, opportunities, and threats. Most people who have learned about strategic planning are familiar with the SWOT model. Basic familiarity with a model does not mean it is used correctly, especially when SWOT is carried out at the product or product portfolio level. It is easy to default to the use of company or divisional indicators because there isn't enough sensitivity to the necessity of carrying out *product level* SWOTs. However, in many instances, when working with my clients, I have found that there just isn't enough product-level data. Caveat: A casual attitude or just sheer avoidance of this analysis can result in exposing your product's weaknesses, leaving your product (and perhaps your company) vulnerable to its competition. Collecting this product-level data and organizing it so that you can carry out a SWOT for the product or product line can seem an overwhelming, time-consuming, and exhausting chore, but let me assure you that it is a necessary task.

The SWOT model is typically represented as a quadrant model, as shown in Figure 10.12. In each one of these quadrants, you need verifiable market data, product data, financial data, and operational data. Now, I'll show you how to utilize this model.

When a product exhibits a *strength*, it contributes positively to the portfolio and is strongly differentiated from its rivals. It could be its positive contribution to the revenue stream, its reputation with customers, its competitive position, its unique technology, or its documented quality as perceived by customers and analysts. Because many products exist within a portfolio, you might need to consider the strength of the product portfolio as one of the dimensions in this quadrant. In addition, you can

FIGURE 10.12

A SWOT Model for a Product

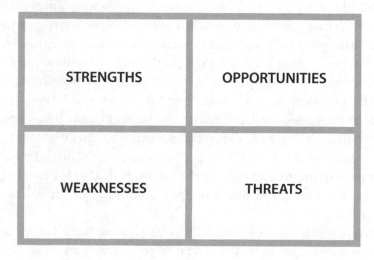

include aspects of the company itself if its reputation or image serves to positively support the product's market position. You need the right level of *documented* and *proven* data to help you define these strengths. This means that you can support the claim.

A *weakness* is the opposite of a strength: the product is not robust, its design or style is outdated, it is competitively inadequate, customers return the product too frequently, or there are too many complaints. A weakness could include a lack of breadth in a product line or eroding market share. You can also consider whether the product detracts from the performance of the portfolio or the company's image causes customers to consider other options. It could also mean that it is not generating a profit for the product line. All of these, and more, can contribute to a poorly performing product.

A *threat* is typically felt from outside of the organization. Threats leave the product vulnerable to a competitor's attack. For example, if your competitor has introduced a competing product with a more attractive value proposition and greater benefits and is telling potential or current customers that your business has problems (whether this is true or not), such a competitor could succeed in taking market share from you. A threat can also connote that your product is in danger of losing customers because it no longer meets the needs of the customers within your chosen market segments.

Opportunity is the last and most important quadrant to be worked on. It is the culmination of your research and the focal point for the strategic product planning process. The reason is that "opportunity discovery" is part of the inspiration and ideation process. Your analysis and interpretation of the product's strengths, weaknesses, and threats can be the catalyst for generating fresh and innovative ideas for new products or enhancements of existing ones. Opportunities or possibilities could include the creation of a product that fills what you have perceived to be an unmet need or a product enhancement that beats the competition. It can help in redesigning a product to make it more attractive. It can suggest investments in promotional or channel development to stimulate demand and deliver the product to a wider market area. It can include a change in a production technique or an operational support system.

The opportunity quadrant of your SWOT analysis is linked to your product's future success, and that is why you need to work on all of the other SWOT quadrants first—before you put anything into the opportunity section.

The guideline for populating any quadrant is that it should be *backed up by actual, verifiable data*. The content in any quadrant should be populated in a way that allows it to be ranked or prioritized in order of importance. Then, when your team members need to draw a conclusion from the data, they are more easily able to put that conclusion into some sort of perspective that is based on the relative importance to the product or portfolio.

Therefore, the *content* of each quadrant will require the answers to three critical questions:

1. What is the specific item that is to be called out?
2. Why is this specific item so important?
3. What data was used to support the statement?

Each quadrant would therefore look like what's shown in Figure 10.13.

Here's how you might go about assembling your product SWOT by using some different examples for each quadrant.

Suppose you are the product team leader for a well-known digital music player and you wanted to write about the product's strengths. In Figure 10.14, one of the product's key strengths is highlighted and defended with data.

FIGURE 10.13

Quadrant Layout for the Product SWOT Model

WHAT?	WHY?	SUPPORTING DATA

FIGURE 10.14

Defining a Strength

What is the strength?	What is the data source?	Why is it important?
85% market share for all products in the line, 45% profit across all products in the line	• Financial records • Industry analyst reports • Stock market analyst reports	Strong market share & robust product profitability allows us to be flexible and agile in keeping ahead of the competition.

Now, suppose you are the product group director for a child's toy action figure sold in markets around the world and you are to describe a product line weakness. Figure 10.15 shows you how this weakness is described.

In the third example, you are now a product line manager of a business software application and you are going to describe a threat, as depicted in Figure 10.16.

Each of these examples is designed to show you how you should be applying the vast amounts of data you have collected and how to reflect

FIGURE 10.15

Defining a Weakness

What is the weakness?

The product line is built in China, and a lack of quality oversight allowed the contract manufacturer to use lead paint in its production process.

What is the data source?

The ABC consumer organization and national trade commissions carried out random product tests. Our research labs also sampled more than 85 product batches. Finally, a team of scientists was sent to the contract manufacturer took paint samples from the warehouse, and found the source of the problem.

Why is it important?

Our reputation as a provider of child-safe toys—a reputation unblemished for more than fifty years—has now been tarnished, and our customers are returning our toys and our other products as well.

on, analyze, and process this in your own mind—and with your cross-functional team members—to come up with a landscape of new opportunities that can be considered for the future.

In the threat sample, the situation for your organization may be formidable, but not as dire as you may think. When two competitors merge, they may actually become vulnerable. Mergers tend to be disruptive within organizations because they are bringing two cultures together, rationalizing multiple technologies and operational infrastructures, and dealing with a host of other issues. It can also be confusing for existing customers because they may not know exactly what to expect and may actually hold off on purchases.

I've purposely left the Opportunity quadrant as the last one to be addressed. When using the SWOT technique, you address the other quadrants first, before examining potential opportunities. For example, in Figure 10.17, I've decided to link the opportunity back to the threat.

FIGURE 10.16

Defining a Threat

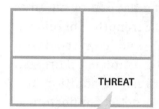

What is the threat?

Your two nearest competitors just announced a merger, explicitly to bring together the products you compete with. Those two products have 65% combined market share. Not only that, they plan to merge their software architectures into one flexible platform. Your product platform is 5 years old.

What is the data source?

The industry analyst and stock market analysts provided this data for you in a market briefing. You and your team members have also read this in industry publications. No one expected this merger.

Why is it important?

While you play platform catch-up, this newly merged competitor is going to take market share away from you, asserting that its technical prowess and flexibility will allow it to meet customers' needs more rapidly and at lower costs. Since your platform is older, it is not as flexible or robust.

FIGURE 10.17

Defining an Opportunity

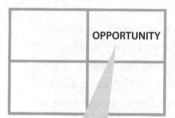

What is the opportunity?

Get working on the platform migration as soon as possible. (Deprioritize the next release.)

What is the data source?

Past merger activity like this has never delivered the promised benefit to customers. Analysts say that customers wait too long for "futures" but have problems to solve now.

Why is it important?

When competitors merge, they may take their eyes off the market as they try to integrate their product lines, systems, and cultures. There is no proof that their platform has been proven and tested. They are highly vulnerable.

Of course, a vast list of opportunities can emerge from each category. Your goal when you are carrying this out for your product or product line is to create a direct linkage between what's happening in any quadrant and what you could actually do about it. Strengths therefore are capitalized on. Weaknesses can be overcome and converted to strengths, or you might evolve appropriate defensive strategies. Threats (being vulnerable) usually require defensive postures. In addition to offering the prospect of fresh possibilities for your product, opportunities can be enlisted as "attack" or "defend" strategic postures to create the best possible position for your product. As noted earlier, opportunity analysis is integral to the ideation process and may help to remove ambiguity around what is often referred to as the "fuzzy front end" of product innovation.

Prepare to Tell a Story About the Product

Data can have more meaning and value if you know the story the data is revealing. What does it all indicate? What should be done, and how do you deal with it? These are the vital questions product managers need to answer. Data translated and synthesized into useful information allows the team to arrive at the most appropriate conclusions, which can then be factored into the most suitable strategic actions for the product. Here are some thoughts to consider when you're drawing conclusions from the data:

1. How important are the product's strengths in relation to its contribution to the business? Some products are "must have" products in the product portfolio, even though they may be commodity-like on their own. Some products contribute positively to the cash flow of the firm. No matter what the data reveals about the current position of the product, it should be put into the most appropriate context.

2. How could the weaknesses affect future product and market success? For example, if the technology places your product at a disadvantage, you'd want to be sure the company's executives recognize that the product needs some strong innovative engineering resources in order to overcome this Achilles' heel. Whatever weakness you uncover, you need to be able to explain its meaning and impact on the future of the product.

Extrapolating meaning from the data and a subsequent analysis of its significance should be translated into a story about your product as a business. Telling a story about your product and its current "state" provides comprehensive and incisive insight to you, your team, and management. Like the dinosaur skeleton I described earlier, you will have bits of "bones" that you must infill with "clay" to produce your result. In other words, you have to mold your data and conclusions into a cogent story—a narrative that can be conveyed to your teams and your management.

One more point in relation to the baseline template shown as Figure 10.11: If one of the cells is missing some data, try to obtain the data or make a judicious assumption about what may have happened.

One last thing. If you feel that only you are responsible for this entire assembly process, you may want to think about taking full advantage of your cross-functional product team and how this kind of work structure can benefit you when you are assembling and interpreting the data.

The State-of-the-Business Product Strategy Review

It's time to meet with the leadership team so you and your cross-functional product team can present your "product as a business" story. In this meeting, your job is to narrate the path the product has taken and then describe how you're going to march forward.

In a novel, themes, characters, and events are knitted into a plot that is carefully unraveled and driven to a conclusion. The *state-of-the-business* product strategy review reveals the storyline, which is skillfully guided by the product manager and the team. To prepare and create a meaningful product strategy review, follow the outline and sequence as shown in Figure 10.18.

Staging the product strategy review serves an extremely important purpose. It inspires management's confidence in your capabilities as a guardian of the company's investments. In addition, your peers and members of your cross-functional team will more fully appreciate the expertise you have brought to gathering the data, interpreting it, and weaving your conclusions into the cogent story you are presenting to show how things are going with your product as a business. There is

FIGURE 10.18

Product Strategy Review Template

SECTION	TITLE	CONTENT
1	Cover Page	• Product Name • Product manager name & names of cross-functional team members • Date of Presentation
2	Introduction	• Executive Summary • Key points to be covered • Support that will be needed from management
3	Mission & Vision	• Current product purpose or mission • Current perspective on the product manager's vision
4	Market Review	• Industry and competitive activity and important trends and your product's current situation • Product's current market positioning (Is the product leading the competition, lagging behind, or is it about equal?) • Current market segments • Customers and usage patterns • Changes that are anticipated for the future and implications for the product's business
5	Financial Review	• Unit volumes and prices • Cost of goods sold • Gross margin/product profitability • Controllable expenses • Explanations of variances • Future financial expectations, funding requirements, etc.
6	Marketing Mix & Business Performance Review	• Product evolution (functionality, changes, technologies, etc.) • Pricing activity (discounting, special bids) • Promotional program and campaign performance • Channel activity (sales, distribution, etc.) • Brand and reputation indicators • Operational performance analysis and evaluation • Service and support analysis and conclusions
7	Integrated Perspective on the Product's Business	• KPIs and a discussion of cause and effect • Linkages between business indicators and explanations ("because we reduced our prices and raised our quality, we increased market share by 10% and overall profitability increased by 6%") • Discussions on positive business contributions, areas for improvement, and desired future competitive positioning
8	Future Sales Opportunities	• Short-term: needed management support and financial guidance • Mid-term: budgets and approvals that may be needed • Longer-term: roadmaps and required investments
9	Recommendations to Move Forward	• Concluding comments • Recommendations • Required support from management • Discussion of risks • Action items

great satisfaction in being a product manager who knows the product's business inside and out, who can converse about its current situation, and who can depict a future vision to management and to the team. It is also tremendously gratifying when you meet your CEO in the elevator and she says, "How's your product doing?"

Step B. Recast the Vision for the Product

Refer back to the model in Figure 10.3. Product managers are usually expected to have a vision for their product—a vision of what they want to see for their "business" at some point in the future. This is a powerful statement for a powerful requirement. *Vision* is considered one of those "non-negotiables" for CEOs, and is often a non-negotiable for product managers.

In all my years of being a Product Management leader and in all my experience working with my clients, conveying—or trying to convey—the importance of vision is often quite frustrating. One reason is that not all product managers have the innate sense of a vision for the product. If you inherit a product, vision isn't a genetic transplant. So, if you are a newer product manager or if you've inherited the product, it's likely that you may not "see" that vision right away. Vision stems from passion for an idea, a cause, a goal. Think of Richard Branson's Virgin Group or Steve Jobs's legacy at Apple. Think of Steven Haines and his vision to professionalize Product Management. To me, vision is the dream you have for your product or business.

But what do you do if you aren't a mystic visionary? As an alternative, picture your product as realistically as you can and try to answer this question: In two or three years, if you needed an industry analyst to portray your product, or if you wanted a customer to write the most incredible testimonial about the product, what would you want them to say?

Or try this: Think about all of the product's virtues. List how its use makes life or business better. List any other positives you can think of. Use this method to articulate your vision when it isn't passionately engraved in your heart. And, remember, not every product can inspire passion, and some temperaments don't access emotion easily.

Based on my experience with thousands of product managers in my workshops and working with hundreds of my executive-level clients, I have learned that cultivating product vision can be difficult because by its very nature it defies definition. After wondering how to help those who have trouble developing vision, I came up with these exercises. People learn to list their good qualities when they can't envision themselves realistically, and it works for a product as well.

Continue to maintain a deep sense of where you want to take your product, new or otherwise, and that force that will help you drive your product and establish your position of leadership.

A couple of other secrets to innovative future product success reside in your efforts to uncover problems customers don't know of, or in solving problems with resourcefulness and creativity. However, creativity and innovation are not available on demand. Chapter 8 on market segmentation offers some procedures you can use to learn about customer anthropology. These techniques may give you clues that assist in your quest for the next new thing while making sure the ideas you evolve remain true to your strategic future vision.

Step C. Identify Strategic Options

Now that you have gone through the entire baseline exercise and considered your vision, your next challenge is to mull over each and every category of data you have analyzed and develop a going-forward, *integrated strategy* for the product as a business. Based on the product's market, financial, and operational performance and a new perspective on the vision, what's next?

The work that you do to get your baseline and recast your vision is all about being able to figure out what's next. This chapter is placed where it is in this book for a reason.

The outcomes from the strategic product planning process are designed to provide one of the key inputs to the front end of the Product Management Life Cycle Model—specifically, the area called Discovery and Innovation. The categories of work you carried out in collecting the data to form your baseline—where the product is now—are generally the same categories that you will use in recasting opportunities for the future as you define which opportunities you might pursue and why, and over what future time frames.

This is where the template shown as Figure 10.19 comes in. This template can be used to guide your future strategic options for the product as a business. As in many of the templates used in this chapter, it contains descriptive categories and a series of cells. Each cell has to be populated with a piece of data, an activity, or action. In this case there are six main categories (listed below) supported by a host of subcategories, as well as three columns that represent specific future time frames. For your product, you'll want a matrix like this, with the proper level of detail, to establish your strategic intent

1. Dimensions of the market on which you'll focus
2. The resources you'll need
3. Product roadmap elements
4. Other marketing mix elements
5. Product life cycle performance indicators
6. Strategic operational performance

I have an expression I use to describe the integration of these six categories. I call it the "strategic mix." The expression is useful because it extends the metaphor of the marketing mix into the entire suite of interrelated business elements that, when taken together, form a holistic strategic profile for the product.

Review the content of each of the subelements. The cells next to each row should be populated by explicit work activities. In other words, each cell requires action: "What are we going to do this upcoming year, in one to two years, and three or more years out?" Every one of the categories and cells must be interrelated. Using this template simplifies the "game board" for your strategic planning activities because it allows you to see all of the pieces and how each will evolve over time.

This future state set of opportunities and actions cannot possibly be cast in a vacuum. Remember, the product manager leads the cross-functional product team and provides the facilitated guidance to help determine the most plausible, market-oriented opportunities for the next several years.

Beyond this are the action steps that must follow. Strategies for the product require a high level of cross-functional buy-in because the team is responsible for carrying out these strategies. Therefore, Functional Support Plans (FSPs) should always be drafted to answer the question, "If we do these things, what will we need to do to support them and execute?"

FIGURE 10.19

The Product as a Business Strategic Planning Template

Strategic Elements for the Product as a Business			Less Than 1 Year	1–2 Years	3+ Years
Market Focus	Industry	• Industry trends & movement (PRESTO) • Areas on which to focus			
	Competitors	• Who will we face in the market? • What products will we need to compete? • How will we attack or defend our position?			
	Customers	• Which market segments are the most attractive? • Which customer types within a segment are worth pursuing? • How will customer needs evolve?			
Needed Resources	Financial	• Money required for product investments • Money required for marketing programs			
	People, Skills, Capabilities	• What are the technical skills that are required? • Which functional disciplines are most critical?			
	Support (Legal, Regulatory, etc.)	• In each market, what are the legal requirements? • How will regulatory change affect our strategy?			
Product Roadmap Elements	Functional Evolution	• Which functionality will be created or added? • Which attributes/features will support the functionality? • What are the requirements for performance, reliability, etc.?			
	Platforms & Technologies	• What are the key architectures to be deployed? • What technologies will be leveraged across the organization?			
	Designs, Styles, Colors, Models, etc.	• What designs & versions are needed for each segment? • How will these attributes, variations, or versions be produced?			

PRESTO = political, regulatory, economic, social, technolocial, and other

Strategic Elements for the Product as a Business			Less Than 1 Year	1–2 Years	3+ Years
Other Marketing Mix Elements	Pricing	• What value proposition will suit a given market segment? • What list prices & discounts will be established? • How will prices be set with respect to the other mix elements?			
	Advertising & Promotion	• Which programs will be used to generate leads? • Which campaigns will be used to drive website traffic?			
	Sales & Channels	• Which sales people will be deployed to sell the product? • What are the optimal channels of distribution?			
Future Life Cycle Performance Indicators	Unit Volumes	• What are the forecast volumes by product/category? • What is the optimal sales mix? • What production capacity is required?			
	Customer Satisfaction	• What "net promoter score" or equivalent metric will we track? • What items will we track on our customer report cards?			
	Market Share	• What market share will we obtain based on volumes and prices? • How will we grow market share in desired market areas?			
Strategic Operational Performance Indicators	Product Quality	• How will we source and manage our ecosystem partners? • What performance and quality standards will we employ?			
	Service, Repair, & Return	• What are acceptable defect levels? • What service levels will we work toward?			
	Inventory Management	• What are acceptable turnover levels? • What are the decision criteria for safety stock?			

The FSPs are drafted because the alternatives to be considered for the product are not complete, even though the exercise has reached this milestone. The real goal in applying this planning model is the determination of what *could* be done and what the team recommends within the context of the overall strategic vision and goals for the product. Usually, your team will not get funding for long-term projects. However, they may earn placeholder status in the budget so that, at an appropriate time in the future, these opportunities may enter the New Product Development funnel and be analyzed, along with other opportunities, with a Business Case. Some opportunities may receive incremental funding for current projects (products currently in development, products being readied for launch, and the ongoing funding of existing products).

This product as a business strategy model is connected to Step D, which depicts the Product Management Life Cycle Model and the New Product Development process (shown underneath the New Product Planning work area)—not as committed work plans but as new product ideas and product enhancement possibilities.

As you will learn in the next chapter, the product team is going to be considering many opportunities over of the course of the next year. It is not possible for all of those unplanned-for opportunities to be implemented. One of the key determinants of whether an idea or an opportunity is worthwhile to pursue is to decide whether it is tied to the strategy for the product and, furthermore, whether it is tied to the strategy of the division or company. This is why, as you will learn, there are successive phases of product planning that enable the team to consider a variety of ideas and opportunities, not just the ones that were driven out of the strategic planning process.

A Note on Product Roadmaps

If you'd like to learn more about product roadmaps (which are different from *strategy*, although many treat them otherwise), please turn to Chapter 20. There is a lot of variation in the types of roadmaps developed based on the audience—people who are internal or external to the firm. In Chapter 20, I discuss the roadmap as a way to portray a visual *statement of intent* that reflects the broad themes outlined for the product's functional and technical evolution. I'll also discuss why it's a great tool to align the people on your cross-functional team and to set the stage for effective prioritization. I'm sure you'll find that material quite helpful.

SUMMARY

The strategy of a company or one of its divisions is formulated by its executives. It is the game plan that stakes out the firm's industry posture and competitive position. Product managers have the responsibility of creating a vision and strategy for their products, consistent with the division's or company's strategy.

There isn't any magic involved in strategic planning at the product level. What is involved is a lot of hard work in collecting and using data to reveal secrets about the markets within which you operate, the customers you serve, the internal stakeholders who are supposed to deliver the systems and infrastructure elements that support the business, and excellent service and support of customers. The main barometers are the financials, marketing, and other business metrics that are the most relevant and serve to provide the signals that allow you to navigate the turbulent seas of your marketplace.

The game plan is a complex, interrelated group of activities that are related to the market in which the product is sold, the infrastructure supporting the product, and the elements of the marketing mix, all of which, when brought together, create the most advantageous strategic mix for your product as a business.

RAISING YOUR PRODUCT MANAGEMENT EXPERIENCE QUOTIENT (PMEQ)

1. When it comes to strategy, one of the first things to do is determine what's happening in your own company and/or division. Here's a list of information you should collect and understand.

   - What is the company's stated mission and vision?

   - What is the explicitly stated competitive advantage the company strives for (e.g., low cost or differentiation)?

   - What are the primary financial and human resources the company capitalizes on to achieve its strategy?

   - How effective is the current strategy?

2. Keep current on what's happening with other companies. Read business publications such as the *Wall Street Journal, Forbes,* and *Fortune* to learn

about how other companies craft and carry out strategies. Also, take a look at publications such as *The Harvard Business Review* and *MIT Sloan Management Review*. These institutions continually study companies and report on what they learn.

3. Research the product strategies of your competitors. Try to formulate a side-by-side comparison of your product against the competitor's products. How do its products' strategies differ from yours? What outcomes is it achieving and why?

4. Locate any product-related strategic planning documents, roadmaps, and various plans used by other product teams in your company. This will allow you to learn from others—both about their successes and their documented areas for improvement.

5. If you don't have all of the material, devise a plan to secure that data over some time period. Involve people in other business functions in securing some of the data so that you can build a shared purpose for the ultimate use of that data.

6. Create a game board like the one shown in Figure 10.18 to help you establish a historical perspective for the business of the product. If you create a laminated wall poster out of it, when attached to a wall, it will provide you (and other team members) with a birds-eye view of your product as a business.

7. Make sure that you store the documentation you collect. This could be in a Product Master Plan repository, on a Product Management community file server, or other convenient place.

8. Create a SWOT for your product over a period of days or weeks. Use the method suggested in this chapter to secure as much data on your own and then work with people on your team or others who may be associated with the product to come up with the "what, why, and data sources" that will help you create a useful SWOT for the product.

9. If you don't own the vision for the product you're associated with, find out who owns (or created) the vision for the product or product line. Try to discover how the vision came about and how it may have evolved. If you understand this, you will understand the "why" of the work everyone on your team is carrying out—or you will pause to question why the team is heading in that direction.

10. Everyone wants to know where they fit in the bigger picture and why. If you do own your product and the vision for it, and are really able to articulate where you want to go, have you made it clear enough to others so they "get it"? Also, you may wish to talk with other cross-functional stakeholders to get their impression of what they see or intuit from you as the product lead. Taking the strategic pulse of those around you may help you when resetting the strategic vision and reexamining this future state for the product.

11. As a product manager, your job will be to communicate with others about the strategy or strategies you developed with your team. Use techniques from marketing communications such as making up a small poster or laminated card that articulates the mission of your product team, the vision for the product, and the strategic goals. Be sure to use action words such as *deliver, demonstrate,* and *achieve.*

12. After you conduct product strategy reviews for management, think about adding product and market review sessions with the team members from each business function. For instance, have a breakfast get-together before the workday gets started (this means bring food). Create a 20- to 30-minute presentation of the state of your business, and, for reinforcement, emphasize some of the key imperatives that are to be carried out in the future. To instill more interest and greater *esprit,* you could even split the presentation with other cross-functional team members to demonstrate unity and commitment to the strategy.

MODULE 3

THE START OF THE PRODUCT'S JOURNEY: THE NEW PRODUCT DEVELOPMENT PROCESS

INTRODUCTION TO MODULE 3

Plans are only good intentions unless they immediately degenerate into hard work.

—PETER DRUCKER

I have worked with many companies to dissect failed launches and Business Cases gone awry. I've also had my own share of product performance issues during my tenure as a product manager and as a product team leader. Along the way, I've built up a repertoire of reasons why products might fail to perform in the market or miss their financial objectives. You can also find some of these insights among the vast amount of literature written about New Product Development (NPD) and why products fail.

One of the most frequently cited root causes of these problems seems to be lack of attention to detail. Critical details, small and large, were overlooked or passed over during what *should* have been product and market planning. In almost every case, even though plans were formulated, results didn't live up to the plans. There are many reasons for these performance issues, and some of the most conspicuous include the following:

1. Teams are not clear on roles, deliverables, or timing.

2. Market cues and customer needs are misinterpreted.

3. Market sizing models are built on incorrect segmentation models or incorrect assumptions.

4. Customers have unrealistic expectations.

5. Forecasts are inaccurate.

6. Technical problems plague the product through its development and after the launch. In fact, many products should never have been launched at all due to some of those technical problems.

7. Product requirements are incomplete or inaccurately portray the customer's needs, causing a tremendous amount of rework, both during development and product trials and after the launch.

8. No one ever tested the concept with a prototype or model, and there was no evidence of user or customer feedback.

9. Operational systems and infrastructure elements are not prepared (or are ill equipped) to support the product in the market.

10. Salespeople are either untrained or not given correct incentives to sell the product.

11. Value propositions are miscast because they do not capture the benefits from the customer's point of view, or they focus on the wrong customer type.

12. The product is not positioned correctly in the market.

13. Channels are not correctly set up to adequately distribute the product, or the channels cannot accommodate products due to insufficient capacity.

14. Manufacturing cannot produce the product to specifications.

15. Team members do not realize that activities take longer than originally anticipated or are not fully committed to execution.

16. Pricing does not reflect the value proposition or benefits from the customer's perspective.

17. Insufficient money or resources are allocated for advertising, promotional programs, or customer education—or there *are* no promotional programs.

18. The products are not different enough to inspire the purchase.

This list is just the tip of the iceberg. You can probably think of numerous reasons not mentioned here.

After conducting benchmark research and diagnostics for more than two decades, I've noticed that these problems most often stem from issues related to the planning and development process—that is, the NPD process. The NPD process is bound by the period of time from when an idea is first considered up until the resulting product is launched into the market. Some call this "cycle time."

It's not that there is an absence of process. Almost all companies have some kind of phased NPD process. Occasionally, there is no real planning process because the boss or owner just tells people what to develop. Notwithstanding that anomaly, more often, planning processes and methods are poorly understood, resulting in inefficiency, lack of consistency, employee frustration, and, most problematic, an inability to properly execute whatever plans were derived. This incongruity is apparent in different companies, different industries, and even in the same business unit or division. Sometimes processes are so ambiguous that no amount of effort and enthusiasm can fill the gap. Even when a formal process model is used, its interpretation varies widely. Some people take the process as a highly rigid set of edicts and checklists. Some take a more amorphous approach, preferring to skip over needed analyses. Some just don't have the data or resources required to do the work.

By helping you understand these issues, or by validating what you may have experienced, I offer you the hope that there is a way forward. If the root cause of product and process failure is understood, then product managers and their teams can make the changes necessary. This means that you have to understand the work that has to be done and how to do that work. Furthermore, you have to know when to carry out the work as products move from idea to market.

There is a major root cause beneath every one of these reactions to the NPD process: a failure to do the work that is required during the phase so that appropriate decisions can be made. The failure to do the work is related to the fact that people either don't know how to do pieces of the work because of skill or competency gaps, or they don't take the time to do what is necessary. When results don't materialize and the new innovations don't bubble up, management believes that the process is flawed and must be replaced. I have worked with several companies who believed their "new" NPD process model would solve all problems. But in comparing the "old" process to the "new" process, the only differences would be the names of the phases or an increase or decrease in the number of phases and gates.

Furthermore, when a process model is adopted, product leadership often fails to take complete ownership or to establish consistent governance policies. Therefore, the novelty wears off when consultants go home. In many cases, even if the process is supported and maintained, and even when people are trained to use the process, ambiguities drive team members to overanalyze data or to make quick, shallow decisions that don't consider the downstream consequences that will result when (and if) the product makes it to the market.

LIMITS AND BENEFITS OF PROCESSES

Processes are useful to have. Larger, complex organizations have a greater need for standard processes and procedures. A reliable product planning process gives you a *better* set of guidelines from which to organize and carry out work, clarify roles and responsibilities, and improve collaborative decision making in a team environment. However, in product planning and development, any phased process model should only be considered a framework or guide. Markets are too dynamic to apply a rigid linear process for each and every opportunity. Too much rigidity ends up choking the organization, paralyzing team members into inaction, or specifying functional resources that do not have the appropriate skill set or that are simply not available.

A phased process should be adopted for the right reasons. For example, trying to reduce cycle time with structured planning models has achieved, at best, mixed results. Consider Abbie Griffen's article appearing in the *Journal of Engineering and Technology Management* (Elsevier, 1997), "Modeling and Measuring Product Development Cycle Time Across Industries." She undertook a research project to determine if companies actually *could* improve cycle times using a variety of approaches, including a formal product development process. In the conclusion, she states, ". . . higher product complexity *increases* NPD cycle time and using a cross-functional team *reduces* product development cycle time early in the process, before physical development has begun." In the real world, it's nearly impossible to attribute cycle time reduction to the use of a product development process because all projects are different.

Process is not a *source* of creativity, but it is an *enabler* of creative, inventive ideas. A structured process does not infuse your team with creativity and vision. Design, style, service, and unique customer experiences aren't driven by process elements—they come from the minds of astute, market-focused people with a sixth sense for creativity and inventiveness. By standardizing mundane, rote parts of the process and ensuring that the right information is visible to the right people at the right time, a solid planning and development process will make it much easier for you and your team to come up with creative solutions to customer problems. Thus, my ultimate aim for you is to make sure that you *keep everything you do focused on the market,* so that you can ensure that the products you conceive, develop, and introduce have a much higher likelihood of being successful.

A GENERIC PHASE GATE MODEL

For the most part, I am a strong advocate of a *flexible* phased product planning and development, or NPD, process. This series of chapters focuses on the workflow included in the phases, decision gates, and documents related to the areas of work in the Product Management Life Cycle Model called *New Product Planning* and *New Product Introduction.*

By the way, the word *new* should not be misconstrued to mean a brand new product never before seen by the market. The "new" idea might be an enhancement to an existing product, product line, portfolio, or product platform. "New" in this context is meant to convey "different from what we're currently doing." After all, what is a new product? Is it a revolutionary new idea, never seen before by your competitors or your markets? Is it a new product area for your company? Is it a totally new take on a very old product? Or is it a set of features so revolutionary that you completely remake the product? But here's the good news: From the perspective of the Product Management Life Cycle Model, it doesn't really matter whether you're starting with a green field or a huge portfolio of existing products. The thought process behind what you do—and for the most part, how you do it—is exactly the same. Just because you've inherited a mature, stand-alone product, you shouldn't assume that creativity doesn't apply, or that there's no need to consider new ideas. You simply begin to gather and validate ideas that may meet your objectives, without being overly concerned about whether you're working on a new product or some derivative of an existing one.

This holds true for companies that produce tangible products, services, or even software or systems. There may be some variances such as in the pharmaceutical industry, where there is a high degree of experimentation within a scientific community—but even there, if you examine the regulatory process for pharmaceutical development and testing, you'll find a phased decision-making process as well.

No matter what kind of product idea (new or existing), and no matter what form it takes (tangible versus intangible), it is very important to emphasize this point of using the process flexibly, yet consistently, in order to avoid confusion among cross-functional product team members.

PROCESSES ARE LINEAR, MARKETS ARE NOT

NPD process models, as typically presented, are shown as a *linear system* model. They are *linear* because they go along a line from left to right, and they are *system* models because there are definable inputs, activities, and outputs. Sometimes, though, the process looks more like a boiler room operation, as depicted in the amusing diagram shown in Figure M3.1. Perhaps you can identify with this process as well.

A high-quality generic product planning and development process is represented *within* the Product Management Life Cycle Model and is shown with its associated phases and gates in Figure M3.2.

This is the same diagram used in Chapter 1 (Figure 1.8) in the section "How Does Product Management Transform a Product?" Refer back to that chapter and that section to refresh your general understanding about each of the areas of work, as well as the underlying phases and gates. Also a good idea: begin reading each of the subsequent chapters.

IMPORTANCE OF THE RIGHT PACE FOR NEW PRODUCT PLANNING

Proper pace is the greatest planning challenge for product managers and their teams. Essentially, they must work a linear model so that the team can go as quickly as possible yet go slowly enough to cover all areas of concern. Many product managers plan as if seated on a high-speed passenger train reading a book. They can see the book directly in front of their face but cannot really process the rapidly moving countryside passing by the window. Product managers and their teams do *not* need to take the train. Instead, they need to walk along their journey so that they

Product Planning Boiler Room Operation

The Product Management Life Cycle Model (© Sequent Learning Networks)

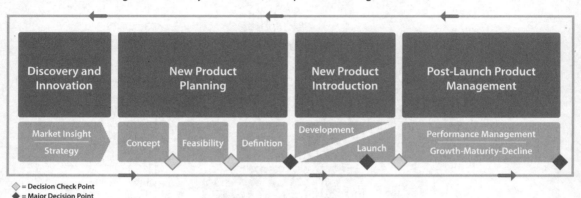

can take in the details. I cannot emphasize this enough: *You must slow down enough during planning so that you can go faster later.* This is exemplified by the size of the rectangle representing the New Product Planning area of work in the Product Management Life Cycle Model. If you overlook an operational detail (such as establishing a product code in an ordering system), you will spend hours or days fixing that problem instead of paying attention to important market signals. A senior product leader in a major bank recently shared her thoughts about this with me when she asked, "If you don't take the time to do things right now, how will you ever have the time to do anything later?"

This need for careful planning explains why New Product Planning spans the largest space in the Product Management Life Cycle Model. Planning *should* take longer, allowing for more purposeful, focused execution later. What you *don't* want to do is spend your time during development and after the launch fixing things you could have anticipated with better planning. That doesn't mean everything will work perfectly, and there will always be some clean-up after the launch—but not a major product overhaul. Once the product is in the market, you should be able to spend the bulk of your time restrategizing and replanning to take advantage of dynamic opportunities.

But wait. If speed and agility are important, are all new product projects the same? No, not all product projects are the same. Brand new product ideas require more thought and robust analysis than an enhancement for an existing product. With an existing product, you (hopefully) already have good industry, competitive, customer, and financial data so the amount of research you need is lowered. This is best exemplified in Figure M3.3, where you can see three different visualizations of the phases of New Product Planning. In the top row for the *new product*, you see the phases and gates organized sequentially, spanning a specific time frame that appears to be longer in duration than that shown in the subsequent rows below, called out as either a major or a minor product enhancement. This portrays the fact that when you have enough market and product performance data about a current product's business, you don't need to do as much research to figure out what to do; you "compress" the phases, moving more rapidly through them. It's a good idea to make sure that you classify your product projects as they come up for consideration. You can classify them by type, as shown in Figure M3.3, and then by other means such as complexity, amount of time anticipated, and financial resources required.

FIGURE M.3.3

Flexible Usage of Phases and Gates During New Product Planning

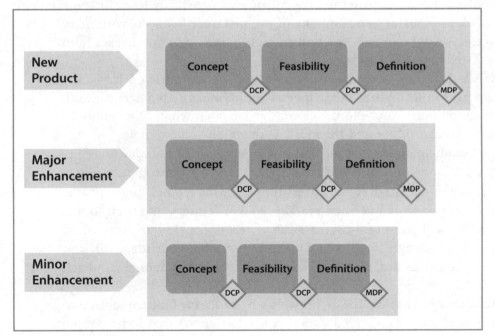

DCP = Decision Check Point
MDP = Major Decision Point

If the team spends the right amount of time planning, then it can execute with ease, speed, and agility, whether it's a complex new product or a simple product enhancement. Thorough planning helps you anticipate and overcome problems and improves your chances of cultivating products that contribute to the economic value and market strength of the company.

FASTER IS NOT ALWAYS BETTER, BUT IT CAN'T HURT

One of the things I learned from starting my own company was the need for laser-sharp focus on vision, purpose, and execution. The only thing that mattered to me was getting to market as fast as possible with a high-quality product that would earn a good reputation. After more than a dozen years, I can tell you that just because I wanted to move quickly didn't mean that the market wanted to move in that manner as well.

In the business environment of the twenty-first century, the word *lean* is frequently used to denote speed or agility. Athletic sprinters with toned muscles and little body fat can jump over hurdles, run fast, and pivot when needed because they are considered physically lean. In some cases, such as in a start-up company or even a larger firm, the word *lean* is sometimes used to mean "in good enough shape" to get to market (and profit) faster than a competitor.

While I am an advocate of moving quickly and efficiently, as any business person is, I believe that speed should be regulated according to certain guidelines. You should carefully consider what "fast enough" means for your product and the markets in which you compete.

As I study businesses, I see definite links between practice and performance. When you think you have a great idea for a product, it needs to be verified and tested. If you spend time creating a mock-up or prototype in the absence of a verified market need or strategy and rush to test the concept, will you make the best use of resources at your disposal? If you are lucky enough to get some customers to like your idea, will you have analyzed your organization's capability to develop, launch, and sell the product?

Take another look at the 18 reasons why products fail, as mentioned earlier. Based on the collected data, I can safely assert that most people who think they have a great idea fail to see a broad picture of market, strategy, technology, and capacity. In other words, they do not see things the way a product manager should see the world. Keep in mind that you must first fully appreciate the dynamics of business before you make decisions to commit resources. If you move too quickly and try to be too lean up front, you may miss the market.

THE VALUE OF FLAWLESS EXECUTION

The Area of Work called New Product Introduction (NPI) requires much less time to carry out than does New Product Planning. As mentioned earlier, you should go slowly during planning in order to move faster later. Well, during NPI, it's later. NPI is the time to move quickly.

NPI depicts two parallel paths: Development and Launch. The Development phase involves the work of the Product Development group itself (which might be called R&D, Engineering, or IT). Development may include the final designs and production of a physical product, software development, or any other type of activity involved in fulfilling the product definition. Launch, the other parallel path, involves the work of people in the other business functions required to get the product to market. Launching involves the work of product managers, marketers, salespeople, and those from Operations, as well as any other organizations who are responsible for making sure that the product can be introduced, ordered, delivered, and billed for.

Both shapes relate like wedges; Development tapers off over time, while Launch ramps up, but each happens in lock step with the other. This is in stark contrast to what is typically portrayed in NPD documents used by most consulting firms and in the available literature about NPD, which shows typical sequencing of design, development, testing or validation, and introduction. This kind of linear sequencing can cause a product to be late to market.

Product managers must also understand how their products are developed, and which techniques are used. Despite the proliferation of rapid product development techniques such as "agile," "lean product development," or other methods, *the product manager must provide oversight during development*, ensuring that the appropriate work is taking place and that launch activities are being carried out from the time the initial project is approved. This is NPI, which is characterized by execution—where the product manager and the team get work done.

ORGANIZATION OF THE CHAPTERS IN THIS MODULE

The most important things to remember as you follow these chapters is that each one sets the stage for carrying out work. Individual phases are separated by decision points. These points are used to determine whether the work done in that phase has yielded sufficient confidence that a decision can be made to proceed to the subsequent phase or to kill the project.

The challenge of writing a book with so many interconnected elements is to make sure that every piece of work is covered sufficiently and in a logical manner. To this end, the chapters in this section are listed as follows:

Chapter 11: Making a Molehill out of a Mountain: The Concept Phase

Chapter 12: Is There Really a Business Here? Assessing Feasibility

Chapter 13: Appearances are Everything: Defining and Designing the Product

Chapter 14: Justifying Product Investments: The Business Case

Chapter 15: Synchronizing the Gears: The Marketing Plan for the Product

Chapter 16: Execution and Oversight During Product Development

Chapter 17: Introducing the Product and Orchestrating the Launch

You will find that a major topical area is handled in more detail in one chapter and mentioned many times in others. However, in real life you will be using the practices, tools, or documents across the entire life cycle. Take *positioning* for example. In the Concept phase chapter, the positioning statement is discussed and a template is provided. In subsequent chapters, and in fact throughout the product life cycle, the product's positioning will need to be reevaluated and updated.

Finally, you will find that the processes, documents, and manner of thought from hereon are dependent on all of the foundational elements discussed in Module 1 and the chapters related to "Making the Market Your Primary Focus," as discussed in Module 2. The earlier chapters have provided you with the basic tools you need to be able to lead any product on its inevitable, profitable journey.

11

MAKING A MOLEHILL OUT OF A MOUNTAIN: THE CONCEPT PHASE

Executive Summary

- New product concepts come from a variety of sources, including intensive market analysis, observation, and even structured ideation activities.
- There are always going to be more ideas than there are resources to commercialize them. Not all ideas will make good business sense. A structured process helps to narrow down the field, quickly and efficiently.
- The Concept phase is really a fast-paced business decision–making process.
- Without a solid strategic plan for the product, product concepts are difficult to put into perspective.

Ideas are a dime a dozen. Good ideas are harder to come by. Product and service ideas that will make it in the marketplace and produce a profit at the same time are the rarest of all. Every day you're bombarded with a barrage of opportunities and product ideas, and from those, you cull a number of those ideas that seem to be promising. But how do you decide which of those have enough merit to be appraised further? How do you recognize the truly workable, relevant ideas to build a product on?

Finally, how do you decide which ones go through to the work-intensive Feasibility phase and which ones get pushed off the table as time goes on? This chapter will put all of these questions into perspective as we explore the Concept phase, which is the first phase of the New Product Planning Area of Work.

THE BASIC PROCESS

I don't want to overstate the obvious, but it's impossible to evaluate, in detail, all of the ideas for new products or product enhancements that come across your desk. The Concept phase is designed to help you rapidly vet a large number of ideas so a more manageable number of ideas can be evaluated in the subsequent phase. The main idea is to drive the concepts that have the best chance to achieve success in your chosen segments. The inputs, activities, and outputs of the Concept phase are shown in Figure 11.1

Starting with viable ideas from a variety of sources (Inputs), the product manager assembles a small core team to assess the worthiness of each possible candidate (Activities) and to discuss (and document) its intent in an *Opportunity Statement* (Outputs). When an opportunity is considered worthy of additional analysis, the product team usually presents its findings to the product portfolio review board with its recommendation and a request for additional funding to support further analysis in the Feasibility phase.

FIGURE 11.1

The Concept Phase Process Profile

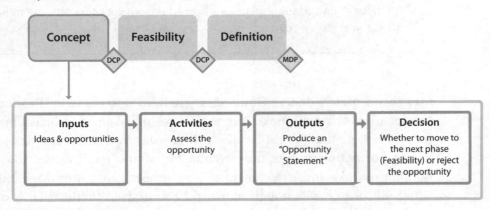

DCP = Decision Check Point
MDP = Major Decision Point

IDEATION: WHAT'S THE BIG IDEA?

As quarterback of the cross-functional team, the product manager's mantra should be "What's next?" What signals can you spot? What is the source? How significant are they to your product? Always keep in mind that every source of useful information about your product is also a source of potential opportunities. Whether you're developing strategy, reporting on the state of the business, studying your industry, scoping out the competitive environment, or segmenting markets, you will encounter clues to customer or market problems that haven't been solved or could use a fresh approach to improve them. New products or enhancements can be developed to solve new problems as the unmet needs of existing ones are discovered; or a fresh approach can be used on evolving problems as they arise from the market's reactions to existing products. Either way, you need ideas to solve these problems—ideas that have "staying power"—which we define as ideas that will capture and hold market share while producing a profit.

Ideation is the term used to define the methods and techniques that generate ideas through market sensing, market exploration, and other discovery techniques. Ideation is often associated with innovation, which seems a natural connection. Product managers shape the future state of a product with their vision, and that vision is shaped by their knowledge of the relevant markets.

For this discussion, I am referring to active ideation, not some process of sitting back and waiting for inspiration to come. You and your team must point your ideation "telescope" at the marketplace and adjust the lens properly to scan the market for signals. As you scan the market horizon with your ideation telescope, adjust the focus for both near and far away to scope out details and the bigger picture. Just as you'd use a telescope, move your lens carefully. Scrutinize all facets of patterns, trends, and other signals attentively. Don't zip past vital signs, or you may miss something without even knowing it.

Market-based patterns and trends are the first places on which to focus your ideation lens because they contain a lot of material to take in. Delve into and research the many sources of market information: review trade journals and business publications, visit customers, scan your daily informational feeds, read synopses from your competitive intelligence group, review relevant blogs, and check into any other sources you can think of. Doing this will help you identify many useful indicators.

Furthermore, you should be sharing the knowledge you gather with your cross-functional team on a continuous basis. After all, the product manager is not the sole contributor to the ideation process. Each and every team member is a source of ideas and opportunities.

As a matter of fact, for ideation, it is vital that you draw on people from Marketing, R&D and/or Engineering, Materials Research, Operations, Technology, Product Design, and Market Research, to name just a few. Bring these people together for some storytelling and brainstorming. Here's why:

- Storytelling allows people to express what they've seen, heard, or read in a way that builds context. These stories can, of course, include visuals, diagrams, and mind maps to connect ideas to implications, issues, systems, people, or other random topics that may emerge.
- Brainstorming helps stimulate "so what?" questions, allowing the team to identify potential answers that may clarify problems or inspire solutions.
- Many consultants and facilitators are good at carrying out this kind of end-user research and translating it into compelling product ideas that solve customer problems in unique ways. You may find it useful to get some support from one of these expert resources.

A few years ago, an article appeared in a business periodical that talked about a project undertaken by a large, multilocation hospital and a design firm. In a time of increased attention on improving the quality of health care, the hospital's strategy was to *attract more patients and reduce costs*.

The initial meetings involved nurses, doctors, and facilities managers from the hospital along with social scientists, designers, and architects from the design firm. Teams from both organizations observed patients making their way through the hospital's medical facilities. At times, team members even played the role of patients themselves. Together, they came up with some surprising insights. The design firm's team revealed that patients and their family often became annoyed well before seeing a doctor because checking in was a nightmare and waiting rooms were uncomfortable. The design firm's cognitive psychologists pointed out that while many people—especially the young, the old, and immigrants—bring a parent or friend along, that second person is often not allowed to stay with the patient, leaving the afflicted individual alienated and anxious. Patients hated the examination rooms because they often had to wait alone for an extended period of time in a cold room with nothing to do, surrounded by threatening needles and other medical items. The two teams concluded that the patient experience was frequently awful, even when people left treated and cured.

The study led to the following conclusion: The hospital needed to overhaul the patient experience. All parties learned that seeking medical care is much like shopping—a social experience shared with others. The hospital needed to offer more comfortable waiting rooms; a lobby with clear instructions regarding where to go; larger exam rooms, with space for three or more people and curtains for privacy, to make patients comfortable; and special corridors for medical staffers to meet and increase their efficiency.

Notice that the experts on the team were from unrelated fields. They were social scientists, psychologists, facilities managers, doctors, and nurses. A mixed group of experts (a true cross-functional team) all brought different perspectives to the problem, based on different paradigms and experiences. They all had their ideation lenses focused and filtered with a strong dose of the human element.

This is why real market and customer focus is vital to the success of your products. The most important takeaway is this: It doesn't matter one bit how good your process is if you can't come up with some ideas that make your product unique, separating it from its competition. And if the product can't be differentiated because the market has commoditized it, than hopefully your company has either a respected brand, great service, or some really great way to inspire sales.

EXPERIMENTATION AND DISCOVERY

Most companies have an organization called Research and Development, or R&D. Most often, firms focus on the "D"—that is, the development and commercialization of products. Unfortunately, many organizations do not pay close enough attention to the "R"—the research. In pharmaceutical companies, the discovery of new compounds through research is usually guided by the firm's strategic intent. For example, a company that wants to focus on immune system ailments won't usually invest in research for heart disease. Research is important, and I suggest that you think about this as you progress through your careers.

While most product managers are not scientists, they should have a good sense of the domain in which they operate. Therefore, in my opinion, they should be given adequate time to do some of their own discovery. While doing research to write this book, I learned that a number of firms actually encourage product managers to spend some time "offline," not involved in the day-to-day management of their product's business. Instead, they may travel to observe or interact with customers, visit laboratories, or do their own research. Indeed, these creative adventures may not result in big "aha" moments. However, they may inspire you to think about a customer problem in a new way—and yes, maybe lead to an idea for a new product, enhancement, or technique to improve user experience.

In the firms that permit this work, small teams of people may be involved in the creation of a prototype, working model, design, or other representation of an idea. In some cases, they may be able to test the concept with certain customers who have been vetted for such purposes. In other cases, the ideas may be shown to leaders of a product portfolio board who sanction this work.

If the executive leadership team or an associated product portfolio review board believes this work is worthwhile and wants to devote funds to further experimentation and discovery, it may choose to put the opportunity into the standard phase gate process within the Concept phase. Alternatively, it may decide on a faster track to market outside of the phase gate process. Either way, I strongly recommend that product managers and their leaders provide for this work and engage it on an ongoing basis. If you feel that this work is not officially sanctioned, know that it is still within the realm of your responsibility to take some time for creative thought and ideation. Whether it's an hour a week to read articles related to areas of interest, industry association information, or research from a university, you can and should take a time-out and allow your mind to think of what's possible.

CATEGORIZATION OF PRODUCT "PROJECTS"

When I carry out diagnostic activities in a company or facilitate a workshop, I usually ask participants about their product ideas. Everyone is enthusiastic about their ideas until I ask the question, "Where do you keep those ideas?" Answers range from "on my laptop" to "in a spreadsheet" to "in my head." These are not the most nurturing places for ideas to germinate. In fact, many better mousetraps have never seen the light of day because they got lost in a drawer full of "stuff." Some companies have idea repositories, which in itself is a great idea. I like the suggestion box metaphor. Any interested party, whether inside or outside of the company, should be able to submit ideas. Suggestion templates on websites and e-mails to a suggestion inbox are just two methods for collecting ideas.

Once collected, these ideas have to be processed. First, all ideas should be classified by the idea type:

1. A minor enhancement to a product, such as a new feature or attribute
2. A major enhancement to a product or a grouping of features or attributes
3. A brand new product or a derivative
4. A new or upgraded product platform
5. A breakthrough product unlike anything that exists in the category

Classifying ideas is useful because it quickly determines the amount of work needed to follow up on the idea. Too often, product ideas and opportunities are focused on the first two—minor or major product improvements or enhancements. New products, platforms, and breakthroughs tend to provide better prospects for the longer term.

The next categorization is the idea source or motivation for the idea. Figure 11.2 contains many of the most common idea sources. To the right of the figure is an arrow with a question mark meaning, "What do we do with this?"

SORTING OUT OPPORTUNITIES

The ideas and opportunities collected, categorized, and listed will continue to accumulate until the product manager and team decide to do something further with them. Because there are usually many concepts, they tend to build up like drops of water in a bucket. If your "bucket" gets too full, it will overflow and good ideas may get lost. An *opportunity inventory* will help you keep track of what you have in "stock." If you use a standard repository, at least it's easier to check what's in your

FIGURE 11.2

Idea Categories

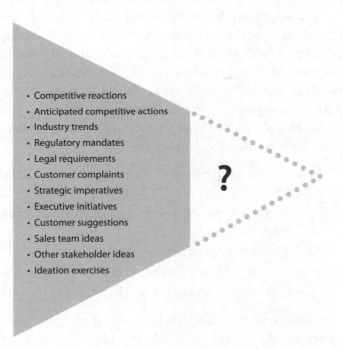

- Competitive reactions
- Anticipated competitive actions
- Industry trends
- Regulatory mandates
- Legal requirements
- Customer complaints
- Strategic imperatives
- Executive initiatives
- Customer suggestions
- Sales team ideas
- Other stakeholder ideas
- Ideation exercises

opportunity inventory. It is important to review the material in the inventory on a regular basis. If the inventory builds up too much before you process it, then you may feel overwhelmed by the task and miss a vital market opportunity.

However, processing is easier said than done. With so many opportunities, you can't possibly have enough time to thoroughly investigate each one. Therefore, the initial screening of ideas, or rapid opportunity assessment, is the purpose of the Concept phase. "Rapid" means a couple of hours to a couple of days, depending on the level of complexity and perceived importance to the business. The document called the Opportunity Statement, shown as a template in Figure 11.3, is a great tool to use to capture these ideas.

The product manager doesn't evaluate ideas in a vacuum. I cannot overemphasize this point. Every idea, or perhaps "bundle" of ideas, needs to be evaluated by a subset of the cross-functional team, including the product manager, a technical person (e.g., developer, engineer, scientist, or technologist), and a marketing representative. I call these meetings

FIGURE 11.3

Opportunity Statement Template

Name of Opportunity: _____   Name of Product Manager: _____

Idea Type/Category: _____   Name of Engineer: _____

Source of the Idea: _____   Name of Marketing Manager: _____

Date of the Original Evaluation: _____   Name of the Other Evaluator: _____

Situation Summary: What is the customer's problem? Describe how this need was uncovered.

For Whom: Market segment of customer type

How would this opportunity solve the customer's problem?

How is this opportunity aligned with the division's or company's strategy?

What are the characteristics of this market that make this an attractive opportunity?

Who are the primary competitors?

High-Level Financials. Provide a rough estimate of unit volumes, pricing, revenue, and possible cost targets.

Recommendation: Should we request funding or approval to move to the Feasibility phase or should we reject and file?

"opportunity review sessions." An opportunity can usually be assessed in one or two short sessions (perhaps an hour or two each). Keep this team small to allow for a rapid appraisal. When a full team is present, there may be too many opinions in the room and the pace will slow markedly. The idea inventory is usually pretty much backed up, so these small core sessions are intended to relieve that pressure by allowing the small, agile team to quickly assess the perceived importance to the business. Figure 11.4 describes some of the roles and responsibilities of this smaller cross-functional team.

Because this is a cross-functional initiative, with a possible decision to move the opportunity to the next phase, each member of this small core team works together on the Opportunity Statement, giving input and a recommendation. Each function should estimate the level of resources they believe their team would need to commit to the product from development through discontinuation. A full Functional Support Plan (FSP) isn't necessary (yet) because the opportunity is merely being

FIGURE 11.4

Cross-Functional Team Membership During the Concept Phase

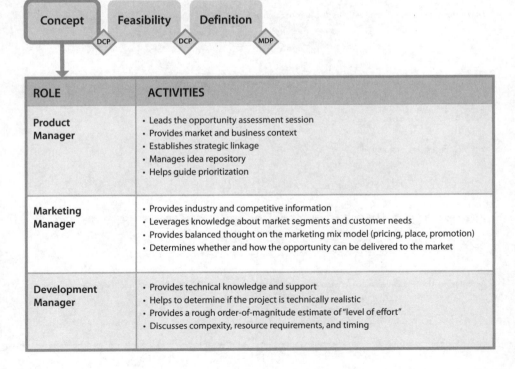

ROLE	ACTIVITIES
Product Manager	• Leads the opportunity assessment session • Provides market and business context • Establishes strategic linkage • Manages idea repository • Helps guide prioritization
Marketing Manager	• Provides industry and competitive information • Leverages knowledge about market segments and customer needs • Provides balanced thought on the marketing mix model (pricing, place, promotion) • Determines whether and how the opportunity can be delivered to the market
Development Manager	• Provides technical knowledge and support • Helps to determine if the project is technically realistic • Provides a rough order-of-magnitude estimate of "level of effort" • Discusses compexity, resource requirements, and timing

evaluated based on what is actually known by the participants in the evaluation.

Another key to rapid assessment relies on each small core team member's own storehouse of knowledge and expertise. All functional representatives must be able to discuss the opportunity based on the functional discipline they represent. If one member has to do a vast amount of new research before final discussion, it slows down the process, and the other participants will tire and lose momentum. Eventually they will stop bothering to evaluate ideas. Team members' strong familiarity with the current products, industries, customers, and technologies will speed the process. Ask more experienced team members to produce drawings, sketches, models, user interface mock-ups, or anything else that can help the team better visualize the idea and the solution.

Also, keep in mind that one of the essential items in the Opportunity Statement is a high-level financial projection that generates estimates of market sizing and revenue potential. These estimates are dependent on two fundamental practices: finance and forecasting. The process will probably slow down if you or your marketing counterpart hasn't at least a rough idea of the market size and cannot estimate potential volumes for the opportunity.

LOOKING DOWN THE PRODUCT PIPELINE

A given opportunity may be important enough to be classified as a single product "project," or it may represent several different projects. It's also possible that the opportunity may enhance (or inhibit) existing product activities. The dynamic mix of opportunities during planning has to be viewed as part of an "up-front portfolio" of opportunities. The faster the industry activity, and the faster the overall product life cycles, the more dynamic the up-front portfolio. This continually evolving up-front portfolio needs to be evaluated in light of the entire product portfolio, as depicted in Figure 11.5.

Underneath each product group are three boxes: products being planned, products being developed, and existing products. These three categories comprise the entire product portfolio. Detailing the box called "Products Being Planned" is a representation of the three phases of product planning—a visualization of the winnowing process. Planning, for the product manager, amounts to evaluating a lot of opportunities and striving to find those few that demonstrate the best business and financial attributes for the company.

FIGURE 11.5

The Up-Front Product Portfolio

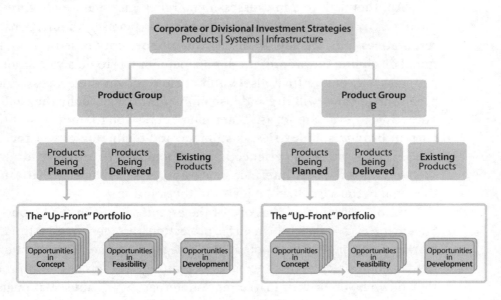

The flow of opportunities through the phases of product planning represents the dynamic product "pipeline" of new product projects. Even while you're evaluating new ideas, the speed with which product projects are moving through that pipeline must be carefully considered within the context of the entire product portfolio, not just your team's portfolio of new opportunities. In other words, even though you're still evaluating ideas, you have to look down the pipeline to see what else is "in process" and "in market."

Some call this activity "pipeline management," and it serves to govern the speed with which product projects can be considered. You can't push too much through the pipeline, or there won't be enough resources to develop, launch, and eventually manage the products in the market. In the pharmaceutical industry, the pipeline is judged by industry and market analysts to determine the chance that the company will be able to introduce a blockbuster product. (Stock analysts refer to the drug company's "new product pipeline.") Figure 11.6 illustrates the common viewpoint that the number of opportunities shrinks as the process proceeds. Ultimately, budgets dictate that only a small number of incremental projects can actually be carried out. The progressive, graduated funneling visualization

FIGURE 11.6

The Graduated Funnel

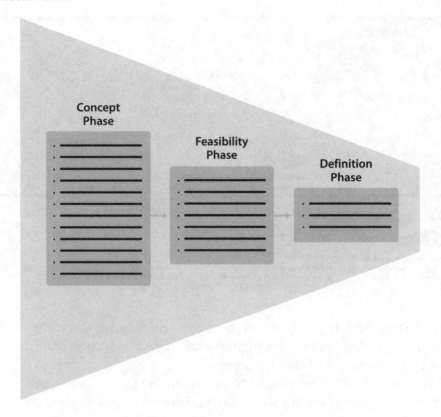

helps to make a connection. Even if you have 100 ideas, only two or three may end up coming out of the funnel.

The progressively narrowing or graduated funnel reduces the number of opportunities, thereby helping Product Management and Development practitioners apply the planning process. I'll explain why.

Think of the planning process as the on-ramp to a high-speed highway or motorway (Figure 11.7). The traffic moving on the highway itself (at high speed) is used as the representation of the existing products presently being supported in the marketplace—the existing product portfolio. The speed at which products can move along the highway is used to determine the company's product capacity. If there are too many products on the highway (in the market), then the products being launched or slated for launch may consume all the remaining capacity.

FIGURE 11.7

The Product Manager's Motorway

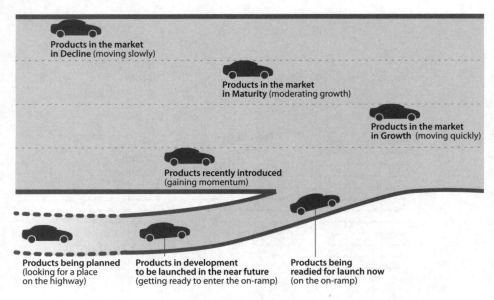

Therefore, when too many products are planned without consideration of what's already on the highway, a higher level of risk may affect the product and the reputation of the company.

As you contemplate new products or enhancements to existing products, your strategic thinking about the current situation of all the products in the market must get ample consideration. This is another reason product portfolio management is so important.

PRODUCT ENHANCEMENTS AS A GROUPED OPPORTUNITY

New opportunities are often challenging because a change in a product rarely consists of a single enhancement with a single feature. More often, a group of features or attributes are clustered together as a single product enhancement. Most product projects in companies are enhancements or upgrades to existing products.

The uniqueness of an industry often determines how enhancements are grouped. In the software or technology industry, for example, product changes are accumulated in a "release" or "version," including additional features, bug fixes, performance updates, and user interface adjustments. Consumer products may introduce a "new and improved" product, which usually involves a new package design with a new formulation. Banks may introduce a new card product with enhanced security and an easier-to-read statement. No matter what industry you work in, the product planning process is an ideal mechanism for assembling elements or groupings of product characteristics into a single opportunity. In another approach to planning, the elements of the opportunity (combinations of features, designs, content, attributes, etc.) can be adjusted for the most optimal mix.

"SO WHAT?": THE VALUE PROPOSITION FOR THE OPPORTUNITY

One of the most significant determinants of the potential success of a product opportunity is whether it brings benefits that customers value and appreciate. The true test is whether they will actually purchase the product. Such an assessment is not contingent on whether or not the customer considers the product worth buying. Questions such as, "Would you buy this product?" often yield misleading answers. Customers may give an affirmative response if asked in a survey or presented with an explicit question. What they may not do, though, is actually part with their money when faced with the decision. One reason could be that they have other purchasing decisions to make; the need the product meets is just not "urgent enough." Another could be that the idea seemed appealing when presented, but the actual product doesn't meet the customer's needs. This is why it is vitally important that the product manager, marketers, and entire team strive to identify and verify the target customer for the product and grasp what that customer needs and values most at the moment the need arises.

Information about several things is necessary to derive an effective value proposition. Equipped with the proper amount of needs-based segmentation data, four questions must be answered:

1. Who is the target customer?
2. What is the validated problem or need of that customer?
3. What would solve the problem or meet the need of that customer?
4. How can the solution's benefit be proven, either quantitatively or qualitatively?

If these questions cannot be answered substantially, it's not an effective value proposition and the opportunity should not be pursued. Perspective may help you avoid shallow, check-box answers. Try putting yourself in the customer's shoes, and ask yourself the following questions:

1. Who am I? (If a person, what age, gender, occupation, and so on? If a business, what industry, how large a firm, what products do we sell? Where do we do business?)

2. What is happening in my (personal or work) life that tells me I have some sort of problem or need? What exactly is that problem or need? Do I care enough to go further for answers?

3. What would help me solve my (explicit or implicit) problem, and how would I benefit?

4. If I were going to purchase something, how would I justify that purchase given my budget, my dissatisfaction with the present state of affairs, and my overall situation? Is it worth it to me within the context of other problems I have to solve and my limited budget?

I strongly recommend this approach when developing value propositions. It is very effective.

Here's an example. Suppose I was offered a persuasive story to convince me to purchase office automation software. The sales rep demonstrated to me that this software would save 10 hours per week for one $25 per hour employee, and I could save 500 hours a year (valued at $12,500)—wouldn't that be a great deal? Assuming I'm offered a good price of, say, $2,000, that would mean it would pay for itself in just under two months. What a great value proposition!

Or is it? What if I had to take two weeks to learn the software and another week to assimilate it into my business and some time for staff to learn it? What if I still needed the $25 per hour employee for other tasks and saving an hour a day would not matter much? Would it be something that really interested me? The software salesperson probably knows nothing about how I spend my time. I might not have two weeks to learn the software. Perhaps I'd rather spend $2,000 on advertising instead, hoping to get more sales leads.

Good value propositions require a solid understanding of customers' needs and the benefit they would derive from the solution, in their terms. Good value propositions also help you consider your customers' options and trade-offs. However, even well-constructed value propositions, with the right math, may be inapplicable.

Value propositions for businesses should always focus on the values that businesses generally seek. All businesses just want to make money, reduce costs, and be efficient. Anything that can be proven to achieve these purposes may get your product onto their product evaluation list. But even then, it must always be connected to an unequivocal and explicit need of that customer type who is in the position to strongly influence the purchase decision or who actually makes the decision to make the purchase.

Value propositions for consumers differ from those of businesses. Consumer preferences differ widely, and their purchasing decisions are based on an assortment of variables. They buy diverse products for differing needs and desires. They buy staple goods regularly (e.g., eggs, milk, rice, soap); they buy to replace old with new (e.g., clothing, computers); they buy the next new thing (e.g., music players, tablets, high-definition televisions); they buy emergency products when needed (e.g., plywood before a hurricane); they buy impulse products at their whim (e.g., ice cream, music downloads, luxury watches); and they buy durables to fulfill longer-term needs (e.g., cars, washing machines).

Each customer, regardless of type, goes through a varying number of motivational states, some persistent and some transient. The product manager and the team have to be experts on each market segment, and understand the underlying needs that ultimately drive the customer's value proposition. This can then be portrayed in the Value Proposition Template, shown as Figure 11.8.

The proofs are the most important.

- How would you defend the idea to management or your portfolio review board?
- How would you defend it to yourself?
- And here's my favorite: Would you bet your bonus on it?

Here's another way to test your proof: ask. Find a friendly salesperson or a colleague who is less familiar with your product area, and read your value proposition to him (and later, your Positioning Statement). If he has difficulty understanding your point, or simply doesn't get it, then you may have to go back and work on it some more until it is clear to people who are not involved. You must get the value proposition right in order to set the stage for positioning the product. To sum up, these four questions must be answered in the product description for it

FIGURE 11.8

Value Proposition Template

Describe the product/opportunity: _____

Characterize the customer and the verified need for the target customer:

Role	Name/Title	Need
Buyer		
User		
Influencer		
Decision Maker		

Narrative: (include information about motivational state)

The main validated (economic or non-economic) proof points for each customer type (buyer, influencer, or decision maker):

(increases revenue, reduces cost, saves time, more efficient, quality of life, etc.)

FIGURE 11.9

Linking a Need to a Feature

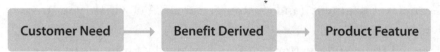

to be meaningful, and as a result, the answers will make their way into the marketing collateral.

Finally, each need must be linked to the product's functionality or features that bring that functionality to life. Use the diagram shown as Figure 11.9 to visualize that linkage.

CLARIFYING YOUR IDENTITY WITH A POSITIONING STATEMENT

Value propositions are important, but in order to be most effective, they must be wrapped in a Positioning Statement. In their book *Positioning: The Battle for Your Mind,* Al Ries and Jack Trout describe how positioning is used as a communication strategy to reach target customers in a crowded marketplace. Positioning slogans are used regularly as building blocks in marketing communications in all media. You hear or see this every day in advertisements and reading materials, on the radio or television, and on whatever other devices you use. Keep in mind: Products can be positioned. Brands can be positioned. Companies can be positioned.

Product positioning is an important output of the product team, not only during the phases of New Product Planning but also across the entire life cycle. It is used to describe how you want your product to be perceived by the target customer and allows for comparison with other available products offered by your competitors. The emphasis must be on competitive differentiation. Why should anyone want to buy your product versus that of the competition? What makes your product so unique? Product positioning also provides a solid foundation for consistent communication about the product, whether it is internal to the firm or used externally in marketing communications.

Positioning is often recognized by a slogan or saying. This is really great fodder for advertisers, but not necessarily for all product managers. Like the value proposition, useful product positioning cannot be established unless all of the foundational pieces are in place. These include:

1. The market segment (and customer target) on which you are focusing
2. The need states, motivations, or problems of the target customers
3. The environment of the industry
4. The competition and how each of their products is positioned.
5. The aspects that differentiate your product from its competition

To craft a successful Positioning Statement, make sure you have your value proposition in hand as you work with the template shown in Figure 11.10. This template provides the basics of what you need to effectively position the product with the target customer in mind. As you gain experience, creating this sort of content becomes easier. The template should also be used as a tool to collaborate with people who work in creative functions (the preparation of a creative brief, for example), either in your own Marketing department or with outside agencies, who can take your Positioning Statement and shape it for market consumption.

POSITIONING MEANS MAKING A DIFFERENCE

A word of caution: it's much too easy to produce meaningless Positioning Statements. Filling in the blanks of a template with nothing to support the prose is not good business. Pay special attention to the messages on television commercials and in magazine advertisements. See if you can pick out the key messages, especially when they say ". . . unlike _____, ours is different. Here's why. . . ." Most products tend to commoditize over time, and, unfortunately, weak positioning causes this to happen much sooner. The longer a product is on the market, the more likely competitors will take it apart and attack its shortcomings (or exploit its own product's strengths) to build up their own products. Before long, products look the same and the marketing materials sound the same.

Some companies claim they differentiate their product by providing greater levels of service. But, in reality, they don't follow up and do so. They pay lip service to the idea and delude themselves into thinking they have improved. Sometimes products can't be differentiated because they *are* the same or are considered "complete" because no new functionality

FIGURE 11.10

Product Positioning Statement Template

Name of Product/Enhancement: _____   Name of Product Manager: _____

_____   Name of Engineer: _____

Date Prepared: _____   Name of Marketing Manager: _____

Life Cycle Phase: _____   Name(s) of Other Team Member(s): _____

This product is designed for (a specific customer target group or market segment):

A specific customer	...with this proven need	...is satisfied by this feature/attribute
User	1. 2. 3.	1. 2. 3.
Influencer	1. 2. 3.	1. 2. 3.
Decision Maker	1. 2. 3.	1. 2. 3.
Buyer	1. 2. 3.	1. 2. 3.

BASIC ELEMENTS OF THE VALUE PROPOSTION

The customer (target) will benefit from using this product because it helps them:
(How will the customer be able to acheive some value, either in qualitative or quantitative terms?)

_____

_____

The product is unique because:

_____

_____

It compares favorably to available competitive products because:

_____

_____

is required. In such a case, a company is capitalizing on its brand and reputation. There is no one silver bullet for this. People visit the TD Bank in the United States because it's open until 8:30 p.m. and on Saturdays and Sundays. That's a vital service differentiator. So when it says its "America's Most Convenient Bank," it can prove it. If you're going to be different, you need to be sure you understand what that actually means. You also need to know that your target customer knows it, too. Not everyone can be the "leading solutions provider of mission-critical, end-to-end systems."

NARROWING THE FIELD: CHOOSING AMONG OPPORTUNITIES

When a product team is considering multiple opportunities, a structured decision matrix should be prepared to compare the opportunities being considered. A simple decision matrix (as shown in Chapter 5) can be created and scored. As decision criteria, I recommend you include items such as: resource availability and capability; strategic significance; financial viability; the degree to which the solution meets the needs of a given customer type within a validated segment, competitive posture; and complexity. You can certainly create your own criteria or add those that seem to be relevant for your situation, as each company and each industry has different decision-making criteria. In any case, no more than six criteria should be used to evaluate concepts.

Quantitative scores can guide your choice but should probably not be your only basis for making decisions. There may be other important factors that aren't apparent or scorable.

- If a new product is needed to round out the product line from a competitive standpoint, then scoring it may be unnecessary.
- If, during the strategic planning process, budgetary line items and resources are already committed, then those don't need to be vetted either.
- If a product enhancement is needed to meet a regulatory requirement, that project will usually take precedence.

These nonscorable items may radically change the priorities on your list, and the most likely impact overall is that fewer people and financial resources will be available.

The decision matrix is also useful when evaluating trade-offs for product content or features. For example, if a major enhancement for a technology product contains many different possible features, then the team can evaluate a variety of feature groupings. Each "opportunity" is a grouping, vetted against criteria such as complexity, time, cost, resource availability, competitive importance, and other market and organizational criteria that might be applicable.

In Figure 11.11, four different opportunities are profiled. Column A shows the weight for each individual criterion. For this grouping of opportunities, competitive viability is more important than technical achievement. Strategic importance is weighted higher than acceptable market size. These weights are usually determined within the organization, depending on current financial and market position. The number of evaluative criteria will increase as the opportunity evolves through the planning process. What we are building up to is a decision about which opportunities to pursue. If we have four now, we may only want to accept two and reject two. In the Feasibility phase, a larger team will do more extensive research, and will prepare more documentation on the opportunity.

Suppose you could only select two projects to move to the Feasibility phase: which ones would you choose and why? You can use the decision matrix as a guide, but it should not be the only input to your decision. Numbers tell a story, but your job is to determine which variables have the most weight and then evaluate this data in the context of your market, customer, and organizational awareness. In reviewing the scores for the opportunities in Figure 11.11, one might just pick opportunities 1 and 4. An astute product team will focus on other variables. And by the way, one of the decisions might be to pass on all of them. You don't have to say "yes" if you feel that these are not worthwhile investments after all.

MANAGING REJECTED OPPORTUNITIES

Each rejected Opportunity Statement should be filed away. It should be categorized, stored, and available for review at some point in the future by members of your team or others. Suppose you decide to take another job, and two years in the future the team in place wants to carry out a strategic planning session to identify new opportunities. By having archived the opportunities and ideas in a single repository (e.g., in your Master Plan) your successors will know what you and your team were thinking about and acting upon.

FIGURE 11.11

Concept Phase Weighted Decision Matrix

	A	B₁	C₁	B₂	C₂	B₃	C₃	B₄	C₄
		OPPORTUNITY 1		OPPORTUNITY 2		OPPORTUNITY 3		OPPORTUNITY 4	
DECISION CRITERIA	Weight 1–5	OPP 1 Rating	OPP 1 Score	OPP 2 Rating	OPP 2 Score	OPP 3 Rating	OPP 3 Score	OPP 4 Rating	OPP 4 Score
Strategically Aligned	4	9	36	5	20	7	28	1	4
Acceptable Market Size	3	6	18	8	24	2	6	10	30
Financially Attractive	4	7	28	9	36	9	36	9	36
Competitively Viable	5	8	40	6	30	9	45	9	45
Understood Needs	3	8	24	5	15	3	9	9	27
Technically Achievable	2	5	10	5	10	1	2	9	18
TOTAL SCORE			156		135		126		160

SECURING APPROVAL TO MOVE TO THE NEXT PHASE: THE CONCEPT REVIEW

One of the main benefits of the work done during the Concept phase is that your product team has a chance to govern itself and decide if any ideas are worthy of pursuit. Not all opportunities have to be presented to the portfolio team for review. If the idea clearly does not have merit, it should not be brought to management's attention. If you are not sure, then it would be advisable to have some conversations with senior-level stakeholders to determine if there is an appetite for such an investment.

When several realistic opportunities are to be considered in the Concept phase, the team needs to present its findings to a product portfolio review board or similar group, staffed by a cross-functional group of senior managers or executives who have the authority to allocate investment money within the organization. A formal review session should be attended by key stakeholders on the product team, and these members should be prepared to defend the investment or to recommend its rejection, especially if an executive sponsor had asked for the team to review the opportunity. The session may be brief, but presentations to executive portfolio groups are often mixed sessions where new opportunities are only one part of the agenda.

It is important to demonstrate to the review board that you have carefully thought out the opportunity within the context of market, customer targets, ability to develop, and financial viability. Concept reviews should represent your team's knowledge, experience, and efforts. You must display confidence as you discuss opportunities that your team assessed. Ask directly (and with equal confidence) for money, resources, and time to do additional research to determine whether the opportunity is worth pursuing. Before going to the review board, make sure you have a Concept phase checklist as exemplified in Figure 11.12. It will serve not only as a reminder to look at all business and technical issues prior to your review but also to set the stage for a go or no-go decision. You want to answer one key question for the review board: should the project be rejected or moved to the next phase?

FIGURE 11.12

Concept Phase Checklist

- The idea has business merit.
- It has been tested for strategic fit.
- The market need is understood.
- The investment will help us be more competitive.
- The technology is available and/or adaptable.
- The financial projections are realistic.
- Resources are available for the next two phases.
- Market research can be done for the Feasibility phase.
- The decision review is scheduled on [_____ date].
- This project is approved to move to the Feasibility phase.

SUMMARY

The Concept phase is used to narrow down a vast number of ideas for new products or product enhancements, within the context of a phased product planning process. These ideas and opportunities surface continually from market observations, customer input, and the strategic planning process. Product managers and their teams should make time to assess these opportunities frequently enough so that their idea inventories don't accumulate and cause important opportunities to be missed. The name of the game is speed. The primary stakeholders in Product Management, Development, and Marketing should have enough common data and knowledge about the product and the marketplace to be able to quickly evaluate the opportunities using an Opportunity Statement template. The best opportunities should be recommended to management in a formal Concept phase review meeting, during which the ideas are either rejected or moved to the next phase, Feasibility.

RAISING YOUR PRODUCT MANAGEMENT EXPERIENCE QUOTIENT (PMEQ)

1. Try to get a copy of your company's New Product Development (NPD) process documentation, and try to align what has been discussed in this chapter with what happens in your company. What is similar? What is different? What are the standard documents called (e.g., Opportunity Statement)?

2. What is the name of (or who are members of) the executive group that makes decisions about allocations of money and resources for new product investments? Establish relationships with those individuals to better understand what types of product investments are important, and why.

3. Is there a formal review process? Is there an opportunity for you to observe an idea (or concept) review session?

4. What do you do with your product ideas? Find out if there is an idea repository or an equivalent storehouse of ideas or opportunities. Who is responsible for working through those ideas?

5. Do some research on how to carry out an ideation session, and try one with a small group of people with whom you work.

6. Try to carry out a lunchtime opportunity review session with a couple of people—one from Engineering and one from Marketing—to see if you could work through an Opportunity Statement.

7. Observe and/or participate in several opportunity review sessions.

8. For your product, or for the product line group in which you work, try to map out an up-front portfolio and lay out the "product manager's motorway."

9. Choose an existing product in your company with which you are most familiar, preferably one that has several versions or models. Compare the features across versions/models, and try to determine how much one product release varies from another. Try to determine whether the release is brand new or is a grouping of enhancements. You can then try to learn about the history of the release or new model by talking to the product manager who brought it about.

10. Construct a value proposition for an existing product in the product line group in which you work. Try to determine if it is complete within the context of what was discussed in this chapter. Is it aligned methodologically? How would you change it if you needed to?

11. Try to "reverse engineer" the value propositions and Positioning Statements of your competitor's products. Compare them side by side to see if there is anything you might be able to exploit. Also, use this type of exercise to see if you should be updating your own value proposition and Positioning Statement. Use the templates and suggestions mentioned in this chapter as your guide.

12. Strive to gain experience leading several opportunity sessions such that you can evaluate several using a decision matrix. Decide among your small team what you would want to recommend to management and why. Then, present the series of opportunities to your management or portfolio board with a recommendation to take one of those and move it to the next logical phase for a more detailed analysis.

13. Make sure you are documenting all of your work and archiving it in the Product Master Plan.

IS THERE REALLY A BUSINESS HERE? ASSESSING FEASIBILITY

Executive Summary

- In the Feasibility phase, a cross-functional product team decides if there is a realistic business worthy of pursuit.
- Product managers must align the cross-functional team to make sure that the product can be developed, launched, and sustained in the market.
- Four key documents begin to come together and evolve during Feasibility: the Business Case, Product Marketing Plan, Product Requirements Document, and the Product Launch Plan.
- By the time the opportunity reaches the Feasibility phase review, most of the key "business" questions about the potential product should be well understood.

The goal of this chapter is to describe the Feasibility phase, which starts after the successful completion of the Concept review. Based on a go-ahead by the portfolio review board to secure financial and human resources, the cross-functional team is expanded to carry out a more comprehensive review of the opportunity. In this phase, the product team focuses on gaining a deeper understanding of everything needed to

develop, launch, and manage the product in the market, with heavy empha-
sis on Functional Support Plan (FSP) development. You will learn that
the most important document that evolves in Feasibility is the Business
Case. However, because the Business Case is such a complex document,
I've decided to dedicate an entire chapter to it, along with a case example.
You will learn more about the Business Case in Chapter 14. The other key
documents that evolve, starting in the Feasibility phase, are the Product
Requirements Document (PRD), covered in Chapter 13, and the Marketing
Plan for the product, covered more thoroughly in Chapter 15.

To get the full force and effect of the activities that take place in this
phase, it is important to study both this chapter as well as Chapter 14.

From my research, I've learned that feasibility studies tend to focus
on a few key aspects of financial and market viability, coupled with a
cursory "can we build it?" assessment from R&D. Feasibility, in the way it
is described here, represents the deep-dive analysis necessary to validate
the strategic, business, and financial viability of the opportunity. In fact,
the core thrust of the Feasibility phase within the Product Management
Life Cycle Model is perhaps the most difficult work carried out by the
product manager, mainly because of the level of effort required. The
chances of choosing and developing profitable ideas go up immensely
when the cross-functional team really digs into the details during the
Feasibility phase. I strongly recommend maintaining a high degree of
diligence when carrying out the research and developing the critical
documents that capture how the product solves the customer's problem
and how the business will support the product.

Figure 12.1 shows that the membership of the cross-functional team is
focused on carrying out a significant amount of analysis during this phase.

Specifically, the team develops the preliminary Business Case and
supporting documentation to assess whether the new product or enhancement has enough business, market, and financial merit, and whether it can
be operationally implemented and supported. The product team members
must also take the time to evaluate what commitments they would need to
make to one another—and to the overall team—in order to develop,
launch, and manage the product in the market.

During the Feasibility phase, clarity around roles and responsibilities is paramount. As team members closely collaborate, they can more
easily determine if the product investment has merit. If the product
manager does all of the work, then the purpose of the cross-functional

FIGURE 12.1

Cross-Functional Team Membership During the Feasibility Phase

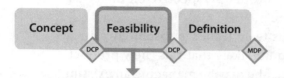

ROLE	ACTIVITIES
Product Manager	• Orchestrates the complex cross-functional interactions to produce the Business Case and other relevant documentation • Prepares the initial sales and demand forecasts • Drafts the initial version of the Product Requirements Document (PRD)
Marketing Manager	• Augments industry and competitive information • Validates market segmentation model and target customers • Ensures that initial Marketing Plan is produced • Works on the initial version of the Launch Plan
Development Manager	• Works with the product manager to translate high-level requirements into a Product Specifications Document (PSD) and/or design document • Evaluates the best technologies or platforms to be utilized • Provides cost estimates, quality guidelines, test plans, and designs for manufacturability (if required) • Commits to support early trials, beta tests, etc. • Prepares preliminary project plans
Finance Manager	• Supports the creation of financial models and forecasts • Creates product level budgets • Evaluates various scenarios and conducts sensitivity analysis • Provides corporate/divisional financial guidelines to assist the team
Customer Service Manager	• Deals with current and future service-related activities such as call center staffing, complaint or case handling, and order taking • Plans for customer self-service programs • Drafts guidelines for service management programs
Sales Manager	• Collaborates with product managers, marketers, and finance in the support of sales forecasts, volume commitments, and revenue targets
Operations Manager	• Defines operational infrastructure elements required to launch the product and to support the product while it is actively sold in the market
Supply Chain Manager	• Determines sourcing needs, evaluates ecosystem partners and contracts • Ensures that the procurement, logistics, and other supply chain elements are available
Manufacturing Manager	• For tangible products, capacity plans and the demand forecasts must be linked to ensure that the product can be produced
Legal & Regulatory Manager(s)	• These advisory team members are consulted to ensure that the team's plans are consistent with rules & regulations for each market area
International or Global Organizations	• Provides local market input to the product team to ensure that the product can meet the needs of regional market areas

product team is lost and important evaluative information is left out. For this reason, the Functional Support Plans (and associated negotiation) serve the team well. Figure 12.2 offers a proper perspective on the Feasibility phase inputs, activities, and outputs.

The role of the product manager as team leader is absolutely critical in the Feasibility phase. However, it is quite likely that this "new product" is not the only project she must work on. She may be managing an existing product or other product projects and may even be working on or leading other teams. All team members are also working at fulfilling obligations in their own departments.

Given the workload, synchronization of team activity becomes more complex. When pressures build in an organization due to excessive workloads and scarce resources, team members may find it difficult to communicate about problems they may have fulfilling their commitments. Further, they may need to dynamically reprioritize their current workloads as they consider what it will take to gear up for incremental work. For this reason, performing due diligence during the Concept phase is crucial to making good decisions about what's truly important for the

FIGURE 12.2

Feasibility Phase Process Profile

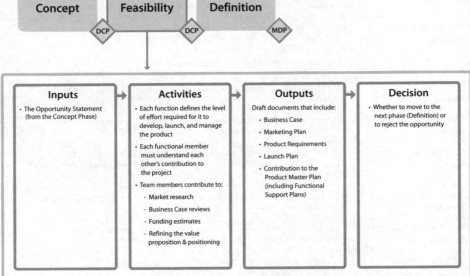

DCP = Decision Check Point
MDP = Major Decision Point

future of the business and to ensuring that efforts expended during the Feasibility phase are worth the time and effort. This is also true of subsequent phases, provided that the team decides to continue and given that the appropriate approvals are secured for the team to continue its work.

Despite the complexity, the team's work will be simplified if you can influence the cross-functional negotiations that are required to pave the way for the team's work plans. You can earn your way to the "table" and have an impact on the negotiations by demonstrating your thorough understanding of market dynamics, as described in previous chapters. However, during the Feasibility phase, the team may still have to ramp up its efforts and find additional resources that validate existing research or seek additional market.

USING FUNCTIONAL SUPPORT PLANS TO CLARIFY ROLES, RESPONSIBILITIES, AND DELIVERABLES

FSPs are developed during the Feasibility phase. These plans are critically important because they establish the fundamental pattern for negotiation and communication across the team. The FSPs are also crucial for focusing the team on the sequencing of deliverables, determining cross-organizational dependencies, and identifying possible risks. Ultimately, the team is responsible for ascertaining that the product can be successfully managed in the market across its in-market life cycle and within the context of the entire portfolio of products.

During the Feasibility phase, product team members negotiate with one another (and to the team as a whole) to analyze and agree upon the level of effort that would be needed to develop and launch the product. FSPs serve as horizontal contracts between dedicated team members and the product team leader. Team members may not fully understand how to prepare FSPs. It is therefore up to the product team leader to instruct them in the methods. They probably have a general idea of the necessary work activities but may not know which of the team members is meant to receive a deliverable.

This first step in the cross-functional negotiating process allows for the pairwise discussions to take place. Figure 12.3 is a diagram that shows how two people in different functions might discuss their roles and responsibilities.

The product manager should lead the two functions in the discussion, which is intended to be a cross-functional negotiation session. A first-pass output from the negotiation resulted in the content shown in Figure 12.4.

FIGURE 12.3

The Pairwise Relationship as a Basis for the Functional Support Plan

Function A (e.g., Marketing)

- The role
- Key responsibilities
- Major deliverables produced
- Other consumers of the deliverables
- Timing (when are the deliverables needed?)
- Possible risks
- Agreed-upon escalation paths (how to communicate to executives if there's a jeopardy or a missed deliverable)

Function B (e.g., Sales)

- The role
- Key responsibilities
- Major deliverables produced
- Other consumers of the deliverables
- Timing (when are the deliverables needed?)
- Possible risks
- Agreed-upon escalation paths (how to communicate to executives if there's a jeopardy or a missed deliverable)

FIGURE 12.4

High-Level Functional Support Plan

Marketing FSP Summary

Joseph from Marketing agrees to provide the following to Angelica in Sales in 30 days:

- A market profile with explicit market segment information
- Need-state descriptions and personas for each customer target

This information is also to be used by the product manager for inclusion in the Business Case. If the market profile is not provided on time, the assumptions in the Business Case will not be validated. The SVP of Marketing understands this and approves of this work effort.

Sales FSP Summary

Angelica from Sales agrees to provide the following to Joseph in Marketing:

- A list of 30 key executives to interview in each of 3 major segments within the next 14 days
- A draft unit volume forecast for each segment within 30 days

This information is vital to Marketing so that the lead generation program can be established. The Supply Chain organization needs the unit volume information to prepare its cost estimate for the Business Case. The SVP of Supply Chain secured agreement from the SVP of Sales on the deliverable.

To provide greater context and a more formal way to frame the negotiation, each team member in this negotiation should be provided with an FSP template as shown in Figure 12.5.

The product manager can have brief meetings with individual functional team members or small groups to define work tasks, hand-offs, and deliverables as called out in the template.

The more precisely the roles and responsibilities are defined, the higher the probability that the team will be able to fulfill its obligations—and that will ultimately contribute to the success of the product. If there is a project manager on the team, that person must absolutely be present to document the project activities.

After all the possible pairwise sessions are completed, team members will find that there are other cross-team deliverables and dependencies that still require resolution. A good way to handle these open items is for the other "pairs" of functions to set up offline negotiating sessions.

The final cross-functional negotiation takes place in a full team meeting, which will probably last many hours. All functional representatives review their FSP, including their deliverables, timing, and dependencies, with the entire team. Other team members, especially those who would be affected by a necessary deliverable that was omitted or unnamed, will call attention to the omission of that deliverable. Figure 12.6 shows the way the interactions may evolve.

Questions will invariably arise:

- Can the receiving function actually absorb the deliverable?
- What should they do with it once they have it?
- How long will they have to complete their task(s)?
- Are they supposed to respond with another deliverable, and can they do so in the expected time frame?

After a while, when more of these questions arise, it becomes apparent why this interaction is so complex.

The quality and tenor of this interaction ripples across the remainder of the life cycle. During subsequent phases, especially during Development and Launch (Execution), and in Post-Launch Product Management, it will be apparent why these cross-team dependencies and interactions are so important. Setting up these plans is the fundamental, crucial approach to help the team track performance and to minimize ambiguity with clearly

FIGURE 12.5

The Functional Support Plan Template

DATE: _____   VERSION: _____

Team Member Information:

Function Represented	
Product Name	
Product Life Cycle Phase (feasibility, development, etc.)	
Project Name/Number	
Team Member Name/Role	
Team Member Contact Info	
Name of Manager	
Manager Contact Info	

Deliverables required by this function TO another function

Deliverable Required	For whom? In what function?	Date Promised

Deliverables required by this function FROM another function

Deliverable Required	For whom? In what function?	Date Promised

Resources provided

Names	Titles/Roles	Skills/Expertise

Funding needed by this function to support its deliverables

Funding Category	This Year	Next Year	Year After
Money already allocated			
Incremental start-up money needed			
Money needed as incremental to ongoing budgets			

Supporting Information:

- Key dates and milestones
- Risk assessment (complexity, time, resource, etc.)
- Performance measurements

The terms of this Functional Support Plan are Agreed:

_____   _____

Manager Name, Signature, and Date   Manager Name, Signature, and Date

FIGURE 12.6

Cross-Functional Negotiation

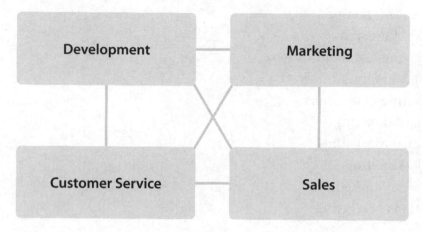

defined roles and responsibilities. It won't hurt either if you use basic goal-setting tools, such as SMART objectives or the RACI model, discussed in Chapter 4.

One of the best methods to track these cross-team deliverables is a project management tool. I do not endorse one automation tool over another, but I strongly embrace the methodology. Whatever tool is used, it must be used consistently and updated as frequently as needed. It should be used as a way to communicate status and risks. I'll talk a little more about project management controls in the next chapter.

FSPs can evolve when people from within each function have a good sense of their responsibilities and deliverables. The following descriptions and bullet lists can be used as guides to begin your discussions with each person from each function. They may not be complete because of the nuances and practices of your own organization, but they should serve as a suitable starting point.

THE MARKETING FUNCTIONAL SUPPORT PLAN (THE MARKETING PLAN FOR THE PRODUCT)

The Marketing FSP (Marketing Plan) is a complex document. As an FSP, especially during the product planning phases, it serves as an *integration document* because it may contain contributions (or even subplans) from other marketing-related organizations.

Specifically, the Marketing Plan is the place to capture commitments from:

- Product Marketing
- Market Research
- Marketing Communications
- Event Marketing
- Marketing Operations
- Global Marketing
- Regional Marketing
- Field Marketing
- Strategic Marketing
- Solutions Marketing

This does not even include all the related functions, such as people in marketing who maintain relationships with advertising and creative agencies, industry analysts, and public relations firms. Not only are there many related marketing groups that typically fall under the Chief Marketing Officer, but there may also be marketing plans that stack up hierarchically through an organization.

The format and flow of the Marketing Plan for the product will be more fully discussed in Chapter 15. For now, what I want to emphasize is the primary documentation from the "Marketing" person who represents all of the marketing-related functions to the product team during the phases of product planning. Therefore, the Marketing function must be able to:

- Describe the work activities that will contribute to solid descriptions of the market segments, customer targets, and the underlying needs of each grouping.
- Commit to the maintenance of data about the general marketplace.
- Make sure the right research data is available to support market sizing, competitive positioning, and segmentation for the Business Case and other documents such as the Launch Plan and marketing collateral.
- Assess the capabilities and vulnerabilities of competitors.
- Collaborate on the creation of the value proposition and positioning.

- Work together on pricing models.
- Clarify the most appropriate distribution models.
- Determine possible creative needs for integrated advertising and promotional programs for the product during the launch phases and after the launch.
- Articulate the need for public relations support.
- Specify the requirements to communicate with industry analysts.
- Align marketing plans and programs with other corporate initiatives.
- Resolve possible issues related to cross-elasticity with other products (either complements or conflicts).
- Estimate marketing resources and budgets.
- Provide estimates for the creation of sales collateral, your internal website, and other documents that are seen in your market area.
- Ascertain needed training (e.g., Customer Service, Sales).
- Identify efforts to support the product's market introduction, including market trials and controlled introductions, as well as the overarching launch plans.

PRODUCT DEVELOPMENT/IT/SYSTEMS FUNCTIONAL SUPPORT PLAN

The Development FSP for a new or enhanced product describes the activities, responsibilities, and deliverables of the Development organization. In many organizations, Development may be called R&D, Engineering, or IT (Information Technology). In other organizations, IT may be a separate organization responsible for operational systems and infrastructure, while Development refers to product development. For the purpose of this FSP, I am referring to the technical organization responsible for designing, developing, testing, and maintaining the product.

The Development FSP focuses on the sequence of activities and interactions with other functional departments. In addition to the FSP, Development prepares its own internal plans and documents that guide its work activities. As with each FSP, the Development FSP will ultimately have project schedules, deliverables, hand-offs, milestones, and budgets that can be integrated with the other FSPs. Development is usually expected to:

- Identify resources and skills that are needed to design and develop the product.

- Specify and validate technologies to be considered.

- Define or validate product platforms or architectures to be used.

- Interpret product requirements from Product Management so that product design documents and/or specifications can be drafted and negotiated with product managers.

- Prepare to meet industry standards if needed, by market area and/or country.

- Assemble initial drawings for manufacturing so that product prototypes can be created, and to verify that the product can actually be produced.

- Work with the supply chain organization so that bills of materials can be created and that procurement activities can be supported. Bills of materials are also used by cost accounting to estimate product costs.

- Determine if additional tools or facilities are needed.

- Estimate project costs, resource requirements, and time frames for project plans and align with other functions.

- Define quality guidelines and product testing plans.

- Design the product to be manufactured or work with external suppliers to manufacture it.

- Determine if offshoring is needed for programming support.

FINANCE FUNCTIONAL SUPPORT PLAN

The Finance department's FSP is one of the most important because it describes the activities, functions, and tools that help the product team focus on financial viability and future product profitability. It also helps provide the linkage to other interconnected functions, such as compliance, governance, and reporting, to support the business of the product. The Finance FSP is primarily focused on the economic evaluations, financial models, forecasts, and any other financial data that will ultimately be used by the product manager and the product team. Generally, Finance must be able to:

- Conduct economic and financial analysis for product investments.

- Make sure that product and market forecasts have the right supporting data and assumptions to ensure they are financially achievable, believable, and realistic.

CHAPTER 12   Is There Really a Business Here? Assessing Feasibility

325

- Provide support for Business Cases, including discount rates for net present value calculations and other required financial standards.
- Set up the appropriate systems and tools to track and report on product financial performance.
- Set capital budgeting parameters for equipment, facilities, etc.
- Support the derivation of market-based pricing models working with Marketing and Product Management.
- Prepare financial statements used for the Business Case.
- Collaborate with the Supply Chain group (or procurement) and Development on the bill of materials so that cost-of-goods estimates can be formulated.
- Develop revenue and gross profit estimates based on pricing models, unit volume forecasts, and cost estimates.
- Establish contact with and prepare to provide input to the regulatory and reporting organization so that product financial data complies with all necessary standards.

CUSTOMER SERVICE FUNCTIONAL SUPPORT PLAN

The Customer Service FSP for a new or enhanced product describes the activities, responsibilities, and deliverables of the Customer Service organization. Customer service may be a combination of order taking (which can be inbound sales over the phone, outbound telesales, or a combination of both) and service (which can include inbound complaints and problem handling and/or case management, or outbound services such as following up on service quality and customer satisfaction surveys).

Modern businesses pay close attention to the positive customer interactions and the overall customer or user experience. Therefore, the Customer Service FSP should address the major issues and evolving trends related to servicing and supporting customers. The entire range of support channels should be considered: telephone, Internet, teller machines, kiosks, e-mail, and so on. The commitments of the Customer Service function should help the team:

- Determine what is actually needed to carry out support activities in terms of training and staffing based on required service levels.
- Ensure that customers can contact the company (inbound) to report problems or lodge service requests (case management or trouble handling).

- Estimate the combined inbound and outbound human resources that are required to support blended interactions and a variety of programs (e.g., up-sell, cross-sell programs).
- Confirm that systems and resources will be available so that customers can call in or log in to submit orders (usually in conjunction with IT or other systems organizations).
- Ascertain the feasibility of different interaction channels through which service, sales, or support might be provided.
- Verify that the supporting infrastructure can facilitate and measure the desired customer experiences.
- Secure training from Marketing for Customer Service personnel.
- Staff the contact center.
- Define necessary IT or operational systems availability and capacity for contact systems and web infrastructure.

SALES FUNCTIONAL SUPPORT PLAN

The Sales FSP is a highly important document because it paves the way for the product team to communicate and negotiate with Sales. Good product ideas will remain only product ideas unless the Sales team agrees to supply enough qualified people to sell the product. Sales also needs to bring to the table a willingness to be trained and a capacity to compensate salespeople for their efforts. Without these pieces of the selling puzzle in place, the product will probably fail to meet its business objectives. The Sales FSP can serve to minimize the risk of product failure because it enables the product team to secure commitments from the Sales team for items such as:

- Sales forecast estimates
- Market size validation—working with Marketing
- Sales operations activities
- Well-established relationships with the Human Resource department for alignment on compensation plans
- Partnerships with Marketing to ensure training is carried out at the right time
- Methods to report progress so the product team can monitor performance

CHAPTER 12   Is There Really a Business Here? Assessing Feasibility

327

OPERATIONS FUNCTIONAL SUPPORT PLAN

The Operations FSP, especially during the product planning phases, serves as another integration document because it may contain contributions originating from many organizations. Think of the operational infrastructure of a firm that enables everyone else, in every function, to be able to carry out their work. These areas might include:

- Facilities
  - Site management
  - Building maintenance
  - Laboratory setup
  - Plant setup
  - Equipment management
- IT and its supporting systems such as:
  - Customer ordering systems
  - Billing systems
  - Customer management or contact management systems
  - Company website
  - Accounting systems
- Installation and maintenance
- Field operations (repair, infrastructure surveillance)
- Quality and productivity programs
- Human Resource Management
  - Training and development
  - Organizational development

Each subfunction in the operations department could provide an FSP, but not every department is a core team member. The most critical questions about Operations support are usually as follows:

- Can the product be set up in a system so that it can be ordered, billed, and posted to the right accounts?
- Can products be put into the electronic product catalogs and showcased on the company website?
- If installation is required, can installation and maintenance programs be put into place?
- Can related field operations and activities be carried out?

SUPPLY CHAIN FUNCTIONAL SUPPORT PLAN

If the product requires components or materials that must be procured from outside suppliers or vendors, an FSP is needed from the supply chain team. This FSP describes the activities, responsibilities, 328 and deliverables that are needed to:

- Have a vendor-selection methodology to support the product as needed
- Be able to work with product development on designs and drawings and in the creation of bills of material for the product
- Support the sourcing of product components or entire products from external suppliers or ecosystem partners
- Collaborate on material logistics to ensure that the materials are available on time and that finished goods can be transported to and through distribution channels
- Coordinate with Finance to make sure that vendor payment terms are agreeable and that monies will be available to pay vendors according to those terms
- Carry out vendor negotiations on pricing—work with Finance to ensure that cost of goods can be captured
- Work with Finance on standard or target costing programs

LEGAL/REGULATORY/COMPLIANCE FUNCTIONAL SUPPORT PLAN

The FSPs from Legal, Regulatory, and/or Compliance provide advice and guidance to the product team on the regulations, guidelines, and timing set up by governmental bodies and by corporate standards. It also provides advisory support, oversight, and governance for intellectual property management, including trademarks, copyrights, patents, and, in some cases, antitrust laws. Based on this FSP, these functions should commit to:

- Support contracts that may arise from vendor agreements or sales
- Work with Marketing to make sure that all copy is in accordance with corporate guidelines
- Provide filings for any legal documents

MANUFACTURING FUNCTIONAL SUPPORT PLAN

If tangible products are to be produced, a Manufacturing FSP is needed to describe the activities, responsibilities, and deliverables of the Manufacturing organization. Parts and components can also be secured from outside the company, so a tight relationship with the Supply Chain department is necessary. The Manufacturing representative to the product team is responsible for ensuring that the product can be manufactured and deciding whether it should be done internally or externally. The overall goal of this function is to make sure that physical or tangible products can be produced. If a product analysis has to be performed to determine if it should be made internally versus purchased or sourced externally (make versus buy), Manufacturing and Supply Chain work closely with Development and the product manager in order to carry out that analysis. This is discussed in more detail in Chapter 13.

The responsibilities of the Manufacturing organization relevant to the FSP should include:

- Evaluating manufacturing capabilities to make sure the product can be produced
- Determining alternate sources of supply, if necessary
- Ensuring that all parts and components are available on time (in partnership with the Supply Chain organization)
- Assuring the team that plants and facilities will be set up to meet demand through effective design and implementation of the manufacturing process
- Creating all purchasing requests for capital expenditures with sufficient lead time to allow for approvals, order processing, delivery, setup, and testing on the production line
- Ensuring that quality control systems will be in place to meet established quality standards
- Collaborating on all product drawings such that the most appropriate and efficient production methods can be employed
- Designing serialization procedures for product tracking, if needed
- Setting up procedures to ship and receive defective products and support repair and return policies, in partnership with the Customer Service department

- Committing to maintain product drawings and to adhere to established documentation and archiving standards
- Examining methods for improving plant throughput and increasing efficiency

INTERNATIONAL (OR GLOBAL) FUNCTIONAL SUPPORT PLAN

The International FSP for a new or enhanced product is negotiated between the product manager and the associated organizations located in geographic regions outside of the home market. Some of these organizations may provide in-region sales support or may be involved in market surveillance. Others may provide a more complete in-region business presence that encompass sales, marketing, development, production, delivery, and support where a regional general manager is responsible for regional business profitability.

In some cases, companies deploy a regional product manager or someone with an equivalent title. This person is responsible for keeping an eye on local market trends and ensuring that the provided products suit local requirements. However, this can become problematic for some companies when people who work in local geographies forge independent paths. This is because of the increased chance for duplication of efforts or other inefficient product operations. Companies that manage product portfolios on a global basis tend to supply what's needed for local markets. In such cases, the regional product manager might actually be a regional market manager.

The reason I'm describing this here is because the International Functional Support Plan must account for how people in charge of global businesses "interlock" with people in various locations, as well as a centralized Product and/or Portfolio Management organization. There is much to lose if the numerous gears that connect concerned stakeholders do not operate effectively. Product managers who work in global organizations must be aware of how important it is to cultivate and maintain solid working relationships with all constituencies.

In my first Product Management job, I was the international product manager and the product team leader wanted absolutely nothing to do with international requirements. He claimed they distracted the team and took away needed resources. This created an egregiously ineffective structure because without product modifications for the local market (in my case, Japan), there was no way that the product could be sold there even if it was halfway dressed up for the local market. The sales-people knew it, the marketers knew it, and the competitors knew it very well. The product didn't even last two years before we folded our tents.

A globalization strategy begins at the top of the company. The product team, working closely with its international counterparts, defines and delivers the product to the chosen markets. The International FSP therefore should include commitments for the following responsibilities, as a minimum:

- Ensure that any international market information and product requirements are provided to the product manager.

- Consider each product for each market based on the needs it meets and the market environment in which it must survive.

- Develop pricing models consistent with the value proposition for the local market.

- Make any adjustments to the Positioning Statement needed to reflect the local competitive environment.

- Work with marketing to create market-specific programs for lead generation, awareness building, etc.

- Derive country-specific sales and volume forecasts.

- Evaluate currency risk and exposure, consistent with corporate guidelines.

RESOURCE PLANNING AND SUMMARIZATION

During the product planning phases, each business function must provide documentation regarding the resources required to support the team in the current and future phases, as well as those that would be required to support the product in the market. This is an important determinant of whether a product project can be authorized to proceed to the next phase or must be rejected. I recommend that each team put together a Resource Estimate and Approval document (Figure 12.7) as part of its FSP input. This is also a great tool to use when considering the ongoing management of existing products and for defining resources that should be used when the product is in the market (during Post-Launch Product Management).

FIGURE 12.7

Resource Estimate and Approval Template

Name of Function	
Date	
Name of Team Member	
Email Address	
Name of Product	

UPCOMING PHASE ACTIVITIES			UPCOMING PHASE RESOURCES		
Activities		Due Date	Person Days/Weeks	Expenses	Capital

Reason this funding is needed and why these activities are so critical:

APPROVALS:
Functional Department Agreement:

Signature of Authorized Department Executive (Agree or Deny)

After all Resource Estimate and Approval forms are collected, the product manager should have a snapshot view of all resource commitments. This not only is important for the current phase but could also capture subsequent phase estimates. A suggestion might be to use the Product Team Resource Summary template as shown in Figure 12.8. By the way, this is a great tool for the product manager when providing summary reports to management.

The FSP is a great tool to establish the cadence for securing data from other team members, highlighting their commitments, determining the dependencies, and identifying any risks. This approach gives team members

FIGURE 12.8

Product Team Resource Summary Template

Product Name	
Product Manager	
Date	

Function	Current Phase Headcount	Current Phase Expenses	Current Phase Capital	Next Phase Headcount	Next Phase Expenses	Next Phase Capital
Product Manager						
Marketing						
Development						
Finance						
Customer Service						
Sales						
Operations						
Supply Chain						
Legal/Reg/Compl.						
Manufacturing						
International						
Other						
TOTAL						

a guide that tells them what they need to do, whom they work with, what they are responsible for, the time frame within which to work, and if there are any risks that may stand in the way of this work getting done. This also allows the product manager the opportunity to look at the bigger picture and act as the team's "quarterback." As it is, product managers have a heavy workload. If, in addition, they must fill in on jobs others are responsible for, important details could be missed and such oversights would likely jeopardize the success of the product.

Once all FSPs are assembled and agreed on, an integrated set of FSPs should be created. In project management terminology, this would

FIGURE 12.9

Integrating Functional Support Plans into One Integrated Plan

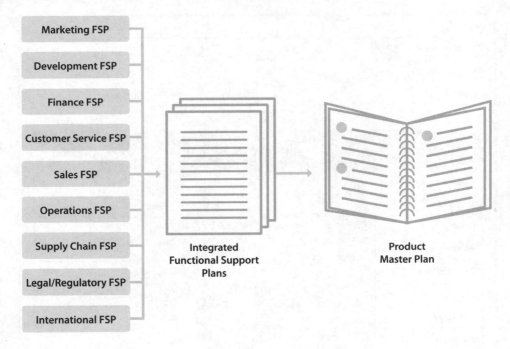

Marketing FSP

Development FSP

Finance FSP

Customer Service FSP

Sales FSP

Operations FSP

Supply Chain FSP

Legal/Regulatory FSP

International FSP

Integrated
Functional Support
Plans

Product
Master Plan

be the program plan, represented pictorially in Figure 12.9. For the rest of the chapters on planning, when I refer to FSPs, it is not necessary to repeat the entire list or rework it. Refer to the lists in this chapter, and use the FSP format as shown as a summary in Figure 12.3 (or as a more detailed template in Figure 12.5) to guide your work as you reach out to people in other business functions.

DOCUMENT EVOLUTION DURING FEASIBILITY

Many documents are prepared during the Feasibility phase, and most of them are in a constant state of evolution. Even at the end of Feasibility, they are merely preliminary or draft documents. I am often asked about how long a preliminary document should be. Aside from the "it depends" answer, I try to provide an order-of-magnitude estimate. For a Business Case, the preliminary Business Case may be about 5 to 10 pages and the final would be approximately 25 to 30 pages. It's not a hard-and-fast rule, but it can act as a gauge for level of effort.

The main documents being prepared during Feasibility include:

1. *Business Case.* This document represents the primary investment justification for the project through its description of the history, the problem to be solved, and how this investment contributes to the strategic, market, and financial well-being of the product line. It also defines the benefits to the organization within which the product line exists, based on a given set of assumptions. The Business Case is discussed in greater detail in Chapter 14.

2. *Product Launch Plan.* The Launch Plan begins its evolution here. Although probably not completed in exhaustive detail, a solid first pass should be completed before the product investment is finalized. Many launches start too late, and then everyone must scramble to finish the work of the launch. Meanwhile, they miss other critical work activities. If the team can stir up some interest in the product's launch-worthiness early on, it may influence the ultimate decision to move ahead with the project.

3. *Product Requirements Document.* The PRD is used to clarify the actual functionality and features of a product. The PRD is initiated during the Feasibility phase so that the product's characteristics and capabilities can be articulated. The PRD is discussed in more detail in the Definition phase chapter (Chapter 13), which contains a more comprehensive protocol for eliciting, defining, organizing, and managing the product requirements.

4. *Marketing Plan for the Product.* The Marketing Plan, as described earlier, is treated as an FSP for the product. It represents the holistic interconnection of the marketing mix elements (product, pricing, promotion, and place or distribution channel). In essence, it's the roadmap for getting the product to the target market segments. The Marketing Plan is discussed in Chapter 15.

PLANNING TO MONITOR THE FUTURE PERFORMANCE OF THE PRODUCT

If a product is going to be introduced or enhanced, its performance in the market (and results achieved) should be tracked against the plan already established. Many companies call these tracking metrics, results indicators, or even key performance indicators (KPIs). The Business Case should be able to articulate the expected returns to the business in the form of future metrics, results indicators, or KPIs. The product manager and other key stakeholders should be responsible for establishing product-specific performance goals and the requirements by which actual performance will be tracked.

Although they are established during the phases of New Product Planning, performance measurements may change as the complexion of the business changes. I want to stress the importance of setting up useful mechanisms, such as product scorecards, that will help the team run the business of the product while the product is in the market. If the product manager fails to make sure adequate performance-monitoring capabilities are set up, there is a chance that the data will not be available when it is time to restrategize.

Most performance metrics for products are generic to the product team, although some may originate within a given business function. The following list represents the typical indicators used to run the business:

- Unit volumes
- List prices
- Average unit price
- Average revenue per customer
- Cost of goods (e.g., material, labor, overhead)
- Expenses by department (if controllable)
- Customer satisfaction
- Quality measurements (e.g., number of defects, number of complaints)
- Inventory levels
- Repair and return levels
- Mean time between failure rates
- Warranty claims
- Warranty costs
- Win rates
- Sales by channel
- Sales cycle
- Order-to-fulfillment cycle
- Order-to-cash cycle

In Chapter 19, I will cover, in more detail, how to evaluate the performance of the product when it's "in market."

THE POWER OF THE PROTOTYPE

If you were going to build a house, you would start by working with an architect to create the initial design and layout. As you familiarized yourself with each successive rendering, you would imagine yourself living in your future home. You wouldn't spend any money on materials or labor before you finalized that drawing. In the same vein, you shouldn't spend a cent on a product until there is proof that a customer will find it desirable and that your team will buy into your vision.

In an era when successful innovations are enthusiastically sought after but risk management is the watchword, it's important to be as confident as possible about your product investments. If you use eye-catching physical models, mock-ups, wire frames, or any other early-phase assessment, you will gain valuable insights from lead users, potential customers, or others in a similar capacity. The more the model actually works, or portrays how the product should work, the greater the chance you'll be able to evaluate how potential customers will react to the product—and whether they'll buy the product.

Prototyping is important for all product investments. Products that have particularly short life spans (such as mobile applications or games) benefit from immediate feedback from users about their experience trying the product out. The sooner you get those prototypes done, the better! And even longer-lived products, from enterprise software-as-a-service applications to heavy industrial products, greatly benefit when you are able to demonstrate their value (to targeted customers) and defend your investments to your leadership.

I have also used storyboards and animations to portray a day in the life of the customer. This is especially useful when you get other cross-functional team members to join you as you sketch these out—especially if they've been derived from a shared customer visit! I also like to use these methods to determine if sales or marketing people would get excited over the idea.

In a nutshell, prototypes are a must-have in almost any product area to validate the product with prospective targeted customers. If you do not have the time or resources to create the prototype, you probably don't have the wherewithal to take your product idea to the next phase.

THE DECISION MATRIX FOR THE FEASIBILITY PHASE

I have brought in the decision matrix from the Concept phase to show how the number of opportunities that were considered can be reduced from four to two, as shown in Figure 12.10. I took the highest-scoring

FIGURE 12.10

Feasibility Decision Matrix

		OPPORTUNITY 1		OPPORTUNITY 2	
	A	**B₁**	**C₁**	**B₄**	**C₄**
DECISION CRITERIA	Weight 1–5	OPP 1 Rating	OPP 1 Score	OPP 4 Rating	OPP 4 Score
Strategically Aligned	4	9	6	1	4
Acceptable Market Size	3	6	18	10	30
Financially Attractive	4	7	28	9	36
Competitively Viable	5	8	40	9	45
Understood Segment Needs	3	8	24	9	27
Technically Achievable	2	5	10	9	18
NPV Meets Threshold	3	4	12	7	21
Preliminary Business Case Shows Positive Outcomes	5	4	20	6	30
Acceptable Risk Levels	3	6	18	3	9
Functional Groups Have Requisite Expertise	4	9	36	2	8
TOTAL SCORE			**242**		**228**

opportunities from the Concept phase as examples and expanded the list of decision criteria, adding four more criteria. The ratings from the initial matrix are unchanged in order to keep the models consistent.

It is important for you to either locate a current scoring model from your own company or derive a model that can be used by all stakeholders that contains the most appropriate criteria or variables for your company and your specific project types. The main areas you are scoring are business (or market) and technical areas. The job of the product team is to sift through the main documents, discuss them thoroughly, and think critically about the *feasibility* of transforming this investment into a product reality. This is the reason the phase is so appropriately named.

While studying the decision matrix, consider a few questions: What would you want to know more about? Do you think that you could make a real decision based on those numbers? Would you feel comfortable going to the product portfolio review board without a good story? Will all the business functional leaders buy into the program and commit their resources?

The scores will often guide the decision, but in some cases, subjective business judgment and other business drivers may steer the decision to go forward with either project—or to kill both projects. Remember, just because you have gone through the analysis doesn't mean you have to carry out the project. There is plenty of other work to do!

PHASE REVIEW: FEASIBILITY

Once you have your rationalized, integrated collection of FSPs in hand, all the relevant product documentation, and an updated decision matrix (Figure 12.10), you're ready to prepare for the Feasibility review. Most people who research and write about product development seem to focus on the "gate review." This approach forces the team to work toward a gate with a checklist in hand. Ultimately teams need to focus on the *work* to be done during the Feasibility phase, and only when the phase work is done should the team decide to review its findings and recommendations with the portfolio review board or management team.

Keep in mind that the organization is looking to the product manager and the team to define new investment opportunities. If it was your money and you were going to invest it, what information would you want before doing so? Obviously, you'd want to know the outcomes of the Business Case. Therefore, a phase review is really an intensive review of the preliminary Business Case. One thing you don't want to do is make it an all-day extravaganza. You should take no more than 30 to 60 minutes to make your case to management.

Summarizing the Business Case, the content for the phase review presentation must be able to present and answer the following questions:

- What is the opportunity?
- How did it come about?
- What are you asking for?
- Why is it strategically important?
- What is the market and/or customer problem being addressed? Can you adequately describe the segments and customer targets?
- How will the problem be solved? What products, services, or solutions will be needed?
- What is the value proposition for the customer? How will you prove that the value you deliver is the benefit they will buy?
- How will it be positioned competitively? How will you prove it?
- What technologies, platforms, techniques, methods, or science will you depend upon?
- How does the investment look from a financial and operational perspective? Can we make the product, market it, operationalize it, launch it, and manage it as part of the overall portfolio? How will all this be confirmed?

- What will happen and when? Is there a project schedule? Is there cross-functional buy-in?
- Are there any legal or regulatory issues? Are there any intellectual property issues? Are there international issues?
- What are the risks? How significant are they? What are the mitigation plans for each risk category?
- Where is the supporting data?
- What is the recommendation? Is it to move forward or reject?

It's a long and thorough list, but it is not a good idea to schedule the review unless you can answer each and every question.

To prepare for the review, I have two suggestions:

1. Socialize the work you're doing with leaders in different departments. Leaders do not want to be surprised by new initiatives. Often, through this quiet politicking (that's what you're doing here), you'll know whether the organization has an appetite for the investment. Most likely, you will also pick up some helpful feedback that may have you fine-tune the presentation. You'll be happy you did this when you get the nod.

2. When you're more confident about having buy-in from senior leaders, you should rehearse with your team. One option is to role-play the review session with someone who acts as a demanding CEO. The product manager should never go alone to the review. Key stakeholders from Marketing and Development should also attend, and perhaps one or two other very relevant team members. This phase review is an important decision-making session. Bottom line, it means you go in armed with the knowledge that what you recommend is crucial, whether it is to move ahead or to cancel any future efforts. Rejecting the project is a viable option if you and your team members believe the risks outweigh the return, or if the investment doesn't make business sense.

Another important point to remember: in a Feasibility review, other projects may also be presented, some of which were done within your team and some which originated with other team members. In the next phase (Definition), you learn that you cannot manage a huge number of projects and expect to get meaningful work done on all of them. Another consideration is that different projects may be making claims on the resources already committed to various other projects.

When functional team members claim they "could" do the work (because it's within the realm of their expertise), it doesn't mean the budget would include the head count needed to get the work done. That's why the Resource Estimate and Approval form is so important. In the final analysis, it forces the functional team's management to consider all of its resource commitments.

At the end of each phase, your team should have prepared a checklist to make sure anything and everything related to the investment proposal was considered. An example of this checklist is shown in Figure 12.11. I suggest constructing the checklist over time, especially if you are newer to this process. Most companies have pretty robust checklists already, so it's also worthwhile to check into your corporate process.

SUMMARY

The Feasibility phase started with an approved Opportunity Statement, which was the output from the previous Concept phase. The purpose of the Feasibility phase is to evaluate, in greater detail, those product concepts. This is accomplished by getting a better sense of its business, market, technical, and operational viability. This phase focuses on intense data gathering and research by each of the business functions working on the cross-functional product team. FSPs are drafted in a pairwise manner and then expanded across the landscape of the team. The product manager and the team then examine all of the contributions required by all team members holistically (the integrated FSP) to see how it all fits together. These inputs are then knitted into the fabric of the supporting product documentation.

Therefore, the emphasis during this chapter is on the work that people from the business functions carry out and how that work contributes to the evolution of the Business Case, Marketing Plan, PRD, and Launch Plan for the product (which, as stated earlier, is covered in subsequent chapters). Additionally, metrics are developed that would be used to track the product's performance, if it ultimately makes it to the market. Based on these documents, a decision matrix is rendered and evaluated. When everything is in place, a Feasibility review is carried out with the appropriate review team (such as an executive portfolio review board) to either allow the

FIGURE 12.11

Feasibility Phase Review Checklist

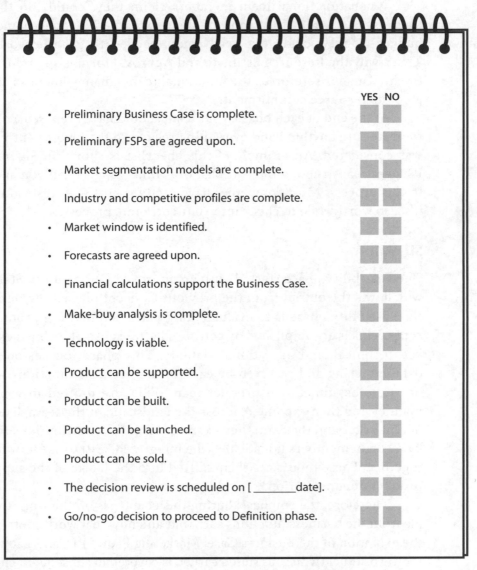

	YES	NO
• Preliminary Business Case is complete.	☐	☐
• Preliminary FSPs are agreed upon.	☐	☐
• Market segmentation models are complete.	☐	☐
• Industry and competitive profiles are complete.	☐	☐
• Market window is identified.	☐	☐
• Forecasts are agreed upon.	☐	☐
• Financial calculations support the Business Case.	☐	☐
• Make-buy analysis is complete.	☐	☐
• Technology is viable.	☐	☐
• Product can be supported.	☐	☐
• Product can be built.	☐	☐
• Product can be launched.	☐	☐
• Product can be sold.	☐	☐
• The decision review is scheduled on [_____date].	☐	☐
• Go/no-go decision to proceed to Definition phase.	☐	☐

opportunity to go on to the next phase or to reject it altogether. Regardless of whether you have decided to reject or forward the opportunity, it's necessary to carry out the Feasibility review to report on the extensive work that has been done to evaluate the opportunity.

RAISING YOUR PRODUCT MANAGEMENT EXPERIENCE QUOTIENT (PMEQ)

1. During the Feasibility phase, one of the most important things you may need to do is facilitate a negotiation between two or more business functions. This is important because you need to clarify roles and responsibilities for subsequent phases and to help set the stage for work that has to be carried out. If you have not "brokered" these pairwise discussions at some point in your career, seek the counsel of a manager who has experience negotiating work activities between different business functions. To enhance your own experience, schedule one-on-one meetings with the individuals from the relevant business functions in order to lay the foundation for this discussion. Provide them with an FSP template and ask them to work on as much of it as possible. Next, review their deliverables *to* one of the functions and then bring that other function into a brief meeting to review that which is to be provided. Have each person try to clarify the other's deliverables, timing, and dependencies. After you hold some of these sessions, you will appreciate the degree of complexity involved.

2. Consult with the members of your cross-functional team to determine how they expect to validate their ability to commit to a given project. Explain the idea of the FSP and share the template. Find out what elements of the template are more difficult to pin down, and begin working on ways to discover the needed data.

3. Bring in a project management specialist to help you capture commitments, deliverables, resources, and schedules for each of the FSPs.

4. If you have not created a prototype or a model for a new product or an enhancement, talk with other product managers in your organization to find out who has. Find out how they did their prototyping project, who funded it, and how it contributed to their feasibility evaluation.

5. Much of the work carried out in the Feasibility phase is related to content discussed in Module 2, "Making the Market Your Primary Focus." Industry and competitive research, segmentation, forecasting, and strategy all play a vital role in guiding this work. You may need to look ahead to Chapter 14, on the Business Case, to get your template for action.

6. Review the New Product Development process that may already be used in your company. (There may be a process organization or equivalent function.) There may even be an internal website you can visit to find out about your company's processes. This phase may or may not be called "Feasibility" in your company; it would be the phase that follows an initial idea phase. Review the relevant documentation and checklists to make sure that the work you are doing is aligned with your process model.

7. Find out about the product proposal process in your company. To which group or board are new product feasibility studies presented? What are others' experiences in dealing with this board? What can you learn that will help you enhance your chances for having a successful review?

8. For any research, investigations, or other work carried out, don't forget to keep updating the Product Master Plan in relation to these efforts.

APPEARANCES ARE EVERYTHING: DEFINING AND DESIGNING THE PRODUCT

Executive Summary

- A solid definition of the product from the customer's perspective improves the product's chances of achieving its market goals.
- The Definition phase is the most important linkage between the needs of customers and the designs and capabilities of products.
- The Definition phase serves to not only clarify the product's content but also complete all planning documentation, including the Business Case and the Product Launch Plan.

This chapter describes the important work activities and associated documentation that need to be finalized in the Product Definition phase. During this third and final New Product Planning phase, the Product Requirements Document (PRD) must be completed, along with the product's overall design. Other work activities that product managers should focus on during this phase include the make versus buy analysis and the Product Launch Plan.

An opportunity that has reached the Definition phase has successfully progressed from the Feasibility phase review. The team has demonstrated to the portfolio review board that it has carried out sufficient research and prepared the appropriate documentation, and as a result it has received approval to invest time and resources to finish up the plans for the product. Important decisions made during this phase have profound impacts on later phase investments in the actual development, launching, and marketing of the product.

In the Feasibility phase, the team had more flexibility in deliberating about features, content, and trade-offs. However, during the Definition phase, the debates about product content, function, and design become more focused because the definition needs to be clearly understood by all team members. The Definition phase buttons up all of the planning work done in previous phases, with the end result being the completion of all product and business documentation.

In the Definition phase, the main documents to focus upon include: the PRD, the Business Case, the Marketing Plan for the product, and the Launch Plan. This chapter will cover the PRD and the Launch Plan. I discuss product launch execution in Chapter 17. The other documents, the Business Case and the Marketing Plan for the product, are handled as separate chapters so that they can be referenced as stand-alone documents, and because they are very dynamic in nature. Finally, there is one topic that is often neglected in the Definition phase. It involves a make versus buy analysis. This area is often neglected because of the belief that the product should be built or developed in-house. This is a vital topic to address because oftentimes the product is neither built nor developed in house—it is outsourced.

As in the other phases of product planning, there are inputs, activities, and outputs as the team drives for a go or no-go decision on the product, as represented in Figure 13.1.

Typically, companies associate product definition solely with product requirements, features, and the few business activities that couldn't be previously completed. Nothing could be further from the truth. Team activity continues to intensify and expand in the Definition phase, as Functional Support Plans (FSPs) solidify, and roles and responsibilities are clarified. The business documents such as the Business Case, Launch

FIGURE 13.1

Definition Phase Process Profile

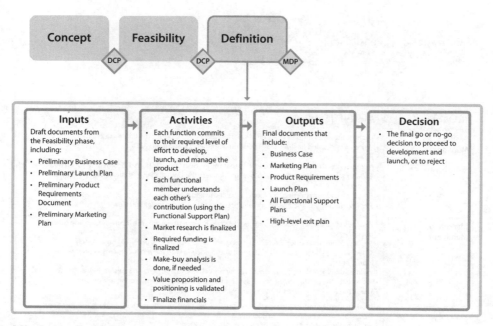

DCP = Decision Check Point
MDP = Major Decision Point

Plan, and Marketing Plan evolve as team members continue to negotiate and finalize their commitments for related activities during the phase. The more technically focused Product Specifications Document and design documents are also finalized during this phase. Most important, this is the phase where all team members agree to the fulfillment of their commitments during development, launch, and Post-Launch Product Management. As with the preceding phases, the work during the Definition phase is characterized by a matrix, shown in Figure 13.2.

Hopefully, the lessons learned thus far have demonstrated that a flexible, phased process offers a guiding framework for evaluating product opportunities. However, this represents only part of the product definition puzzle. Creativity and vision—the notion of what *could* be—cannot be taught. Think of the phases of product planning as the highway on-ramp, and as we gather speed, the product Definition phase helps us accelerate onto the highway with a solid set of interpretable, realistic, descriptive product requirements. The process also allows us to choose to decelerate and do other productive work.

FIGURE 13.2

Cross-Functional Team Roles During the Definition Phase

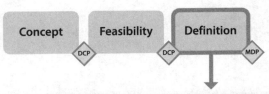

ROLE	ACTIVITIES
Product Manager	• Orchestrates the complex cross-functional interactions to produce the final Business Case • Writes, reviews, and finalizes the Product Requirements Document (PRD) • Reviews and approves the final product design • Negotiates with Development to ensure that the Product Specifications Document (PSD) is completed • Collaborates with Marketing and others to complete the Launch Plan and the Marketing Plan for the product • Ensures that the marketing mix model is balanced and realistic • Finalizes remaining documentation and prepares the team for the gate review
Marketing Manager	• Finalizes all customer, industry, and competitive research to support the Business Case and other documents • Secures commitments for promotional programs for the product launch and post-launch • Lines up early adopters or lead customers in conjunction with the product manager and the sales manager • Ensures that market trials and other preliminary activities are in place to support prelaunch programs • Works with the product manager on synchronizing and balancing marketing mix model • Leads the work to finalize the Marketing Plan for the product
Development Manager	• Works with the product manager to take the final PRD and provide the final Product Specifications Document (PSD) and/or design document • Finalizes the best technologies or platforms to be utilized • Provides cost estimates, quality guidelines, test plans, and designs for manufacturability (if required) • Commits to support early trials, beta tests, etc. • Agrees to provice resources for product support after the launch • Prepares final project plans
Finance Manager	• Helps validate and finalize financial models and forecasts • Creates final product level budgets and ensure that all functional budgets and plans are consistent with the Business Case • Provides corporate guidelines to help with team decisions
Customer Service Manager	• Assures the team that future service related activities like call center staffing, complaint or case handling, and order taking can be accomplished • Is responsible for the creation of tools to help customers serve themselves in web transactions • Ensures that service programs are integrated within the operational infrastructure of the organization • Puts in place programs to support service level agreements
Sales Manager	• Finalizes commitments with product managers, marketers, and finance in the support of sales forecasts, volume commitments, and revenue targets • Makes sure that targets and compensation programs are in place to incent sales people and ensure that volumes can be supported
Operations Manager	• Finalizes operational infrastructure elements required to launch the product and to support the product while it is actively sold in the market • Links operations plans with other functions such as customer service and IT so the product can be properly managed
Supply Chain Manager	• Finalizes sourcing, ecosystem partners, and contracts • Ensures that the procurement, logistics, and other supply chain elements are synchronized
Manufacturing Manager	• For tangible products, commits to final capacity plans and assures that the demand forecasts are linked to ensure that the product can be produced
Legal & Regulatory Manager(s)	• These advisory team members are consulted to ensure that the team's decisions are consistent with rules & regulations for each market area
International or Global Organizations	• Finalizes local market input to the product team to ensure that the product can meet the needs of local/geographic market areas

PRODUCT DEFINITION DOCUMENTS

Product Definition is not only the name of the phase but also a guiding force in the product planning and development process. If the Business Case is one of the most important documents for Product Management, the product requirements are the bridge between the activities of product planning and the actual designing and building (or producing) of a sellable product. Success of the Definition phase is measured in terms of a product whose purpose is fully understood and whose features and attributes actually solve (or contribute heavily toward solving) a customer's problem or enable the customer to take advantage of an opportunity.

The Business Case is the primary *business* document for product definition. The product description section of the Business Case should contain major elements from the product requirements. It should clearly reflect the research and findings carried out throughout the phases of product planning. The elements of the Business Case that directly influence the product definition include:

1. The degree to which the product is aligned with the strategy of the product line or business division within which the product is situated

2. A solid understanding of customer needs, including the needs of users, influencers, and decision makers

3. A clear perspective on the competitive environment and how the product will help the company to win in the market

4. A recognition of the political, economic and regulatory environment and its impact on the product in its chosen markets

5. Explicit positioning in the market and in relation to the competition

6. Demonstration that the product's features and attributes were derived using structured qualitative and quantitative prioritization within the context of customer needs and market requirements

7. Solid risk assessments and mitigation strategies

8. A valid, balanced marketing mix model (product, pricing, promotion, and distribution)

9. Project resource availability to carry out the work in development and operational execution

10. A committed cross-functional team that shares the vision and purpose for the product

Getting the product definition as right as you can and as soon as you can really does matter. A properly constructed product definition will help you communicate and negotiate with Development, which will help make sure that you have what you need, when you need it. The document used to carry out this negotiation is the PRD. The PRD is one of two types of documents used as the product definition evolves. The other is the Product Specifications Document (PSD), which should contain the technical parameters for the product. PSDs may include a section on the product's actual design (physical or otherwise). It may also be augmented by a separate product design document that characterizes or portrays physical specifications, user interfaces, and other relevant items. The terminology your firm uses will likely vary, but here is the bottom line: *The PRD is a business- and market-driven document* that describes the functional and non-functional characteristics of a product that reflects business, market, or customer needs. This document is owned by a product manager and may be written or documented by a business analyst, systems engineer, or technically proficient product manager (depending on the complexity of the product). The PRD should be considered the document that takes the business perspective and covers market issues, customer challenges, and other problems that require a solution. The evolution of the PRD across the phases of New Product Planning is shown in Figure 13.3.

The PSD is written by people who work in Product Development, which can be R&D, Engineering, or an equivalent technical function.

FIGURE 13.3

Evolution of the Product Requirements Document

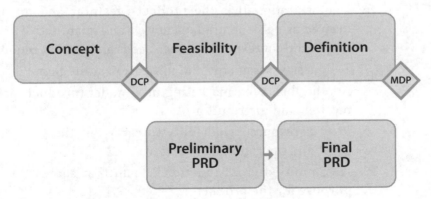

The PSD answers the question of how the product requirements will be fulfilled. Of course, the technologists want more specificity from the business people, and the product managers or business people want innovative, cost-effective designs that yield a product that works as defined in the PRD. Additionally, the product's physical design must be explicated. This may include the design for a tangible product, the delivery model for a service, a user interface for an application, or other aspect where the product's appearance or ease of customer interactivity is critical.

Problems emerge when it comes to interpretation, especially when product managers want more and the developers cannot or do not want to commit to the work, usually because of issues related to ambiguity. Other challenges can emerge when the designers and developers cannot come to terms.

When I was a product manager for a telephone system, the PRD indicated the size of the phone system control unit. This was based on the environment where the device would typically be mounted. With that information, the developers designed an appropriate housing for the control unit. When the developers created the drawings and models for the housing, our team agreed to continue with the program. However, we ran into an unanticipated problem. The space allocated in the control unit for a power supply did not account for the actual size of the power supplies available at the time. You can only imagine how we all felt. I realized that I had overlooked one of the critical steps in the process—that is, to ensure that all elements of the physical design were completely worked out among the product manager, designer, and developer.

When the product manager has comprehensive market knowledge and communicates the proper parameters in the PRD, the chances are that the PSD and design documents will reflect the intended result. In Figure 13.4, you can see how the PRD, PSD, and design document must evolve as the product manager inspires the appropriate level of collaboration among these vital team members.

As the product definition moves forward, the foundational market and strategic intent must be accounted for. Therefore, the more market oriented and customer aware the product manager is, the greater the chances that the PRD will be complete and will fulfill the customer's value proposition. This increases the probability that the PSD and the product's ultimate design will reflect that intent.

FIGURE 13.4

Evolution of the PRD, PSD, and Product Design

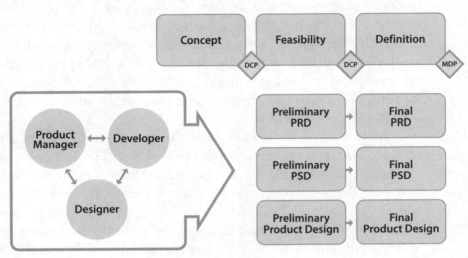

In many organizations, an issue arises when the technical community wants more specificity from the product manager. In this case, I strongly advise that boundary conditions be established between the product manager and the developer. The PRD represents business and market drivers, problem statements, scenarios, and stories. The PSD represents the development community's intent to solve for the issues and conditions as communicated in the PRD. In fact, I recommend that a fixed line between the business-driven PRD and the technically oriented PSD be maintained (Figure 13.5) and that negotiations between the product manager and the developers follow the format used in the FSP, as I discussed earlier in the book. The other reason the PRD must remain a pure business- and market-driven document is that people in Marketing should be able to utilize its content for sales collateral or other marketing materials. They won't be able to do so if the content is too technical and engineering oriented.

THE PRD OUTLINE AND TEMPLATE

Most PRDs should follow a fairly standard outline. The sections in the template shown as Figure 13.6 are listed here for quick reference. However, further reading in the chapter will provide more context for you.

FIGURE 13.5

The Boundary Between the PRD and PSD

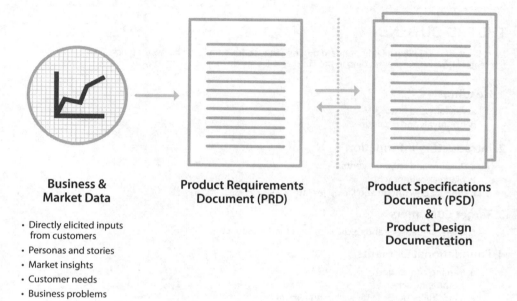

Business & Market Data

- Directly elicited inputs from customers
- Personas and stories
- Market insights
- Customer needs
- Business problems

Product Requirements Document (PRD)

Product Specifications Document (PSD) & Product Design Documentation

MANAGING REQUIREMENTS

The product manager needs a systematic approach to shape the product definition. The product requirements process is fairly well documented, especially for the technology industry. Because of this, I will provide a general overview of the requirements process so that you can get your bearings if you are relatively new to the product definition process or need the guidance of a standard process. The general steps in requirements management consist of the following:

1. Eliciting requirements
2. Defining requirements
3. Organizing documents
4. Managing requirements from beginning to end to assure that there is complete traceability

A primary result of this effort is the creation of clear documentation that defines the functionality, features, and/or attributes of products.

FIGURE 13.6

Product Requirements Document Template

THE PRD OUTLINE

Most PRDs should follow a fairly standard outline. The sections are listed below for quick reference. However, further reading in the chapter will provide more context for you.

1. Headings
    a. Versions and history
    b. Approvals and signatures

2. Introductory Information
    a. Purpose and strategic context
    b. Market environment
    c. Product description and life cycle state

3. Target Customers
    a. Users, influencers, and decision makers for the product

4. Foundational Elements
    a. Naming conventions
    b. Numbering schemes
    c. Rationale or purpose for each requirement
    d. Dependencies (and how those will be called out)
    e. Conflict resolution process
    f. Diagram standards used to describe work flows, clarify intent, etc.
    g. Traceability and references

5. Functional Requirements and how those should be shown to reflect the basic intent or what the product should do.

6. Non-Functional Requirements that describe characteristics, properties, or qualities, and described as features or attributes. Non-functional requirements can also be divided into a number of categories and subcategories. These include:
    a. Areas associated with customer usage or usability
        i. Efficiency or speed
        ii. Transaction turn-around times
        iii. Learnability or ease of recall (for usability and simplicity)
        iv. Acceptable errors that a user or customer could make
        v. Feedback (as in a sound, "click" or otherwise)

    b. Areas associated with physical characteristics
        i. Size
        ii. Appearance
        iii. Weight
        iv. Styles
        v. Colors
        vi. Designs

6. CONTINUED

    c. Areas associated with performance and quality

        i. Speed
        ii. Response time
        iii. Precision
        iv. Number of simultaneous users
        v. Reliability (or mean-time-to-failure)
        vi. Capacity
        vii. Scalability
        viii. Durability
        ix. Longevity

    d. Areas associated with operational support or integration

        i. The physical environment
        ii. Interfaces and compatibility with other products or systems
        iii. Hardware requirements
        iv. Software requirements
        v. Release or launch plans
        vi. Operational environment integration

    e. Areas associated with maintenance and support over the life of the product

        i. Documentation required
        ii. Maintenance or maintainability
        iii. Adaptation or migration from the current environment
        iv. Auditing or monitoring the performance of the product or system
        v. Access: physical or remote

    f. Areas associated with data

        i. Data elements
        ii. Fields (size, alpha, numeric, alphanumeric)
        iii. Ranges
        iv. Constraints

    g. Areas associated with safety and security

        i. System or product access
        ii. Verification
        iii. Privacy
        iv. Safeguards

    h. Areas associated with laws or regulations

        i. Local or country specific
        ii. Time frames required
        iii. Standards body compliance

    i. Areas associated with global or international usage

        i. Local packaging or design
        ii. Local performance
        iii. Local materials

There are two main types of requirements, both of which focus on the customer or user: *functional* requirements and *non-functional* requirements. Functional requirements reflect the basic intent of the product, or "what it's supposed to do." Functional requirements are often articulated using the word *shall*. Non-functional requirements describe characteristics, properties, or qualities that the product "should" or "must" exhibit. These are sometimes called *behaviors* of the product, usually related to the product's desired characteristics, usability, or maintainability (and sometimes, performance).

Whether the requirements are functional or non-functional, they must meet the customer's need and the manner in which those problems are to be solved. Therefore, the PRD cannot even be started without an understanding of the market segmentation models and the underlying needs of the customer targets within those segments—those needs for which the product is being defined. The big question is, "For whom are we building this product, and why?"

Eliciting Requirements

Elicitation is the process of drawing out a response from someone (a customer), either through questioning or observing. The process of eliciting requirements for a product can be informative and interesting—and sometimes fun. Elicitation allows the product manager to dig for each and every customer or market motivation that will help to produce a product requirement. Successful products reflect requirements that are derived from known data and from a variety of sources—sources reflected as customer targets (e.g., users) within the segmentation models. Once these sources have been identified, the product manager should have a way to systematically obtain, synthesize, and rationalize the data. Rationalizing helps to reduce the number of requirements that may be in conflict or redundant.

Eliciting requirements is aligned with many of the approaches I've discussed thus far, such as needs-based market segmentation and ideation. The techniques that work best in collecting requirements include:

- *Highly structured interviews from customers or other experts.* I'm not talking about questionnaires, but direct interviews. The kinds of questions I like to use are similar to those that might be used in consultative selling. These types of open-ended questions serve to guide the customer, allowing the interviewer to gain perspective from the responses and other descriptions provided by the customer. This technique is especially helpful in uncovering needs customers don't even know they have. When I ask a question about a customer's environment, it can be as simple as, "Can you explain to me how you process an order?" which allows me to listen to the customer talk and explain. It also allows me to gain a better context and to craft other open-ended, context-free questions.

- *Conducting working sessions.* In my last corporate job, I participated in a customer advisory group composed of users and decision makers for a customer service application. On one of the days that we all met, we spent about three hours in a fairly intense brainstorming session during which we captured dozens of ideas. We divided the larger groups into smaller groups, gave each group a fictitious budget, and then sent them into breakout sessions with instructions to allocate money to each of the feature areas. When we brought them all back together, we were able to come up with a good list of things to work on—not that we were going to include each and every wish into our product, but we were going to use each idea to explore further and elicit greater levels of requirements. Again, you cannot create the requirements if you cannot get to the underlying needs.

- *Customer surveys.* Often, product managers deploy surveys to current customers or to customers who might be possible targets in the hope of learning about their attitudes, preferences, work practices, and other aspects of their personal or work lives.

- *Information gathering from the cross-functional team.* People in Marketing, Sales, Customer Service, and other functions, or corporate experts, are a great resource because of their evaluations of customer interactions or market activity.

- *Conversations with industry analysts.* Industry analysts are very insightful because they carry out conversations with competitors, economists, and other market or domain specialists. Customers often tell analysts things they don't tell vendors.

- *Reviewing competitive product features and attributes.* An important element of competitive analysis is to reverse engineer or extensively analyze the competitor's product, or to use the competitor's product as a source of requirements. This can reveal interesting competitive strengths or weaknesses as well. At one point in my corporate career, I did a feature comparison with a competitor's product and was surprised at how the competitor implemented some of its product's functionality. The product didn't perform exactly as indicated in its marketing materials nor did it do what had been reported in the feature comparison prepared by industry analysts. The teaching point is to avoid being fooled by functionality or features with the same identifier or name in competitive comparisons by industry analysts. You can use this type of detailed competitive product profiling to add some unique competitive advantages into your own product definition.

- *Potential customers or current customers or product users.* Customers who are familiar with your product can be a great resource. There may be many users of the product in one company (in a business-to-business company) or there may be many consumers who are willing to talk to you. They all probably have opinions and would make great candidates to interview or observe.

- *Brainstorming.* This unstructured, free-form facilitated technique is a great way to elicit and capture customer needs and potential requirements. You can brainstorm with your cross-functional team, with customers, or with other subject matter experts. Along with brainstorming, *mind mapping* is also a great technique that helps people create visual connections or linkages between thoughts, ideas, and expressions to reveal potential solutions that may not have been explicitly apparent through general interviewing or observing.

- *Architectural reviews.* Many of today's products are part of larger systems or solutions. As such, any new product or enhancement to an existing product must consider the complexity of interfaces, whether electronic or manual, and the workflows that drive intersystem processes. When you understand and can specify the inputs, activities, and outputs of any product in a "system," or when you can clarify interplatform dependencies, you minimize risk and ensure that the product will work properly.

- *Product quality reviews.* When product managers and their teams review technical product performance information, product complaints, product failure data, and the like, they have an important context around which to shape the definition of enhancements or new products

- *Storytelling.* This is a remarkable method for a variety of purposes. Stories can be used to convey what happened in the past and to visualize the future. Product managers who can tell stories that portray the customer's "way of life" can create current scenarios about what people do now and scenarios about what people might do in the future. With many consumer products or consumer applications (e.g., a mobile computing device), "user stories" can drive the product definition. Scenarios as characterizations are also helpful in building customer "personas," as I described in Chapter 8. Scenarios put product requirements in context. However, there is another benefit: scenarios can be used to build assumption sets for forecasts in Business Cases and in crafting meaningful value propositions. Lastly, these stories can be told when providing readouts of anthropomorphic methods as used during customer visits and when capturing observations about customers in their own environments.

Whatever you do in this elicitation process, make sure that it is all being recorded properly so that you can refer to it when writing those requirements at the appropriate time.

Defining Requirements

As just described, product requirements can begin as a story, scenario, or abstraction of a series of events involving a customer or a system. These stories are typically modeled around a desired customer target or persona. Statements that ultimately emerge might include "our day-to-day work demands that we all be able to stay in touch with one another no matter where we are." From this, you might be able to deduce that there is a need for a low-cost mobile device. As the process continues, the requirements might become more specific or they may diverge, ultimately coming up with a statement like "the device must weigh less than three ounces," or "the device must have a display that can be easily read in broad daylight," or "the device should be able to operate for up to 72 hours on a single battery charge." Requirements evolve and become more specific as product managers are better able to explain to designers and/or developers what they want in the product.

Better requirements have the following characteristics:

1. They are *clearly described* and written, which means they are not subject to different interpretations by different readers.
2. They are *complete*, which means they cover all the pertinent points.
3. They are generally *consistent* because they do not conflict with other requirements in the document. I say "generally" because you might want to examine seemingly contradictory needs to look for potential linkages, which may help you solve a customer's problem in a unique way.
4. They are fully *traceable*, which means that the source of each requirement is identified and linked back to the original customer requirement that was elicited.
5. They are *testable* by quality engineers or other people (including product managers), with an underlying intent for the product to be maintained, serviced, and supported in the future.

Moreover, PRDs should include additional information. Such information may include contextual statements, tables, and glossaries. Actual requirements should therefore be highlighted by a unique text size or color or with boldface text. Writing requirements is like writing a how-to book. This kind of a book has sections, chapters, and subchapters that may have some repeated thoughts or activities. The requirements author has to collaborate with many specialists (editors) to make the book whole.

Let's look at some examples of functional and non-functional requirements. Functional requirements describe what the product should help the customer to achieve. I'm going to use the simple example of an automated teller machine (ATM) at a bank because it is something we are all familiar with, plus it has physical attributes and technical attributes.

The ATM's purpose is to help banking customers who have a secure identification key (personal identification number [PIN], etc.) to authenticate themselves and to enable them to carry out a variety of self-service banking activities, including getting cash, checking balances, and transferring money in a secure, safe environment. One element of the product's functionality may be described with a *scenario* or a chain of events as follows:

A customer walks into the bank's vestibule to use an ATM to get cash. The customer inserts her card, which prompts the ATM to send a signal to the bank's computer system that someone is ready to sign on. The computer then sends an instruction to the customer to enter her PIN. After the PIN is entered, it is securely conveyed back to the computer system, which then looks up the PIN in its database. The result is either an authorization or denial of access to the customer's account. If authorized, the customer can carry out her desired transactions.

The functional requirement is a reflection of this short story and contains, at a minimum, the following sections:

1. A *requirement number* (e.g., FR 1.0, for functional requirement 1.0), which allows for hierarchical organization and traceability.

2. A *description of the requirement* so that it is put into perspective:

   The ATM must be able to authenticate the customer when the customer inserts the identification card into the card slot of the ATM.

3. The *reason for the requirement,* which tells a more concise story about why the requirement is important:

   It is critical that customers be able to securely establish their identity when they choose the self-service option in dealing with the bank. The bank's strategy is to drive more and more people to the self-service option to reduce teller staffing.

4. *Assumptions* that may be helpful in a requirement so that the author can put the requirement into perspective. Assumptions may not always need to be expressed, but if they provide additional context beyond the reason for the requirement, they should be included:

   It is assumed that the ATM is placed in an area that is safe and secure for customers to transact their business.

5. A *requirement source,* so that any clarification of intent can be traced back to the person or group who suggested the functionality:

   Joe in the Marketing department and Audra in the IT department came up with a more robust authentication scheme. This is due to the bank's recognition that customer security is an increasingly important factor in whether a customer does business with our bank. This was made clear in hundreds of recent customer interviews.

6. *Dependencies* on any other products or systems:

   The ATM is connected to a banking network, which links back to different parts of the bank's computer system and perhaps various databases (such as a PIN database, an accounts database, and a customer database).

7. *Reference documents* or materials that help the author to relay to the reader that this requirement may not stand alone:

> Refer to PRD 45 from the ABC Security Company and XYZ Bank regarding the mandatory ATM interfaces to the banking network.

8. A *profile or history of changes* so that the adds, updates, or deletions can be tracked.

Non-functional requirements help set the parameters for customer usage and interaction. If functional requirements assert what a product *shall do*, the non-functional requirements define what qualities or characteristics the product *should have*. The more technology oriented the product, the more attention that needs to be focused on these requirements. For example, software-oriented "systems" need to have requirements describing configurability, scalability, modifiability, throughput, response times, and so forth. Non-functional requirements tend to focus on the following:

1. The external product design elements or styles the product should follow (how the product should look, feel, sound, etc.)

2. How the product should perform under a variety of conditions

3. How the product should be maintained (if it requires maintenance)

4. The kinds of safety or security elements the product should have to protect the customer

5. Any regulatory or governmental requirements the product should be able to meet

Using these five general non-functional requirements categories, here are examples that put each category into better perspective:

■ External design:

> The ATM should have a screen that can be seen from the angle of a person who is from 4 feet 10 inches tall to 6 feet 8 inches tall and should have a viewing area measuring 12 inches in width by 10 inches in height.

■ Performance:

> The ATM should be able to operate in a temperature range of 0 degrees Celsius to 40 degrees Celsius.

■ Maintenance:

> Preventive maintenance for the keyboard should not be required more often than once per year for ATMs averaging 144 transactions per day.

- Security and safety:

    For security purposes, transactions should be completed within 30 seconds of the last customer interaction (button push or screen entry) or else the authentication process should restart.

- Regulatory:

    All ATMs must conform to the rules for placement and security as described by the state banking department.

Most non-functional requirements establish boundaries for the product—or what some designers and developers call *constraints* on the product. A constraint on an ATM might be whether the network can handle a specific number of ATMs or whether there are even enough skilled developers to carry out future computer programming for system upgrades or maintenance. On the same plane, a functional requirement might end up restricting an ATM to a specific number of transactions per day because it's all the network can handle.

With this context for functional and non-functional requirements, I want to turn your attention to the next category within the complex set of activities related to product definition, namely, organizing the necessary documents.

Organizing Documents

In order to clarify and justify the requirements, product managers and representatives from the technical community (Development, IT, etc.) need to collaborate and negotiate. Product managers need to be able to explain the requirements, while Development needs to be able to interpret and understand them, so it can respond accordingly. Many products are treated as a system, structured from a variety of product elements, so there should be a document hierarchy that organizes the requirements according to the product's overall design. In a system, there may be a list of requirements for software as well as for the physical hardware (as described earlier); there could also be a series of documents focusing on performance, maintainability, and security.

I cannot provide you with an explicit set of guidelines that tell you how many types of documents should be used, because the documentation is dependent on the type of product and its degree of complexity. The critical takeaway is this: requirements should be organized so that you can easily isolate specific requirements that may need to be considered separately. For example, if you plan to evaluate subassemblies as they are completed, it would be highly inconvenient to have requirements for those subassemblies scattered through many sections of several documents.

Managing Requirements from Beginning to End

Requirements start their lives when the first opportunities are connected to customer assessments, articulated in this chapter as requirements elicitation. Requirements can take on a life of their own due to their interconnectedness and their propensity to cascade from one level to the next, just like an outline for a book. In other words, once the requirements are captured, they evolve. The rough evolutionary path of any changes needs to be documented so that at any time the requirement can be traced back to its source.

When I learned computer programming in college, I learned that the programmer's responsibility was to place documentation in sections of the programs so that anyone called upon to debug the code could have a context for the reason for a specific routine within the code. Having such traceable requirements allows the product manager, analyst, and development teams to manage the project's activities and tasks and, furthermore, helps to manage project risks. Usually, some kind of a hierarchical diagram between documents can help with visual traceability.

The second key to requirements management is related to the management of change. Even if a team member (especially a developer) has an idea for a feature, don't build it in until it has been agreed upon by the owner(s) of the product definition. Change in the input to product definition is a constant imposition on the product team. If changes are made too hastily, critical features or attributes may be left out, or the analysis of the impact of a change may evoke conflict, leaving the team vulnerable to a variety of influences.

This is why the need for traceability cannot be emphasized enough here. Even if the PRD is frozen, some inputs will change, be added, or need to be dropped, based on complexity, cost, and time. Traceability affords the product manager and the team the ability to ensure that they can trace back the requirement to its source, as well as the reason for the requirement, and a linkage to other related requirements. This way, if a requirement needs to be left to "version 2.0" of the product, the changes in the PRD can be monitored and efficiently managed so that the functionality can be realized and brought to market later.

The longer the Development phase, the more likely that product changes will emerge from all of the business functions as they evolve their FSPs. Even though there is strong advocacy for freezing the definition and baselining the product requirements at the major decision point between New Product Planning and New Product Introduction, it may be unrealistic. If you hold the line on very-long-duration Definition phase activities (development lasting more than 9 months, for example), the product may lose value because markets, technology, and team dynamics experience inevitable changes.

If long-duration development projects are overexposed to possible changes, you should note that very-short-duration development projects might not contain enough content to be meaningful. This is especially true in software and technology projects, and less prevalent in consumer goods or other tangible industrial products. Many software or technology firms use fast-track releases or develop their products in short iterations that put the product managers on a definition treadmill, leaving in-market products in the unmanaged care of salespeople or unskilled marketers.

Successful projects seem to allow for selective change, mostly related to new competitive information or other unanticipated market factors. Some are "in-bound" changes, which are typically related to the management of scope of the project. Some of these are "out-of-bounds" and must be deferred. The key to change management is to formally capture and document these changes. The change documents may be called Engineering Change Requests (ECRs), Modification Requests (MRs), or something else. One of the key problems to avoid is, of course, scope creep or feature creep, especially without appropriate adjustment of critical documents.

The cross-functional team, using decision matrices to look at the relative importance of scope adjustments or change requests, approves any such changes. Any major trade-offs requiring a shift of the investment or a major change in the project should be brought to the product portfolio review board (or equivalent) for approval. After all, if it approved the investment, it should be able to approve major changes. Some companies freeze the requirements (no changes at all) instead of waiting for a major enhancement that may not be scheduled. To avoid missing the market window, they send out essential changes in a retrofit kit to customers after the launch. Companies with no formal change management philosophy struggle with scope creep demons, which ultimately lead to higher levels of product failure in the marketplace.

Without traceability, inevitable changes cannot be managed during development, and certainly not when the product is in the market. With traceability, changes can be managed in an orderly manner, because the product manager or business analyst can follow the bread crumbs (the path of the relationships between product requirements) across the established document hierarchy.

PRIORITIZING REQUIREMENTS

As mentioned earlier, you're not going to get everything you want, and you will have to figure out what to do and what not to do. In Chapter 5, I discussed the importance of decision making and provided you with a way to vet various options based on specific criteria. Further, in Chapter 11, I showed you how to use a decision matrix to evaluate different product investment opportunities. In a nutshell, because you have to make trade-offs, you should use a decision matrix that contains various criteria. These must be vetted against agreed-upon criteria, as shown in the sample matrix in Figure 13.7 You'd insert a score based on a scale of 1–10 in each cell in the matrix, with 10 as the most significant contributor and 1 as the least. When you total the scores, from left-to-right, you can more easily rank and prioritize the requirements.

FIGURE 13.7

A Decision Matrix to Prioritize Requirements

	Aligned with Strategy	Fulfills the Customer Value Proposition	Contributes to Desired Product Positioning	Technology Is Available	Total Score
Requirement 1					
Requirement 2					
Requirement 3					
Requirement 4					

INSPECTIONS AND PEER REVIEWS

PRDs may be authored and owned by product managers. However, like a manuscript for a book must be reviewed and edited prior to publication, so must the PRD. Every product manager has a different writing style, and it is important that what has been written can be correctly interpreted by the intended audience. Further, product managers have varying levels of experience and understanding of the product.

Earlier in my career, I worked in an environment where PRDs were considered so important to the success of a product that a group of people, including peers and managers, met to review and discuss my work. This peer review process is important to ensure consistency, clarity, and completeness in the product definition process.

Lastly, due to various cultural norms and perspectives, authors may use the same words but with different intended meanings. To overcome this challenge and to ensure that the requirements are consistently written and presented, a group of peers and others may wish to conduct PRD review sessions and inspections before an agreement is reached on the final, or baselined, PRD. Firms use many different types of reviews, including the following:

1. *Inspections*—a systematic, rigorous review to look for areas of ambiguity, inconsistency, and achievability. Inspections also include discussions of risk, especially when technologists are part of the process. Inspections are also used in the negotiation with the technical community as it crafts its PSD.

2. *Team reviews*—where developers and product managers (sometimes augmented by members from other areas) look for clarity of intent or purpose and consistency in language. Team reviews are also great ways for teams to exchange ideas about how problems are solved in other areas. These reviews are like extra sets of eyes to help edit the PRD.

3. *Walkthroughs*—where the product manager presents the essence of all the sections of the PRD to a group of peers or others, or sometimes customers, to ensure that the logic, intent, and desired outcomes are understood by all stakeholders. Walkthroughs also can surface gaps and problems that may have eluded the product manager or other contributors.

Peer reviews and inspections are attended by a wide range of people, and their outcome is dependent on a variety of factors. Consider reaching out to your peers or others to get a better understanding of this process. You should make sure that the process and protocols are documented in the Product Master Plan repository. Note: it's helpful to use a roles and responsibilities matrix for any type of review. For example, inspections may include:

- The author—the product manager who created the PRD.
- The facilitator—a person who uses a standard checklist of areas to review and facilitates or moderates the session. Facilitators should prepare participants in advance so they can effectively play their role during the inspection session.
- The reader—a person who may be called upon to recite specific sections of the PRD so that questions and comments can be elicited.
- The recorder—a person to act as the scribe, record issues, and support the moderator in the preparation of the inspection report.
- The inspector—the person who examines the PRD prior to the inspection session to look for problems. The inspector will prepare information for the facilitator. Inspectors also serve to identify further issues or problems and challenge assumptions as the session progresses.

When peer reviews and inspections are carried out, the product manager should ensure that outcome reports are prepared or work with the recorder and facilitator to keep track of issues and suggestions in an "issues log" or equivalent document. This is important because the product manager will have to provide updates to the inspection team to keep the team apprised of actions taken to address the issues.

REQUIREMENTS MANAGEMENT AND THE PRODUCT LIFE CYCLE

In today's business environment, some product life cycles move at breakneck speeds, and some products last for decades. The definition process must be adapted to suit the product environment. No doubt you will encounter various product development terms such as "agile," "rapid application development," or "waterfall." In addition, some development processes are linear while others have various iterations.

It is clear to me that development methods will continue to evolve and that product managers must have an astute sense of the process so they can ensure that product definition documents have the optimal content and provide developers with the guidance needed to produce the product, whether in increments or in one major program.

An application for a portable computing device may be developed iteratively at break-neck speed. In this case, the collaboration among the product manager, developer, and others will be very quick, and iterations may be done over hours or days. These products tend to have short life cycles and are enhanced on an ongoing basis. In an enterprise software environment where a major application is delivered as a subscription service, product upgrades may be built over weeks or months, but the full release takes place once a year. In such a case, the PRD may be worked on as user or business scenarios are brought to life in the product—with major integration points. In addition, there are long-lived industrial products driven with electronic controls to automate given actions. Those tend to be software driven. As with the subscription-software model, the main product is launched at a given time, even though aspects of it are built incrementally or iteratively.

No matter which environment you find yourself in, make sure that the PRD is properly baselined and that the requirements are easily prioritized so that work can proceed. I'll talk more about this in Chapter 16.

THE EVOLVING PRODUCT DESIGN

People in the development organization are responsible for the PSD. The PSD may contain elements of the product's design. Often, a separate group, either from within the company or brought in from the outside, assumes responsibility for the physical design of the product. As I mentioned earlier, there are three different documents that might come together—the PRD, PSD, and product design—and they evolve as the product planning phases progress (see Figure 13.4). In some cases, the PSD or the product design might need to be changed after the project is approved because of unanticipated problems.

Even if a prototype was built during the Feasibility phase, real product "construction" issues will invariably arise. I recall watching a documentary on television about the Airbus A380's development. It showed how the development team struggled with the operation of the landing gear. The gear is supposed to "drop" under its own weight even if the motor that actuates the lowering of the gear fails. It took a lot of work for the engineers to figure out why the landing gear door kept getting in the way. They ultimately fixed the problem, but it was one of the flaws that just couldn't be uncovered in a design document. The experience had to be gained by the actual building of the first product. Whether the product is tangible or intangible, of an advanced technology nature or not, the design will change. Therefore, some allowances need to be made for reevaluation of the product's design early in the Development phase.

In Chapter 8, I discussed the importance of understanding customer needs and market segments. I'd like to expand on that discussion now by using the example of Thomas Edison. It cannot be refuted that Thomas Edison's invention of the incandescent light bulb was a major contribution to the world. Unfortunately, without an entire infrastructure or power grid to support this invention, the light bulb would be rendered unusable.

When you can understand the broad implication for how customers do what they do or how they interact with their environment, you're well on your way to the creation of something truly great. However, sometimes we don't have the time, wherewithal, or experience to understand these environments in the way Edison did. That's why *we may need specialists, other than product developers, to help us with the product's design during the product definition phase.*

The field of *design thinking* embodies this environmental perspective for products and services. Design thinking is a methodology or approach that helps people (such as product managers or product designers) think holistically about the product's business by considering a broad spectrum of customer needs. This approach examines the world in which customers interact, helping to refine the product's look, feel, and operation. Additionally, design thinking centers on what is technically feasible and what appeals to the value system of a customer.

The benefit to you and the team when adopting this type of mindset cannot be underestimated. For instance, the management of a product, once in the market, requires a significant amount of data and the ability to evaluate various infrastructure elements that support the product. If the complete environmental perspective was not considered during the definition phase, you and your team may end up spending unanticipated time fixing problems and reworking the product.

As you gain experience writing PRDs and negotiating with developers, you'll want to ensure that the suite of documents supporting the product's definition and design reflect the world in which your intended customers operate.

LINKING THE PRODUCT DEFINITION TO "BUILDING" THE PRODUCT

As product definition evolves, the cross-functional team has to decide how the product will be "built." Building the product could mean software development, the actual manufacture or assembly of tangible products, procurement (external sourcing) and distribution, or staffing to deliver a service. More and more, products are being built beyond the four walls of your building—often in other countries. The product may be built in another location by your own company, or you may have to have someone build it for you. Building in-house just might not be the right decision for a variety of factors, including cost, time, market proximity, supplier proximity, local regulations, or current capacity.

Outsourcing is the word used when a function that may normally be carried out by your company in-house is actually carried out elsewhere by another party. Whatever the condition you and your team encounter, you have to be able to carry out a "make versus buy" or "build versus buy" analysis. In the next section, I'll describe how to carry out a make versus buy outsourcing analysis.

MAKE VERSUS BUY

In order to establish a methodology for making the make versus buy decision (see Figure 13.7), the product manager and the team should have a clear understanding of the following:

1. The estimated cost of goods, or cost to produce the product, from all internal resources, which includes:
   a. Material costs—you need a detailed bill of materials from the Cost Accounting department and Supply Chain group.
   b. Labor costs—you need to have bona fide estimates from internal resources responsible for production.
   c. Overhead costs—you need the actual overhead rates applied to the product from the Accounting or Finance department.

2. When the product is actually needed to be in the market.

3. Whether there are enough of the right resources to build the product.

4. The degree to which intellectual property (such as patents or trade secrets) would be used in the product.

5. The degree to which product quality must be built in and maintained.

6. The contractual oversight needed from the Legal department, especially in the case of a technology transfer to the outside supplier.

7. The support of the Purchasing department or Supply Chain organization.

CARRYING OUT A MAKE VERSUS BUY ANALYSIS: AN EXAMPLE

Because you will likely face a make versus buy or build versus buy decision at some point in your career, here is an easy-to-navigate example to help you put this into perspective.

Consider the following situation: It is February. You are the product manager for Zoltar, an electronic toy robot that responds to voice commands. Based on testing with kids aged 10 to 13, you and your team think the product will be a smash for the next holiday season. The product needs to be in the retail channel by mid-summer to make the holiday rush. It's a premium product that will ultimately have a retail price of $595.00.

The Business Case asserts, and Sales commits, to selling a minimum of 35,000 units at a discounted wholesale price of $250.00. The product design is complete, and the physical requirements and the software requirements are complete. Your company's factory recently went through a downsizing but then received a directive from the CEO that it had to ramp up capacity to produce another product on the same production line. The plant representative said your product could not be built until September, with deliveries into the warehouses by late October. You also know this plant is always late and seems to be short a robust quality control staff.

Your job is to figure out the best alternative to get the product built and into the retail channel in order to be on the shelves by September 15.

Your product team is working with your Supply Chain organization and identified two suppliers who have some experience in building this type of product. Part of the analysis is in making a structured comparison between the sourcing from your company and the other outside sourcing options. Your team was able to assemble a build versus buy matrix.

Based on this matrix, there are some questions you should consider as part of a quick analysis:

1. What is the total cost per unit at volumes of 20,000, 25,000, 30,000, and 35,000 units?
2. What makes one vendor better than another?
3. Is there any data that is not presented here that you would want to know about?
4. Do you think that you could construct another alternative?
5. Which alternative would you choose and why?

FIGURE 13.8

Example Make Versus Buy Matrix

	INTERNAL	OPTION 1	OPTION 2
Material Cost	$50.00	n/a	n/a
Labor Cost	$32.00		
Overhead Cost	$17.00		
Total Cost Per Unit	$99.00	$119.00	$104.00
Software Development	$475,000	n/a	$150,000
Monthly Unit Inventory Carrying Cost	$4.00	$4.00	n/a
Lead Time (Order to Ship)	120 days	90 days	60 days
Minimum Factory Order Quantity	10,000	7,500	4,000
Minimum Total Contract Quantity	n/a	25,000	30,000
Date Needed	June 14	June 14	June 14
Date Available	October 22	June 14	June 14
Cost of Product Documentation	$75,000	$32,000	$32,000
Level of Vendor Experience with this Type of Product	High	High	Moderate

There are just a couple of additional thoughts for you to consider regarding building versus buying. Additional thoughts are presented in the form of questions you might want to ask, including:

1. Does the vendor have enough experience to inspire confidence?
2. Does the vendor have references with whom we could speak?
3. If we source externally, do we have resources to maintain the relationship with the vendor?
4. Will the vendor be able to work with Product Management over the long run for product updates or upgrades?
5. Will the vendor allow periodic inspections of its facilities and processes?

Finally, as with any decision, the risks for each alternative should be evaluated. These "what-ifs" can guide you and your team. Using a risk matrix, you can decide which variables in the decision are the most important and, of those variables, which ones carry the most weight.

THE COUNTDOWN STARTS NOW: LAUNCH PLANNING

Oftentimes in the many Post-Launch audits I've carried out, a Launch Plan was found to be late or deficient in terms of tasks, activities, and cross-functional deliverables. The downstream impacts of poorly planned launches include products that miss their market window, don't have the supporting documentation or marketing materials, or are introduced before testing is completed. *Product managers are responsible for the product launch and should seriously consider starting their planning as early as needed.* Although I'll be talking about what happens during the Launch phase in Chapter 17, I'm positioning the Launch Plan as one of the key output documents of the Product Definition phase. Generally speaking, the Launch Plan should be started somewhere during the Feasibility phase and evolve through the Definition phase as shown in Figure 13.9.

Other factors for crafting a successful Launch Plan are described as follows:

1. All the appropriate business documentation for the product needs to be incorporated into "everything launch," which includes a focus on the chosen market segments, Business Case assumptions, value proposition, and other supporting documents.
2. It's a team effort. The Launch Plan is a cross-functional effort and requires an integrated project plan. A launch team leader, who can be

FIGURE 13.9

The Evolution of the Launch Plan

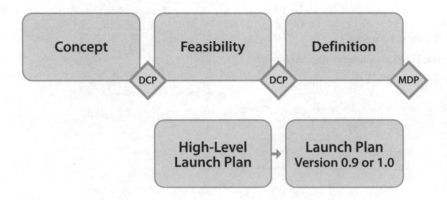

a product manager, a marketing manager, or other executive, must be the champion for the launch. The planning actually starts somewhere during the Feasibility phase and evolves through the Definition phase. I prefer the designations "version 0.9" or "version 1.0" of the Launch Plan. This allows for many inevitable changes and modifications after the product's funding is allocated for the subsequent phases of New Product Introduction, which include Development and Launch.

3. Measurements should be established to determine launch success. These are the initial business metrics to determine whether the business of the product is being carried out as planned. These measurements are different from other Post-Launch questions, such as "did we get the brochure done on time?" (Post-Launch audits are covered in Chapter 18.) The metrics on which the plan should focus set up the team to look for the following:

   a. Forecast versus actual units sold

   b. Average price compared with plan

   c. Time to first order after launch

   d. Average amount of time to fill an order

   e. Duration of the sales cycle

   f. Percentage of shipments sent on time

   g. Degree to which discounts have to be used

   h. Customer satisfaction ratings

FIGURE 13.10

Simple Launch Functional Support Plan

Business Function: _____

Name of Launch Team Representative: _____

Deliverables	Start Date	End Date	Needed Information from Other Functions		Risks to the Launch
			What	When	

By having this perspective of "setting up the business for success," all of the people associated with the relevant business functions who have a role in the launching sequence should be able to assemble their FSPs to support the launch. You can refer to the general FSP template in Chapter 12, or for early launch planning just use a simple template such as the one shown in Figure 13.10.

COUNTING BACK: HOW TO MEET THE LAUNCH GOAL

The launch, like any project plan, has an explicit end goal (the market window). It's practical to look at work activity planning for specific launch goals from the perspective of the end point and *count backward*. I'll share with you an example: the creation of a product brochure. By breaking down the tasks of this launch deliverable from the end-point back to the start point, you will be able to see the importance of this approach. First, you have to sequence the project as if you were starting from the beginning, using the following tasks:

1. Write and edit content.
2. Have content reviewed by subject matter experts from Product Management, Marketing, Product Development, and so on.

3. Make sure that the positioning is clear and consistent with established guidelines.
4. Have content reviewed by Legal and/or Regulatory.
5. Have the brochure layout done.
6. Have brochure artwork completed.
7. Review the design, artwork, and layout.
8. Locate printers and get quotes for the print job.
9. Get Purchasing involved to get a purchase order for the print job.
10. Order the print job.
11. Ship to a central location for collateral fulfillment.

From these eleven start-to-finish steps, we now construct a project profile of "finish-to-start," with the finish assumed to be August 15. This is visualized in the Gantt chart shown in Figure 13.11, using the counting

FIGURE 13.11

Counting Back Launch Plan

TASK/DELIVERABLE	NOV	DEC	JAN	FEB	MAR	APR	MAY	JUN	JUL	AUG
Launch Date										▲
Ship from printer to collateral fulfillment center									■	
Order print job from printer								■		
Get purchase order for print job							■			
Design & Artwork Review					■	■				
Brochure Layout				■						
Legal Review			■							
Check for Positioning			■							
Content Edits by SMEs		■								
Content Creation	■	■								
Start Project	◆									

back method. This tells the team when they have to start working on the brochure. In this case, it's November of the prior year. This could be a big shock, especially if you found yourself in February and you learned how far behind you already are.

OTHER PARAMETERS FOR SUCCESSFUL LAUNCH PLANNING

There are a couple of other characteristics of successful Launch Plans. First, if your product launch is significant for the company, an executive sponsor or champion should be identified before the end of the Definition phase. This helps with a variety of factors, including making sure all cross-functional team members are doing their jobs. It's also important if there are industry analysts or others who are watching your company because only some executives have the authority to carry out those interactions. This may be outside of most paradigms, but launches should actually have a series of phases in order to be executed appropriately and on time. These launch phases (early, middle, and late, for example) may help the team in setting expectations about specific launch goals and deliverables. I'll discuss these phases of launch execution in Chapter 17.

Next, it's a good idea to think about things like beta trials and market tests as important activities in support of Launch Plans. Although this may not fully coincide with the Launch Plans crafted during the Definition phase, placeholders should be put into the plan with action items to find the beta customers or market trial locations in the early phases of launch execution.

Like every plan involving resources, time, and people, considerations should be made for launch budgets. The Launch Plan budget should be established early to make sure that there is enough funding to support all the launch activities.

Identify your cross-functional team counterparts early as well. Launching a product to the market also means you're launching it to the Sales force. Hopefully the FSPs included this, but just in case, put in a checklist item to make sure that Sales is on board and able to "carry the bag" and get paid.

SETTING THE CONDITIONS TO RECOGNIZE FUTURE LIFE CYCLE STATES

One of the last topics to be discussed during the Definition phase has to do with planning the future of the product. As will be discussed in the section on Post-Launch Product Management, once the product is introduced it will typically follow a curve that includes growth, maturity, decline, and, at some point, be discontinued. You don't want to just let the product meander through the market; you want to establish "look-out" points, which are typically financial or market indicators. This helps set the stage for the most appropriate responses to changes in the market, which will trigger optimal marketing mix investments as those conditions warrant.

The product's forecast revenue or profit should be plotted on a graph, showing the future trajectory of its performance. Regardless of whether you are in charge of the product in the future or someone else is, a signal needs to be established that communicates that a strategic action is needed. Another way of setting a look-out point for this is called "setting a future state condition" for the product. Therefore, we provide conditional statements in the product's planning documentation: "If sales go up at a rate of 20 percent per time period, then the product should be considered as being in growth," is a good example. The graph in Figure 13.12 depicts the future life cycle curve for a product whose sales are going up 20 percent per time period.

FIGURE 13.12

A Product on a Growth Trajectory

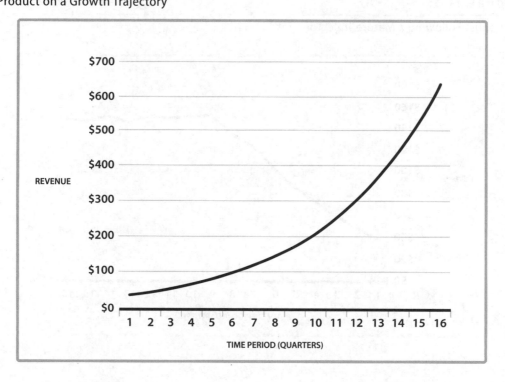

The next question is, "What do I do with this?" First of all, you'll want to use it to solidify your product's investment position. Product managers who can legitimately say that their product is in a state of growth can secure higher levels of marketing or product investments than managers whose product doesn't grow as quickly or is maturing.

However, what if the growth condition is no longer encountered? Following the conditional logic of "if–then–else," the product manager needs to set up a subsequent set of potential strategic options that states, "If sales are flat or modulate slightly (plus or minus a few percentage points) over some time period, the product is probably in some phase of maturity." Figure 13.13 depicts that trajectory.

This whole business around setting up some kind of future state condition is predicated on the fact that product managers may not be in their jobs two or three years from now. Conditional statements help establish the "what the product manager was thinking about then" perspective for the product manager who's on the job in the future. It's like leaving a legacy, so the future product managers don't need to try to figure out what

FIGURE 13.13

A Product Following a Mature Trajectory

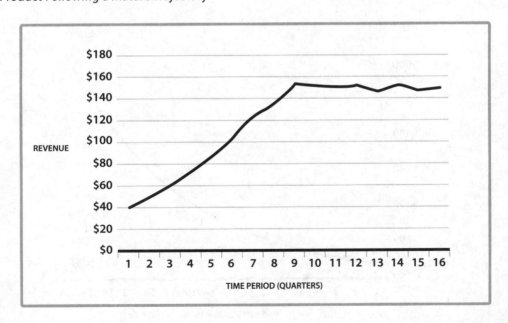

you and your team were thinking about years before. It will also save future product managers from misspending because their perception of the actual life cycle state is out of line with what was originally intended.

THE EXIT PLAN

When entrepreneurs start up new companies, they have a specific goal they want to achieve. When authors write novels, they build characters and a plot and ultimately direct the story to a conclusion. When a product is conceived, it is envisioned to evolve across its own life cycle. The Product Management Life Cycle Model is a representation of that holistic, beginning-to-end point of view for the product. During the phases of product planning, it is up to the product team to establish the market conditions that would trigger a decision to withdraw the product from the market.

A Product Exit Plan (or Discontinuation Plan) should be made a part of the Product Master Plan *before* the product investment Business Case is presented to the portfolio review board. This Exit Plan does not have to be more than a short paragraph. It should clearly state the market conditions and key performance indicators that would signal the need to begin discontinuation procedures to the future product team. The exit process will be described in more detail in Chapter 22, on product discontinuation.

THE PRODUCT DEFINITION PHASE REVIEW

After the activities and documents have been completed for the Definition phase, the product team must prepare for the Definition phase review with the product portfolio review board. One of the documents that should be completed prior to the phase review is called the Product Team Concurrence Form, which is the actual sign-off "cover page" for any documentation used to present the final investment proposal to the portfolio review board. An example of this type of template is shown in Figure 13.14.

At this critical meeting, the team makes its recommendation to go forward with the project or reject the investment. The Business Case is generally the foundational document used in this session, so it should be complete, realistic, and believable. All team members must agree on

FIGURE 13.14

Product Team Concurrence and Program Approval Template

Name of Product: _____

Name of Project: _____

Functional Organization	Name of Authorized Team Member	Phone	Signature	People Resources Committed	Financial Resources Committed

AGREED TO by the Portfolio Review Board

By: _____

Date: _____

DENIED by the Portfolio Review Board

By: _____

Date: _____

the investment (and have signed the Product Team Concurrence Form). The Definition phase checklist shown in Figure 13.15 serves to make sure that the team has covered all aspects of this important review meeting.

SUMMARY

The Product Definition phase is the keystone set in place by the product manager and the team because it marks the point between the plans being set in place and the actions and activities that will bring the product to life. The idea, whether it was for a new product or an enhancement, made it into this phase because of its business and strategic

FIGURE 13.15

Definition Phase Checklist

	YES	NO
• Final Business Case is complete.	☐	☐
• The PRD is complete.	☐	☐
• The PSD is complete.	☐	☐
• The Product's design is complete.	☐	☐
• Market segmets and customer targets agreed upon.	☐	☐
• Market window is established.	☐	☐
• Forecasts and financials fit with corporate guidelines.	☐	☐
• Financial calculations support the Business Case.	☐	☐
• Make-buy analysis done, as needed.	☐	☐
• Technology is available and agreed to.	☐	☐
• Intellectual property issues addressed.	☐	☐
• Resources committed for development and launch.	☐	☐
• Functions (Operations, Service, etc.) are aligned.	☐	☐
• Sales agrees to goals, compensation, and training.	☐	☐
• Executive launch sponsor is identified.	☐	☐
• Launch Plan is complete.	☐	☐
• The decision review is scheduled on [_____ date].	☐	☐
• Go/no-go decision to proceed to Development.	☐	☐

merits. The work carried out during the Definition phase focuses on the remaining research and legwork used to finalize all of the necessary planning documentation, including the Business Case, the PRD, the Product Launch Plan, and the Marketing Plan for the product. This chapter focused specifically on the PRD and the Launch Plan with supporting activities such as make versus buy analysis and setting up future life cycle states. All of these documents set the stage for developing and launching the product.

The next two chapters will turn your attention to a more comprehensive discussion of the Business Case and the Marketing Plan for the product.

RAISING YOUR PRODUCT MANAGEMENT EXPERIENCE QUOTIENT (PMEQ)

1. Spend some time learning the requirements development process and documentation for your company. Compare it with the process described in this chapter. Specifically, map out any differences in how nontechnical documents are updated and/or finalized during the Definition phase.

2. Locate actual PRDs and study their formats and content. You will find that they are written in a variety of styles with varying levels of completeness, depending on who wrote the requirements and how. It is suggested that you talk to the authors, if they are available, to learn the process they used.

3. Are there any elements missing from your own process? Are the Business Case, FSPs, and Launch Plans updated or evolved as a standard part of the process? If not, can you devise a way to incorporate these missing steps into your own work without creating organizational issues or confusing your management?

4. Meet with your Development or Engineering counterparts. Ask them about their satisfaction with the product definition process. Find out what they like and dislike about their perceived quality of interactions with other product managers as well as with the PRD/PSD contracting or negotiation process. They may have some biases, so you might want to use their comments as a reference point as you figure out how to position yourself with them.

5. In order to keep the market in your "sights" during the Definition phase, make sure you continue to review and update the industry, competitive, and customer research documentation. Maintain contacts with people in the market research area or those in the area of industry analyst relations. Remember that the insights you gain from ongoing market analysis will help you in characterizing the product's definition as it evolves.

6. Stay actively involved in the customer visit process.

7. Review previous customer interview guides to see how some of the questions are formulated. Talk to others who have led formal customer interviewing sessions to learn what they believe are effective or ineffective interviewing techniques.

8. Take a class on consultative selling techniques so that you can improve your approach to data gathering, observation, and questioning. Along these lines, go on the road with salespeople to observe their interactions and to get on site with customers so that you may have an opportunity to cultivate some customer relationships.

9. Coordinate a customer advisory board, advisory council meeting, or user group.

10. Practice writing customer usage scenarios so that you can perfect the technique in creating PRDs.

11. See if your organization supports a formal requirements review or inspection process. If it does, meet with the facilitators, talk to other product managers, and learn how this process works. You'll surely want to participate when you have to review your PRDs.

12. If your firm uses an internal or external design group, arrange to meet with its members and find out if you can accompany them on a customer site visit. You may learn much from their anthropomorphic approach.

13. Find out who in your organization has carried out a make versus buy analysis. You may need to visit someone in Procurement or the Supply Chain group, since they may have been involved in the process at some point in the past. The goal is to learn what may have taken place and why, and what some of the outcomes have been. Ask to review any documentation that may exist in this area.

14. Carry out your own make versus buy analysis in the next Business Case you work on, if it is warranted.

15. Review the launch planning documentation and compare it with some of the guidelines discussed in this chapter.

16. Work on a launch planning project team. Observe the dynamics throughout the planning process and take special note of aspects such as project planning and scheduling of tasks. Refer to SMART goal setting and RACI (as mentioned in Chapter 4) to determine just how roles and responsibilities are assigned and agreed upon.

17. Take the opportunity to lead a team with the responsibility to plan for a launch.

18. Work with your manager to make sure you have the opportunity to continue your experiential development in leading small teams preparing product planning research and documentation.

19. Attend a Definition (or equivalent) phase review session.

20. Evaluate planning process activities and performance based on your increasing experience by looking for opportunities for improvement and in streamlining planning activities. Use what you learn to help product managers who have less experience so that their learning curves are shortened.

21. Lead product planning review sessions for your teams so that they are up to date on process planning methods, documents, and so forth. Become one of the "go-to" resources for product planning expertise.

CHAPTER 14

JUSTIFYING PRODUCT INVESTMENTS: THE BUSINESS CASE

Executive Summary

- A Business Case is a standard method used to justify investments in new products, product enhancements, and major marketing programs.
- The Business Case is a dynamic document that evolves from the Concept phase, through Feasibility, and is baselined in the Definition phase. Its assumptions are continually reevaluated throughout the product's life
- Business Cases are assembled as a collaborative effort of the cross-functional team. Its believability is tied directly to the realistic achievability of its intended outcomes.
- Within the context of the Business Case, product managers take on an investment management role. Therefore, they must protect the invested capital of the company and must accordingly manage its exposure to risk.

Throughout the other chapters of this book, I've referred heavily to the Business Case as a vital underlying document contributing to the success of products. That's absolutely true. During New Product Planning, the Business Case is a principal vehicle for decision making at each of the appropriate decision checkpoints. Business Cases can be used for other investment decisions, which include vendor selection or carrying out make versus buy versus partner analysis. They are also used to justify investments in equipment, business unit expansion, movement into new markets, or other internal projects. This chapter provides you with the formal structure and guidelines for the Business Case as well as a sample case study to reinforce the key points.

THE PURPOSE OF THE BUSINESS CASE

Business Cases are generally designed to answer the question, "If there is a business or market need, and if I could meet that need by making an investment, what are the business and economic impacts if I choose X or do Y?" In order to accomplish this goal, a good Business Case shows expected *financial and business* consequences of the decision over time, and it includes the rationale for quantifying benefits and justifying capital and operating expenditures.

It also describes the overall impact of the investment opportunity in terms that every financially astute manager or executive seeks: net cash flow, discounted cash flow, payback period, and internal rate of return. Business Cases can even be used to validate the value or benefits of an investment from a customer's point of view. I call this the Customer's Business Case. To put this in context, if the customer was evaluating an investment in your product, would the justification made by the customer be equivalent to the value and benefits you asserted to your own management in the Business Case?

While it isn't the *only* important document, it *is* a living (continuously updated) document that spans the life of the product. Because this document is so important, it seems appropriate to take a more detailed look at it, as well as provide you with an example, presented as a situational case. First, let's take a look at a few important characteristics of a strong Business Case.

CHARACTERISTICS OF GOOD BUSINESS CASES

At the outset, you should clearly understand that the Business Case alone is not a management accounting report or financial document. It seeks to qualitatively and quantitatively rationalize an investment, while considering elements of market needs, proposed solutions, and economic outcomes. It is based on varied assumptions about the current state of the market and possible future state scenarios. It also establishes a consistent paradigm for rationalizing investments across the product portfolio.

That said, Business Cases must be believable. The executives who oversee the product portfolio have limited resources and, often, limited patience. If you and your team appear with incomplete Business Cases, poorly crafted assumption sets, erroneous forecasts, or wild, unsupportable claims, you will probably not be asked back. Product managers must always think about building their credibility horizontally and vertically within the organization—and the Business Case is a primary tool for doing so.

Business Cases vary in size, scope, and level of effort, depending on the amount of investment and degree of risk involved. Business Cases should be sufficient to put the point across. They don't always have to be excessively long and verbose. Regardless of length, however, Business Cases usually undergo several iterations before you have just the right blend of information.

Business Cases absorb input from different people including the most appropriate cross-functional team members. Before you begin the Business Case, ground rules for document sharing and version control methods should be agreed upon by the team building the case. The product team leader may assign a Business Case project owner, which may be the product manager or the product team leader. It is the responsibility of that team leader to maintain control of the versions. By the way, all Business Cases should be archived in the Product Master Plan.

In assembling a Business Case, the product team or an assigned *project* team is responsible for the collection of data, associated analysis, and completion of the case. The team should be cross-functional, with clearly defined roles and responsibilities, an underlying project plan for carrying out the work activities in preparing the case, and a target completion date. There is never enough time to be as precise as you and your team members might prefer. Team members must therefore be comfortable with the risks associated with making assumptions about unit volumes, market share estimates, resource capabilities, and deriving forecasts. Many Business Cases are often unnecessarily extended over many months because of the quest for more and more accurate data. In those months, the competition can introduce a product that beats you to market. The team should attempt to strike a balance in terms of data collection, assumptions, risks, and recommendations.

FIGURE 14.1

Line of Sight to the Market

Because the Business Case helps to justify an investment that influences the future of the product, the Business Case team must have what I call a "line of sight to the market" (Figure 14.1).

When the team has a line of sight to the market, it can clearly articulate how the product will be not only developed and launched but also integrated with the current portfolio of products. The team has to be able to answer questions such as: Will Sales sell it? Will Marketing market it? Will Operations integrate it? Will Customer Service be equipped to take calls? Will we make money? Every one of these questions must be asked and answered with clarity if the Business Case is to be meaningful and useful.

ACTIVITIES AND SEQUENCING

The Business Case *evolves*. When I talked about Functional Support Plans (FSPs), I explained that FSPs evolve across the phases of product planning. The Opportunity Statement, developed during the Concept phase, is the first pass at the Business Case. In the Feasibility phase, the Business Case is still a draft document, but it becomes more comprehensive as the team does more research. During the Definition phase, the Business Case is further updated to what can loosely be termed a "final" state. Figure 14.2 helps to visualize this sequence.

FIGURE 14.2

Evolution of the Business Case

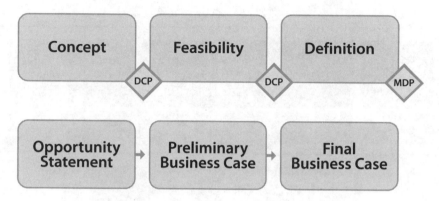

I use the term *final* loosely because decision making does not stop after the Business Case is approved and the investment is authorized, and, actually, neither does the Business Case. While Figure 14.2 is a representation of the evolution of the Business Case during the three phases of product planning, it could lead you to the conclusion that once the Business Case is completed in the Definition phase, it's filed away. This would not be correct.

The assumptions, forecasts, and actions that flow from the Business Case will invariably change. Market conditions change, competitors act, technologies evolve, and people change jobs. With so *much* change, the team must ensure that the Business Case is re-examined at relevant intervals, just to make sure that the investment still makes sense. In fact, the Business Case should be reviewed periodically during the phases of New Product Introduction, as represented in Figure 14.3 (Development and Launch). The Business Case should also be reexamined throughout the life of the product.

I would say, unscientifically, that more than 95 percent of my clients cannot produce an original Business Case (in text format) for an existing product. Couple this with the fact that incremental changes to products are typically not well documented, and it's usually very difficult to tell how well the product performed against the original Case.

When you invest in financial securities, you want to know how well you did so that you can invest more in one area and divest from others—which is essentially portfolio management. When you make investments

FIGURE 14.3

Evolution of the Business Case Across the Product Life Cycle

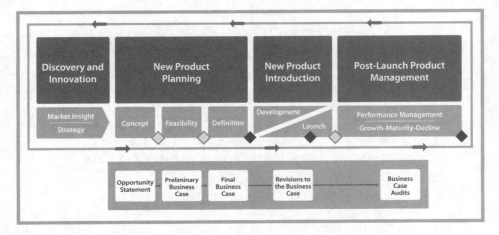

in products, you will want to know how well those investments achieved your investment goals. Therefore, I suggest that the Business Case be used as the *audit platform* for running the business. Depending on your business and the velocity with which your products move through the market, a Business Case audit should be carried out so that new investments can be put into better perspective.

ORCHESTRATION OF THE CASE

Product managers should have extremely keen insight into their firm's strategic goals, organizational dynamics, and political climate. They must lead the cross-functional product team to secure the cross-organizational buy-in required to support the investment. Just like an entrepreneur would pitch a venture capitalist, the product manager must paint a portrait of achievable possibility.

When you understand this simple context, you can then begin to work the organizational backchannels. This includes having informal conversations with leaders in other functions as well as your own management chain. Regardless of whether you have a great idea, it will not see the light of day unless you can convince the bosses that the signing on to your program is worth risking their own reputation. Mere persistence and brute force are insufficient when it comes to securing funds for your project. Keep in mind that your idea is competing with a number of other initiatives whose champions feel that their project is most important.

In addition, it is crucial that you understand how your leadership team or the portfolio board reviews the cases at hand and, ultimately, makes decisions. This means that you have to figure out what their "hot buttons" are and how their decisions align with the New Product Development (NPD) or gate process, or the portfolio allocation process. You can do this by talking with others who have been through the process, including your boss. You should document the process you follow and record your notes in the Product Master Plan repository so that others can learn from your experience.

BUSINESS CASE STRUCTURE

In this section, I am going to review the major sections of the Business Case. If you just need a template, refer to Module 6. Following this section, I am going to show you a "mini-case" so that you can get an idea of some of the language you can use as you prepare your own Business Cases.

Cover Page

Every formal business document needs a cover page. A cover page identifies the document (Business Case) and serves to communicate to the audience the name of the product, a project name (if needed), the names of the team members, a version number, a date, and anything else that may be helpful.

Executive Summary

The executive summary is used to capture the essence of the entire case in one or two pages. It describes the purpose of the case and sets up the formal investment request. It achieves this by summarizing the business and market environment and describes how the customer's needs are being met. Furthermore, it presents the assumptions made, culminating in a high-level financial profile. It is prepared as the *final* step, when the rest of the Business Case is complete.

Framing

Every good story needs a strong context, and this section of the Business Case is where you set the context for everything you want to say to management. In fact, this is the perfect section to tell a story about what you've observed, what's happened that caught your interest, and why you're interested. This material allows the team to express two things: a *chronology* of events that led up to building the case, along with the overall business situation; and a formal funding request that describes what is needed now, next year, and in subsequent years.

Additionally, this section should set out in clear terms exactly what is requested from the product portfolio review board. A clear statement is needed, such as "We are requesting $350,000 this year and $175,000 next year to support the development and launch of the ABC product enhancement."

Business Need and/or Strategic Fit

The goal of this section is to describe how the product line or product portfolio will benefit from the investment. You should describe the opportunity based on the business or market need and define the different alternatives that were considered when coming up with your approach. Most organizations focus on revenue improvement, cost savings, and operational efficiency. These are usually structured as investments that increase market share, improve customer satisfaction and loyalty, or improve efficiencies of the internal operational infrastructure. Of course, this context also supports or validates the value proposition for the intended customer or customers.

Think about the Business Case as one of the opportunity documents that may emerge from the organization's strategic plan. With this context, the investment opportunity is part of a larger puzzle, so you should always be able to state how the opportunity complements the organization's strategy. Highlighting the team's understanding of strategic issues makes it easier to explain and justify the requested investment. Part of this explanation probably involves describing the way your idea fits with other products or services in the portfolio. When you're describing the fit with other products in the portfolio, you're going to have to describe whether this investment is complementary to other products. Alternatively, there may also be potential overlaps in the product line, leading to cannibalization of sales. These issues need to be uncovered and addressed.

Market Assessment

This section of the Business Case provides the context around which the case is built. Included are the data about the industry, the competition, the market segments on which the investment is focused, and the needs of the customers in those segments. This should be expressed in a way that shows a clear understanding of customer needs such that the investment can be defended to management. Additionally, this is where the market window may be discussed; namely, what market conditions abound that make this an important, timely investment? When does the market need the product or enhancement, and when is it right for the company to release the product? (Refer to Chapters 7 and 8 for a detailed discussion on this topic.)

Product Description

A product description is needed to convey the characteristics of the product that are connected to the needs you've uncovered. The description includes the following elements:

- Features, functions, and attributes
- Unique designs or styling
- Performance characteristics
- Technologies or platforms being recommended

One of the most useful documents for this purpose is the Product Requirements Document (PRD). Product requirements represent customer needs, competitors, technologies, and other standards that help shape the product's functionality and positioning in the market relative to the competition. (The PRD is discussed in more detail in Chapter 13.)

The level of detail for the product description in the Business Case may vary. For a brand new product it may be more comprehensive, while for an enhancement it may be brief. My recommendation is this: if the description is too long, capture the major highlights in the body of the Business Case, and put the details in an appendix. Regardless of the level of detail, of course, the product description should clearly reflect the value proposition and the intended positioning.

Project Proposal

The project proposal reflects the level of effort required to develop, launch, and manage the product in the market. The cross-functional team assembling the Business Case creates it. Often, a *project plan* is created that focuses only on the work necessary to develop and launch the product. Consequently, many product investments fail to meet their targets because they don't consider the investments required to support the product when it's in the market. There have been many instances in my work with companies where the "line of sight to the market" is not established, so the product fails.

A project's success is defined by its ability to meet its objectives, within the specified time frame, on budget, and with the right level of quality. The project proposal must clearly identify the following, as a minimum:

- The resources needed from each functional department
- The deliverables for which each function is responsible
- The timing for each deliverable
- The dependencies of those deliverables on other deliverables
- An implementation and operational plan
- A plan to support product, field, or market testing
- A high-level launch support plan

Avoid including extensive details, as they can make this section of the case too long and difficult to follow. You should have sufficient detail in the body of the Business Case so that the portfolio review board understands the complete picture; relegate the details to an appendix.

Assumptions, Forecasts, and Financials

Scenarios are stories about the future. A variety of scenarios should be portrayed because the Business Case is essentially a well-thought-out story that proposes an investment that will affect the future of the business. Useful sentences for scenario building may start with, "What if . . . ?" As you develop your scenarios, each story may be changed, or altered slightly, to reflect adjustments in forecast volumes, pricing, costs, and expenses—that is, your assumptions about the future. For each scenario, change only one or two variables at a time so that outcomes can be compared against a financial "base case." The variables that are usually changed in the Business Case center on pricing, volumes, costs of goods, cash flow projections (getting paid), selling cycles, discount rate, and expenses by department.

Ultimately, the Business Case should demonstrate an incremental benefit to the business. After all, the investment is adding to the portfolio of products in some way. The Chief Financial Officer and your CEO are particularly interested in the incremental portfolio impact, which is considered in "before" and "after" scenarios. The *before* scenario is your base case. (Some people use the term *as-is* to describe the current situation.) Think of the base case as business as usual: if you didn't make an investment, how would the business look now and in the future? To highlight your proposal, select a scenario showing how the business would look in the future with more units, different prices, different market timing, and other variations that the forecast assumptions might suggest. (Some people use the term *to-be* to describe these future states.)

Take the example in Figure 14.4. In the base case, the volumes are assumed to increase by 25 percent each year. In scenario 1, the unit volume is assumed to rise at 40 percent per year. Just by changing one variable, unit volume, the outcomes for subsequent years will change. Your Business Case should consider a variety of similar assumptions. Some are better than others, but it is up to the team to determine which scenarios reflect cases that are realistic, believable, and achievable.

FIGURE 14.4

Examples of Scenarios

	"Base Case"				Scenario 1			
	CY	CY + 1	CY + 2	CY + 3	CY	CY + 1	CY + 2	CY + 3
Unit Volume	100	125	156	195	100	140	196	274
Unit Pricing	$25	$25	$25	$25	$25	$25	$25	$25
Total Revenue	$2,500	$3,125	$3,906	$4,883	$2,500	$3,500	$4,900	$6,860

Financial analysis is one of the most important parts of the case. Frequently, the executive leading the review will go straight to the numbers. The numbers *do* tell the story, even though the rest of the case needs to portray the *complete* story. The financial analysis should include:

1. A profit and loss (P&L) projection based on the team's agreed-upon assumptions.

2. A cash flow projection, showing when money is being spent and when money is expected to arrive. Just because you think a sale is made in November doesn't mean that revenue can be recognized in that year or quarter. Your Accounting or Finance department can help you with "revenue recognition" rules.

3. The capital expenditures needed to start along with any ongoing or additional capital expenditures.

4. The operating expenses needed to start and sustain the business incrementally.

5. The discount rate used to discount cash flows. You get this from your Accounting or Finance department.

6. The payback period, defined as the amount of time it takes to have enough money coming back into the business to cover the initial costs of the investment.

7. The net present value (NPV) or the amount of the total value of the future cash inflows in today's dollars.

8. A break-even analysis, which is an important measure of investment effectiveness that shows where the cash inflows equal cash outflows. Break-even can be expressed in time or units of volume as well.

Operations and Implementation

In order to put the investment into action, several puzzle pieces must come together to meet the market window, the time when the product needs to be in the market. The first part of this section explains how you plan to implement elements of the marketing mix. This means that pricing systems should be in place to manage pricing models for different segments or different product combinations, or even discount structures based on promotional programs. Promotional programs must be ready to be launched and tracked as well. And distribution channels should be set up for fulfilling orders, handling complaints, managing returns, and dealing with other logistics issues—in close harmony with the Supply Chain organization.

Systems to support human resource planning and management, facilities, procurement, and an operational infrastructure must come together in a synchronized way to make the machine of the business work. If there are international issues, there may be local procedures for selling, distribution, and localization. If any one issue is missed, the product's market entry could be delayed. Although the project plan should be the framework for organizing work, the team should have a clear operations and implementation plan so that the product can be sold, ordered, billed, shipped, and supported.

Risk Analysis and Contingency Plans

The Business Case should represent the best possible proof that an investment will deliver the promised return to the business as established by key performance indicators (KPIs) and other metrics. One way of assessing risk is through both qualitative and quantitative (statistical) analyses of the major project elements or deliverables. A qualitative risk statement is, "What if Development slips their schedule by two weeks?" Upon review of the FSP's elements, the team then looks at all the cross-functional dependencies to see who else is affected and what happens with their deliverables. Again, this is the argument I make for good project management methods and tools that help track these dependencies. An answer to the question could be, "a day-for-day slip in the end date for the project," because all other functions are dependent on Development's deliverable.

Quantitative risk assessments might also be made. Using a decision matrix, each milestone from each business function can be evaluated against specific probabilities of a problem occurring.

What kinds of problems can actually occur? I'll give you some examples of the issues I've encountered and had to address:

1. *Management support risk*—because not all managers will buy in based on their affinity to supporting certain kinds of projects and their veto power on the portfolio board.

2. *Technology risk*—because engineers often think the new architecture or new tool or technique will solve all problems, only to find that the technology was untested.

3. *Deadline risk*—because management imposes sometimes arbitrary deadlines and the team cannot possibly do the real work necessary to validate the investment; and if a "go" decision *is* reached, the project may immediately be in jeopardy.

4. *Resource risk*—because sometimes a function says "sure we could do this," but when the project is approved, the resources aren't available.

5. *Project risk*—because there isn't an experienced project manager who can oversee the complexity of the program and keep all stakeholders to commitments.

6. *Team risk*—because sometimes the team doesn't work well together.

7. *Complexity risk*—because sometimes the project is so large and cumbersome that assigned resources cannot see all of the work that has to be done or don't have the skills to complete the work once it's identified.

8. *Requirements risk*—because sometimes the requirements are incomplete and unclear.

These items represent just the tip of the iceberg. I've encountered many of them both before and after Business Cases were approved.

One of my career and life lessons has been this: the more you know about what can go wrong, the more careful you become about the Business Cases you commit to doing. Part of this lesson rests not in quantitative data but in the "gut feel" for the business, which is why the Business Case is such an important decision-making tool.

Recommendation

Every Business Case ultimately comes to a conclusion, and that conclusion is the recommendation. "Should we invest or not?" If so, why; and if not, why not? This is one of the most important decisions that product managers and their teams make, and it is the reason you've been invited to present your Business Case. Here's a hint: *don't* say "yes" when you mean "no." So many of the people I have interviewed over the years have made this mistake. They did so much work on the analysis that even if the decision seemed to point to "no," they recommended going ahead anyway. The idea behind the Business Case is to "green light" the right projects and to reject the wrong ones, regardless of how hard it was to arrive at that decision.

Appendices

The Business Case is built upon vast amounts of data. It would not be reasonable to put every piece of data into the Case because it would end up being too long. The appendix holds exhibits, charts, and anything relevant that serves as proof for representations, estimates, and assumptions presented in the case.

KICK START THE BUSINESS CASE

As you might surmise, the Business Case process can be complex and sometimes takes longer than you would prefer. It may also be a bit more difficult to get team members into a room for this kind of a project. It doesn't mean they don't care; it just means that corporate realities sometimes force us to veer from the path a little to get the good jobs done. Here's an idea I've used to help get things moving.

First, do a little homework. Take the Opportunity Statement and begin to populate your Business Case template on your own. You should always have a lot of research material around, so capitalize on that as well as other available content. The goal is to try to sketch out a great storyline for the investment. Therefore, it's smart to do a lot of work on the framing section—the history and chronology—to put the opportunity in perspective. Also, put some of the forecasting templates together, even if they're very rough. You want to demonstrate to your colleagues that you have the vision. If you can show them that some of the work has already been done, it's easier to engage them. Your job as the product manager, in this case, is to do enough work that you can get the main stakeholders into a first meeting. This first step could also be used to rally the bosses to dedicate resources to your team.

Next, meet with each needed person individually and discuss the project and some of the up-front work you're doing. This helps build consensus in advance. After you have a good draft, get a few close colleagues into the room (usually from Development, Marketing, Finance, and sometimes Sales) and have a go at the Business Case. Although Feasibility is often about bringing a larger team together, there are times when you want to take the Business Case a little farther with a smaller core team. Because I tend to be somewhat conservative, I use this interim step to check out my gut feel and to put some better data together.

Before the group meeting, provide a list of "things to look into." In reality, that implies your call for help from the other team members. What you're trying to do is gauge the level of their excitement; for political reasons, you may need the functions to spread the word upward to their management. The collective bosses are usually the portfolio reviewers, so if their subordinates (your peers) aren't excited, you can probably say goodbye to the case, even though it might be worth a chance.

CASE STUDY: CREATING A BUSINESS CASE

Now that I have provided you with the Business Case structure, I will tell you a short story about a product manager named Elizabeth and her job at a local bank. Then I'll then ask you to follow along with me as I take you on the journey of the Business Case.

Elizabeth is the product manager at the Regal Bank of Ohio. The bank is based in a small, growing suburb outside Columbus, Ohio. Elizabeth is responsible for the profitability of automated teller machines (ATMs) and online banking. Regal has ten branches. There are two ATMs in the vestibule or lobby of each branch. The original cost of each ATM was $30,000, and each has been fully depreciated. Each of the 20 ATMs generates 233 transactions per day for the bank, broken down as follows:

- 70 withdrawals from current depositors generating no income
- 45 cash withdrawals from other banks' customers (foreigners) at $2.00 per transaction
- 27 balance requests at $1.00 per transaction
- 41 transfers within the ATM network at $2.50 per transaction
- 50 bill payment fees at $.50 per transaction

Elizabeth's management is interested in finding more ways for customers to self-serve. They also want to draw traffic from other banks and improve foreign transaction revenue. The bank's strategy is to improve market penetration in the region and capture new customers while retaining and delighting existing customers. Elizabeth's boss told her that she had to increase her annual revenue by 30 percent per year for the next two years.

Recently, she decided that it would be a good idea to spend a couple of hours in and around the branches to observe foot traffic and talk to the branch manager and customers. She asked her colleagues in Branch Operations, IT, and Marketing to accompany her on some of her visits because she realized the value of other "eyes" for observing customers on customer or field visits. In some cases, they visited the same branch several times, at different times of the day. Elizabeth and the team noted the movements and patterns of customers, both at the machines and as they were waiting for tellers. She even had one of her colleagues "act out" by trying to annoy other customers who were waiting in line, taking a long time at one of the machines, making a withdrawal and checking her own balance, all the while watching the expressions on customers' faces as she lingered. The customers were always in a hurry and seemed unhappy to be at the bank.

Elizabeth and her colleagues observed a lot of construction of new shopping centers, condominiums, apartments, and housing developments around every branch. She also noticed that automobile traffic was very heavy and people at the drive-up window seemed impatient. During morning visits, the team observed that most customers had a piping hot cup of coffee picked up from the new coffee house across the street. She made it a point to have everyone read a regional report issued by her Economics department, which stated that there were 2,000 new building permits issued last year and 2,500 issued this year. For a town of 20,000, that meant at least 2,000 new families in the area.

During inclement weather, people had to run to the bank from the parking lot. They were soaked by rain, blown by the wind, and frustrated by the time they got to the vestibule to complete their transactions.

Elizabeth thought that a makeover was due because the vestibules looked a little drab and customers seemed unenthused by the experience of going to the bank. On two of the outings, she decided to drive over to the competitor's bank to see how it was doing. She noticed some construction in its vestibule and saw a crate containing new machinery, along with some outside construction next to the night drop box.

FIGURE 14.5

Business Case P&L—Current Situation

	Daily (Avg) Transactions	Fees	Per ATM Per Day	Per ATM Per Week	Per ATM Per Year	20 ATMs Per Year (Now)
Revenue						
Withdrawals from Regal customers	70	$0.00	$0.00	$0.00	$0.00	$0.00
Withdrawals from foreign customers	45	$2.00	$90.00	$630.00	$32,760.00	$655,200.00
Balance requests	27	$1.00	$27.00	$189.00	$9,828.00	$196,560.00
Transfers	41	$2.50	$102.50	$717.50	$37,310.00	$746,200.00
Bill payment fees	50	$0.50	$25.00	$175.00	$9,100.00	$182,000.00
TOTAL REVENUE			**$244.00**	**$1,711.50**	**$88,998.00**	**$1,779,960.00**
Direct Expenses						
Fees to banks 5% of foreign revenue			$4.50	$31.50	$1,638.00	$32,760.00
Networking and communication			$21.00	$147.00	$7,644.00	$152,880.00
Electricity			$11.00	$77.00	$4,004.00	$80,080.00
Paper and supplies			$9.00	$63.00	$3,276.00	$65,520.00
Maintenance			$0.00	$100.00	$5,200.00	$104,000.00
Banking ops overhead 5% of revenue			$12.23	$85.58	$4,449.90	$88,998.00
TOTAL DIRECT EXPENSES			**$57.73**	**$404.08**	**$21,011.90**	**$420,238.00**
Depreciation and amortization			$0.00	$0.00	$0.00	$0.00
Corporate allocations 25% of revenue			$61.13	$427.88	$22,249.50	$444,990.00
NET PROFIT BEFORE TAXES			**$125.65**	**$879.55**	**$45,736.60**	**$914,732.00**
Profit %						**51.39%**

During a team meeting, Elizabeth asked the Financial department's representative to the team to provide the team with the ATM P&L statements (Figure 14.5), indicating revenue, expenses, allocations, and net profit before taxes. As the entire team could see, the ATM business was still very profitable.

Elizabeth's boss said that the product portfolio review board needed a Business Case to support the growth of the ATM business, and that he wanted it, along with her recommendation, in three weeks. She called a meeting of her cross-functional team, including her good friends in Marketing, IT, and Branch Operations, to brainstorm some ideas. Here's what the team came up with:

- Add a new ATM in each vestibule as a free-standing machine, avoiding any construction costs.
- Remodel two of the vestibules and add a new machine to each of two branches.
- Add one new ATM in a sheltered drive up at each of two branches. In addition, remodel the vestibules in each of ten branches. Branches will also provide morning coffee, pastries, and install a television so that customers can catch a glimpse of the local news.

THE SAMPLE BUSINESS CASE

Although this is not a very complex situation, I am going to select the third option and create a sample Business Case analysis for you so that you can see how I went about assembling this case. Here's how my Business Case might look:

Cover Page

Business Case
ATM Expansion Project

ATM Product Team
November 21, 2xxx
Version 1.0

Submitted by:

Elizabeth—Product Manager
Max—IT and Systems
Sherry—Marketing
Roberta—Branch Operations

Executive Summary

ATM Expansion Project

Introduction

The purpose of this Business Case is to request funding for an additional 10 ATMs (one at each branch) for an expansion and modernization project at all 10 branches. Our team seeks a decision to go ahead based on an investment of approximately $1 million.

Description

Our goal is to drive up service revenue and increase customer activity. Through the placement of 10 new ATMs that will be strategically positioned either in drive-ups or vestibules, plus refurbishment of the ATM vestibules at all 10 branches, we believe at the very least, traffic and transactions will increase at least 10 percent, which is what this case is based upon, with upside potential of 22 percent. Customers will be greeted with hot coffee each morning, and a television will be placed in each vestibule. The goal is to provide greater levels of convenience for our customers and to accommodate the additional traffic anticipated due to explosive regional growth.

Market Overview

The market area is growing rapidly. The local economy is expected to grow at 4 percent per year. With more than 2,000 families moving in, a 20 percent increase in highway traffic, and new shopping centers, the market area needs additional banking capacity. Our research department provided data that indicated a preference for our personal service over the competition. Although there continues to be consolidation and escalating competition in our industry, our community bank niche remains robust.

Assumptions

Our team met with the most appropriate internal resources as well as external vendors. We secured quotes and commitments that will quickly mobilize all resources, should we get the go-ahead within the next four weeks. We assume volumes will increase at a minimum of 10 percent and networking fees will be reduced by 10 percent. Our IT group committed to a vast improvement in transaction speed.

Financials

Capital expenditures would be between $830,000 and $996,000 (best/worst), with initial expenses of $71,000. The estimated payback period is between 18 and 20 months. Incremental profit between years 1 and 5 is approximately $2.3 million.

	Current	1st year	2nd year
Revenue	$1.8M	$2.4M	$2.9M
Profit	$.9M	$1.2M	$1.4M

Recommendation by team is to approve.

Framing: History and Formal Funding Request

For several years, our bank's position and stature in the community has grown, and according to our quarterly preference survey, our positive reputation continues to grow. We have 10 branches and an increasing number of depositors, and what looks like an increasingly diverse set of ATM transactions. Our community focus draws people from other banks into our lobbies to withdraw money, pay bills, and make transfers. They also come on their way to work because the number of shopping centers, coffee shops, and the other destination stores is increasing. The growth rate in the community is 10 percent per year. There are 3.5 members per family and 2,000 families are moving in this year alone, swelling our population. In order to capitalize on these trends in population size, residential and commercial building, and a strong jobs market, our team is proposing an expansion program for our ATMs.

Therefore, we are requesting funding of between $830,000 and $996,000 for capital and $71,000 for expenses for this year and next year for this project.

Strategic Fit

Our corporate economist and our executive team have formally described other programs for deposits, credit card issuance, small business lending, and mortgage lending that will capitalize on improving our market presence and the number of depositors. The strategy of the bank clearly states that we will focus on market share growth and new customer acquisition in all banking areas. In fact, if growth continues, the bank's strategy is to build several new branches and perhaps consider a merger with another neighborhood bank. This ATM investment capitalizes on this trend with a modest, low-risk, high-return scenario. We want to ensure that this investment garners the appropriate growth.

Market Assessment

The market environment is quite dynamic in our town, as it is throughout the country. Competition is everywhere. Bank of the Midwest is purchasing our local competitors and is building selectively. The local economy is flourishing with residential and commercial construction. Our mortgage business is strong. We require 20 percent down payments on all mortgages, so our lending profile minimizes our risk. The regulators know that we are conservative and our practices are above reproach. Our bank's financials are strong, and even if we lose some of our current customers, our gains will far surpass our losses because our branches are in the neighborhoods being built up now. One of the things that our customers tell us is that they love our personal service. They cannot believe that when they call, they talk to a person, not a machine. We represent what banks are supposed to represent. Even when people are harried in the morning, they don't dislike coming to the bank, despite some of the facial expressions we saw upon observation. Finally, people are more informed today. The idea of having a television on in the vestibule with news, and of course with coffee, will bring our customers closer and will foster loyalty. Besides, if they know the coffee is free in the morning, they're more likely to stop by, and we'll have their attention for potential up-sell and cross-selling opportunities. We think this is the right time to expand our ATM business. Our window of opportunity is now. If we are successful, we will begin to consider an ATM strategy for supermarkets and malls because foot traffic is growing everywhere.

Project Plan

Our customers, who value their time and place a premium on convenience, will benefit because screens on the ATMs will be brighter and easier to navigate. Since they're always in a rush, customers will appreciate the speed with which each machine cycles through each step of the transaction. Each complete transaction should take 30 percent less time than the average 100 seconds per transaction today. Moreover, each customer will be greeted with a bright, welcoming vestibule, and each morning they'll have a fresh cup of coffee waiting for them in travel cups that they can take with them in their cars.

Increased networking throughput and lower networking costs are transparent to the customer, except that they will notice the increase in the speed of their transactions.

Finally, customers will certainly appreciate the drive up window with the new ATM, and customers who are on foot and just want to complete their transactions outside will have a safe place to stand in the covered walk-up area, even if a car is in the drive-through area.

IT development on networking and related activities will proceed until early January. Upon approval of this Business Case, purchase orders (which are ready now) will order ATMs, construction services, and other relevant functions. Two construction crews would work sequentially, so that one new machine could be online every three to four weeks until October of next year. We commit to a project review after the fifth machine is installed, with a six-week waiting period to test for results and customer activity.

Assumptions and Financials

We worked with the facilities manager and the contractor, and met with the designer we worked with on the last branch decorating project. Because we all met together, we were able to secure these rough estimates. Our team believes they may be a little low, so we are going to add 20 percent to all of the costs. We will ask for the amounts quoted but will ask management to hold the 20 percent in reserve.

The main elements of this project focus on the following activities and impacts:

- Retrofit the branches with a new or modified drive-up lane and one new ATM. Construction is estimated to be $24,000 per facility plus $3,500 for a walk-up area. A new ATM is $37,500, including installation.
- Redecorate 10 vestibules, assuming design fees of $25,000 overall plus construction, carpet, and paint for $18,000 per vestibule.

  1. Programming. When we met with the IT department, we discussed the process improvements for a 50 to 75 percent improvement in system response times. We believe that will shorten customer wait times by 25 to 35 percent, allowing us to move more people in the lobby. The IT department is hiring an outside contractor for this project, which will take two months and cost $46,000, which is spread out over ten machines, at $4,600 per machine.

  2. We are going to add morning coffee service to each new lobby. We will make arrangements with the local coffee shop to deliver an urn containing 75 cups of coffee plus condiments. On Friday and Saturday, we will serve cake, cookies, and fruit salad. This will add $500 per week per branch, but we think it will add to the customer experience. For each lobby we will add a high-definition television broadcasting cable news.

  3. Marketing and cross-sell. By keeping the people in the lobbies, not at the machines but preparing coffee and watching the news, we will have the opportunity to put out additional marketing collateral and show bank advertisements on the television. For this, the marketing group has agreed to provide funding out of its budget, and there will be no impact on the project.

4. Time frames. One branch every three to four weeks starting in January. Total time = 30 to 40 weeks.

5. We assume that each ATM, including current ATMs, will increase its transaction volume by 12 to 22 percent, but for this case, we are considering only a 10 percent increase for each ATM as a worst-case scenario.

6. Our communications costs are going to be reduced by 50 percent because of higher-security internal network usage and ATM network usage. The telephone company lines are being disconnected now. Although this was already happening, it only adds to the financial attractiveness of this program.

7. Electric usage will be neutral. New ATMs are more efficient, which will offset slight increases in rates by the local utility.

8. Maintenance will be reduced by 10 percent due to more stable computer programs and networking equipment.

9. Transaction fees are not expected to change for at least the next two years. As a matter of fact, our competitor just raised its foreign transaction fees from $2.00 to $3.00.

10. Funding request summary and accounting impact:

    a. Machines: $375,000, depreciated over 6 years, equivalent to $6,250 in annual depreciation per ATM

    b. Construction: $455,000, depreciated over 10 years, equivalent to $4,550 in annual depreciation per ATM

    c. Design services: $25,000 to be expensed this year, and programming services: $46,000 to be expensed this year and paid for out of the controller's special expense budget.

    d. Total investment directly related to the ATM product group includes $830,000 capital + 20 percent contingency ($166,000) = total of $996,000

TABLE A

Business Case Financial Profile

	First Year of Expansion	30 ATMs Per Year (Future)	20 ATMs Per Year (Now)	Change	Change %
Revenue					
Withdrawals from Regal customers	0.00	0.00	0.00	0.00	n/a
Withdrawals from foreign customers	891,800.00	1,070,160.00	655.200.00	414,960.00	63.3%
Balances requests	273,000.00	327,600.00	196,560.00	131,040.00	66.7%
Transfers	1,023,750.00	1,228,500.00	746,200.00	482,300.00	64.6%
Bill payment fees	250,250.00	300,300.00	182,000.00	118,300.00	65.0%
Revenue totals	$2,438,800.00	$2,926,560.00	$1,779,960.00	$1,146,600.00	64.4%
Direct expenses					
Fees to banks 5% of foreign revenue	44,590.00	53,508.00	32,760.00	20,748.00	63.3%
Networking and communication	95,550.00	114,660.00	152,880.00	−38,220.00	−25.0%
Electricity	100,100.00	120,120.00	80,080.00	40,040.00	50.0%
Paper and supplies	81,900.00	98,280.00	65,520.00	32,760.00	50.0%
Maintenance	117,000.00	140,400.00	104,000.00	36,400.00	35.0%
Banking ops overhead 5% of revenue	121,940.00	146,328.00	88,998.00	57,330.00	64.4%
Total direct expenses	$561,080.00	$673,296.00	$420,238.00	$253,058.00	60.2%
Depreciation and amortization	54,000.00	108,000.00	0.00	108,000.00	
Corporate allocations 25% of revenue	609,700.00	731,640.00	444,990.00	286,650.00	64.4%
Net profit before taxes	$1,214,020.00	$1,413,624.00	$914,732.00	$498,892.00	54.5%
Profit %		48.30%	51.39%		

Operations and Implementation

Our teams are ready to go. Prior to the final review of this case, all cross-functional stakeholders met, including those from Branch Operations, Field Operations, Maintenance, Telecommunications, and even our community outreach groups. A detailed project plan and local impact statement were reviewed with the township committee. No objections were made. Adding ATMs to our network is not a complex activity because we have made sure that all departments know what is going to happen and when.

Of particular note are the efforts from Marketing, which is focusing on in-branch announcements, direct mail, and radio spots to tell our customers about the added convenience in dealing with us over the competition. We think that this is a win–win situation!

Risk Analysis

One of the most important things to realize with this investment is that we are carrying it out sequentially, one branch at a time, so that we can closely monitor the progress of the project and manage cash expenditures. Here are some of the risks we feel warrant attention:

1. If there is a building construction slowdown, the number of new families coming into the community will slow. This might affect our number of transactions and, hence, our revenue may slow.
2. If our machines do not ship on time, we will be late. RCM company, where we get our machines, has not met its delivery commitments lately.
3. If the transactional mix changes negatively (meaning we have more of our own depositors carrying out non-fee-based transactions), we may not make our revenue targets. Conversely, if our depositors do come into the vestibules and are "up-sold" via brochures and other advertisements (because they'll be in the lobbies longer with coffee and the news), other product areas may actually benefit.
4. If the IT project focused on faster transactional speeds does not yield its intended result, we may not be able to achieve the appropriate throughout.

With all of this said, we believe that this investment should go forward. If, after five branches are converted, we do not see material positive results from the first few installations, then we will revisit this case and reevaluate our assumptions, thereby minimizing some of the risks associated with this investment.

Conclusion and Recommendation

The ATM product team stands ready to support the strategies of the bank through this lower-risk, high-potential-return project to expand market share, improve customer activity, and improve revenues. We have proven that even our worst-case scenario yields positive benefits to the product portfolio, and we respectfully request funding for this case.

CONCLUDING COMMENTS

This simple case example is designed to show you the general flow and thought process behind an investment proposal, harnessed within the format and flow of a Business Case. It is also written in terms of the business so that it allows the product manager and the team to express what they will do and how the investment will affect the results. The product team shown here could benefit from understanding about the kinds of investments other product teams are doing so that they have an understanding of how competing investment requests might affect theirs. Furthermore, it is possible the other product team activities might even complement this investment.

You can use the template in Module 6 or just follow the general sequencing here to create your own Business Cases within the context of the phases of the Product Management Life Cycle Model.

SUMMARY

Each and every investment opportunity for a new product, product enhancement, platform, or related item in a company should have a formal Business Case. The Business Case documents the facts leading up to the investment request and presents the business, market, and financial rationale behind the investment.

Business Cases are not produced autonomously by a product manager, but in harmony with the cross-functional team members who can commit human and financial resources to carry out the actual activities that are the focal point of the investment. Therefore, the Business Case is, in reality, a true representation of—and the documentation for—the three phases of New Product Planning: Concept, Feasibility, and Definition.

The Business Case should not be created and developed as a graphics presentation, but as a text document first. The document evolves as various inputs are collected and synthesized into a meaningful story, which can be readily told by any team member who helped develop it. The contents, intent, and impact should not be a surprise to anyone, so it becomes a perfect vehicle for communicating across the business functions. Long-term, the Business Case produced for a product or product portfolio should be kept in the Product Master Plan so that it can be referred to over time and used as a learning mechanism for new employees and new team members.

RAISING YOUR PRODUCT MANAGEMENT EXPERIENCE QUOTIENT (PMEQ)

1. Consider the case study of the Business Case presented in this chapter. Try building a similar case for one of the other options or another option you might have recognized when you read the case.

2. Find out what kind of Business Cases or other investment decision tools your organization routinely uses. What steps seem to be missing? How can you include this type of Business Case in your own work, without minimizing the normal process?

3. What additional process steps and/or interlocks does your company utilize? How can you integrate them into your own Business Cases? Based on these answers, try to identify the closest event to a Business Case review and gather examples of documentation for past reviews. Study these to determine how best to improve your own presentation of ideas to the relevant decision body.

4. Consult with the various individuals and departments that justify investments (either product investments or non-product investments) within your own company to see how they prepare, socialize, improve, and present their Business Cases.

5. If possible, locate a Business Case for an existing product, along with any notes that may have been generated from it. Gather additional research from your own sources: industry, competition, market research, observation, periodicals, industry analysts, and the like. Compare your research with the actual product's performance, and see if you can determine how well the product is doing against the assumptions of the original case.

6. Observe several Business Case review sessions, if you're allowed to do so. How could you adapt the process described here to those cases and your own situation and environment?

7. Try the "kick start" approach if you're having trouble getting team members to buy in to the case.

8. If you have a project that passed a Concept review and you have completed an Opportunity Statement, take the team to the next level by working through a preliminary Business Case in the Feasibility phase. Coordinate the research and investigations, and help team members through the

functional support planning process. Use this experience to lead the team into the Feasibility review. Afterward, conduct a post-Feasibility phase review to learn where you and the team did well, and what areas could be improved.

9. As your experience grows and you are managing other product managers, establish an environment for coaching and support so that all product managers can learn from one another, and that a "storehouse" of Business Cases and other important documentation becomes a repository of professional growth.

15

SYNCHRONIZING THE GEARS: THE MARKETING PLAN FOR THE PRODUCT

Executive Summary

- The Marketing Plan for the product is a Functional Support Plan (FSP) from the Marketing department supporting marketing investments for the product.
- One of the most visible areas of the Marketing Plan is the marketing mix, but the plan requires the integration of many other well-thought-out elements to be complete, effective, and actionable.
- Unlike other FSPs, the Marketing Plan may be subject to more scrutiny at higher levels within the organization because marketing activities are the main ways that companies influence customer purchasing decisions.

Everybody has a Marketing Plan, right? The Marketing Plan sounds like it should be a simple document. There are certainly enough books, outlines, and resources that provide you with templates for Marketing Plans. Nearly every company that does business has people spending time on a Marketing Plan of some sort. However, the Marketing Plan is subject to varying interpretations by different types of practitioners in different organizations. The Marketing Plan is often confused with a Business Plan or Business Case because it contains common elements such as strategy, segmentation, industry and competitive analyses, along with forecasts. In some organizations, the Marketing Plan is owned by a marketing manager; in others, a product marketing manager takes the reins; and in still other organizations, a product manager owns the plan. Given this inconsistency, it's important for me to be clear about the *purpose*, *ownership*, *content*, and *structure* of the Marketing Plan for the product, which will be described in this chapter.

THE MARKETING PLAN FOR THE PRODUCT IS A FUNCTIONAL SUPPORT PLAN

The Marketing Plan is nothing more than an FSP, *from* Marketing, *for* the product. What's most important for you to take away is that the Marketing Plan for the product, like any plan, sets up an outline for explicit marketing work activities that have to be carried out at various points along the product's life cycle. Product teams use the Marketing Plan to map the product's pathway into the market. It describes a variety of investments that need to be made and sets up a marketing budget for the product as well as metrics that can be used to compare actual performance in the most important areas of the plan.

GETTING ORGANIZED

The Marketing Plan is prepared in a collaborative manner between the designated representative from Marketing (or Product Marketing) and the product manager. Sometimes, the responsibility for the creation and management of the plan will end up in the hands of a product manager. At other times, some of the work will be carried out by a marketing manager, product marketing manager, or someone who works in another subfunction within the marketing department. By the way, in many companies, the product managers and marketing managers report to the same person.

Additionally, because this is an FSP, there are going to be deliverables to and from people in other functional organizations. These cross-team dependencies may not be the same for a general Marketing Plan,

FIGURE 15.1

Marketing Plan Hierarchy

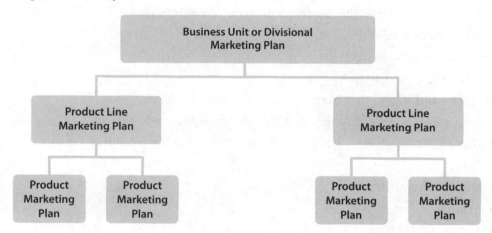

but they are common for product Marketing Plans. You know about FSPs based on what you've garnered from other sections of the book. You'll need to make sure you have articulated these cross-team deliverables and dependencies within the body of this plan.

In the same way products are organized hierarchically in an organization, so, too, are the Marketing Plans that support those products. Figure 15.1 shows this hierarchy.

The Marketing department and its varied subfunctions help shuttle this along. Sometimes, however, the Marketing department can be a confusing place to navigate. Because of this, one of the first things product managers should understand is the "who's who" of the Marketing department and how the people in those subfunctions affect the Marketing Plan. The Marketing department is not just the place where promotional advertisements are created, events planned, and strategies hatched. Marketing departments are complex, and they vary from company to company. Just so that you are familiar with some general Marketing organizational structures, I've prepared a brief outline to portray the typical functions and subfunctions you may find in a general Marketing department:

- Chief marketing officer (CMO)
- Strategic marketing management
- Global marketing management
- Product Management (sometimes)

- Inbound marketing management
  - Competitive intelligence (CI)
  - Competitive product analysis or reverse engineering
  - Industry analysis
  - Customer research
  - Regulatory research
- Outbound marketing management
- Integrated advertising, promotion, and customer education
- Direct mail
- Print
- Digital or multimedia
- Events
- E-mail marketing
- Public relations
- Industry analyst relations
- Event planning and management
- Creative management
- Agency relationships
- Art and design
- Social media
- Search engine optimization
- Production
  - Channel management
  - Web marketing
  - Solutions marketing
  - Corporate and/or divisional branding

What's really interesting, and quite helpful, is that when you secure the organization chart for the Marketing department, you actually have a *blueprint* for activities that can be mapped out in the Marketing Plan for the product.

Another way of thinking about the Marketing department is from a systemic point of view. All systems have an input; they process what they take in, and there is an output. An interesting way to view this "system" of marketing is through the visualization shown as Figure 15.2.

FIGURE 15.2

The Marketing System

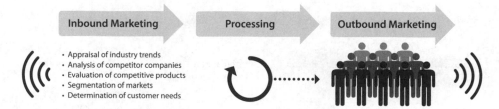

The marketing function can be easily divided into two meta-activities:

1. *Inbound marketing* refers to the efforts devoted to securing data and information from a variety of sources so that it can be used to guide Marketing Plans and programs. Inbound marketing subfunctions include customer research, CI, and industry analysis. Inbound marketing is the radar of the organization. People who carry out inbound marketing activities are constantly scanning the horizon of the marketplace to identify market-based issues such as general trends, economic signals, and competitive activity. Inbound activities are described in Chapters 7 and 8.

2. *Outbound marketing* encompasses the work activities carried out to create programs that communicate your message to customers and analysts, using advertising, public relations activities, events, and other avenues that are described later in this chapter.

Lastly, I want to reinforce one of the key points about the importance of a close relationship between Marketing and Product Management, as shown in Figure 15.3. This figure suggests that there is a broad team in place that should be able to support the product. The product manager and the marketing representative to the team need the Marketing Plan for the product as the way to link all the other marketing subfunctions to the work that must be done to support the product. Furthermore, it is the product manager's responsibility to know who's on the overall team. If the product manager becomes either a collaborator or the actual author of the Marketing Plan for the product, he knows what elements should be included and who to go to in order to secure support for the activities from that subfunction.

FIGURE 15.3

The Marketing Organization's Relationship to the Product Team

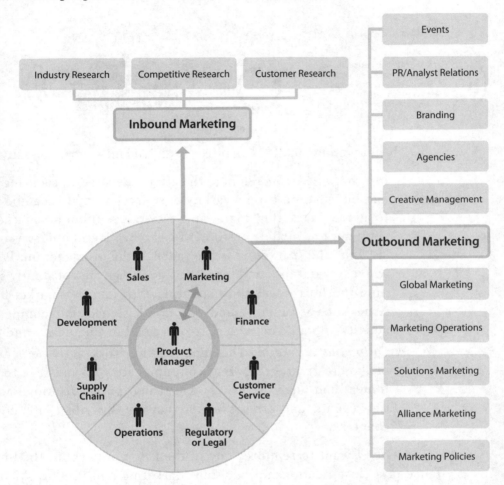

MARKETING PLANS ALWAYS BEGIN WITH STRATEGY

Foundational elements for the Marketing Plan are set within the strategy that should be formulated for the product as a business. Whether it's been developed for an individual product or a product portfolio (remember, this is a hierarchical model), strategy is the starting point. Chapter 10, on strategy, helped put the past into perspective so that a future-state marketing mix and other associated business elements could be envisioned and mapped out to be executed at the right time. To put strategy and the Marketing Plan in perspective, the strategy describes where we are going, and the Marketing Plan *contributes* to how we'll get there.

The Marketing Plan is a contribution toward the future business of the product because it typically focuses on elements of the marketing mix, expressed as strategically driven tactical plans and programs. As I've frequently mentioned in this book, there are other organizations that need to participate and contribute to the success of the product, such as Operations, Customer Service, Manufacturing, and Supply Chain. Each of these organizations also develops FSPs, but their work is not usually listed in the Marketing Plan. However, there may be deliverables from Marketing that are needed for other departments to do their work. For example, Marketing may need to train customer service agents or organize sales training events.

BUILDING A HISTORICAL MARKETING PROFILE

To construct a Marketing Plan, you can begin by formulating a historical marketing program profile. You want to check what's already been done, from both inbound and outbound perspectives, as far back as reasonable. Your work on this is similar to organizing your data for strategic product planning. As the plan evolves, you will be turning to the various Marketing subfunctions whose input is necessary for the creation of a successful Marketing plan (as shown in Figure 15.3).

Because this is a big data collection project, you will need lots of room, physically or virtually, to store the physical data and artifacts being pulled together. Keep in mind it is not a one-day project. The data is accumulated over time and updated on an ongoing basis—it will always be a work in progress. If you make this a once-and-done effort, you will lose the benefit of the emerging insights you and your team can gain from this amazing repository over the long run.

Historical Inbound Programs

The best way to begin the project is by delving into the various types of historical inbound data. There may be organizations within your company that can help. However, in some cases, you may have to do a lot of the research yourself. Either way, the goal is to get the most complete background possible. What follows are some key areas to consider:

Competitor Research

Many companies have a CI group. But whether they do or not, it can be helpful to reach out to anyone in your company who may be carrying out competitor research. You can also search your own archives and discover what other people in your department have accumulated. The idea is to gain the best perspective about the competition and its products, past and present. Think of how sports teams review videos of past games to learn from them. They observe games and strategies in retrospect; they check how they interacted with their opponents and how the opponents reacted to their strategies. For your research, you will want to include things such as:

- Competitor data sheets and any marketing collateral you can find for all competing products.
- Data on each product taken from competitor websites.
- Diagrams to show competitor product line hierarchies.
- Actual products—if you can purchase your competitors' products, display them so that you can see how they look, feel, how they're designed, and so on. If they are not tangible products, find as much descriptive visual information as you can get. For virtual repositories, pictures taken from different angles may provide a similar realistic impact.
- Competitors' integrated advertising and promotional programs. List those you know about, and scour industry publications, press releases, and events in which they participate. Find out about how they invest their money in communicating with the market-place. From this, you can discern how they are positioning, to whom, and with what value propositions. You want to know what you're up against, don't you? Some companies go so far as to engage market research firms to travel to different cities and watch television and read local newspapers to see if your competitors are doing regional or local advertising.
- Competitor brand data should be captured to learn about the strength of their branding activities and how this might contribute to the success of their products. This can be achieved either by procuring second party research or through research activities carried out by your CI department.

Field Research Data

You or others in your company may have taken trips to see competitor products displayed in retail or wholesale outlets. You may have tried to call a competitor's call center to request information. You could measure how long you were on hold or in the interactive voice response (IVR) queue, or how knowledgeable or helpful the customer service representative came across. I have many clients who hire outside research companies to shop the competitors.

Market Segmentation and/or Customer Research

In Chapter 8, it was suggested that you find out about your customers, namely who your company sells to now and why they buy. What benefits do they derive, and why do they select your products over competing ones? This information can be found in reports from customized research projects, customer satisfaction surveys, loyalty studies, field visits, voice of the customer research projects, and any other pertinent data you can locate. Such records create a perspective for the team to understand the motivation for research studies carried out by your company, its outcomes, and how those outcomes were applied toward the evolution of your marketing mix.

Industry Research Reports

Your company may subscribe to industry research providers who create profiles on the industries in which you operate. If these reports are available, relevant content related to the product line should be made available for inspection and evaluation. If your company engaged the services of outside research firms for customized industry assessments, these too should be displayed. If you can, have some of the market sizing forecast charts enlarged, put onto poster board, and hung on walls. Charting your market share is a great way to visualize your product's performance and to help everyone see the trajectory of your product's market movement.

Checking for Inbound Data Sufficiency

The purpose of this inbound data compilation project is to help you see what kind of data was collected in the past, and why. Does what you've gathered represent enough data to allow you and your team members to form the insights needed to determine why specific outbound plans and programs were created by those competitors? Furthermore, is there sufficient information already, or does this raise a flag to the team suggesting that greater levels of research investments are required in order to facilitate better outbound program decisions? For example, I recently asked one of my clients if he had actually purchased the competitor's product. He replied that he had not. He explained that he hadn't thought of it but couldn't get funding for it even if he had. "How could this be?" I asked. Could you imagine an automobile company not buying each and every competitor's car?

To complete the picture, attention should be paid to the other part of the data collection project: historical outbound program data.

Historical Outbound Programs

The next step in preparing for your Marketing Plan is research directed at past outbound programs. Historical outbound program data helps the team to "see" the methods used to communicate with the marketplace and to learn about the effectiveness of such past investments. For this research, you'll most likely be reviewing more archival data than actual research. Every company has many outbound initiatives, but many of them are not easy to categorize. Nevertheless, here are a few common areas to consider.

Advertising, Promotion, and Customer Education Program Information

Find out about each advertising and promotional activity undertaken by your organization, specifically product-related promotions. Advertising and promotional activity can include direct mail, e-mail, trade publications, conferences and/or general advertising specialties (pens, pads, etc.), press releases, spec sheets, product information, television commercials, radio spots, and so on. (A detailed discussion including examples is provided in Chapter 20.) In addition, your firm may provide programs to improve customer awareness or engage customers through advisory groups and other customer education programs. Try to find out about the targeted customers, budgets allocated, and associated response rates for each of the programs. If your product has no direct advertising or promotional program investments, relying only on sales force, website, or retail outlet, it may be more of a challenge to understand what actually motivated the customer's interaction with your firm.

Sales Information

Accumulate any and all sales or sales mix data (products, services, etc.), including direct sales, indirect sales, web sales, and so on. This gives you data about what you sell, through which channels, and to which customers. Often this is the hardest data to gather. Many companies structure this data into multiple databases, separated by geography, product line, or division. Sometimes the customer profiles are kept separately for security purposes, and at other times, customer names and sales volumes are very closely held for competitive reasons. For products with long life cycles (several years), sales data usually reside in one or more generations of systems, requiring that you extract and compare data from different sources. Regardless of the level of effort needed, however, these sales data are crucial to developing a strong Marketing Plan.

Marketing and Selling Collateral

Accumulate your sales collateral, positioning information, or other product-oriented data to help you have a full and complete understanding of how you communicate about your products. When you collect your competitor's corresponding collateral and place it alongside yours on a bulletin board or display wall, you'll have a great visual and maybe will get some good ideas for attacking the competition.

Using the Historical Profile

The outcome of this project is not only what you learn but also potentially a series of fun, team-building experiences. Everyone is focused on the goal of the project and, to that end, is getting a better perspective on the plans and programs of the past. As you proceed, people will begin to get excited about their role in the future. This historical profile is a great vehicle for earning higher levels of credibility as a product and market expert. Once the data is assembled and showcased visually, you will have equipped your team with a solid base of information with which to assemble a Marketing Plan for the key upcoming time period (e.g., the next fiscal year).

PUTTING THE MARKETING MIX IN PERSPECTIVE

The Marketing Plan is only as valuable as the team's ability to carry out that which is articulated in the plan. In my experience, especially reviewing past Marketing Plans from some of my clients, only a small portion of the programs envisioned in the Marketing Plans is ever carried out. The typical Marketing Plan seems to be more of a wish list or things to think about doing rather than an explicit roadmap for calculated tactical marketing investments seeking a desired outcome. In order to be successful with your Marketing Plan, you cannot fall into this trap.

Granted, planning to execute is usually more complex because of the interrelationships between the marketing mix elements. The elements in the mix cannot operate independently—they are highly *interdependent*. Imagine launching a product without a promotional program to communicate to the marketplace about the product's benefits. Imagine introducing a product without a price. Or could you have a successful product if it couldn't be delivered? Figure 15.4 shows the interdependencies between the marketing mix elements.

The second part of the marketing mix equation is, "Who is responsible for each marketing mix element?" This is a tremendous challenge in many organizations. Very often the responsibilities rest not with one person or group, but with many people and many groups. This is not always optimal, but if we understand that each marketing mix element must be considered from both strategic and tactical points of view, then the product team has a better chance to set the product up for success. If the product's success hinges on the performance of the product team, then anything affecting the product's performance should be managed

FIGURE 15.4

Marketing Mix Interdependencies

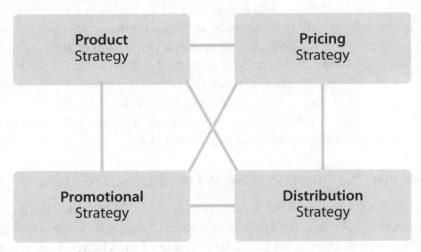

by the team led by the product manager. This can sometimes become problematic due to organizational structures. Some these issues are as follows:

- Product Management and Product Marketing are often in separate groups and report to different functions.
- There are separate groups for pricing, promotional mix management, and distribution. In many companies, integrated promotional program management is not centralized.
- The marketing communication group for products is separate from the advertising and promotional organization in the Marketing department.

Despite the melting pot of organizations you may have to deal with, remember that one of the key skills of the product manager is *leadership*. As I have explained elsewhere in the book, leadership is about influence. Although the marketing representative to the cross-functional team may be responsible for leading these marketing elements, it can't hurt you to get involved. For example, it might be a good idea to attend a marketing meeting, or a marketing group planning session, led by the marketing representative but *influenced* heavily by the product manager.

To harness the skills and capabilities of key owners of different mix elements such as pricing and promotion, use the FSP as a blueprint to negotiate who does what with whom and when.

OUTLINE FOR THE MARKETING PLAN

In order to get you started on your own Marketing Plan, let's look at the most important components of the plan. There is no such thing as a perfect template for this kind of plan because every company has its own spin on marketing. That said, most Marketing Plans should consider the same general elements. Because I have had the chance to review many Marketing Plans from many different companies, I've been able to isolate four things that will increase your ability to be successful:

1. The data you use as your input should be collected on an ongoing basis.
2. The Marketing Plan should have some place to call for resources needed for ongoing research and data collection activities. You may encounter a major shortage of structured, archived marketing data,

or there may be people who have it and don't make it available for others. This could take some extra effort to find, but it is worth it. I cannot emphasize this enough.

3. This *particular* Marketing Plan should only cover the product or product line (or that small product portfolio). It is not a divisional or corporate plan. This brings up an important point: you may need to review higher-level plans to see where yours needs to "tie into the system."

4. Some programs in the plan may not be new programs, but continuations of prior year or prior period plans. The team needs to recognize that incremental programs may be limited depending on what is actually happening within the organization and across the team's spectrum of committed-to, previously budgeted work activities.

To begin assembling the Marketing Plan, I suggest utilizing the basic outline and flow shown in Figure 15.5.

SETTING THE TEAM UP WITH A REALISTIC MARKETING PLAN

Like many of the documents on which we focus, this plan should be assembled with the help of the most relevant cross-functional team members. The product manager, product marketing manager or marketing representative, someone representing the Sales organization, and someone representing the Customer Service function should be participating in the development of the Marketing Plan. Every company is different, but what I've learned from my own corporate career, as well as consulting with other companies, is that the Marketing department tends to silo itself. If you're not careful, Marketing tends to focus much more on broad-brush programs such as corporate advertising, corporate market research, events, social programs, and non-product-oriented marketing activities—sometimes leaving Product Management to fend for itself.

For example, when Global Marketing is planning a big industry event (such as a trade show), they enlist the individual product groups, so that each group is able to display and demonstrate its products. As a result, the *corporate* marketing group controls the budget and manages the event as a project. In that case, each product team must make sure that it has the means to support that event, including adequate budget, resources, and time for the event. This would go into the Marketing Plan for the product.

FIGURE 15.5

Marketing Plan Outline for a Product

PRODUCT MARKETING PLAN TEMPLATE

1. Executive Summary

2. Strategic Context

3. The Market Environment for the Product
   - Industry and Competitive Activities
   - Market Segments and Target Customers

4. The Marketing Mix
   - Product strategies
     - Value proposition and positioning
     - Relevant roadmap information (as needed)
   - Pricing strategies (tied to value proposition)
   - Advertising and promotional programs to drive demand
   - Corporate program that require mandatory participation (e.g., trade show)
   - Distribution channel strategies to sell and deliver products (including incentive compensation)

5. Marketing Alliances used to gain access to other markets

6. International or Regional Marketing Programs

7. Product Launches to Be Scheduled

8. Sales Training Programs

9. Customer Service Training Programs

10. Any other programs to be provided by Marketing to other functions and other deliverables needed by Marketing from other functions

11. Integrated Budgets for All Programs

12. Metrics to Gauge Success

13. Risks

14. Appendices and Supporting Material
    - Includes location of documents in various repositories, schedules, contacts, etc.

ESSENTIAL SECTIONS OF THE MARKETING PLAN

The essential sections of the Marketing Plan are clarified below. You will also find a Marketing Plan template in Module 6.

Executive Summary

The first section of the Marketing Plan should be a short (but comprehensive) executive summary. Like all executive summaries, it should be completed after the entire plan is assembled. The major elements of this summary focus on:

- Summarizing the market environment and the strategic marketing imperatives.
- Linking any plans and programs to corporate or divisional strategic goals.
- Summarizing the programs to which the team is committed.
- Describing how new programs synergistically fit with existing programs.
- Identifying the human and financial resources required to achieve success.
- Capturing any risk factors about which management should be aware.

Strategic Context for the Marketing Plan

Each and every tactical marketing activity should be aligned with the strategic goals established by senior leaders, either at the enterprise or divisional level. You will need to reach out to key leaders to ensure that you understand their objectives, and you will need to communicate those objectives to all team members. If you are successful at this, when you and the team provide the plan to the executives, they'll clearly recognize the connections between each part of the plan and the strategic intent they've set forth for everyone. In other words, the Marketing Plan must explain exactly how your proposed marketing activities for the product are strategically aligned with those of the product organization and its "next-higher-level" strategies. Remember that the vision for the product needs to be translated into action-oriented goals. Essentially, this section should clearly explain why you want to carry out the specific activities that help in achieving that vision. Management needs to know how your plan will explicitly guide the efforts of team members in confronting competitors, serving specific market segments, and delivering benefit-laden products to your chosen markets.

The Market Environment for the Product

Next, you should provide a general summary of what's going on in your marketplace, told as a short story. The market environment is shaped by the industry in which the product is sold, the competitors that are confronted, and the customers who *should* be the focus of marketing activities. Your explanation should make it clear to management that the team understands the general direction of the market. Specifically, include information such as the size, demographic makeup, and descriptors that make the market attractive or relevant.

Recognize that this summary of the market environment also serves as proof that the team has a thorough understanding of the industry and competition. Discussion in this section should highlight how the product's attributes are shaped by the targeted customer's needs, within the confines of the chosen market segments. If you're having trouble with this part of the plan, review Module 2, "Making the Market Your Primary Focus," where I explore in detail the rationale and methods for evaluating industry and competition, choosing market segments, and creating market share forecasts.

Ultimately, this section sets the stage for the justification of incremental marketing investments that you're asking management to make. Not every investment is going to be approved. Therefore, significant marketing investments—just like product investments—will need to be vetted with a Business Case.

This discussion about the market environment should identify any opportunities agreed upon by the product team members as outputs from any strategy formulation activity carried out. Remember, this Marketing Plan represents the output of the research and analysis performed by the team, including key business issues, market drivers, and motivations for evolving the marketing mix.

The Marketing Mix: Strategies and Tactics

Many Marketing Mix models are based on the four P's: product, price, promotion, and place (or channel). These should be your *control levers for marketing execution*. This section of the plan should provide sufficient detail for management to be able to clearly and directly understand your planned activities in order to approve them. Many of these elements have been called out in the documentation evolved for the strategic plan for the product. Therefore, in addition to clarity and completeness, this part of the Marketing Plan should be consistent with that documentation.

However, before delving into the Marketing Mix, I wanted to share some thoughts with you on the topic. I have encountered a variety of situations where poor outcomes were traced back to ill-conceived marketing mix models or mix models that didn't consider all elements of the mix. Furthermore, Philip Kotler, one of the masters of marketing academia, introduced four C's (customers, costs, convenience, and communication) as a variation on a theme. I have even heard a CMO say that the traditional marketing mix is ineffective.

So often, desired business outcomes fail to materialize because the various business functions throughout the entire organization don't operate as if they share the same objectives and do not work together to mesh in a synchronous manner. In fact, as I've stated throughout the book, the cross-functional team and FSPs truly offer an optimal opportunity for everyone to focus on the same goals.

Lastly, marketers today are determined to integrate many different types of marketing communication vehicles into a holistic program ("integrated marketing"). With this type of emphasis, the marketing mix may be thrown out of balance because the emphasis is on reaching a vast array of customer types through a plethora of methods (e.g., young mobile consumers using mobile devices).

With all mix forces vying for resources, it's important to remember to focus on the achievement of balance across and between all marketing mix elements, regardless of which ones you use. A more comprehensive discussion about using this model can be found in Chapter 20. I'll now review each element.

Product

Let's get back to basics. Throughout the discussion of plans and promotions, we need to focus on the object of this marketing effort, which is the first P, for product. There are many dimensions that need to be articulated in this section of the plan:

- Your comprehensive description of the product (derived from the product requirements or other relevant descriptive material) is needed so that the object of the marketing mix strategies can be put into context. Also, major elements of product features or functionality should be called out to reinforce explicit linkages to the benefits that are to be delivered to the chosen market segments and associated customer targets.

- Forecasts and financial projections for the product are essential. Volumes and revenue should be characterized by product variant (if appropriate) and channel through which the product is to be sold. This financial profile can also be graphically depicted, which may provide a visual for the life cycle state of the product.

- The value proposition for the product (especially for each market segment and/or customer type) must be stated clearly. In addition, the product's Positioning Statement should be included. Related to the Positioning Statement, there may be a series of unique selling points (USPs) that need to be called out. This information will be used in promotional literature and in training salespeople. Some of the distinctions that may be highlighted include design, style, performance, reliability, and ease of use. Additionally, there may be service distinctions that focus on a unique customer experience. Remember, products that are perceived as being unique have a better chance of commanding more advantageous prices.

Value-Oriented Pricing

The price of any product reflects the targeted customer's willingness to buy the benefit. Price setting represents a tremendous challenge because of its dependency on the correctness of the *value proposition*. Even if the value proposition seems correct, there may be other intermediating factors that customers simply will not accept. For the Marketing Plan, the pricing strategies need to be called out in the following ways:

- The list price(s) for the product.
- The linkage of the pricing rationale to the value proposition.
- The linkage of the pricing model to the unit volume and revenue forecast for the product. This is critical because price and volume are inextricably linked. If the price is too low, you may sell too many units, and if the price is too high, you may sell too few. As stated earlier, the more unique the product, the higher the perceived value and the more likely that you will be able to charge more.

■ Any discounting programs that would be acceptable. This means that "floor pricing" should be established so that salespeople know how much they can discount in a competitive situation.

Pricing Strategies will be covered in more detail in Chapter 20.

Advertising, Promotion, and Customer Education

In this section, the team focuses on promotion: the plans and programs that will communicate the value and benefits you can bring to your customers (or intended customers) about your products. These promotions drive demand, interest, and, hopefully, customer action. Mandatory corporate or divisional programs should be listed first so that the team knows, at a minimum, what it must support. As suggested earlier, the kinds of promotional programs that are possible may actually be limited by the organizational structure of the Marketing department, so it's wise to check.

Think of promotional programs as an integrated mix of tactical activities that can be divided into discreet individual campaigns. Therefore, a campaign is a mini-program that directs promotional marketing investments to achieve a desired result. Each campaign is called out with its focus on a particular market segment with a specific goal, call to action, budget, and metrics. Articulating a host of campaigns in your plan doesn't automatically mean they will be carried out or funded. Some of them could be placeholders that can be carried out at some point in the future if the market conditions warrant the investment. Figure 15.6 shows how campaign plans might be organized.

Place: Sales and Distribution Channels

A product takes many and varying paths from its point of origin to the customer's hands. These paths are called distribution channels.

FIGURE 15.6

Promotional Campaign Plan Matrix

Name of Campaign	Potential Date	Targeted Group	Goal of Campaign	Message or Call to Action	Budget	Campaign Metrics

One path to a customer is via a direct sales force. Another path is through indirect means such as a distributor, wholesaler, or reseller. A third path is through a web channel, where products are sold via the firm's website. Any channel or combination of channels can be referred to as a "channel mix." Each firm's channel mix is guided by the strategy of the company and its investments to move, sell, and deliver products.

Sometimes, it's helpful to visually portray the product's path to market through the use of a channel map, as is represented in Figure 15.7. The channel map is a great way to communicate to the team how a product will make its way to a customer. It's important to establish clear lines of communication to ensure that any sources of conflict or confusion are avoided. Further, if different pricing tactics are used for different channels but similar products, these need to be called out in the Marketing Plan.

FIGURE 15.7

A Channel Map

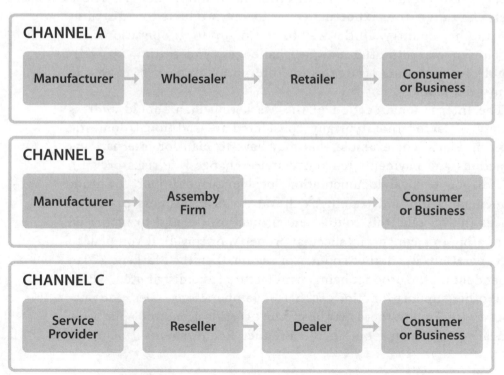

Marketing Alliances

Very often, companies need to team up with other firms that have access to a desirable market segment or geographic area, unique operational expertise, or a larger sales force. Complementary business objectives form the common ground of alliances or joint ventures.

Forming alliances may be easy, but managing alliances is extremely difficult and time consuming. Make sure that your team realizes the effort, time, and money involved in these efforts. Furthermore, there may be publicity that needs to be called out in the promotional plan section. If this is part of your go-to-market strategy, or part of your market penetration strategy, this should be articulated in the Marketing Plan.

International Marketing Activities

You may be successful at home, but that doesn't guarantee success with customers who are located in different countries. Always keep in mind they have distinctly different tastes, needs, and customs. International marketing is different from marketing in your own country and can entail the use of a host of different business models. These models can range from exporting your current products to a distributor in another country, all the way to setting up local operations. All your chosen markets offer unique challenges, and setting up well-thought-out marketing strategies for international markets is among the most demanding.

The International section of the Marketing Plan should address a variety of factors not typically considered in traditional domestic Marketing Plans. For example, you may have to plan for international transactions and payments (currency and exchange rate risks prevail), import/export or local documentation, local language support for product documentation and training, cultural or local business practices, alliances (if you take this route), and protection (related to increased risks relating to payment, intellectual property, or travel). If you plan to set up operations in another country or region, then the Marketing Plan is dependent on the product being manufactured and distributed, with a host of other support functions such as field operations, sales, and customer service. Finally, there may be product certifications and approvals, which are to be called out in the Product Requirements Document

(PRD). All relevant issues related to these activities should be included in this section of the plan.

Product Launches Being Planned or Being Carried Out

Your product launch may not be the only launch on the radar. There may be several launches during the same month or quarter, or your product may be bundled with others in a division or business unit launch. There may be product launches that are in the process of being carried out, or there may be launches on the immediate horizon that may complement, or detract from, messages you may be preparing. Furthermore, there may also be prelaunch activities taking place in the form of market trials, beta tests, and so on. Your planned launch activities should mesh with each of these existing activities. This is vital if you are resource constrained. It is important to be able to characterize the work and any risks that may affect the on-time delivery of a product to the market. You can refer to Chapter 13, in which launch planning is discussed, and Chapter 17, where launch execution is explained.

SALES SUPPORT AND TRAINING PROGRAMS

Sales teams are dependent on product managers and marketers for marketing support and training. Training programs usually focus on how to sell the product, but adding *other* kinds of training to your agenda can foster stronger ongoing relationships with sales teams. For instance, training sales teams on the industry, the competition, and evolving trends in customer tastes and preferences is *extraordinarily* helpful and is usually met with a high level of appreciation by those sales teams. Training salespeople to sell more consultatively helps them to foster greater partnerships with customers. There may also be sales guides, sales kits, sales briefs, and other meaningful documents that support the sales teams that you furnish them or guide them to find.

Training activities can be carried out at sales kick-off meetings, regional update meetings, or at other events where you have the chance to build strong bonds with sales teams. Lastly, it is important to make sure that the appropriate "negotiations" take place that will ensure that sales management has made available the right compensation packages to encourage salespeople to be motivated to sell your products.

Customer Service Training

You may find that marketing programs call for the migration of customers from one version of a product to another. Or maybe you want to tell current customers about another product that your company has for sale—your product. These are situations in which Customer Service is integral. Often, customer service representatives are equipped with scripts to offer discounts, promotions, and other incentives to drive another purchase, either as an upsell or cross-sell program. If your goal is to upsell or cross-sell to certain customers, you may have to negotiate an agreement (e.g., as in an FSP) between yourself, a marketing person, and a customer service manager, ensuring that agents are trained, scripts developed, and metrics put in place to track progress.

Additional Research Programs Needed

Additional research funding may be needed for primary or secondary research. Such research investments should be articulated in this part of the plan. Furthermore, other corporate organizations may need to be involved, such as Corporate Competitive Intelligence. Each research request should be summarized, by source and needed resource, with an approximation of the funding needed. Customized research projects may require a Business Case as a justification for those expenditures, even if they are earmarked in the Marketing Plan.

Cross-Functional Deliverables and Dependencies

This section of the Marketing Plan for the product cements the intent that makes this an FSP. As I have discussed throughout this book, one of the characteristics of an FSP is that it describes what people from one function commit to delivering to others across the organization. For example, Marketing might provide deliverables to Sales or Customer Service in the form of training or supporting marketing documentation. In return, those functions should provide adequate staffing and timing for the training. There may also be deliverables due between subfunctions within the Marketing organization, and these should be clearly articulated. In this case, the marketing lead might need to orchestrate interactions between the promotional mix manager and the pricing manager to ensure that they are synchronized in achieving specific goals related to tactical marketing mix initiatives.

Integrated Budgets

Budgeting for the Marketing Plan's elements should be set up to show what funds will be needed within identified time frames. My preference is to lay out these expenditures as funds are needed, by month, being careful to point out the funding that would be authorized by management if it approves the plan. Other funding categories might require separate authorizations or Business Cases. In any event, the marketing budget is an important tool that affords you the ability to plan and track marketing investments.

One of the particular differences between a *product* Marketing Plan and a *general* (divisional or corporate) Marketing Plan is that product investments are handled differently. Investments in product development, testing, and other cross-functional supporting work are captured in the Business Case for the product. In many companies, the marketing budget, although called out explicitly in a Marketing Plan like this, allocates a share of marketing cost to each product based on some predetermined percentage of an overall budget line item. In these cases, marketing expenses then become uncontrollable direct expenses for the product team.

Measurements and Metrics

Marketing managers are increasingly being held responsible for making sure that marketing funds are being productively invested in the business. How will the efficacy of marketing programs be measured? Modern marketing measurements talk a lot about return on investment (ROI). Marketing program ROI for the product is highly dependent on the effectiveness of company or divisional promotional program expenditures. It's difficult to measure the return on market research or on product launch programs. Product-level investments are outside the purview of this plan because they are considered from the point of view of sustaining activities. Similarly, new product development investments are vetted through Business Cases.

Marketing program measurements are, for your plan, promotional return metrics. An event like a trade show may represent one of those investments. If the expected outcome of the event is an explicit number of new orders or new sales leads, and those orders or leads guide the team to accomplish agreed-upon goals for new or incremental business, then the ROI for that event (as a campaign) would be considered positive. Additional metrics might include the following:

- Advertising program effectiveness, such as increased call volume after an advertisement or visits to a unique landing page

- Event analysis, meaning to what degree an event like a webinar, trade show, or other activity resulted in increased sales or expressions of interest
- Brand awareness, as measured through brand preference surveys

Risks

Every plan is filled with potential problems. What could go wrong? Each and every dimension of the plan should have some kind of risk assessment. The plan should express to management "what if" scenarios that demonstrate the team's desire to protect company investments. Risk profiles show not only the marketing activity but also the probability that outcomes will yield (or not yield) the desired result. This can be represented in a list or a table, depending on the complexity of the plan and the number of activities that create risks. Examples of risk factors might include the following issues:

- A campaign's investment might not yield the desired number of leads.
- An economic downturn might reduce the number of units sold.
- Excessive discounting, due to unanticipated competitive actions, could lead to reduced product profitability.

It isn't possible for me to give you a concrete list of all possible risks, as these vary not only by company but also by division, business unit, and product line. Simply be aware that you must carefully and realistically evaluate all major or visible risks that you can imagine might affect the plan.

Appendices and Supporting Material

Each Marketing Plan should have a good supply of back-up data, statistics, charts, and anything else that may serve to explain that which is communicated within each section of the plan. Sources should always be called out within the relevant area of the plan, with a reference to the page or section of the appendix where the source document can be found. The goal of these sections is twofold: they must call out any detailed evidence that proves or supports your recommendations, and they should absorb any material that seems too detailed for other sections of the plan. A few trips to other Marketing

Plan reviews (at least, those that involve your management) will help you gauge the right level of detail for the main document and supporting material.

SUMMARY

The purpose of this chapter was to provide you with a formal structure and guideline for creating a Marketing (Functional Support) Plan for the product. I wanted to make sure that I clarified the purpose of the Marketing Plan so that it was actionable and realistic within the context of the work needed to support the product in the market. I have two important closing thoughts for you to consider. First, you can't predict exactly which marketing elements will be needed for a product unless you thoroughly understand the market. The industry environment, competitors, and market dynamics have to be internalized before you can establish succinct goals and then write a realistic plan. Second, if you take the time to really understand your markets in this way, you'll find it relatively easy to assemble a strong Marketing Plan, using this chapter simply as a reminder list of things to include. Ultimately, the purpose of the Marketing Plan is to convince management that you are in a position to do meaningful things that will influence customer purchase decisions, besides just building the next best mousetrap.

RAISING YOUR PRODUCT MANAGEMENT EXPERIENCE QUOTIENT (PMEQ)

1. Try to locate a Marketing Plan for a product or product line. If there is one, see how it compares with the outline presented in this chapter.
2. Try to assemble all of the historical inbound and outbound data so that you can start assembling a Marketing Plan for your product.
3. Pay attention to the cross-functional deliverables and dependencies within the Marketing Plan outline. Use this as one of the key distinguishing characteristics of this plan from the others in your organization that may be more corporate or at a higher level.
4. Is there a hierarchy of Marketing Plan documents as suggested by Figure 15.1? Finding out about this will help you put marketing planning as used in your organization in perspective.

5. If you happen to be working on a Business Case, try to build a Marketing Plan to support the product investment being justified in that Business Case. This presents an ideal opportunity to put a real product-level Marketing Plan together. If this isn't possible, try to take a retrospective view on a previous case and see if you can build a Marketing Plan for that product investment.

6. Gather some typical Marketing Plans from other products within your company or organization. How do these differ from the suggestions in this chapter? What steps seem to be missing? What additional process steps and/or interlocks does your company utilize?

7. How can you include elements of the suggested Marketing Plan in your own work without modifying the normal process? What new marketing activities do you feel you should integrate into your own plans?

8. Find out when some Marketing Plans will be under review, and see if you can attend to take notes. When you attend, try to determine ways to improve your own presentation of ideas for the relevant decision body.

9. Consult with the various individuals and departments that justify investment decisions within your own company to see how they prepare, socialize, improve, and present their Marketing Plans.

16

EXECUTION AND OVERSIGHT DURING PRODUCT DEVELOPMENT

Executive Summary

Product managers are responsible for making sure that the product is developed according to the PRD and Business Case, and that the product is produced on-time, within budget, and with the desired level of quality. This means:

- Keeping all business functions focused on meeting their commitments.
- Facilitating and synchronizing the work of many functions across the organization.
- Surfacing risks in a timely manner.
- Adjusting priorities and making trade-offs based on what's learned during development.
- Managing one or more projects.

Up to this point in Module 3, I've discussed the three phases of New Product Planning—the first area of work within the Product Management Life Cycle Model. As you know, planning involves an array of forward-looking activities resulting in the preparation of the documentation that will guide the work of others. All of this is done so that the product can be built, launched into the market, and managed successfully. Earlier I mentioned that, during planning, you should go slowly at first so that you can go faster later. Now, it's later. The Development phase within the area of work called New Product Introduction (NPI) is the subject of this chapter. During this phase, *the product manager leads the team to bring the product to life.*

As I explained in the introduction to Module 3, NPI provides the umbrella for two parallel phases: the Development phase and the Launch phase, shown as two wedge-shaped forms in Figure 16.1. During the Development phase, any remaining design issues are resolved such that the product can be fashioned from the requirements, tested to assure that it works as envisioned, and handed off to production, or an equivalent area, so that it can be delivered to the market. The Development phase is shown to start out broadly and then taper off to reflect the intensity of work, while the Launch phase is shown as starting out slowly and ramping up. Figure 16.1 reinforces this key point.

Within the Development phase, as with other phases, there are inputs, activities, and outputs. Figure 16.2 summarizes this workflow.

During the Development phase, many different interactions are taking place between people in other business functions. At the same time, team members fulfill many of the pairwise commitments made to one

FIGURE 16.1

The Product Management Life Cycle Model Emphasizing New Product Introduction

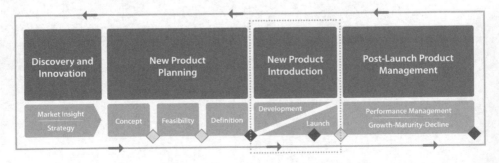

FIGURE 16.2

The Development Phase Work Flow

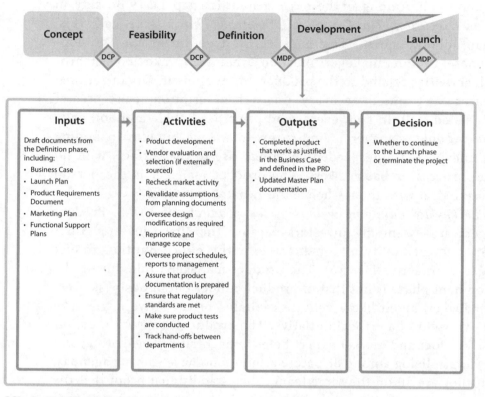

DCP = Decision Check Point
MDP = Major Decision Point

another in the Functional Support Plans (FSPs). Before continuing, I'm providing you with a visual that will give you a high-level view of some of these interactions, using the wedge shape of the Development phase.

THE PRODUCT MANAGER'S ROLE DURING THE DEVELOPMENT PHASE

The product Development phase requires strong execution management and oversight as well as true team leadership. This oversight is critical because changes in the marketplace may necessitate changes to the product as it's developed. It can be easy for product managers to be distracted during Development by exigencies of the moment because they assume other teams are adequately executing.

Execution doesn't always fit neatly within the NPD process mold with so many processes, organizations, teams, divisions, business units, and so on. Among all these dimensions is a gap. Larry Bossidy, in his book *Execution: The Discipline of Getting Things Done,* calls this, "the gap nobody knows." This is especially true during the Development phase. Product managers must do "whatever it takes" to synchronize all activities related to the product's development. Organizational structures can't anticipate everything; job descriptions can't predict every needed skill. In fact, events and priorities bubble and boil daily for the product manager trying to execute. Like bubbles in boiling water, unexpected, unprecedented things rise to the surface, with no defined process or pat answers. The product manager is the person who has to deal with them—hence the "whatever it takes."

The key to managing well is vested product ownership. Product managers are essentially investors because they have invested their budget, their credibility, and their career in this effort. But the product manager is an active investor. The product manager's role during the Development phase is not that of product builder but of business oversight manager, much like a venture capitalist or executive might take direct oversight of a critical initiative. The product manager's credibility as a product and market expert helps in negotiating, mediating, and facilitating a dialog among disparate groups who have varying agendas, even if they are all on the same team. This is additional proof that the product manager needs to use skills similar to those of a general manager or CEO.

From this description it is obvious that the product manager can't handle everything alone. In fact, the cross-functional team shares oversight responsibilities (and, if appropriately constructed, shares the incentives and rewards as well). FSPs and the project plans they contain represent the key to good team mechanics. The FSP represents the binding thread that holds everything together. As you move deeper and deeper into Development, it becomes clear that all the planning work to get these reciprocal commitments right is going to pay off.

Even with FSPs, of course, product managers shouldn't be clueless about other functional areas. In order to develop a strong relationship with their cross-functional team, product managers should comprehend precisely how work gets carried out within and between business functions. In fact, one of the secrets of execution is asking "how" questions, a topic I'll cover in just a moment.

THE PRODUCT MANAGER AS FACILITATOR, PARTNER, AND ORCHESTRATOR

During Development, the relationship between the product manager and the Development function is *especially* important because the people in Product Development, Design, Quality Assurance, or Product Testing, and any other supporting function are vital to the successful creation of the product. Product managers walk a fine line in this relationship while they keep the Development team focused and on schedule. Simultaneously, the product manager must make sure that the product's progress is tracked against the Product Requirements Document (PRD), the Business Case, and any project plans that were established and approved.

You can imagine, then, that the product manager's relationship with Development goes beyond just teaming. The product manager must help the Development team finesse some of the aggravating issues and administrative trivia that may arise. For example, the product manager must make sure that the appropriate hand-offs take place at the right time. Did Development send the right bill of materials to Procurement and Cost Accounting on time? Did the hand-off take place between Development and Manufacturing? Is Logistics, or Shipping, or Fulfillment aware that a product is on its way, and are they ready to handle it? Figure 16.3 shows some of the types of hand-offs that might take place in the creation of a tangible product. I recommend that you work with your team members to come up with your own version of this diagram. Remember, this visualization is one of the ways to rationalize what is included in the relevant FSPs.

Similarly, the product manager must manage external requirements that may affect development efforts. For example, the product manager must ensure that regulatory approvals and/or certifications for local or international product deployments get done in order to make sure that the product can be marketed, sold, and supported domestically or internationally. This might include the laboratory tests for electrical safety, a financial product's regulatory compliance, food or pharmaceutical safety regulations, and type approval for communications equipment compliance.

FIGURE 16.3

Development Phase Interactions

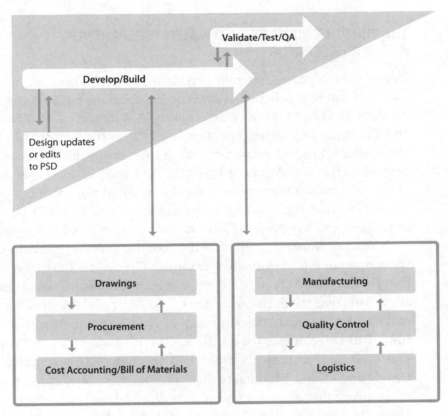

TRUTH MIXED WITH COMPASSION

Execution requires a healthy dose of realism. Product managers should surface realities and address them as effectively as possible. However, this realism can't be harsh. The product manager must finesse relationships, which requires "soft" (a.k.a., people) skills. Soft skills come very naturally if you can empathize, that is, if you know how other people tend to think and feel. Part of this empathy requires that you understand the other person's environment and the typical situations to be contended with. Such familiarity is built up over time and through years of experience working with product developers and in working in a cross-functional setting.

Beyond environment, however, it helps if the product manager can understand developers. This means you need to take time to find out how developers and engineers think. There is much to be learned from the great minds of engineers, and there is much they can learn from the product manager about business and markets. It may not seem like a necessary activity, and from a pure project management point of view, it isn't part of the typical work breakdown structure—but it is essential. Open up the dialog, visit the laboratories and the work spaces devoted to design, and spend some time getting to know your developers and making sure they get to know you.

PRODUCT MANAGERS MUST UNDERSTAND EXECUTION AND MITIGATE CONFLICTS

In short, the product manager must clearly understand execution, which is about getting things done. If there were no conflicts, everything would be done as soon as possible, on time, and flawlessly. Once the dependencies for a given task have evaporated, two types of conflicts prevent immediate and swift action: conflicts of understanding and conflicting agendas. Very often, both types of conflicts emerge during both Development and Launch, occurring between functions or even within one function. And the product manager must surface and deal with these conflicts right away—it's the only way to prevent them from throwing the project off track.

SURFACING CONFLICTS AND REALITIES WITH "HOW" QUESTIONS

Earlier in the chapter I discussed why "how" questions are a secret to strong execution. It's simple but true: if you ask "how" questions until you have a clear understanding of the path between here and there, you've greatly reduced the risk of missing the target. How will the new feature be implemented in a week, when the previous record for such features is two months? How will customer feedback from the beta program be handled? How will the limited number of engineers on the project be able to handle both development and testing during a very short project timeline? Product managers may find it more comfortable to sit idle in development reviews and project meetings, trying to soak up information and figure out how things are really going to come together. It isn't easy to speak up and question things that aren't clear, but it's a lot easier than dealing with project cost overruns and failed products later.

This kind of questioning is also useful in resolving both misunderstandings and conflicting agendas. When two team members from different functions aren't moving in lockstep, it's very important to bring it up. How are the two of you going to coordinate this activity? How are you going to verify that it can be done, given these changes? How can we both get on the same page? This doesn't mean that there won't be conflicts, especially when it comes to differing agendas. Sometimes team members or functional representatives won't or can't hold to their FSP commitments for some reason. If it's an unforeseen problem that makes the commitment impossible to fulfill, it's a "how" question: How can we change this requirement with minimal impact on the product plan? If it's anything else, you may simply have to hold a hard line or use a predefined escalation path. Hopefully, well-crafted FSPs will help you avoid most of these situations.

Regardless of what kind of conflict has to be resolved, it's important to put together some kind of special follow-up activities to make sure things are getting fixed.

RAPID PRODUCT DEVELOPMENT

Many product managers work in organizations that create software products or tangible products with software components. Consistent with corporate goals to achieve shorter cycle times to get to market faster, many firms use rapid product development techniques to cycle through short development intervals. Because of this need for speed, as well as speedy validation, the term *agile* has been adopted. This rapid approach to product development can be especially helpful when it's vital to ensure that the product meets customer expectations, as in consumer-oriented mobile applications or IT environments. It is also used to test and validate the functionality or performance of product components (e.g., a control system for a machine). This section provides some guidance to help you adapt to this environment without being unduly drawn into the whirlpool of product development.

Figure 16.4 portrays the iterations that are used to develop products or product enhancements in short cycles (sometimes called "sprints").

This method is helpful in a couple of areas. One might include the development and deployment of a new consumer electronics product or mobile application. This is especially important when a user's opinion will contribute greatly to the final product—or validate an improvement. It can also be used to update a large-scale enterprise business application.

FIGURE 16.4

Product Development Iterations

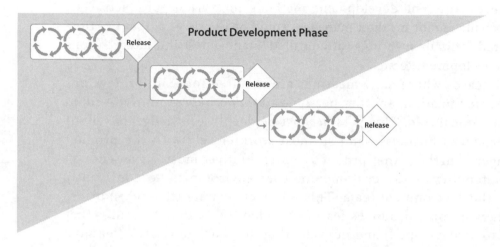

Some of these short development cycles result in an output that is deployed immediately and released for a broad base of customers to use (e.g., a mobile application). Many of these releases are imperceptible by customers, while others significantly alter the customer experience. Other short-interval software development projects are completed and "saved up" to be released in a major update or launch. In either case, the product manager is responsible for the oversight of this release process.

In certain environments, products are built in a series of parallel steps that have both hardware and software components. Consider a heart pacemaker, which requires software that works in harmony with its hardware. In this case, the software components can be built in short cycles. However, at some point, all of the product components need to be integrated and tested prior to launch. In this case, a product manager will have to ensure that multiple development work streams are seamlessly brought together.

Many who operate in this environment of rapid development know it can be quite time consuming. Many development-centric organizations draw product managers (or in some cases "product owners") into what I call the *vortex of product development*. In this situation, product managers may lose sight of the business of the product. When the product's business performance indicators are not monitored, undesirable outcomes may result.

Product managers must be cognizant of, and work effortlessly with, those who work in the development shop in their company, even if their firm uses different development methods for various products. The main challenge for product managers could be the sheer amount of time required for daily meetings (often called "stand-ups") and interventions with development teams.

In cases where daily meetings are required for work or development prioritization, another person—a *product representative*—could play a tactical role. This person must be deeply knowledgeable about the product's business—and so must work closely with the product manager. Further, the product representative must have enough understanding of the customer or user environment to confidently guide the development team. This is especially important when prioritizing work on a product's feature backlog (i.e., a list of features that need to be developed) and in evaluating the "burndown list" (features that have not yet been developed), as used in an agile environment. Finally, the product representative must have the political and organizational savvy to ensure that the team produces or develops a product that is competitively positioned. In one firm I studied, the product manager and the product representative shared the same office and were able to achieve the desired level of communication.

Regardless of development methodology, it's important to remember that the product manager is in charge of the product's business, not just the product's functionality, design, or features. Therefore, the product manager must always be cognizant of the following:

1. Vital industry, competitive, and customer drivers so that the direction of the product's business is understood by all.

2. The strategic direction of the product. This ensures that decisions and trade-offs are made with the strategy in mind.

3. The foundational constructs of the Business Case that justified the investment for the product.

4. The precepts used in the PRD to ensure that developers and designers have the right guidance.

5. The roles and responsibilities of others in the organization who work on various aspects of the product's business so that all of the gears of the organization operate in harmony, not just with the pace of development.

PROGRESS TRACKING

Keeping close tabs on Development status at all times actually helps *prevent* many of the stickier conflicts. Keeping track of the work of product developers helps the product manager monitor progress, evaluate emerging risks, and prepare to make decisions that can influence the outcomes of the product. Most of the time, continuous feedback and good preparation can keep projects running smoothly enough to keep big headaches to a minimum.

You've probably heard that what gets measured gets done. Some of the best measurement tools are the planning documents approved moving into the Development phase. While they are generally not static because the market is not static, they still serve as a very handy yardstick. Listed here are four critical tools I've discussed, and how their content contributes to progress tracking:

- The project plans within the Business Case contribute to the tracking of development progress, helping the product manager see whether the product that's coming together actually matches what the market seems to want.
- In organizations that utilize agile development, a burndown report will assist the team in comparing its progress against plans, resource utilization, etc.
- The PRD serves as a yardstick for product functionality, features, and attributes. The question, "Will the product do what it's supposed to do?" is always on the mind of the product manager. The PRD also serves to control scope and other unexpected change requests. (More on change control and "scope creep" shortly.)
- Product specification and design documents move in lockstep with the PRDs. Also, the developers maintain internal project plans that usually become visible only when product managers attend development status meetings.

And, by the way, markets change their minds, even while you're developing a product.

That's correct. Market changes may cause you to adjust the Business Case, Launch Plan, Marketing Plan, or even product requirements *before* you can finish the product and get it to market. Customer needs, which are the definitive inputs to the requirements, may change in the space of a development cycle. The longer the development cycle, the more likely changes will occur. This is why, in some firms, shorter cycle times contribute to greater certainty. Customer needs that drive market segmentation models should be checked to make sure that motivational states have not shifted and that your value proposition is intact. And customers are not the only movable boundary. Industry influences should be verified to determine if there are any changes in the signals or trends that supported the business justification. Competitive actions in the markets (and competitor product changes) should be carefully reevaluated, so that your proposed competitive advantage, represented in the product's positioning, remains compelling.

Periodically, the entire planning document set should be checked against the market drivers that contributed to its creation. As things change, the realities should be surfaced, along with any resulting conflicts (as described earlier), and then addressed as rapidly and effectively as possible. Diligent oversight of development, combined with continual review of market dynamics, may uncover discrepancies in requirements. It certainly reduces misunderstandings, and it definitely reduces scope creep, as I'll describe momentarily.

FREQUENT STATUS UPDATES ARE ESSENTIAL

Diligent oversight requires frequent status updates, and these updates are one place where the cross-functional team can really contribute. As I've mentioned, product managers don't review progress in a vacuum. Frequent status meetings of the cross-functional team are needed during the Development phase so that each team member can stay informed. This is where FSP commitments make a great yardstick, because they can (and must) be monitored, along with the associated project plans and budgets. Using the cross-functional model effectively means that each team member will own the primary reporting responsibility for his or her function. Those same team members should be expected to keep their functional management in the loop. Frequent management updating is needed, so this forum is the means to communicate status, outcomes, and emerging risks to management.

MANAGING PROJECT PLANS HELPS MANAGE RISK

Many product managers lament that they are just managing projects most of the time. This may be true because product managers must follow up on the work (tasks) or projects of other people in different business functions. There is no way around this.

Whether you enjoy project management or find it tedious, the fact is that you should know something about it. Years of experience in managing projects has shown me that well-structured project plans track development progress very well. Good project management is pivotal. Most project deliverables and results are only as good as the project plans themselves. Managing these work activities, deliverables, and dependencies—and their relationships—has already been codified in a standard body of knowledge (described in the next paragraph). By implication, the product manager must know *project* management. Understand that the product manager doesn't always have to do active project management but may have to play the role as needed. In some companies, there is a *Program Management Office* staffed by able project managers who are dedicated to teams. In other companies, another capable person can be assigned from a related business function.

One of the reasons that project management is so important to product managers, especially during the phases of NPI, is because the quality of project management affects the readiness of the product, based on all of the FSPs. Project management has a standard protocol and methodology defined by the Project Management Body of Knowledge or PMBOK˚ (pronounced "Pim-Bok"). It defines a project as "a temporary endeavor undertaken to create a unique product, service, or result."

Projects are managed under what is called a "triple constraint," composed of project scope, time, and cost. Each constraint is like a variable in a mathematical equation. If one variable changes, then the entire outcome of the formula will change. Successful outcomes from the Development phase are dependent on several simultaneous, ongoing projects being completed on time, on budget, and with the specified functionality, features, and desired level of quality. If costs go up or the project takes too long, a different set of less than desirable outcomes will result.

In my experience working for a defense contractor, there are usually cost and schedule control system criteria that establish acceptable quality constraints for project outcomes. When I held that job, the U.S. Air Force was the customer and the product went into fighter jets. The firm couldn't just complete a project on time and within budget; the product had to work with the highest levels of quality and reliability. Each constraint had to match military specifications.

In order to summarily clarify some of the elements of project management, here are a few key points.

- A project plan is made up of many tasks that are organized and grouped under an umbrella called a Work Breakdown Structure (WBS).
- All tasks have a start point and an end point, so by default, each has a duration attached to it.
- Some tasks must be completed before other tasks can start (predecessors), and some tasks are dependent on the completion of others (successors).
- Some tasks can be carried out simultaneously, while others can be carried out autonomously.
- Each task has assigned human resources and budget items.

Project management literally provides a structured method for planning and carrying out work—which is what execution is really about. As a product manager, you should be intently concerned with how activities are defined so that the path from start to finish is crystal clear—hence the "how" questions.

An example of a WBS for a customer-service training project (within a larger system implementation program) is shown in the ensuing list. I've set it up this way just to demonstrate a hierarchical project. Each WBS element has a series of tasks associated with it, but all of the tasks from all of the WBS elements must come together in order for the project to be successfully completed. In this example, if the Marketing department doesn't have the resources for the training, the project will either be late or incomplete.

WBS 10.0—Customer Service System Turn Up

    10.1—Customer Service Agent Training

        10.1.1—Secure facility

10.1.2—Order materials

10.1.3—Send out invitations

10.1.4—Process registrations

10.1.5—Notify marketing department of training date

10.1.6—Distribute product literature for agents to study

10.1.7—Distribute preclass test

Incidentally, much of this WBS information should already be captured in the FSPs developed by members of the cross-functional product team.

The visual for the above task progression is shown in Figure 16.5, where Task 1 is the predecessor of Task 2, and Task 3 is a successor of Task 2. Each task must be completed in sequence.

Figure 16.6 introduces the idea that some tasks are carried out simultaneously by people in different functions, and that there are hand-offs and dependencies between different departments. As you can see, three are three separate sets of workflows (i.e., series of tasks) that must be brought together to complete the project.

FIGURE 16.5

Basic Sequential Task Progression

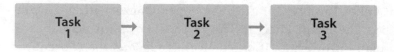

FIGURE 16.6

Task Progression with Dependencies

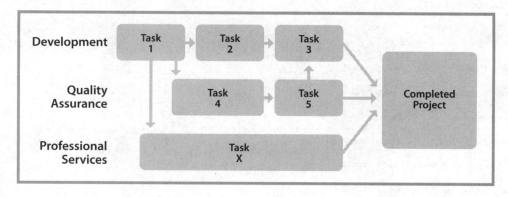

FIGURE 16.7

Task List in Tabular Format

WBS Element	Responsible Person	Start Date	End Date	Dependency on Other Function?	Risk Factors
Task 1					
Task 2					
Task 3					
Task 4					

Work activities can also be represented in a table that describes tasks, responsibilities, start and end dates, dependencies, and risks. Figure 16.7 shows how to represent tasks in a tabular format.

ADDITIONAL PROJECT MANAGEMENT TOOLS

There are some additional tools used to show how projects are organized, which include the Gantt chart and the network diagram. These standard methods bring all of the human resource, timing, and cost variables into plain sight, ready to be tracked. It's worthwhile to take a quick look at each of them.

A Gantt chart is used to portray tasks as a series of horizontal bars, sequenced and linked to show duration and dependencies within the context of the WBS. The Gantt chart in Figure 16.8 shows the sequence of steps taken to plan a workshop. If one deliverable is late, the subsequent

FIGURE 16.8

Simple Gantt Chart

ID	TASK NAME	START	END	JANUARY					FEBRUARY				MARCH			
				Week 1	Week 2	Week 3	Week 4	Week 5	Week 6	Week 7	Week 8	Week 9	Week 10	Week 11	Week 12	Week 13
1	Secure Facility	Jan 1	Jan 21													
2	Order Materials	Jan 22	Feb 1													
3	Send Invitations	Feb 1	Feb 7													
4	Process Registrations	Feb 11	Mar 14													
5	Distribute Pre-Class Work	Mar 14	Mar 16													
6	Carry Out Training	Mar 24	Mar 28													

dependent tasks will slip, either causing the project to be late or, as often happens, a lot of people to work more hours to put the project back on schedule.

The other commonly used task representation is a network diagram. There are two network diagram techniques. One is called the Program Evaluation Review Technique (PERT), and the other is the Critical Path Method (CPM). These are good tools to visualize where a delay might cascade through the project. Each representation has nodes and lines (pathways) that connect the nodes, intended to graphically portray project duration and completion of tasks.

What generally differentiates these methods is the location of the task (on the line or in the node). In the CPM, the critical path is the longest distance of the most critical tasks through the network diagram, so a slippage along the critical path becomes a time period for time period slippage. Figure 16.9 shows this simple visual of a network diagram for a project. Node 5 is right on the critical path, so if a predecessor task deliverable is a day late to node 5, the project deliverable (node 6) slips day for day.

The intent of this section of the chapter is not to make you an expert on project management. However, you should have enough familiarity with project planning and management that you can effectively use these tools to track progress and manage risk.

Project plans identify risks because they point out physical impossibilities and unlikely estimates. For example, if a single resource is needed for two different tasks in a project, and those tasks must take

FIGURE 16.9

A Network Diagram for a Project

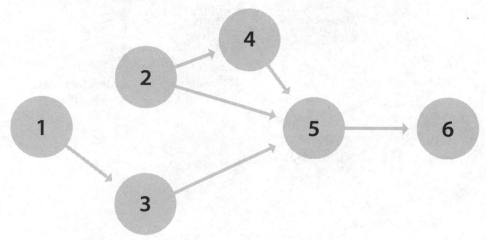

place simultaneously, the project is at risk. Likewise, if the first five engineering operations each take 50 percent longer than expected, the product manager can quickly compute—and communicate—the associated schedule risks. As you work with project plans, you'll quickly discover that they make great project status dashboards for various aspects of the Development phase.

As a matter of fact, these plans can be combined to create a much larger dashboard when you use the Product Master Plan as a project plan repository. The diagram shown in Figure 16.10 visualizes how three FSPs and their associated project plans are integrated so that all the project elements can be assessed. This "giant dashboard" means risks that affect overall product readiness for the market can be more quickly recognized and managed.

FIGURE 16.10

Functional Support Plan Project Integration

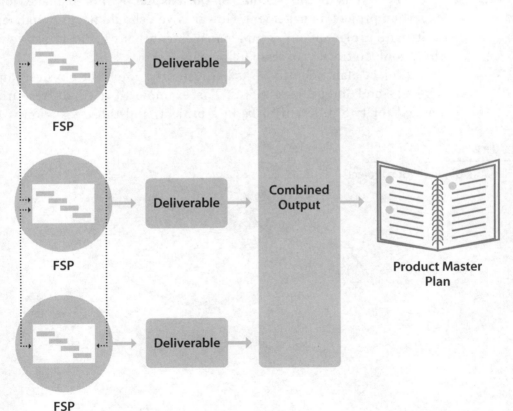

PROGRESS VALIDATION IS ESSENTIAL

Recall again that all deliverables by designated staff members from a business function represent the completion of each of their own projects. This is why the product manager and the cross-functional team should know (and oversee) *all* of the general project deliverables from *each* business function and should understand how all deliverables relate to one another. When the product manager and the team are working together during development, they can review their progress against those plans—ideally every week—and provide the needed readouts and status updates to management. This proactive project/program review process will contribute greatly to the team's credibility and will demonstrate the product manager's leadership.

When I worked for a defense contractor, we had a room with a wall that must have been more than 100 feet long where massive project graphics were viewed by project teams so that everyone could view the project's status. These visuals made it easier for project managers to keep the plans and status reports up to date.

But project plans are only as good as the input. What if the input is underestimated, or optimistic, or premature? What if unstated assumptions go into a status report, or unexpected issues don't get surfaced and compared with the plan?

This is where the product manager and the team should insist on tangible proof of development progress. Nothing against the development team—they're almost always doing the best they can with the constraints they're given. But there is no substitute for clear, visible proof of development progress. For example, some of the outcomes of early Development phases include models, mock-ups, or prototypes. Getting the cross-functional team together to pick apart these simulated products usually pays big dividends in understanding. A 10-minute session with a prototype can save weeks of rework by catching misunderstandings before they become deeply embedded into the product.

Management by walking around (MBWA) can also help you keep tabs on progress and spot flaws in requirements-to-product translation. MBWA is generally credited to have been developed by David Packard, of Hewlett-Packard fame, during the firm's early development. Managers were encouraged to get up from their desks, get out to the offices, cubicles, and laboratories, and find out what was going on in real-time—eyeball-to-eyeball. MBWA is a powerful tool in this regard. It can give progress validation in a fraction of the time it takes to evaluate some-one's accuracy on the phone or in a report. It is vital that product man-agers visit the laboratory, shop floor, factory, or any other area where developers build what they build. Product managers must be able to see the physical product, assess its functionality to determine whether the intended features are included, and form an even deeper connection with the product they "own." Even if it's software that is being developed, a user interface can be navigated, or an administrator's panel can be viewed when sitting next to a programmer. Beyond just improving progress readings, MBWA also helps managers develop the kind of empathy that dramatically improves soft skills.

PRODUCT TESTING

The product manager and the team must verify that the product works and will be built according to the product requirements. Making sure that the product actually works as designed is the function of testing. At this juncture, it is appropriate for the product manager to be involved in oversight of testing (to make sure it's being carried out), as well as do some actual testing to make sure that the functionality and features are actually working as planned. Every company has a variety of testing pro-tocols as well, so make sure you're familiar with those. Testing is crucial in assessing the product's integrity. Here are some of the types of testing situations or protocols you may encounter:

- *Functional testing* considers whether the product is actually doing what it is supposed to be doing. For example, if your com-pany is building automated teller machines (ATMs), you might enter the amount on the ATM screen, press the enter button, and see whether the ATM gives you the right amount of cash. If it doesn't, then the ATM doesn't function as required.

- *Use testing* allows the product to be tested under the actual con-ditions for its usage. An employee of the company could be asked to use the prototype, or it could be tried out in a laboratory envi-ronment. Some critics of use testing say that it just delays the product introduction because it takes too much time. I truly believe that some kind of tangible testing of the product must take place to verify whether it looks, feels, and works as envi-sioned by the product manager.

- *User or customer interface testing* is another key test. User interfaces could apply to anything from toys to electronic games to computer applications. How a user or customer interacts with the product to bring about the desired experience is the goal of this type of testing.

- *Stress testing* usually means that the product has to withstand certain conditions. It could include materials testing or just functional testing under severe conditions.

- *Systems interface testing* is important for products that are parts of larger systems or contain many subsystems. For example, IT systems may pass data between dissimilar systems, using compatible or standard formats. Extensive testing is required to ensure that the data isn't corrupted because of a faulty interface.

- *Structural or material testing* may be required for components or parts of products. Sometimes these tests are carried out by outside companies. Product managers may not be involved directly with this type of testing, but it's useful to understand and plan for this activity.

- *External testing* and approvals were mentioned previously. Some products cannot be sold unless they comply with specific standards as established by regulators. For example, electrical testing, fire safety testing, and a host of other approvals may be used. Visit the Underwriters Laboratory website (www.ul.com) to get a sense of these kinds of approvals. The most important thing is to start very early in the development process. A certification not carried out in time to allow for potential rework or laboratory time availability can delay a launch by many months and put you at a competitive disadvantage.

The product manager must ensure that Development integrates testing protocols into its project plans and allows for the appropriate hand-offs and hand-backs (if a test fails, for example). Most often, there is a quality assurance (QA) group within the Development organization. QA is responsible for structuring and carrying out product tests. It also works with Development and Product Management to report findings so that problems can be identified and fixed. Finally, the QA group should make sure that the product's quality is sustainable while the product is in the marketplace. Unless QA sits directly on the cross-functional team (and has its own FSP), these sustaining quality evaluations should be a commitment in the Development FSP. As always, your organizational structure may vary.

THE BETA TEST

Certainly, testing the product in the laboratory, or even with some "users" inside your own company, yields interesting or helpful results. But such "alpha" trials only go so far. At some point in the development process, you should be able to test an actual customer's experience with the product. One of the most powerful validation tools for this type of customer testing is beta testing. Making sure that Development and other relevant groups support and execute early customer testing using a beta trial will put a great deal in perspective. Nothing forces performance against deadline like formal, active, in-market testing by a small group of actual customers. A beta trial has its roots in the technology industry, but it's used in a variety of other industries as well (such as scientific equipment or small-scale industrial machinery). Even consumer products are beta tested (e.g., Polaroid used to beta test cameras and film packs).

Each beta trial is a short-term customer test of a product to determine if it works the way it should and provides the desired customer experience. It allows the customer to identify defects or problems so that Development can fix them early. This test is not designed to determine whether the market segmentation is right or the customer needs are valid. Therefore these tests should use a select customer or customers and be carefully controlled. In a business-to-business setting, a beta trial should normally include the following controls:

- A small group of "friendly" customers should be identified. Sometimes these groups are known by the terms *lead customers* or *lead users*.
- A project plan should be constructed, identifying key roles and responsibilities for Product Development, Marketing, Sales, and Product Management. The project plan conforms to the duration of the trial and the disposition of results after the trial.
- A contract between the customer and the product company should guide the project so that the customer understands the goals, duration, and any compensation to be received. A confidentiality clause

should also be included. There must be a definitive end date to the trial.

- The customer should be educated about what will be tested and how to report results. The team needs to make sure they collect the customer's data, conduct any final interviews, and take the product back to the laboratory.

And, of course, a beta trial is no good if the results are ignored. Many companies do beta trials as a way of debugging products but plan them so poorly that the defect fixes have to ship in a Post-Launch update. This doesn't convey the right impression. Under such circumstances, it's hardly worth doing the beta testing to begin with. In Chapter 17, covering launch execution, I'll talk about the use of a market trial, which represents another step toward a full market roll out.

PRODUCT DOCUMENTATION

Product documentation is literally how you communicate with customers when describing how to use a product. If it is not completed on time, or merely left for a later phase during development, it may jeopardize the product launch. As evidenced by the high percentage of less-than-useful product manuals (both paper and electronic) on the market, documentation is often poorly written and, frequently, not tested. Ensuring that the product's documentation is complete and accurate is another key responsibility of the product manager. Don't get caught up on the word *manual*, imagining a bulky three-ringed binder. The main idea is to provide adequate documentation for different customer types that may include users, administrators, and so on. When planning, remember that product documentation sets may include:

- Customer or user guides
- Online help guides
- Installation instructions
- Repair manuals
- Troubleshooting guides
- Administration manuals
- Operating manuals
- Care and maintenance manuals

The writing, editing, testing, publication, distribution, and updating of product documentation is usually done by a documentation manager. Sometimes this is managed within the Product Development organization, but other times writers report to different departments. Product documents must be accurate, readable, and helpful. Whether the documentation is published in paper or digital format, it must meet the needs of the intended audience and, most often, meet a corporate standard or guideline for format and structure. The documentation must also be usable by the customer! How often have you searched for help on the web only to find inadequate results?

In one of my jobs leading a software product team, the documentation manager actually reported to me. One day she came to me with a problem. She told me that the documentation her team was creating was inaccurate. She said this was because she didn't have the most current system from which to create the product user and administration guides. We called upon our team of developers, product managers, and documentation writers and set up a room with screens and projectors. Then we projected the image of the documentation on one side of the room and projected the system administration screens on the other side of the room. Step by step, we went through the current system and found many errors both in the system (found by the product managers) and in the documentation (found by all). The major lesson to be learned from this is to make sure that all cross-functional team members are synchronized so that they can carry out their work and give the product a fighting chance to fulfill the product definition.

MANAGING SCOPE AND BUDGET CREEP

Scope creep refers to unanticipated change requests, embellishments, or "great ideas" for the product that surface after the PRD has been baselined and frozen. One big problem with scope creep is that it represents additional work, by the same people, with no additional budget and no additional time. It's also a problem because it means straying from the PRD and, therefore, deviating from the team's understanding of customer needs. It may also cause the product to fit poorly into the product line or incorporate a value-added feature into a lower-cost model, distorting the marketing mix. This undesirable state of affairs is a plague to product managers and the team because it's distracting and unproductive.

Say what you will about innovative, maverick geniuses who go their own way with product requirements, but the hard truth is much simpler. The three main causes of scope creep are

- Poorly conceived requirements
- Incomplete product specification and design documents
- Excessively long development projects

Poorly conceived requirements force engineers to interpret what's being requested, which may or may not lead to the features that were intended. Incomplete or overlooked design details are discovered as prototypes and mock-ups are created, causing the team to have to "go back to the drawing board," which puts the project at risk. Excessively long development projects cause the time for understanding to get murky and cause the turnover to put too many hands on the work—not to mention the changes in market conditions over a long span. The product manager has to create crisp, clear requirements and keep projects on track, efficient, effective, and short. If things get fuzzy or take a very long time, engineers may, out of sheer necessity, stage a coup and take control of the project.

It isn't possible for the product manager or the team to catch all mistakes or all scope creep work items, but bad requirements must be fixed when they're found. The product requirements may be incorrect, inexact, or just may not adequately reflect customer needs. The features being developed could be less important to the targeted customer groups than originally thought, or the market may have moved, as alluded to earlier. Whatever the reason, the team must fix unclear, confusing, or inaccurate requirements. The PRD, PSD (Product Specification Document), FSPs, and Business Case are all good guides for resolving requirements errors.

Scope isn't the only thing that can creep. The product manager leads the team in keeping the product on budget as well. The goal must be to assure that the development of the product meets all cost and financial targets established in the Business Case. Accomplishing this means carrying out periodic reviews of financial data, work schedules, and estimates to complete the product, which implies a continuous data-gathering process, and a continuous financial reporting process.

Sometimes products get so far away from the original scope, or so far over budget, that they just have to be canceled. Even if a change in market conditions compromises the product (by changing the assumptions of the underlying Business Case), then a decision to halt development may need to be made. Rather than continuing to thrash alternatives and reorganize projects indefinitely, it's better to set some clear conditions under which a product would be canceled. At that point, if you've done everything reasonable within those conditions to salvage things, then it is up to the product manager to consider a decision to kill the project—which is why we have decision points factored into the New Product Development process.

MANAGING CHANGE: TRADE-OFFS AND PRIORITIZATION DECISIONS

Partway through development in many projects, the Product Development group discovers that some product features are more complex to develop than originally estimated. Other features may have crept in because of post-PRD requests. Sometimes key features are simply overlooked during the Definition phase. In this case, the product manager and the cross-functional team should decide whether to make feature trade-offs. The earlier these trade-offs can be made, the better. The more involved the product manager is in development meetings, the more likely these items will be caught early.

Engineers believe they know trade-offs very well. Engineers or product developers in many companies have an uncanny knack for proving that they know the most about the product and that they are in the best position to deal with technical trade-offs. But as good as they are, they may not have the market, strategy, or business perspective to select just the right adjustment to the product requirements. This means that product managers will have to explain the business basis for any given trade-off. You'll need to be equipped to defend the product through your market and customer knowledge and experience. Sometimes, you will need to defend customer needs and justify market-derived features.

Market knowledge helps product managers when feature prioritization is called for. There will always be trade-offs and other work reprioritizations that need to be considered within the context of cost, schedule, resource availability, and skills. As the engineers get to know you, it will become apparent to them that market knowledge sets the stage for optimal change decisions and that clear, needs-based requirements are essential to document the product's functionality and features.

Should the product require changes during the Development phase, there are usually formal change request protocols within each organization. These documents are variously referred to as engineering change notices (ECNs), engineering change requests (ECRs), modification requests (MRs), software bug reports, and so on. In addition, as products evolve and get tested, they also generate defect notices (DNs) or some other document noting problems that need to be fixed.

All of these change requests are typically numbered and categorized according to some kind of severity, based on complexity, impact on a system, and so on. The problem with this approach is that the categorization is usually made by the person who files the document. That person's view may not be the product manager's view or the product team's view. Categorizing a problem's severity should be made within the context of complexity, impact on the product's success, time, cost, market impact, and strategic significance. Using a decision matrix (see Chapter 5, on decision making) can be especially helpful in listing change requests or other problems. Figure 16.11 shows a simple decision matrix for a bank ATM development project, identifying seven different problems.

Frequently, the entire content of development meetings may revolve around these particular issues, so it's worthwhile for the product manager to become intimately familiar with these processes and documents.

One of the key messages is that the product manager should attend development meetings, as observer or participant, but not as a leader of the meeting. Note that participation is usually earned based on experience and knowledge, not on job title. The goal of attending is twofold: to keep a strong read on the pulse and progress of development and to be readily available to deal with feature trade-offs (and prevent scope creep) in real time. It also sends a positive message to the developers that you are interested, listening, and involved in the project. In addition, by attending, you will continuously improve your understanding of engineers and developers. Remember to use "how" questions and hone your soft skills as you go.

By the way, newer product managers should attend these meetings to get their bearings and to learn as much as they can. They will quickly learn the importance of attendance, and also learn about the product in ways they might never have considered.

To communicate the benefit of attending a development meeting, here is a short story about one of my first experiences in attending one:

FIGURE 16.11

Decision Matrix for Prioritizing Development Changes

RELATED REQ'T NUMBER	CHANGE NUMBER	REPORTED PROBLEM	COMPLEXITY TO FIX 1=Low 3=Medium 5=High	INCREMENTAL COST IMPACT 1= < $10K 3= < $50K 5= >$50K	SCHEDULE IMPACT (IN WEEKS) 1= < 2wk 3= < 5wk 5= >5wk	COMPETITIVE IMPACT 1=Low 3=Medium 5=High	MARKET WINDOW IMPACT 1=Low 3=Medium 5=High	TOTAL SCORE
R 009	12	Sceen readability obscured by person over 5'11"	1	2	3	1	3	10
R 231	21	Too much pressure required to push buttons	2	3	3	2	2	12
R 093	34	Touch screen accuracy problem	5	5	3	5	5	23
R 131	55	Currency counter inaccuracy	2	1	3	5	4	15
R 205	61	Machine is 10 lbs over the maximum 55 lb limit	4	3	3	1	2	13
R 077	71	Customer database interface problem	3	4	3	3	3	16
R 022	93	Customers want more color options	1	2	5	1	1	10

The first development meeting I ever went to took place when I was fairly new to Product Management. My product—the Japanese version of a made-for-U.S. office telephone system and a new telephone set—was being readied for market along with its North American counterpart. Because I took over the product midstream, I only knew what I knew based on the limited scope of the product requirements documentation.

I heard about a Bell Laboratories "architecture review" meeting that was to take place in Middletown, New Jersey, and asked the department head of R&D if I could attend as a fly on the wall. He agreed to my request. (I had done a fair amount of research on the competitive products in the market and knew about designs, functionality, and other characteristics of the competitor's products, having recently returned from Japan where

I attended a communications industry trade show and saw a vast array of stylish, full-featured competitive products.)

In the meeting, I sat in the back of the room as the engineers made presentations and reviewed their specifications. The product director for the entire product line was also present. As the meeting progressed, the engineers began a discussion about the display on one of the telephone set models. They argued that the two-line display was too costly and would force the engineers to redesign the housing and make new molds, among other changes. Therefore, they agreed that the two-line display would have to be eliminated until some future time. Even the lead product manager for one of the United States–based telephone sets was nonplussed by this decision. Politely, I raised my hand and asked if I could make a comment. The 20 or so people in the room all looked at this new guy from International Product Management, and the room got noticeably quieter. I started by saying, "In Japan, the market leaders, Panasonic and Toshiba, already have two- and three- and four-line displays on their telephones. Some displays are in color with cool little animated characters." I asked, "Is there any way you can reconsider this decision? The only place we can sell these is in small professional offices, and that's not our intended market segment." Then I stated that "International" needs a multiline, bright turquoise color display (i.e., LCD) and we need to fulfill a forecast of at least 10,000 units, and this change would put us at risk because we would not have the product needed for the market. I had been polite, but the Bell Labs department head quickly shut me down. He said something to the effect that no one really used the second line of the display anyway. I thought, "How did he know?" When I was in Tokyo, our distribution partner took me to visit different offices there. I noticed that three or four people shared a phone, and they could view the caller information and other data on the bigger, multiline displays. Bottom line: the product was never delivered with a two-line display—and I ultimately shut down the business in Japan.

THE DEVELOPMENT PHASE REVIEW AND CHECKLIST

A Development phase checklist should be prepared prior to the review meeting and takes a form similar to the one that follows in Figure 16.12. Certainly, the checklist you create for your own organization may be more complex. Notice that the last item on the checklist is the go/no-go for

FIGURE 16.12

Development Phase Review Checklist

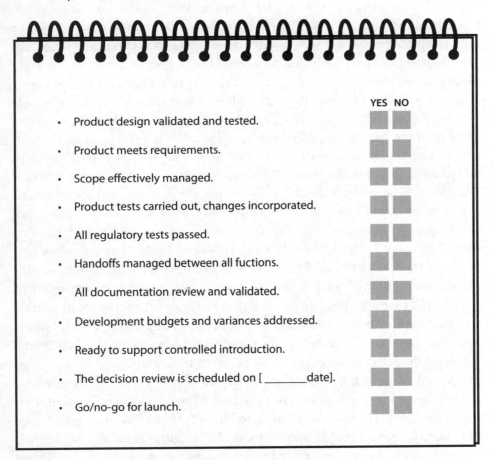

	YES	NO
• Product design validated and tested.	▢	▢
• Product meets requirements.	▢	▢
• Scope effectively managed.	▢	▢
• Product tests carried out, changes incorporated.	▢	▢
• All regulatory tests passed.	▢	▢
• Handoffs managed between all fuctions.	▢	▢
• All documentation review and validated.	▢	▢
• Development budgets and variances addressed.	▢	▢
• Ready to support controlled introduction.	▢	▢
• The decision review is scheduled on [_____ date].	▢	▢
• Go/no-go for launch.	▢	▢

launch readiness. This signals that the product is ready for either early-phase limited market availability or to support a full-scale product launch.

At the conclusion of the Development phase, the product team presents its results, listing all activities that focused on the design, development, testing, and validation of the product. The primary presentation at the review includes members from the Design, Development, Manufacturing (if required), and Quality organizations, with strong support from the product manager. The key decision sought is to make sure that the product is ready to be introduced to the market. The Development phase review actually precedes any reviews regarding launch readiness. The reason is that the Development organization must prove that the product was created under the guidelines of the product requirements and resulting design and specification documents.

SUMMARY

The product manager's role during the Development phase is to oversee the work of people who create or build the product. This could mean designers, developers, programmers, and people who test the product. There are also other cross-functional team members who are involved in a variety of activities and hand-offs. These activities put the product manager in the role of facilitator, motivator, negotiator, and, often, project manager, because the main goal is to make sure that the product is created as envisioned in the product requirements, that it can be efficiently produced, and that it can be delivered to the market on time, within budget, with the appropriate level of quality.

As the competitive environment continues to accelerate, many products are developed at breakneck speed. Regardless of the development method utilized, product managers cannot neglect the product's business. That can be hard to do when you're pulled in many directions and the developers want more of your time. Therefore, you have to consider the cadence of your markets and the speed with which your organization moves so that both are kept in harmony. There's no use in pushing products into markets that cannot digest them.

Your success in the work as orchestrator during this phase will add to your credibility as a market-focused, actively engaged business leader. It will also contribute to your standing as you take on a more complex portfolio as your career evolves.

RAISING YOUR PRODUCT MANAGEMENT EXPERIENCE QUOTIENT (PMEQ)

1. Investigate the business management structures for oversight of development within your own organization. How is it done? Who is involved in oversight? What are the gateways or sign-offs that transition the product from planning to development?

2. Talk to peers or others who work in your organization to gather some historical information from past projects and see how the planning and introduction areas of work compare with each other. How much effort is expended in planning? How much effort and time goes into development? Can you find a correlation between planning effort, development time, and product success? Is there a "sweet spot" for your organization, and if so, why?

3. Investigate your own company's development activity. What are the standard inputs? What are the typical activities? What are the outputs? What decisions are made along the way? How are they made?

4. Compare your company's process to the process described in this chapter. Can you find or suggest ways to improve the development activities for your own product without creating unnecessary conflict?

5. Review a few past development projects and talk to experienced product managers, program managers, and development team leads within your own organization. How many nonstandard, unexpected, or hard-to-assign tasks and responsibilities tend to crop up during development? Are there some that crop up consistently? How do these other team leads tend to handle them? How could you apply what you've learned from this chapter to handle them more effectively?

6. Evaluate your own product situation. How can you clearly communicate vested ownership and leadership of product success without appearing to make a "power play" or trying to "wrestle away control" of the product? How can you show more interest and enthusiasm in a way that will be accepted and appreciated by the developers and engineers?

7. Take time to learn about the functional areas that participate most heavily during product development. Are there meetings you can attend? Are there managers or team leaders you can get to know? Are there interfunction processes that you should know about, and possibly even assist in smoothing out or redesigning?

8. Find out what kinds of development meetings are held, and arrange to attend as many of them as possible, within your own time constraints and the comfort level of the developers. Of course, building relationships and trust with your Development counterparts is essential to establishing the comfort level of your being in those meetings. Find out in advance how the meetings operate, so that you can participate in a constructive, helpful way. How could you use "how" questions and leadership soft skills to make these meetings go more smoothly, if it's appropriate to get involved?

9. What external requirements are placed on your products, in terms of certification, exports, independent testing, licensing, and so on? When do these requirements have to be met, and how long is the lead time for each of them? Did you include all of those items in your PRD?

10. Find out what kind of progress tracking is normally done within your own organization. Get some historical progress reports, if they're available, and compare them with your own Business Case, requirements documents, and other components of the Master Plan. Will the typical progress reporting mechanisms give you a clear understanding of how development work relates to the Master Plan, or do you need to meet with developers and other team members to design a more complete reporting system?

11. If you work in an agile development organization, learn about the techniques to evaluate burndown trends and understand burn rates and how resources are utilized. You might want to "shadow" an experienced product owner or product representative to learn effective techniques to manage in this environment.

12. Make sure that you are actively continuing your market surveillance during development. When you're running your team meetings, make sure that everyone has a chance to do a customer and/or market review. Market updates are captured and used for updating your product documentation, including the Business Case, Marketing Plan for the product, etc. This will also help you when it comes down to managing change requests and reprioritizing work. Keep the Product Master Plan updated.

13. Investigate your own company's project management methods. Compare these with the Project Management Institute's (PMI's) approaches and the PMBOK® disciplines. How can you improve your own project management skill set? If necessary, how can you integrate better project management into your own Development phase activities? If you have no formal project management training, take at least a basic PMI or equivalent course that uses the PMBOK®.

14. Find out whether your company assigns trained project managers to development and other product efforts. If so, how can you get one assigned at the earliest possible opportunity? If not, how can you get one involved in your team or take care of the work yourself?

15. Develop a plan for validating progress that includes several elements: prototypes, models, mock-ups, or early alpha versions; the freedom to visit laboratories and development work areas frequently; and participation in

testing. Share this plan with your team and with the developers to let them know you are interested, involved, and aware of product development progress.

16. Gather testing plans, beta test processes, and documentation plans for several past projects within your organization. Review these for depth, comprehensiveness, completeness, and timing. How could you improve on these plans within your own product life cycle? Work with the relevant team members or team leads to adapt these plans as necessary.

17. Look at the proposed and "as-built" feature sets for several products similar to yours, within your own company. Talk to others or examine other product documents to see how changes were introduced and managed. Try to determine how priorities were managed by talking to those who were associated with the project. Add their learnings to your own list of things to watch out for.

18. Evaluate budgets and actuals for previous products similar to yours. How did Development perform with respect to financial plans? Are there common, recurrent trends that you might want to expect and be ready to forestall?

19. Work with your development team leads to understand the change control systems used in your organization. Make sure that you are added to both the "pushed" information (change reports, notices, etc.) and also added to the relevant systems as a user, so that you can asynchronously monitor change activity.

INTRODUCING THE PRODUCT AND ORCHESTRATING THE LAUNCH

Executive Summary

- Product launch is one of the most visible and most important activities within the product's life cycle.
- The product launch is not a one-time event. It is a series of activities carried out over a period of time, culminating in a final announcement to the market.
- Successful launches work toward a competitively attractive market window.
- The launch is not a short-duration, high-intensity event that is concentrated near the end of product development; instead, it's a longer-term activity that starts during product planning and gradually ramps up to a successful, on-time launch, based on full readiness of many disparate elements, systems, and organizations.
- Product teams should feel comfortable canceling a product launch at any time if it becomes apparent that the product's strategic goals will not be attained.

The product launch is one of the most visible activities for any company. It's the chance for the company to showcase the product's unique value proposition. For Product Management, it represents the pivotal transition between the structured New Product Development (NPD) process and the less structured activities of Post-Launch Product Management. Because the launch is so visible and often accompanied by much fanfare, its success or failure quickly becomes apparent.

To ensure that you have the best chance to achieve success with your product launches, this chapter is designed to provide you with a context that will reveal vital information for you so that you can understand the challenges you might face. Then, I'll equip you with a clear-cut set of recommendations to improve your launch success, which, of course, will bolster your credibility as a product manager.

LAUNCH BENCHMARKING OUTCOMES

For many years, my firm has benchmarked a variety of companies across many industries, including medical devices, scientific instruments, retail banking, pharmaceuticals, transportation services, technology products, and heavy industrial equipment. These benchmarks evolved through structured launch audit diagnostics, organizational diagnostic sessions and interviews, interactions at professional association events, and informal conversations with executives and workshop participants. Issues revealed through this benchmarking seem to be common among all companies; there do not seem to be any industry-specific indicators. The most frequently seen issues related to product launches include the following:

1. Firms fail to establish clear market windows for the introduction of products.
2. Executive champions are not assigned to lead important launches. Even when they are assigned, they do not keep close enough tabs on the progress of the launch.
3. Launch plans are not synchronized with the Business Case or are not included in Marketing Plans.
4. Sales force and channel organizations do not have the capacity to sell the product and, in many cases, do not have their compensation plans adjusted to encourage the sale of new products.

5. Sales and Marketing collateral is incomplete, inaccurate, or late.

6. Sales training is not carried out on a timely basis, or the training is not sufficient to equip salespeople to sell the product.

7. Operational systems and infrastructure elements within the business are not ready to support the launch, either because they are brought into the process too late or are not sufficiently staffed.

8. Launch metrics are missing, incomplete, or ignored.

9. Product teams are reluctant to kill a product mid-launch, even if that's obviously the right thing to do.

Just because these outcomes were identified does not mean that all companies did not carry out launches. In fact, most did, despite many challenges. The benchmarking suggested that even when some of these mistakes were made, products went on to be successful.

However, what did become apparent was that when the launch-related documentation was not completed around the time the product definition was completed, or if other business documentation was not updated (e.g., Business Case or Marketing Plan) while conducting launch activities, other consequences emerged. These included product rework, product material rewrites, and resubmission to certifying authorities, all of which added more time and costs than planned. If problems were deprioritized, then Post-Launch problems appeared in the form of negative analyst opinions and customer dissatisfaction.

The launch is often seen as a separate and distinct exercise, as if carefully developed strategic planning for the product never took place. I have reviewed actual launch planning documentation, and when I compared such data with other product strategy documentation and Business Cases, I found differing market data and differing strategic positioning data. In these cases, the Launch Plan was found to have been completed by the Marketing department, and the product strategy or the Business Case was completed by Product Management. Results were no different if Product Management reported to the head of Marketing or if it reported to Development. There tended to be insufficient communication and synchronization of activities between the two groups, and work plans were inadequately coordinated. These are major mistakes because the product launch is not a new strategic initiative. *The launch is just one dimension of the continuous execution of the product strategy.*

These findings, and the issues they represent, are very troubling. Product managers and marketers profess that they do not have guidelines and templates. However, even when they do, launch results seem to indicate that teams don't always fulfill their commitments on time. This leaves executives sorely troubled, especially when large product investments have been made. Yet every problem listed earlier can be capitalized upon and converted into an asset. If you look at each item in the list, you'll see clues to more effective launch efforts. Let's see how these clues lead us to better results.

THE PRODUCT LAUNCH PHASE WORKFLOW

The Launch phase has one objective: to successfully get the product into the market so that revenue will begin flowing into the company as quickly as possible. This phase is visualized by the triangle highlighted in the Product Management Life Cycle Model, reprised in Figure 17.1. You may remember that the Development phase overlaps launch activities, hence the two triangles. Launch execution actually starts when development work begins. For the launch, the shape of the triangle is depicted with an upward slope to indicate that launch activities ramp up as development proceeds, and also to remind us that launch is the product's on-ramp to the market.

In Chapter 13, on product definition, it was suggested that the Launch Plan be in a "version 0.9" state, which is a good way to say that the Launch Plan should be just about complete at that point. With the approval of the Business Case, along with the availability of the other product and marketing

FIGURE 17.1

The Launch Phase Within the New Product Introduction Area of Work

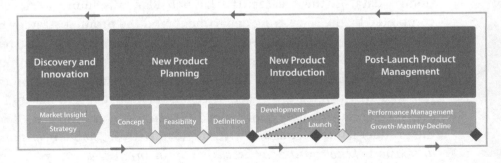

documentation, the cross-functional team members should spring into action. Early Launch Plan completion signals that all launch activities will be staffed and carried out, with achievable work tasks, milestones, and deliverables.

One of the methods I used—one that clearly provided a benefit for my teams—is a multiphase launch model. Don't forget, the launch is a *phase* within the New Product Introduction work area, and this means that the team is executing on the Launch Plans. If the Launch Plan is just being started at the beginning of the Launch phase, as is typical in many companies, the launch may already be in jeopardy. The three phases of the launch workflow I recommend can be categorized as *early, middle,* and *late.* Whether your company has an existing launch process or not, I strongly suggest that you try to divide the launch into smaller, easier pieces that have more identifiable work activities.

Sequencing the launch in this way has additional benefits. First, it allows the product team to make go/no-go decisions, at any stage, about whether to proceed with the launch. Such an outcome can happen because the product manager and the team are continually able to validate market signals, reassess the strategy, test the assumptions of the Business Case, or respond to any other jeopardy conditions that may be encountered. Second, phased launch execution helps maintain strong communication among cross-functional team members, so that launch work can be carried out and completed with a minimum of frustration and headaches.

The Launch phase has the systemic elements of inputs, activities, and outputs, as do all phases within the Product Management Life Cycle model. Figure 17.2 summarizes this workflow and contains the multiphase visualization in the "activities" section.

However, I want to provide you with a slightly different view on the launch, viewed through the three launch subphases mentioned above. These subphases will help you be a better launch orchestrator because they follow a sequencing of thought and action. I refer to the three launch phases as the "three A's." The three A's are activities that allow the product manager to:

1. *Arrange*
2. *Activate*
3. *Announce*

FIGURE 17.2

Launch Phase Workflow

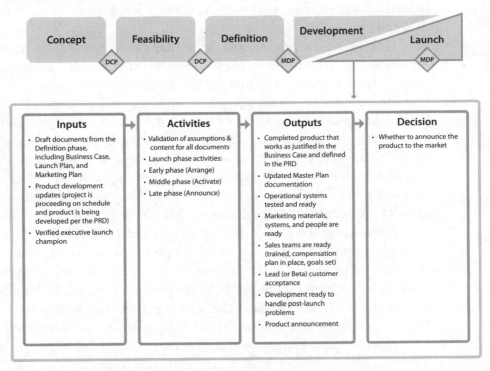

DCP = Decision Check Point
MDP = Major Decision Point

The three A's provide a slightly more granular roadmap for you so that you can have an opportunity to improve the outcome of the launch. The three A's are depicted in Figure 17.3. All arrangements are made in the early phase. The activate phase initiates the tangible work required to integrate and operationalize the product in the business. The later phase involves the culmination of all work activities such that the product can be announced to the market. Furthermore, this triple-A roadmap lays the groundwork for most of the topics that will be discussed in this chapter. I strongly recommend that you create a template of your own for your product so that the launch roadmap can be clearly communicated to all stakeholders. Functional Support Plans (FSPs) help to ensure everyone knows who's doing what, with whom, and when, to properly execute the launch.

FIGURE 17.3

The Three A's of the Product Launch

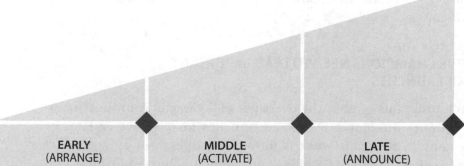

**EARLY
(ARRANGE)**

- Meet with senior executive sponsor to ensure alignment on Launch Plan.

- Confirm market window and agree on announcement date.

- Synchronize all activities with Development and QA to make sure all testing activities will be supported (lead user, Beta, market trial, etc.).

- Update any changes to Launch Plan as required.

- Secure final dates and deliverable from all functions.

- Review and validate all business documentation and assumptions.

- Work with Development to resolve any technical or design issues.

- Review & agree on dates for provision of product or prototypes to regulatory bodies or product safety organizations.

- Align any creative organizations who will provide copywriting, design, or other related work.

**MIDDLE
(ACTIVATE)**

- Recheck & update any business or market information for consistency with original Business Case assumptions.

- Validate value proposition and positioning.

- Ensure that Sales teams are available for training and secure training dates.

- Get sales and marketing materials written & approved.

- Plan for any internal & external launch events.

- Conduct market tests and Beta trials.

- Contact analysts or journalists and make appointments for interviews, articles, and other coverage.

- Secure product codes and update product catalog.

- Work with Operations to make sure that all internal systems will support the new product or any product enhancements.

- Make sure that Customer Service is prepared to process service requests (complaints, returns, etc.).

**LATE
(ANNOUNCE)**

- Carry out sales training.

- Conduct customer service training.

- Process pre-orders (if required).

- Secure testimonials from early adopters.

- Ensure that the product works or performs as required.

- Confirm all regulatory approvals are secured.

- Check to see if all product codes & prices are loaded into the required systems.

- Turn up & test all operational support systems.

- Assign product availability codes to allow for orders and fulfillment.

- Provide test versions and samples for sales people or channel partners.

- Recommend go or no-go for final announcement.

- Announce the product to the market.

Building on this foundation, I'm going to identify some of the important launch activities and provide a synopsis of things to consider. To reiterate, your own company probably has some sort of Launch Plan process, so please take care to integrate that plan into your own Launch Plan.

EXECUTIVE CHAMPIONS NEED TO LEAD IMPORTANT PRODUCT LAUNCHES

All launch programs require the oversight of someone. A product manager or product director can oversee launches for product updates or enhancements. All of this work is ultimately supervised by a product portfolio review board or equivalent council. However, important launches require an executive champion. This should be decided before the end of the product Definition phase and be committed when the Launch phase commences.

When so much money is riding on a successful launch, a key executive will make sure that all functions carry out their work and can also provide more timely intervention when problems arise. These key executives are usually appointed as corporate spokespeople and are able to interact with analysts, guide public relations activities, and be a face to the market, according to established corporate protocols. If the product is not being launched in a domestic geography, additional, local executive sponsors may need to be engaged for the product's transition to the market.

CONFIRM THE MARKET WINDOW

Successful product introductions require a clear market window. The market window is defined, very simply, as the *best* time to launch a product into the market. It's the point at which the product is strategically positioned as sufficiently unique or differentiated versus the competition. Some organizations have a standard launch time frame (quarterly, semiannually, or annually), sometimes as collective launches of every new product offering, gathered up from all the divisions or business units.

Clustered launches like this are done so that a large company can make predictable announcements to the market and to analysts. I characterize this as the "launch train," where all the product teams race to get their products completed and marketing documentation finished, otherwise they'll have to wait for the next train, which may not be for another three or six months. Products *released* this way are often launched without regard for an explicit market window.

There may be a good reason to launch a *specific* salable product at a specific time. Very often, a trade show might be the motivation for a launch. When product managers race to meet deadlines of structured, clustered, or interval launches like these, they are forced to make the assumption that the organization will be fully prepared to sell and support the product. And, of course, all this hinges on the market's unverified willingness to drop everything, pick the product out of dozens of other clustered offerings, and buy it according to the forecast.

Real market windows are apparent when:

1. There is nothing as unique in the market.
2. The main competitors are inactive.
3. The customer need you have uncovered and solved for has no rival.
4. Seasonal market movements are well understood (fashion, holidays, model year changeover).
5. Large company budgeting and buying cycles are easily identified.
6. Major industry events take place (such as the U.S. Consumer Electronics Show each January in Las Vegas).

The strategy for your product should be closely tied to the launch by making sure that you answer the question, "When do we need to be in the market, and why?" What should also drive the identification of your market window is your familiarity with the industry, your market segmentation models, and your competitive situation. Very often the outcomes of beta tests or market trials help the team determine the best time for the product announcement (more on this shortly). By the way, by this point, the Product Master Plan should be a treasure chest of knowledge to contribute to improved launch performance.

Take a look at Apple and other firms that do a great job creating market excitement for their products. Their launch plans are hatched far in advance to ensure that they can achieve maximum market impact. Business publications and the media do a wonderful job following major market movers. Make it a point to use these examples as benchmarks as you build momentum and excitement in your product team and bring your product to market.

SYNCHRONIZE YOUR DOCUMENTATION (THE BUSINESS CASE, MARKETING PLAN, AND LAUNCH PLAN)

The Business Case, Marketing Plan, and Product Launch Plan must be carefully synchronized, and more important, they must remain in lock-step. If they don't offer all team members the chance to "sing off of the same song sheet," you may miss important details. As suggested earlier, the main documents often are assembled and owned by different people under a variety of conditions, using different assumptions. What is important is to make sure that you are all focusing on the same set of objectives. It is up to the product manager as the leader of the team to make sure that these documents are explicitly linked and the related work activities are integrated and synchronized. Ongoing team status meetings and a forum for communicating project plans, resources, deliverables, and dates will contribute to better launch outcomes and outstanding harmony among the team members.

The Business Case, which served to justify the investment in the product and its associated marketing expenditures, is the guiding document. The Marketing Plan for the product sets the tactical wheels in motion, and, as mentioned in Chapter 16, if a launch is to take place, the Launch Plan's elements will be included in the Marketing Plan for the product. Think of the Launch Plan as a project plan that lays out the tasks and activities to introduce the product to the market. When thought of in this way, the launch activities, along with other FSPs, are easier to isolate. All of these documents are housed in the Product Master Plan, so there is always an integrated plan of record for the product.

Vigorous cross-checking between all supporting documents is an excellent way to mitigate risk, as Figure 17.4 indicates.

REVIEW MARKET AND BETA TESTS—OR CONDUCT THEM IF NECESSARY

Launching a new product without a market test is like riding a bicycle in New York City while wearing a blindfold: it's something you would never think of doing because it's so dangerous. If the team has invested so much time and money to get this far, then it should do a limited test or "soft launch" for the product. When a new restaurant opens, it really doesn't open to the public during the first few weeks. Even if you walk by and see people at the tables, waiters bringing food, and lots of other activity, you may not be able to simply walk in and eat. In this case, the

FIGURE 17.4

Multiple Documents, One Target

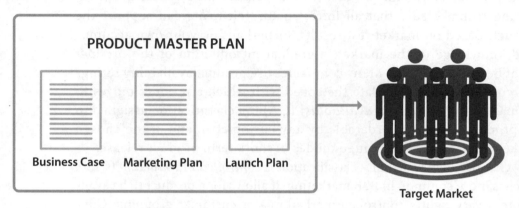

PRODUCT MASTER PLAN

Business Case   Marketing Plan   Launch Plan

Target Market

restaurant is going through a *soft opening*, in which friends, kind individuals, and others are helping the restaurant owners test every dimension of the business. Every operational aspect of the store is scrutinized and adjusted, including seating, order taking, order processing (cooking), delivery (serving), billing, payment processing, and even the dining experience.

Market tests help to achieve the same goal. More typically suited to consumer products, the market test validates the market segmentation models by answering the question, "Do those customers we selected really need this, and will they buy it?" Market tests also validate forecasts by answering a key question: How many can we sell on a limited basis, and when those results are extrapolated, will they approximate the forecast? Finally, market tests help the team understand what customers actually think of the product.

In Chapter 16, I discussed the use of beta trials. The beta trial seeks to achieve similar kinds of results in the business-to-business (B2B) domain as a market test would achieve in the consumer world. The goal is to take the product to your intended customers (or lead users), have them use it in the way in which it is intended to be used, monitor the results, and determine whether you should proceed to a complete launch of the product. Even if you arrive at a no-go decision at first, market test and beta trials may increase the odds of identifying changes that could make the product viable—changes that you might be able to implement within the time and budget constraints for launch.

PRODUCT AVAILABILITY RATINGS

Market testing allows the product team to validate the need for the product and to make sure that all infrastructure elements can support the product. Based on market test results, or perhaps on your own accumulated knowledge of the market, a gradual introduction of the product might be the right thing. Many companies use product availability ratings as a control valve to regulate the speed with which a product moves to the market. While *general availability* (GA) is a classification assigned to the product when it is orderable by any customer in any of the chosen markets, there are more limited modes of short-term product release.

One product availability classification is *controlled introduction* (CIN), which is more common in B2B marketing. It allows for a product to be available to a very tightly controlled market area or customer grouping. Controlled introduction ratings are used when a product is in a beta trial state, or perhaps being test marketed in segments or geographical areas that are easily "readable." If the controlled introduction phase exposes the organization to any undue risk, or the product does not work properly, successive launch phases can be canceled and the product investment can be curtailed.

Limited availability (LA) is another rating classification, and one that allows for a slightly wider audience to purchase the product. LA ratings permit marketing efforts and operational support systems to be fine-tuned. It also gives a wider market audience or geographic area a chance to experience or use the product. Close attention is focused on the product and on these customers or customer targets to ensure that the product works as represented, that the value proposition is valid, and that the benefits reported by the customers are those intended by the strategy. LA is also a classification that can be used as products approach the decline phase of the in-market product life cycle, when sales need to be restricted because support structures are being slowly decommissioned—especially if there is a replacement product being readied or already available. One prominent risk of the LA classification is tipping your hand to competitors before you have an opportunity to reach your larger target market with an updated or brand new product.

PROVIDE ADEQUATE SALES TRAINING

Sales teams need to be educated in the most appropriate manner for the industry in which your company operates. In some companies, sales training is incomplete or does not happen beyond the issuance of a new spec sheet or Sales Brief. In some cases, that's all that salespeople have available. Some sales training teaches salespeople to sell features and technology—an approach that is quite distinct from more engaging, consultative methods. Worse, sales compensation programs are sometimes not changed to provide adequate incentive for salespeople to sell the new product. You can do everything else right, but if your sales teams don't understand how to properly position and present the product, it will fail.

Sales training can take many forms. Training of sales teams in faster moving, consumer product categories tends to be more structured and frequent than training in B2B companies. Programs should be planned far enough in advance to match the speed of your industry. Training should coincide with periodic "kick-offs," followed by more formal, scheduled programs. Product managers and their marketing counterparts should jointly plan training events and make sure that the salespeople can be educated via the most effective methods.

Salespeople are generally auditory and visual learners—they may not like to read as much as they like to observe or listen. Whatever method you choose, though, sales documentation should be organized to make sure that the following kinds of information are imparted:

1. The characteristics of the customers who are ideal targets for the product, including buyer types, influencers, and decision makers
2. The primary, proven needs that drove the development of the product
3. The benefits and associated features of the product
4. Methods to ask questions, using consultative techniques
5. Demonstrations, models, and other visual aids that will help salespeople retain as much as possible

Successful launches depend on well-trained salespeople to carry the product's messages to the market. Sales teams must understand the product and know exactly why each segment would want to buy it. Lastly, they *must* be fairly compensated for their efforts.

SALES GOALS AND COMPENSATION

Most salespeople are provided with goals or quotas. In such environments, sales goals are integrated with the sales forecasts in the Business Case. Without these goals, it will be more difficult to fulfill those assumptions. Product managers need to make sure that they negotiate with leaders of the Sales organization early enough to get their products into the "bag" of products carried by the sales force. However, a quota or sales target is useless if the salespeople are not compensated to sell the product. Therefore, part of the negotiation is related to volume commitments, and the other part is to make sure that salespeople will be incented to make the sale! Well-trained salespeople without an incentive will, at best, sell products incidentally—not with purpose.

ENSURE READINESS OF MARKETING COLLATERAL, WEBSITE, AND INTEGRATED PROMOTIONAL PROGRAMS

Sales and marketing collateral should be prepared in a timely fashion, which means preparations should be made early in the launch sequence. Midsized to large corporations tend to demonstrate consistency in their use of style sheets to portray and maintain the corporate brand, which is a good thing. Still, there is a tremendous amount of variability across organizations, within organizations, and across industries in terms of the actual *effectiveness* of collateral, including its visual appeal, messaging, and readability. Here are some suggestions to make sure that sales and marketing materials are appropriately created:

- Product managers and marketers should work closely together by clearly defining their roles and responsibilities when preparing sales and marketing materials.

- The product manager should ensure that there is a highly skilled subject matter expert who writes some of the detailed material. However, you need a good creative copywriter to make sure that the documents are clear, readable, and not full of technology speak, especially when unwarranted.

- Inspections and reviews of sales and marketing documentation (including websites) should take place to ensure that they are readable and understandable. Creative copywriting and editing are required. An executive once said to me regarding his favorite assumption about the marketing collateral and creative copywriting, "They're in Marketing, they *must* know how to write collateral."

- Make sure that product requirements are truly business requirements and that they are easily understood and interpreted by those who need to write marketing materials. People in Product

Marketing are often provided with product requirements under the assumption that they'll be able to distill the benefits and features from those requirements. Likewise, technical documentation writers are often assumed to be able to write sales training materials, and they too may not have the creative ability to translate those technical terms into the language of the customer.

■ Allow enough time to prepare sales and marketing documentation not just for creative writing but also for artwork, layout, legal reviews, printing, and fulfillment.

It is critical that product managers and marketers negotiate the deliverables for each of the documents that have to be created. Try creating a mini-project plan for each item of collateral that needs to be prepared. In most companies, there are standard sets of documents for the sales force, including some kind of sales guide, sales briefs, frequently asked questions (FAQs), objection handling documents, and so on. *Every* piece of collateral should be prepared as if it were going to be used to support sales training. The relevant FSP should be used as a guide to carry out and document any negotiations that take place between Product Management, Marketing, and other related stakeholders.

Positioning statements, supported by valid, needs-based market segmentation models, must feed the sales and marketing documentation. Demonstrated proofs used in the Business Case should be the basis for writing about the business and market environment, the situations customers find themselves in, and how the product provides the most compelling benefits to those customers. Ideally, you should use the already-derived segmentation models to support robust integrated marketing communications documents and activities. (Integrated marketing is a newer term used to represent a "portfolio" of marketing communications vehicles and programs that go from traditional advertising and promotion to digital, multimedia programs.) All vehicles used to communicate to customers, from sales collateral to your websites, should communicate your compelling value proposition. Again, I cannot emphasize too strongly that all marketing collateral and any other related documents, electronic or paper based, must be easy to read, point out key benefits, and allow salespeople and customers to stay as informed as possible about the products—and the value those products create.

ARRANGE COVERAGE BY INDUSTRY OR MARKET ANALYSTS

In many industries and in large firms, product announcements to the market are often coordinated by people who work in public relations or media relations groups. Large-scale announcements are sometimes used for major product launches, but not all firms use these methods to launch products. Yet, it's important to make sure that people who watch goings-on in your industry are aware of your team's major product releases or launches. Your job as a product manager is to figure out what techniques your company uses to create visibility for new products. If you don't have a way to communicate with those who ultimately communicate with your customers, you won't get the exposure required. The only bearers of your message will be your salespeople and, perhaps, your website.

Industry or market analysts will greatly benefit from face-to-face meetings with designated leaders in your company. Their job is to evaluate your company and its products, especially those that are being launched. All analysts monitor industry or sector trends as well as competitor firms and the products they offer. However, different types of analysts have different parties who depend on them. For example, some *industry analysts* are actually paid by a community of members so that better informed procurement decisions can be made. Some *market analysts* operate in a brokerage firm and serve the interest of their clients who are financial investors. Other market analysts work for a business television station, publication, or other media outlet; their job is to communicate with viewers or readers for a variety of reasons.

In any case, your company and its products are constantly under someone's microscope. It's up to you to make sure that you work with your senior leaders, marketers, and analyst relations people so that they know you and your product, what your product does, and how it contributes to the company's strategy and business results.

MAKE SURE DISTRIBUTION CHANNELS ARE ABLE TO SELL AND DELIVER THE PRODUCT

Sales and distribution channels must be able to sell and deliver the product. Often, too many products are simply pushed into retail and/or wholesale channels, and the channels often don't have the capacity to

FIGURE 17.5

The Channel Capacity Problem

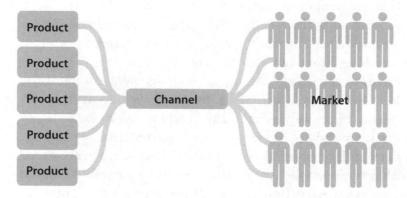

carry the product to the final destination. This can result in a lack of "shelf space" for the product with distributors, or a lack of real mind-share on the part of salespeople. This undesirable situation is referred to as a channel capacity problem (Figure 17.5).

My benchmarking results have shown that when capacity issues exist, forecast volumes are not realized within one or two months after the launch and sales volumes tend to be negligible. Worse, however, are the results of product portfolio reviews that show thousands of inactive stock-keeping units (SKUs) with virtually nonexistent inventory turn-over for tangible products.

In many cases there is no intermediary between the product team and the channel organization, meaning there is no one to resolve capacity issues, even when they work for the same marketing executive. A *channel capacity manager* or similar job category, supervised by the product port-folio review board, would be a good way of minimizing this risk. Further-more, if the capacitance issue could be surfaced as a decision-making criterion earlier in the product planning process, some product invest-ments might be curtailed. This would leave room for product investments thought of as having a greater probability of achieving success.

Introducing a product to the market involves a complex array of activities. The cross-functional team is supposed to grease the skids of the organization by making sure that the product can actually reach the market via the chosen distribution channel and be sold by those who are believed to be able to sell it. In retail banking, for example, there are a host of deposit-oriented products, each with terms and conditions and new features that are supposed to stimulate demand. If the retail bank branches are short of staff, there is the likelihood that salespeople in the branch will not have the capacity to even read the internal product release notes, let alone effectively sell the product.

Because channel capacity planning and management is one of the most overlooked issues, it represents a tremendous opportunity for product managers to improve product viability when they're formulating product and marketing plans. From a channel perspective, it's worthwhile to look back at the historical performance of each and every product or SKU within the portfolio, trying to determine how well it sold, in what volumes, and over what time frames. If the product and portfolio strategies are more closely aligned, and if the opportunities vetted through the New Product Planning process take the channel perspective into consideration, some products (even some sure winners) might be reconsidered before too much money is invested.

ENSURE READINESS OF OPERATIONAL SYSTEMS

Many firms may be able to finish the development of the product on schedule, but this doesn't mean that operational infrastructure elements are always activated on time. One of the reasons for this failure is poor operational planning. Operational infrastructure elements for the launch are often not clearly documented because too much emphasis for the launch is focused on marketing and selling.

The elements of the operational infrastructure that must be engaged, turned up, or activated include:

- Sourcing and logistics, to make sure that tangible products are available, in the channels or warehouses, and ready to ship
- Order taking, order handling, and fulfillment, so that customers can interact with the company, submit orders, and receive product
- Installation or implementation support, which should be readied and handled through the appropriate service organizations
- Repair and return processes, procedures, and actual handling, all of which should be put into place at the right time
- Customer complaint handling via training of customer service agents, appropriate staffing, and adequate IT infrastructure

■ Any other IT support systems, physical plant, or other infrastructure elements required, which should be in place and ready to support the product

It cannot be overemphasized that these operational pieces of the business puzzle *must* be a part of every Launch Plan. Moreover, as the product moves through the market, product managers and product teams must evaluate the effectiveness of these operational systems and methods and look for greater cost savings and efficiencies.

PREPARING FOR THE INTERNAL LAUNCH

I was working with a senior leader in a major multinational firm. It was about to introduce a product that would reshape how its customers worked—a true game changer. He asked me a simple question: "With such an important announcement about to take place, why aren't people in the company more excited?" I asked him this question: "How are they supposed to know?" I could tell by the look on his face that he was perplexed. This sparked a conversation that served to enlighten and energize him. It exposed something critical: the internal product launch is often overlooked.

The internal product launch can be an amazing vehicle to communicate with people inside the company. I attended a major launch for a company during which the atmosphere was filled with much fanfare. Executives made speeches, food and music were provided, and balloons dropped from above. In this firm, its employees are also consumers of the firm's product. Imagine how hundreds of people can become product messengers to friends and family!

Everyone in the company should be able to rally for the company, but this is possible only when a suitable atmosphere is established. When the proper "buzz" is created, people feel good about the company; they are energized and engaged. It also creates an army of educated people, many of whom interact with customers, vendors, or ecosystem partners.

The purpose of an internal launch is to ensure that everyone is on board and that people are excited that their company is an active, recognized competitor! And by the way, the leader in the firm I mentioned has actually started carrying out internal launches and even keeps a large billboard in the lobby of the corporate headquarters. Everyone at his firm knows what's going on.

LAUNCH METRICS MUST BE ASSEMBLED AND READY TO TRACK

On a related note, launch metrics are critical operational measures of how well the business is executing on the plans that were set down. For example, each business has its own unique cycles for sales activities, from actual announcement date to the time of the first order. Another relevant sales measurement might be from first order until the time the invoice is sent, or from invoice to payment receipt (order-to-cash). Other metrics might involve time required to fill an order, or even call center response times. Each company in each industry should have a set of relevant measurements, meaningful from the time the first public announcement is made, to ensure that all business systems and functions seamlessly execute.

Product managers should track the launches of not only their own firm but also other firms. I routinely watch business news programs and read business publications to learn about what different firms are doing. For example, I recently noticed an interesting product announcement in a press release. The name of the product executive was mentioned, so I looked up his contact information and made a call. I explained who I was, and that I was really curious about his firm's launch practices, both challenges and successes. He was eager to share, given the context I set. This is an example of something you can do, too. I have learned much from these types of discussions, and you can too. As a Product Management professional, your market focus is as broad as you want it to be. Imagine the insight you could acquire by speaking to a couple of product leaders in other companies who are not competitive with yours!

RISK MANAGEMENT

In Chapter 14, I discussed risk management within the Business Case. The product launch is really an extension of the Business Case, which is why it's worth taking another look at your risk exposure before you make your final go-to-market decision.

Every organization has a lot of gears that need to mesh and turn at the right time, at the right speed. In addition, there are external market factors that must be given a final look. In other words, there's a lot to consider, which can be daunting when all internal forces are gathering momentum to go to market. If you're effectively tracking all these factors, take a good look at these vital aspects of the product launch process:

1. Ensure that the product works as intended, both from the technical and the customer's perspective.
2. Check in with all stakeholders with respect to the forecasts and financials.
3. Evaluate all ecosystem partners to make sure they're moving in lockstep.
4. Verify that all training for all departments has taken place, including Sales, Service, and Operations.
5. Double-check with management so that it can intervene if escalations are required.

These last-minute check-ups will give you peace of mind, knowing that all dimensions of the launch have been covered. When the team meets to conduct the final go or no-go for the launch, you'll have the confidence required to make the appropriate decision.

BE WILLING TO RECOMMEND GO OR NO-GO FOR LAUNCH

One of the reasons for the use of a phased decision process is to make sure that decisions are actually made. Unfortunately, many product projects, especially later-phase, funded projects, continue as if there were no checkpoints and no possibility of cancellation. That's a mistake, because many things can go wrong, even at the last minute: The product could have a quality or material problem. The software could have too many bugs. The salespeople might not be able to get essential samples. Whatever the problem, the work on the launch might just need to stop. It doesn't always work this way. Once a product has been built, or even *nearly* built, teams don't usually consider a cancellation or postponement of the launch. The cause of this denial is usually behavioral. Stakeholders have so much invested that they assume the product couldn't possibly be in jeopardy.

Not long ago, I was in a client's office building when the head of Product Management ran out of his office to usher me inside so he could tell me a great story. During the summer of that year, a grand launch was planned for a product that was to redefine an entire category of products. With a big smile on his face, he said, "We had to postpone the launch!" He explained that the product manager, who had done a great job on the product's definition, validation, and everything else, had a sneaking suspicion that something wasn't right. The product was a home security system that worked via the Internet and could control lights, locks, security cameras, and heating systems. It was designed to be easily set up by any homeowner. Even though the product worked as designed, the home user set up and test had not been verified. So the product manager arranged for 50 employees to take the product home over the weekend to install and set up. On Monday morning, everyone was surprised that there were so many issues with the set up. These had to do with things such as switch position, color coding, and other items related to usability. The leadership team was appraised, and the launch was postponed by 90 days until the problems were fixed. Imagine what would have happened if this astute product manager had not taken this "last look" before such an important product launch!

I very strongly suggest that go/no-go decision reviews be taken very seriously. When products are introduced and customers begin to use them, the *last* thing they want is a product that doesn't work as advertised or a customer service representative that can't answer a basic question when the customer calls. Product work can be stopped at *any* point along its journey. Like the emergency stop cord on a train, anyone on the cross-functional team should be able to pull the cord, call a timeout, and reassess the state of the product to make sure that *any* problems can be discussed and solved.

THE ANNOUNCEMENT

One of the most critical milestones in the launch sequence is the announcement. The announcement date is synchronized within the context of the market window established in the Launch Plan. The product portfolio review board in its role as overseer of all product investment activities makes sure that there aren't any other launches taking place that might confuse the market.

The announcement date is agreed upon by the cross-functional team and represents the time when all launch work activities have been completed. It means that official notices to the market will be provided via the agreed-upon media, PR, and other marketing communication and promotional channels. In the end, the announcement signals to the market that the product is ready to be ordered or purchased. Amid much fanfare, the sales teams hit the road, ready to challenge the competitors, and customers await the arrival of the latest and greatest. The announcement could not be achieved without careful launch planning, which began early in the phases of New Product Planning. Successful launches bring the product to life and fulfill the strategic, operational, and financial goals of the firm.

THE LAUNCH CHECKLIST

Each phase along the product planning and development spectrum is punctuated by a go/no-go decision. At the conclusion of each phase, a checklist is prepared to make sure that all actions have been carried out. For the launch, this checklist is *very* important, because if a specific checklist item is overlooked, the product may fail to meet its targets. Some of the most important launch checklist items, which reflect the items I've highlighted in this chapter, are shown in Figure 17.6. Of course, you will want to create your own company-specific checklists that you can expand and modify as you gain additional experience.

SUMMARY

One of the most important facts to remember about the product launch is that it is made up of many different activities that are carried out over a period of time. These activities are governed by a Launch Plan that should be "almost final" at the end of the product Definition phase and be synchronized with the completion and/or revision of the Business Case. Furthermore, because the launch is a cross-functional initiative, it requires the skilled guidance of a launch project leader, capable creative resources, and a sales force that can be trained to carry the most important positioning messages to the market—and of course, be paid for their efforts. And this needs to be achieved with the appropriate corporate and executive support.

There are certainly company- or industry-specific nuances in every launch; however, the most important fact to remember is that you have to start early enough in order to carry out all of the work required to

FIGURE 17.6

Launch Phase Checklist

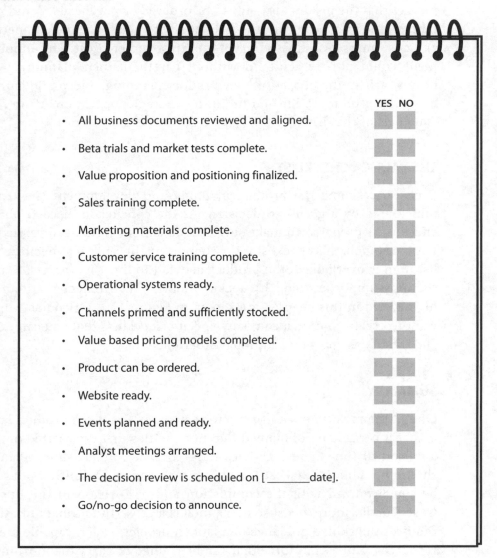

	YES	NO
• All business documents reviewed and aligned.	☐	☐
• Beta trials and market tests complete.	☐	☐
• Value proposition and positioning finalized.	☐	☐
• Sales training complete.	☐	☐
• Marketing materials complete.	☐	☐
• Customer service training complete.	☐	☐
• Operational systems ready.	☐	☐
• Channels primed and sufficiently stocked.	☐	☐
• Value based pricing models completed.	☐	☐
• Product can be ordered.	☐	☐
• Website ready.	☐	☐
• Events planned and ready.	☐	☐
• Analyst meetings arranged.	☐	☐
• The decision review is scheduled on [_____date].	☐	☐
• Go/no-go decision to announce.	☐	☐

complete the launch, introduce the product to the market at the right speed, and finalize the announcement within the company and to customers, industry analysts, and others who need to be informed. Finally, any plan requires that the most appropriate set of metrics be used to determine the level of success of the launch.

RAISING YOUR PRODUCT MANAGEMENT EXPERIENCE QUOTIENT (PMEQ)

1. As early as possible, obtain many examples of prior launch plans, successful and unsuccessful, from within your company. Study them to determine how the sequence, along with the presence or absence of various activities, seems to relate to product performance against forecast.

2. Talk to product managers and people who worked on launch teams for several different products within your organization. Try to determine how launch plans and execution differ, and what aspects of execution may need better documentation.

3. Attend launch project review meetings to learn how they are carried out. In fact, find out how you can play an increasingly active role in carrying out launch-related activities within the context of an established Launch Plan.

4. Obtain and review available launch planning documents and templates.

5. Secure as much knowledge as you can, through meetings or interviews with key executives in Sales, Marketing, and other areas regarding how some of the following work is planned and carried out:

   a. How are launch plans and activities synchronized to market windows? What are the official launch policies for the organization? Is there an internal launch website?

   b. What is the process to secure executive launch sponsorship? What level of sponsorship seems to be applied to different types of products and launches? Ask some of the leaders of launches what they have done in the past.

   c. How are products assigned within the sales force before the launch? Are these assignments changed after launch?

   d. How are incentives structured for salespeople? Speak to the managers in charge of the Sales department to find out. Use this information and any contacts you have the next time you are trying to figure out the launch worthiness of a product.

   e. Do there seem to be rules about or conditional behaviors for the sales force with respect to launches? For example, are salespeople given an incentive to "push" a product for a quarter or two, and then move on to something else?

f. How are launch plans and activities synchronized with annual business plans, Business Cases, and Marketing Plans for each product you're considering for launch?

g. How is operational readiness ensured? What elements of operational readiness seemed to be missed or ignored?

h. What launch metrics seem to be commonly used, and how do they relate to forecasts, strategy, and the Business Case?

6. Take the three-phase launch plan and design your next launch around the three A's. Use the diagram (Figure 17.3) to characterize the work of other cross-functional team members and to draw those people together in the launch planning process.

7. Who is responsible for the development of marketing materials? Is there a process to follow? Brand standards to abide? What are the lead times required to produce and distribute sales and marketing materials (collateral)?

8. Find out how creative resources are engaged in your organization for copywriting, artwork, and other promotional activities. What are the rules or procedures used to secure these resources? What happens if these resources are not available for a future launch? What would you do?

9. Find out how you ensure that the product meets all safety and regulatory requirements. When do you need to start this work, and how is the work carried out?

10. How is sales training carried out in your company? Try to attend several different presentations by different product managers to see how they train salespeople. Also, work with the leaders within the Sales organization to identify issues where salespeople need help so that future sales training can be more effective.

11. When you have an opportunity to lead your own launch team, try to be involved with analyst review meetings to learn the protocol and methods so you can prepare and carry them out in the future. You will probably need to work with an executive sponsor for this.

12. What seems to be the common practice for canceling a product launch? How can you set conditions for your own product that will result in a go or no-go decision that is more likely to be accepted later in the launch process?

MODULE 4

CONTINUING THE JOURNEY: POST-LAUNCH PRODUCT MANAGEMENT

INTRODUCTION TO MODULE 4

The journey thus far has provided you with a great foundation. This foundation is captured in chapters focusing on leadership, decision making, and finance. The journey has also helped you learn to focus your attention on the market—a focus that leads to meaningful insights and realistic strategies. Equipped with the right tools, you were then led through the process of driving a product from idea through design and development, and into the market. It's now time to transition to one of the most important areas of work: Post-Launch Product Management.

Throughout this book, I've repeatedly asserted that business is business. To that end, the product manager's job is to "run the business of the product." There is no magical formula for carrying out this work for a product or product line, nor even for a broad, divisional, or corporate product portfolio. Running the business means that the *investments made in the product must deliver the promised results.* Delivering results means that product managers and their teams must fulfill their commitments, monitor their performance using meaningful metrics, and take action to address deviations from their plans. Once the product has been launched, the product manager continues to harness the power of the cross-functional product team to gather performance information, reshape the vision for the product, and set sail for the future.

The purpose of this module is to guide you through the area of work that some product managers describe as "purely chaotic." In my workshops, we humorously refer to Post-Launch Product Management as the time when the product manager is fighting fires and is blocking and tackling. Sometimes, we draw a picture of a product manager who has many arms, like an octopus, and is constantly multi-tasking. The illustration shown as Figure M4.1 represents many of the attributes that are ascribed to the product manager. I'm sure you can relate to what's shown in this picture!

However, if you've done your homework and aligned your team, fires can be minimized. You can learn a more effective approach to the job of running the business by reading the five chapters that comprise this module.

Chapter 18 is appropriately called "Auditing Results after the Launch." In this chapter, I'll offer you a method, modeled on operational and financial auditing, to get to the root cause of problems encountered after the launch. I'll also talk about win–loss audits.

Chapter 19, "Post-Launch Strategic Performance Analysis," provides the perfect context to ask and answer the question, "How are we doing?" I'll introduce you to a construct I call the "product business strategy cycle" that will reinforce what you have learned about the Product Management Life Cycle model. As the chapter unfolds, you will see how the vast, interconnected field of data must be harvested to provide meaningful information. Once collected, the information is evaluated, analyzed, and distilled into options that can be considered by the cross-functional product team. I'll even describe a great way to run a product team meeting!

Chapter 20, "Post-Launch Strategic Mix Management," extends the discussion started in Chapter 19. It teaches you how to determine those important "next steps" to effectively steer your product through turbulent markets. You will learn how to craft an integrated product roadmap with an eye toward delivering the best value proposition, which, in turn, will allow you to derive the optimal price. Armed with this knowledge, you can align your outbound advertising, promotion, and customer education

FIGURE M4.1

A Typical Product Manager

programs, empowering your customers with the information they need to make smart decisions and ensuring that the product is available where customers want to buy it. Additionally, I'll show you how to create an unforgettable customer experience and earn the loyalty of your customers while keeping an eye on the operating efficiency of your product's business.

Chapter 21 provides you with a broad perspective by bringing life cycle product portfolio management into focus. It achieves this by providing you with foundational definitions, so that we can apply the Product Management Life Cycle Model to product portfolio management. I'll then discuss the importance of achieving the proper balance between existing products, products being developed and readied for launch, and products being planned, so that you can focus on the optimal approach to product investment allocations.

Chapter 22, "Enough's Enough! Discontinuing the Product," brings us to the end of the product's journey. One of the most common issues I've heard from clients is that they have a difficult time determining when and how to discontinue a product. This is the chapter that guides you through the discontinuation process. You'll even find a sample discontinuation notice.

When you're finished with these five chapters, you will have brought the entire Product Management Life Cycle Model "full circle," because you'll have seen the full picture of the product's life, from beginning to end.

CHAPTER 18

AUDITING RESULTS AFTER THE LAUNCH

Executive Summary

- The Post-Launch audit, conducted by an impartial auditor, examines the effectiveness of launch activities and Launch Plans.
- The win–loss audit examines the reasons for winning or losing individual sales, in an effort to isolate and correct systemic problems.
- Both types of audits are only as good as the team's willingness to implement changes that mitigate the problems found during these audits.

In many of the earlier chapters, much of the emphasis has been on the planning and execution needed to efficiently bring a product to market. This chapter covers two important "look-backs" that should be carried out after a product is launched to the market:

1. The Post-Launch audit
2. The win–loss audit

Both are critical efforts that could benefit from structure and formality. You'll see the word *protocol* more than once to emphasize this point. These audits are important because they reveal deep insight into organizational, structural, or procedural issues that can be addressed and fine-tuned to the benefit of all product teams. Lastly, audits allow for learning to take place across the organization as new findings emerge, are shared, and are then archived in the Product Master Plan.

AFTERWARD

The product manager and the team worked exhaustively on introducing the product during the launch, and the sales are coming in! Or are they? Over the years, I've engaged in informal dialogs in workshops and structured dialogs with product managers, marketers, and executives, and I've carried out Post-Launch audits for various products. These dialogs have revealed some interesting facts about Post-Launch performance analysis. Specifically, these findings suggest that Post-Launch reviews are generally sporadic, inconsistent, and relatively unstructured. In essence, few teams take a good look back at how well the launch was carried out and how well all of the people, financial resources, systems, and operational support served the business of the product launch.

Executives and product managers alike anxiously await first sales data. They look at other metrics such as web traffic, responses to advertisements and press releases, as well as feedback from salespeople. These are typical and normal reactions to the Post-Launch environment. More often than not, though, companies do not use a standard method, applied at prescribed intervals, to find out what happened, with what result, and why.

In general business terms, an audit is an evaluation or examination of a process, project, or system to determine how well all the internal elements performed together against the original plan. The word *audit* tends to remind people of a financial investigation, so some may be reticent to use it. Nevertheless, product managers, marketers, and executive champions for the launch should have a formal, structured method to audit launch results. The goal is a review of what happened in relation to the plan including what worked, what didn't work, and the results that were achieved.

A Post-Launch audit examines the performance of every business function that committed to support the launch in Functional Support Plans (FSPs). At a minimum, the audit should examine the following aspects of the launch:

1. Market window and timing relative to the window
2. Executive sponsorship and support

3. Synchronization between the Business Case and the Launch Plan
4. Preparation of sales and marketing collateral
5. Sales training
6. Operational system readiness
7. Launch metrics

With these main elements of the Launch Plan in plain sight, the Post-Launch audit can be effectively carried out. I'll talk about each of these presently.

Timing of the audit depends on the type of product. Faster-moving consumer products (of all types) typically hit the market with a lot of advertising and promotion, amid great fanfare. With this kind of investment, the audit has to happen fairly soon after the launch, perhaps within 30 to 90 days. For more complex business-to-business (B2B) products with longer sales cycles, the Post-Launch audit would be effective any time from three to nine months after the launch. This is not to say that any function should ignore problems that arise, prior to the audit, along the product's path into the market. Root-cause problem analysis is one of the reasons for the Post-Launch audit. The time lapse between the date of general availability and the audit allows for the business to run a little while, so that problems appear in the normal course of business. Note that modern systems and business intelligence can provide up-to-the-minute snapshots of many variables, and you should not neglect these if they are available.

USING AN IMPARTIAL AUDITOR

The Post-Launch audit, like any financial or operational audit, should have an impartial auditor. This may seem difficult, but it can actually be a peer of the executive sponsor or even someone from the corporation's quality office or equivalent organization. It must be someone who understands processes, systems, and corporate methods. A formal report from the launch auditor should be the output of this process. As the product manager, you will want to work closely with the Post-Launch auditor so you know what to expect. You should serve as the guide to the auditor, perhaps along with a Marketing counterpart (or whoever led the launch).

This auditor should use the actual Launch Plan as the baseline document. The first order of business on the auditor's list of things to do is to gather all the launch documentation, which would include project plans, FSPs, and anything else that explains the general structure of the work, timing, FSPs, project plans, and deliverables involved in the launch. The auditor will also want a list of everyone associated with the project who had major responsibilities (an organizational chart can be very helpful for this). The auditor will probably want to set up interviews with each of the major stakeholders to determine:

1. How each of them believes they performed.
2. How their organization is currently being affected in relation to their actual agreed-upon commitments to the launch.

The auditor should review each function's project plans to make sure that it fulfilled its commitments and understands what may or may not have happened.

After the initial interviews are held, a series of cross-functional team meetings can be held, with the auditor facilitating the discussions within each of the sessions. The audit sessions should take place with all core cross-functional team members present, so that everyone can learn about the interactions, interdependencies, and "break-points" that contributed to system failures or gaps in response times. In the following sections, I'll detail how some of the key questions can be evaluated. Please note that your own organization or situation may dictate a different set of things to examine.

Market Window Compliance

First on the audit agenda is the market window. The market window should have been established at the time the Business Case was created (which is when the initial Launch Plan should have been assembled). This window may have represented the company's typical launch cycle, or the launch may have coincided with an announcement at a trade show or similar event. Whatever criteria and launch window were established, the window should have been chosen to garner maximum market reaction. The question is, did it? The audit may look at the product availability ratings in an automated system, in relation to the planned dates, in a format like the one shown in Figure 18.1. Discussions about discrepancies (and lessons learned) should actually take place in the audit meeting.

In Figure 18.1 the controlled introduction date was scheduled for April 1, but the product's packaging and instructional insert were not ready on time. In the 40 days between the planned controlled introduction and the actual introduction, valuable operating and product feedback was

FIGURE 18.1

Audited Results: Market Window Compliance

LAUNCH ACTIVITY	PLAN	ACTUAL	VARIANCE & REASON
Controlled introduction date	April 1	May 10	15-day delay due to incorrect logo on packaging and delayed arrival of instructional insert from the printer (because the Document Production department did not have this in its project plan).
General availability date	July 15	September 5	Product defect in early deliveries was found in a sourced component. QA never checked the component because its engineer left the company.

missed. The general availability didn't change at that point, apparently because no one noticed that there was a problem. In fact, there was a component problem that caused a delay of one-and-a-half months. In that time, valuable market momentum could have been lost.

Suppose, for example, that the product was something that college students would have purchased prior to returning to school after summer break. Launching a product after students are back at school would mean that the product would never have penetrated the market at the anticipated rate of sales, so an entire year's sales may have been lost. That one-and-a-half months could be the deciding factor between market success and failure. The audit report, in that case, would have indicated how oversights and quality issues contributed to product and market performance problems.

Executive Sponsorship

Another key Launch Plan element deals with the existence of an executive champion, who should be identified in the Launch Plans. There is a real role for this sponsor in providing oversight to the launch project team, and in removing obstacles so that the team can carry out its work. Often, key decisions need to be made. If the executive in charge is not available, less than desirable consequences may result. In any Post-Launch audit, it is very clear when executive support is evident or lacking.

In Figure 18.2, an audit of a specific activity within the launch sequence reveals that the sponsoring executive was needed at a launch meeting to agree and sign off on a venue. The executive may have had another obligation, but there was a breakdown in communication that

FIGURE 18.2

Audited Results: Executive Sponsorship

LAUNCH ACTIVITY	PLAN	ACTUAL	VARIANCE & REASON
Decision on which venue to use for the launch ceremony and public announcement.	February 5	March 12	Executive champion was not available for the event planning meetings due to previous commitments. The Marketing team did not have the authority to bind the company to the preferred venue and so lost the time slot and venue. Furthermore, the key industry analyst who was available only in the location was then committed by her company to another project.

jeopardized the launch, resulting in a five-week delay in a decision. This, in turn, caused the loss of a favored venue and the support of a key industry analyst. All of these failures happened because the executive in charge may not have thought it was important enough to make the decision, and the appropriate emergency escalation paths were not put into place.

Business Case Synchronization

Another key area for the audit concerns the direct linkage between the Business Case and the Launch Plan. These two documents should be linked early in phases of New Product Planning and kept synchronized throughout execution. The auditor can examine the evolution of both documents, reviewing the revision dates and content of those plans and how revisions may have affected overall outcomes. However, the auditable elements related to the alignment of these documents are probably not as significant as the actual Launch Plans and activities.

Adequacy and Timing of Collateral

Related to the preparation of sales and marketing collateral, the auditor and the team members should examine the launch planning documentation to determine what happened with each sales and marketing document. If the collateral development within the Launch Plan focused on brochures, spec (specification) sheets, website updates, and sales training materials, then each document or subset of documents should have had a project plan associated with it. Figure 18.3 provides an auditor's view of the activities involved in the preparation of a product brochure.

FIGURE 18.3

Audited Results: Adequacy and Timing of Collateral

LAUNCH ACTIVITY	PLAN	ACTUAL	VARIANCE & REASON
Product brochure	March 15	May 30	Several reasons are cited for the delay: 1. Marcomm attempted to write the content but in the end decided it needed a copywriter, which took several weeks to find and secure a purchase order. 2. The product models were never ordered for the photographer because this was not on anyone's project plan. 3. The brochure verbiage review by Legal was overlooked. 4. The team did not know the internal printing department was closed because of cost cutting, and an external printer needed to be located. 5. No one took responsibility to communicate to the printer that final printed copies were to be shipped to the sales offices.

As can be seen, the two-and-a-half-month delay of the product brochure was due to a lack of proper planning and ownership.

Collateral seems to be problematic in many launches. Even though the manager who has responsibility for the launch and the associated projects may have all the plans, these types of miscues seem to occur frequently. Ultimately, much "scrambling around" is done to get the documents finished. Planning marketing collateral far enough in advance helps prevent this very common "schedule killer."

Adequacy of Sales Training

Another key area of focus during the launch audit is to make sure that sales training takes place in a timely fashion with the right materials. Sales training can be delivered through both formal and informal events, usually coordinated between product managers, marketers, and, often, engineers or developers. As Figure 18.4 demonstrates, delays along the launch project pathway delayed sales training by a month in our example. In that month, salespeople could have been learning more about the product and interacting with Product Management and/or Marketing to clarify questions and issues.

FIGURE 18.4

Audited Results: Adequacy of Sales Training

LAUNCH ACTIVITY	PLAN	ACTUAL	VARIANCE & REASON
Sales training: Eastern region	To be carried out between May 10 and May 20	June 12	The e-mail notice to the head of the Eastern region went out on April 20 instead of March 10. The brochures were not ready on time due to writing and publishing delays.
Sales training: Western region	To be carried out between May 20 an May 30	June 19	The product demos that were supposed to be delivered by Development were not ready until the first week of June. The developer in charge missed the second launch meeting and didn't send a delegate.

Reviewing Operational Readiness

One of the reasons for the use of a cross-functional product team and FSPs is to make sure that the product can be inserted into the market so that business can be transacted. The Operations FSP is a complex set of interrelated subplans that may include areas such as Finance, IT, Human Resources, Methods, and other basic business functions. There are complex, interfunction interfaces that need to be maintained, especially if many different databases are located within different operating departments.

The Post-Launch audit should involve a concerted effort to understand all of these interdependencies, which should have been called out in the launch project plan. The auditor may need to interview and investigate each of these areas to isolate any breakdowns in communication and also to accentuate positive activities that were completed, so that future Launch Plans (and Business Cases) can consider these organizational intricacies. As Figure 18.5 demonstrates, seemingly small, interfunction activities can have broad consequences for the launch.

Conformance to Launch Metrics

The last area I'm going to suggest for the Post-Launch audit is related to the preestablished launch metrics. These metrics might include the usual unit volumes, timing of those volumes, revenue, discounting, promotional responses, and even competitive responses, depending on your organization's specific needs and preferences. The auditor should use accounting data and operational data to determine whether the goals have been met.

FIGURE 18.5

Audited Results: Operational Impacts

LAUNCH ACTIVITY	PLAN	ACTUAL	VARIANCE & REASON
Update product codes in the product catalog system	April 15	June 15	The product manager did not know this was needed or how to get a code entered because it was his first launch program.
Train the customer service agents on the product and install up-sell scripts in the CRM system	June 15	July 12	1. The scripts were not developed on time because no one was assigned to it and the scripting tool had a defect in its workflow generator. 2. The training date for customer service also had to be delayed because the sales training (which was also delayed) took place on the dates originally set aside for customer service training. 3. The Customer Service department was to hire three more agents, and has not been able to secure them because HR didn't approve the hiring requisitions because of budget cutbacks.

The auditor will also invariably learn about other issues in the process, which will act as learning to update or revise future choices of metrics. It is strongly advised that product managers and their teams pay close attention to these audited results. The impact on their ability to manage their products as businesses can be profound. Figure 18.6 shows how some of the measurements were audited in our fictional example, and the root causes of those variances.

MAKE SURE TO CAPTURE LESSONS LEARNED

The preceding example scenarios depict various elements of a typical Post-Launch audit. Perhaps you'll identify with some of these depictions. I cannot overemphasize the tremendous benefit of carrying out a Post-Launch audit with an independent or impartial auditor. The auditor's focus on decomposition and diagnosis of the Launch Plan and actual outcomes is invaluable to improve future launch activities. All too often, the Post-Launch reviews end up being one meeting, with biased individuals defending their positions and blaming others for not doing their jobs. This is not effective, nor is just wondering why revenue isn't coming in and why the phone isn't ringing.

The audit is a root-cause analysis that should result in action-based recommendations, some of which should be acted on immediately, especially

FIGURE 18.6

Audited Results: Launch Metrics

LAUNCH ACTIVITY	PLAN	ACTUAL	VARIANCE & REASON
Order processing time	3 days	6 days	The web-based order input system is not always accessible by salespeople so they are faxing orders one or two days after the actual order time. The order processing center is short on staff, so orders are in a state of backlog.
Time from order shipment to receipt of payment (order-to-cash)	43 days	67 days	Several customers refusing to pay until defects are fixed.
Number of customer complaints	250 in the first 30 days after launch	820 in the first 30 days after launch	1. Most complaints are divided into two categories: product performance and product documentation, as determined by statistics filed by customer service agents and in listening to call recordings.
	150 in the next 30 days	1,624 in the next 30 days	2. One of the main problems reported is that the product's functionality doesn't work as represented, and the second is that customers complain that the instructional insert is inaccurate.
			3. They are both related. The more the product was sold, the higher the number of complaints. Customer recordings also reveal greater dissatisfaction as hold times increase due to a rising number of complaints.

when reputations are at stake. Ultimately, the Post-Launch auditor's report should be reviewed with *all* launch team stakeholders to make sure that future launches benefit from what was learned. Probably one of the most important lessons from the Post-Launch audit is how well it serves as a platform for pre-launch activities in the future. As more launches are carried out, past problems can be minimized or (with any luck) not repeated at all. Meanwhile, continual auditing means that new problems and their subsequent resolution can be added to the launch knowledge base. And of course, all of these documents should be archived in the Product Master Plan.

WIN–LOSS AUDITS

Most companies don't just take orders for their products; they are often in competitive bidding situations or may be providing proposals or quotations for customers. These situations are more common in B2B interactions. In these cases, a win–loss audit is another useful form of Post-Launch audit. As a matter of fact, win–loss audits should be carried out on an as-needed basis across the entire life cycle.

Documents used by businesses to invite proposals are often called "Request for Quote" or "Request for Price." For clarity, we can simply refer to it as an RFx (a request for something) by a customer (usually initiated by a purchasing department). When a company submits an RFx, it is said that they're making a bid for business, usually in a competitive situation. Some RFx's are very long and complicated, and some are just a couple of pages long.

Most product managers will be involved in responding to these at some point in their careers. Product managers who have provided excellent product documentation and training for sales teams will usually have minimal involvement in the typical RFx, or perhaps no involvement at all. This is usually an indication that the documentation has been adequately developed or shared and that the salespeople are well equipped to respond.

The object of the win–loss audit, as you might guess, is to figure out why your company won or lost a bid. Typically, though, we only want to find out why we *lost*—and by correlation, we want to find out if the sales process itself is effective. We naturally turn to the salesperson to find out. The response is, more often than not, "price." An official win–loss audit is generally needed because we may not want to accept price as the only sales barrier. As with any audit, a formal protocol or method should be established.

The win–loss audit takes two paths that must ultimately converge: the internal path and the external path. The internal path seeks to understand that which led up to the sale, including identification of the prospect, qualification, and the level of sales and other organizational interaction in support of the sales effort itself. The external path involves customer interviews and debriefings. The goal of all these efforts is to correlate the internal and external observations. You want to understand why you lost the bid but also recommend improvements for the future. Some of those improvements may require change to the product (which is why Product Management should be involved) or to the selling process (which is why Sales is involved).

Internal Win–Loss Auditing

The internal win–loss audit starts out with an understanding of what led up to the sales situation. The salesperson and his manager should be involved in describing the source of the lead and the people with whom the salesperson interacted. This serves to validate that he was working with the right customer and that he understood the motivations of that target customer type (buyer, decision maker, etc.). It also helps the product manager make sure the customer target is appropriately characterized. Additionally, the auditor reviews call reports or notes, which should have been documented, in the sales management or customer relationship management (CRM) system.

One of the most common problems in the internal sales audit is that salespeople don't always record their call notes or reports, so it's difficult to follow the audit trail. The other challenge is to sift through embellishments and potential exaggerations by the salesperson or sales manager, in terms of uncovering actual needs and whether the product actually was appropriate for the customer. Other sales process issues that should be addressed include a discussion of who the competitors were, what they were representing (if known), and how this may have been expressed in conversations with customers. Finally, the salesperson should be asked what he believed were the decision-making criteria for the sale (e.g., benefits, features, installation, service, pricing, references, brand image, and customer's perception of the company). In the end, the auditor wants to know one thing: "Why did we win or lose?"

External Win–Loss Auditing

Once the internal interview and internal data elements are examined and summarized, an outreach to the customer is needed. The customer interview requires an impartial person to initiate contact, just to make sure that the right person is contacted—preferably, the decision maker. Although it may be considered an easy interview to arrange and carry out, it should be taken very seriously. This activity is like an act of diplomacy. Diplomats use formal protocols to interact with other diplomats.

The first step in the process is to open up a dialog with the decision maker. The author of the communication is another executive or an auditor. This may sound old-fashioned, but a letter sets the stage for the formality with which this should be carried out. Appropriate care is necessary even if there is a win, and even if you have a good relationship with the customer. Once the customer responds (via whatever mechanism you wish—phone call, e-mail, etc.), suggest a formal agenda for the meeting. The meeting agenda should be documented and agreed upon in advance, including the duration of the meeting, topics that are off limits, a discussion of how the request for the proposal came about, who the bidders were, how they found out about your company's product, and the overall decision-making process. Another topic that should be on the agenda is the sales process, including the role of the salesperson, and his responsiveness, professionalism, and degree of understanding of the customer's business. Once the interview ground rules are established, the meeting is executed, with the auditor recording detailed notes and highlighting the most important points.

Assembling a Report

Finally, after both internal and external interviews are done, the auditor combines the two sets of data into a report. This will usually consist of a readout of some kind, to either the executive in charge, the product team, or, preferably, both—in the same room. The determinant of report format will largely depend on the degree to which problems may have been personality related. For instance, if the salesperson was found to be ill informed and didn't document his interactions and didn't act professionally or responsively in the eyes of the customer, the handling of this matter will be outside the purview of the product team. Based on the feedback from the report, decisions should be made (as soon as possible) and changes made to the sales process (as soon as *practical*) to improve the odds of winning the next bid.

SUMMARY

The goal of this chapter was to describe two important audit techniques: the post-launch audit and the win–loss audit. These two methods offer invaluable feedback for the product manager and the cross-functional product team after the product has been introduced to the market. Good Post-Launchauditing improves future launch planning and execution. Effective win–loss audits help improve the rate at which sales close while the product is in the market. These audit techniques provide excellent feedback to the product team, but they are only as good as the changes that result from lessons learned. Knowledge is just potential power; only when it's put into action will things improve.

RAISING YOUR PRODUCT MANAGEMENT EXPERIENCE QUOTIENT (PMEQ)

1. Investigate whether your company, division, or business unit conducts some type of Post-Launch audit to determine overall launch effectiveness. Although these are frequently called "postmortem" reviews, discourage the use of this title, because the product should *not* be considered "dead to the world" after it's been launched.

2. Gather some Launch Plans from similar products within your own company and attempt to conduct a mock, impartial Post-Launch audit of your own. Talk to some of the players and review all available documentation. Can you see patterns that you should avoid or adopt in your own launch planning? Can you see better ways to design your own Post-Launch audits?

3. Try to identify an independent auditor within your organization—someone with whom you feel comfortable and who will give you honest, well-researched feedback. Try to find out the "rules of engagement" for her time for a future session. Also, she may be able to provide you with some insight on things you should look out for that might bolster some of your planning activities. In other words, try to find out how to not repeat others' mistakes.

4. Consult with your Sales organization to understand what kind of win–loss analyses may already be conducted at your company. Ask to be involved in several analyses of other deals, strictly as an observer. How can you use this knowledge to design better win–loss auditing processes and contribute more meaningful feedback to your sales force?

POST-LAUNCH STRATEGIC PERFORMANCE ANALYSIS

Executive Summary

- Product managers and their teams are responsible for optimizing the performance of their existing products, consistent with the strategies of the organization.
- In order to optimize the performance of existing products and product lines, product managers must be able to harness data and associated metrics to assess the product's "life cycle state" so that optimal decisions can be made.
- When products are active in the market, the cross-functional product team serves as the "board of directors" for the product, analyzing the product's performance and making the most appropriate strategic and tactical decisions for the product's business.

When you can measure what you are speaking about, and express it in numbers, you know something about it; but when you cannot measure it, when you cannot express it in numbers, your knowledge is of a meagre and unsatisfactory kind.
—BARON WILLIAM THOMSON KELVIN, FROM POPULAR
LECTURES AND ADDRESSES, 1889, VOLUME 1, 80–81

This is the first of two chapters that will guide you through the area of work called Post-Launch Product Management. During this phase of the Product Management Life Cycle model, the product is living its plans and the product team is responsible for optimizing the financial and market performance of the product in the market, consistent with the strategies of the company.

Unfortunately, many business resources refer to this activity as "product life cycle management," which can be confusing. By taking a beginning-to-end perspective of the product's life, we can view one product or many products in a portfolio more holistically, allowing for a more strategic view of all products and how they each contribute to the value of the entire portfolio. This point of view allows for more efficient allocation of product investments to the product lines where invest-ments are needed. This is why product managers and their team should be *optimizing* their product's performance, not *maximizing* perform-ance. Ultimately, product managers should strive to build a durable, long-lived "product business" and a solid reputation. *This chapter is devoted to strategic perspectives on evaluating and measuring the prod-uct's business.* The next chapter will describe ongoing strategic programs that can be deployed for the continued optimization of the product's business.

RUNNING THE BUSINESS

Whether you've launched a brand new product, introduced an enhance-ment, or tried to capitalize on a new market opportunity, a high degree of real business diligence is required to track the performance of the product as it moves through its selected markets. Mindset, behaviors, and activities in this area of work differ from those needed up to this point. For example, the work areas in the Product Management Life Cycle Model that relate to New Product Planning and New Product Introduction are guided activities with linear processes and defined decision gates. There are templates for eliciting product requirements, building Business Cases, creating the Marketing Plan, launching prod-ucts, and evolving the Product Master Plan.

By contrast, Post-Launch Product Management requires a lot more thinking on your feet. This is where the true work of the product man-ager and the team starts, because there isn't a Post-Launch Product Management step-by-step template. The approach you take at this stage needs to be tailored to the situations you encounter, the dynamic nature of markets, and the transactions of the business.

I call this dimension of Product Management "running the business of the product." This is when product managers earn their stripes as business owners, just like successful entrepreneurs and CEOs. In this work area, you're always on the go, and your mind is constantly processing a *dynamic mix of data,* from explicit market signals to implicit market cues. You can't stop for a minute because you are being bombarded from all fronts. Sometimes, you may feel overwhelmed. You may want to put the book down now, feeling that you didn't sign up for this. Don't do that; if you've built out the Product Master Plan carefully as we've gone along, and you have the right strategic context, you can keep your fingers on the pulse of the business. With the right preparation, you will be able to guide your product's business with a subtle finesse that may even surprise *you* at times.

Think of it this way: if you were running a small business, you would always need to respond to the exigencies of the moment because of customer requests, supplier issues, and operational challenges. Product managers run their own small business and will always be pulled by e-mails, numerous meetings, random executive requests, a variety of questions from Sales, customer complaints, and many other demands.

As a matter of fact, if you've had experience running businesses or parts of businesses, you may be familiar with some of what will be discussed here. On the other hand, this might be new material for you. Either way, hopefully you will benefit from learning some new tricks and ideas to help you think about your products as businesses.

There's one thing I'm sure you will discover if you haven't already: most plans have flaws. Some of the work you do is aligned with the plans that were formulated along the product's journey. You will quickly learn that even these carefully prepared documents will have to be updated with some frequency. You can't drive looking *only* at the map, and like driving, you'll find that constant surveillance of the internal and external environments will end up guiding you as much as any advance plans.

THE IMPORTANCE OF MEASURING PERFORMANCE

Thousands of years ago, the ancient Babylonians created the first numbering system. They used tally marks and symbols to create calculations to keep track of time and communicate about quantities and such. During these early times, business people knew they needed a way to determine how their businesses were performing. Today, living without numbering or measuring systems, whether in our personal or business lives, is almost unimaginable. These systems are vital to planning and tracking performance.

Throughout this book, I've talked about why it's important for product managers to have the ability to evaluate markets, strategies, programs, revenues, and expenditures. Diagnostic skills allow you to make connections between independent observations and measurements—or to "connect the dots." Without these skills, you won't have the wherewithal to manage the product's business, and you'll be forced into a continuous state of reactive firefighting.

Without exception, senior leaders say they want product managers to speak the language of business—of efficiency and productivity—and to produce positive returns to the firm. Because product investments account for such large sums of money, this is not unreasonable. But having quantitative and diagnostic skills is only one part of the formula. Product managers need to know *what* to measure and *how* to measure it. In addition, product managers need to know how the metrics enable connections so that conclusions can be drawn. As stated previously, a situation will arise that, when evaluated, is caused by many factors. Rarely is there a one-to-one, cause-and-effect relationship. When you are alert to the many influences on a product's business, you are better prepared to take action that will lead to a positive outcome. With this, I'd like to reinforce an important point: *product managers will earn greater levels of credibility across the organization when they understand and act on proven facts and relevant data.*

Metrics provide the key. Metrics are standards that allow you to quantify, evaluate, diagnose, and explain findings and to consider future options. Some people actually refer to metrics as "measuring systems" because of the inputs required, actions taken, and outcomes produced. Metrics are based on data, and many product managers are challenged by a lack of sufficient data. Fortunately, leaders in many companies are addressing this problem as new and innovative ways emerge to mine data in disparate systems and to secure increasingly available public data. Regardless of the hurdles you face, you will always be "crunching numbers" in order to figure out how well your product is doing. Later on, I'll discuss data and metrics in more detail.

THE PRODUCT BUSINESS STRATEGY MODEL

In spite of the "field-expedient" nature of Post-Launch Product Management, we can structure the product as a business model into several submodels, tools, and analytical techniques. This structure isn't a linear process, per se; it's a cyclical process, and it will give you some "subroutines" you can run when different conditions are encountered. The cyclical nature of this model allows for the consideration of new data and information and creative solutions, and it provides a decision framework. The model is perfectly suited to meet the imperatives faced by product managers, which include:

1. Identifying the "in-market" life cycle state of the product, so you know where your product sits on the product life cycle curve.

2. Defining "what's happening now" with the product as a business, using a variety of scorekeeping aids, since scorekeeping runs as a powerful undercurrent to the business. Your measurement tools are shaped by the data derived from your ongoing review of financial results, industry and competitive movements, operational performance indicators, and customer reactions to the product.

3. Influencing and involving your cross-functional product team, as you lead its evolution into something akin to a small *board of directors for the product*. You will also learn about the importance of frequent product review meetings, replete with a standard agenda and a way to record the results of those sessions.

4. Recasting the *strategic mix*, which links life cycle position, scorekeeping, and cross-functional team action planning, to a variety of new possibilities and actions. *Strategic mix* is an expression I use to embody the business guideposts for running the product as a business. I will discuss the first three items in this chapter, and I will describe how to recast your product's strategic mix in the next chapter.

As described throughout this book, the Product Management Life Cycle model provides the context to visualize the entire life of a product. The Product Business Strategy Cycle (or cycles) runs as an undercurrent to the entire Product Management Life Cycle model. It depicts what happens while products are "in market" and allows you to knit together a host of "things to do" when a situation is encountered.

FIGURE 19.1

Evaluative Cycles as an Undercurrent to the Product Management Life Cycle Model

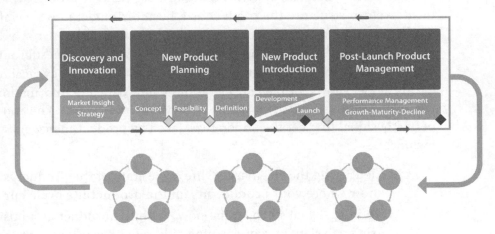

See Figure 19.1 for some perspective on this point. Notice the arrow emerging from the Post-Launch Product Management work area that points to several *evaluative cycles,* which are undercurrents of the product life cycle. Each evaluative cycle is undertaken when a situation is encountered. This is similar to how your mind works when evaluating various aspects of your day-to-day life and the choices you must make. An outcome from any *cycle* might result in a decision to alter a product's strategy, refine an operational process, or augment any other dimension of the product's business.

Using this higher-level perspective, let's now explore the Product Business Strategy Cycle in a little more detail. This cycle offers a way to think broadly about the product's business. It's a "strategy cycle" because it considers a very dynamic, ongoing set of inputs that are collected. These inputs must be evaluated at the speed of the business so that options can surface and you can make decisions that can be acted upon. And as in any cyclical model, you have to continually revise your perspectives. Shown as Figure 19.2, this Product Business Strategy Cycle has five basic steps: Collect, Evaluate, Decide, Act, and Revise. The acronym for these steps is CEDAR. Cedar wood is considered one of the most durable for construction, it's distinctive in how it withstands the harsh forces of weather, and it's beautiful. If you want your model to stand the test of time and your products to have market durability, use CEDAR as a way to establish your strategic perspective for your product. Notice the

FIGURE 19.2

The Product Business Strategy Cycle

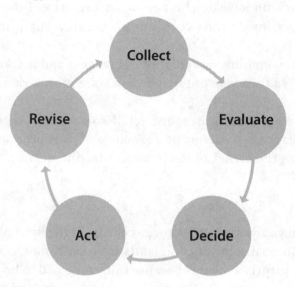

shape of each cycle in the model as shown in Figure 19.2 and how the CEDAR cycle is described here.

If you adopt this cycle and make it part of your everyday thought process, you will improve your organizational and market agility. By association, you will reinforce important foundations of leadership. Because product managers must continually bring disparate data together and then consider creative ways forward, the term *integrative thinking* is an appropriate designation for this dimension of your role. It's the perfect tool to inspire you and your team to consider the question, "What's next?" I'll first briefly describe each dimension and then offer a detailed discussion of the first two, Collect and Evaluate.

Collect refers to the collection of data from various repositories and activities that are related to the product's business, the company, and the market.

Evaluate refers to the analysis of interconnected pieces of data to figure out where the product is situated in the market and to assemble a story about the current state of the product's business. This allows the team to reach a conclusion about what's possible. Much of what is covered in this chapter is devoted to this area. It's also why this chapter is called "Post-Launch Strategic Performance Analysis."

Decide refers to considering various options and ultimately reaching a decision that lays out the path that should be taken.

Act refers to work undertaken by people in the cross-functional product team or others inside the organization to carry out what has been decided.

Revise refers to the ongoing surveillance of business and market situations in order to drive the cycle of further data collection, evaluation, and so on.

Now, I'll review each section in more detail so you can utilize the model as a way to manage the strategic performance of your product and to really take control as the owner of the product's business.

COLLECTION OF DATA

Imagine that you are in your office and you get a call from the head of Customer Service about an onslaught of complaints from customers about a product defect. You're surprised by this because things seemed to be going well. You're taken offline from everything else you had to do, and after a few days you find out that the head of procurement, in a cost-cutting move, sourced a component for your product from a new supplier whose reputation had not been tested. Your product, with a sterling reputation, is now sinking fast, and the industry analyst, who just happened to be doing a product comparison, found out about this and wrote a scathing review—just what you needed! Had you monitored your cost variances in the cost of goods sold (COGS) part of your product's profit and loss (P&L) statement, you might have been forewarned that costs were going up and your gross margin was declining. Or, had you been alert to metrics supplied by Customer Service about an increasing number of complaints, you might have been able to act sooner. But you missed the signals, and someone else, through his actions, caused your product to falter.

Product managers must understand that data is the fuel that runs the product's business. Data is necessary to help you evaluate how your product performs. And data, as is evident in the example above, should be associated with certain triggers that send alarms when a specific condition is encountered.

Data collection may involve many people from across the business. Therefore, it's cross-functional. And any activity that involves the cross-functional product team provides an opportunity for people to share common insights and perspectives. This also allows team members to get ahead of the curve because they will start to knit perspectives in their mind and begin to think of new and interesting ideas. *The role of the product manager in data collection is to ensure that the right data is available and to actively facilitate the integration of myriad data elements.* If the data is not available, then the product manager must "make the case" for the data and work to influence others, such as IT, Marketing, Finance, Sales, and Operations to ensure that the data is collected and made available.

For product managers and their teams, data doesn't always appear as a figure on a financial statement or a graph on a market share chart, although much data comes from market intelligence, sales, or operations. Data can be derived from documents you read, processes you use, customers you observe, or competitors on the market battlefield. Data can reside in many systems inside your company and in publicly available repositories outside of your firm. As a product manager, you have to proactively look at dynamic data indicators (e.g., daily or hourly trouble reports), data that is collected on a routine basis (e.g., customer satisfaction surveys or operational performance reports), and data that is gathered as commissioned special projects. Data is everywhere; you just need to know how to look for it!

Once, while visiting a customer, I was afforded a tour of an operations center. The operations center used my product, which was a software application. The work space was organized such that workers had to get up and down from their chairs many times over the course of an hour to fetch documents from a printer and carry them to others. It seemed inefficient to have a printer so far away. I calculated that they must have spent 10 to 15 percent of their time doing this. When I asked why the printer was not closer to the workers, the customer said that it was positioned near the network connection. If it was my business, and human resources were scarce, I would place a printer closer to the worker to improve efficiency. This would mean that employees could spend more time on value-added analytical work rather than tactical work that adds no value to the business.

You might think that this concern has nothing to do with the job of the product manager. However, you should make it your job to know all aspects of your product's business. If you know that 10 people are doing a particular job, and one simple investment could result in the reduction of employee headcount or the redeployment of a person for a more important purpose, you have an opportunity to create a better value proposition for your customer.

Sources and Types of Data

Data comes from many places. Data sources are mentioned, either explicitly or implicitly, throughout this book, so I won't rehash it all here. What I will do is define some of the most important data categories that you should be very familiar with. These include:

- Market data
- Financial data
- Sales, service, and operations data
- Observational data

Before I review these types of data, I want to point out that some performance measures will only provide you with a context around the *results obtained*. The results you evaluate should focus on areas deemed critical to the success of the product's business. That's where the expression "critical success factor" comes from. Examples of success factors could include:

1. Improve market share in North America by 10 percent
2. Decrease product returns by 25 percent
3. Increase revenue from current customers by 30 percent

Whichever measures you have, they must be evaluated frequently enough to detect patterns and to catalyze action from any member of your cross-functional team.

For example, if you worked closely with Sales to provide training and better product positioning, will the salespeople make more sales calls and close more deals? Or, if you increased your product testing to improve quality and usability, will you have reduced the number of product returns?

Product managers and their teams must have these measurements to both evaluate performance and inspire corrective action to continuously improve the product's business and its contribution to the firm's overall results. Let's now review these data categories and associated measurements.

Market Data

As mentioned in Chapters 7 and 8, the "market" of buyers (i.e., customers) and sellers (i.e., competitors) is multidimensional. The term *market movement* is used to indicate that one or more dynamics of the market is in play at a point in time. Product managers and their teams must be able to take snapshots of market activity and rapidly consider what's going on. The following list is an overview of some of the areas that you might want to understand:

1. *Market share* is a metric that shows how you are faring against your competitors. You might look at revenue by market area or unit volume. To calculate market share, you need to know the revenue your product produces for your company versus the revenue of all available competitive products. Alternatively, calculating unit-based market share requires data about the number of units you sell compared to all of the units purchased in a given market area. As you can see in Figure 19.3, market share charts can help visualize competitor market movements as well as describe who's taking share from whom and why. In this case, a new market from year 1, Competitor 1 has slowly gained share. Competitor 3, on the other hand, has not kept up. Imagine if you could portray your product's life cycle curve of revenue and profit and describe how your strategy resulted in greater market share!

FIGURE 19.3

Market Share Chart

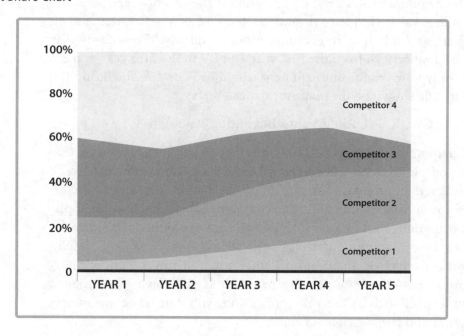

2. *Market penetration* relates to how quickly your product is accepted (purchased) by targeted customers and against competing firms. To calculate market penetration, you need to know how many customers have purchased your product in a given market area or segment against the total population of targeted customers in that segment, including your competitors' customers. (Arithmetically, divide the number of customers by the total number of targeted customers.) This information is also important when you forecast future penetration into current or new markets.

3. *Compound Annual Growth Rate (CAGR)* can help evaluate the year-over-year growth rates (e.g., market penetration) of your product or product line. If you have data about unit volumes, revenues, and/or average selling prices in a given market area, you can calculate your own CAGR. However, what's important is to compare your product's CAGR with the market's average CAGR (e.g., for the industry, sector, or geography). Interestingly, this measurement can be checked against your product life cycle curve to see if your product is leading, lagging, or equal to the market's growth rate. CAGR can be expressed in absolute and percentage terms. Given this, it is easy to confuse CAGR with an annual average growth rate—a method that is not recommended. To calculate CAGR, start with the beginning value (BV, e.g., revenue at the end of year 1) and the ending value (EV, e.g., revenue at the end of year 5). Remember, there are only four intervening years if you have five end-of-year observations, so from the first year-end EV to the fifth year-end EV is only four years; your exponent would be $\frac{1}{4}$ or .25. You'll find the formula shown below in most financial texts:

$$CAGR = (\text{Ending Value/Beginning Value})^{1/n} - 1$$

4. *Customer usage* tells you how often your product is used by targeted customers. There are a host of ways that you can track usage, depending on the type of product and typical frequencies. If you have a product with an online presence, such as an application delivered as a service, you can track *number of simultaneous users, amount of time spent in a transaction,* etc. If you survey users of a computer game, you can find out how many hours per day they use the product. If you have a web-based presence, such as a bank application, you can track *number of visits* and *transaction volume.*

5. *Customer profitability* allows companies to determine which customers add the most value to the business. A related metric, *customer lifetime value*, allows product managers and others to see whether a key customer is active and profitable across the duration of the relationship. Companies may add up all the revenue from a single customer for all products purchased or calculate the sum of individual product revenues. You may find that your product is sold at a discount as a way to cross-sell other products. You may also learn that your product is very profitable and helps your company's other products to be more successful. Either way, it's good to know where your sales revenue is coming from!

Financial Data

In Chapter 6, I discussed the importance of finance and referred to money as the language of business. In the end, your product must produce a profit for the business or be the catalyst for other solutions to bring in solid, positive contributions. The following list defines some common financial metrics:

1. *Unit volumes* provide you with a way to evaluate the number of units you sell or the number of transactions you produce. This helps you determine the contribution value of incremental units. It also allows you to figure out how sensitive your unit volumes are in relation to prices charged. Further, you can use unit volumes to calculate your market share or market penetration numbers and to target advertising and promotion programs that might influence greater unit sales.

2. *Average price per unit* allows you to see patterns based on discounting or competitive activity. In the communications sector, a popular metric is called *average revenue per user* (ARPU). If salespeople have a quota for your product and don't achieve their numbers, they may resort to heavy discounting to beat the competition. As you track average prices over time and link these price movements to other factors, you can figure out which levers to pull to realign and rebalance the product line or when to consider options such as an enhancement or a product discontinuation.

3. *Gross margin and Cost of Goods Sold (COGS)* are important metrics that add to your understanding of your product's business

contribution. As mentioned in Chapter 6, COGS is made up of the materials, labor, and overhead used to produce a tangible product. These costs, when subtracted from total revenue, provide you with a measure called *gross margin*, a rough approximation of profitability, shown both as units of currency (money) and in percentage terms. It's important to understand your product costs because you can equate costs to unit volumes and, ultimately, to revenue and profitability. When you can effectively explain these movements, you are in a great position to help the cross-functional team understand some of the complexities of running the business of the product. In most firms, this is one level of performance where a product manager can influence actions.

4. *Channel margins* are generally considered profits that can be calculated by multiplying the unit volumes sold through a given channel (wholesaler, online, direct sales, etc.) by the unit revenues in that channel. In some industries, a product moves through several layers of the distribution channel before it gets to the final customer. Product managers greatly benefit when they know the price charged as the product moves through each level. This allows you to figure out where each channel provides the best contribution to the business and the actual value as perceived by the customer.

Sales, Service, and Operations Data

One of the areas often overlooked by product managers includes the performance metrics of other departments. Because the people in these departments may be members of your cross-functional team, it's important to know how their measurements affect your product's business. Another way to look at this is to consider the "order-to-cash" process. In a recent organizational assessment, I learned that it took one company over a month to process an order and deliver the product because of paperwork bottlenecks, many intersystem hand-offs, and a lot of mistakes. I also learned that this frustrated the product manager because she said that the product was functionally superior and preferred over competitor products. It frustrated customers because they wanted to have the product in their hands more quickly. You can imagine how a process improvement such as an automated system might contribute to the product's success. Instead, sales were impeded.

From an operational perspective, product managers should ensure that they can meet the demand patterns for customers in any market area at any time. Many operational metrics focus on how effectively distribution and logistics processes work.

Here are some useful metrics that you can use:

1. *Sales force effectiveness* allows a sales leader to assess the performance of a salesperson. These metrics may include the number of calls made, effective contacts (actually connecting with a customer), percentage of sales that are from new customers, and average revenue produced by the salesperson. When I was a product manager, I was very concerned with sales force performance over time to ensure that I could count on increased market share and product profitability. Any product manager is greatly concerned when salespeople do not fulfill their objectives. This limits market potential, penetration rates, and growth rates for products.

2. *Out-of-stock metrics* are important to determine whether the inventory held for tangible goods is sufficient to fulfill demand. From a logistical perspective, you have to make sure that the business can get your product to the place where a customer needs it, when they need it. If not, they'll go elsewhere and you'll lose any good will you've earned to that point. A frequently used ratio is known as the "stock-out" ratio, and is calculated with the following formula:

$$\frac{\text{Lost Revenue} \times 100}{\text{Lost Revenue}} = \text{Stock-Out Ratio}$$

This information can help ensure that you don't run out of inventory, allowing for replenishment at given trigger levels.

3. *Inventory turns* refer to the number of times inventory is sold and replenished (for tangible products) during a given time period. This metric is calculated on the basis of sales of the product and the inventory held. Divide the revenue of the product by the average inventory level. As inventory turns increase, you know that your product is selling at an increasing velocity. An associated metric, *days of inventory* may provide visibility into how quickly inventory moves. If you divide the number of days of the year by the number of inventory turns, you'll come up with the average number of days a product is kept on hand. More turns means that

there is greater velocity in volume—a good indicator. If you compare your turns over various time periods and against industry norms, you'll know where you stand and can make appropriate adjustments. Too much inventory ties up working capital. Too little inventory may cause a stock-out, which means some customers will be unhappy when they are unable to purchase your product.

4. *Customer quality of service* metrics focus on how customers feel about their experience interacting with your company. For example, you've probably interacted with many companies on the phone or online and have been asked to fill out a survey after your interaction.

5. *Customer satisfaction* indicates whether your product is fulfilling the customer's need, providing value to that customer. It is also measurement that can provide an indicatation as to whether the product will be repurchased. This widely used measure contributes to your ability to predict future purchases by customers. Generally, you want to focus on a large number of customers, establish acceptable targets, and then have those targets exceeded.

    Product managers and their teams should also secure sufficient feedback from their customers about their level of satisfaction with their experience in using the product. I recommend that you check with people from Marketing or Customer Service to find out how customer satisfaction surveys are constructed and conducted at your firm. Many firms use *customer quality of service metrics*, such as a postservice survey, to gauge the customer's experience. Try to determine the measures used in your company in relation to your product. There are a lot of easy-to-use tools that can be utilized to survey your customers.

6. *Incident-based metrics* are those that allow you to gauge how effectively your organization engages with customers when they contact your company to resolve a problem. Your firm may interact with customers over the phone, via e-mail, through social channels, and the like. For example, if your company operates any type of interaction center, you'll want to measure *average hold time* or *average time to respond to an online request*. As you know from personal experience, you become less satisfied when you cannot get in touch with a customer service person or when it takes too long to solve a problem. The *incident handling time* metric may help you find out how long it takes to solve a customer

problem. When these are tracked, you can help the Service or Operations department to fine-tune their own functional efficiencies. You'll then be able to compare some of these numbers with levels of customer satisfaction or customer sentiment, and even sales volumes, to determine how well you're doing.

Observational Data

If there's anything that has motivated me throughout my career, it's been to create more value, either for my own product's business, for a customer's business (in the B2B world), or for consumers in how they carry out their lives. With this in mind, consider that *product managers must always hunt for the next value proposition*!

Some of the best lessons are learned through observing people. Observing takes many forms. You can observe a customer in a retail environment. You can observe employees who work in a customer company. And you can observe people who work in your own company. Hunting for value is a challenge; you have to make it a part of your life.

Recently, I visited two retail stores on the same day while shopping for a portable computing device. In one environment, the salespeople were personable and highly knowledgeable. In the other, there weren't enough salespeople, they weren't well trained, and the environment was not customer friendly. I'm sure you've encountered these situations numerous times. As a consumer, you know how you make decisions, and you know what you value. If you were the product manager of a product sold in each environment, what would you do? Do you know what your customers think about their purchasing experience?

An examination of the creation of value requires two perspectives— that of your company and that of your customer. First, consider your company's mission, processes, and people. What do you need to do to be more profitable, and how could you best satisfy your customers? Then consider your customer's point of view. In a B2B firm, customers want to know how a product will make them more efficient or more innovative.

When I probe clients during diagnostic interviews, two of the questions I invariably pose are these: what do you do to solve customer problems better than competitors do, and what inspires a customer to buy once and buy again? I usually get a host of answers, but none really hits the mark for me. The reason is that many people, including product managers and their leaders, don't fully understand the interconnected processes of their own company. They may be able to describe a workflow, but they never take the time to actually observe and study the actual work. The solution is simple: get out and look around, take good notes, and equate your observations to other metrics such as COGS, customer satisfaction, or market share. If you have an order fulfillment department, find out how an order is presented, who handles it, how long it takes, what documentation is provided, how inventories are adjusted, and so on. Determine if the order fulfillment process times have improved over time, and if that has resulted in positive perceptions by your customers. You can create workflow diagrams that identify each step, time needed, and how work is handed off from one person, or one system, to another until the process is complete. Too much time spent is often equal to value lost, either for your firm or in the eyes of the customer!

EVALUATE THE DATA: WHAT'S HAPPENING NOW WITH THE PRODUCT?

As you might surmise, data is like a precious metal. In an organization, product managers must harness troves of data in order to manage their products proficiently. However, individual data elements do not provide enough value. Interrelated pieces of data must be knit together so that they can be evaluated and so that options can emerge. That's why I recommend that product managers actively integrate data with the help of their cross-functional team members. The evaluation of disparate data elements can be a challenge, unless you figure out how to create the connections—or, to use an expression mentioned earlier, "connect the dots." One of the great benefits of having a cross-functional product team is that you have an able-bodied group of people who can help one other make sense of the numbers.

To start connecting the dots, visually associate various data elements or metrics so that you can create a storyline or conversational thread. This visualization can be done with a Data Association Map, as portrayed in Figure 19.4.

With a Data Association Map, you can construct the following story:

> Our product unit sales were in line with our forecast until a competitor introduced a new product. While the competitor achieved greater sales numbers for three months, it had some product quality problems and could not ship on time. We created a marketing campaign to talk about our high levels of customer satisfaction and then launched a major product replacement that easily beat our goals for new product revenue during the year. Overall, we had a great year!

FIGURE 19.4

Data Association Map

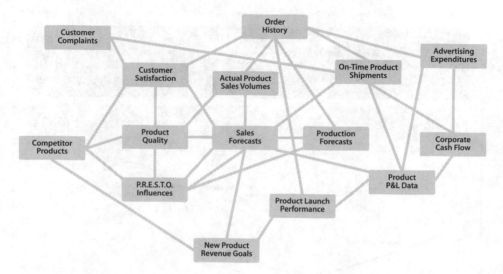

Now that I've set the stage with a discussion of data collection, let's dig into some of the more important dimensions used to evaluate your product's performance. For the proper evaluation to take place, you must be able to:

- Identify the in-market life cycle state of the product
- Answer the question, what's happening now with the product?

Identify the In-Market Life Cycle State of the Product

From time to time I ask product managers and other product stakeholders to tell me if they have products in the market that are in the Growth phase of the product's life cycle. Many say that they do, but when I ask how they know it, most of them answer that their products are in "growth" because *revenue* is growing. When asked *how* revenue is growing, and over what period of time, many provide responses such as, "sales are up 7 percent for the past two years." This may or may not be the product's actual revenue trajectory. Who decides what the Growth phase looks like, and is revenue the only determinant of growth? These are important questions for us to answer.

A product life cycle curve can be represented by any or all of these: the product's revenue, gross profit, or cash flow across its entire life

FIGURE 19.5

A General Product Life Cycle Curve

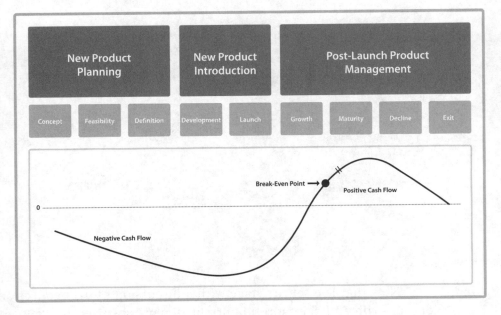

cycle. As shown in Figure 19.5, the cash flow curve suggests that during the Planning, Development, and Launch phases, the product is using up cash but not generating any.

When a product is in the Growth phase, the cash flow is increasing at an increasing rate. It further depicts the fact that positive cash flow must "pay back" the initial investment, hence the "break-even point" notation on the curve.

Mature products, on the other hand, have revenue that is either increasing at a decreasing rate or is relatively flat. There are some products that can be mature for extended periods of time with stable revenue and predictable profit contributions. Some mature products can even contribute higher gross profits than they did earlier in the life cycle, mainly because of operational improvements to the business. Finally, Decline phase products have sales decreasing at an increasing rate with eroding profits and vanishing customer bases.

There are even more granular views you can take in characterizing a product based on subphases, such as early growth, middle growth, and late growth. It depends on how granular you want to get and the speed with which you need to respond to the market signals of each life cycle state.

FIGURE 19.6

Revenue and Gross Margin

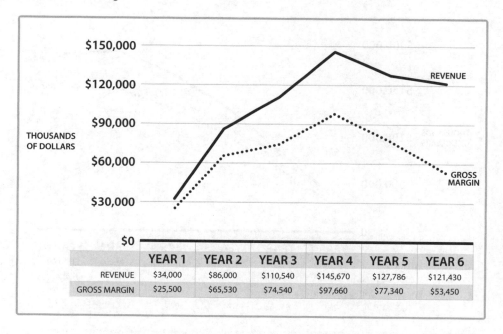

	YEAR 1	YEAR 2	YEAR 3	YEAR 4	YEAR 5	YEAR 6
REVENUE	$34,000	$86,000	$110,540	$145,670	$127,786	$121,430
GROSS MARGIN	$25,500	$65,530	$74,540	$97,660	$77,340	$53,450

Each of these curves, either for planning purposes or showing actual performance, is the result of data points that are graphed and plotted. Every product has a unique set of characteristics and thus may have a curve that does not follow a standard shape. Each curve tells a story about the business of the product, and all of the data points collectively (the life cycle curve) tell a more complete story.

Using these curves can be a little complex, though. Take the representation of two different curves depicted in Figure 19.6. Notice that the revenue curve stays higher for a longer period of time and slopes down gradually, while the gross profit curve descends at a more rapid rate. A product manager who believes that sales are going up in year three is not wrong—if that's the only observation point.

As can be seen, though, by year three, the gross margin is already under pressure. Perhaps salespeople are discounting prices and pushing higher volumes, while raw material costs continue to soar. There could be a host of scenarios that might explain such data. The main point, though, is that the life cycle curve for a product in the market is not really one curve, but many that have to be assembled as a storyline. Even more important, that storyline needs to be put into perspective—a perspective

FIGURE 19.7

Revenue and Gross Margin Curves: Actuals Versus the Business Case

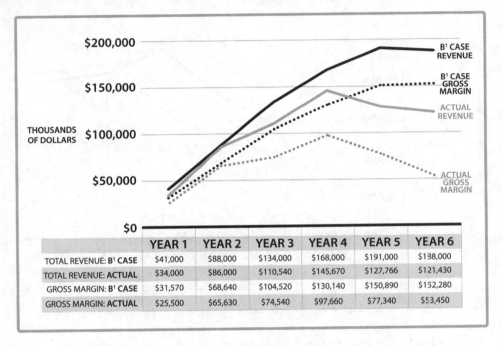

	YEAR 1	YEAR 2	YEAR 3	YEAR 4	YEAR 5	YEAR 6
TOTAL REVENUE: B¹ CASE	$41,000	$88,000	$134,000	$168,000	$191,000	$138,000
TOTAL REVENUE: **ACTUAL**	$34,000	$86,000	$110,540	$145,670	$127,766	$121,430
GROSS MARGIN: B¹ CASE	$31,570	$68,640	$104,520	$130,140	$150,890	$152,280
GROSS MARGIN: **ACTUAL**	$25,500	$65,630	$74,540	$97,660	$77,340	$53,450

provided by the original Business Case for the product. Figure 19.7 gives you an idea of how you might acquire this perspective.

If you examine Figure 19.7 closely, you'll see that there are now four curves. Two curves represent the revenue and gross margin from the original Business Case, and the other two represent the product's actual performance. The original Business Case identifies the projected revenue and gross margin for the product over a six-year period of time. Now the story changes, because we know that the original Business Case was more optimistic, and the business is not doing as well as originally expected. Suddenly, what seemed like a rapidly growing product may actually be showing signs of slightly slower growth. This could be an indication of revenue and gross margin pressure. As you follow the curves, you can see the overall result.

Using the Business Case or another similar planning tool allows product managers, in close partnership with their Finance and Marketing counterparts, to set the stage for managing the product in the future. A good method to pave the way for better Post-Launch Product Management is to predetermine and document what the future life cycle state *should* look like. For example, one could state in the Business Case that "the product in 'growth' should exhibit sales increases of 8 percent year over year with a gross margin of 70 percent." Then, when the product manager and the team review the product's performance at some point in the future, they have a standard against which to measure its lifetime performance, not just performance based on an in-year budget that offers no historical perspective. If the Business Case and other supporting financial forecasts are archived in the Product Master Plan, the product manager (current or future) can immediately gain the most important perspective on where the product is in its (in-market) life cycle state.

Finally, when you pinpoint the product's correct life cycle state, you can choose the most appropriate investment strategies for the product. If you believe your product is really in the Growth phase, you will likely be investing in product improvements and promotional programs. However, if you misunderstand the product's life cycle state and invest heavily in a mature product (that you believe is in Growth), you probably won't reap the kinds of returns you're expecting, and you would also be using up valuable resources that could be applied to other endeavors. Once the product manager has a view of the product's place in the market, graphically portrayed, the team's efforts can be more effectively focused on the most appropriate future strategic options.

Answer the Question: "What's Happening Now with the Product?"

Suppose you, the product manager, met up with the CEO of your company in an elevator, and she asked you, "What's going on with your product?" What would you say, and how would you inspire the confidence of the CEO in your role? Well, the simple answer is "money" (that is, you'd express results in financial terms). Financial and other business and market-based measurements give you the best read on product performance. This is the reason that finance is one of the foundational practices for Product Management. Without finance, there is no way to assess how well the product is performing against established plans. Having a good product performance scorecard graphically depicts the product's financial situation. Monitoring the product's financial performance is critical at each phase in a product's market life. Therefore, it is vital that financial reporting systems be tuned to report product-specific financial data.

In many companies, the actual expenses from organizations such as Marketing, Operations, and R&D are not always driven directly to the

FIGURE 19.8

A Standard Financial Scorecard for a Product

Original Business Case	Revised Business Case	Current Year Plan	Y-T-D Plan	Y-T-D Actual	Y-T-D Variance		Month Plan	Month Actual	Month Variance
						Units			
						Average price per unit			
						Total Revenue			
						Cost of Goods Sold			
						Gross Margin			
						Gross Margin %			

individual product's P&L. Instead, these expenses are allocated to each product by the corporate Finance department, according to predetermined formulas. Because these are generally uncontrollable by the team, I am going to leave these out of the formula and focus solely on unit volumes, pricing, total revenue, cost of goods, and gross margin. Gross margin is a broad yet acceptable measure of product profitability, as I discussed in Chapter 6.

A simple financial scorecard should be used not only for standard monthly and year-to-date analysis but also to show the data from the original (or revised) Business Case that justified the product's original investment. This provides the most relevant way to compare the data to indicate whether the financial assumptions of the Business Case are being fulfilled. Figure 19.8 provides a snapshot of a simple spreadsheet you can use to track product financial performance.

If you have more than one product (or even one product sold through multiple channels), you will need to construct a more detailed financial statement, such as the one shown as Figure 19.9. As long as you are able to break down the unit volumes and unit prices by channel, you will be able to create a robust financial profile for the product. Of course, you will need to work with your Finance representative to make sure you can extract this data from your company's accounting systems in order to prepare a report with the right level of granularity. In a nutshell, you must have the right financial data, at the right level of detail, in order to effectively analyze product results against plan and take the correct remedial action.

FIGURE 19.9

A Standard Financial Product Scorecard for Two Products

Original Business Case	Revised Business Case	Current Year Plan	Y-T-D Plan	Y-T-D Actual	Y-T-D Variance		Month Plan	Month Actual	Month Variance
						Units Product A			
						Average price for A			
						Total Revenue for A			
						Units Product B			
						Average price for B			
						Total Revenue for B			
						Total Revenue A + B			
						Cost of Goods for A			
						Cost of Goods for B			
						Gross Margin A			
						Gross Margin % A			
						Gross Margin B			
						Gross Margin % B			
						Gross Margin Total			
						Gross Margin % Total			

The product manager needs to do more than keep track of the financial score for the product. There is other work to do as well. First, the team needs to recheck the trends that shape the industry, the ongoing actions of competitors, and the evolution of customers' needs. Second, there are some *business indicators* that should be tracked for the product. While the product is rapidly moving through the market, you need a way to capture what's going on. In Figure 19.10, there's a table that you can use to keep track of, and portray, industry and competitive activities, as well as set the stage for future opportunistic action planning and/or restrategizing. For example, if you are a product manager for a line of midmarket plumbing fixtures used in home remodeling, and the

FIGURE 19.10

Evaluating Industry and Competitive Activity

OBSERVED INDUSTRY/ COMPETITIVE ACTIVITY	POSSIBLE STRATEGIES	POSSIBLE ACTIONS
• Housing remodeling industry is slowing due to a downturn in the economy. • Competitors are selling another lavatory design to the distributors. The distributors told the sales team that they are concerned about reduced sales to remodeling contractors.	• Investments in a new technology lavatory design might be put off for a short time. • Reevaluate sales forecasts, inventory positions, and other key business indicators. • Minimize expenditures in product design for the next six months by suspending the contract of the design consultant.	• Slowing down expenditures • Waiting to see what happens with the economy • Managing inventory levels to protect company assets • Maintaining gross margins by managing product costs

economy is heading toward recession, what possible short-term strategies might you pursue and to what end?

After examining industry and competitive influences, the team should examine the effectiveness of its segmentation models, based on how well the product sells and to whom. The goal of this analysis is to see how well the product's attributes satisfy the needs of customers in the targeted segments. The main question to ask is, "Are the people who buy our products now the same as we originally thought, or are they different?" Suppose a company that sells customized, made-to-order computers creates a line of high-performance portable gaming devices whose original targets are teenage gamers. As sales progress, the company collects product registrations and finds that the actual buyers are not only teens but business travelers as well. The team would quickly learn that product promotions to teen gamers were either ineffective or that the gamers could not afford the devices. In either event, it would mean that promotional expenditures were probably ineffective, and furthermore, that the market segmentation model should be reevaluated. The associated marketing mix elements would also need to be fine-tuned.

As part of running the product's business, the team should review the outcomes from all available metrics, voice of the customer research projects, observational data, or other feedback that serves as a means to

FIGURE 19.11

Promotional Campaign Tracking

CAMPAIGN DESCRIPTION	CUSTOMER TARGET/ TARGETED SEGMENT	GOAL OF CAMPAIGN	MEDIA/ CHANNEL USED	CALL TO ACTION	BUDGET	EXPECTED NUMBER OF QUALIFIED LEADS	EXPECTED FUTURE BUSINESS	ACTUAL RESULTS
Trade show	CEOs & COOs	Lead generation	Speaking slot plus booth	Come to the booth and enroll in a raffle to win a free trip	$45,000	20	Close 5 deals at $30,000 each ($150,000)	Got 30 leads, closed 6 at $30,000 ($180,000)
E-mail blast	Purchasing Agents	New orders	Email	Visit website, reorder early, and get 10% off	$12,500	150	Close 20 at $5,000 each ($100,000)	Closed 30 at $4,000 each ($120,000)

validate customer needs. This is very important, because needs-based segmentation models require constant surveillance to ensure that all investments are focused on the most strategically viable market areas.

Similarly, customer responses to promotional marketing and sales activities should be evaluated. In order to determine the effectiveness of some of these programs, promotional campaign tracking tools should be used that capture the campaign's goal, budget, call to action, and results. A sample tracking tool is shown in Figure 19.11. Although Marketing may be responsible for promotional campaigns, it cannot work in a vacuum. These programs must be purposefully aligned and tracked with the appropriate metrics, just as other product-related investments are tracked. This way, the team can determine where to best invest its promotional funds in the future so that value can be communicated to customers and positive results accrue to the product's business.

The last two groups of evaluative measurements focus on marketing mix performance measurements and operational performance. The marketing mix represents the combination of investments in the product, its pricing (value creation) schemes, promotional programs (value communication), and paths to the end customer via the most efficient channels of sales and distribution (value delivery). As the product moves through the market, various combinations of marketing mix options are devised, put into place, and tracked. The questions, "What did we do?" and "How well did we do it?" should be constantly asked by the product team, so that new strategic actions can be considered and taken. Figure 19.12 shows a variety of marketing mix and marketing performance indicators. And Figure 19.13 depicts a way for you to evaluate operational performance.

FIGURE 19.12

Evaluating Marketing Mix and Marketing Performance

MARKETING MIX & MARKETING PERFORMANCE	PRIOR YEAR	Y-T-D PLAN	Y-T-D ACTUAL	Y-T-D VARIANCE OR VARIANCE %	REVISED GOAL
Pricing actions and discounts	No actions	Promotional discounts of up to 10% to encourage 5% increase in unit volumes	Promotional discounts averaging 12% encouraged 10% increase in unit volumes	Higher discount percentages improved profits revealing a higher degree of elasticity than thought	Use selective discounting for the first six months of next year
Promotional campaign expenditures		$67,500 in a trade show & postcard campaign	$67,500 in a trade show & postcard campaign	N/A	No additional promotional expenditures
Channel performance data	31% indirect 45% direct 24% web	28% indirect 42% direct3 0% web	29% indirect 35% direct 36% web	3.6% indirect 6.7% direct 20.0% web	28% indirect 28% direct 44% web
Campaign return on investment	21%	23%	23%	N/A	24%
Market share	37%	42%	40%	(4.8%)	41%
Unique web visits (monthly average)	32,000	47,000	36,000	11,000	41,000

YTD = Year to Date

Unlike a financial table that uses similar headings, when dealing with tables similar to Figures 19.12 and 19.13, the content of each cell can confirm both quantitative *and* qualitative data. This helps the team discern the plan, *evaluate* its results, and *analyze* variances against the plan. This kind of quick variance analysis provides an excellent perspective for figuring out what happened, so that adjustments can be made (some call this a "replan") or so that future opportunities may be capitalized on. (By the way, when a variance between two percentages is noted, the variance is taken as the percentage difference between the plan and the actual, not the

FIGURE 19.13

Evaluating Operational Performance

OPERATIONAL MEASUREMENTS	PRIOR YEAR	Y-T-D PLAN	Y-T-D ACTUAL	Y-T-D VARIANCE OR VARIANCE %	REVISED GOAL
Order Processing Time	7 days	6 days	6 days	N/A	5 days
On-Time Shipments	95%	96%	94%	(2.1%)	96%
Repair & Return Data	1 in 500	1 in 550	1 in 500	(50)	1 in 600
Inventory Turnover	6 times	6 times	4.5 times	1.5 times	6 times
Customer Trouble Reports	730/month	620/month	790/month	(120/month)	600/month
Customer Satisfaction	91%	94%	88%	(6.4%)	93%
Plant Utilization	77%	81%	81%	N/A	83%

YTD = Year to Date

absolute percentage. For example, if the plan is 50 percent and the actual is 60 percent, the variance is 10 percentage points. The calculation of the variance in that case would be (60% − 50% = 10%)/(50%) = 20%.

The evaluation of data shown in Figure 19.12 can be highly insightful because it is set up to tell a story about what's happening. In this example, sales channel performance is shifting to the web. If direct sales activity is slowing, perhaps the team might recommend that sales workforce adjustments (reductions) be considered. On the other hand, this shift could mean that salespeople are processing orders on the web, so a more detailed analysis is probably the right thing to do before you make a final decision.

As I discussed in the Data Collection section earlier, when the team is evaluating the current state of the product, it should also focus on the degree to which the operational infrastructure is efficiently supporting the product. Operations usually encompass areas such as procurement, service, information technology, logistics, and others. All companies are organized differently, so you should have a good understanding of your own company's operational infrastructure, as discussed at various times throughout this book.

One of the most important aspects of the business covered by Operations is the efficient sourcing of materials and production of products. Products also need to be moved efficiently from the point of production to distributors, or to end customers. Collectively, these operational elements are referred to as a *supply chain*. There should be a supply chain participant on the product team to make sure that the team's strategy is executed through the most efficient sourcing, handling, logistics, and physical distribution.

As an example, a company that sells customized computers requires an efficient, responsive supply chain to make sure that customer orders can be fulfilled and shipped rapidly. On-time shipments would be one supply chain metric that the team would want to manage. If that computer company ships defective products, then repair and return data would reveal these problems, as would a variety of customer complaints. What's shown in Figure 19.13 could help this hypothetical team to examine a variety of key performance indicators (KPIs), all related to operational dimensions of the product.

Reviewing these financial and nonfinancial indicators should be standard practice for product managers and their teams. By having a broad perspective about how product performance depends on different aspects of the business, the product manager and the team are in a much better position to revise their plans, *consistent with the life cycle state of the product.* With the right data and thoughtful evaluation, the team can readily make both short-term and long-term decisions and think about strategic and tactical options to adjust the business to the conditions of the market.

"What's happening now?" is a question the product manager should always be prepared to answer. After all, the product manager is accountable for the performance of the product. A product performance report card is an excellent vehicle to use and should be on the monthly agenda for every product team. The product performance report card should include, at a minimum:

- Financial results (unit volumes, average prices, gross profit)
- Major sales activity (key wins and losses)
- External KPIs (industry and competitive activity)
- Operational KPIs
- Marketing mix performance (pricing movements/discounting, promotional campaign performance, and channel performance)

FIGURE 19.14

A Product Performance Dashboard

There are also some interesting visualization tools that you might want to use to create product dashboards, which can accompany the product performance report cards. An example is shown in Figure 19.14.

LEADING THE CROSS-FUNCTIONAL PRODUCT TEAM

The cross-functional product team should remain in place across the entire life cycle, acting as a board of directors for the product. The team should manage the product as a business, according to agreed-upon roles and responsibilities and as articulated in Functional Support Plans. The team should review the data regarding the product's market progress, uncover tactical alternatives or new strategic options, and decide on the best course of action. In essence, the team has to decide what's next, based on signals from the market and new data from within the organization, such as newly reprioritized projects, downsizing, or reorganizations.

Product Team Meetings

The team should meet as frequently as needed or a minimum of once a month. As discussed throughout the book, I recommend a formal protocol for these critical product team meetings. The meeting should be guided by a standard yet flexible agenda that enables effective review of results and general business issues related to the product. Furthermore, the team should be governed by rules of attendance, discussions on progress, and decision making. Nevertheless, the team should allow some flexibility in handling nonstandard business and product issues as well. If complex cross-team issues emerge during these review meetings, it is suggested these be taken offline, with resolution presented and discussed early in the subsequent meeting. As with other phases, it is critical to make sure that primary core team members are present for each meeting and maintain strict rules for substitution. Typically, substitutes may not be authorized to act or make decisions for the functions they represent.

Each team meeting should take approximately 90 to 120 minutes, which is achieved more readily by having a strong, agreed-upon agenda, prepared far enough in advance so that participants are ready when the meeting takes place. Some of the standard agenda items may include those in the following sample agenda for a product team meeting. Your team should decide on whatever standard meeting agenda is appropriate for your environment.

For each product team meeting, the product manager (or a person designated by the product manager) should be responsible for recording the team meeting minutes. These minutes should be distributed within 24 hours of the conclusion of the team meeting. A suggested template for these team meeting minutes is shown in Figure 19.16. You can always devise a template that is most appropriate for your team, but please consider the suggestion that you use the format consistently and that you keep a copy of the template *and* each set of minutes in the Product Master Plan repository.

FIGURE 19.15

Agenda for a Cross-Functional Product Team Meeting

1. Agreement on the current agenda with recognition that there may be a need to review nonstandard items.

2. Issue resolution from the prior team meeting (refer to the team meeting minutes)

3. Market review by product and/or marketing managers.

4. Customer reviews, including wins and losses, major sales, and other customer-related issues requiring team attention.

5. Financial review, provided by the Finance representative and the product manager.

6. Functional team member readouts. All team members must provide a 5–15 minute overview of their status of activities and deliverables. Readouts of more than 15 minutes might require special handling or a separate meeting.

7. Project updates and satuts reports from any special projects being carried out by the team.

8. Nonstandard issues that are not part of the regular team meeting.

9. Action plan review, in which each person from the respective business functions reads out what action plans he or she intends to complete before the next meeting.

SUMMARY

If you're like most product managers, you want your product to be exemplary. However, when you really think about it, there's a lot of work to do to make this happen. As I mentioned, this is the first of two chapters devoted to helping you optimize the performance of your product. Earlier in the chapter, I presented you with a model—the CEDAR model—and I discussed the most important initial dimensions of it: *Collect* and *Evaluate* the data.

FIGURE 19.16

Template to Record Cross-Functional Product Team Meeting Minutes

Product/Product Line Name: _____

Executive Sponsor: _____

Date of Meeting: _____

Role/Function/Names of Participants

Product Manager	
Engineering or R&D Manager	
Marketing Manager	
Service Manager	
Supply Chain Manager	
Operations Manager	
Finance Manager	

Product Business Review

Issue/Data/Observations	Source of Issues & Person Who Raised It	Significance, Impact on the Business, and Plan of Action

Cross-Functional Review

Functional Department	Notes, Comments, Issues, etc. from This Readout

Product Financial Review

Category	Budget	Actual	Variance	Explanation

Action Item Register

Action Item	Date Assigned	Function/Person	Risks	Outcomes

To be able to collect and evaluate data, you need to know what data and metrics exist and in which departments or systems you can find them. As you begin to harness and evaluate product performance measures, you'll quickly learn that you'll need both historical and current measures to produce meaningful perspectives; single data observations just won't do. Further, as you evaluate various measurements, you'll soon discover that additional data is required to help you in your evaluations. As the product manager, you are responsible for integrating various data elements and leveraging your cross-functional team to continually evaluate the product's measurements so that you and the team gain the most complete perspective on the product's performance. This is vital so that you can point your product's business in the right direction.

RAISING YOUR PRODUCT MANAGEMENT EXPERIENCE QUOTIENT (PMEQ)

1. If you are unfamiliar with how current products are managed in your company, make it your first priority to find out what procedures are used. You can reach out to other product managers who are responsible for the management of current products. Use the Product Management Life Cycle Model and what was discussed in this chapter to gain important perspectives.

2. Find out how product performance results are reported and how frequently they are reported—and to whom. You may need to speak with people in Finance and Marketing.

3. Ask your manager if there is a portfolio review board or equivalent leadership team. Find out who is on it and how often it meets. Ask the board if it would be receptive to your observing several of its review meetings to learn how it evaluates product lines and product portfolios.

4. Make sure to connect with all functional department leaders to understand their key workflows and the data they produce and act upon.

5. Create a list of all data and associated metrics available for your product based on what you learn from each functional leader. This "data inventory" can be used to create a Data Association Map, as described earlier in this chapter. Follow the categories mentioned in this chapter, including market, financial, operational, and observational data.

6. Produce your own Data Association Map. Bring your cross-functional product team members together to review it and to create a cause-and-effect matrix that allows the team to bring about a common understanding of the interrelationships between the data.

7. Locate a product life cycle chart for your product. Ensure that it represents a plot of revenue, costs, and profit. Create a retrospective analysis that describes why the life cycle curve moved up and down and what the influences were. Consider some of the key metrics that are mentioned in this chapter, and review the other market influences such as PRESTO and the actions of competitors. If you cannot locate the life cycle chart, then plot one on your own and bring your team members into the discussion to validate what happened over the course of the product's life.

8. Find out from your leadership about the types of systems or tools that are used to create product dashboards. If none exists, create one for your own product based on specific data elements from various sources. Leverage the Data Association Map to bring about thoughtful discussions and debates among cross-functional team members so that more insightful analyses can take place.

9. If there is no cross-functional product team designated to act as the "board of directors" for the product as suggested in this chapter, you may wish to arrange your own meeting to discuss the business of your product. The first step in this process is to identify the people from the business functions that you believe are important to this endeavor and share the idea with each person's manager in a one-on-one meeting. If you can secure their agreement to participate or to have a delegate participate, share the agenda with them (use the agenda from this chapter) and see if they agree. You will also want to make them aware of the kinds of data that will be required. Then, schedule your first meeting. Explain how the meeting was planned in advance and that they all agreed to attend and participate. Make sure you are fully prepared with financial and market data. If you really want them to participate, ensure that they have prepared their status report and that you've secured their agreement to do this in advance. You want to make sure you make the meeting a productive "safe harbor" for the team to, in a matter-of-fact way, discuss the business of the product.

POST-LAUNCH STRATEGIC MIX MANAGEMENT

Executive Summary

- To optimize the performance of their products, product managers and their teams must focus on value-oriented solutions.
- Integrated roadmaps provide product teams and others with strategically relevant direction that minimizes confusion and maximizes productivity.
- When customers are properly educated about the benefits of your products and solutions, you'll build greater market credibility—especially when you deliver on the value proposition.

Every day you may make progress. Every step may be fruitful. Yet there will stretch out before you an ever-lengthening, ever-ascending, ever-improving path. You know you will never get to the end of the journey. But this, so far from discouraging, only adds to the joy and glory of the climb.

—WINSTON CHURCHILL

After you've gained the proper perspective on the product's business performance, as depicted in Chapter 19, it's time to drive your product's business forward. However, merely knowing what got you here doesn't guarantee future success. As I've learned, there are many obstacles that can stand in the way of a product's future success. These barriers are a result of limited market insights, ill-conceived strategies, and poor organizational execution. Even if some problems are addressed with temporary fixes (a quick research project, an updated roadmap, etc.), root causes are often ignored.

Through the research I've conducted over the years, I've learned that well-run companies set their goals and craft their product line strategies based on an interrelated, balanced mix of business items. In these firms, senior leaders insist on and enable the following:

1. A continuous stream of data that promotes deep market insights
2. Clarity of purpose based on well-defined strategies
3. A balanced marketing mix model whose levers are synchronized by a product manager, regardless of ownership of the various mix elements
4. Timely product business and financial results that are integrated, evaluated, and acted upon by product managers and their teams

This chapter is devoted to the aspect of the CEDAR Product Business Strategy Cycle that helps you *Decide* on options for your product's business, *Act* swiftly to execute, and continue the cycle with relevant *Revisions*. Some of the options that you can consider for your product's future success include the following:

1. Upgrading or replacing the product
2. Repositioning the product in current markets
3. Reducing costs
4. Improving the customer or user experience
5. Expanding into new market areas
6. Educating customers so they can manage risk and make good decisions
7. Fine-tuning business operations

Whatever option you select, there are six *strategic mix* elements (see Chapter 10 for additional context) that must be integrated and aligned in order to guide the product's business. These include the following:

1. Markets on which to focus
2. Required human and financial resources
3. Product roadmap elements that must be assembled
4. Other marketing mix components that support the product's business goals
5. Future product life cycle performance indicators
6. Operational capacity requirements

As you harness the power of your cross-functional product team, keep in mind that the product's business is guided by the strategic mix model. However, from that model, a more finely focused marketing mix will emerge. To keep all of this in perspective and to clarify what I will discuss in this chapter, refer to the diagram in Figure 20.1.

FIGURE 20.1

The Strategic Mix and the Associated Marketing Mix Model

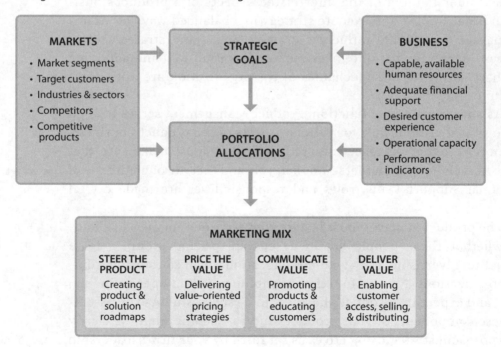

As shown in the lower part of Figure 20.1, the items covered in the marketing mix model will be described next. To summarize, I'll describe how to:

1. Produce an actionable, integrated product and/or solution roadmap
2. Create value-based pricing strategies
3. Orchestrate programs to advertise, promote, and educate so that you can effectively communicate your value to chosen customers
4. Enable customer access through the best pathway or channel to your chosen customers

After I describe how to utilize these marketing mix elements, I will guide your thoughts so that you are better able to:

- Create unforgettable customer or user experiences
- Protect the brand
- Garner customer loyalty
- Operate more efficiently

Lastly, to complete the CEDAR cycle, an action plan must be created and carried out.

As has been discussed throughout this book, you should have a holistic understanding of the interrelated aspects of a product's business in order to plan and execute strategy in a balanced way. For example, market movements influence strategic goals, and strategic goals direct product and portfolio investments. This is all well and good in a flowchart. However, the mechanics of the organization are not always this fluid.

As an organizational function, Product Management serves to align people who are responsible for various aspects of the product's business. Therefore, product managers or product leaders must make sure that people in each function understand their role and that, through the use of Functional Support Plans, roles and responsibilities are made crystal clear.

The product manager must inspire conversations among stakeholders—whether those people are in a separate pricing group, a team devoted to advertising and customer education, or in sales or distribution organizations. No one function or subfunction can operate in "silo mode" and expect the product's business to be successful. As you assemble these components of your product's future, keep in mind the clarity of purpose and strategic objectives as set forth by your firm's leadership team.

STEERING THE PRODUCT USING AN ACTIONABLE, INTEGRATED ROADMAP

If you haven't been called upon to produce a product roadmap, rest assured, you will be. In my research, I've found various types of roadmaps; some outline the functional evolution of a product, while others point out the planned development of product features or attributes. The challenge is that there is much variability in how roadmaps are created, what they contain, and how they are presented. During my corporate life, customers demanded to see our detailed roadmaps so they could make decisions about their own businesses. Industry analysts wanted our detailed roadmaps in order to make comparisons between what we planned to develop and what our competitors planned to develop. Salespeople wanted them to sell futures.

Roadmaps are not, and should not represent, a commitment to any external party (customer, analyst, or otherwise). Otherwise, you will expose your firm to unnecessary risks. Furthermore, in some companies the roadmap is integrated with the Marketing Plan or even a sales plan. Again, this is not a good business practice because it makes the assumption that all facets of the roadmap will be delivered. In many instances, people across the organization see the roadmap as the strategy. The most important thing to understand is that *the roadmap is not the strategy; it is a method to portray, visualize, and integrate the elements that encompass the evolution of a product or a complete solution.*

The roadmap is deeply rooted in the strategy of the firm or the business unit in which you work. I refer to a product roadmap as a *statement of intent* to describe, in broad themes, the future of the product's business. The roadmap is a wonderful tool to:

1. Link market movements and strategic goals to the products, platforms, and technologies required to execute on the strategy
2. Represent the functional and non-functional requirements to the technical community and other concerned stakeholders
3. Align cross-functional team members so they can deploy the resources needed to support the product's business

In short, roadmaps are good planning tools that integrate business and market information with the evolution of product capabilities, technologies, and platforms. When used consistently, they can set the stage for more effective prioritization and can set the cadence for the work to drive the future of the product's business. This perspective is portrayed in Figure 20.2.

FIGURE 20.2

Influences on the Integrated Roadmap

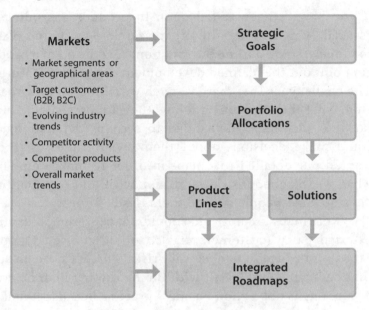

You'll note that I refer to products *and* solutions. You may recall Chapter 1, where I described what a market "solution" might entail and provided a diagram to portray this idea. When you boil it all down, any product should solve some problem for a customer (or customers) within a market segment. Many people get confused because they think that a "solution" or a "system" isn't a product. For clarity, *a solution is a grouping of products and/or services that, when collectively assembled or integrated, offers a compelling value proposition for a customer or group of customers.* The integrated roadmap provides the holistic perspective to portray how many of the elements of the product's business will be assembled to address the needs of customers and the challenges of groups of customers within broad market segments or geographies. To ensure you have the best context, you and your team should be able to answer these questions:

1. How will we move with or define the direction of the industry?

2. What do we need to do to competitively gain market share?

3. What are the elements of the customer or user experience we need to enhance?

4. What are the specific aspects of the product's functionality that should be addressed?

5. Which functionality provides the greatest competitive advantage?

6. How will the functionality be provided for—which features or attributes?

7. Are there different features or attributes required for different customer types?

8. What are the required technologies or platforms required? Are they available?

9. Is there sufficient intellectual property within the firm, or must it be licensed?

10. Does the firm have capable resources in its technologists, engineers, and designers?

11. Is there sufficient development and or production capacity?

12. Do the envisioned product capabilities meet local requirements?

To simplify things, I've created two templates that you can use as a guide to create your own integrated roadmap. First, you'll want to prepare an "annual roadmap input matrix," shown as Figure 20.3, to *justify* each element of the roadmap. This is why the headings in this matrix ask you to identify what it is, why it's important, and the supporting data. When you have this context, it will foster cross-functional communication and portray just the right amount of information on the roadmap. Once this is done, you can populate the integrated roadmap template,

FIGURE 20.3

Annual Roadmap Input Matrix

Roadmap Element	What	Why	Data
Main Market Drivers			
Functionality			
Features/Attributes			
Design			
Platform			
Technology			

FIGURE 20.4

Integrated Roadmap Template

Roadmap Element	Year 1	Year 2	Year 3
Main Market Drivers			
Functionality			
Features/Attributes			
Design			
Platform			
Technology			
Components/ BuildingBlocks			

as shown in Figure 20.4. In this template, you will be able to insert content in each cell. Once done, you can draw lines between each of the elements to demonstrate where each product element is connected, or is dependent on another. For example, if a product's functionality is dependent on a technology platform or building block, you'll need to ensure that people in the technology area are willing and able to support this. As the roadmap evolves, you'll be able to translate those elements into the PRD. Refer to the PRD template in Chapter 13 to make sure you incorporate aspects of the roadmap into the product's definition.

Ultimately, an executive, an analyst, a salesperson, or someone in Development will want to know what's on the roadmap. That should not ever be a problem because you'll have one ready to go when you need one. However, roadmaps don't conform to a one-size-fits-all model. You need to have variations for different audiences. You'll need, at a minimum, an internal version and an external version.

The *internal* version is used to communicate with cross-functional team members, including Sales, Marketing, Service, Development, and Operations. As Functional Support Plans evolve, the roadmap can become a great tool to help negotiate roles and responsibilities. Executives also have an interest in this roadmap because it's used to portray a product's evolution as part of your product line strategic plan.

The *external* version may be used for analyst presentations and customers. Analysts may represent an industry group or equivalent organization. They use roadmap information that they collect from many firms and create comparisons that are often sold to researchers and others. If you expose too much, then you might contribute to product commoditization because all competitors feel they ought to have products with equivalent capabilities. On the other hand, you may be criticized for not having sufficient evidence of your future work. In this case, work with your leadership team to ensure that the company's position can be made clear and that messages are consistent.

Customers often want roadmaps so they can create budgets or other plans. However, very often, the people who want to know are not necessarily the decision makers for future expenditures. In some cases, they're doing their own "shopping" based on a perception of future promises. Unfortunately, if they believe it's on the roadmap and want to buy it, but you didn't make it, you'll not garner favor with those customers, who may go elsewhere. As with all communications to customers, make sure that your leadership has sanctioned what will be communicated.

To conclude this discussion on roadmaps, consider this: roadmaps are vital expressions of strategic intent and the way forward for your product and for your team over an explicit period of time. Further, roadmaps assist you and the team in setting realistic targets that help you compete. When interruptions occur, as they usually do, the team can rally around and contribute to a reprioritization of work or a necessary pivot.

DERIVING VALUE-BASED PRICING

A number of years ago, I was consulting with a Chief Marketing Officer at an industrial company in the United States. We were discussing his product line strategies, and I asked him some questions about customer and product profitability. He had some great, colorful charts that showed stable share and gross margins and slightly eroding profits. When I asked him about what his customers thought of his company and of his products, he said that his firm had great long-term relationships with its customers and that things could not be better. Then I asked about the last time that prices had been increased. He said that it had been about eight years. My eyes widened, and he asked me what was wrong. I indicated that he had great products, offered tremendous value, and provided superb customer service—and that his firm probably left several million dollars on the table. He knew what I was talking about: a price increase! He said that if they raised their prices, they would lose customer trust. I told him that I tended to disagree, and that a carefully considered analysis of sales and other business data might offer evidence to support some targeted adjustments. I also suggested that increased product and company profitability would open the door to new investments to grow the business.

After a few weeks of data analysis, across-the-board increases were put in place. The result was not as he anticipated. Ultimately, his customers made statements such as, "It's about time!" and "I was wondering when this would happen!" He learned that his fear of undermining customer trust was not realistic; instead, he was able to leverage the good will and reputation his firm had earned over the years. The analysis of business and market data provided the clarity needed to support the pricing strategy. In the end, the value offered by his firm and his products was greater than perceived by the entire leadership team.

Pricing strategies are incredibly important across the entire life cycle, because they are so visible to the customer. Pricing strategies change as products and markets mature. Pricing is the one way that customers validate that the product delivers the promised value or benefit. This is where the value proposition is put to the test on a daily basis. Often, product managers, marketers, and salespeople fixate on prices because pricing is the most visible barometer of success. When the sales team says, "We lost that deal because our price was too high," it evokes one set of feelings, and when they say, "We won because our price was so low," you experience another, similar set of feelings. Incorrect pricing when a sale is easily made can leave a team wondering whether money was left on the table.

On the other side of the counter, pricing sets in motion a series of post-purchase analyses for customers. After they purchase a product, customers actually have to own and/or operate it. Some of the truths about *total value of ownership* begin to settle in. Customers begin to ask, "Was it worth the price paid?" Products cost money to own and operate. Electronic gadgets require an endless supply of batteries. A new car may require higher insurance fees, premium fuel, frequent maintenance, and very expensive tires. A new software system may require annual maintenance fees, administrative overhead, training, and customization. All customers, at some point, may question the Business Case they constructed (on paper or in their heads) when they decided to buy the product.

Pricing challenges abound, and the internal deliberations seem interminable. Some of these challenges include the following:

1. Poorly conceived value propositions can result when customer needs are misunderstood.

2. Cost reductions are sometimes engineered to help produce greater profit, regardless of the benefit provided to targeted customers.

3. Products intended to be differentiated don't always command a premium price.

4. Customer demands and budgets are thought to represent their "voice" without regard for the value provided.

Market-oriented pricing strategies must be revisited across the product's life cycle. Market pricing strategies are the antithesis to traditional, inefficient, cost-plus models. *Cost-plus pricing* is invariably dangerous because it disregards the most important variable of all—that of volume or quantity. The impact of cost-plus pricing can be highly positive or highly negative, depending on the base assumptions and the outcome. Suppose you have a product that costs $30,000 to produce 1,000 units, so the cost per unit is $30. Now suppose that you decide to mark up the product by 50 percent, selling it for $45 per unit. Your assumption is that you will sell 1,000 units at $45, generating total revenue of $45,000. You made $15,000 in gross margin! But what would happen if you only sold 700 units and you already set your price at $45? You have to spread the $30,000 in costs among 700 units, which raises the cost per unit to $42.88 per unit. If you are selling them for $45.00 per unit, your gross margin is only $2.12 per unit or $1,484 in gross margin. That's a far cry from the $15,000 in gross margin that you might have made if you sold 1,000 units. The lower your volume, the worse off you are. The higher your volume, the better off you are. The issue is that cost-plus pricing is the result of inside-out thinking and doesn't really consider the conditions of the market.

Another unsatisfying pricing model is created when all pricing is done in *reaction to the competition*—especially when that pricing yields little or no profit. Commoditization often forces this to happen; however, of late, offshore manufacturing, software development, or other factors such as support and production have become the competitive weapons of many global companies. If your product is produced in a high-cost country and sold at a heavy discount to win the business, then your company may be doing some downsizing very soon—unless your product offers a tremendous incremental benefit over the competition. Companies that pursue contract manufacturing and assembly should be able to do a better job of facing lower-cost competitors.

Market-oriented pricing can result in better returns to the business. This means that the product manager and marketing counterparts continue to evaluate industry trends and competitive actions. Of course, the most effective updates to pricing models will only be as good as the product manager's evolving understanding of customers and their ever-changing need states, motivations, and preferences. Fundamental to almost everything in this book is the need for a basic understanding of what motivates customers, the challenges they face, and the needs they exhibit, whether implicit or explicit. This is why it's so important to have up-to-date market segmentation models and associated customer value drivers. With these in place, value propositions are easier to prove and pricing models have the best foundations.

Strategic Context

Consistent with much of what I discuss is the fact that any pricing strategy begins with market insights, business information, and historical transactions that are based on relevant facts and data. In the diagram shown as Figure 20.5, you can see the influences on the strategy of the firm—and how they cascade all the way down to the pricing strategies. Notice how similar this diagram is to Figure 20.2, which was used to describe the impacts on the roadmap!

As the product travels on its path across the life cycle, different strategic pricing options will need to be chosen, depending on the situation. Of course, there are advantages and disadvantages of each.

There will be times when pricing needs to be calculated based on a *one-time, competitive bid*, in which case costs should probably be considered in relation to the price. While easy to calculate, it completely disregards other market indicators. There may also be times when the price can be used to drive away customers that you wish would *migrate to another product*, in which case you might raise prices of the current product until you achieve a specific behavior. If you're introducing a brand new product, you might try *competitive parity* pricing, which could easily align with customer expectations but limit your ability to differentiate later. Other

FIGURE 20.5

Influences on Pricing Strategies

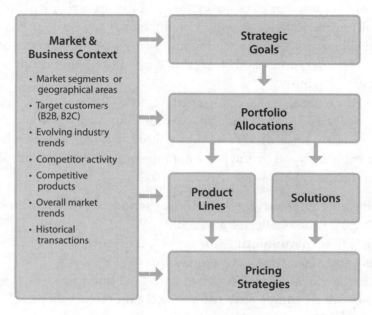

pricing strategies might include those that are adjusted to build or defend market share, and yet other strategies are used for highly differentiated, luxury goods. The point about pricing strategies is that they not be crafted and carried out in a vacuum. They need to be closely tied to the other marketing mix elements and based on a desired business outcome.

Value Orientation

The key to all of this is delivering value to customers in a way that your competitors cannot. While this may sound like a complex undertaking, it's really not. Instead of creating a feature that you think a customer can use, try to figure out more about what the customer is trying to do. If you can help that customer do something more easily or faster, make a better decision, or save money, you could create an algorithmic formula to convince them. For example, if a customer takes an hour to complete a task, but your solution cuts it down to 10 minutes, what's the value of that additional 50 minutes? Can you use this leverage to bolster a higher price?

From another perspective, some people target a market segment that they feel is attractive based on its size, growth potential, or geography.

Instead, think about which customers in a given segment would be most likely to recognize value in what you provide. In this case, if your business-to-business (B2B) firm pursues large businesses and has focused mostly on relationships with procurement and supply chain people, try working with key decision makers or influencers who would recognize the benefits of time efficiencies, fast decisions, and streamlined operations that result in lower costs of doing business.

In each of these areas, there are specific *value drivers* that you can harness in order to create value propositions for your customers. In some cases, it's fairly simple to create the arithmetic for each driver. In other cases, the value is found through the enhancement of the firm's reputation or brand image. These value drivers focus on:

- Improving customer service or technical support response times
- Increasing up time or service availability
- Reducing the turnaround time for repair and return
- Extending the mean time between failures (MTBF)
- Shortening key businesses processes with fewer people
- Expanding the customer base and retaining more customers
- Abridging the time it takes to make a business decision
- Creating a profoundly unique experience for the customer or user
- Decreasing the time to market for new product introductions
- Focusing on sustainable products
- Enhancing the positive feeling a customer gets for using a product
- Reducing risk
- Minimizing losses
- Enhancing safety and security

Consider these value drivers in relation to the "critical success factors" that I discussed in Chapter 19. You will notice that these value drivers fit very nicely within that context. I also recommend that you *use these drivers as contextual areas for your product requirements document* (PRD), as discussed in Chapter 13.

In this discussion on value-based pricing, I do not want to give you an entire treatise on pricing strategy; there are plenty of good resources that offer plenty of good formulas to follow. What I do want to leave you with is the notion that you can, and should, consider the value that you provide to your customers (in a B2B or a business-to-consumer [B2C] firm) or the value that you can help your B2B customers achieve when they operate as a B2B2C or B2B2B company.

I recently spoke to a senior executive in a consumer goods firm that spent so much time trying to figure out the value proposition for its customers (i.e., buyers who represented retail firms) that it forgot to focus on the value for the end customer—the consumer or user. The firm lost significant market share because of this oversight. It bears repeating that each *customer type* in the value delivery chain has a unique value orientation. It's up to you as the product manager to create a value map that taps into each customer type along that delivery chain, so that your product or solution adds a compelling benefit that no other competitor can touch!

CREATING PROGRAMS TO ADVERTISE, PROMOTE, AND EDUCATE CUSTOMERS

You can develop the most innovative product on the market, but if you cannot communicate its value and benefits to the people who are most likely to listen, you're not likely to sell very much of anything. The world of advertising, promotion, and customer education is designed to communicate or explain the value proposition and to reinforce your competitive position to stimulate business.

If one were to take a snapshot of the general state of promotion or advertising at any point in time, the number of methods used (or recommended) would overwhelm anyone! I've watched this for many years. Every method is guaranteed to earn you more visibility, more site visits, and better return on investment (ROI). Unfortunately, there isn't any one technique that works well all the time. Just like you create a balanced portfolio of products to produce a solid return to the business, a portfolio of adequately funded outbound programs is needed to support creative development, program (or campaign) deployment, and performance management. The *promotional mix* is the combination of programs used to achieve one or more of these goals:

1. Establish and maintain visibility with targeted customers
2. Drive business transactions, whether it's through your website, call center, retail store, or other places where people can learn more or purchase products
3. Create or reinforce your brand image or company reputation
4. Create leads for salespeople

Like other areas I've discussed in the previous chapter and in this chapter, business and market indicators drive strategies, which in turn

FIGURE 20.6

Influences on the Promotional Mix

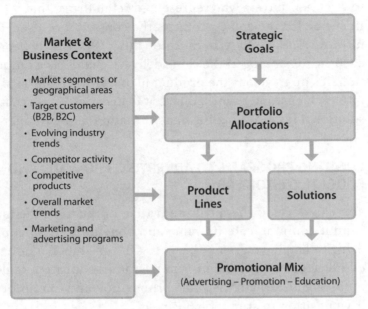

influence allocations to the product and solutions portfolio. When strategic objectives are clear, the resulting plans and programs are more purposeful—and so it is for the promotional mix, as shown in Figure 20.6.

Most advertising, promotional, and customer education programs are articulated and synchronized in the Marketing Plan (refer to Chapter 15). Sometimes, the plans are *not* synchronized, well coordinated, or balanced. This is because Marketing leaders often distribute the work among marketing subfunctions. These groups act like functional mini-silos. For example, the advertising and creative subfunctions often don't integrate their work or messages with those created by the cross-functional product team. This break in communication presents a challenge for product managers who wish to promote their individual products or product lines. Therefore, promotional planning and execution must be threaded back to the marketing mix strategies and the overall strategic mix. This is required to make sure that *integrated* marketing communications activities (the entire promotional mix) are strategically aligned for efficient execution and measurement. As I indicated in the beginning of this section, there are many different types of programs that can be undertaken. Here, I'll focus on the foundations that will survive the test of time. If you can gain a solid understanding of the following areas, you will gain a strong foothold in your drive to influence or catalyze promotional programs for your product. These include:

1. Fundamental advertising, promotion, and customer education programs
2. Understanding what your company is currently promoting
3. Action plans to promote your own product and educate your customers

Fundamental Advertising, Promotion, and Educational Programs

Advertising, promotion, and education programs are, as mentioned, designed and deployed for a specific purpose and an anticipated return to the business. Many people use the expression *integrated marketing* as a way to describe the promotional mix and to ensure that messages to targeted customers are consistent.

As consumers, we notice how advertisers battle for the money in our wallets through television, radio, and print. Because we are so mobile, and because customer data is so ubiquitous, we are also bombarded with recommendations and promotions on our portable devices. The number of places where advertisers find customers is growing more rapidly than is humanly possible to absorb. Because of this challenge, the chance that the message is received, processed, and acted upon is greatly diminished. Adding to this complexity is the fact that distribution channels (direct, online, retail, etc.) are diverse, and often the lines between *promotion* and *channel* become fuzzy.

Product managers should be mindful and up to date on the latest promotional methods. You can do so when you follow the efforts undertaken by advertising agencies, programs used by your own company, and from what you observe as a consumer. However, at the most fundamental level, promotional programs are grouped into two main categories: *traditional* and *digital*. These are shown in Figure 20.7.

I'll leave it to you to expand and maintain your knowledge about these methods as you gain experience. As a point of interest, some of these are used by firms that operate on a B2C model. You see these every day as a consumer. However, many product managers operate in the B2B world, and in this area, there are some efforts that you can undertake to promote your product or product line using both traditional and digital methods. I'd like to provide you with guidance so that you can become more directly involved in the successful promotion of your products.

FIGURE 20.7

Methods Used in Traditional and Digital Promotion

Traditional Promotion	**Digital** Promotion
• Print (publications, brochures, newsletters, etc.) • Outdoor (a billboard) • Indoor (on a shopping cart) • Television • Radio • Direct mail • Press releases • Data sheets or sell sheets • Sales briefs • Events, demonstrations, and trade shows • Seminars or educational workshops • Customer advisory councils • Customer education programs • Banners • Premiums • Thought-leading publications or research • Samples	• Provocative website design • E-mail of special offers • E-mail with links to newsletters • Search engine optimization • Pay-per-click advertising • Social networks • Blogs • Online video • Online forums • Webinars • Online content creation and sharing • Direct advertising (e.g., instant coupon) to mobile customers • Content provided to customers on portable devices

A number of years ago when I was a product director, I received a call from the VP of Global Marketing. He said that he needed me to write the data sheet for one of my product lines, and it had to be submitted in two days. I'm sure that you've received similar calls. I wasn't happy because my staff was very busy, and I didn't think they did a great job writing promotional copy. Product managers are not advertising copywriters, and when they play that role, two things happen: First, they are taken away from other important work. Second, they tend to write about features, not about benefits and value from the customer's perspective.

Regardless of the type of outbound promotion, each must have:

1. A strategically driven goal
2. A targeted market segment or customer type
3. Clarity around the motivations or needs of those customers
4. Evidence (data) to prove that the targeted customer would be available to "listen" (e.g., hear or see) at a time when you want them to listen
5. A method or media that will be used to fulfill the goal

FIGURE 20.8

A Template for a Promotional Program

Goal	Customer Target	Customer Need	Evidence	Method or Media	Message	Metrics & Monitoring
Improve visibility for your company and your product. Bring 100 new customers to your website to download the paper and create 20 qualified leads for the sailes people and bring in 10 new deals.	Money managers who work at midsized and large banks.	Greater visibility into transaction volumes so that decisions can be made more quickly, and for higher levels of profit to be made on each transaction.	Customer complaints about speed and performance.	Present the findings from your research and thought leading white paper at a trade show.	Demonstrated proof that beta customers achieved 50% savings in time and efficiency. Proved the value proposition.	After the conference, monitored web traffic and found that 200 new prospects downloaded the white paper, 32 qualified leads resulted in 12 new deals.

6. A message that is clear enough to inspire the customer to act, based on the value proposition and competitive advantage

7. Realistic metrics to determine if the promotion helps achieve the goal

In Figure 20.7, you can see how you might work with relevant people on your cross-functional team to plan a specific program that produces a desired outcome. As an example, suppose that you work in a firm that provides software for banks and you are to present findings from a white paper at a professional conference. The paper concerns the deployment of a new technology that saved your early-adopter customers time and money. Study Figure 20.8 to discover the logic behind the program.

Understand What Your Company Is Currently Promoting

What does your company say or do? How do you know? I was recently reading an article about integrated marketing in a well-known business periodical. The thrust of the article was that a certain demographic, characterized as young and mobile, did the majority of its shopping in retail stores, not online. This was backed up by data that indicated the poor results from online advertisements made to that audience. The lesson is this: even if you're not directly responsible for the promotion of your product, you will greatly benefit from understanding how things are done in your own company.

A number of years ago, when I was the product manager for a small business product line, I knew that it wasn't the kind of product typically advertised in the mass media. Advertisements were made for the broad category of small office products into which my product was grouped. However, I wanted to know who made the decisions about what was to be promoted and why?

One day, I decided to make an appointment with the head of Marketing for the business unit in which I worked to learn about the marketing programs that were being worked on. My 30-minute appointment extended into about an hour and a half! What I learned was nothing short of extraordinary. The entire Marketing Plan was shared with me, and I understood what was planned and how the campaigns were synchronized with corporate programs. I also found the cross-functional collaboration engendered by the plan to be very interesting. For example, when the firm ran a national campaign, the person who ran the call centers had to staff up for peak loads. Out of further curiosity, I arranged to meet with the woman who ran three very large call centers that, during normal times, employed about 1,200 people but doubled staffing during major campaigns. She indicated that the people in the Operations and IT areas had to ensure that they could handle the volumes, process the orders, and ship the products. It was a great indoctrination to the art of promotion as a dimension of cross-functional strategic execution.

While you might not be directly involved in large-scale programs, it would be a good idea for you to become friendly with people in Marketing who are responsible for these outbound promotional programs. Think about having the marketing representative on your cross-functional team make a presentation to the team about the types of campaigns and programs being planned. To broaden your team's experience, perhaps a blank template, as exemplified in Figure 20.8, could be used to create a retrospective profile of programs to learn about what works and what doesn't—even if it's not at the product level. These perspectives will surely put some ideas in your mind about what is possible. Being clued into marketing programs should also contribute to your notions about what's to appear on your roadmap. For example, if you plan to bring out a major enhancement to a product and there isn't any money allocated to promote the product, your great enhancement may not generate the desired revenue.

Action Plans to Promote Your Own Product and Educate Your Customers

In my broad B2B experience, most of my products were not promoted under the big corporate banner. I had to find a way to creatively promote my products, both internally and externally. I'll use some types of programs extracted from Figure 20.6 to explain how to achieve promotional success.

One of the first steps you should take is to create an inventory of promotional material and programs used to promote your product or educate your customers. If your firm has a Master Plan or central repository, this information could be stored there. You'll have to do some investigating and probing by talking to a lot of different people—some of whom may be in different roles but who might have produced or worked on promotional materials in the past. Your inventory could also be placed in a small "war room" or conference room where you can lay out the physical copies of data sheets, pictures from trade shows, sales training materials, and similar items. Also, review your firm's website to see if it contains the proper information that competitively positions your product and explains your value proposition. If it only lists features, you're not going to inspire customers or prospects to read further. Keep a list of the items you collect and identify when they were created and by whom. See if the artwork is up to date and if the material fits modern standards for creative presentation.

The next step is to work on the materials that you can absolutely create and control. However, you should first consider what well-run companies do before undertaking any promotion or customer education programs: they write a *creative brief*. Interestingly, the creative brief is built on the foundation of work you should already be doing, as elucidated in Module 2. The creative brief answers the following questions:

1. What's generally going on in the market (e.g., the market story)?
2. What is the purpose of the promotional program or campaign?
3. Which customer population is to be targeted and why?
4. What are the key messages that must be conveyed?
5. What response or action do you want to evoke?
6. What creative resources are needed and when (e.g., a designer, photographer, copywriter, editor, agency, etc.)?
7. What budget is required?

You'll notice that promotion isn't always about a brochure or an advertisement. Often, you can promote your product through the subtleties of customer education. For example, there was a clothing chain that once used a slogan in its television advertisement that stated, "An educated consumer is our best customer."

In the pharmaceutical industry, product managers are deeply involved in educating physicians about the benefits of their products. They also are involved in educating patients so that patients can make better choices and ask more probing questions to prescribing physicians. Education is crucial in the pharmaceutical industry because physicians and patients must make important decisions that compare risks and benefits. When you grasp this concept of customer education, you can factor this into the materials you write or the programs you create.

With this in mind, here are some documents and programs that you can personally influence to promote your product and educate your customers.

- Your product's brochure, either in print or online
- The sales training materials you produce
- Sales training that you carry out
- Customer case studies, references, and testimonials
- The product's information on your firm's website
- Demonstrations at trade shows or conferences
- Thought-leading white papers you write
- Thought-leading presentations you deliver
- An online discussion group with your customers
- A customer advisory council
- Customer education programs
- Data from research that proves the customer value proposition (e.g., better decisions, greater efficiencies, reduced risks, and improved profit)

In a nutshell, there are a number of actions that you can take to ensure that your product's benefits stand out to prospects, customers, and salespeople. Now, I'll talk about sales and distribution channels, or the "Place" dimension of the marketing mix.

IMPROVING CUSTOMER ACCESS BY SELECTING THE BEST PATH TO YOUR CHOSEN CUSTOMER

"Place" is usually the designation in the marketing mix strategy that describes *how a product moves from the point of creation to the point of use.* The term *place* can describe a *sales* channel (as in direct to a customer) or a *distribution* channel for the physical transfer of goods or the delivery of an intangible service or solution. Some products travel the path directly from company to customer (e.g., Dell Computers), some travel via the industrial wholesale channel (e.g., Kohler plumbing fixtures), some through consumer retailers (e.g., Best Buy), and some are sold directly over the Internet (e.g., Amazon). Some companies use intermediaries such as sales agents, resellers, professional services companies, systems integrators, and the like. Many firms now use a combination of all channels. Realizing that there isn't a "linear pathway," such firms meet their customers where and whenever it's convenient for the customers. Every firm hopes to hear their customers say, "Your company is easy to do business with!"

Any product must move through some channel to reach its final destination. This implies that the customer is the primary actor and "pulls" the product through a selection process. However, it's interesting to note that the customer doesn't always have the options required to create the best purchasing experience. Therefore, you should consider a customer reaches out (or has access) to your company in the manner that is most appropriate to them at the time that is most suitable. Timeliness and immediacy are central considerations.

Sometimes, a number of intermediaries may contribute to better access. Local networks of retailers help to locate a product through a shared inventory system (e.g., automobile dealers), while distant retailers work with shippers to get a product to your door—sometimes the very same day or even within hours! If you visit any modern airport, you will probably notice that they've become quite a shopping destination! Major retailers and restaurants have set up outposts for people who arrive early and want to do last-minute shopping or enjoy a good meal. *Increasing access means giving customers more choices to get what they need, when they need it.*

Product managers and their teams appreciate the value of these access points or channels because they help products (in many cases) reach more customers with fewer direct selling resources. Some intermediaries help in the value delivery chain because they purchase your products, stock them, process orders, and deliver products to end customers. Some intermediaries are merely selling and billing functions that don't hold any physical inventory. Service businesses, such as investment companies and insurance companies, sell their products directly to customers with their own brokers but usually have a complex array of resellers who are made up of independent agents, broker-dealers, and financial planning specialists. These intermediaries serve the purpose of promotion and distribution!

This is why it is so important to have the data about not only past channel performance (which products sold through which channel) but also about the future needs of customers who are shopping, ordering, and taking delivery of physical products or using intangible services. Product managers and their teams can avail themselves of different types of channels, depending on the strategic approach desired to get products to the customers in chosen market segments. Future state distribution strategies are dependent on the preferred source of supply by customers in those segments.

The Internet has created a whole new marketing mix area I call a "marketing mix hybrid." This marketing mix hybrid is strongly employed by businesses that use the Internet as a distribution channel, a product, and a promotional tool. Consider the website of any bank. When a customer (business or consumer) logs on to the bank's website, the entry page provides many access points for each customer type, whether business, consumer, or investor. Log on as a consumer, and you can manage accounts (open checking accounts and purchase certificates of deposit), pay bills, or apply for a mortgage. When you log on as an investor, though, you may have a range of visible financial products and analysis tools that the consumer banking customer would not see.

The bank website is a showcase for many products: deposit products, credit card products, mortgages, and so on. Each product team has a chance to put its "storefront" on the Internet. Now, add in the fact that someone needs to manage the bank's website as a product. The Internet product manager needs to make sure that the portal works, is easy to navigate, and provides storefront merchandising support for the product teams. Finally, the bank's website also provides space for special promotions, which encourage further interactions by customers of the bank. The product manager and the team should seriously consider this kind of hybridized marketing mix model, because portable, Internet-enabled devices continue to proliferate. The more devices there are, the greater the chance that these devices will afford your company the chance to promote your products, invite immediate calls to action, and encourage inquiries, product searches, and order processing.

As the product continues on its journey, the product manager orchestrates the product's path to the market via these indirect or direct channels and continues to monitor performance of unit volumes and revenue through each channel. The product manager is able to use a variety of promotional mix elements to stimulate volumes in a particular channel, depending on desired future state strategies.

DECIDING ON THE BEST PATH TO TAKE AND CREATING AN ACTION PLAN

In our discussion of the CEDAR product business strategy model introduced in Chapter 19, we have reached the point where we must now consider product business investment options. The four major areas discussed to this point relate specifically to the forward-looking marketing mix model. Refer to Figure 20.9 as a reminder. These four elements taken holistically can produce positive returns for the product's business. The challenge for the product manager is to:

1. Ensure that the mix model is properly integrated, even without complete control of all aspects of that model.
2. Harmonize the efforts of the cross-functional team to bring about that integrated approach to the management of the product's business.
3. Make optimal decisions based on specific decision criteria.
4. Keep management informed through ongoing performance monitoring.

Although this mix model makes a lot of sense, you may still feel that it will be difficult to implement. I can assure you that this model has been successfully deployed in many firms where all stakeholders understand their role and there is solid leadership. However, if executives do not see the evidence of product team leadership, solid decisions, and positive results, they will quickly act to disempower the product manager. This does not have to be the case. If you've earned credibility by following the suggestions throughout this book, you'll have built a collaborative environment in which to produce recommendations based on logic, facts, and evidence—so much so that your leadership will defer to your team's decision! As a reminder, in the CEDAR model, the D stands for Decision.

FIGURE 20.9

Marketing Mix Model

MARKETING MIX			
STEER THE PRODUCT	**PRICE THE VALUE**	**COMMUNICATE VALUE**	**DELIVER VALUE**
Creating product & solution roadmaps	Delivering value oriented pricing strategies	Promoting products & educating customers	Enabling customer access, selling, & distributing

One way to lay out the mix model is to present it as a table that describes each mix element in relation to both the current market position (i.e., leading, neutral, or lagging) as well as your team's desired future market position. When you have the metrics that provide indications of your results (see Chapter 19), you'll be able to expose options or actions that can be taken. Refer to the example in Figure 20.10.

Using this type of table, you can construct a decision matrix (see Chapter 5) that will allow you to evaluate each option based on specific decision criteria. These criteria must answer the following questions:

1. Does it contribute to the strategic objectives set forth by your leaders?
2. Is the customer value proposition fulfilled?
3. Will the mix model contribute to a better competitive or market position?
4. Are the right resources available to plan and carry out the required work?
5. Can the business have the operational capacity?

FIGURE 20.10

Future Marketing Mix Options

Mix Element	Current Market Position *(Lagging, leading, or neutral to the competition)*	Desired Market Position *(Lagging, leading, or neutral to the competition)*	Actions to Take
Product & Solutions	Lagging	Leading	• Enhanced user interface • Faster set-up time • New technology platform
Value-Based Pricing	Neutral	Leading	• Raise prices to reflect new value proposition
Advertising, Promotion, and Customer Education	Lagging	Neutral	• Deploy advertising on mobile platform • Present new case studies at conference • Extend new customer advisory panels • More frequent sales training
Customer Access and Distribution	Leading	Leading	• Continued improvements to e-marketplace • Enroll more retailers in Europe

Some companies have deployed marketing mix modeling tools that are, at their heart, highly sophisticated mathematical algorithms that consider different variables and probabilities. Universities also teach these in their business programs. However, as I mentioned in Chapter 5, no matter how much you tweak your decision formula, you've got to be able to put a stake in the ground, make a decision, and, as I usually say, "run for the wall!"

INTEGRATING OTHER ASPECTS OF THE STRATEGIC MIX FOR THE PRODUCT'S BUSINESS

Creating Unforgettable Customer or User Experiences

A few years ago at a Product Development and Management Association (PDMA) International Conference, the director of engineering planning and the product development office director from Harley Davidson gave a presentation called "100 Years of Great Motorcycles." In that presentation, the director stated that "Harley Davidson customers don't just buy a motorcycle; they purchase an experience and a family membership." The director went on to talk about how the employees of the company were "Stewards of the experience . . . that the responsibility to preserve a rich heritage does not allow for complacency."

If a company is serious about creating unforgettably positive experiences, then these experiences need to be planned, just like every other dimension of the business of the product. Designing for the customer or user experience means that you will be able to *measure* the actual experience against that plan and gain the most meaningful customer insights. *Measuring*, in turn, means that you can audit and analyze what happened, and set new plans in place to improve.

Unfortunately, this aspect of the business of the product is more often than not an afterthought. To remedy this situation, the product manager may act as the advocate for the customer or user in three areas across the life cycle: as concepts evolve, as products are readied for market (e.g., prelaunch early adopter or lead user testing), and while the product is in-market. Alternatively, this role can be played by another member of the cross-functional product team. In some firms, someone in the Customer Service function may have an ancillary role in obtaining customer feedback through formal surveys or informal conversations that are recorded in call notes. However, there should be a customer experience or customer/constituent insight owner, and that person must recognize that customers experience the company and the product (across marketing mix and operational areas) in the following ways:

- The overall experience users have as they interact with the product can be positive, negative, or anything in between.

- The advertising and promotional experience and the responses evoked by those advertisements may yield the following response: "I don't like the music in the television advertisement."

- The ordering experience, including ease of website navigation, the interaction with a customer representative, order confirmation, and so on, may evoke the following: "The website was slow and then froze up. Then I called the call center and was put on hold for 20 minutes, and then the agent couldn't answer my questions. Then, I didn't get an order confirmation via e-mail, as promised."

- The price may evoke a response such as: "How could they charge that much?"

- Distribution channel actions may evoke a response about the delivery experience, as exemplified in the comment: "Every time I order your product, it's late."

- The customer education process might serve to delight customers, as in: "I really learned a lot from the webinar on how to use the product."

- Packaging experiences are based on both the physical design and ease of opening or closing the package. A customer may lament: "Every time I pick up a new device from the store, it takes me 10 minutes to cut through the plastic without cutting my finger."

- Product quality experiences are shaped by ease of operation, ease of interpreting instructions, ease of interacting with or using the product, or other "look and feel" attributes.

- Cognitive experiences are shaped by repeated, persistent interactions with a company, which might involve a reaction to the logo or the brand, as well as the feelings customers experience when using the product.

With all this in mind, what does it take to make sure that your customers have an unforgettably positive customer experience for the future?

Much of the work that goes into planning for the customer experience is based on knowing what customers do, why they do it, and how they do it, as discussed in Chapter 8. This research is based on proven needs and motivations of customers at the time the customers exhibit the needs.

Because need states are transient, it is often challenging to put your finger on the pulse of that customer. No one company can claim to create an outstanding user experience unless its product managers know the particulars of the experience valued by that customer and the benefit derived. This is consistent with what I discussed earlier about the marketing mix and its focus on value creation and delivery. In other words, a consumer needs to know that the product works as advertised. A procurement manager needs to know that the order will be processed and handled correctly. Each and every interaction customers have with your company or with your product forms an indelible image in their mind. Therefore, you should think like a customer to ensure that they can have the most positive experience. Apply this approach in the following situations:

1. Navigating a website
2. Operating a mobile application
3. Buying a product in a retail store
4. Speaking on the phone to a service person
5. Logging onto a website to search for help
6. Dealing with a field technician at your home or office
7. Having a product installed for you
8. Installing a product by yourself
9. Operating a product

Each time you travel with an airline, for example, your experience is shaped by the reservation process, the check-in procedure, the boarding process, your seat, the food, the flight attendant, in-flight technology (e.g., internet service or entertainment system) whether the flight is late, and when your luggage arrives. One negative experience can dismantle all of the good will developed by other positive experiences along the way.

Figure 20.11 is representative of the type of customer experience management tool that you should consider using for your product. The key elements include:

1. An experiential category you wish to measure
2. Realistic, measurable experiential objectives you wish to achieve

FIGURE 20.11

Customer Experience Management Tool

Experiential Category	Date of Experiential Objective(s)	Actual Experiential Outcome	Variance from Objective	Reason & Action Plan
Telephone ordering process	Less than 2 minutes on hold or in a call queue	Averages of 3 minutes from data derived from the telephone switch	One additional minute due to short staffing in call center	Review staffing reports and call arrival and disposition data
	Speaking with a knowledgeable, pleasant agent	Listened to call recordings and found satisfactory performance	Agents are handling calls with the right attitude	Continue agent monitoring and training
	Processing the order in 2 minutes or less	Reviewing timing through IT records and learning that the average order processing time is 1.4 minutes	Positive .6 minute variance	Continue to monitor
	98% compliance by agents in asking a survey question at the end of the call	91% compliance by IT records and call recordings	7% negative variance	Continue agent monitoring and training to improve compliance
On-time delivery of a product	Product delivered according to the delivery promise, e.g., "next business day by 10:00 a.m."	Products delivered on time and as promised, according to point of delivery data from the delivery management system	No variance	Continue monitoring deliveries not completed, e.g., when customer is not available to accept delivery. How does this impact customer experience ratings?

3. The outcome versus the objective, meaning that you can use system data, follow-up surveys, and account management data to validate whether the objective was met

4. The quantitative or qualitative variance or gap versus the objective

5. An explanation of the variance and an action-oriented improvement plan

In many cases, product managers and their teams may feel that the customer or user experience is out of their hands, mainly because other departments are responsible for service and experience delivery. This does not have to be the case. By rationalizing this into the scope of responsibility and accountability of the product team's work, the product manager can lead others toward the reality that *the user experience is both the starting point and the ending point in the customer life cycle.* Customers will stay with you for a long time if you consistently deliver on the experiential promise, but they will go somewhere else when you violate the promise, even if your product is the best product in the world. With this in mind, the product manager and the team should increasingly factor in revised plans for managing the customer experience, so that you can stay on the road to the creation of unforgettable customer experiences.

Protecting the Brand

The product manager and the team are guardians of the brand. Their product may *be* the brand, or it may contribute to the company's brand image as perceived by customers. The word *brand* is open to many different interpretations, using words such as *name, sign, symbol, promise, pledge,* and *perception.*

Whatever words you choose, the brand image of the company or the product is formed in the mind of the customer over repeated, highly positive interactions (e.g., I like Starbucks coffee), through inheritance (e.g., my mother always used Tide laundry detergent), or referral (e.g., many of my friends drive Hondas). Customers who are loyal to the brand continue to buy because the product and the company fulfill an expected promise. Whether customers choose the Intel processor versus the AMD processor in their computers, the Volkswagen versus the Mercedes, or the Samsung versus the Sony television, they do so because of what the brand represents to them: quality, design, an experience, a feel, or a look. Future strategies for the product and related marketing mix elements must stay true to the company's brand strategy through the attributes expected by customers. Nurturing the company's brand is a corporate responsibility. If your product doesn't fulfill that brand's promise, no degree of advertising or pricing changes will lure those precious customers back.

Garnering Customer Loyalty

Many companies assert that customer loyalty is an integral part of their strategy. Sometimes customer loyalty is confused with customer satisfaction.

Satisfied customers generally like doing business with your company, like your products, and like the collective experiences they have both with the company and the product, as described in the earlier section about creating unforgettable experiences. Loyalty refers to a customer's ongoing desire to do business with your company or to continue to use your products. You won't have loyalty if you don't have satisfied customers who continue to have unforgettable experiences with your company *and* with your product. You can always have satisfied customers, but if they don't continue to buy from you or recommend you, then they don't exhibit behaviors of loyal customers.

It is no secret that it costs more to acquire a customer than to keep the customers you have; many books and articles have established this fact. If you have a bad experience in a restaurant, even if the food is good, you likely won't go back. For the product manager and the team, planning to satisfy the customer by creating the desired experience is an important element in the strategy for the product and the supporting marketing plans.

Happy customers may not always come back for more when competition is intense. The more competition there is, the more difficult it is to retain customers' interest. Contractually binding customers to your company for an extended period of time is one way to skirt this issue. For example, the current U.S. wireless communications companies do this by capturing the customer via a low-priced wireless device, accompanied by a two-year service contract. Sometimes customers feel they don't have a discernible choice, such as might be the case with a choice of cable television service versus satellite service. Customers know that the relative experience of being a customer of either company is generally the same, so they default to rational ignorance, becoming reluctant to switch unless given a compelling reason or inducement. When competition is rampant, such as with airline travel or credit cards, then people may switch based on the best deal. Longer term, however, when products are distinctive, based on perceived quality, usability and design, preferred brand, or some other visible attribute, then customers will typically come back for more.

When customers are voluntarily committed to a company or its products, there may be simpler ways to track their purchase levels for extended periods of time. This is easier said than done, but if your company *can* track the frequency with which your product is purchased across the customer life cycle (the time in which they are associated with your company or product), then you can track the lifetime value of those customers. For example, airlines keep track of how many miles you fly in their loyalty programs, and credit card companies keep track of the value of your purchases. With this in mind, it's easier for you to know which customers you really want to keep. And it's also a way to validate why these customers choose your product over other available options.

From a quantitative point of view, some companies may use scoring models to enable you to segment your customers into groups. The data can be gathered using surveys, which might determine the degree to which customers are satisfied, their intent to buy your product again, or whether they would recommend your product to others. These surveys are also useful in validating whether your current customers' needs have shifted and in coming up with creative ways to maintain relationships with those customers.

Operating Efficiently

Every executive team wants to make sure that the firm operates efficiently to support its products and services. I use the term *operational infrastructure* to describe the "machine" of the company whose gears need to move synchronously in order to plan, develop, launch, and manage products. Product managers must always think about this to ensure that the business of the product can be carried out and evolve as the product's business expands. As discussed in various parts of this book, the multitude of operational areas that support the business is rarely the first place that product managers and their teams look for opportunities to improve the financial and market performance of the product. Nevertheless, operational efficiency is worth considering and often yields compounding results.

If you refer back to Chapter 19 and look at Figure 19.13, you'll notice that it represents an analysis of some of the most frequent operational performance areas that directly support products. Each operational area can (and should) be considered for potential operational improvement. This means understanding each and every step involved in the process. Such an examination allows for closer inspection and root cause research, which may help reveal new and better ways to carry out various types of operational activities. For example, if you were to look at order processing time, you would want to understand every step of the process, from the source of the order (e.g., phone, web, salesperson) to shipment completion. You might then want to examine how the order form goes to the Ordering department, how Accounting handles the orders, how inventory is picked, and how other related activities are carried out. Flowcharts, activity timing, and the like become the baseline for examining cost-sensitive effects: the degree to which costs accumulate, the number of people involved, and anything else that might offer an opportunity for streamlining and cost cutting.

SUMMARY

Both Chapters 19 and 20 are devoted to the management of current products. The Product Business Strategy Cycle, as discussed in Chapter 19, is referred to by the acronym CEDAR. As a reminder, it stands for Collect, Evaluate, Define, Act, and Revise.

One of the most influential people in the study of quality was W. Edwards Deming. Deming was noted for his PDCA model, which stands for Plan, Do, Check, and Act. The main idea behind Deming's model is that business processes should be exposed to ongoing measurement and analysis to uncover the reasons behind a product's failure to meet the needs of customers. In essence, the PDCA is a "continuous loop" that allows for this thorough, ongoing evaluation. The Product Management Life Cycle Model and the associated Product Business Strategy Cycle have close ties to Deming's model. The reason is simple. It's a model for continuous improvement of a product's business. The R in the CEDAR cycle is the linchpin to the effective, ongoing management of a product's business.

When products are in the market, the product manager and the team should focus on the optimization of the product's business and market position. This chapter brought into focus the kinds of work that product managers must undertake with their teams to decide what to do and to create an action plan to do it.

The most exciting part of managing a product is when it's competing in the market! Simply stated, when your product makes money, it earns you and your team the credibility and trust of management. That earned empowerment provides you with the wherewithal to set the future state vision and the strategy to achieve that vision.

The strategic mix is offered to you as a way to look at a product's business from a holistic perspective, enabling you to create more value than your competitors do. This is embodied in a cohesive, integrated roadmap. With that roadmap in hand, your value proposition can be brought to life because your customers realize that the value and experience are worth paying for. When the product's value is realized, it's easier to gain buy-in from those in the organization who support the communication of value as well as the delivery of value.

When the gears of a product's business are synchronized, it feels like you're driving a well-tuned automobile that handles flawlessly and easily absorbs bumps in the road.

RAISING YOUR PRODUCT MANAGEMENT EXPERIENCE QUOTIENT (PMEQ)

1. Look for examples of product roadmaps that are being used by, or have been used by, people in your company. Notice any differences in both appearance and content. Based on what has been discussed in this chapter, see if there are any variations between internal and external roadmaps.

2. To extend the exploration of product roadmap usage, talk to people in Product Development, Sales, and Marketing to hear their thoughts on roadmaps that have been prepared by product managers. Try to refine their comments into key points that can be used to improve how roadmaps are created in the Product Management organization.

3. To further enrich your perspective, try to take a retrospective view on a roadmap that was done for your product in the prior year (if applicable). See if you can create linkages between the strategic intent that was documented, what was placed on the roadmap, and what the actual results were. Then, analyze any variances to determine what might be done to improve future roadmaps.

4. Meet with people who are responsible for product pricing. Your goal is to ascertain how prices are derived and how well they're linked to the customer value proposition. As discussed in this chapter, see if you can create the arithmetic behind the model.

5. Arrange to meet with some customers to determine if the prices paid are a reflection of the value proposition. Try to understand their motivation and how they evaluated the purchase of your product versus other alternatives.

6. As suggested in this chapter, evaluate the programs that are used to advertise, promote, or educate customers. Find out if the program's results are in line with the objectives.

7. If your firm has a Creative department or a group of people who work with external agencies, see if you can review a creative brief. Then, if possible, try to write your own creative brief.

8. Talk to people who work in marketing communications or others who play an equivalent role to learn about their perspectives on prior contributions by product managers. Look for opportunities to enhance your contribution based on a balanced view of the marketing mix model.

9. Consider the creation of a customer meeting to understand more about customers' interactions with people in your company in relation to your product or product line. This may help establish a better foundation for future customer education programs.

10. Create a customer advisory board (or council) or an equivalent type of structure. These boards are made up of various customers (users, influencers, etc.). These boards can work collaboratively to help you validate product direction, consider service and support options, and provide valuable feedback. If you have no experience with this, seek out others in your organization who have experience in this invaluable method, and who can provide helpful advice.

11. Review your firm's sales structure. You can meet with sales leaders to find out about what they know—or don't know—about your product. See if you can find out how they feel about the product training they've received, and build a collaborative environment to support them so that they can sell more of your product.

12. Create a channel map or an equivalent diagram to show how your product moves from the point of creation to the point of purchase or usage.

13. Work with your team to carry out a user experience research project to learn as much as you can about how customers use your product or how they interact with it. Enhancing a user experience may involve a change to the product, which might ultimately appear on the roadmap.

21

LIFE CYCLE PRODUCT PORTFOLIO MANAGEMENT

Executive Summary

- The performance of all products within an organization's portfolio is a major variable in the strategic planning process.
- All products represent investments by the firm and must be managed holistically to achieve optimal performance outcomes.
- A product portfolio review board should ultimately provide oversight of the company's product investments.
- Product portfolio management requires that decisions be made to ensure that the firm's resources are optimally deployed.

Savvy investors avidly monitor the performance of their investments. They chart historical activity and review prices every day—sometimes many times during the day. They make every effort to determine where the markets are headed in order to determine how they can make the most money. They continually rebalance their investment portfolios by judiciously selling off some investments, buying others, while holding on to a core of solid, productive, profitable investments.

Managing a portfolio of products is no different from managing an investment portfolio. Products are simply investments made by the company. Good management of your product portfolio *requires* close oversight, constant review of historical and current performance, and the courage to rebalance and rationalize the portfolio when necessary while aligning your actions with the overall strategy of the firm. Whether you're managing a small product line or commanding several product categories that go across the firm, you must decide how to allocate limited funds to many possible product investments. In this chapter, I'd like to show you how to do this kind of simple, strategic portfolio management, using a straightforward method called *life cycle product portfolio management*.

There are some great resources available, including the Boston Consulting Group's BCG Growth Share Matrix and the GE/McKinsey Model. These are good corporate portfolio and strategic planning tools, and they can be adapted to product portfolio management—especially when analyzing existing products. What you really need, though, is a practical way to examine every product, wherever it sits in its life cycle, to decide where to invest and where to *stop* investing. By showing you some real-world ideas for implementing this method in your organization, I hope to help you simplify portfolio evaluation so that you can invest your product resources wisely and productively.

DISPELLING SOME MYTHS ABOUT PRODUCT PORTFOLIO MANAGEMENT

It will be easier to grasp the life cycle method if you're not harboring any "modern misconceptions" about portfolio management. Over the past several years, much has been written about product portfolio management, mainly in academic and consulting circles. A lot of this literature advocates a strategy that, frankly, just doesn't work. Current thinking seems to suggest that portfolio management means constantly adding new products, rather than slowly evolving the mix of products across the life cycle. Popular methods would have you focus on "product pipelines," encouraging a very high volume of products being planned, developed, and readied for launch—all of which absorb working capital.

This emphasis on *new product development project portfolio management* can lure you into a false sense of security, because it feels like you're expanding a continuous stream of new, innovative products. However, if you create a huge flow of new products, and the product catalog contin-ues to swell, you will eventually overload the capacity and comprehension of your sales force, your market, and even your own infrastructure. Stock-keeping units (SKUs) start to proliferate, the number of products skyrock-ets into the thousands, and your inventory becomes an unfocused jumble of idle working capital. Like the day trader who takes on too many stocks, you end up with all your capital invested in a jungle of overlapping, unre-markable products that you really don't understand and can't evaluate.

Let me offer a couple of relevant examples. Retail bank product portfolios are filled with hundreds of unsold (or undersold) products. There isn't enough physical space in the branches to make customers aware of all these products, nor can branch personnel garner enough mindshare to sell them effectively.

I remember one meeting with executives in a multibillion dollar company who actually acknowledged this problem yet didn't have the fortitude to attack it. Solving the problem would just take too many people, too much time, and too much money. In truth, there wasn't enough incentive to change (enough pain), because profits were good, but overly ambitious product development had created hundreds of product variants resulting in thousands of idle SKUs. Can you imagine how that weak working capital position would affect the company's abil-ity to seek a merger or guide itself through a market downturn?

Likewise, computer hardware companies often produce far too many models, submodels, and revision numbers. One recent visit to a major computer firm's website revealed more than 13,000 unique part numbers in a single product line, many of them differing in impercepti-ble ways. Customers calling the support hotline typically spend an inor-dinate amount of time just trying to specify exactly which model they own. This "portfolio overflow" hurts profits in at least two very visible ways. First, the firm's customers reach the point of *rational ignorance* in choosing models, so they default to the cheapest products. This means the purchase decision defaults to price, which means a commodity sale. Second, these same customers spend an exorbitant amount of telephone support time discovering that the feature they really need requires a dif-ferent model that costs more money. This means that customers view the firm as less than ethical, when in fact they just have too many products. In short, huge investments in constant portfolio expansion have caused customers to see this firm as a shady commodities broker—a reputation neither deserved nor intended.

Incidentally, the proliferation of product portfolio planning and management software only encourages this "stuff the portfolio" thinking. Portfolio management software promises comprehensive insight and wonderful visualization tools for new product development and project portfolio management. Granted, there's a real need to manage the "input side" of the portfolio, but it's problematic that these tools *only* focus on inputs. Companies are easy prey for this one-sided thinking because they are always desperately searching for the best practices to grow the product pipeline.

Improving pipeline performance isn't a bad objective, it's just incomplete. I contend that a back-to-basics business model gives much better results. Figure out how well your current products are doing, and you can more easily achieve your desired strategic and financial goals. A little focused, concentrated, creative thinking will help you see what really needs to be done, especially if your thoughts are grounded in a clear understanding of the current situation.

So as I go forward, keep in mind that you need to focus on portfolio *optimization*: inputs *and* outputs, investments *and* divestitures, new products *and* discontinuations. I'm going to start by giving you a long, somewhat complex definition—but don't worry, I'm also going to break it down. When I'm done, you should be able to use the long definition almost like a checklist for good portfolio management.

WHAT IS LIFE CYCLE PRODUCT PORTFOLIO MANAGEMENT?

Life cycle product portfolio management is an ongoing, multidimensional, multiphase, decision-making methodology that allows a business to achieve strategic, market, financial, and operational balance across each and every product in an organization, across all life cycle phases. Embedded in that definition are the most important messages about life cycle product portfolio management:

1. *Ongoing.* Product portfolios should not be analyzed just once a year, or just when things break. They must be analyzed frequently enough to fine-tune the mix of investments at the speed of the market.

2. *Multidimensional.* Solid business management practices always consider many strategic market factors, as well as a variety of internal factors (e.g., core competencies or technologies) at the product line, group, division, and corporate levels.

3. *Multiphased.* A comprehensive view of the portfolio considers all products across the entire life cycle. This includes opportunities being analyzed (i.e., new product projects being planned), products being developed, products being launched, and products that are being sold in the market.

4. *Decision-making methodology.* Best-in-class Product Management practices ensure that you make the best possible strategic and financial decisions, even when allocating investments across the entire portfolio of products.

5. *Achieving balance.* A diverse product portfolio balances investments by considering how much is being invested in every product, across its life cycle, considering the risks associated with each of those investments.

In other words, decisions about products should be made within the context of the entire budget for all products within the portfolio. When it comes to your own money, you can't just look at one security in your portfolio and ignore the others, or your net portfolio performance could take a huge loss. Similarly, you can't just ignore monies allocated to the other products in your product line, your division, or your company. Otherwise, you'll end up with a great product from a bankrupt company. You have to have a sense of what kind of Product Management activities are going on at every level in the organizational chart: in your group, in your division, and in the company as a whole. You have to simultaneously take care of the products for which you are directly responsible while keeping an eye on all of the other product lines and portfolio groupings in your organization. The company needs to ensure that the overall corporate portfolio—and each product in that "big" portfolio—are strategically significant for the firm, competitively positioned, and capable of providing the optimal return.

A PORTFOLIO REFERENCE MODEL

In the world of finance, an investment portfolio is composed of the number and type of securities held in an account. Most people know the three rules of investing money: "diversify, diversify, diversify." Say what you will, a diversified mix of investments is critical to the achievement of portfolio balance, within the context of the investor's goals and individual tolerance for risk. If you were an investor, and you had a portfolio of financial instruments (stocks, bonds, mutual funds, etc.), you would probably want to examine that investment portfolio on a fairly frequent basis. Human nature even has us looking more often when times are good and the portfolio is growing. Conversely, we tend to "cover our eyes" and not look as often when the markets are not doing well. Most financial planners suggest that investors take a look at their portfolios once or twice a year and see how well the portfolio is performing against the goals they established. At that time, you would rebalance the portfolio by selling underperforming investments, possibly taking some profits, and reinvesting in other, more promising areas.

If the world of personal investing seems so simple, then why wouldn't we do this with our product portfolios? It's only a *short* leap of faith to suggest that products represent investments by a company, and in return, the company should expect a reasonable return on those investments. Furthermore, the product portfolio manager has a fiduciary responsibility to the organization to protect the investment against unwarranted risks and to pursue prudent incremental investments consistent with the organization's overall strategy.

THE IDEAL WORK STRUCTURE FOR PRODUCT PORTFOLIO MANAGEMENT

In many companies, the area of product portfolio management is seen as an isolated set of business activities that are done "somewhere else." This should never be the case. Product portfolio management must be woven into the complex fabric of the organization's other business activities in order for its true value to be realized. The linkage between product portfolio management and the strategic planning process cannot be emphasized enough. Important threads connect mission and vision to the manner in which specific product work is structured and carried out. This linkage is critical, because if the portfolio strategies are not properly cascaded down and communicated, then the product managers will misinterpret or fail to act on those portfolio directions. This kind of linkage is what strategic alignment is all about.

Beyond this, however, the organization should be structured such that cross-functional analysis and decision making can take place, because possible decisions and future plans must take into consideration the work required by other business functions. Without a cogent, collaborative, cross-functional approach, key decisions affecting different business functions and product groups will not be carried out efficiently—and may even fail. Logical, cascading workflows will help *any* company carry out *any* kind of product portfolio management in a more collaborative, cross-functional group. On the other hand, without an understandable corporate or divisional strategic context or appropriate organizational structure, product portfolio decisions simply can't be made. The glue that holds this cascade together is the culture of the organization and the people who carry out the work. As my extensive benchmarking shows, *many companies do not adequately consider the connection between top-level strategy and lower-level execution.* In corporate benchmarks associated with product portfolio management, the greatest implementation problems I've uncovered have to do with communication, collaboration, and establishing a common purpose for product portfolio management.

The Cross-Functional Product Review Board

Once all strategic, structural, and cultural issues are in sync, then the most important work structure can be implemented: the cross-functional product portfolio review board. This board is an executive-level team established as a forum for ongoing, periodic reviews of product line portfolios within a division or business unit. The product portfolio review board is the overarching decision-making governing body, guiding and prioritizing product investments for existing products, products in development, and product projects in various planning phases. It is important that this group has overriding approval or veto authority on all product investments. Figure 21.1 shows the makeup of a typical cross-functional product portfolio review board. Notice the similarities to the cross-functional product team structure shown in Chapter 4 (Figure 4.2). The main difference between them is the level of seniority; that is, the product portfolio review board is staffed by senior business leaders.

This senior leadership group is accountable to collectively make cross-product and cross-functional decisions, especially in the allocation of funding for products and product projects. Ideally, it should oversee cross-functional product teams that are working on the product lines within the review board's span of control. For the product portfolio review board to operate most effectively, it should have frequent, consistent interaction between its members and the members of the cross-functional product teams it oversees. (See also Figure 24.1 in Chapter 24, "Organizing for Product Management," showing how this leadership team can also provide oversight in chartering cross-functional product line teams.)

FIGURE 21.1

The Cross-Functional Product Portfolio Review Board

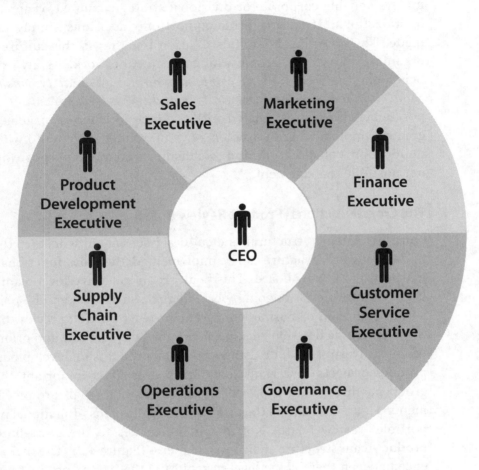

A LIFE CYCLE PRODUCT PORTFOLIO MODEL

The Product Management Life Cycle Model (PMLCM), shown in Figure 21.2, can be used as a reference model for not only individual products, as described throughout this book, but also the entire product portfolio.

The PMLCM sets the stage for dissecting the portfolio into its requisite elements so that each piece can be assessed. The areas of work serve as a good way to take a first cut at dividing up the portfolio into chunks, which I call "meta-buckets." Figure 21.3 shows how the main areas of work, or meta-buckets, are divided up.

FIGURE 21.2

The Product Management Life Cycle Model

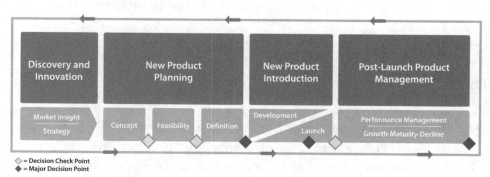

FIGURE 21.3

Product Portfolio Work Area Buckets

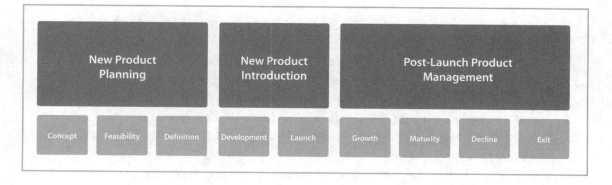

Compared with the initial PMLCM, the first difference you will notice is that I've removed the Discovery and Innovation work area. For our discussion on product portfolio, we want to focus on areas where money is being spent. Next, notice the size and configuration of the areas of work or meta-buckets. In this model, Post-Launch Product Management is represented as the largest work area. New Product Planning is represented as smaller than Post-Launch Product Management but slightly larger than New Product Introduction. New Product Introduction is represented as the smallest because there may be fewer products (in various phases of development or introduction) involved in this work area.

Another difference in this model variant is that it shows smaller boxes, seemingly arranged in a linear manner. These I call "product buckets." This lets me create a simple visual into which we can classify *all* of the products, no matter where they are in the phases of planning, introduction, or in-market. This gives us three meta-buckets and nine total product buckets.

Although the PMLCM has appeared frequently throughout this book, I want to distinguish the meta-buckets and product buckets so that they can be used as intended for portfolio management. The meta-buckets include the following:

- New Product Planning serves to distill many ideas for new products or enhancements to a small number of "product projects" that have the best chance of achieving market success. There is a constant stream of activity as new ideas continually flow through the system, each supposedly better than the next, vying for scarce financial and human resources. *Product projects in this bucket absorb resources; they do not contribute any money to the company.*

- New Product Introduction covers the development and launch of new products or enhancements. For portfolio management purposes, I like to think about this as "work in progress." This means that the company has decided to invest financial and human resources in developing those enhancements or new products and is readying them for market. *Products in development or being launched also absorb resources and do not contribute any money to the company.*

- Post-Launch Product Management refers to the products that are in the market in various phases, characterized by market position, revenue, and profit contribution (or lack thereof) to the business. Current products usually *contribute positive cash flow to the business* to finance operations and pay salaries. They also provide money for reinvestment so that the business can grow.

With these descriptions in mind, turn your attention to the visual provided in Figure 21.4. It shows the major product portfolio work area buckets and overlays a cash flow curve. The image captures two important statements asserted earlier: work carried out in New Product Planning and New Product Introduction do not contribute cash to the company, and the investment doesn't typically achieve a break-even point until some time after the product is introduced, even after the cash flow turns positive. With this viewpoint, you can begin to see why it's so

FIGURE 21.4

Portfolio Work Area Buckets with Cash Flow Overlay

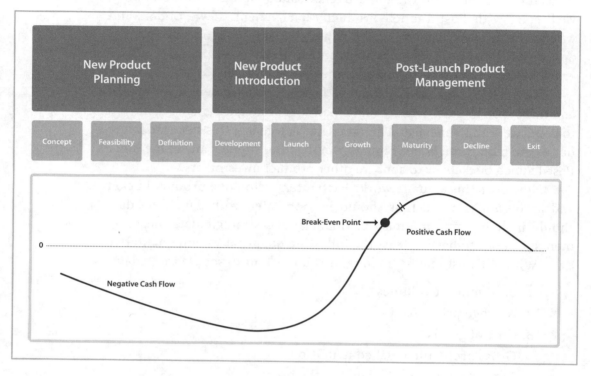

important to look across the entire life cycle when thinking about product portfolio optimization and balance.

METHODOLOGY

Most corporate financial analysts view the corporate portfolio in terms of divisions, business units, or even wholly owned operating subsidiaries. They manipulate these entities like chess pieces on a chessboard, based on the historical and current performance of those businesses. Although we are not looking at business entities, we can think about products like pieces on a chess board and consider past performance and current performance in the same manner we might create a strategic baseline. In fact, this thinking is exactly the essence of life cycle product portfolio management—the *strategic management of groupings of products.* Just like any strategy, we need to know where we are, where we're going, and what options we can reliably choose to get there.

CONSIDERING EXISTING PRODUCTS

Instead of starting with the meta-bucket called New Product Planning, we'll start with Post-Launch Product Management. If we understand where the money is coming from and synchronize our investment opportunities toward value creation and strategic positioning, it will be easier to figure out how to invest money in other areas.

Figure 21.5 takes the Post-Launch Product Management meta-bucket and turns it on its side. This reveals a matrix or strategic framework for you to populate with financial and market data. The goal of this step is to figure out where money *might* be coming from to either support any of the other Post-Launch buckets or to apply to other product investments.

How does this actually work? Each intersection of a product bucket and a column is a cell that should be populated with data. The data should include a minimum set of financial and strategic data measurements. I prefer to have at least the following quantitative and qualitative data. While this list may seem long, it is important to secure these data:

1. Product unit volumes
2. Average prices paid
3. Cost of goods
4. Gross profit/financial contribution
5. Total expenses as allocated to the product

FIGURE 21.5

Post-Launch Product Management: Existing Products in All Phases

	Where are we NOW?	Where are we GOING?	What could we DO NEXT?
Growth			
Maturity			
Decline			
Exit			

6. Earnings before interest, taxes, depreciation, and amortization (EBITDA)

7. Depreciation and amortization

8. Net profit

9. Market share

10. Inventory levels

11. Inventory turns

12. Repair and return statistics

13. Strategic value to the firm

14. Customer satisfaction

15. Competitive positioning

16. Industry situation

Based on the physical size of the model in the book, this won't all fit in that tiny cell. But a value for the cell can be determined through collection and compilation of the data. Without this present data, it will be impossible for you to figure out how to allocate future investments across any of the products within this meta-bucket, whether for enhancements or ongoing product and marketing management.

Without getting caught up in an exhaustive amount of detail, I'll place an imaginary magnifying glass over the cell corresponding to the column "Where are we now?" and the row entitled "Growth." This shows us that we are examining the performance of two products that are thought to be in the Growth phase. This is depicted in Figure 21.6 as a callout to show you the contents of the cell. In the callout, I've inserted spreadsheets for Product A, sold in segment X, and Product B, sold in segment Y. Each product's individual financials are included, along with some general operational metrics.

Given this information, the team is equipped to carry out some analysis. With only two years of data, you may not get the complete picture, but in the example above (Figure 21.6), there are two different products, with different profiles, being sold in two different market segments. Product A grew at 9 percent, while product B grew at 5 percent. Product A's gross profit is up, its inventory turns are improving, customer satisfaction has improved, and market share has improved. Product B's gross profit is down, inventory turns have worsened, customer satisfaction is down, and market share is down.

FIGURE 21.6

Past Performance for Two Growth Phase Products

	Where are we NOW?	Where are we GOING?	What could we DO NEXT?
Growth			
Maturity			
Decline			
Exit			

Product A Segment X	Prior Year	Current Year
Units Sold	32,100	34,989
Average Price	$24.30	$26.50
Total Revenue	$780,030	$927,209
Cost of Goods	$214,508	$242,001
Gross Profit	$565,522	$685,207
Gross Profit %	72.5%	73.9%
Inventory Turns	4.5	5.1
Customer Satisfaction	75.6%	81.4%
Market Share	15.6%	16.9%

+

Product B Segment Y	Prior Year	Current Year
Units Sold	61,320	64,386
Average Price	$18.30	$19.12
Total Revenue	$1,122,156	$1,231,060
Cost of Goods	$353,479	$393,939
Gross Profit	$768,677	$837,121
Gross Profit %	68.5%	68.0%
Inventory Turns	5.5	4.8
Customer Satisfaction	55.8%	48.3%
Market Share	12.9%	11.8%

=

Total Products A + B	Prior Year	Current Year
Total Revenue	$1,902,186	$2,158,269
Cost of Goods	$567,987	$635,941
Gross Profit	$1,334,199	$1,522,328
Gross Profit %	70.1%	70.5%

In this case, investment decisions in the next analytical box called "Where are we going" will have some interesting options. The team may wish to question whether product B is actually beginning to mature and whether the level of investment may need to be cut back. On the other hand, maybe it's just in need of a competitive adjustment. These are the issues that the product line team needs to address with the product portfolio review board. However, the board will require something concrete from the product line team: a contextual analysis for future options. This analysis would need to be based on the most important business practices discussed in this book, namely, industry and competitive analysis, market segmentation, finance, forecasting, and strategic planning. Do you see how it all starts to tie together? The product portfolio review board will review all of the products and their performance profiles, whether they are in Growth, Maturity, Decline, or the Exit phase. To achieve this, they will depend upon a solid set of data and analytics provided by each product line team.

The meta-bucket called Post-Launch Product Management—and all of the products in that bucket—provide a context to the review board for all income and outflows supporting those existing products. With these product line performance outcomes, a collective view of the business of all the products in the market helps the review board see where money is being spent, how well it's being spent, and what the returns are for current products. It also alerts them to problems that may necessitate revival strategies or the withdrawal of the product from the market. All current, in-market product strategies provide the proper backdrop and perspective for reviewing the rest of the portfolio.

PRODUCT PROJECTS IN NEW PRODUCT INTRODUCTION

The next stop on our product portfolio journey is the list of products being developed and readied for launch. Products in the Development phase and the Launch phase are typically new product projects or product enhancement projects. These projects should have been approved by Business Cases and other business and marketing documentation. Because these are work-in-progress investments, the portfolio review board is going to need a readout on how well financial and human resources are being utilized, whether projects are slated for on-time completion, and if there are any problems.

Figure 21.7 shows the two product buckets called Development and Launch with the associated status of three example projects. Two projects are development related, with one in launch. It shows that $1,095,000 has been authorized for the three projects, and as of now, $780,000 has been spent. Project 1 is a month late and Project 3 is two months late. If the portfolio review board were to consider the resource availability for other projects, they would, in fact, find that current projects 1 and 3 are understaffed and late. If some competing resources were needed for other projects, the portfolio team would not be able to authorize funding for these late projects.

PRODUCTS BEING PLANNED

Finally, the product portfolio review board must examine the product projects across the three phases within the meta-bucket called New Product Planning. Figure 21.8 provides a profile of five fictitious projects being proposed, showing how they have either progressed through the

FIGURE 21.7

Product Projects in Progress

	Where are we NOW?	Where are we GOING?	What could we DO NEXT?
Development			
Launch			

		Authorized Amount	Actual	Variance	Target Date	Revised Date	Risk Factors	Mitigation Plans & Recommendations
PROJECT 1:	Product C Enhancement							
Headcount		12	11	1	12 - Aug	9 - Sept	Staff shortage	Hire contractor
Funding ($000)		$375	$280	$95			None	
PROJECT 2:	Product D Upgrade							
Headcount		9	9	0	1 - Oct	1 - Oct	None	
Funding ($000)		$500	$400	$100			May need new sewer	None
PROJECT 3:	Product Y Launch							
Headcount		4	2	2	15 - Sept	12 - Nov	Need marketing support	May need to hire consultants
Funding ($000)		$220	$100	$120				Consultant fee is $90k

FIGURE 21.8

Product Project Proposals in New Product Planning

	CONCEPT				FEASIBILITY				DEFINITION			
	Presented	Cost	People	Go?	Presented	Cost	People	Go?	Presented	Cost	People	Go?
1	June 3	$500k	4	No								
2	June 10	$600k	6	Yes	July 12	$800k	7	Yes	TBD			
3	June 17	$275k	3	No								
4	June 24	$870k	8	Yes	July 17	$750k	6	Yes	Aug 29	$990k	10	No
5	June 24	$480k	5	Yes	July 17	$480k	5	Yes	Aug 22	$480k	5	Yes

phases or have been rejected. Of the five, only project number 5 was approved to move into the Development phase.

CREATE YOUR OWN PRODUCT PORTFOLIO MODEL

Mentioned briefly early in the chapter, many of the other "matrix" methods for corporate portfolio management are worth considering as you navigate the complex waters of life cycle product portfolio management. There are actually several matrix models you can learn about, including:

1. The BCG Growth Share model
2. The GE/McKinsey model
3. The Shell/DPM model
4. The Product Market Evolution Portfolio model
5. The ADL Life Cycle model
6. The Risk-Return model

No one model is perfect, but you can consider using elements of each of them to derive your own integrated matrix model that would be the most useful for your organization or product line. Of course, I prefer the areas of work within the Product Management Life Cycle Model as the primary buckets.

Whatever you choose to do, think about which matrix you like and the number of cells within your own grid (e.g., 2×2, 3×3, 5×3) that you wish to have, based on axis definition and cell content. Be careful how many cells you have because you'll have to name them and populate them with the data you ultimately select. For example, you may have your x axis defined as the product's competitive position and the y axis portray market segments or target customer types.

The major challenge is to identify the decision criteria you wish to use. This is really the most difficult part. Some of the criteria used by many well-run firms include:

-   Strategic alignment or fit
-   Product/solution attractiveness to current target market segments and customers
-   Value to the line, the division, or the company
-   Importance to the brand

- The product's time in market (e.g., some companies want to have some percentage of revenue coming from products that are less than three years old)
- Time to market (for new products)
- The product's growth potential in selected markets
- The degree to which a product complements others in the portfolio
- Whether a product cannibalizes sales of other products
- Whether the right core competencies are available
- Whether the product leverages existing technologies or platforms
- Amount of R&D funding used
- The degree to which existing technologies or platforms are used
- The market areas where the products are sold
- The degree to which a product meets current customer commitments
- The degree to which a product positions the firm to attack competitors' vulnerabilities
- How well a product defends against a competitor's forays or protects market share

PORTFOLIO DECISION MAKING

Now that you have had a high-level glimpse of the type of product and project analyses and status information that needs to be brought in front of the product portfolio review board, what's next? Portfolio decisions are made based on the careful analysis of the current situation and on what needs to be done to help the organization achieve its strategic objectives. Decision options can be categorized by posing questions and considering outcomes:

- Should products in development be canceled?
- Should a mature product be revived?
- Should we focus on investments to increase market share?
- Should we invest in a more diverse set of products so that we minimize our exposure to risk in a given product category?
- Should we invest in improving the product's name recognition in a limited geography?
- Should we invest in cost cutting for a product line?

- Should we invest in other marketing mix elements, new distribution channels, or more advertising and promotion?
- Should some products be discontinued?

When people are evaluating their financial investments, they ask three questions: Should we buy? Should we sell? Or should we hold? These are the decisions that the portfolio review board must consider.

The board is a decision-making body, so what guides their decisions? They make decisions by evaluating each existing product, each product in progress, and each product project proposal from three *broad* perspectives: economic value, strategic impact, and available resources.

As I discussed in Chapter 5, on decision making, and as reviewed in the chapters where decisions have to be made at the end of phases, decision "screens" should be used. The decision screen should not have to be the definitive decision-making tool. Some criteria are more important than others, and each should be weighted accordingly in a standard decision matrix. I recommend its use as a reference model so that a significant number of evaluative criteria can be considered, whether quantitative, qualitative, subjective, or objective.

Challenges emerge when multiple products or new product projects compete for the same resources: people and money. In some of these cases, a risk "score" must be added to the calculation. Furthermore, it is the responsibility of the product portfolio review board to not make decisions in a vacuum, but to carry out discussions with key stakeholders. Often, a product's profile can be enhanced by those team members who are more committed to the success of one product over another. These qualitative angles cannot be ignored.

Other helpful evaluative methods that serve as a good balance to weighted decision matrices may include:

- Financial measurements, which might include the anticipated return on investment (ROI) for the product, or the current ROI. Products can be ranked by the financial resources used and returns provided to the firm.
- Basic checklists, such as whether a product meets certain criteria. For example, "Is the product uniquely positioned in the market?" A yes or no answer is needed. The board will then tend to respond positively to the number of yes responses.

■ Decision trees can also be used, as described in Chapter 5, to determine the other possible outcomes that might emerge—or other decisions that might have to be made if one path is chosen over another.

In order to make progress, product portfolio decisions must be made. If the appropriate go/no-go decisions are not made, then products will proliferate and the portfolio will remain out of balance, exposing the organization to unwelcome competitive attacks.

AVAILABILITY OF DATA IS CRITICAL

For the product portfolio review board's product line reviews to be viable and effective, there must be ready access to detailed project and product data. The most efficient way to get this data is through standard corporate financial and other "back office" systems. Complementary data sources might also include sales pipeline data and quotas. These will help the review board visualize the kind of business that may be coming into the company. This view may, in turn, help the board weight some of the decision criteria that will be scored to determine the best possible avenues for product investments.

Ultimately, the product review board is there to take action. However, even when equipped with the right tools and data, the board often fails to make the most appropriate decisions. Some boards allocate money to projects that don't perform but then don't terminate the projects when they discover these are problems. Other boards don't allocate money to products for needed improvements. Many get lured into rosy, 30 percent growth rate projects and then get disappointed later because those returns are not realized. The point is this: even with data, product portfolio decision making can be a challenge.

SUMMARY

Product portfolio management is a critical business practice. Many organizations would do well to nurture their core competencies in this critical business area. Still, today more than ever, executives are at a loss when they try to efficiently manage portfolios that consider all products across all phases of the life cycle. The marketplace will continue to churn, and economic uncertainty will always prevail; this only underscores the importance of elevating product portfolio management within the organization.

Portfolio management must also be stitched into the corporate fabric. If not, companies will miss important opportunities because they will be focusing on cost cutting, eliminating resources, and betting on a host of new products to build top-line growth. The more effective answer is a holistic approach to the practice and methods of life cycle product portfolio management, tightly connected to the strategic directives of the business. These methods will improve the chances that the business can grow and prosper.

RAISING YOUR PRODUCT MANAGEMENT EXPERIENCE QUOTIENT (PMEQ)

1. Try to determine how product portfolios are currently managed within your own firm. Doing so may require your understanding of how strategies cascade from upper to lower levels.

2. Investigate whether specific portfolio management tools are used to collect and evaluate portfolio data within your company.

3. Reach out to one or two key executives in your division or at the corporate level. Ask them to explain the methods they use to devise your company's product portfolio strategies. How can your comprehension of the material from this chapter improve that approach?

4. If your company doesn't currently have a high-level review board, consider proposing such a board at the highest level that makes sense for your products. For example, can you propose to your manager that she create such a board with immediate peers? Consider creating a Business Case for such a board and presenting it to your management. In this case, you could underscore its importance and propose a pilot implementation.

5. Evaluate your own products and the portfolios in which they reside. Are you currently forced to invest resources in underperforming or unused SKUs? Can you work at reevaluating and eliminating underperforming products to improve the effectiveness of your own portfolios?

6. Try to mock up a portfolio evaluation of one or two major portfolios that envelop or touch your own products. Can you identify the meta-buckets? How would you report status on these products and/or portfolios to a review board? Could your mock-up results be useful insight for you, your peers, or your management?

22

ENOUGH'S ENOUGH! DISCONTINUING THE PRODUCT

Executive Summary

- Nonviable, noncritical products within the portfolio use vital resources that could be used for other product investments.
- Product disinvestment should seriously be considered for some products as an option during the life cycle product portfolio planning process.
- Product discontinuation may involve selling the product to another company or group of investors or the sale of intellectual property, designs, or technologies as a means of recouping losses.

We struggle with the complexities and avoid the simplicities.
—NORMAN VINCENT PEALE

This last chapter in the series of chapters that focus on Post-Launch Product Management represents the end of the journey for the product. *End of life, sunset, exit,* and *discontinuation* are terms used to describe the time in the product's life when it is no longer viable in the market because it no longer fills a need or because it has been replaced by another product from your company or from a competitor. As every product needs to be managed across the active phases of its life cycle, so does its discontinuation and eventual withdrawal from the market. This chapter is designed to help you recognize those market signals and guide you through the product discontinuation and market withdrawal process.

BARRIERS TO DISCONTINUATION

For some reason, this natural conclusion to the life of a product seems to be a major challenge for many firms. Product and portfolio managers don't take product discontinuation seriously, nor do they typically make it an important part of product life cycle management decision options. The reasons for this include the following:

1. They don't pay close enough attention to the financials or market performance indicators.
2. They aren't attuned to this part of Product Management or may think the responsibility belongs elsewhere.
3. They feel that if they lead the exit, they'll lose their job and that others in the organization will lose their jobs as well.
4. They feel that the up-front investments have already been spent. Why bother removing it from the market if it doesn't cost anything to keep it there? You might hear, "Who knows? Maybe someone will order one."

If good life cycle product portfolio management provides for the investment in a steady stream of products across all phases of the life cycle, then it should stand to reason that the portfolio management process should actively consider discontinuation, not prevent it. If we get past the psychological factors for avoiding discontinuation and adopt a controlled exit process as a best practice for Product Management, perhaps we can look at product discontinuation as a logical conclusion to the product's life.

First of all, product discontinuation does not just happen because customers stop buying the product, although lack of sales is a good reason to discontinue one. Product discontinuation is part of the normal portfolio evaluation cycle. The life cycle product portfolio management process recommends evaluation of all of the products in the portfolio. The approach defines which products are currently in the market, what is being primed for launch, what product projects are in development, and which product projects are in various planning phases. Second, product discontinuation doesn't occur on a given date. Just like the launch that phases the product *into* the market, the discontinuation process phases the product *out* of the market. You can't just pack up your tent and go home. Because discontinuing products is a natural part of the life cycle, it's worthwhile to explore the decisions and processes for doing so.

THE DISCONTINUATION DECISION

The discontinuation decision process (versus the actual decision itself) should not be difficult to initiate, especially if end-of-life signals have been pulsing onto the cross-functional team's radar for some time. With due diligence, the product team should have noticed explicit, Decline phase indicators. Understand that sales don't just automatically drop off the chart, unless you're selling some style-oriented or fad product. A number of signals point to a product's readiness for discontinuation:

- The product is no longer strategically viable or valuable to the firm.
- Sales volumes and revenue are declining rapidly or have evaporated.
- Market share of your product is falling precipitously.
- Customers have been encouraged to switch to another product that your company sells.
- Customers have switched to a competitor's product that is less expensive or more attractive.
- Production or maintenance costs are escalating, and the product is losing money.
- Team members are disinterested and unmotivated by a sinking product.
- Salespeople aren't willing to sell the product.

Even though, in the past, there may have been some reticence on behalf of the product manager to bring up the topic with management, these signals tell you the time is right to take action. But what is that action?

PRODUCT DISCONTINUATION DOCUMENTATION

In order to appropriately structure the necessary decision making, a formal decision document should be created. This document tells the life story of the product, describing why it's probably time for it to enter the retirement phase of its life cycle. This document is called a *Product Discontinuation Document* (PDD).

The purpose of the PDD is to build a case for the discontinuation of a product and its withdrawal from the market. The PDD describes the business, financial, and market situation of the product. Then, it describes the roles, responsibilities, and necessary communications among stakeholders within the company, as well as communication plans to reach customers, suppliers, and partners outside the firm. It is also an important document that describes the existing contractual relationships that the company may have with those customers, suppliers, or partners. For example, if there are multiyear withdrawal provisions in contracts with certain customers, those liabilities need to be surfaced, funded, and managed. Ultimately, the PDD becomes a formal means for cross-functional product team members to understand their roles and responsibilities throughout the discontinuation and market withdrawal process. A typical PDD is depicted in the template outlined in Figure 22.1 as follows:

THE CROSS-FUNCTIONAL TEAM

Throughout the life of the product, the cross-functional team provides effective guidance regarding the product. During the discontinuation phase, the team is no less important. Perhaps team members wish to devote their time to other, more enriching endeavors; however, their participation cannot be discounted. Team members need to be fully engaged in the discontinuation process and must commit to carry out vital activities that are related physical disposition, facilities, systems, legal activities, and so on.

Because this cross-functional team may have been exposed to team member displacement and changes over the declining phases of the product's life, team members may feel that their jobs are in jeopardy. "Once I'm finished here, what's next?" The same can even be said for the product manager. Therefore, product managers should make sure that they reach out to management to ensure that there are indeed other opportunities waiting for team members. Although this isn't always the most pleasant topic, the one thing I can recommend is that communicating to management in advance is critical. In Chapter 23, I'll talk a little more about managing your career.

Just one quick note: some companies actually provide additional bonus monies for employees who stay with a less-than-pleasant task or set of activities related to a product discontinuation and market withdrawal. This is a very good idea—and a topic you may want to bring up with your management for discontinuation of high-profile or deeply embedded products.

OTHER TYPES OF "DISCONTINUATION"

A number of years ago, I was part of a team that acquired another company. One of my roles was to rationalize that acquired company's portfolio of products, within the context of the strategies already formulated for the portfolio. One of the products was a software system that was being sold to small- and medium-sized companies. There were only about 100 U.S. customers for that product, so I had my team go through a discontinuation process that took approximately two years. That was the easy part. The complex part involved a South American reseller of the software and other professional services. With the dismantling of the support infrastructure, another way had to be figured out to eliminate my company's responsibility for that product. We ended up selling the reseller perpetual rights to resell and modify the software, limiting its territory to South America. In exchange, we received royalty payments for three years, after which time we would no longer own the base code or any other rights, title, or interest in that software.

This is one example of what some companies do when they need to divest themselves of nonstrategic products. This is especially significant when a company can no longer make any money on the product because the overheads and corporate allocations become untenable. For example, the following types of strategies are often considered for discontinuation:

- A company might outsource the labor force for a product or sell off the product to another company.
- There may be intellectual property rights or patents that may be of value, and those can be sold as well.
- For products significant enough to be small companies by themselves, a management group from inside the company (or even a separate outside company) might purchase the product as a business and set up its own operation with the product and the customer base. Just because a product doesn't make strategic or financial sense to one company doesn't mean it won't make sense to another.

FIGURE 22.1

Product Discontinuation Template

Name of product:

Date of original introduction:

Name of product manager:

Date of this document:

SECTION 1. EXECUTIVE SUMMARY

As with any Executive Summary, it is completed after all of the work is completed. This summary should tell, up front, what course of action should be taken, over what time frame; what remaining commitments must be managed; and any financial, human, or operational resources needed to support discontinuation. The Executive Summary captures everything discussed in the plan, including explicit statements or recommendations to management.

SECTION 2. HISTORY AND CHRONOLOGY

Providing a historical chronology or retrospective helps to put the product's performance and its associated metrics into perspective. You will describe how the measurements have been tracked over time, and which market signals were acted upon. Some of the data that might be offered include the product's functional evolution, competitive place in the market, financial history, market share, and anything else that would characterize how and why the product has reached this phase.

This section should also provide descriptive data about what actually happened to the product and why its performance waned, explaining carefully what led to its decline and loss of business. Alternatively, if the product is being discontinued because it's been replaced, this, too, should be mentioned. Further to this point, this would have been included in the replacement product's Business Case, so you will also want to refer to that documentation.

SECTION 3. PRODUCT DESCRIPTION AND RELATED ORGANIZATIONAL OR PORTFOLIO IMPACTS

This section describes the product, explaining its purpose, the market segments on which it focused, the needs it addressed, and how those needs may have either changed, or possibly how competitors were able to take away market share. As suggested in the previous section, you should reinforce the point if another product is replacing the product being discontinued and talk about any migration planning.

Other portfolio impacts may also be important to discuss. The team's job is to make sure that the removal of this product would not cause other products in the portfolio to be exposed to undue risk, and this section should show how the team plans to address these risks.

SECTION 4. BUSINESS ASSUMPTIONS

As products are considered for discontinuation, there may be some residual sales activity. Additionally, some expenses are probably being incurred, and some operational support activities are taking place. In this section, a forecast should be derived that estimates any anticipated future product sales. Other financial assumptions should also be considered, including pricing, costs, and any other expenses directly attributable to the product.

Furthermore, and if applicable, a list of customers should be assembled so that all contractual relationships are uncovered and all terms and conditions for all customers are fully understood. These become part of a plan for a critical subproject, designed to find out when these customers can be communicated with, how long you have to maintain spare parts or telephone support, and any other commitments that would keep you from shutting down support mechanisms.

If your product is made with outside parts or components, or sold with partners or distributors, all of these business relationships need to be understood so that all contractual situations can be reviewed, and so that termination conditional clauses might be triggered. For example, a "last-time" stock order might be a restrictive condition with a supplier.

SECTION 5. FINANCIAL DATA

The assumptions derived from the previous section related to any near-term revenue and expenses, plus the costs of maintenance and support, need to be put into standard financial P&L statements. If there are asset positions that need to be liquidated, Balance Sheet data must indicate items like remaining book value and possible write-offs. Additionally, there may be inventory positions that require consideration for disposal, or that may have to be set aside for spare parts. Conversely, final builds may be needed in order to shut down assembly lines or to avoid having to set up a line in the future (which could be very costly).

Anything of a financial nature that requires sustaining resources, facilities, or other expenses must be included in this financial profile. These results should be distilled and reported in the Executive Summary.

SECTION 6. PROJECT PLANS AND SCHEDULES

The discontinuation process is carried out over time. A phase-out plan is very helpful to guide a cross-functional team's activities during this time because it provides exhaustive detail about what happens and when. The following list of tasks may help you construct and describe the phase-out plan:

1. Write letters to customers describing the intent to discontinue, in the time period allotted. Some customers may require one- or two-year notifications and multiyear support arrangements after that period (it can actually take five years to discontinue support on certain kinds of business infrastructure products).

2. Determine how long inventory can be held prior to its disposal.

3. Develop an inventory disposition plan.

4. Determine the spare parts stocking requirements, according to contract provisions, usually starting when the discontinuation notices are sent out.

5. Determine if any regulators have to be notified, and when.

6. Determine the shutdown process for operational support systems, possibly including the following subtasks:

    a. Turn off ordering and billing systems.

    b. Remove part numbers and descriptions from catalogs.

    c. Recall any software from escrow accounts.

    d. Recall all product and sales documentation from sales offices.

    e. Develop internal communication plan and set dates for notifications to be transmitted.

    f. Develop communication plan for partners, suppliers, or customers, and set dates for notifications to be transmitted. Make sure to secure Legal department approvals.

SECTION 7. RISKS AND CONTINGENCIES

Not every discontinuation is going to go exactly as planned. Situations will arise where a customer may take legal action to prolong support for the product. It may also be learned that components for this product are used in other products in the company (e.g., a memory card, a wiring harness, etc.), so if you discontinue your product, it might cancel critical supplies of another, active product. On a product's bill of materials, shared components or product elements should always have some kind of indicator where the component is shown to be used on another product.

SECTION 8. RECOMMENDATION

Just like any planning document intended for management authorization, a clear recommendation should be provided.

Finally, sometimes a truly undesirable situation arises where a product becomes harmful or unsafe and requires a complete discontinuation and market withdrawal. In this case, the most important thing to do is to figure out how to mobilize quickly and bring all the products back to the company for disposal. Rapid discontinuation and recalls don't qualify for formal product discontinuation case studies. However, if you work in an industry where a recall is a possibility, emergency procedures should be documented so that if the situation arises, the organization knows how to mobilize and deal with operational and logistics issues and, of course, the public relations and other controlled communications to the market.

THE DISCONTINUATION NOTICE

If you have not had the opportunity to prepare an official discontinuation notice (for example, to send to a customer or distributor of your product), it might be helpful to use the following simple template.

Sample Discontinuation Notice

Dear North America and Europe Customer or Distributor:

This letter is to confirm to your company that OUR COMPANY, INC. is discontinuing the manufacture of a number of PRODUCTS and SPARE PARTS as listed on Exhibit __ to this letter. In accordance with OUR COMPANY's product discontinuation policy, we are hereby giving notice of these product changes in order for your company to adjust its product purchasing records or to make any final lifetime purchases of the discontinued products that are still in supply.

This notice only applies to OUR COMPANY, INC. customers and distributors in North America and Europe. OUR COMPANY's customers and distributors in Asia, Latin America, and other regions will receive their product discontinuation notices from OUR COMPANY's regional account management organizations responsible for such international locations.

While Exhibit __ covers an extensive listing of discontinued end-of-life part types, it represents a small percentage of the OUR COMPANY product portfolio. Many of these products have had little or no recent sales history and may cover a number of versions or selections of the same basic product. We are including these items in this notice to insure that our customers and distributors are informed of the obsolescence of these products.

Part Types to Be Discontinued

If you are the primary contact within your company to receive this notice, a record of your company's known direct purchases of the discontinued part type(s) from OUR COMPANY during the past twenty-four (24) months is included with this letter as Exhibit __. If OUR COMPANY has no record of your company's purchase of the referenced parts in North America or Europe during the past twenty-four (24) months, an Exhibit __ purchase record will not be enclosed. Additionally, if you are receiving this notice under one of OUR COMPANY general customer or distributor mail lists, you will not receive an Exhibit __ purchase history.

Last-Time Buy Conditions

General: Last-time ordering conditions may vary by product. Refer to Exhibit __. The Last-Time Buy Date automatically expires when the final available inventory quantity or production unit has been scheduled and sold.

Dates: Last-time delivery conditions vary by product. Refer to Exhibit __. The code "LA" in the "Last Buy Date" or "Last Delivery Date" column indicates a limited availability part type. Refer elsewhere in this notice for further description of limited availability condition.

Order Placement: Discontinued product orders placed with OUR COMPANY in North America or Europe must be clearly identified as a "Last-Time Buy." Each Order must: (a) reference control number LTB-____; (b) contain your company's requested delivery dates per this notice; (c) be within the minimum order quantity requirements in an existing volume purchase agreement or meet OUR COMPANY's standard minimum order policy; and (d) otherwise conform to all other applicable conditions in this notice.

Pricing: Standard rules for minimum order quantities apply based on the existing agreement with OUR COMPANY. If you have an expired volume purchase agreement (VPA), OUR COMPANY will honor the discounts from the previous VPA if an order was placed with us in the past 18 months.

Acknowledgment and Delivery: OUR COMPANY will acknowledge each acceptable discontinued product order in writing or by electronic data interchange (EDI). We will attempt to meet your company's requested delivery date(s) wherever possible. However, OUR COMPANY's acknowledged delivery date(s) are deemed to be approximate because of the special circumstances associated with last-time product manufacturing conditions.

Except as stated above, the applicable terms and conditions of sale for these discontinued products will be the unmodified provisions in our standard order acknowledgement form or, as applicable, the terms and conditions contained in a duly executed contract in force between our companies.

OUR COMPANY ACCEPTS NO LIABILITY FOR EXCESS REPROCUREMENT COSTS OR FOR ANY SPECIAL, INCIDENTAL, OR CONSEQUENTIAL DAMAGES WHATSOEVER ASSOCIATED WITH THIS NOTICE, WITH ITS PRODUCTS, OR WITH THE FINAL MANUFACTURE AND PERFORMANCE AGAINST ANY LAST-TIME BUY ORDERS RELATED TO THE DISCONTINUED PRODUCTS COVERED BY THIS NOTICE.

We regret the inconvenience and impact this notice may cause your company. OUR COMPANY sales, marketing, and distribution personnel stand ready to assist you in placing your company's final orders or in providing product information you require.

On behalf of OUR COMPANY, we appreciate your understanding and assistance in helping us to help you minimize the impact of this product discontinuation on your company. We look forward to OUR COMPANY's continued support of your company's product requirements in the years to come.

SUMMARY

The purpose of this chapter was to provide you with a perspective on product discontinuation and a structure to discontinue a product. The initial decision to create a product is guided by a Business Case, which justifies the investment and describes how the product should perform in the market. As described, just like a Business Case is used to invest, a formal method, along with clearly thought out documentation is required to disinvest. Just like the launch was shown as a gradual ramp-up to the market, when a product is discontinued, there is a gradual ramp-down. This ramp-down allows customers to migrate to other replacement products or make other arrangements. It also allows you the opportunity to put whatever sustaining infrastructure in place to support the ramp-down, including the procurement of spare parts, service staff, or other extended support activities required to fulfill the company's obligations to customers and to ensure that the company's brand is fully protected.

RAISING YOUR PRODUCT MANAGEMENT EXPERIENCE QUOTIENT (PMEQ)

1. Investigate whether your company has a product discontinuation team, group, or initiative within the firm. This team may be labeled as a "sunset," "exit," "discontinuation," or "shutdown" team. If there is such a team, you will want to connect with the members to understand the discontinuation process.

2. Begin to decide what conditions or indicators will cause you to evaluate the possibility of product discontinuation as a potential strategy. Discuss these criteria with your management to determine which ones would be acceptable for a product discontinuation plan.

3. Obtain any discontinuation plans previously used for similar products in your company. How do these plans compare with the recommendations in this chapter? What additional information would you include to strengthen the Business Case for discontinuation, should you have to make that decision?

4. Develop an outline for your Product Discontinuation Document as a standard part of your Product Master Plan, even during the planning phase of the product life cycle. Discuss with your cross-functional team how discontinuation will be handled and how commitments will be maintained over the exit period.

MODULE 5

PROFESSIONALIZING PRODUCT MANAGEMENT

INTRODUCTION TO MODULE 5

Whether you have had the opportunity to read through this entire book or have only encountered this module as you thumb through its pages, I invite you to get comfortable for a short while to absorb some of the support and guidance contained in the next two chapters.

This book provides a perspective for professionalizing Product Management, inspired by my vision for this profession. One of the ways the book achieves this goal is by helping readers understand the foundational knowledge, skills, and experiences required for people engaged in this amazing profession (or considering the job).

In this light, I'd like to discuss two dimensions regarding the topic of Product Management professionalization. The first deals with the product manager—and the evolution of the body of knowledge and portfolio of experiences that are needed to excel in this job category. The second focuses on the role of the managers of product managers: the leaders and executives who are responsible for the organization.

These topics are very important to me. In the years that followed the publication of the first edition of this book, I wrote two other books that explored these topics in greater detail. *Managing Product Management* was written to help senior leaders organize more effectively for Product Management. *The Product Manager's Survival Guide* was written for people who are either new to Product Management or who want to recalibrate their career. I hope you'll become familiar with those books as well.

Chapter 23 is called "Charting Your Career." Every person engaged in the profession has a starting point. As I discussed in the Introduction, most people in Product Management come into the position from "somewhere else." I've provided you with a brief skills assessment that should give you some data to help you get your bearings and work with your manager to define (or redefine) your work activities so that you can approach your development in a more deliberate, efficient manner. I've even included a career-planning template to help you keep track of your progress. You can also use this template for working with your manager as you continually revise your work plans and raise your product management experience quotient (PMEQ).

Chapter 24, entitled "Organizing for Product Management," is aimed at the bosses. It is envisioned as a work tool for business leaders in structuring the organization and in guiding product managers. The chapter sets the stage for organizing a leadership-level, cross-functional oversight group that serves many functions, including that of portfolio supervision, product team staffing, team empowerment, process ownership, building a community, and other helpful, needed executive leadership. I've also addressed the issue of, and need for, ongoing coaching. Coaching is an important part of management because people usually need support in validating their goals and in carrying out their work.

I sincerely hope that you find these chapters helpful. If you are a product manager and you read Chapter 24, you will come away with an appreciation for some of the challenges your bosses face. This appreciation may help you in "stepping up" to the challenge of improving your own capability. On the other hand, if you're one of the bosses, reading Chapter 24 may give you a better appreciation for the type of guidance that you can provide for your employees. In both cases, everyone comes out a winner.

23

CHARTING YOUR CAREER

Executive Summary

- Planning a career in Product Management requires an understanding of where you've been, where you are, and where you want to go.
- To achieve success as a product manager, you need to formulate the professional strategy that will work best for you.
- Encountering unexpected experiences and situations is common in Product Management. Therefore, product managers are always in a state of learning.

Leaders who learn continuously will enhance their value to the business and reduce risk.

—STEVEN HAINES

Before I started working on the second edition of *The Product Manager's Desk Reference*, I wrote a book entitled *The Product Manager's Survival Guide*. Its purpose is to help newer product managers become as productive as possible, as fast as possible. It also serves as a handy guide for those who want to reboot their careers.

Over the years, Product Management leaders have explicitly told me that they want to improve the time to proficiency for newer product managers (which I read as "shorten the learning curve!"). They also want product managers to expand their horizons through new experiences and earn greater levels of empowerment to drive business results. This book can help as a building block for any product manager because it is a dynamic resource designed to help you raise your game.

At the outset of this book, I stated that I wanted to transform this largely accidental profession called Product Management into a recognized discipline. To achieve this, I developed two general themes: one theme is related to a product and its journey across its life cycle, from beginning to end; the second theme is the journey of product managers across their career. Throughout the book, at the end of most chapters, I have provided some suggestions for "Raising Your Product Management Experience Quotient (PMEQ)." I hope that you have been able to use some of these ideas in carrying out your own job.

In this chapter, I provide you, the Product Management practitioner, with some additional support in charting your career. In Chapter 24, I offer some additional guidance for the bosses—the managers of Product Management. Furthermore, because "business is business," if you happen to find yourself reading this chapter and you're not a product manager, I urge you to read on. You will come away with an understanding of the business skills that are most essential to Product Management, product marketing, marketing, and general management.

IT'S UP TO YOU

Early in my corporate career, one of the guidelines communicated to me by management was that "your career is up to you." The same holds true today. The pendulum of the business cycle swings rapidly in response to volatile business conditions. Because of this volatility, management development—the professional grooming of managers—may, from time to time, take a backseat to short-term corporate performance goals. In some firms (but not all), managers are formally developed by providing them with experiential opportunities. They may stay in each of a variety of jobs, some for several years, under the guidance of experienced coaches. Some are assigned mentors who are not their bosses.

There are many exemplary leadership development programs in companies all over the world because these companies realize that they must have a steady stream of executive talent from which to choose. However, based on my experience in working with hundreds of companies and talking to thousands of product managers in my workshops, it doesn't seem that companies pay as much attention to this today as they did in the past, especially with increasing emphasis on Product Management.

It's frustrating to hear from many product managers that their bosses don't buy into the best practices for Product Management and that there's no time for implementing any practices to improve the product's business. Therefore, my message to you is this: no matter what your management says or does, if you want to cultivate your experience in this profession, you need a plan. You need to create a professional development strategy that is tied to action plans that will build your skills and experience, because, in fact, your career will always be up to you.

A CAREER STRATEGY

When you studied the strategic planning process earlier in the book, you learned that you must understand where you are, where you want to go, and how you are going to get there. If you follow this sequence for products, you can follow this sequence for your Product Management career as well. To achieve this, you need to devise learning strategies for yourself so you can set yourself up for success. You need to be able to create linkages to your annual goal-setting process so that you can describe to your manager the kinds of things you believe you should be working on. Your initiative in figuring some of this out will likely be rewarded.

One way to develop your own learning strategy is to emulate what entrepreneurs do. Entrepreneurs may not know everything they need to know, but they have a spirit and a drive to do as much as they can in order to achieve their vision. From this, the message is that product managers need to possess a vision for *themselves*. Whether it's a grand vision or only what you can see for the next two years, you need an end point to aim for. The more you can bring this about on your own, the more you're actually contributing to your own leadership development— an important competency discussed in Chapter 3.

WHERE ARE YOU NOW?

A career can be thought of as a series of jobs that a person holds during her working life. The jobs you've held thus far have, in some way, influenced your current situation. You may find that you are thinking of a job in Product Management, have a couple of years' experience, or have been doing the job for many years. In Chapter 1, I provided you with basic information about what product mangers do, so I'm not going to rehash those responsibilities here. Subsequent chapters described each of the work categories that relate to the roles and responsibilities of product managers, which you will want to leverage.

Finding out where you are right now begins with an honest appraisal of what you know, what skills you have, and what experience you have amassed. With this assessment, you can determine, either through your own efforts or working with your manager, what you can do to improve your effectiveness as a product manager. This is Product Management career planning in a nutshell.

ASSESSING KNOWLEDGE, SKILLS, AND EXPERIENCES

To begin your work, I'm providing you with a basic diagnostic tool. It is a self-assessment survey that may help you figure out where you are and help you think about where you would like to be. After you carry out the self-assessment, I'll give you an action-planning tool you can use. The assessment is *not a test*. Its goal is to help you establish a benchmark in major Product Management practices. Generally aligned with the flow of the book, the following broad categories will be used to create an assessment:

1. Leadership and collaboration
2. Cross-functional product teams
3. Making decisions
4. Financial management
5. Industry and competitive analysis
6. Market segmentation and customer needs
7. Forecasting
8. Strategic planning
9. New Product Planning and New Product Introduction
10. Post-Launch Product Management

I am going to provide you with a series of assessment forms corresponding to each Product Management category. The assessment form uses a rating scale of 1 to 4. Here are the descriptions of each rating for you to use as a guideline:

- A score of 1 means *no evidence.* In your career, you haven't had the opportunity to establish sufficient skill or experience. Don't think of this as a negative. It's just a way to understand what you've done and not done.
- A score of 2 means there is *some evidence* of experience you've gained along the way. However, you may not have had sufficient opportunity to develop the acumen you need.
- A score of 3 means *evident.* You've demonstrated actions frequently enough that you feel comfortable with the work and that others with whom you have worked generally have confidence in your ability. However, you may not have perfected the practice.
- A score of 4 means *very evident.* Your experience is recognized by others, and you are considered a subject matter expert or role model with an ability to coach others.

There are two dimensions to this assessment; the first is based on your self-assessment score and the scale above. In the table that is used for the assessment, the right-most column contains a space for you to identify the possible actions you could take. This is an important opportunity for you and your boss to review and validate your current skill or experience. It also helps to set up a collaborative environment in which you and your boss are more closely aligned on the factors that will contribute to your success. This evaluation helps determine areas where you might require additional coaching or, when your experience is evident, even areas where you might be able to coach others!

This assessment protocol is a representation of what's possible to evaluate. To develop a more in-depth profile, you can scour this book and the others I've written. In the next chapter, written for the managers of product managers, I'll discuss the importance of your manager's relationship with you as well as with leaders across the organization.

To use the assessment, place a check in the box that corresponds to your current skill level. Next, in the cell, write some short notes indicating the actions you might take. This way, you can better prioritize the work areas on which you might want to focus.

Once you've carried out your self-assessment and identified areas on which you would like to focus, the next thing to do is to create some developmental goals. You can do this independently, with your manager, or both. You probably should work closely with your manager because it will demonstrate that you are sincerely focused on proactively managing your career. It will also involve your manager in ongoing professional development and guidance. In addition, your manager may be able to help you identify other "go-to" resources who can act as coaches who can help you when it comes to carrying out different kinds of work. Your active collaboration with your manager will enable you to integrate your work activities with your company's annual goal-setting process. You can use the career action planning template and the applied learning project template shown later in this chapter.

Finally, this process of self-assessment and professional action planning contributes to the overall professional stature of Product Management. Product Management leaders, as you know, must possess a wide variety of skills to achieve targeted strategic, financial, and market results.

With respect to any of these attributes, your acquired knowledge may not necessarily equate with your experience. *It's always best to avoid painting an inaccurate portrait of your experience*. Studying the structure of a profit and loss statement in an accounting class does not equate with the experience of evaluating cost variances in a production environment. Or, if you represent yourself as adaptable and flexible but are seen by others as rigid and inflexible, you'll quickly be "discovered," and your role will be marginalized.

Having such results orientation is critical to your success as you evolve as a Product Management leader. In Figure 23.1, the basic self-assessment template is shown, followed by the actual assessment, shown as Figure 23.2.

FIGURE 23.1

Basic Self-Assessment Template

ELEMENT	1	2	3	4	POSSIBLE ACTION PLANS

If you do this assessment every year or work with your manager to complete this evaluation, you will clearly see how a path of continual improvement contributes positively to your career growth. If you are in a position to manage or coach others, you'll find deep satisfaction in using this tool with them.

Once you carry out your self-assessment, you will see a number of developmental possibilities. These will surely help you improve your effectiveness as a product manager. An outgrowth of the opportunities you identify in this template will be work projects. Therefore, I'm going to provide you with two additional templates.

1. *Career action planning template.* This is used to map out, at a high level, the projects you will undertake or training you will pursue. This is what you can use when establishing performance goals with your manager.

2. *Applied learning project template.* This template is used when you want to propose and secure the buy-in from your manager, and others, to carry out a comprehensive, sometimes complex work project. For example, if you haven't led a product launch team, this would be the template you would use to describe your work plan to your manager. The evidence, in this case, would be an on-time, successful product launch.

CAREER ACTION PLANNING

One of the best ways to apply the data you develop through your assessment is to create a learning roadmap. In Figure 23.3, this learning roadmap is embodied in a *career action planning template* to help you focus on some specific objectives.

YOUR APPLIED LEARNING PROJECT

An applied learning project is one that builds a specific set of skills or competencies. You may be able to carry out several of these each year. When this kind of work plan is integrated into your goal-setting or performance planning process with your manager, it helps you carry out more purposeful work activities and cultivates a good rapport with your manager. Use the Applied Learning Project Template in Figure 23.4 to guide your work and negotiate with your manager.

FIGURE 23.2

Product Manager Self-Assessment

LEADERSHIP AND COLLABORATION (CHAPTER 3)

ELEMENT	1	2	3	4	POSSIBLE ACTION PLANS
Develops a network of contacts inside my company					
Earns credibility through actions					
Engenders trust among team members					
Meets commitments					
Helps others					

CROSS-FUNCTIONAL PRODUCT TEAMS (CHAPTER 4)

ELEMENT	1	2	3	4	POSSIBLE ACTION PLANS
Recognizes the phases of team development					
Clarifies roles and responsibilities					
Establishes team participation across the life cycle					
Negotiates Functional Support Plans (FSPs)					

MAKING DECISIONS (CHAPTER 5)

ELEMENT	1	2	3	4	POSSIBLE ACTION PLANS
Solves problems					
Evaluates options					
Uses a decision matrix to establish priorities					

FINANCIAL MANAGEMENT (CHAPTER 6)

ELEMENT	1	2	3	4	POSSIBLE ACTION PLANS
Knows the "numbers" of the product's business					
Evaluates product profitability using a P&L					
Works easily with the finance department					
Calculates discounted cash flow					
Prepares product budgets					

INDUSTRY & COMPETITIVE ANALYSIS (CHAPTER 7)

ELEMENT	1	2	3	4	POSSIBLE ACTION PLANS
Classifies the industry in which the firm operates					
Completes P.R.E.S.T.O. analysis					
Puts industry indicators into perspective for others					
Compares competitor strengths and weaknesses					
Creates competitive profiles and shares with others					

MARKET SEGMENTATION AND CUSTOMER NEEDS (CHAPTER 8)

ELEMENT	1	2	3	4	POSSIBLE ACTION PLANS
Has an up-to-date market segmentation model					
Plans and carries out customer visits					
Creates customer or user personas					
Updates customer need state models					

FORECASTING (CHAPTER 9)

ELEMENT	1	2	3	4	POSSIBLE ACTION PLANS
Prepares market share forecasts					
Has Total Addressable Market (TAM) forecast model					
Develops or collaborates on demand forecasts					
Creates top-down and bottom-up volume forecasts					
Devises robust assumptions for product forecasts					

STRATEGIC PLANNING (CHAPTER 10)

ELEMENT	1	2	3	4	POSSIBLE ACTION PLANS
Uses the strategy formulation process					
Assembles a baseline "state of business" model					
Envisions the product's future					
Prepares product-level SWOT analysis					

NEW PRODUCT PLANNING AND NEW PRODUCT INTRODUCTION (CHAPTERS 11-17)

ELEMENT	1	2	3	4	POSSIBLE ACTION PLANS
Uses a phase-gate process to make decisions					
Applies business criteria to decision gates					
Creates a positioning statement for an opportunity					
Prepares a value proposition for an opportunity					
Writes product requirements					
Negotiates with developers and others					
Write a Business Case for product investments					
Oversees the product's development					
Creates a Product Launch Plan					
Leads a product launch team					
Assembles a Marketing Plan for the product					

POST-LAUNCH PRODUCT MANAGEMENT (CHAPTERS 18-20)

ELEMENT	1	2	3	4	POSSIBLE ACTION PLANS
Performs a post-launch audit					
Conducts a win–loss audit					
Uses metrics to gauge the product's life cycle state					
Evaluates product performance measures					
Regularly reviews product results with others					
Determines future markets for the product					
Assembles an integrated roadmap					
Defines value based pricing strategies					
Synchronizes promotions and customer education					
Optimizes sales and distribution					
Calculates operational capacity					

FIGURE 23.3

Career Action Planning Template

Name	
Date of Plan	
Manager's Name (Coach)	
Summary description of your goals that you would like to achieve in the upcoming year and why these are important:	

Competency or skill to develop.	Work program, projects, or developmental actions planned.	Estimated duration of project and target completion date.	Others you plan to work with or resources you plan to utilize.	Date completed and evidence of work provided to management.

FIGURE 23.4

Applied Learning Project Template

Name:
Project title:
Importance:
Skills and experience you plan to develop:
Project goals:
Techniques and methods you will apply:
People with whom you plan to work:
Requested support from management:
Evidence you will provide:

When you complete this applied learning work project, you should write a complete report comprising approximately 8 to 12 pages. It should contain the following elements:

1. The challenge you took on
2. The concepts, skills, techniques, models, or tools you used and how you used them

3. The process you followed

4. The people with whom you worked

5. The obstacles you encountered and how you overcame them

6. The decisions you made and how those decision were made

7. The measurements you established and how you achieved these results

8. The overall outcome of the project and the impact on the business of the product or portfolio

9. Why you should have this made part of your permanent record

10. Your manager's signature and others' recommendations

SUMMARY

Product managers are always in a state of learning. Sometimes the learning is purposeful, and sometimes it's by accident. I happen to have learned a fair amount by accident. The goal of this chapter has been to help you better focus your efforts so that you can be as efficient as possible in guiding your own development. Using a structured, data-driven approach can be very helpful as you take the reins of your career as a product manager. Hopefully, with the simple assessment tool I've provided, you can put your skills and experience into perspective. This should help you to pinpoint the areas on which you should focus. Finally, when you have "applied learning projects" active throughout your career, you will grow more quickly. Moreover, you can use this type of tool to help others who may end up working for you at some point in the future.

24

ORGANIZING FOR AND MANAGING PRODUCT MANAGEMENT

Executive Summary

- Product Management is not a job title; it is a horizontal, integrative business function that should be part of the organization's design.
- A Product Management governance board or equivalent group should be chartered by the executive leadership team to ensure that the function of Product Management survives for the long term.
- Good, experienced product managers enable the company to be more efficient and productive.
- Leaders must ensure that product managers have accurate, timely data, usable processes, and a complete toolset to effectively do their jobs.

To reach a port we must sail, sometimes with the wind, and sometimes against it. But we must not drift or lie at anchor.

—OLIVER WENDELL HOLMES

This chapter is written for managers of Product Management and those who are responsible for leading and guiding the Product Management organization. I focus on this because it is the job of those who lead the function of Product Management to ensure that the firm can achieve competitive advantage from two perspectives:

1. To guarantee that there is a sufficient organizational infrastructure so that Product Management can thrive
2. To equip the organization with a solid base of competent product managers and product team leaders

As I prepared to write the first edition of this book, I interviewed dozens of senior leaders across a vast landscape of companies and a diverse set of industries. Through conducting this research, I noticed that senior leaders faced many challenges to organize effectively for Product Management. To help them, I wrote a book entitled *Managing Product Management*. That book has been a faithful adjunct to the suite of resources called upon by senior leaders. However, these executives continue to encounter a number of challenging questions, including the following:

1. How will we ensure that our products and portfolios receive the proper level of investment to support our growth targets?
2. Who will we rely upon to drive discovery, innovation, and Product Management excellence in our firms?
3. How do we capitalize on our organizational strengths to align leaders and support vital strategic imperatives?

Just like the journey of a product across its life cycle, and the journey of product managers across their careers, each organization follows a journey as well. Sometimes the map is difficult to read, and sometimes the road isn't well paved, but if you and your executive colleagues are equipped with the right set of tools, you will be better able to contribute to the organization's success. I am certain that you will be enlightened by what's contained in this chapter.

GETTING ORGANIZED

There are several organizational problems I want to talk about. I've discovered these problems over many years of benchmarking and interviewing key business leaders.

First of all, some business leaders don't buy into the view that Product Management is (or should be) a critical element of the company's business model. Instead, many of them think of Product Management as:

- A cadre of people in Marketing who create marketing collateral, train salespeople, and staff demonstration booths at trade shows
- Those people who write product requirements and crank out volumes of product definition documents—without ever interviewing a customer
- So-called product owners who work with developers and designers (with customer input) to rapidly build and release a product without regard for the business consequences of their decisions
- Surrogate sales specialists who help perform demos, answer customer complaint calls, or help close deals

It may be true that product managers will be involved in each of these areas from time to time. However, too often these narrow sets of responsibilities become the paradigm for how business leaders think about how Product Management operates within a given environment. Yet, when there is a defined structure for Product Management excellence (as I have reinforced in all of my books) with the potential to have a powerful impact on the business results of the organization, it seems to me that upper management should not accept less.

My firm has collected and validated a significant pool of data that points to vast seas of variability in organizational performance due to:

- A lack of agreement among senior leaders about the function and purpose of Product Management
- An absence of clarity around roles and responsibilities
- A lack of appreciation for the fact that strategies for products and portfolios depend on the life cycle state of the product
- A shortage of financial and market data
- Insufficient understanding of key product-related processes across functional boundaries

These are directly related to the fact that the organization's leadership does not have an appreciation for both the purpose of Product Management (see Chapter 1) and the true role of the product manager. One of the root causes is that they have not had sufficient experience or positive examples to learn from.

However, the most troubling issue has to do with the fact that too often product managers are ill equipped for the job. Either they don't have sufficient skills or experiences, or they don't have a supportive infrastructure. Instead, they are relegated to the role of herding cats and project work, thereby leaving a product leadership vacuum. In response, the organization attempts to right itself by having other people—from other functions—carry out the work that rightfully should be orchestrated by a product manager. Often, this vacuum is filled by people from Engineering, Operations, or Marketing or designated by the leaders in organizational functions who feel they have the strongest product knowledge. This leads to a lopsided, inside-out view of how to successfully manage a product.

The end result speaks for itself: some companies push ideal products to customers who do not understand why they need the next best thing. They don't see what is wrong with the old thing and aren't willing to part with their money simply because a technologist insists it's a good idea.

Even where Product Management is an established function, those who work as product managers report to different leaders—some to Marketing and some to Development. However, what's quite encouraging to me is that the Chief Product Officer has emerged as a recognized executive leader with a "seat at the table" in the C-suite! In the final breakdown, product managers should, at a minimum, be required to:

- Understand the function and purpose of Product Management.
- Establish credibility to lead a cross-functional product team.
- Make effective, fact-based decisions.
- Apply financial techniques.
- Develop, use, and share market insights that include the evaluation of the industry, competitors, competitive products, and customers.
- Envision a realistic future for the product or product line and derive the most appropriate strategies based on financial, market, and business data.
- Make the most appropriate business decisions in a collaborative manner with the cross-functional product team, consistent with the product's position in the life cycle.
- Create achievable forecasts of sales, market share, and production levels.
- Utilize a New Product Development (NPD) process consistently to narrow down a large field of ideas and opportunities to the ones that make the most business sense.

- Use Business Cases to effectively justify and guide product-related investments.
- Evaluate the product's performance at any moment using relevant data and metrics so that new plans and programs can be put into place.
- Leverage product portfolio management techniques to help the company fulfill its financial and competitive objectives.

Hopefully the list shown above, coupled with all the material presented throughout this book, can help to establish a standard set of skills that support the body of knowledge for Product Management.

In Chapter 23, I provided a framework for product managers to better equip themselves in managing their careers. As much as I believe that career management is up to the individual, product managers require strong executive sponsorship and coaching. All executives understand that change starts at the top. Therefore, the balance of this chapter is devoted to helping the collective "you," as the executive team, to nurture and cultivate Product Management as the most important element of your organization's business model. My thoughts also apply to those who are directly responsible for leading the team of product managers.

LEADING PRODUCT MANAGEMENT

No matter how an organization is structured, the general population of employees looks to executive leaders for guidance so they can have clarity of purpose. They want to know what's expected, how they'll be evaluated, and how their bosses will support and help them. Easy enough.

The problem is that executive teams don't necessarily do a good job of guidance. Often the cause can be attributed to a lack of harmony in the leadership team. Every team, no matter what level, seems to suffer from the typical team behavioral issues, including lack of alignment on priorities, mistrust, and lack of accountability for business results. The implication is that members of executive leadership teams may not mesh well together. All members believe their function is the most important, and this lack of harmony trickles down to lower-level employees. This leaves the responsibility for cross-functional product team success up to the leadership and influence of the product manager—and again, because the job of the product manager is often inconsistently defined, results are, at best, uneven.

Compounding the problem of disharmony among executives, there are some leaders, especially Product Management executives, who have never *done* Product Management jobs. As a result, these managers don't have a direct appreciation for the complexity of the job. Furthermore, when an executive team is considering a shift in the organization's focus to Product Management, those who don't fully understand the role of the product manager don't understand why any change is needed. Especially if business is "okay," these leaders tend to prefer other solutions. Many executives have expressed to me their unease with being in charge of Product Management, for fear of losing control over their *own* domain. Many of these problems can be solved through a committed organizational transformation. This means organizational change. I'm probably overstating the obvious when I say that most people in organizations resist change because they don't understand what to do with the change, how to lead it, or how long the change process will take.

Performed correctly, Product Management serves as a *unifying function that spans all functions.* Unlike the shared-service horizontal functions of Finance or Human Resources Management, a firmly entrenched and chartered Product Management function must have a direct stake in guiding and directing the corporation's product portfolios. Therefore, Product Management itself must be governed—and governed in a sustainable way—for the long term. To achieve this, an executive-level team or governance board must be established for Product Management. A firmly entrenched and chartered Product Management governance board provides a structure to ensure that policies and procedures, protocols, and general rules of engagement are clearly spelled out and flexibly adopted. The board achieves its broad objectives through the following:

1. Focusing the organization on high-performance products and product portfolios
2. Maintaining a capable, competent staff of product managers
3. Enabling Product Management through effectively utilized processes
4. Supervising systems and tools used to monitor the performance of portfolios, people, and processes

For the balance of this chapter, I'll focus on these areas and others to help you in this endeavor. You can find a deeper exploration of all of these topics in the book *Managing Product Management.*

TRANSFORMING THE ORGANIZATION

The first step in transforming the organization is for the executive leadership team to carefully consider the requirements to guide Product Management. Within this context, the executive leadership team should be responsible for the following items:

1. Chartering and supporting cross-functional product teams
2. Acting as the product portfolio review council and directing product investments
3. Assigning an owner for all Product Management processes and documents
4. Providing data for product managers
5. Resolving problems as they are escalated by product teams
6. Utilizing staffing strategies for product managers
7. Ensuring ongoing professional development of product managers
8. Supporting the building of a Product Management community
9. Creating an environment for establishing and maintaining customer partnership councils or advisory boards
10. Investing in market research to support the product teams

Let's take some time and look at each of these in some detail.

Chartering and Supporting Cross-Functional Product Teams

If your organization wants to take advantage of the benefits of Product Management, chartering, supporting, and empowering a cross-functional product team is vital to the success of your program. In Chapter 4, I described the generic, cross-functional product team and its role as the mini–board of directors for the product, with a product manager as the team leader.

One of the keys to the effective implementation of this model is delegating the right people to the team. Therefore, the executive leadership team (or Product Management governance board) must be able to agree on who those core team members should be. All delegated functional team members should have the authority to act on behalf of their own business function and ensure that they generate the appropriate Functional Support Plans to help them plan and manage their commitments.

With this level of authority and accountability, you don't want to put novices at the table. Product team leaders must have several years of demonstrated leadership experience and be trusted and respected by their peers (the other core team members) and by management. Job titles such as senior product manager, group product manager, or product director would probably be most appropriate for this role. The team should generally be in charge of a significant product or a product line. It's hard to describe the absolute parameters, but you can use product revenue or product complexity as gauges to determine the scope of business responsibility the team will carry.

Another desirable characteristic would be for the team to stay together across the entire life cycle of all the products within its scope of responsibility. This is very important, because it allows for the team to maintain a high degree of familiarity with the product line and support the cultivation of quality, long-lasting relationships among team members. Teams in place for longer periods of time are more efficient, and they perform better, especially when it comes to the adept allocation of investments across products within the line.

Cross-functional teaming should also be part of the organizational structure for associate product managers or product managers. Cross-functional teams at those levels tend to be more transient, as people move from project to project. These teams are better directed by the higher-level cross-functional product line team, where functional members are assigned as needed for a variety of purposes, such as the evaluation of a new product opportunity or even to oversee a minor product launch. An illustration of this team hierarchy is shown in Figure 24.1.

Empowerment

Organizing teams is one challenge; empowering them is another. The word *empowerment,* as with many terms used in business today, is subject to a variety of interpretations. First off, empowerment is not merely bestowed on a product team leader, let alone a team. If the executive leadership team believes that the product team is able to handle the tasks at hand, and the team discharges its responsibilities accordingly, with positive results, then the team will have earned some empowerment points. However, good behavior and good results don't always mean empowerment remains an earned asset. For example, if the product team doesn't take calculated risks and misses market opportunities, then it will not have earned empowerment.

FIGURE 24.1

Product Team Hierarchy

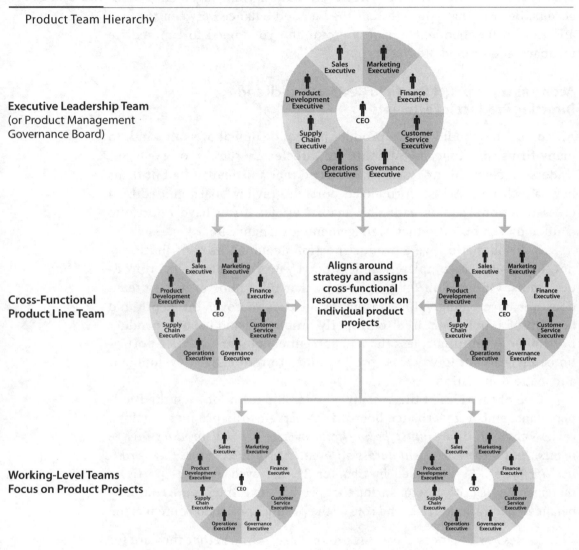

Executive Leadership Team
(or Product Management
Governance Board)

**Cross-Functional
Product Line Team**

Aligns around strategy and assigns cross-functional resources to work on individual product projects

**Working-Level Teams
Focus on Product Projects**

Empowerment also means that the product team will have adequate resources at its disposal to get its job done, so if the right people and an adequate budget are not made available, then the team will have failed. There also needs to be a synergy among team members in creatively solving problems and making decisions. The better the decisions, the more empowerment points they earn. These are the fundamental elements to think about when empowering product teams. And one last point about empowerment: teams who are actually empowered will tolerate significant levels of stress—and there is plenty to go around in today's corporations. Be aware, however, that micromanagement is dangerous. Be sure that you've established a good balance between the creation of an independent business group and your need for immediate feedback and immediate results.

Acting as the Product Portfolio Review Council and Directing Product Investments

All companies should have a product portfolio council of some kind. In many firms, portfolio investments are directed by the senior executive leadership team. In my research, I learned that a little over half of firms have a well-entrenched, formalized portfolio review board guided by a cross-functional senior leadership team. Very few firms have a portfolio council driven by a Product Management governance board.

In firms that utilize a product portfolio council, its contribution is not fully visible or completely understood by product managers or product teams. One reason for this may be that the senior executive team does not have enough time, resources, or data to cover the depth and breadth of activity required to properly rationalize and balance product portfolios. For example, less than 40 percent of companies *with* a portfolio council do *not* look across product lines to rationalize development and avoid duplication.

One of the roles of the executive leadership team (or even the Product Management governance board) is to serve as the product portfolio review council. *There must be portfolio oversight of all product investments: that means oversight across all products situated across their product life cycles.* As discussed in Chapter 21, life cycle product portfolio management is critical to ensuring that product investments are routinely balanced and rationalized. The role of the product portfolio council is to:

1. Review Business Cases for *product projects*, whether they are for new investments or major enhancements. These reviews are driven out of the phase gate New Product Development (NPD) decision-making process.

2. Audit the outcomes of prior Business Cases to ensure that the assumptions, forecasts, and anticipated contributions to the business are being fulfilled. By association, the portfolio council will also want to ensure that post-launch audits are part and parcel of the audits of Business Cases.

3. Evaluate the product portfolio's acquisition targets to ensure that new product lines can be strategically interwoven with the existing lines.

4. Prioritize or reprioritize the dynamic mix of incoming funding requests.

5. Determine which products or product lines should be discontinued based on the firm's portfolio strategy.

Several times a year, each product line team should provide a strategic review to the board. This review is needed to ensure that the product teams stay focused on their strategic objectives and achieve their explicit strategic results. Chapter 10 provides a strategic review template for product teams. On a regular basis, usually monthly, each product team should present its business performance results to the designated leaders on the product portfolio council (or equivalent) leadership team, including comprehensive market and financial readouts, major business wins, project status reports, and other information related to initiatives and activities. A standard reporting format and agenda should be used for all teams. When creating the agenda, a few extra minutes should be allotted to allow for those nonstandard agenda items that never fit into templates. Written documentation should be maintained by the product team in the Product Master Plan.

Assigning an Owner for All Product Management Processes and Documents

Product Management activities are guided by many processes and subprocesses. I won't go into a detailed discussion about these overarching Product Management processes here because they have been discussed throughout this book. However, to establish the right context, I will refer to what I call "meta-level processes" that are directly linked to the Product Management Life Cycle Model, including:

1. Development of market insights
2. Formulation of product and portfolio strategies
3. Efficient product planning and development
4. Targeted, timely product launches
5. Effortless product performance management

Unfortunately, many companies do not treat these Product Management processes with the degree of formality needed to *achieve consistent, predictable usage.* When there is a lack of focus on critical Product Management processes, it follows that there may be a lack of direction for product managers and others they work with. When they do not fully understand their roles and responsibilities, important work activities may be completed inadequately. The result is that either product managers have to complete the work of others, or others have to complete the work for which product managers are responsible. This can be a great challenge to efficiency and product profitability. And you may find it problematic if your objective is to sustain Product Management for the long term.

There is nothing more wasteful and less efficient than creating an NPD process or document and then putting it on the shelf. Processes and documents constantly evolve, especially because process improvement is one of the ongoing mantras in modern companies. Therefore, it is absolutely vital to *assign an owner for all Product Management processes and documents.* The process owner should be a highly experienced leader who has lived through the wars of Product Management. The critical thing about process ownership is this: the executive leadership team must realize that the longevity of that group is vital to the success of the Product Management transformation (regardless of where you are now) and, optimally, should be a continuing entity.

To get started, a process owner would produce an inventory of the workflows, documents, and other items for each of the five *meta-level process* areas described earlier. I like to organize these into "process libraries." This central repository makes it easy to evaluate and improve the library's contents and to learn about what works well and what doesn't. For example, if you are performing a post-launch audit (see Chapter 18) and the product launch process has been captured and evaluated, you can easily identify what went well and what didn't so that future launches go more smoothly!

Having an owner ensures that the process documentation and related business documents (e.g., Business Cases, Product Requirements, Customer Visit Plans, and NPD guidelines) are updated and made available to the Product Management community. Furthermore, the group ensures that processes, practices, and documents are used consistently and that there is a common Product Management vocabulary.

Process owners and their staff can also be a major go-to resource for the community at large. This is especially helpful because this team can provide in-house professional development support, coaching, and team facilitation. In short, the process oversight group can be of tremendous help to the executive leadership team by ensuring that there is a staff of experienced professionals who can provide guidance and advice for the evolving profession in the company.

Providing Data for Product Managers

Some firms have formal structures for data collection and presentation, and some do not. The absence of relevant data can have a negative impact on the effectiveness of product managers and the performance of the products they manage.

When product managers have good data, their decisions tend to be superior; when they do *not* have good data, their decisions tend to be suboptimal. Therefore, it should be the board's responsibility to the cross-functional product teams and to the product manager population to ensure that a constant stream of relevant data is made available and accessible.

All product managers should be provided with data and information from which they can derive insights and make decisions. Without necessary data and other indicators, it is virtually impossible to run the products' business with any degree of precision. Further, just as the senior leadership teams are able to examine all aspects of the firm's performance, so should cross-functional product teams be enabled to do so.

Data comes in many forms. There are sets of data that come directly from embedded corporate systems. These sets include data related to plans and outcomes of business functions such as Supply Chain, Operations, Sales, Production, Development, and Service. They are also linked to explicit processes that are used to guide these functions. Product managers should routinely examine a host of data elements (see Chapter 19) that include the following:

1. Key indicators to evaluate each function's contribution to the product's success.

2. Important figures and reports from financial systems that include budgets, forecasts, and other allocations. These outcomes can and should be compared to original plans so that variances can be analyzed and addressed.

3. The suite of important market data that needs to be planned for, captured, organized, and analyzed. This includes customer research, industry analysis, competitor information, and competitive product evaluations.

Data is the fuel required to manage a product's business, and there is nothing more frustrating than product managers who cannot tell you how much money they're making on their products. In this modern time of advanced business automation, I am amazed to find that a vast number of product managers cannot articulate their gross margin numbers. Integrated back-office systems should provide vital statistics on unit volumes, pricing, revenue, and P&Ls at a glance through visual dashboards and other reporting tools. Moreover, sales force automation systems provide indications of sales pipeline activity so that product forecasts can be validated or updated in a timely fashion. Additionally, project accounting systems enable project status reporting on incurred costs and estimates to complete on major project categories related to the products.

Leaders are responsible for making sure that all data sources are known, catalogued, and made available as needed by product managers and other cross-functional team members. Moreover, leaders must understand that every process produces data in areas such as cycle time, time to launch, order to cash, and others. *The product manager sits at the intersection of data and process and is called upon to capture what's relevant, connect the dots, and take action.* Without the right data at the right time, it's impossible for product managers to do their job.

Creating a Repository of Templates and Tools

Over the years, I've talked to a lot of product managers and product leaders. One of the more troubling things I've discovered is that product managers are often required to use a template that just doesn't fit the situation. This rigidity stifles efficiency and innovative thought. There is doubt that many of the processes utilized in your firm are supported by a variety of templates and guidelines.

Templates are great business tools. They can help organize thoughts and structure work as well as synchronize the work of others. *When properly used, templates can be modified or varied based on application or situational precedents and saved in an archive of "fit for purpose" templates* (e.g., in the Product Master Plan repository).

The downside of template usage in many firms is that product people and others will often just "fill out the form" without giving proper thought to the content. There are two very simple reasons for this. The first is that some people who fill out the templates do not have the requisite knowledge and/or experience to provide the appropriate content. The second reason is that the requisite data is not available, making it impossible to properly utilize the template. This gap can be so severe that a template can be considered completed even though it contains flawed data and assumptions. This situation creates what I call a "checkbox" culture in an organization.

There are dozens of templates used throughout this book. They are catalogued in a section at the front of the book. I've also included many of them in Module 6. These can be used as your foundational library and updated as required. I strongly suggest that your leadership team agree on a consistent set of templates and make them available to product managers and their teams.

Resolving Problems as Escalated by the Product Teams

The responsibility of the cross-functional executive leadership team or governance board is to address and resolve problems that are escalated from the product teams. In order to achieve this stature, the rules for escalation must be established so that the product team knows the conditions under which escalation is warranted. Usually some kind of external event, project jeopardy, or customer issue will require a leadership team intervention.

However, some thresholds should be established so that the product team can maintain its autonomy, meaning that most issues should be resolved by the product team. This is important because you want to cultivate an environment of collaborative problem solving and decision making. In the event that there is confusion regarding the level of urgency, ask the team to think through the issue and come up with some options for action. If the team needs help in this area, you may wish to engage the services of a consultant or coach to help the team through the process. These lessons are an important part of the team's earned empowerment, as discussed earlier. With a better set of tools, the team will know exactly what to communicate in terms of the severity of the problem, what specifically to ask for in the escalation, when action is needed, and why. As with all "lessons" in the team's evolution, leaders should allow time for postevent analyses and continued coaching.

Staffing Strategies for Product Managers

How a company hires and places product managers and how its leaders enable them to excel as strategy-minded business managers can have a major impact on whether that company merely survives or flourishes. Similar to CEOs and general managers, exceptional product managers catalyze action across the organization.

Product managers don't mysteriously materialize when needed, nor are they found through sheer serendipity. Therefore, all senior product leaders will find value in practices that result in the proper placement of product managers.

Staffing strategy, like any strategy, begins with an evaluation of the current environment. Just like you would perform market research to segment markets, you must create a segmentation model for people who are in product roles. Segments can be made of various elements, including the following:

- Title
- Time in role
- Areas of responsibility
- Aspects of products managed (e.g., new products, existing products, mature products, components of a product, and a product line)
- Degree of product complexity
- Extent of customer-facing interactions
- Domain expertise or technical area of specialty
- Job level or band
- Salary
- Work activities performed (or task frequency)
- Competencies in all Product Management work areas

Once the segmentation of the population is accomplished, managers or other leaders in the product organization must identify areas of strength and weakness. One tool you can use is a SWOT analysis for the product organization. Try to uncover the positive contributions and results (with the right data) as well as areas that contribute to unfulfilled goals (refer to Chapter 19 for examples of metrics). You may need to work with other cross-functional leaders to gain their perspectives. As a by-product of these cross-functional consultations, a more collaborative environment is often created.

Now that this is done, consider the contributions required from product managers. This should be fairly straightforward when you *use the Product Management Life Cycle Model as your reference.* Next, find out what's not being done in regard to the unmet goals, and try to understand what the root causes might be. For example, if a product manager fails to adequately monitor his product's performance, is it because he doesn't have financial skills? Is it because he lacks adequate data? Or is it because the task is not within his scope of responsibility. Use this type of analysis to determine what's needed for individuals based on where they are and where you need them to be. In addition, job descriptions can be rationalized based on this analysis. Here are some areas that should be considered to normalize the product manager job description:

1. Reporting relationships (manager of the product manager, etc.)
2. Principal focus areas of the job
3. Key processes utilized
4. Core competencies and experience required
5. Results and objectives
6. Cross-functional interrelationships
7. Decision rights
8. Budget authority
9. Performance standards required for promotion

Your firm's product manager staffing strategy can—and should—be fine-tuned through the continuous evaluation of product managers and their contributions. However, as you will discover, product managers will fall into different categories based on their knowledge and experience. At times, you will find that people are miscategorized or in an inappropriate job level, either because of too much experience or not enough experience. You're not likely to immediately adjust their level, so you may have to alter your strategic time horizon to make changes. One way to think about your forward-facing strategy is the tradesperson analogy and its three phases of initiation: apprentice, journeyman, and master. You can apply this method to newer populations of product managers and utilize levels such as associate product manager, product manager, and senior product manager.

When the evaluation of the population is complete and the job descriptions and levels are updated, leaders will need to concentrate their efforts on performance management of the product managers. The main areas of focus should concentrate on:

1. Guiding product managers to think and act holistically and systemically about their product's business
2. Motivating product managers to be conscientious about the performance of their products
3. Inspiring product managers to make informed, fact-based decisions
4. Making sure that product managers can effectively influence and lead others

The progress you make in these staffing strategies will ultimately result in targeted professional development programs for the product manager population.

Ensuring Ongoing Professional Development of Product Managers

One of the key activities of the leadership team should be to establish and maintain professional development programs for product managers. One way to think about this recommendation is to compare the professional development of product managers with the programs used to cultivate high-potential leaders. Not all product managers make it into the program, but there should be development pathways for all staff members. For all product managers, there should be comprehensive job descriptions for multiple job levels and criteria for moving from one job level to another, based on experience and/or time in that level. Finally, there should always be an "on-deck" plan for evolving product leaders so that the organization is prepared to take on new challenges and grow its field of solid product team leaders.

In another vein, adequate learning and development opportunities should be instituted for product managers. One of the best ways to achieve this is to analyze the profiles of all the product managers in the community as often as possible, as I discussed in the previous section. This can certainly be a part of the annual or semiannual rating and ranking routine, but I'm talking about something a little more detailed. There should be an ongoing effort to maintain competency profiles for each product manager so that experiential gaps can be tightened up and so that continuous, targeted learning and development programs can run as an undercurrent to the daily work of the product manager.

In Chapter 23, there is a brief assessment that I provided as an example for product managers. Profiles like these should be kept up to date. Moreover, explicit experiential development projects should be factored into the performance development plans or annual goal-setting programs for product managers. In Chapter 23, I also provided the product managers with both a career action planning template as well as a framework for an applied learning project.

In line with this overall focus on professional development, which is based on skill gaps, it would be a good idea to consider creating a curriculum for product managers and find targeted programs such as instructor-led training (such as those offered by Sequent), coaching (which I'll discuss later), and mentoring. Mentoring can be arranged through formal or informal contacts in your organization, usually with your executive peers or other leaders who may have a specific set of skills or characteristics.

Mentors help develop the "person," so there are no job performance goals attached to the relationship. For example, a product manager could have a leadership mentor and an engineering mentor or a work–life balance mentor. You can also encourage product managers to find their own mentors. Very often, the Human Resource department can be a helpful source of this information.

Support the Building of a Product Management Community

Because Product Management is a dynamic, interconnected living system, the firm will benefit greatly from a dynamic, interconnected, knowledge-based community of product managers. Furthermore, a well-organized Product Management community can enhance creativity, deepen understanding, and sharpen collective problem solving.

I am a strong advocate for the establishment of a vibrant Product Management community. Such a community would bring together product managers and those they work with through mutual collaboration, shared knowledge, and collective experience. These communal processes would go far to help everyone involved build on and improve their competencies and collective cognizance. The value derived from the formation of this type of community cannot be overestimated. However, deciding to build community is one thing. *Continuing and sustaining the community is another.*

The community of practice I suggest for Product Management would utilize some of the tools and techniques described throughout this book. This Product Management community of practice should serve to ensure that product managers, and others with whom they work, have a way to share knowledge, understanding, experience, and insights.

Building a community of product managers should be sponsored and supported by the executive leadership team. A community can meet in person, in video conferences, and in online forums. A community also needs a designated website where standard Product Management documentation can be kept (e.g., templates, tools, brand information, marketing guides, and style sheets) as well as for document management (for active documents and archives). Needless to say, the community website could easily house Product Master Plan virtual binders.

Part of the responsibility of community building is to cultivate an environment that reflects the mission and values of the organization. This should not be taken lightly. A collaborative culture can be encouraged and nurtured and should be rewarded. The basics of team building and leadership include behavioral attributes such as integrity, doing right by customers, clear communication, helping one another, striving for innovative ideas, and always looking to improve a process or a method. These can be instilled into the team through the leadership team's direct observable actions. This puts key leadership team members, such as the CEO or general manager, chief marketing officer, and others in a position of role model for others within the community to observe and, hopefully, emulate.

In order to build this community of practice and have it survive for the long-term, these foundational building blocks must be in place:

1. A charter and purpose
2. Proper leadership and guidance
3. An appropriate venue (i.e., an environment that promotes interaction)
4. Events and activities (e.g., lunch and learns, brown-bag meetings, webinars, and all-hands meetings)
5. Resources and funding
6. An environment that promotes learning and sharing, inside and outside of Product Management
7. Showcases and examples of best practices that include product people and cross-functional team members
8. Rewards and recognition

The Product Management community of practice should be an ongoing element of any organizational strategy. In other areas unrelated to Product Management, communities of practice are catalyzed and perpetuated in a fluid, dynamic, unplanned manner. They are held together by their members' passionate interest in learning and sharing. The benefits of this type of approach cannot be disputed.

Establishing an Environment for Creating and Sustaining Customer Partnerships

This is a critical program. Customer relationship building can be a priceless asset to companies whose executives provide the resources for this unique structure. An example of this would be to have your most important customers come together twice a year to help in the shaping of product and portfolio priorities. If your company is global and your customer's travel expenses are limited, hold regional partnership meetings instead. These are generally more easily carried out for business-to-business organizations. The closer your relationship with your customers, the greater your ability to gain access to different customer target groups for extended anthropomorphic research. Moreover, this helps you build closer partnerships with your Sales organization and account managers.

Investing in Market Research to Support the Product Teams

The investment in a robust Market Research or Market Intelligence function would be an invaluable investment to support product managers and marketers alike. In the Introduction to this book, I described how the benchmarking I carried out suggested that best-in-class companies religiously focused their efforts on the marketplace. Enabling an outside-in view of the world can serve as an inspiration to product teams. However, it is unwarranted to place the entire burden of all industry, competitive, and customer research in the laps of the product managers. Certainly, the product managers are responsible for making sure they're in touch with the markets in which they operate, but there are times they can use a little help and some additional resources. Market analysts should be assigned tasks related to uncovering industry trends, competitor product analysis, and customer segment research. They can also help in securing syndicated research or in securing research reports from the corporate Competitive Intelligence organization (which is sometimes not fully accessible to product managers).

Market research at the product-line level is more difficult to carry out and requires that analysts have more product-specific knowledge. Doing reverse engineering on a competitor's product is not something that can be performed by analysts, but they would benefit from seeing the parts on the table, the bill of materials, and other "parts" that would help them in better understanding your products as well as those of the competitors.

Also, corporate or divisional research projects are often undertaken by the Marketing department. That would include brand studies, mystery shopping programs, and other in-market voices of the customer research. I urge the leadership team to make sure that product managers are aware of the existence of these programs and are apprised of the outcomes. All this information should be made available on the product managers' community website.

Lastly, I need to talk about supporting customer or field visits. I am a big proponent of these visits. When carried out appropriately (meaning, in small, cross-functional teams), with specific objectives and expert guidance, these can be extremely valuable. When I hear that there is no money in the travel budget for customer visits, I feel that the business is at a big disadvantage. There is a routine and a protocol for carrying out these visits (refer back to Chapter 8 to find out more) so that your teams can be advantaged by this unique experience.

COACHING PRODUCT MANAGERS

Coaching is important in every organization. It's especially important in Product Management because in most companies, even with the best processes and documents, people and culture seem to take a front seat. When people don't help one another or don't share knowledge or experience, everyone suffers. When people don't think they're part of a bigger picture, the organization suffers. In today's busy companies, managers do so much "work," they often neglect the development and growth of their employees. It is very troubling for me to see these omissions, having worked in more nurturing environments earlier in my career. Therefore, I urge you to support and guide people, especially the product managers.

However, there are several things that help. People generally improve their performance when they know *why* they're doing what they're supposed to do, and they learn best when they see *how* work is done. This means that if you're the boss of the product managers, you have more experience than your employees, and you can demonstrate and guide their work. What you want to inspire is a culture of action and doing, not overanalyzing and discussing.

Coaching is complex, and it's hard work. That's why many managers avoid it. The other reason is that they don't know how. I'm going to provide you with a few ideas that you might be able to utilize so that you can become more effective and thereby improve the effectiveness of your product managers. It should be noted that coaching is not a one-time event—it's ongoing and is part of your job responsibility. You may need to coach from time to time, or you may need to coach daily. More often than not, the need for coaching usually comes about when you notice an undesirable behavior or poor result or you receive a complaint from another colleague about your employee. Unfortunately, this is usually when managers put their coaching hats on. This should not be the only time you coach. For example, if you set aside five to ten minutes a week with each employee, you would be able to do quick check-ins to make sure that work is proceeding, to provide a short lesson, or to learn if an intervention is needed. Just think, that's only four to eight hours per year per person.

Think of it this way. Coaching helps you guide employees. When you're coaching, you're in position number two and the employee is in position number one—which is often out of most people's paradigms for the manager–employee relationship. Coaches receive their reward from building a success in their employee. To achieve optimal outcomes they should always seek to fine-tune their coaching methods.

Because coaching is situational, the following situations may arise when coaching is needed the most:

1. If there are behavioral problems with the employee, you should try to understand what's happening, determine the root cause, and make suggestions to rectify the problem.

2. There may be the general coaching of your own employees or other manager's employees so that others can gain from your insight, experience, or suggestions. (By the way, this is the most rewarding coaching that you can carry out and should be carried out with the greatest frequency.)

3. You may need to provide remedial training and guidance if you notice weakness in a specific competency or just to keep the employee focused on performance objectives.

4. You may need to coach a person out of the organization for consistent underperformance or other behavioral actions.

Good coaches of product managers are what I call "product therapists." They listen well and ask really good questions. This, of course, gets product managers to think about situations and to develop the brain wiring that enables them to learn more. In other words, they help product managers to be better learners. However, the real ideal in coaching is to change something in the employee, set a goal, and then measure the goal, which is why coaching must be ongoing.

And as the fourth entry in the list above states, sometimes you need to coach employees out of their job. One of the key facts is that being a product manager is not right for everyone. If a person is not cut out for the task at hand, keeping him in his role offers little benefit to him, the department, or the company. It's an unfortunate but real corporate reality.

Overall, though, coaching is a rewarding, gratifying part of being a leader of product managers. When others learn that you're a good coach (word does get around), you may have more people knocking on your door. Just make sure you put a sign on your door that says "Product Therapy—Please Make an Appointment."

At the Heart of Business: Product Management Matters

In the business climate of the twenty-first century, companies must hone their operations to become more strategic, agile competitors. I firmly believe that the best approach to achieving this goal is through an enhanced utilization of the function of Product Management. As reinforced throughout this book: *Product Management is the systemic, holistic business management of products and services.*

Most leaders have an extensive background of corporate experiences and perspectives, all of which have contributed to their unique understanding of Product Management and organizational dynamics. You have witnessed the effects of new strategies, leadership changes, organizational realignments, and other structural adjustments. Therefore, you know that many corporate changes and reorganizations are fraught with challenges and unfulfilled expectations. In such cases, the changes have detrimental impacts that include the following:

- *A chain reaction that leads to more changes.* This compounds the challenges for employees (including product managers) as they struggle to understand their roles and responsibilities.

- *A static effect that leaves daily work activities unchanged.* As a result, product managers and others see radically increased workloads

■ *A degradation of continuous learning.* By not appreciating the path taken in the organization, newer leadership teams tend to repeat the mistakes of the past.

In the face of all this, I believe senior leaders can be a force for positive change by properly aligning and strengthening the function of Product Management within the organization. To achieve this, all senior leaders must agree on a unified definition of the function of Product Management and the organizational design required to bring this about. When this is done, leaders will notice that:

1. Functional silos are minimized.
2. Team members focus on markets and on defeating the competition rather than one other.
3. Strategies are clearly understood so that everyone marches in the same direction
4. The stage is set for continuous improvement of all business practices that support or enable the creation of innovative, successful products.

No matter where you are in your firm's spectrum of organizational development, *if you are serious about achieving greater levels of market success* with a robust, optimized portfolio of products, then you need an aligned senior leadership team and an army of product people with the right skills and experiences to carry out these jobs. These people should be organized into effective cross-functional product teams who have the resources and budgets to do what's necessary to run their products and product lines like businesses. Furthermore, to ensure success, product managers and their teams need a good toolbox filled with processes, templates, and other guidelines. Bottom line: the role of senior leadership is to ensure that product managers and their teams have every advantage to contribute to the results needed to achieve market victories.

MODULE 6

THE PRODUCT MANAGER'S TOOLBOX

A toolbox, by definition, contains the tools to help improve any project or undertaking. Consistent with the entire theme of *The Product Manager's Desk Reference (PMDR)*, I have included a variety of tools throughout the book: templates, tables, figures, and other useful diagrams. Their purpose has been to illustrate principles, demonstrate usage, and provide you with the formats that will help in carrying out your work and building your career.

CUSTOMER VISIT PLAN TEMPLATE

Name of customer's company _____

Address of customer _____

Customer contact information _____

Account manager's name and information _____

Product manager's name and information _____

Date of planned visit: _____

Objective or purpose: *[Why is this visit being carried out? What do you want to learn? Is this visit a singular visit to one customer, a series of visits to one customer, or is it one customer visit in a series of multiple customer visits?]*
_____
_____

Customers to be visited: *[Names of people, job titles, etc.]*
_____
_____

Guidelines and ground rules: *[e.g., voice or video recording, picture taking, security rules, nondisclosure]*
_____
_____

Team members who are attending: *[Names and titles (e.g., product manager, engineer, marketing manager, account manager). Also, what role will each play (e.g., observer, interviewer, video recording, workflow diagrams, photography, etc.)?]*
_____
_____

Agenda and structure: *[How will the visit be structured (e.g., introductory session, presentations, tours, on-site employee visits, interviews, observations, etc.)?]*
_____
_____

Capture the visit: *[Use this space to write down what you heard or observed. Note workflows, skills used, timing, difficult activities or actions by different customer types or users as they "do what they do."]*

_____

_____

Debrief: *[Capture all observations based on what all visitors learned, observed, or inferred. Use this data to prepare a final visit report or presentation for cross-functional team stakeholders.]*

_____

_____

Additional notes, actions, or follow up: *[e.g., thank you note for customer and for team members]*

_____

_____

CUSTOMER VISIT PLAN TEMPLATE

FUNCTIONAL SUPPORT PLAN TEMPLATE

Function		Date	
Product Name		Business Unit/Division	
Project Name		Project Number	
Name of Team Member		Role (core/associate/advisory)	
Phone (office)		Alternate Phone	
E-mail Address		Alternate Contact Info.	
Manager's Name		Manager's Phone	

Other Pertinent Information to Describe This Functional Support Plan

Life Cycle Phase	
Planning *[Specify Feasibility, Definition]*	
NPI *[Specify Development or Launch]*	
Post-Launch *[Specify Growth, Maturity, Decline]*	

Deliverables Provided by This Function to Other Functions

Describe the Deliverable	To Whom Is the Deliverable Due?	Date Promised

Deliverables Provided to This Function From Other Functions

Describe the Deliverable	From Whom Is the Deliverable Due?	Date Promised

Resources to be Provided
[Include names, skills, and any other important clarifying information]

Name and Core Competency to Be Provided	Time Allotted (e.g., Hrs/Wk, Duration)	Other Information

Additional FSP staffing information to clarify the resource requirements:
Budget or funding needed

Funding Category	This Year	Next Year	Year After

Critical dates and milestones:
Risk assessment:
Performance

OPPORTUNITY STATEMENT TEMPLATE

Name of customer's comp. _____

Name of this opportunity _____

Idea type or category _____

Source of the idea _____

Date of the original evaluation _____

Product manager's name _____

Name of engineer _____

Name of marketing manager _____

Name of other evaluator _____

Situation summary: *[What is the customer's problem? Describe how this need was uncovered.]*
_____
_____

For whom is this opportunity intended? *[Market segment or customer target type.]*
_____
_____

How would this opportunity solve the customer's problem?
_____
_____

How is this opportunity aligned with the division or company's strategy?
_____
_____

What characteristics of this market make it an attractive opportunity?
_____
_____

Who are the primary competitors?
_____
_____

High-level financials: *[Provide a rough estimate of unit volumes, pricing, revenue, and possible cost targets.]*
_____
_____

Recommendation: *[Should we request funding or approval to move to the Feasibility phase, or should we reject and file?]*
_____
_____

PRODUCT POSITIONING STATEMENT TEMPLATE

Name of Product or Enhancement: _____   **Name of Product Manager:** _____

_____   **Name of Engineer:** _____

Date Prepared _____   **Name of Marketing Manager:** _____

Life Cycle Phase _____   **Name(s) of Other team member(s):** _____

This product is designed for (a specific customer target group or market segment):

_____

_____

A specific customer	. . . with this proven need	. . . is satisfied by this feature/attribute
User	1. 2. 3.	1. 2. 3.
Influencer	1. 2. 3.	1. 2. 3.
Decision Maker	1. 2. 3.	1. 2. 3.
Buyer	1. 2. 3.	1. 2. 3.

BASIC ELEMENTS OF THE VALUE PROPOSITION

The customer (target) will benefit from using this product because it helps them:
(How will the customer be able to acheive some value, either in qualitative or quantitative terms?)

_____

_____

The product is unique because:

_____

_____

It compares favorably to available competitive products because:

_____

_____

COMPETITIVE ANALYSIS DOSSIER

Competitor Name: _____

Company URL: _____

Date of this profile: _____

Address information (primary location) City, State, Country, Province	
Phone Numbers	
Key Executives	
Contact information for relevant divisions — including key executives.	

Introduction to the company (provide sources and links)

_____

_____

Industry (industries) in which this company participates (sector, sub-sector) and any pertinent descriptors: _____

_____

Identify and discuss the brand image, market posture, or reputation of this company (provide sources and links)_____

_____

Summarize analyst opinions or other people who refer to this company and what they say.

_____

_____

COMPETITIVE ANALYSIS DOSSIER

Strategic Posture

Data Needed	Data Source	Implication (Intelligence)
The stated mission for the company and for each division.		
The stated vision for the company and each division.		
The stated strategy for the company and each division.		

Customer Profiles

Data Needed	Data Source	Implication (Intelligence)
Primary value delivery model (B2B, B2C, B2B2C, etc.)		
What are their current primary B2B segments (verticals, geographies, etc.)?		
Who are their current primary customers (B2B)? • List of major accounts (top 10, top 50) • Have major accounts moved to other competitors?		
What are their primary B2C market segments (demographics, geographies, etc.).		
Who could be prospective customers? Why? Are you at risk?		
What products do these customers buy?		
Why do they buy those products?		
What is the purchasing process?		
Through which channel do they purchase? Or repurchase?		

COMPETITIVE ANALYSIS DOSSIER

Customer Satisfaction/Customer Experience

Data Needed	Data Source	Implication (Intelligence)
Do you have any insight on the degree to which customers are satisfied or dissatisfied?		
Identify vulnerabilities to exploit.		
What is it like to do business with this company? When you contact the call center? Send an email? Work with a technician?		

Positioning

Data Needed	Data Source	Implication (Intelligence)
What is the stated positioning?		
Write their positioning statement		
Are their claims defensible?		
Main source of competitive advantage (e.g., technology, innovation, people, geography, quality, supply chain, systems, etc.).		

Market Share and Coverage

Data Needed	Data Source	Implication (Intelligence)
Market share for the company.		
Geographies where they do business.		

Financial Data

Data Needed	Data Source	Implication (Intelligence)
Current company profit and loss, cash positions, and balance sheets.		
Signals of financial strength or vulnerability (trends in cash flow, equity, share performance, etc.).		
Divisional finances or product line financial data.		
Key ratios - Liquidity, efficiency, profitability		
Amount spent on R&D		

Their Competitors

Data Needed	Data Source	Implication (Intelligence)
Name each of this company's competitors and the degree to which each competitor is a threat.		
What does this competitor feel threatened by?		

Marketing Mix — Product

Data Needed	Data Source	Implication (Intelligence)
What are the products in their portfolio?		
What is the stated or understood strategy for each product or product line?		
Draw a product line hierarchy for each product line in each division (as is relevant for this profile). Name each product, including version, release number, or other identifier.		

COMPETITIVE ANALYSIS DOSSIER

Data Needed	Data Source	Implication (Intelligence)
Number of product lines.		
Number of products within each line.		
Provide pictures, designs, diagrams, UI's, etc. of each relevant product.		
Provide pictures or designs of packaging, box styles, colors, etc.		
What is the value proposition for each product?		
How is each product positioned?		
Technologies		
Architectures/platforms		
Development methods/tools		
Performance		
Standards or regulatory guidelines they comply with		
Unique packaging methods		
Manufacturing methods		
Where are components sourced?		

Marketing Mix — Pricing and Value Creation for Customers

Data Needed	Data Source	Implication (Intelligence)
Pricing for each product		
Known discounting activities		
Sales person discretion at setting discounts		

Marketing Mix — Advertising, Promotion, and Customer Education

Data Needed	Data Source	Implication (Intelligence)
Types of promotional activities used (trade shows, advertising, thought leadership articles, executive speeches).		
Known advertising programs and methods (traditional, digital, integrated programs).		
Known agency or creative relationships.		
Brand management programs.		

Marketing Mix – Sales and Distribution Channels

Data Needed	Data Source	Implication (Intelligence)
Moving goods or services from point of origin to end customer (direct, indirect, re-seller, broker agent). Create channel maps.		
Web presence and the degree to which the Web is a channel.		
Sales force size and expertise.		
Sales methods (consultative, selling boxes)		
Sales compensation.		
Distributor compensation.		
Distributor stock positions (hold inventory?).		

ALLIANCES OR JOINT VENTURES FOR MARKETING, SELLING, PRODUCTION, ETC.

What are they saying on the Internet?

Data Needed	Data Source	Implication (Intelligence)

What do you hear from former employees?

Data Needed	Data Source	Implication (Intelligence)

What are you reading about in the media?

Data Needed	Data Source	Implication (Intelligence)

Competitor SWOT

Strengths (what, data, why?)	Opportunities for you (what, data, why?)
Weaknesses (what, data, why?)	Vulnerabilities/threats (what, data, why?)

Intelligence Summary — Write a summary of key findings and overall intelligence you've gleaned from the data in this dossier.

_____

_____

Conclusions and Strategic Actions — What do you think this competitor's next move will be?

_____

_____

BUSINESS CASE TEMPLATE

Cover Page

Business Case Title or Subject

Product Team Name	
Project Title	
Product Manager Name	
Project Manager Name	
Category or Classification	
Business Unit or Division Name	
Date	

Product Team Members

Name:	Title, Dept./Function:
Name:	Title, Dept./Function:
Name:	Title, Dept./Function:
Name:	Title, Dept./Function:

Approvals:

Name:	Title, Dept.
Name:	Title, Dept.
Name:	Title, Dept.

Version Control Information:

Version Number	Date	Document Owner	Notes/Reasons

SECTION 1—EXECUTIVE SUMMARY

Introduction: *[Brief overview of the purpose of this case and the desired outcome or decision required.]*
_____
_____

Description: *[Describe the project and the reason for this investment and the major issues that will be addressed.]*
_____
_____

Industry, market, and customer attributes: *[What are the major customer or market needs that are addressed through this case? State the market size, revenue potential, targeted segments, etc.]*
_____
_____

Assumptions and Risks: *[What are the major assumptions, including financial, operational, technological that are discussed in detail and which could impact the probability of success?]*
_____
_____

Key Financial Indicators

	Year 1	Year 2	Year 3	TOTAL
Revenue				
Cost of Goods Sold				
Gross Margin				
Gross Margin %				
Expenses				
EBITDA				
Net Present Value				
Headcount Estimates				
Capital Purchases				
Payback Period				
Cumulative Disc. Cash Flow				

SECTION 2—FRAMING THE CASE

History, Chronology of Events, and/or Current Situation

Part 1: *[Framing is the first part of the investment justification process. The purpose is to discuss the purpose of, or reason for, the Business Case and the factors that led to its creation. This section should also contain any data to confirm when the product needs to be in the market—the market window—and why.]*

_____

_____

Part 2: *[Each Business Case should contain a funding request. This should be a carefully crafted statement that clearly articulates exactly how much money is being requested initially, and in the future.]*

_____

_____

Funding Required	Year 1	Year 2	Year 3	Total
Expense money (people, supplies, etc.)				
Capital expenses (equipment, facilities, etc.)				

SECTION 3—BUSINESS NEED AND/OR STRATEGIC ALIGNMENT

Describe how this opportunity contributes to the goals of the organization in terms of strategic fit and overall benefits to the business, either economically or qualitatively:

_____

_____

SECTION 4—MARKET ANALYSIS

Describe the industry environment and the competitors that operate within the industry. Include detailed data that demonstrates your understanding of the dynamics of the industry, why it is attractive, and how your product will take advantage of the industry situation:

_____

_____

This section should further provide a *comprehensive competitive analysis* to describe each competitor, the products they sell, and how the investment for this product will help your company to win against the competition. The table below may help you in this activity.

_____

_____

Name the competitor and the products with which you intend to or already compete.	What is the source of this competitor's advantage?	What are its main weaknesses?	How do you capitalize on what you know and have researched to beat the competition using this investment?

Describe the *market segments* and the *customer types* within those segments. Make sure that you describe the characteristics based on demographics, geography, and other parameters, depending on whether the segments focus on businesses or consumers. Describe the underlying needs of these customer types and how those needs were validated. You will need to demonstrate that the product can meet the needs of these customers better than any other competitor's product:

_____

_____

SECTION 5—PRODUCT DESCRIPTION

This section conveys the description and characteristics of the product or service. You may describe or reiterate the main needs of customers within each segment and the targets within those segments so that you can show how those needs will be met. Helpful sources to complete this include existing marketing collateral, the product requirements document (PRD), and the product positioning statement.

Write the product description:

Diagrams and other descriptors: *[If needed, add pictures, diagrams, or reference models that will add clarity to the product description.]*

SECTION 6—THE PROJECT PROPOSAL

When new or enhanced products and/or services are developed, or if non-product projects are undertaken, a project plan is created to show how multiple organizations will participate, with what deliverables and committed dates. The project leader (which could be a product manager or project manager) will need to articulate the goals for the project, articulate the deliverables, commit to specific dates, and call out any cross-team dependencies. Define critical path items and make sure you have suggested ways to mitigate risks of delays or how to fill slack time.

Prepare a project description and summary:

What is being carried out and why?

Who will be working on the project?

How are the project's activities going to be carried out?

Provide a project schedule as a table indicating major milestones and deliverables. Also, provide any visualization that indicates key activities, durations, deliverables, and interdependencies.

BUSINESS CASE TEMPLATE

Project Resources Required:

Describe the number of people needed across all functional organizations. Each function should provide a statement of its commitment to the product team should the investment be approved. Each department, in effect, supplies a Functional Support Plan (FSP) for the Business Case.

Each FSP should describe the number of resources, skill sets, timing, budgets, and any other characterization required to indicate what will be done, by whom, and when. A table may be used to summarize this with detailed FSPs as an attachment or appendix to the Business Case.

Task or Deliverable	Person Responsible	Start Date	End Date	Dependency	Task Budget	Possible Risks

Launch Support

Since all product projects need to be launched, it might prove helpful to include a high-level Launch Plan in this Business Case. It should spell out the dates, resources needed, and any other pertinent information to ensure that the product hits the market at the right time with the right amount of executive support.

SECTION 7—ASSUMPTIONS, FORECASTS, AND FINANCIALS

Every Business Case contains a set of assumptions that guide the forecasts of unit volumes, pricing, revenue, and cash flow. Scenarios can be used to provide the right context for a variety of outcomes under varying assumptions. In this section, identify each scenario and the assumptions for that scenario. Provide back-up data in the Appendix as needed.

Scenario 1:
_____
_____

Scenario 2:
_____
_____

Financial Analysis

In this section you'll be preparing estimates and forecasts based on the scenarios built earlier and the described assumptions. The assumptions should be clearly stated and include rationale for choosing a specific forecast. Make sure to include best case, worst case, and most likely case. There are two financial templates that you can use to capture your "base case" and subsequent scenarios. Use as many as you need to portray the scenarios you created. The following major categories should be included in your financial analysis and forecasts:

1. Profit and loss (P&L) estimates
   a. Unit prices and volumes (sales mix)
   b. Cost of goods
   c. Expenses by function

2. Cash flow
   a. Timing of inflows and outflows
   b. Capital expenditures needed (amount and timing)
   c. Discounted cash flow (and NPV)

3. Balance sheet impacts to consider
   a. Asset additions, retirements, depletion, or write-offs
   b. Facilities added or taken off-line
   c. Cash needed to fund the project or notes/debt to finance the project

4. Cost of capital (the discount rate) for discounting cash flows (check with Finance dept.)

5. Financing alternatives (make/buy, lease/buy) for capital equipment (if needed)

6. Depreciation and amortization factors

7. Study period (number of months or years covered by this case)—when does the investment have to start, and when does it end? Also, make sure to identify whether the case covers calendar years or company-specific fiscal years.

8. Break-even point (volume, currency, and/or time)

9. Tax rates, if appropriate

10. Sensitivity analysis (price, cost, volume) and impact on profitability

11. Cost/benefit analysis for specific projects (including goals of cost savings, avoidance, or increased revenue)

Base Case Financials—Business as Usual (or Base Case)

Use this financial profile to show how the business might perform if no investment is made.

	Current Year (CY)	CY + 1	CY + 2	CY + 3
Forecast Unit Volume				
Unit Price				
TOTAL REVENUE				
Cost of Goods				
Gross Margin				
Gross Margin %				
DIRECT EXPENSES				
– Marketing				
– Sales				
– R&D/IT/Dev				
– Customer Service				
– Operations				
– Finance				
– Other				
TOTAL DIRECT EXPENSES				
EBITDA				
Depreciation & Amortization				
Corporate Allocations				
Other Indirect/ Uncontrollable Expenses				
Taxes				
NET INCOME				

Business Case Financials—Scenario 1

Use this, and successive financial profiles, to show how each scenario will influence the business and financial outcomes.

	Current Year (CY)	CY + 1	CY +2	CY + 3
Forecast Unit Volume				
Unit Price				
TOTAL REVENUE				
Cost of Goods				
Gross Margin				
Gross Margin %				
DIRECT EXPENSES				
– Marketing				
– Sales				
– R&D/IT/Dev.				
– Customer Service				
– Operations				
– Finance				
– Other				
TOTAL DIRECT EXPENSES				
EBITDA				
Depreciation & Amortization				
Corporate Allocations				
Other Indirect/ Uncontrollable Expenses				
Taxes				
NET INCOME				

BUSINESS CASE TEMPLATE

After a thorough financial analysis is carried out, comparing scenarios and outcomes, any further information to clarify the information provided in this section should be provided here.

SECTION 8—IMPLEMENTATION AND OPERATIONAL ACTION PLANS

This section addresses the practical realities of the Business Case. Essentially, it describes what is to be done if the investment is approved, when, and how. This section can include any information regarding production, facilities, timing, people, systems, supply chain, logistics, and anything required to support a new product or an enhancement to an existing product. Action-oriented Functional Support Plans can serve as a useful way to think about operationalizing the business of the product and in supporting the product after it's in the market.

Use the following table as a way to describe what happens across the product development, launch, and post launch phases:

	During the Development phase	As the Launch is being carried out	After the product is launched (Post-Launch Audit)
What work is being carried out?			
What are the dates or milestones (when)?			
How will the work be carried out?			
Who will carry out the work?			

SECTION 9—RISKS AND CONTINGENCY PLANS

If one were to examine the constraints, dependencies, project plan elements, and a host of other variables, it would become clear that any Business Case can be plagued by a variety of risks. Using all available data, the team needs to view the project very carefully to identify the risk areas. What are the specific risks involved? You may look at any dimension of this case, or any functional area, and ask the question: What if? By understanding what can go wrong, you'll have a better understanding of how to mitigate those risks or to have a tactical plan to counter the situation if it arises.

Referring to the table used in Section 8, two rows have been added to identify and address possible risks.

	During the Development phase	As the Launch is being carried out	After the product is launched (Post-Launch Audit)
What work is being carried out?			
What are the dates or milestones (when)?			
How will the work be carried out?			
Who will carry out the work?			
What could happen?			
– Probability?			
– Magnitude?			
– Impact?			
What will be put in place to address the risks? (the mitigation or contingency action plan)			

Clarify any additional risks or any important contingency plans here:

BUSINESS CASE TEMPLATE

SECTION 10—RECOMMENDATION

One of the last activities for the Business Case is to communicate to management your opinion about the project. To achieve this, you will need to draw appropriate conclusions and include your recommendation for go or no-go. It is important to remember that the positive outcome you might envision as you begin to assemble this case may indeed be different from what the facts, data, and assumptions reveal. Remember, just because your team invested a considerable amount of time in developing the Case does not mean it should be a go. That would obviate the need for the Case; therefore, if the Case just does not make good business sense or doesn't fit with the profile of investments expected by management, then incorporate good business judgment and do not recommend.

SECTION 11—APPENDICES

- Charts, graphs, etc.
- Detailed supporting data
- Citations and references
- Consultant studies

PRODUCT STRATEGY TEMPLATE

The purpose of this template is to summarize the basic steps in the formulation of a strategy for your product or product line. Many templates provide you with a fill-in-the-blanks form. The strategy formulation process is more complex and requires a fair amount of research, data collection, analysis, and thoughtful insight. In essence, it is a complex exercise that should be done as often as required for the product. To carry out the exercise, the product as a business strategy model is used represented by the diagram shown here and referenced in Chapter 10.

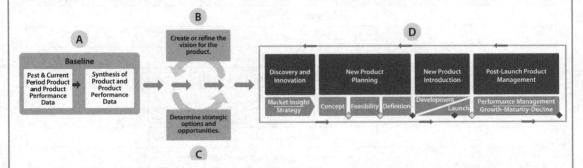

This model is divided into four major areas as indicated by the letters A, B, C, and D. However, for the purposes of this template, only areas A, B, and C are included. The template is essentially a summarization of the steps used, and the data collected to achieve three major goals:

A) Identify where you are with the product.
B) Refine your vision or end state for the product.
C) Determine future strategic options and opportunities.
D) This area is not covered in this template because it represents the outcomes and opportunities that are outlined in C, which are fed, along with other inputs, into the New Product Development (NPD) funnel.

Captured from the essence of Chapter 10, steps A, B, and C are summarized here:

Step A: Establish a baseline for the business of the product. This gives you a focal point that allows you to compare where you've been to where you are so you can determine where you want to go. Setting the baseline demands that you have the most relevant product and business data available because such data is to be synthesized into a product snapshot.

Step B: Formulate or reformulate your vision for the product. To establish your vision as the driving force for the product or portfolio, you must be sure you know where you intend to focus your efforts and the reasons *why* you chose that focal point. You may not have to *create* your *why* from scratch if you have an existing product. You may just need to refine where you want to go.

Step C: Identify strategic options. You can achieve this by identifying the possible future elements of the marketing mix, the desired industry and competitive postures, and any other supporting business functions, which need to be brought into the future state equations.

The work involved in Step A is detailed and complex because of the level of data required to be collected. However, a simple diagram provides the basis from which to plan your work and organize your data.

The main focal point is the data element shown roughly in the center of the matrix. Your goal is to identify a cell and get the data that would occupy that cell. Although it is not realistic or physically possible to put the data in this small cell, the actual data would be collected in many other documents. Think of this as a map to guide you in that data collection. The current year is to the right of the product element, and the prior two years are to the left (CY – 1 represents the prior year, and CY – 2 represents the year before that).

CY – 2	CY – 1	Product/Market Element	Current Year
		External Indicators	
		– Industry activity	
		– Competitor activity	
		– Customers/market segments	
		Internal Indicators	
		– Company financial situation	
		– Skills/capabilities	
		Retrospective Roadmap Information	
		– Features	
		– Models or versions	
		– Designs or styles	
		– Colors or sizes	
		– Technology used	
		– Performance levels	
		– Safety elements	
		– Competitive positioning	
		Product Life Cycle Performance	
		– Revenue	
		– Gross margin	
		– Market share	
		– Pricing programs	
		– Promotional activity	
		– Distribution channel activity	
		Product Operational Performance	
		– Product quality	
		– Customer satisfaction	
		– Repair and return data	
		– Inventory turns	

PRODUCT STRATEGY TEMPLATE

DATA SYNTHESIS

After you've completed the data collection project, you have to synthesize all of the data and analyze it. To do this, you use a SWOT analysis for the product or product line. Refer to Chapter 10 to learn more about why the product level SWOT is most important. The most important thing is to make sure that yje information you populate in each quadrant can be substantiated.

Your subsequent analysis, both using the SWOT as a guide and in extrapolating meaning from the other data elements, will provide you with a perspective on how your product is doing. Now you're ready to share this with your management in a formal strategic review. The product strategy review should be organized as follows:

1. Introduction to the product (including name and vision statement)
2. Market review
3. Financial review
4. Marketing mix and business performance review
5. Key performance indicators and their significance to the product
6. Future opportunities and considerations

Step B involves recasting the vision for the product. If you believe you collected enough data and are going to update your vision (or where you see the product several years into the future), you can report this in the strategic review. You can also leave the vision as is.

Step C involves considering future strategic options. This is set forth in a similar fashion as the Step A process; that is, you can use a matrix as your guideline to propel your vision for the product into the future. In this case, the future is divided into three segments: opportunities to pursue in one year or less, opportunities in the next year or two, and opportunities three or more years into the future. Each cell in the table can be populated with information and action plans.

Product/Market Element	Less than 1 year	1–2 years	3 or more years
External Market Focus			
– What industries will you focus on?			
– What products will you compete with?			
–Which segments or customer types will you pursue?			
Internal Support			
– How much money will you need?			
– What skills will you need?			
Product Roadmap Elements			
– How will you evolve the product's functionality?			
– Which models or versions will you introduce?			
– How will designs or styles change?			
– What technologies or architectures are to be used?			
Other Marketing Mix Strategies			
– How will pricing strategies change?			
– What type of promotional strategies will be needed?			
– How will channel strategies evolve?			
Future Life Cycle & Strategic Performance			
– What unit volumes and revenues are anticipated?			
– What market share will you obtain?			
– What quality guidelines will you follow?			
– What customer satisfaction metrics do you seek?			
– What is the accepted level of inventory turns?			

Once you assemble the future state plans within each cell, you will likely need to focus on selecting from a variety of opportunities. Each opportunity will have financial, human resource, and higher-level strategic implications. This is where the product manager and the team will begin making decisions about what to pursue and why. Some elements will wind up in the annual budget or business plan for the product, and others may end up as place-holders, which, when appropriate, will require a Business Case as the document to justify the investment.

PRODUCT STRATEGY TEMPLATE

PRODUCT MARKETING PLAN TEMPLATE

The Marketing Plan for the product is a Functional Support Plan from the marketing department. Its purpose is to identify explicit activities and deliverables to support the product at various phases of its life cycle, both domestically and internationally. For new products or product enhancements, this Marketing Plan maps the product's pathway to the market. You will find that many of the sections of this plan capitalize on work you carry out to support other documents as well. This means that the data collected in support of other product-related activities can be used here or updated as required.

You can use this plan for new products or existing products, even if its preparation doesn't coincide with your annual budgeting cycle. However, you may be called upon to update this plan during your annual or semiannual budgeting process.

Even though this Marketing Plan is different than a standard divisional or corporate Marketing Plan, it must link to these plans in a hierarchical manner, as shown in the following diagram and as depicted in Chapter 15.

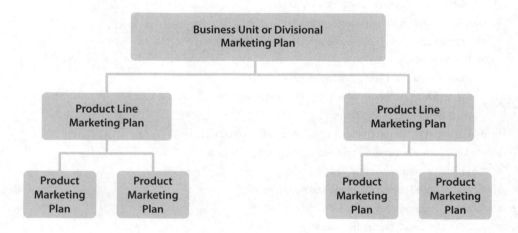

Finally, it is up to the product manager to know how the marketing function is organized. This is important because there may be sections of the product Marketing Plan that may require input or support from other marketing subfunctions, including:

- Competitive intelligence
- Industry analyst relations
- Corporate marketing
- Solutions marketing
- Creative organizations
- Public relations

- Event planning
- Global marketing
- Strategic marketing
- Alliance marketing
- Marketing policy

Marketing Plan Outline

The first step in the creation of the Marketing Plan for the product is to have a general outline. You may wish to change this for your own organization's structure. This outline is a good starting point.

1. Executive summary
2. Strategic context
3. The market environment for the product
   a. Industry and competitive activities
   b. Market segments and customer targets
4. The Marketing Mix strategies and tactics
   a. Product (description plus value proposition and positioning documents)
   b. Pricing strategy
   c. Promotional plans and programs to drive demand
      i. Corporate programs which require mandatory participation
      ii. Product-specific programs
   d. Place or distribution channels to deliver products & services
5. Marketing alliances used to gain access to other market areas
6. International marketing activities
7. Product launches being planned or being carried out
8. Sales training programs needed
9. Additional research programs needed
10. Any other deliverables required to be provided by Marketing to other functions, and other deliverables required by Marketing from other functions.
11. Integrated budgets for all programs
12. Measurements and metrics
13. Risks
14. Appendices and supporting material

SECTION 1—EXECUTIVE SUMMARY

Describe the market environment for the product.

Marketing Program Summary: *[List or describe each of the major marketing activities that will be used to support the product. This is not just for promotional programs. It should include any investments that will have to be sustained by the Marketing department.]*

_____

_____

Alignment: *[How do these marketing investments fit with the strategy of the division or company, and how are they linked to other Marketing Plans and programs? (This may include other product lines or divisional activities.)]*

_____

_____

Assumptions and Risks: *[What are the major assumptions being used within this plan?]*

_____

_____

Key Marketing Investments and Expected Returns:

	Current Year	Expected Returns	Next Year	Expected Returns
Product Investments				
Promotional Programs				
Inbound Research				

SECTION 2—STRATEGIC CONTEXT

Marketing Plans represent outcomes from strategy formulation activities. In this section, describe the overarching strategy for the product and how the marketing plans contained in this document are linked to that strategy.

SECTION 3—THE MARKETING ENVIRONMENT FOR THE PRODUCT

This section describes the three main elements that comprise the market: the industry, competitors, and customers.

Section 3.1—Industry: [The environment of the industry should be described. In which industry areas is the product sold? What are the trends that have been observed? Why is this industry attractive? Refer to elements such as industry size, industry growth rates, and other relevant facts.]
_____
_____

Section 3.2—Competition: [Describe the competitive environment for the product. Which products, from which competitors, do you compete with? What is the market share for each competitor's product? What differentiates your product from the competitors? How will you win in the market with this product? Use the table below as a guide.]
_____
_____

Name the competitor and the products with which you intend to or already compete.	What is the its this competitor's advantage?	What are its main weaknesses?	How do you capitalize on what you know and have researched to beat the competition using this investment?

Section 3.3—Market Segments and Customer Targets: [Describe the characteristics based on demographics, geography, and other parameters, depending on whether the segments focus on businesses or consumers. Describe the underlying needs of these customer types and how those needs were validated. You will need to demonstrate that the product can meet the needs of these customers better than any competitor's product.]
_____
_____

SECTION 4—THE MARKETING MIX

The marketing mix is represented by product, pricing, promotion, and place or channel. These are the control levers of a marketing machine that controls marketing execution. This section is divided into those four subsections of the marketing mix. However, there are some general guidelines to follow. One mix element is not usually changed on its own. It is changed within the context of other mix elements, depending on the strategic intent for the product and for the organization overall.

Section 4.1—The Product: [*Provide a comprehensive description of the product. Make sure to articulate the most important needs addressed by the product and indicate the specific market segment or customer target for which this product was created.*]

_____

_____

Now, relate the specific needs of that segment or target to the features within the product. Then describe the value or benefit for that customer. This must be in the customer's terms because it sets the stage for the value proposition and how the product will be positioned. Use the table below as your guide.

Segment or Customer Target	Need	Feature	Benefit

Diagrams and other descriptors: [*If needed, add pictures, diagrams, or reference models that will add clarity to the product description.*]

_____

_____

Product Forecast: [*All products have sales forecasts for the upcoming year. Alternatively, if an incremental product investment is to be made, this Marketing Plan should identify that increment. This will also serve to link this section to others where explicit activities are called for.*]

_____

_____

PRODUCT MARKETING PLAN TEMPLATE

	Existing Product	New Product or Enhancement	Total Existing + New
Unit Volumes			
Average Prices			
Total Revenue			

The Value Proposition for the Product:

_____

_____

The Positioning Statement for the Product:

_____

_____

Section 4.2—Pricing: [Provide the pricing guidelines here and relate them to the overarching strategy as well as to the value proposition.]

_____

_____

Product Descriptor or SKU	List Price	Allowable Discounting	Floor (Lowest) Chargeable Price

Section 4.3 – Promotional Programs: [Describe each promotional program as a unique campaign. Use the table that follows to list out, organize, and possibly prioritize the expenditures]

_____

_____

Campaign Number	Expected Date(s)	Segment to Be Targeted	Goal of Campaign	Media Channel to Be Used	Call to Action	Budget	Campaign Metrics to Be Used

Mandatory corporate or divisional programs: [In this section, list any programs or events that require the participation of the product team or which will require financial or human resources. If there are any issues, make sure to list them here and to cite them in the risks section of this plan.]

_____

_____

Section 4.4—Distribution channels to be used: [Describe the path of the product from point of origin to its final destination. Use a channel map or other visual to portray this information. Make sure to call out any incremental costs required for channel development.]

_____

_____

SECTION 5—MARKETING ALLIANCES

If partners or alliances are to be used, the reason should be articulated here. Some reasons could include the access of market areas that are new (international geographies) or perhaps to support an evolving solutions business. (If international alliances are used, link this discussion to the next section.)

SECTION 6—INTERNATIONAL MARKETING

Your international marketing activities may require a unique regional marketing mix. You may have to alter the product's platform, change packaging, consider a variety of pricing issues and exchange rate variations, and rely on different distribution channels (including sales agents, resellers, etc.). Furthermore, each organization is different. Some companies use local sales offices, and some have joint ventures or alliance partners.

SECTION 7—PRODUCT LAUNCHES BEING PLANNED OR BEING CARRIED OUT

Since all product projects need to be launched, it might prove helpful to include a Launch Plan. If a new product or enhancement is being readied for market, then this section should be linked to the launch profile presented in the Business Case.

SECTION 8—SALES TRAINING

One of the most important activities to ensure success is to make sure that the product can be sold. This means that there need to be salespeople who are able to sell the product, and they need to be adequately compensated. Training programs are dependent on the type of product. Some products are complex and need to be sold in a consultative manner. Therefore, sales training needs to focus on the customer's business operations as well as the attributes of the product. Other products require that the salespeople be familiar with the overall benefits and features. Describe the training in terms of dates, needed resources, and budgets.

SECTION 9—ADDITIONAL RESEARCH PROGRAMS NEEDED

There may be times when the product team requires research materials or consultative research services to validate market assumptions or to support other product team activities. If additional market research programs are required, they should be articulated here.

Research Required	Purpose	Budget

SECTION 10—CROSS-FUNCTIONAL DEPENDENCIES OR DELIVERABLES

Since this Marketing Plan is a Functional Support Plan, it must articulate any tasks or deliverables that are to be provided by any of the marketing functions to other business functions. For example, Marketing might need to provide updates to the Customer Service department for call center scripts and in return, the Customer Service department is to provide adequate resources to collaborate on the script flow and agents to be trained. The table below is a good way to articulate each deliverable. It can be expanded to suit your own environment.

Task or Deliverable by Marketing	Function to Which the Deliverable Is Due	Purpose	Due Date	Dependency on Any Other Functions	Budget Impact	Possible Risks

SECTION 11—INTEGRATED BUDGETS FOR ALL PROGRAMS

All marketing activities cost money. In many companies, the marketing budget is handled at the corporate or divisional level, and then expenses are allocated to products at a predetermined rate. However, a product team may require explicit expenditures in order to carry out its work programs. The table below can be used to articulate any of these budgetary expenditures to support the product.

In some Marketing Plans, more detailed financial information may be required. For example, you may need to integrate the product forecasts from the product section above with the marketing expenditures here. In other organizations, the Marketing Plan for the product may need to contain the profit and loss (P&L) for the product. You may need to rename this section "Financials" or something similar if your company requires this level of detail or if your product team deems this important.

Budget Category	Current Year Existing Programs	Current Year New Programs	Next Year Continuing Programs
Advertising			
Advertising Specialties and Premiums			
Merchandising			
Publicity/Public Relations			
Analyst Relations			
Event Support—Product Level			
Event Support—Corporate Mandate			
Endorsements			
Sales Incentives			
Sales Support			
Sales Training			
Customer Service Suppor			
Creative Services			
Copywriting			
Publishing/Printing			
Fulfillment			
Website Design			
Website Maintenance			
Corporate Program Support			
Product Design Services			
Consulting Services			
Customer Visits			
Customer Councils/Advisory Boards			
Beta or Field Trial Support Programs			
Other Marketing Services and Expenditures			
Design and Packaging Services			
Branding Support			
TOTAL FUNDING REQUIRED			

PRODUCT MARKETING PLAN TEMPLATE

SECTION 12—MEASUREMENTS AND METRICS

This section of the plan identifies the relevant metrics that are to be put into place to track the performance of marketing activities and investments. Each organization usually has a different set of standards. However, one way to view measurements is by examining each line item where money is to be invested. In Section 11 of this plan, there are a variety of budget line items. Further, the marketing campaigns shown in Section 4.3 also call out specific investments and metrics. Use a table like the one below to set out each investment category and its desired metrics. Leave a column for results so that as the product evolves in the market, you can use the gathered results as a benchmark for future marketing investments.

Marketing Investment Category Outcome	Desired Investment to Be Made	Qualitative Outcome	Quantitative Outcome	Results Versus (Metric)

SECTION 13—RISKS

This section should identify anything that could go wrong and why. It should also contain any plans that would be put into place to compensate for the risk.

Risk (What Could Happen?)	What Action Would Be Taken to Mitigate This Risk?

PRODUCT MARKETING PLAN TEMPLATE

SECTION 14—APPENDICES

- Charts, graphs, etc.
- Detailed supporting data
- Citations and references
- Consultant studies
- Voice of the customer research
- Other research findings

PRODUCT LAUNCH TEMPLATE

This template provides you with a context for planning and carrying out a product launch. Unlike other templates in this category, this template focuses on two dimensions: planning for the product launch and carrying out the product launch (executing).

The Product Launch Plan

The Product Launch Plan is essentially a project plan that helps the product team identify the critical resources, activities, and timing required to carry out a product launch. It evolves from the early phases of New Product Planning and should be just about final when the product investment (or the product project investment) is authorized. With this context, it may be useful to synchronize the Launch Plan with the Business Case.

The Launch Plan will probably need to be updated as product design and development activities commence. The Launch Plan can be prepared as an independent document, or it can be embedded in the Marketing Plan and/or Business Case for the product. The reason for establishing these linkages is to avoid rework and having to craft another lengthy document. You will use content from other documents to set the strategic context for the launch and describe the market environment (industry, competitors, and market segments).

The most important factor is to make sure that launch planning starts early enough so that the plan can be carried out on time, within budget, and with enough forethought to achieve the goals set out in the plan.

The Launch Plan is dependent on the following steps:

> *Step 1: Determine exactly what is being launched, and describe the goal or desired outcome for the launch.* [In this section, it should be clear as to whether this is a new product or an enhancement to an existing product. The product description can be used here as well or referred to in the appropriate planning documents. Further, the launch goal should be articulated such that its linkage to the overarching strategy can be clearly understood by all launch team members and to management as well.]
>
> _____
>
> _____

> *Step 2: Define the market window.* [The plan should identify the time period when the product must be available for purchase by the intended customers. For some industries, a buying season sets the stage. For others, a key industry event or trade show may be the right time.]
>
> _____
>
> _____

Step 3: Identify the launch team and the launch team leader. [The Launch Plan is a cross-functional initiative that requires a team leader (a product manager, product marketing manager, or other project manager). An executive sponsor or champion is important, especially if this is an extremely critical product launch or if the launch is being bundled in a launch of several products. The launch team membership list can be recorded in table such as the one that follows.]

Launch Team Roles	Launch Team Names and Contact Information
Executive Sponsor	
Launch Team Leaders	
Product Manager	
Marketing Manager	
Marketing Communications	
Creative Manager	
Legal and/or Regulatory Compliance	
Early Adopter/Market Testing Manager	
Manufacturing/Supply Chain/Logistics	
Operations (Billing, Ordering, etc.)	
Finance	
Sales	
Customer Training	
Intellectual Property Management	
Human Resources	
Customer Change Management	

[Additionally, since the Launch Plan requires resources at specific times, the perfect document to clarify roles and responsibilities is the Functional Support Plan. Use a form like the one that follows for each business function (Marketing, Development, etc.).]

Deliverable	Start Date	End Date	Information or Work Needed from Other Functions (What/When)	Risks to the Launch If This Deliverable Is Not Completed on Time

Step 4: Develop a clearly mapped out project plan. *[Every launch team should use project management techniques to clarify the work tasks for everyone contributing to the launch. It is recommended that Functional Support Plans be used (see Step 3) and that they be integrated into one document with all interfunction dependencies called out. A critical path chart should be prepared to show the absolute longest duration of all tasks, collectively. This way, the launch team will know how delays or problems with one deliverable might affect the entire end-date (or announcement date).]*

_____

_____

Step 5: Establish launch metric. *[Launch metrics are important to ensure that the product can and will be sold. Sales-related metrics are typically most important, although operational metrics will be important as well. Sales metrics might include the number of new sales leads generated, the time it takes from order to shipment, the number of new customers purchasing, the time it takes from getting an order to getting paid, the amount of each sale (to make sure the pricing is right), advertising effectiveness, etc.]*

_____

_____

Carrying Out the Product Launch (Executing)

When the Business Case for a new product or an enhancement is approved, the design and development of the product commences and the launch team begins its work. These work activities are aligned with what was agreed to in the Launch Plan. The following activities, as a minimum, should be carried out during launch execution. You should also work closely with any existing launch organizations, processes, or procedures used by your company to ensure that your plan integrates well with the normal way of doing business in your company. Think of launch execution as a multiphase process:

Early phase launch execution:
- Meet with executive sponsor to make sure that you're aligned on the Launch Plan.
- Confirm the market window with the cross-functional launch team.
- Synchronize all activities with Development (e.g., on testing or trials, timing, etc.).
- Review/update other important documents (Business Case, Marketing Plan, PRD, Value Proposition, Positioning, etc.).
- Align with any creative groups that need to be engaged.

Middle phase launch execution:
- Prepare sales training.
- Assemble sales kits or equivalent documents.
- Arrange sales training dates.
- Get marketing materials written.
- Make arrangements for specific events.
- Carry out market tests.
- Get product codes.
- Make sure the supply chain organization is carrying out its work.
- Check factory production schedule (if needed).
- Assure that all regulatory or standards testing is completed.
- Finalize pricing (if needed).
- Put together any demonstration kits or demo packages.
- Load ordering and billing systems.
- Make sure that distributors or resellers are trained and ready.
- Make arrangements for industry analyst meetings or PR.
- Recheck documents.
- Review status with executive champion.
- Set the final announcement date.

Later phase launch execution:
- Carry out sales training.
- Train customer service agents.
- Train distributors and resellers.
- Carry out internal announcements.
- Distribute marketing materials.
- Finalize market tests.
- Verify that all regulatory approvals have been secured.
- Assign product availability ratings.
- Load up internal websites.
- Turn up all operational support systems.
- Carry out executive final go/no-go for the launch.
- Make the announcement.

PRODUCT DISCONTINUATION OUTLINE

When a product's sales head into decline, one of the possible strategies is to discontinue the product and withdraw it from the market. The product discontinuation process begins with an evaluation that resembles a Business Case. The Business Case justified the investment for the product, so the discontinuation case describes the reasons to disinvest in the product, or simply, to divest.

The following outline can be used as a method to evaluate the impact of possible discontinuation on the portfolio. You may need to include issues that are germane to your business or industry; this is a good place to start.

1. Executive Summary

2. History and Chronology—describe the business conditions and market drivers.

3. Business Assumptions—to make sure that all issues are being addressed.
   a. Unit volume assumptions
   b. Pricing strategy until the product becomes unorderable
   c. Time required to service and support customers
   d. Funding required pre- and post-discontinuation
   e. Asset write-offs to be considered (if any)
   f. Legal or contractual issues remaining
   g. Customer issues/competitive issues
   h. Regulatory notification
      i. Operational issues
      i. Spare parts or inventory requirements
      ii. Required facilities
      iii. Plant capacity requirements
      iv. Final order dates to be considered
      v. Stock liquidation timing

4. Financial Data—including financial history and future prospects
   a. Profit and loss (P&L) projections

5. Project Plans and Schedules
   a. Human resources required
   b. Tasks involved in the discontinuation
   c. Budgets for each function during discontinuation
   d. Vendor or partner notifications
   e. Customer notifications
   f. Internal notifications

6. Risks

7. Recommendations

PRODUCT MASTER PLAN OUTLINE

The Product Master Plan is the official plan of record for a product, product line, or portfolio. It is a living, evolving collection of other plans and documents that evolve and are collected over time. The Product Master Plan can commence its life when a new product is conceived, developed, or introduced, or it can be constructed retrospectively for an existing product.

Its main purpose is to act as the single storehouse of everything having to do with the product so that all documents have a place to reside that can be handed to successive generations of product managers and that can serve as a learning tool for any member of the cross-functional product team.

The Product Master Plan will certainly evolve. It may start as a single binder and expand to many binders. Each tab in your binder may end up being a single binder or set of binders. The goal is to make sure that no one ever has to look for product-related documentation because it's all located in one place.

This outline is provided to encapsulate most of the major sections of the Product Master Plan into a unified list. You can take this and start your own Product Master Plan as a three-ring binder with tabs, on an internal website, or both.

Product name:
_____
_____

Product team leader name and contact information:
_____
_____

Product Team Protocols
– Membership rules
– Meeting guidelines
– Meeting documentation and distribution
– Attendance guidelines and rules
– Decision making rules
– Meeting reporting and action planning
– Escalation rules and escalation paths
– Conflict resolution rules
– Communication rules

Product Team Member Functional Support Plans
– Each team member's name
– Team member's management information
– Functional Support Plan (FSP) documents and integrated FSPs
– Other project plans supporting the product

Product Specific Data
- Product/product line name(s)
- Product descriptions
- Product Requirements Documents (PRDs)
- Value propositions
- Positioning
- Diagrams and visual retrospectives
- Fit within the portfolio

Other Product and Marketing Specific Documents
- Business Cases
  - Opportunity statements
- Product Strategy
  - Product vision
  - Product roadmaps (retrospective/future)
  - Marketing mix strategy
- Marketing Plans for the product
  - Inbound programs and research
  - Outbound programs
  - Product launch data
- Forecasts

Market Specific Data
- Market segments
- Target customer types
- Customer visit reports and "needs" documents
- Industry categories and characteristics
- Industry research documents
- Competitive product analysis
- Competitor information and data

Product Performance Data
- Financial data
- Product life cycle data
- Marketing statistics
- Operational support metrics
- Post-launch audit reports

Customer Specific Programs
- Beta trials
- Customer testimonials
- Customer advisory programs

– Customer case studies and references
– Bid/RFx history
– Win–loss audits
– Special pricing programs
– Important customer communications
– Service–level agreements

Sales Documentation
– Sales kits
– Sales training
– Sales briefs
– Demonstration packages
– Bid boilerplates
– Sales events

Officially Submitted Documents
– Budgets
– Business Cases
– Strategies
– Marketing Plans
– Strategy reviews

Other Product Documentation
– Customer presentations
– Product presentations
– Alliance contracts
– Product discontinuation documents
– Historical research reports

PRODUCT REQUIREMENTS DOCUMENT (PRD) GUIDELINE AND TEMPLATE

Headings

Version and History

Version Number	Date	Revision Owner	Reason for Revision

PRD Approvals

Approver Name	Role	Signature	Date

Introductory Information

1. **Purpose and Strategic Context:** An introductory series of statements that provide adequate perspective for a reader to understand the reason for the PRD. Further, it should assert any key statements of strategic intent so that all stakeholders understand some of the main motivations for the project or projects that will stem from this PRD.

2. **Market Environment:** This section contains a contextual description of the marketplace. The main areas focus on the industry or domain and its overall evolution, the competitive landscape, and the market segments and associated customer targets. Also included in this section are the main market driven motivations or drivers for the creation or upgrade of the product. Areas that might be covered:

3. **Product Description and Life Cycle State:** If the PRD is for an entirely new product, the PRD must contain the vision and strategy for the product. IF the PRD is for an enhancement or upgrade, the essential descriptors should be summarized or amended as needed. Furthermore, readers will want to understand whether the product is in the growth, maturity, or even the decline phase of its life cycle. As may be surmised, work undertaken to extend the life of a growth-phase or mature-phase product may impact the level of effort, cost, and schedule.

Customer Target Constructs

The PRD will require significant detail to enable clear focus on the current or future customers or users of a product. For example, with consumer products, different users may include various family members. For B2B products, a customer may be a person who frequently encounters or experiences a problem, a person's manager, or other people who benefit from work done by someone who works in a given environment.

Therefore, customer types must be clearly identified so that the people who must interpret the PRD can understand more about the problems presented.

The PRD can begin as a story, a scenario, or an abstraction of a series of events that involve one or more customer types. Many people classify these customers or users with a generalized "persona" that may represent a "day in the life" scenario or a usage situation that will help form an image or visualization that can be shared with stakeholders. The PRD stories, representations, and visualizations should provide the right level of specificity so that the key problems or issues faced by the target customers are clear to all stakeholders.

PRD Foundational Elements

1) **Naming Conventions:** The PRD will be used by different people or stakeholders in the organization. In order to have a high degree of understanding, all definitions should be clearly spelled out in advance. In some cases, where a lot of data may be used in a software or software/hardware system, a data dictionary may be needed, either at the start of the PRD, or as an appendix.

2) **Numbering:** Each requirement should have a number. Each number may have an associated hierarchy that serve as points of clarification. A requirements number may only be used once.

3) **Rationale:** Any individual requirement or group of requirements should have a clearly understood rationale or purpose, tied to the overarching goal of the document, linked to the purpose and/or strategy for the product.

4) **Dependencies:** There may be a number of dependencies between requirements. These should be called out in any requirement.

5) **Conflicts:** All requirements must be evaluated and reviewed to ensure that they are not in conflict with one another.

6) **Diagrams:** Where needed, drawings and diagrams should be used to help communicate and clarify intent.

7) **Traceability:** Individual requirements may refer to other documents or other requirements. Requirements numbers should have appropriate references to allow for adequate cross-references or associated documents.

Functional Requirements: Functional requirements reflect the basic intent of the product, or "what it's supposed to do." Functional requirements are often articulated using the word *shall or should*.

Some examples of functional requirements are shown below:

Number	Functional Requirement Statement
FR 01-001	The cash machine shall dispense cash to a verified bank customer.
FR 01-002	The cash machine shall accept cash deposits from a verified bank customer.

Non-Functional Requirements: Non-functional requirements describe characteristics, properties, or qualities that the product "should" or "must" exhibit. These are sometimes called *behaviors* of the product, usually related to the product's desired characteristics, usability, or maintainability (and sometimes, performance). These are often called "features" or "product attributes."

The word "must" is typically associated with high priority requirements and the word "should" is often associated with lower priority requirements. If needed, a third category that can be called "nice to have" would refer to requirements that are not needed but could add some value, time permitting.

Some examples of non-functional requirements are shown below:

Number	Non-Functional Requirement Statement
NFR 02-001	The cash machine must have a numerical keypad with numbers 0–9.
NFR 02-002	The cash machine keypad must have 2mm raised numbers to provide tactical verification.
NFR 02-003	After a customer enters their personal identification number (PIN) no more than 3 seconds should elapse before they are able to begin their transaction.

There are many categories of non-functional requirements. These categories and subcategories are listed below.

Areas associated with customer use or usability:

1) Efficiency or speed
2) Turn-around time for a transaction (stimulus/response sequence)
3) Learnability and ease of recall in how a product is used (so that users don't forget how to use the product)
4) Acceptable errors or mistakes that a user can make
5) Feedback (as in a sound or acknowledgment that an action results in an outcome — like the *click* of a key on a keyboard)

Areas associated with physical characteristics:

1) Size
2) Appearance
3) Weight
4) Colors
5) Styles
6) Design

Areas associated with product performance and overall quality:

1) Speed (of a transaction or interaction)
2) Online response times
3) Precision or accuracy
4) Number of users
5) Reliability
6) Capacity
7) Extreme environments or stresses
8) Scalability
9) Durability
10) Longevity

Areas associated with operational support or integration:

1) The physical environment
2) Interfaces with, or compatibility with other products or systems
3) Hardware requirements
4) Software requirements
5) Releases or launch plans

Areas associated with maintenance or support over the life of the product:

1) Documentation required
2) Maintenance or maintainability
3) Adaptation or migration from a current environment
4) Auditing or monitoring the performance of the product or system
5) Access — physical or remote

Areas associated with data:

1) Data elements
2) Fields (size, alpha, numeric, alpha-numeric)
3) Ranges
4) Constraints

Areas associated with safety and security:

1) System or product access
2) Verification
3) Privacy
4) Safeguards

Areas associated with laws and regulations:

1) Local or country specific
2) Time frames required
3) Standards body compliance

Global or international (refer to each of the areas mentioned)

1) Local packaging or design
2) Local performance

Reviews and Inspections

PRDs may be authored and owned by product managers. However, like a manuscript for a book must be reviewed and edited prior to publication, so must the PRD. The reason this is so important is because product managers have different writing styles, and therefore, what is meant may not be properly interpreted by the audience of readers. Further, product managers have varying levels of experience and understanding of the product. Lastly, different cultural norms and perspectives may have authors use words that do not have the same meaning. To overcome this challenge and to ensure that the requirements are consistently written and presented, a group of peers and others may wish to conduct PRD review sessions and inspections before an agreement is reached on the final, or baselined PRD.

The Appendix

Appendix 1: Definitions, acronyms, and abbreviations.

Appendix 2: References to other documents or information.

Appendix 3: Traceability matrix that can be used to relate a given requirement to another requirement or system, either in this document, or in another document.

GLOSSARY

Acceptance test—A structured methodology used to determine if a product is fit for a purpose, use, or deployment. Users or customers may apply specific decision criteria to determine whether a product fulfills the customer's need. Internal product testers will also use similar techniques to evaluate the product prior to launch.

Accounts payable—The debts owed by a business, usually in relation to goods or services, inventory, or supplies.

Accounts receivable—The money owed to a business by its customers for products and services delivered to a customer.

Activity-based costing—A technique that logically allocates overhead to products based on actual usage of factory facilities or machinery.

Advisory (cross-functional) product team member—A cross-functional product team member providing consultative support on an as-needed basis. Advisory team members may come from Legal, Regulatory, Governance, or similar functions.

Agile—A product development methodology that utilizes a series of iterative development steps and incremental deliveries of products or product updates. The iterations themselves depend on a high degree of customer or user involvement to validate usability and fit. Techniques used to develop products in an iterative manner will often be subject to interpretation and may be adopted differently across firms.

Allocation—The apportionment or assignment of a business function's expense to an income statement (P&L) of a product.

Amortization—The systematic write-off of costs incurred in the purchase of an intangible asset such as a patent or copyright.

Analysis paralysis—An expression used to describe the ongoing analysis of a problem without making a decision.

Announcement—The product announcement is the formal notification to the marketplace that a product is available for purchase by customers.

Apprentice—A person who is learning from a more experienced person. For example, just as apprentice electricians learn their skill from a journeyman or a master electrician, a product manager can learn from more experienced product managers or product leaders.

Architecture—See *Product architecture*.

Area of work—Within the Product Management Life Cycle Model, there are three major groupings of work activities carried out by product managers and their teams. These areas of work focus on three main items: New Product Planning, New Product Introduction, and Post-Launch Product Management.

Assets—On the Balance Sheet, an asset is something owned that has value, including cash, marketable securities, accounts receivable, plant and equipment, and inventory.

Associate (cross-functional) product team member—These are cross-functional product team members who are typically part-time team members. An associate member can also be an authorized delegate or a subordinate of a core team member.

Assumption—When used in a Business Case, forecast, or other planning document, an assumption is a statement that relates to a potential future state or future situation.

Attainable market share—The market share you could potentially or realistically achieve (attain) in volume and/or revenue.

Attribute—A characteristic of a product that can include a color, design, style, form, shape, or feature.

Audit—An inspection of the plans, procedures, or records of a part of a business to determine whether a plan was followed and if a desired outcome was achieved. In this book, an audit looks into various aspects of a product launch or a bidding situation (win/loss).

Availability rating—See *Product availability rating.*

Backlog (as in product backlog)—A list of planned features or product capabilities. These undeveloped product capabilities are continually evaluated by a set of decision criteria.

Balance Sheet—A financial statement that provides a snapshot of a company's overall financial health. The Balance Sheet is composed of assets, liabilities, and owner's equity (or net worth).

Barrier to entry—A condition that exists in a market that makes it difficult for another business to establish a foothold. A barrier can include intense competition, governmental regulation, a shortage of skilled labor, or other obstacles.

Base case—When creating a Business Case, the base case is the starting point. The base case represents the current business-as-usual situation. A base case allows for other investment assumptions to be evaluated and then compared with the base case.

Baseline—A set of data or information about an aspect of a business (or product) that provides a point of perspective from which future options can be evaluated. A baseline analysis during the product strategy formulation process allows a product manager to assess the past and current business and market environment for a product so that future strategic options can be considered.

Benchmark—A study that compares the actual or observed performance of a business activity, process, method, or function to a standard of competence.

Benefit—Something of value as perceived by a customer.

Best case—When analyzing investment options or creating forecasts, the best case is usually the most optimistic scenario.

Best practice—A business practice that has been codified, endorsed, and improved over time and is proven to contribute to positive business outcomes.

Beta test (or trial)—Testing of a product by a friendly customer or customers who are willing to use the product as intended so that any issues or problems can be uncovered and resolved.

Bill of materials (BOM)—A list of materials or components that are used to assemble a product. A bill of materials can be arranged hierarchically, from a simple parts list to a complex set of lists of subassemblies and sublists.

Bottom-up forecast—This type of forecast method begins with the determination of the demand for a product by a single customer and builds the forecast upward based on multiple customers and so on.

Brainstorming—A creative technique used to come up with ideas or concepts. In Product Management, brainstorming can be used for product ideation or general problem solving.

Brand—Although definitions abound, a concise description of the brand may be represented by this statement: a brand represents the shared or combined set of perceptions formed in the minds of a market segment about a company and/or a product.

Brand manager—In many companies, a brand manager's role is equivalent to that of a product manager. Found more often in consumer goods companies, the brand manager influences the marketing mix for a product, a group of products, a category of products, or even for a market segment or segments.

Break-even point—In general terms the break-even point is the point in a product's life cycle when the total of all investment costs are equal to the profit generated by the product. Additionally, a break-even point can be measured in units (how many do we have to sell to break even?) or in time (how long will it take to break even?). The accounting definition takes into account fixed costs, variable costs, quantity, and time. Check with your Finance or Accounting department when the actual calculations need to be made.

Budget—An estimate of product sales, prices, costs, and expenses over a specified time period, which is typically a year. Another way to think of a budget is to refer to it as a spending roadmap.

Bug—An error in a computer program that may have an adverse impact on the performance of a product. Bugs can also have a negative impact on the overall customer experience.

Bundle—A grouping of products sold to a customer that, together, seek to solve a customer's problem or fulfill a specific need. Customers who are offered bundles may have an opportunity to shop the different parts to get the best deal. However, many businesses use bundling as a way to sell a solution. See *Solution.*

Business Case—Within the context of this book, it is a formal document used to justify investments in new products, product enhancements, and marketing expenditures.

Business Intelligence (BI)—A method used to analyze and interpret business performance data so that fact-based business decisions can be made. The business data referred to in BI is usually extracted from a variety of domains and databases and presented in a way to bring about more efficient analysis.

Business-to-business (B2B)—A business model where a company (a business) sells its products to other businesses.

Business-to-business-to-business (B2B2B)—A business model where a company (a business) sells its products to other businesses, which in turn sell those products to other businesses.

Business-to-business-to-consumer (B2B2C)—A business model where a company (a business) sells its products to other businesses, which in turn sell those products to consumers.

Business-to-consumer (B2C)—A business model where a company (a business) sells its products to consumers.

Business rule—A general policy or guideline that defines or constrains some facet of a workflow or procedure in an organization. Often, business rules or business logic sets the stage for the Product Requirements Document (PRD).

Buyer—A customer type in a business who becomes the ultimate purchaser (e.g., a procurement manager) of a product. In consumer products, the buyer is usually the ultimate purchaser, too.

Campaign—An outbound marketing activity orchestrated to bring about an explicit business result. For example, an advertising campaign may be created to generate sales leads.

Cannibalization—When products from a product portfolio are sold in the market together, and one product draws sales away from the other. In this case, one product is said to cannibalize the potential sales of the other product. Overall, this may have a negative impact on the portfolio.

Capability—Within the context of this book, a capability refers to the knowledge, skills, experience, and overall abilities of cross-functional product team members. In this light, all team members must be able to understand and fulfill their commitments to the rest of the team. Therefore, a capability is the proven ability of an individual or group to perform a specific type of work.

Capacity—See *Production capacity.*

Capacity Management—As used in this book, capacity management refers to the ability of a distribution channel to be able to take the product from its source and deliver it to the intended customer. A lack of capacity in this case means that there are usually too many products that need to be sold and delivered but not enough capable resources.

Capital expenditure ("Cap-ex")—An investment in equipment, facilities, or other tangible asset that is used in the creation of a product.

Cash flow statement—A financial statement showing the inflows and outflows of money. Cash flow is important in creating forecasts, Business Cases, and in analyzing the financial impacts of product investments. Cash flow is the basis for deriving discounted cash flow (DCF).

Champion—A person in an organization, usually a senior manager or executive, who provides the oversight, vision, or unbridled enthusiasm for an initiative.

Channel map—See *Distribution channel map.*

Channel(s)—See *Distribution channel.*

Checklist—A list of items reviewed by a product team at the end of a product development phase. Checklists are used by a product team to make sure that all work items and tasks have been completed.

Collateral—See *Marketing collateral.*

Competency—A set of knowledge, skills, and experiences required to carry out a job.

Competitive advantage—The relative advantage that one product or product line has over those products offered by other companies.

Competitive intelligence (CI)—That which is derived from the analysis of data about competitors. Competitive intelligence helps product teams transform data into information that can be used to strategically guide a product through the market.

Competitive positioning—Ensuring that your product can be favorably compared with your competitor's product.

Competitor profile—A document that characterizes a competitor, its products, and other competitive attributes.

Complementary products—Products in a product portfolio that are sold together in the market, where one product's existence may induce the sale of the other product (the complement).

Component—A subassembly, piece, or part used in a product that allows a product to achieve the desired level of functionality. A fuel injector is a component used in an automobile engine.

Concept—An idea for a new product or product enhancement.

Concept phase—The first phase within the area of work called New Product Planning in the Product Management Life Cycle Model. In the concept phase, a small group of product team stakeholders evaluate many product ideas or market opportunities so that a smaller number may be selected for further evaluation.

Concept screening—The process carried out during the Concept phase to sift through many product ideas and help derive decisions as to which concepts are worthy of moving to a subsequent planning phase—namely, the Feasibility phase.

Condition—As used in this book, a market condition is a business situation, either planned for or encountered, as a product moves through the market. Therefore, a market condition may trigger a market action. For example, if competitors lower the price of their products, it may trigger a response from other competitors.

Consultative selling—A technique used by salespeople to uncover customer needs and business problems. It is based on building a solid understanding of the customer's business through a structured, sometimes hierarchical, questioning or probing method.

Consumer—Typically used in defining an individual or household that will benefit from using a product or service (e.g., B2C).

Core competency—Work or activities that are unique or core to an organization, such as a company or a division in a company. Core competencies can be an important part of a company's strategy if the competencies are unique enough to distinguish it from its competitors.

Cost of goods sold (COGS)—The total cost of raw materials, labor, and overhead used in the creation of a tangible product.

Cost-plus pricing—A technique that adds a fixed percentage to the product's cost (as a mark-up) to derive the product's selling price.

Criteria—Conditions that enable a decision to be made, especially at a decision point within the areas of work related to New Product Planning and New Product Introduction.

Critical Path Method (CPM)—A project planning technique that optimizes the sequencing tasks that are needed to complete a project. The *critical path* is usually the longest path taken to complete those activities.

Cross-functional product team—A cross-functional product team is made up of delegated representatives from their respective business functions. It is (or should be) the primary mechanism through which an organization initiates and executes product strategies and plans. This team is responsible for the strategic, market, and financial success of the product across the entire product life cycle, from concept through discontinuation.

Cross-functional project team (see also *Functional project team* and *Project*)—A cross-functional project team is made up of appointed team members. These teams are only in place for the duration required to carry out the tasks and activities associated with a defined deliverable. Once the project team's work is finished, the team members disband and are available for carrying out work on other projects. Within the context of this book, the product team will carry out many projects and will spawn many different cross-functional projects (such as a product launch).

Customer Business Case—The process undertaken by a customer that helps the customer justify investments in products and services.

Customer experience management—An element of the strategy of an organization or product team that seeks to bring about favorable perceptions across every type of interaction a customer may have with a company and/or product.

Customer focus—The extent to which a company, division, or product team seeks to fully understand the needs, motivations, and way of life of customers.

Customer insights—That which is discerned from understanding a variety of customer needs and behaviors. Insights can be used to influence strategies, guide product development, validate segmentation models, and prepare creative briefs. Insights are also used for guiding the creative process, which is used to drive advertising and promotional activity.

Customer loyalty—The degree to which customers continue to buy or recommend products from the same company.

Customer relationship management (CRM)—A strategy devoted to the development and management of close relationships between customers and the company. In many cases, CRM is referred to as the automation tool that helps bring about this strategy.

Customer segments (also customer type or customer target)—In segmentation, many people may be considered the "customer" and may therefore be involved in a purchasing decision. This can include a buyer, a user, an influencer, and a decision maker. This is important because the true value proposition should be based on the needs of a specific customer type.

Customer visit—A formal structured excursion to a customer's location or to a location where it is feasible to observe customers carrying out activities that may provide clues as to their needs.

Customer visit plan—A formal document used to establish the goal for a customer visit, the team members who will participate, and other particulars that are relevant to guide the customer visit.

Cycle time—The speed with which an operation takes place from beginning to end. In product development, cycle time is often the time it takes from concept to product launch.

Decision checkpoint—A point during the product development process when a general decision is taken as to whether a product investment (opportunity or idea) is to be brought forward to a subsequent phase.

Decision criteria—A set of formally established and agreed-upon parameters used to judge or evaluate an opportunity. As an example, an opportunity might have three criteria against which it is evaluated: strategic alignment, validated value proposition, and competitive positioning.

Decision matrix—A tool or method used to weight and rank multidimensional choices. This is used for new product project selection and product investment prioritization. It can also be used for product feature prioritization.

Decision tree—A decision-making method that uses a branch diagram to portray different options and outcomes.

Decline phase—The last phase of a product's life. This phase is characterized by sales that are decreasing at an increasing rate and a rapid loss of market share. Often, the Decline phase is preplanned to allow for the introduction of a replacement product.

Dedicated core (cross-functional) team member—A product team member delegated to represent a single business function to a cross-functional product team.

Definition phase—The third phase within the area of work of New Product Planning where the product documentation is completed prior to recommending a go or no-go decision for the product investment. The output documents of this phase are typically the Product Requirements Document (PRD), the Business Case, the Launch Plan, and the Marketing Plan for the product.

Deliverable—The tangible or intangible work product from a functional team member.

Delphi method—A systematic forecasting practice that seeks input or advice from a panel of experts. All experts provides their forecast input in a successive series of rounds until consensus is achieved.

Demand planning—A forecasting method used to figure out how much of a product should be produced, and when that product should be produced, based on a variety of factors such as the sales forecast, production line scheduling, manufacturing capacity, inventory strategies, logistics, and other variables.

Demographic—The characteristics of a market segment or population. Most often, demographic characteristics include age, gender, income, educational level, etc.

Dependency—When one business function needs another business function to complete a task, series of tasks, or deliverables before completing its own work or fulfilling its commitments.

Depreciation—The value that an asset loses over time—typically, the asset's useful life. An example could be a machine used to produce a product which may have a useful life of five years; therefore, it loses 20 percent of its value each year. That 20 percent appears on the profit and loss statement (P&L) as depreciation.

Derivative—A variation of an existing product. This variation can be an enhancement, improvement, or other update that does not affect the underlying platform.

Design thinking—A methodology or approach to allow people (such as product managers or product designers) to think holistically about the product's business through the consideration of a broad spectrum of customer needs. This approach deeply considers the world in which customers interact so that the product's look, feel, and operation can be provided for.

Development—This term is used in two ways. First, it is the functional department in an organization responsible for designing and building products. Second, it is a term ascribed to the actual creation of the product.

Development phase—A phase within the Product Management Life Cycle Model, specifically within the area of work called New Product Introduction (NPI). In the Development phase, the product's design is finalized, developed (or created), and tested, based on the agreed-upon product requirements.

Differentiation—The act of setting the product apart from competitors in ways that are most meaningful to customers.

Discontinuation—See *Product discontinuation.*

Discount rate—Future cash flows that are discounted to the present (see *Discounted cash flow*) are discounted based on the cost of funds (cost of capital) to the company.

Discounted cash flow (DCF)—A financial expression that considers all future cash inflows and discounts those cash flows to the present (using the discount rate). This acknowledges the fact that money received sooner has more value than money received later.

Distribution channel—A mechanism that allows a product to be moved from its source of supply to the end customer. Channel is the expression that encompasses one of the four Ps of the marketing mix: place.

Distribution channel map—A drawing or visual diagram used to portray the movement of goods through a company's distribution channels.

Documentation—A term that refers to documents produced by product managers or other functional team members. Documents include the Business Case, Product Requirements Document (PRD), Marketing Plan, and Product

Specification Document (PSD). Documentation can also include that which describes the functionality, usage, and method to operate a product.

Duration (task)—The amount of time it takes to complete a task, from the time it begins until the time it is finished.

EBITDA—Earnings before interest, taxes, depreciation, and amortization is the money realized (earned) by a business or a product before taxes, depreciation, and amortization are deducted from those earnings.

End user—The ultimate customer or "user" of a product.

Engineering change notice (ECN) or engineering change request (ECR)—A document used to record a requested change or adjustment needed to a product, either during development or while the product is in the market.

Enhanced product—An upgrade or revision to an existing product through additional features or functionality.

Entrepreneur—An individual who passionately operates a new venture or new business, accepting all risks for the business. Product managers should exhibit entrepreneurial characteristics.

Epic—Broad collections of user stories or a broad scenario into which smaller user stories can be derived.

Equity—In a Balance Sheet, equity is what remains after liabilities are subtracted from assets.

Ethnography—A qualitative customer research technique that seeks to study or evaluate customers in their own environment. Market researchers use this anthropomorphic technique to observe customers in situ to understand their behaviors or culture in an attempt to understand their needs.

Execution—The act of carrying out planned work.

Exit plan—An expression that can be used to describe a plan to discontinue a product or withdraw from a market.

Feasibility phase—The second phase within the area of work called New Product Planning. During the Feasibility phase, the product team carries out the research and analysis needed to determine whether the product idea has business, market, and strategic merit.

Feature—A product capability or attribute that fulfills a specific customer or market need and provides an appropriate benefit. A mobile device battery with a long life (the feature) meets the need of customers who use their portable device for communicating and web browsing (needs).

Financial ratio—The relationship of one financial measure to another, usually expressed as a percentage.

Focus group—A small group of invited individuals (possibly current or prospective customers) who are guided by a moderator to discuss or evaluate a product or product concept.

Forecast—The outcome of a series of exercises and analysis that helps a company, division, or product group to predict the number of units it might sell or produce or the market share it could attain.

Functional area—A business department in a company.

Functional project team—A project team staffed by people from a single business function.

Functional silo—An individual business function that tends to act as a stand-alone function, often formulating its own strategies and work plans in parallel with other business functions. This expression is used when describing an organization whose functions tend to be less communicative and collaborative. Companies with functional silos may have greater difficulty in creating strong, competitive products because they may fail to recognize the benefit of cross-functional teaming.

Functional Support Plan (FSP)—A major document used by members of a business function that describes the activities, deliverables, budgets, dependencies, and schedules for that business function to members of a cross-functional product team, on behalf of a product, across the entire life cycle of the product. The FSP is a major building block of the Product Master Plan.

Functionality (of a product)—Typically, the product's functionality enables the product to do what it's supposed to do. In other words, a product's functionality enables it to address customers' needs.

Functional requirement—A description of the intended behavior of a product under a given set of conditions or constraints.

Future method of operation (FMO)—An envisioned or possible set of procedures, processes, and methods that might be employed by a company, division, or organization to accomplish business objectives that is different than the present method of operation (PMO).

GA (generally available) product rating—A product availability rating that signals to the organization and to the marketplace that a product can be ordered and delivered.

Gantt chart—A project planning and scheduling technique. It uses horizontal bars to portray a project's tasks and depicts each task's start date, end date, and duration. It also can show dependencies on other tasks being carried out within the overall project.

Gate—A decision point within the product development process that determines whether a product opportunity or project should move to a subsequent phase or be rejected.

GICS—Global Industry Classification Standard developed by Morgan Stanley Capital International (MSCI) and Standard & Poor's (S&P) to provide a way to classify different industry sectors. These classifications can be helpful to product managers and marketers in carrying out industry analysis.

Governance board (Product Management)—A Product Management governance board is established by senior executives to oversee and guide the function of Product Management in a firm. The Product Management governance board is most effective when its members work to ensure that the structure and function of Product Management survives for the long term.

Graduated funnel—A graphical representation showing how a large number of product ideas are narrowed down to a small number of ideas during the phases of New Product Planning.

Gross margin—A financial calculation that subtracts cost of goods sold (COGS) from revenue. Gross profit is one of the most realistic measures of product profitability because its inputs and outputs are more easily influenced by a product team. (Some also use the term *gross profit*.)

Growth phase—After a product is launched, it usually enters a phase of rapid growth, characterized by an increasing rate of sales, growing profits, and increasing market share.

Gut-feel decision making—Subjective decision making based on rational thought or experience.

Hand-off—The planned transfer of responsibility of one set of deliverables by one business function to another function. There is a hand-off between R&D or Engineering to Manufacturing when the product design and development are completed.

Holistic—An approach to looking at an organization or a process completely and systemically. The Product Management Life Cycle Model is a representation of the life of a product, holistically, from beginning to end.

Horizontal contract—An expression that reinforces the reasoning for the *Functional Support Plan (FSP)* and that captures the rationale for the negotiation that takes place between two or more business functions.

Idea category—Classification of a product idea or concept based on the idea type or motivation. For example, an idea might be categorized as a competitive response if a product must be modified to meet a competitive threat.

Ideation—A term used to define the methods and techniques that generate ideas through market sensing, customer or market insights, market exploration, and other discovery techniques.

Inbound marketing—The efforts devoted to securing data and information from a variety of sources so that it can be used to guide Marketing Plans and programs.

Income statement—See *Profit and loss statement (P&L)*.

Industry—A set of organizations or companies who focus their selling and marketing efforts on meeting the needs of similar market segments.

Industry analysis—The methodology employed in determining the activities and trends of a set of organizations that bring about business and economic activity by selling and marketing products to similar market segments or customer types. Industry analysis is a vital element of overall market research and analysis.

In-market—An expression that refers to products currently being sold in the market.

Innovation—Refers to the solving of a customer or market problem in a way that is more unique than other approaches that exist in the market. The solution can include either a radical or incremental change to a product or service. An innovation can also be associated with an improved process or business practice.

Interface—An interface exists between different systems or between systems and networks when considered within the context of computer technology. An interface can also refer to the way in which people interact with a computer or other type of device (e.g., a user interface or graphical user interface). An interface can also have an organizational connotation where one organization works closely with (i.e., interfaces with) another. There are other definitions based on the industry context. However, these may be most common to product managers.

Inventory—A collection of or listing of products that are held in storage (in stock) by a business.

Inventory turnover—A measurement of how many times the inventory is refreshed because of ongoing sales.

IT—Refers to the functional department known as Information Technology.

Just in time—A manufacturing method in which product parts and components arrive at the manufacturing facility as needed for production of ordered product, rather than being stockpiled on site. This method requires strong supply chain management.

Key performance indicators (KPIs)—An important set of metrics (see *Metrics*) used to determine how well a product is performing in the market.

Launch phase—The Launch phase is situated within the area of work called New Product Introduction that includes all of the activities required to bring the product to the market. The Launch phase is concluded when the product is formally announced to the market.

Lead users—Companies or customers whose needs are thought to be ahead of market trends. In many instances, current products do not meet the needs of a lead user.

Liabilities—Financial obligations that are represented on the Balance Sheet.

Limited availability (LA)—A product availability rating that limits the ability of a product to be ordered. A limited availability rating can be used as products are gradually withdrawn from a market.

Line extension—A product that is added to an existing product line either as a newer version or derivative of a current product.

Logistics—The activities involved with controlling the movement of goods through a supply chain, from the point of origin to the point of delivery through designated distribution channels.

Major decision point—During the phases of New Product Planning and New Product Introduction, major decisions are made that involve the commitment of financial and human resources for a subsequent phase. Alternatively, the major decision could be to discontinue any additional expenditure on the product idea.

Make versus buy analysis—A structured analytical technique used to determine the optimal manner in which to produce a product. The alternatives include developing and building the product in-house versus having the product developed by another company.

Market analysis—The activity involved in translating data gathered from market research to yield information on which product and marketing decisions can be made.

Market attractiveness—The appeal of a market area based on the customer types in that market area or market segment. Furthermore, an attractive market can be identified by the ease of access (limited competitive activity).

Market focus—A strategic orientation of an organization or product team that holistically considers the dimensions of the industry, the dynamics of the competitive environment, and customers' needs in determining the appropriate product portfolio investments.

Market penetration—The degree to which a product is being sold in a given market area. Higher penetration means that more people in a currently pursued market area are purchasing the product or that the product is being sold in other market areas.

Market pricing—Pricing strategies that consider customer needs, the value proposition, strength of the brand, and other market forces.

Market research—The formal and informal methods used to learn about the industry, competitors, and customers, enabling an organization or product team to achieve the optimal market focus. Also the activities related to the systematic, ongoing efforts aimed at gathering and capturing data about industries, competitors, and customers.

Market segment—A group of customers (or potential customers) that share common needs or buying behaviors.

Market segmentation—The classification method that helps product managers identify customer types based on specific categories such as common needs or similar buying behaviors

Market share—The amount of market demand that can be captured by a product or product line. Market share is expressed as a percentage of the total addressable market (TAM).

Market target—See *Target market.*

Market window—The ideal time to introduce a product to the market. This can also be referred to as a window of opportunity or a launch window. For a product, the market window could be seasonal or targeted at an industry event. It can also be the optimal time to surprise a competitor.

Marketing collateral—The collection of documents and media used to support selling and marketing activities. These documents can include brochures, data sheets, sales kits, web content, and sales scripts.

Marketing mix—A combined set of strategic or tactical tools, often referred to as the "four Ps." The mix elements include the product itself, its pricing, the promotional programs that support the product, and place (meaning distribution channel).

Marketing Plan for the product—A Functional Support Plan that defines the inbound research and analysis needed to set the stage for outbound plans and programs to support the product in the market. It provides the appropriate rationale that defines the work required and resources needed to carry out these plans. Marketing Plans for the product are slightly different from corporate or divisional Marketing Plans. It is incumbent on the product team to make sure that the Marketing Plan for the product considers corporate mandates or obligations for the product team's support of those programs.

Marketing return on investment (ROI)—The returns or measured outcomes of a marketing program as a percentage of that marketing investment.

Master Plan—See *Product Master Plan.*

Mentoring—A technique used to help less skilled or experienced people learn from more experienced people. The mentor is the experienced person, and the protégé is the person who is guided. Product managers will benefit throughout their career by establishing relationships with others deemed to have a comprehensive set of skills and experiences.

Metrics—A metric is a measurement. When a plan is put into place, a way to measure the outcome is needed. When a market share forecast is created and the outcomes are measured at a future date, the planned metric is compared with the actual metric to determine the degree to which the metric was met. From this data, strategies can be revised and tactical options can be reconsidered.

Migration—The systematic shift of customers from one product version to another. This can be part of a purposeful product strategy aimed at discontinuing an obsolete product.

Module—A product element that can be a component or subassembly.

Morphological box—The visualization of the decision-making technique known as morphological analysis. It can be helpful when there are many different decision-making options and many different outcomes.

Motivational state—That condition (or need) existing in the mind of a customer that drives the customer to purchase a product (see also *Need state*).

Myers Briggs Type Indicator (MBTI)—A personality evaluation tool designed to identify personality types and psychological differences.

Narrative—Any descriptive or prosaic method of explaining forecasts, projections, or results, generally used to augment numerical or financial data.

Need—As defined for markets, a specific, recurrent requirement experienced by a given market segment or group of target customers. Needs are sometimes complex and not easily related to primal or basic human needs as defined in Maslow's hierarchy of needs.

Need state—A basic human need or requirement, at a specific point in time. Basic needs can focus on safety or security. However, need states (or motivational states) are generally transient. For example, when a consumer's car is beyond repair, she enters a new need state that motivates her to evaluate different types of new cars to purchase that will help her achieve her objectives (e.g., commute to work, shuttle children to sports activities, or transport many passengers).

Net income—Excess (or deficit) obtained when total expenses are subtracted from total revenue. Generally computed over a standard accounting period, such as a month, quarter, or year. In the case of a product, this may be computed over a portion of the product's life cycle as a means of evaluating the performance or health of the product.

Net present value (NPV)—The value of some future (financial) outcome stated in today's dollars, taking into account the fact that a dollar (or other unit of currency) today is worth more than a dollar in the future. It includes the effects of the cost of those funds, typically computed by compounding using a stated discount rate.

Networking, network effect—The tendency of ideas, products, and opportunities to increase as increasing numbers of people socialize, purchase, or use it. Also used to refer to the process of making organizational and social connections by traversing networks of mutual acquaintances.

Net worth—Assets, less debts and obligations (liabilities). Also referred to as owner's equity or just equity.

New Product Development (NPD)—Within the Product Management Life Cycle Model, NPD encompasses activities covered under the two areas of work referred to as New Product Planning and New Product Introduction. In these areas of work, many product concepts and ideas follow a general, phased decision process model (NPD process) and are transformed into products that are considered to have the best chance to achieve market and financial success, consistent with the strategies of the organization.

New Product Introduction (NPI)—The area of work within the Product Management Life Cycle Model during which the product is simultaneously developed and launched into the market.

New Product Planning (NPP)—The first and usually most extensive area of work within the Product Management Life Cycle Model, which consists of three phases: Concept, Feasibility, and Definition. It is called *new*, but it really encompasses both brand new product ideas as well as ideas for enhancements of existing products. Within this area of work, many product concepts are generated and are progressively narrowed. This process requires considerable market research and documentation. The outcome from NPP should be a product idea that is worthy of the investment sought and has the potential to achieve strategic, market, and financial success.

No-go—A decision to cancel a product or product project at a specific point from its inception up until its launch.

Non-functional requirement—Descriptions of characteristics, properties, or quality that a product "should" or "must" exhibit.

Nonprofit—In the broadest sense, an organization in which no part of any net earnings can accrue for the benefit of any private shareholder or individual. The U.S. Internal Revenue Service defines a nonprofit via section 501(c) of the United States Internal Revenue Code (26 U.S.C. § 501(c)), listing 27 types of nonprofit organizations exempt from federal income taxes.

Nonviable—A product, idea, concept, or opportunity that cannot meet its intended strategic goals or expectations.

North American Industry Classification System (NAICS)—The NAICS is a highly granular, standard numerical classification system that assigns six-digit codes and standard titles to every possible business type. NAICS is used by the U.S. Census Bureau, U.S. Department of Labor, and other economic organizations to compare organizations and economic activity across North America when deriving statistics or locating businesses that can provide specific products or services.

North American Product Classification System (NAPCS)—NAPCS is a comprehensive, demand-oriented product classification system designed to provide a statistical framework for comparing products for various economic and competitive analyses. To date, 12 categories of products have been coded into the system, comprising the service offerings associated with NAICS categories 48 through 81. NAPCS and NAICS are intended to be coordinated databases.

Obsolescence—The stage of a product's life cycle in which it is no longer viable or competitive from the point of view of its primary market segments.

Offshoring—A special case of outsourcing in which business operations or overhead activities are moved to other countries to reduce costs. Sometimes referred to euphemistically as globalization of operations.

Operating expenses (OPEX)—Refers to ongoing, usually variable costs of operating a business; contrasted with capital expenses, which refers to the plant and equipment needed to support operations.

Opportunity—An idea or a concept derived from a variety of methods such as strategy formulation (see *SWOT*) from market research activities or ideation.

Opportunity assessment—The process of evaluating an idea, concept, or opportunity to determine whether there is sufficient strategic, market, and financial merit for continued consideration and possible development into a product. Generally results in the recording of an Opportunity Statement.

Opportunity Statement—A brief (one- or two-page) evaluation of a product concept or idea to determine if the idea is worth pursuing, especially within the context of many other ideas and opportunities.

Optimization—A state in which all inputs, components, elements, and processes are working together to produce the most desirable, viable, and sustainable outcome possible given the current operating conditions. As referenced in this book, products and product lines should be optimized within the context of the portfolio of products so that the best combinations of product investments produce the most desirable, sustainable market, financial, and strategic outcomes.

Order-to-cash cycle—The activities and processes that take place from the time an order is placed by a customer until payment is received and credited. It is used as a reference point for assessing future cash inflows, especially for forecasts, Business Cases, and budgeting.

Organizational culture—The set of attitudes, activities, and behaviors that, collectively, tend to give an organization its personality.

Outbound marketing—Encompasses the work activities carried out to create programs that communicate messages or position products to customers and analysts, using advertising, public relations activities, and other events.

Outsourcing—The practice of moving business operations or overhead functions to businesses or subcontractors that are independent of a company's normal operations. Outsourcing may be important for product managers and their teams as they determine the optimal way to produce or support a product.

Overhead—Expenses incurred in the production of a product that are indirectly related to the cost of the product. Overheads might include rent, electricity, fuel, and similar expenses. Overhead in service businesses relates to similar types of expenses, which are often categorized as "general and administrative" expenses.

Pairwise—The practice of building larger consensus by seeking a series of one-on-one agreements between people from two different business functions. A pairwise negotiation or agreement is the starting point in developing Functional Support Plans. Generally followed by gradual inclusion of more and more functions or parties, one at a time, until comprehensive consensus is reached across all stakeholders or interested parties.

Payables—See *Accounts payable.*

Payback period—The amount of time it takes to recover an investment's initial outlay.

Penetration (or market penetration)—The degree to which a product has saturated (or propagated within) a given market segment or target market. For example, a 40 percent market penetration would imply that approximately 40 percent of the target customers in a given segment have actually purchased the product at least once within a given time period. Related to but not equal to market share, market *penetration* measures the percentage of possible target customers who have actually purchased a product, while market *share* compares actual product revenue with the total possible revenue available for that product in a given market. For example, market share recognizes the contribution of multiple purchases by the same customer, whereas market penetration generally does not.

Persona—A customer archetype or model created to represent a common set of characteristics or motivations, as with a customer type within a market segment or demographic. It is typically a representation of a group of people as opposed to a singular individual. A persona is a useful reference model for market segmentation and for cultivating useful value propositions. However, a persona is also a helpful guide in crafting meaningful, relevant product requirements.

Phase-gate process—A general product planning and development decision-making process that enables a structured evaluation of product opportunities (e.g., new products and enhancements). Work tasks and activities are structured into phases or groups of activities that allow the opportunity to be progressively analyzed and researched. When a set of analytical activities is completed, a decision is required that determines if the opportunity is to progress to a subsequent phase or be canceled. Also see *New Product Development (NPD) process.*

Place—See *Distribution channel.*

Plant and Equipment—The physical production assets of a manufacturing company.

Platform—The underlying foundations, technology frameworks, base architectures, and interfaces upon which products are built.

PMBOK (Project Management Body of Knowledge)—A standard approach to project management espoused and promoted by the Project Management Institute. For the most current details, see www.pmi.org/Resources/Pages/Global-Standards-Program.aspx.

Policy—A general, usually strategically focused statement, rule, or regulation that describes how a particular activity, operation, or group of operations will be carried out within a company.

Portfolio—See *Product portfolio.*

Positioning Statement—The document used to competitively position a product in the market by identifying the target customer or market segment, clarifying the product's benefits, describing its unique characteristics, and comparing it to equivalent competitive products.

Post-Launch audit—A formal review (or series of reviews) designed to determine how well a product launch was carried out, and how well all of the people, financial resources, systems, and operational support mechanisms were applied to the product launch. The Post-Launch audit provides insight into organizational, structural, or procedural issues that can be addressed and fine-tuned to the benefit of future launches.

Post-Launch Product Management (PLPM)—An area of work within the Product Management Life Cycle Model. PLPM is characterized by a collection of (largely asynchronous) tasks, activities, and tactics that are required for running the business of the product after it is launched into the market. There are several subphases for every product. Generically, these phases characterize the product's growth in the market, its maturity, and ultimate decline and discontinuation.

Practice—As related to business, the actual work performed by people as part of a process. (Also see *best practice.*)

Present method of operation (PMO)—In essence, the current way of doing things, that is, the collection of procedures, processes, and methods currently employed by a company, division, or organization to accomplish business objectives.

PRESTO—A useful, macroscopic view of a market, segment, or market area, constructed by examining the political, regulatory, economic, social, and technological factors affecting that market (or geographic area), also considering other factors that do not easily fit into any other category.

Price—The amount of money charged for a product; one of the four Ps of the marketing mix.

Process—A structured series of activities that are organized and sequenced to achieve a goal.

Product—Something that is offered for sale, either tangible or intangible; defined more fully and completely in Chapter 1, "What Is Product Management?"

Product announcement—See *Announcement.*

Product architecture—The product's fundamental structure or platform that enables the product to achieve its desired functionality. A product's architecture may be built utilizing physical components, specific materials, software and related interfaces, and other attributes that may be shared across many different variations (models or versions) or adaptations.

Product as a business—A Product Management perspective and approach in which each product is treated as an independent investment or entrepreneurial activity, with its own P&L. This expression is used extensively to reinforce the fact that a product should be its own business entity or important part of a product portfolio.

Product availability rating—A classification of a product, used internally to describe the degree to which it can be sold or distributed. For example, an availability rating of GA, or "generally available," means that the product can be ordered by any customer. CMI, or an equivalent term, would support the intent of a "controlled market introduction," which may mean that the product can only be ordered through a special arrangement prior to its final announcement to the market, directly through an account manager, for limited use.

Product champion—An executive or other high-level manager who supports the planning, development, and continued strategic success of a given product or service offering.

Product customization—The process of adding special features or components to an existing platform, product line, or product to meet newly discovered needs of a target market or market segment or of an individual customer.

Product Development and Management Association (PDMA)—A professional organization for those involved in product development and product management. Refer to www.pdma.org for a current and detailed description of the PDMA.

Product discontinuation—The process of removing a product or service offering from a market.

Product elements—Components, subassemblies, or parts of a tangible product. A product element could be a feature or term of use for an intangible product.

Product life cycle—A term to describe a product, from its conception to its discontinuance and ultimate market withdrawal.

Product line—A grouping of products focused on similar markets or on solving a particular type of problem.

Product Management Life Cycle Model—A model representing a product's life, from beginning to end. This model is used extensively as a reference model throughout this book.

Product manager and/or product line manager—A proactive, designated mini-business owner or general manager for a product or product line. The product manager is responsible for optimizing the product's market and financial performance, consistent with the strategies and goals of the firm.

Product Master Plan—A document repository and master control plan for a product or product line. It is made up of many different subdocuments that are historic, current, and strategically oriented. It serves as the plan of record for both current and future product activities. As a collection of plans and information about the product, it serves as an archive, a learning tool, and communication mechanism across the organization and across generations of product managers and product teams.

Product mix—The combination of all products sold within a given portfolio. Very often, the term *product mix* is used for budgeting or portfolio tracking because it describes how many of each product are to be sold or are actually sold.

Product portfolio—Several products or product lines may be grouped into a related collection called a product portfolio. Portfolios may be organized based on segments targeted, their underlying architecture, or even the specific source or manufacturing method used. All products in a business unit or division, or across the entire enterprise, comprise varying views of product portfolios.

Product project—This is a term used to describe any project that may be subordinate to, or chartered by, the product team. Examples of product projects include a project for an enhancement to an existing product, a project undertaken by Development, a market research project, or product launch.

Product positioning—The way in which a product or service is presented or communicated to a particular market or market segment such that a specific perception can be created in the minds of the desired customer types within that segment. Product positioning is important because it asserts a product's differential advantage over competitors' products. A Product Positioning Statement is used to craft this message.

Product Requirements Document (PRD)—A document that describes the functional and non-functional characteristics or attributes of a product that reflect business, market, or customer needs.

Product scorecard—A report that contains data and metrics about the financial and business performance of a product or product line against the guidelines established in a Business Case or in an annual product budget.

Product Specification Document (PSD)—A document written by people who work in Product Development (which may include R&D, Systems Design, Engineering, IT, or an equivalent technical function). The PSD should respond directly to that which is written in the Product Requirements Document (PRD) so that the product can be developed.

Profit and loss statement (P&L)—For product managers, the P&L is a financial statement that helps determine whether a product contributes a profit to the business. The most important elements are *revenue* (units sold × price charged), *cost of goods sold* (material, labor, and overhead), and *gross margin* (total revenue minus cost of goods sold). Gross margin is an effective way of determining if a product is achieving its financial objectives.

Program Evaluation Review Technique (PERT)—A method of depicting, scheduling, and prioritizing a complex set of activities in a way that supports effective project management. This method provides excellent visibility into a project's progress and potential obstacles and risks.

Program management—A meta–project management activity that involves managing more than one project or more than one project team. Related projects may roll-up to a program just as the projects within individual Functional Support Plans (FSPs) are consolidated.

Project—A group of related activities and tasks associated with accomplishing a specific goal or objective. As referred to in this book, projects usually produce a deliverable from a person or persons in a functional department.

Project Management—The act of planning and managing a series of tasks and agreed-upon deliverables. It is based on standard methods and processes. See PMBOK and the Project Management Institute (PMI) for references to additional information.

Project Management Institute (PMI)—An organization that defines, promotes, and provides education in the area of a standard project management. For the most up-to-date information on PMI, see www.pmi.org.

Promotion—One of the four Ps of the marketing mix that involves a variety of methods used to communicate to select customer types within desirable market segments.

Prototype—A model used to demonstrate or refine a product concept.

Push back—The act of presenting data to another person (in another function or in management) to justify why a given course of action should or should not be pursued. Within the context of this book, a product team may need to push back to management when the work load of the product team needs to be reevaluated or reprioritized.

Quality Assurance (QA)—A business function that is responsible for the (often statistically based) evaluation of how well a product conforms to requirements (according to the PRD) and specifications (according to the PSD).

Quality attribute—A type of non-functional requirement that describes a service level or performance characteristic of a product.

RACI—A system for clarifying and/or assigning roles and responsibilities to a variety of members of a cross-functional team, or the constituencies within the departments that support the cross-functional team. For any given activity, it designates who is responsible for carrying out work, who is accountable for its completion, who should be consulted, and who must be informed.

Rational ignorance—A flaw in the decision-making process built on the assumption that no decision will produce an acceptable result, and thus, any decision can be made without the need for reasonable consideration.

Rationalizing—With respect to business systems and products, rationalizing refers to the process of eliminating any duplicates, conflicts, or disconnects in a given set of objects or data. For example, when one rationalizes a product line, one ensures that there are the right number of products in the line to precisely meet the needs of the chosen target markets. This serves to eliminate any internal competition, redundancy, cannibalization, or superfluous features.

Receivables—See *Accounts receivable.*

Regulatory requirements—Product or service requirements that are imposed by an outside (usually governmental) agency that must be met by every product or service under the purview of that agency.

Request for proposal (RFP) or request for quote (RFQ)—A document that invites a vendor to submit a combination of products, services, and other elements (including pricing) to meet a specific set of requirements established by a customer.

Requirements—See *Product Requirements Document (PRD).*

Research and Development (R&D)—The branch of a company or organization that translates product requirements into products. Often this group is made up of engineers, computer programmers, or other technical personnel. In some firms, there is a distinction between the R and the D where Research is the function responsible for experimentation and discovery, and Development is the function used for actual product creation.

Restrategizing—The process of (periodically or continuously) reevaluating the inputs and assumptions that comprise a product strategy and, if changes or new insights warrant, altering the product strategy appropriately.

Results—Business outcomes that are produced as a consequence of specific or purposeful actions. A product's business results might include its contribution to the firm's profit or the achievement of a market share target.

Retrofit—To modify an already fielded product to meet requirements not addressed by the original product configuration.

Return on investment (ROI)—Any method of comparing the amount of money invested in a given initiative with the profitability or financial results of the initiative. ROI calculations are generally very subjective.

Revenue—The amount of money obtained from the sale of products or services. Revenue is calculated by multiplying the number of units of the product sold by the price per unit.

Risk—The consideration of a situation that might arise that would tend to prevent a strategy or objective from being successfully achieved.

Risk mitigation—The act of developing advance plans or taking immediate actions to minimize or prevent known or unknown events (risks) from adversely affecting a strategy or business objective.

Roadmap—A method to portray, visualize, and integrate the elements that encompass the evolution of a product or a complete solution. As used in this book, a roadmap can be referred to as a "statement of intent" to describe, in broad themes, the future of the product's business. It should be noted that the roadmap is *not* the strategy.

Role-playing—The process of considering a particular situation or opportunity from the point of view of another party, such as a customer or persona, and then attempting to emulate and/or imitate the thoughts and behaviors of that party to gain insights that may be useful in developing or modifying products.

Scalability—The capability of a product, service, or platform to be readily enlarged or expanded to handle greater capacity than offered by a single instantiation, whether through replication, customization, or additional supporting elements.

Scenario—A specific sequence of hypothetical events and contingencies, used for planning and forecasting purposes. A scenario can be thought of as a possible story about the future. Scenarios are useful when preparing product requirements, Business Cases, and forecasts.

Scope—The set of features, functions, and attributes associated with a given set of product or service requirements. The scope of work is that work that is to be carried out in order to create or update a product.

Scope creep—When features, functions, or attributes are added to a product during development that goes beyond the agreed-upon product requirements. When this condition occurs, the product is said to be experiencing scope creep. Scope creep is generally considered to be the number one cause of cost and schedule overruns in development projects. (Alternatively, this is sometimes called *feature creep*.)

Segment—See *Market segment.*

Segmentation—See *Market segmentation.*

Sensitivity analysis—The practice of changing a variable in a financial model or forecast to determine how a change in that variable affects the overall outcome. For example, to consider the way in which a change in price might affect the gross profit in a product forecast, one might vary the price in small increments and recompute the figures to see how gross profit changes.

Service-based business—A business that provides services, rather than tangible products, to customers.

Service-level agreement (SLA)—An agreement between a customer and a product or service provider that defines conditions under which the provider will offer support or additional services to the customer, and what level of services will be offered under each of those conditions.

Share—See *Market share.*

Shelf space—A traditional marketing measure that describes the number of inches of store shelf space devoted to the display of a given product. Over time, this expression has been broadened to loosely describe how much mindshare, display space, sales effort, or other proportion of a selling resource is assigned to one product over another.

Silo—See *Functional silo.*

Socialize—Building support for ideas, plans, and strategies by sharing them with various interested and/or influential members of the organization. Socializing is based on the observation that people will tend to show more interest in ideas that are more widely discussed.

Solution—A combination of products, services, and other elements that solve complex problems, have a high degree of integration across disparate elements, and usually require customization for a specific customer type or industry. Compare to *Bundle.*

Sourcing—The process of finding or procuring materials or components for products, services, and other elements needed for product creation, manufacturing, or solution delivery.

Stakeholders—Parties who have a vested interest of some kind in a given product, decision, or activity. In general, all stakeholders should be represented in the RACI matrix (see *RACI*).

Stock-keeping units (SKUs)—A standardized numbering system for uniquely labeling products so that there is no confusion at any point along the value chain.

Stock-out—When a company does not have product available to fill existing orders, the condition is referred to as a stock-out.

Storytelling—A narrative way of describing a scenario, product idea, or strategy intended to provide a real-world context to promote decision making and better understanding.

Strategy—A strategy is a series of planned actions and objectives designed to achieve a specified future outcome. Strategy helps to depict and achieve the end-state, while tactics (such as tasks within projects or projects themselves) contribute to the achievement of strategies.

Strengths—The attributes or characteristics of a product or service that tend to give it a natural competitive advantage.

Subassembly—A subset of a total product configuration that should be separately considered for the purpose of effective Product Management. Also see *Product element.*

Subfunction—Within various business functions are highly specialized subfunctions that should sometimes be considered separately. For example, Quality Assurance may be a subfunction of Development, and Payroll may be a subfunction of Accounting.

Subphases—Recognizable sets of activities within a given product life cycle phase that are distinct enough to be treated as a mini-phase. For example, the product launch phase may have early, middle, and late subphases.

Subsegments—A subset of a market segment that has unique characteristics that need to be considered independently when planning or specifying a product. Equivalent terms would include customer target type or target customer.

Subteam—A subset of the product cross-functional team, convened for the purpose of dealing with a limited or focused subset of product-related activities or tasks.

Suppliers—External companies that provide subassemblies, components, or other product elements.

Supply chain—The supply chain refers to the processes and methods supporting the physical existence of a product from the procurement of materials through the production, storage (creating inventory), and movement (logistics) of the product into its chosen distribution channels. Product managers need to understand how the product is created and delivered from its point of origin to point of purchase. In most companies, Supply Chain is the business function or organization that oversees this process.

SWOT—A general method used as an element of strategic planning. SWOT is an acronym for strengths, weaknesses, opportunities, and threats. Within the context of Product Management, SWOT is used to *synthesize* the many elements of the business environment for a product or product line (as opposed to a corporate or divisional entity). The SWOT model utilizes a quadrant structure.

Synergy—Any relationship between two persons or entities in which the combined effort produces a more useful result than the individual efforts of those entities would produce on their own. Sometimes described by the phrase, "the whole is greater than the sum of its parts."

Tactic, tactical—A group of specific tasks, actions, or objectives that are relatively focused in scope, intent, and procedure. A tactic is associated with a specific, tangible outcome in support of a strategy.

Target customer —Within a given market segment, those customers with common needs who may be likely to benefit from a given product. Some also use the term *customer target*.

Target market—The grouping of target customer types (by geography, demographic, or other segment definition), who exhibit a common set of needs.

Team sizing—Making sure that the cross-functional product team has the appropriate representation at each phase, across the entire product life cycle.

Threats—With respect to SWOT, threats are represented by the competitive products or their characteristics that offer the competition the best opportunity to damage your reputation.

Total addressable market (TAM)—The total amount of possible sales of a given product type within a given segment; generally expressed in dollars (or local units of currency).

Traceability—The degree to which each element of a product can be mapped back to the individual requirement or requirements, which in turn are linked back to the original validated market or customer need.

Trade-offs—The act of selecting alternate product requirements because of new information or because of an inability to meet the original requirements. The trade-off may also have to be made if there is a lack of capability, budget, or human resources. The trade-off process is essentially a decision-making process used by the product manager and the team to reprioritize specific product requirements.

Turnover—With respect to inventory, turnover is a ratio that refers to the number of times that the inventory is replenished. Higher turnover is preferred because it indicates that products are selling rapidly.

Unique selling point (USP)—A feature or attribute that strongly differentiates a given product or service from all other entries in a given category. USPs are built out of product positioning statements.

Upgrade—Additional capability added to a given product or service. Generally, upgrades represent the outcome of product enhancements and are undertaken to improve the product's overall positioning and its value proposition.

Upsell—The practice of convincing a customer to purchase a higher-value product or service than the version currently owned.

Upside potential—The best case scenario for a given opportunity, as in, what is the most we could possibly make from this investment?

User—A person, customer type, or customer target that is identified as using the product or application. A user could also be the ultimate consumer the product.

User requirement—The activities or objectives that a user or group of users should or must be able to carry out or achieve.

User story—Simple descriptions that chronicle the activities or desires of a user or consumer (e.g., "As a shopper, I want to easily select my product, so I can get back to work as quickly as possible.").

Value proposition—Defines the need and proves the economic or qualitative benefit to a specific customer, based on the benefit perceived by that customer. Value propositions must be expressed clearly in the language that the customer understands.

Value-added—Refers to the addition of something else of value to a customer as a vendor attempts to solve a customer's business problem. Value-added services, for example, might include the addition of consulting services or customizing a product explicitly for a customer.

Variance—The difference between a plan (or budget) and an actual (or result).

Variance analysis—The evaluation of a number of variances to determine root causes. Product managers will examine a variety of variances in order to create narratives or explanations as to what transpired and the remedies that will be undertaken to improve performance.

Version control—The process of maintaining strong controls over changes to documents, software, or prototype products to prevent confusion about what changes are the most current.

Vertical markets—Market segments focused on a specific industry, such as pharmaceuticals, telecommunications equipment, or fast food. Often referred to as industry verticals.

Vision—The envisioned end state or optimal future situation. A product leader envisions a product's position in the market at a point in the future. The product leader's vision provides essential guidance to a team as strategies are formulated.

Voice of the customer (VOC)—A technique that captures customer needs either through explicit or direct interactions with customers using surveys, focus groups, or observations as made on a visit to a customer's location. Furthermore, the voice of the customer can be heard by observing a customer using a product or by observing customers doing what they do.

Volume—The quantity of units or amount of money associated with a particular product; can be applied to sales, inventory, production rates, or any product-related quantity.

Vulnerabilities—With respect to SWOT, the characteristics of a product that make it inherently susceptible to unfavorable comparison to competitive products. If a company's product is threatened by the competition, it is considered vulnerable. (See *Threats*.)

Walk-through—The process of evaluating product requirements, documentation, performance, operation, test results, or any development-related aspect of a product, generally for the purpose of validating that the product conforms to some level of specifications.

Warranty—Guarantees or promises made regarding the performance or quality of a product; made by the seller to the buyer.

Weaknesses—With respect to SWOT, the attributes of a product that cause the product to be less than competitive.

Work breakdown structure (WBS)—A structured list of all activities and tasks required to complete a project.

Win–loss audit—An evaluation of a sale (or attempted sale) to determine why a customer did or did not purchase the product.

Workflow—The entire sequence of steps, activities, processes, and tactics carried out in order to transform a given input into a desired output.

Working capital—The amount of liquid assets (generally, cash) that are available to operate or run a business.

Work structure—In this book, the ideal work structure to get Product Management work done is the cross-functional product team.

Worst-case scenario—The least desirable outcome that might result from pursuing a given set of assumptions related to a product investment, forecast, or similar activity.

Write-offs—Monies due a corporation that have become impossible to collect and thus are written off the books. For example, accounts receivable that cannot be collected from a bankrupt customer may have to be written off as a bad debt.

REFERENCES AND RESOURCES

In addition to those references explicitly called out in the book, there are many journals and periodicals I have found to be very helpful. Here are the periodicals I refer to most frequently.

PERIODICALS, JOURNALS, AND ONLINE TOOLS

- *Bloomberg BusinessWeek*
- The *New York Times*
- The *Wall Street Journal*
- The *Financial Times*
- The *McKinsey Quarterly*
- *Strategy + Business* (also visit: www.strategy-business.com)
- *Harvard Business Review* (also visit: harvardbusinessonline .hbsp.edu)
- The *Journal of Business Forecasting*
- The *MIT Sloan Management Review*
- *B2B*
- *Entrepreneur*
- *Forbes*
- *Fortune*
- *ABA Banking Journal*
- *American Banker*
- *Leadership Excellence*
- *Sales & Marketing Management*
- *Treasury and Risk*
- The *Journal of Marketing*
- *Oxford Dictionary of Business and Management*
- *US Banker*
- *Americas Quarterly*
- *Global Business and Organizational Excellence*
- *The Economist*

OTHER GENERAL REFERENCES, INSTITUTIONS, AND ASSOCIATIONS

- Financial Accounting Standards Board (FASB): www.fasb.org.
- International Accounting Standards Board (IASB): www.iasb.org.
- American Institute of Certified Public Accountants: www.aicpa.org.
- Standard & Poor's Corporation: www.standardandpoors.com.
- MSCI (Industry Classifications): www.msci.com.
- Federation of International Trade Associations: www.fita.org.
- International Trade Administration: trade.gov/mas/index.asp.
- International Telecommunications Union: www.itu.int.
- North American Industry Classification System: www.census .gov/epcd/www/naics/html.
- Office for National Statistics (UK): www.ons.gov.uk/ons/index .html.
- North American Product Classification System and Product Lists by NAICS Industry Subject Area: www.census.gov/eos/ www/napcs/napcstable.html.
- Business and Industry Census Bureau Economic Programs: www.census.gov/econ/www.
- Wray O. Candillis, *Commercial Banking Industry Overview–U.S. Industrial Outlook, Annual,* 1992, accessed through the BNET Research Center, www.findarticles.com.
- Enterprise-Wide IT Architecture: www.ewita.com.
- Global Enterprise Architecture Organisation: www.etheryl.net/ GEAO.
- Bad Human Factors Designs is a website that features poorly designed products with suggestions on how products could be more appropriately designed: www.baddesigns.com.
- The Corporate Design Foundation (www.cdf.org) is an interesting organization. You might want to review its newsletter called "@issue" for some interesting stories about product design.
- Capability Maturity Model® Integration Version 1.1, Pittsburgh, PA: Carnegie Mellon Software Engineering Institute, August 2002.
- Survey of Current Business Online from the Bureau of Economic Analysis: www.bea.gov/scb/index.htm.
- Federal Reserve Archival System for Economic Research: fraser .stlouisfed.org.

- Voluntary Interindustry Commerce Solutions Association (www .vics.org/home) works to improve the efficiency and effectiveness of supply chain activities. This organization also sponsors several committees, one of which is the Collaborative Planning, Forecasting, and Replenishment Committee (CPFR®).

- SupplyChainBrain.com—a website dedicated to news and information for people interested in supply chain.

- American Marketing Association: www.marketingpower.com.

- Product Scan Online—a database that has data about consumer packaged goods, used as a resource to find out about new products being introduced and a host of new product innovations: www.productscan.com.

- Project Management Institute website: www.pmi.org.

- European Automobile Manufacturers Association: www.acea.be.

- National Association of Manufacturers: www.nam.org.

- European Commission—Enterprise and Industry—provides material about product standards and conformance, industrial competitiveness, and other useful information: ec.europa.eu/enterprise/ index_en.htm.

INDEX